NESTORIUS

The

Bazaar of Heracleides

NESTORIUS

The

Bazaar of Heracleides

Newly translated from the Syriac

and edited with an

Introduction

Notes & Appendices

by

G. R. DRIVER, M.A.

&

LEONARD HODGSON, M.A.

Fellows of Magdalen College, Oxford

Wipf and Stock Publishers
150 West Broadway • Eugene OR 97401

Wipf and Stock Publishers
150 West Broadway
Eugene, Oregon 97401

The Bazaar of Heracleides
By Nestorius
ISBN: 1-57910-934-9
Publication date: April, 2002
Previously published by Oxford, 1925.

PREFACE

THE present volume is the result of collaboration between two colleagues, the one a student of the Semitic languages, the other of Christian doctrine. After the former had prepared an English translation of the whole work, the manuscript was handed over to the latter, who read it carefully through; the difficulties were then jointly discussed. The editors hope that by this means they are able to offer a reliable rendering of the original text. The absence of any English edition of a work which has given rise to much theological discussion has, in their opinion, justified them in undertaking the task; but, although their edition is based on an independent study of the Syriac version itself, they desire to acknowledge their indebtedness to MM. Bedjan and Nau, the editors of the Syriac text and of the French translation respectively, their reliance on whom is evident on every page of the translation and in almost every note; indeed, if they had not already covered the ground, it is unlikely that the present work would ever have been accomplished.

We wish to express our gratitude also to those whose encouragement and assistance has enabled us to complete our work: to the President and Fellows of Magdalen College and to the Trustees of the Denyer and Johnson Fund for most generous financial grants; to the staff of the Clarendon Press for their courtesy and care; to the Rev. F. W. Green for reading the proofs, and to him and to Mrs. Margoliouth for many valuable suggestions; to Dr. B. J. Kidd for permission to draw on his *History of the Church to* A.D. *461* in compiling the historical section of our Introduction; to the editors of the proposed Patristic Lexicon for putting at our disposal for the purpose of Appendix III the material which they had collected, and to the Rev. T. G. Jalland for his help in drawing up that appendix; and to the proprietors of the *Journal of Theological Studies* for permission to reprint Appendix IV from their pages.

G. R. D.
L. H.

MAGDALEN COLLEGE,
OXFORD.
October, 1924.

CONTENTS

	PAGE
PREFACE	v

INTRODUCTION.
    i. History of *The Bazaar* ix
    ii. The Text xi
    iii. Value of the Syriac Translation xii
    iv. History of the Controversy xvii
    v. The Argument of *The Bazaar* xxix

TEXT.
    The Syriac Translator's Preface 3
    Book I, Part I 7
        „ I, „ II 87
        „ I, „ III 96
        „ II, „ I 186
        „ II, „ II 336

    (N.B.—The following are the chief *historical* sections:
        pp. 96-142, 265-93, 329-80.)

APPENDICES.
    i. Translation of the Syriac Fragments of Nestorius 382
    ii. Critical Notes 398
    iii. The word πρόσωπον 402
    iv. 'The Metaphysic of Nestorius' 411

INDEX 421

ABBREVIATIONS

C = Cambridge. 　　　S = Strassburg.
L = London. 　　　　V = Van.
　　　P = Peshiṭtâ Syriac Version.

INTRODUCTION

i. History of *The Bazaar*.

THE Council of Ephesus met in June, A.D. 431, and was dissolved in September by the Emperor Theodosius II without the two parties, the Orientals and the followers of Cyril of Alexandria, having come to an agreement. Nestorius was bidden to return to his monastery at Antioch, and Maximian was consecrated Archbishop of Constantinople in his place. In August 435 imperial edicts forbade the meetings of Nestorians and decreed heavy penalties against all who should copy, preserve, or read the writings of their master, which were ordered to be burned. By a rescript of the following year Nestorius himself was banished to Arabia, but he was actually sent to Egypt, where from a reference in Socrates he is known to have been in 439.[1] But he was not left in peace in Egypt, for besides being on one occasion made prisoner by Lybian marauders, the ill will of his Egyptian opponents led to his being somewhat harshly treated by the imperial agents responsible for the supervision of his exile.[2]

In 1825 Augustus Neander, in referring to the citations made by Evagrius[3] from a history of his misfortunes written by Nestorius during his exile, wrote ' That the work bore the 'title of "Tragedy" is reported by Ebedjesu, a Nestorian 'metropolitan of the fourteenth century, in his list of Syrian 'ecclesiastical writers in *Assemani bibliotheca orientalis*, T. iii, 'p. i, f. 36. This work of Nestorius has unfortunately not 'come down to us, unless, perhaps, it may be somewhere found 'in a Syrian translation.'[4] As a matter of fact, Ebedjesu mentions six works of Nestorius as extant in Syriac in his day, the *Tragedy*, the *Book of Heracleides*, a *Letter to Cosmos*, a *Liturgy*, a book of *Letters*, and a book of *Homilies and Sermons*,[5] and Neander's prophetic hope has been fulfilled

---
[1] Socrates, *Hist. Eccl.* VII. xxxiv. [2] Cp. Evagrius, I. vii. [3] *Id. ib.*
[4] Neander, *Church History* (Eng. Tr., T. and T. Clark, 1855), vol. iv, p. 207.
[5] See p. xi, n. 4.

by the discovery, not indeed of the *Tragedy*, but of *The Bazaar of Heracleides*.

This work was introduced to English readers by Dr. Bethune-Baker of Cambridge in 1908 in his monograph *Nestorius and his Teaching*.[1] In his preface Dr. Bethune-Baker gives the following account of the work.

The book must have been written by Nestorius in the year 451 or 452, seeing that there are references to the death of Theodosius II in 450, and to the flight of Dioscorus of Alexandria.[2] Dioscorus was at the Council of Chalcedon in 451, but though formally deposed by the Council in October of that year was not condemned to banishment until the following July. On the other hand, Nestorius, though speaking of the triumph of the orthodox faith of Flavian and Leo, does not seem to be aware of the formal decisions of the Council of Chalcedon. It appears, therefore, that Dioscorus must have fled when the Council decided against him, and that when Nestorius wrote he must have heard of his flight, but not of the formal decision of the Council or of the imperial decree by which sentence of exile was pronounced upon him.

Dr. Bethune-Baker identifies this work with that mentioned by Evagrius. He conjectures that the Syriac translation may have been undertaken at the instance of Maraba, Catholicos of the Eastern Church, between 525 and 533, but no absolute certainty can be attained on this point.[3] Apart from the reference to it by Ebedjesu it is not again heard of until the nineteenth century. The original manuscript is at Kotchanes in Kurdistan and for several years its existence has been known to members of the Archbishop of Canterbury's Mission to Assyrian Christians, some of whom obtained copies of it. It was noticed in the last decade of the nineteenth century by two German scholars,[4] and attention was called to it by Dr. Loofs of Halle in his Collection of Nestorian remains published in 1905.[5] In 1908 Dr. Bethune-Baker published

---

[1] Cambridge University Press.   [2] See below, pp. xxviii, 369, 375.
[3] See p. xi, and especially n. 5.
[4] H. Goussen, *Martyrius Sahdona's Leben und Werke* (Leipzig, 1897), and Braun, *Das Buch der Synhodos* (Stuttgart, 1900).
[5] Loofs, *Nestoriana* (Halle, 1905).

History of 'The Bazaar'

his monograph, and in 1910 a Syriac text was published in Leipzig by P. Bedjan[1] and a French translation in Paris by F. Nau.[2]

ii. THE TEXT.

Our translation is based on Bedjan's Syriac text.[3] Nestorius himself wrote his defence in Greek, his works were condemned to be burnt and only a few sermons and letters have survived in Greek and Latin.[4] Now only the Nestorian liturgy and *The Bazaar of Heracleides* are known.

The Syriac translation of the latter work was made about 535 under the patriarch Paul, according to Bedjan[5]; of this there is extant only one mutilated manuscript, which is preserved in the library of the Nestorian patriarch at Kotchanes, in Kurdistan. This manuscript has suffered considerable damage, chiefly at the hands of the Kurds on the occasion of the massacre of Nestorian Christians by the Kurdish chief Bedr Khan Bey in 1843.[6] Of this manuscript Bedjan[7] says: ' According to the blank pages in the manuscripts which I 'have had in my hands, and according to certain brief notes of 'the copyists, I have reckoned that at page 146 of my edition '[*i.e.* Syr., p. 146, as given at the top of each page in our 'translation] there are very nearly 55 pages which have dis-

---

[1] Nestorius, *Le Livre d'Héraclide de Damas, édité par* Paul Bedjan, *P. D. L. M.* (*Lazariste*), *avec plusieurs appendices* (Leipzig and Paris, 1910).

[2] Nestorius, *Le Livre d'Héraclide de Damas, traduit en français par* F. Nau (Paris 1910).

[3] See Bedjan, *op. cit.*, pp. viii–xi, whence our account of the text is drawn.

[4] At the end of the thirteenth century it is clear from the catalogue of the Bishop of Nisibis that most of Nestorius' works in Greek and Latin had disappeared; only a Syriac version of his *Tragoedia*, his *Letter to Cosmos*, his *Liturgy*, a volume of letters and another of sermons, besides *The Bazaar of Heracleides*, survived at that time (*op. cit.*, pp. vii–viii).

[5] This date, however, seems to be at variance with the fact that the translator calls the Bishop of Beroea 'Bishop of Aleppo'; now if, as Nau states on this passage, the name of the see was changed from Beroea to Aleppo in A.D. 638, the translation must have been made *after* that date, provided that the original Syriac manuscript also has Aleppo (see p. 330, n. 1). The new (Eastern) name, however, may have been current long before the name of the see was officially changed.

[6] See p. 192.   [7] *Op. cit.*, pp. viii–ix.

'appeared; at page 161, 42 pages are missing; at page 209,
'36 pages have been lost. One can only make this calculation
'approximately. Further, there are passages where some lines
'have been left blank; other places of no considerable length
'have been obliterated by age.'

There are four copies of this manuscript, the first made in
1889 for the library of the American mission at Urmiyah.
From this two other copies were made: one for the University
of Cambridge, and the other for that of Strassburg. In
addition to these, Bedjan had a copy, written partly at Van
and partly at Kotchanes, from the original in the possession of
the Nestorian patriarch. Of these manuscripts only the last
mentioned, which is the archetype of all the others, is of any
value for the text; Bedjan himself confesses that, where his
text differs from that, the variations are errors or conjectural
emendations of an original which was not accessible to him.

iii. Value of the Syriac Translation.

That the Syriac text is a translation is definitely stated by
the writer of the 'Translator's Preface'.[1] Fortunately, although
the Greek original has been lost, we are in a position to estimate the value of this translation, since the Greek of certain
passages has been preserved in the Fathers. In the first place,
Bedjan[2] is undoubtedly right in seeing in the title 'the *Bazaar*
of Heracleides' a mistake; the original Greek word seems to
have been πραγματεία which connotes both 'business' and
'treatise', which the Syriac translator rendered by *te'gûrtâ*
'merchandise'! There are, however, very few bad blunders
in that part of the Syriac text which can be checked by a
reference to the original Greek, as the following list shows,
while in many cases the cause of the error can be detected:

P. 32: The Syriac translator, in reading ܚܩܠܬܟܘܢ 'in
your parts', appears to have taken μέρους in the original Greek
as plural; the Peshittâ has ܒܕܘܟܬܟܘܢ 'in your place' (1 Cor.
xii. 27).

[1] See p. 3.   [2] *Op. cit.*, p. viii, n. 2.

P. 103: The Greek πάντα κάλων κινούσης, 'straining every cord', is translated in Syriac by 'stirred up all that was fair' (misreading πάντα κάλων as πᾶν καλόν).

Pp. 103-4: The Greek τοὺς διεστραμμένους, 'those who have been perverted', is translated in Syriac by 'those things which are distorted' (reading ܡܚܒܠܐ for ܡܚܒܠܝܢ).

Pp. 269-70: The Greek πάσης συγχύσεως ... γέμοντα, 'filled with all confusion', is translated in Syriac by 'filled with turbulent fellows' (reading ܫܓܘܫܐ for ܫܓܘܫܝܐ).

Pp. 299-300: The Greek ἐναργέστατα, 'very clearly', is translated into Syriac by 'in effect' (misreading ἐναργέστατα as ἐνεργέστατα), and the Greek ἐναργῶς, 'clearly' by 'in operation' (misreading ἐναργῶς as ἐνεργῶς).

P. 297: The Greek προεπάγουσι, 'they cite', is translated into Syriac by 'he cites' (probably owing to the fact that the termination of the masc. plur. in Syriac was silent in pronunciation).[1]

Pp. 299-300: The Greek ταῦτ' οὖν ἀδελφὰ τοῖς παρ' ἐκείνων ὁρᾶτε, 'do you then regard these things as akin to what has been said by them?' is translated into Syriac by 'Do these things then, O our brother, seem to be akin to those which have been said by the former?' (the word ἀδελφά being twice rendered, once as if it were ἀδελφοί, by ܐܚܘܢ, 'our brother', and properly by ܕܡܝܢ, 'akin', a word derived from the same root).

Pp. 323-4: The Greek τὸν ἐκ Θεοῦ φασὶ λόγον γενέσθαι μὲν ἄνθρωπον, 'they say that the Word which proceeded from God became man', is translated into Syriac by 'that the word which proceeded from God became from man' (reading ܡܢ, 'from' for ܡܢ, i.e. Greek μέν, 'on the one hand', which should undoubtedly be restored).

Besides these obvious blunders, there is at least one instance of error through homoeoteleuton,[2] and one where an imperative is translated as if it were an optative.[3]

Secondly, there are a few errors for which no palaeographical explanation can be found:

P. 257: The Greek ὅταν Παῦλος ἐπιστέλλων κηρύττει is

---

[1] The reverse error is found in three passages, on pp. 53, 284, and 378.
[2] See pp. 241-2, and crit. n. on p. 400.   [3] See pp. 302-3.

rendered in Syriac by 'when Paul, who was sent forth to preach, says'.

Pp. 269-70: The Greek περὶ τῆς ἐμῆς βραδύτητος, 'as for my slowness', is rendered in Syriac by 'as for my own Insignificance'.[1]

P. 295: The Greek ἐδιδάχθην, 'I have learnt', is rendered in Syriac by 'we have learnt'.

No reason also can be assigned either for the fact that in the phrase 'he who begins and grows and is perfected is not God, although he is so called on account of the gradual growth' the translator always substitutes 'revelation' or 'manifestation' for 'growth' (Gk. αὔξησις),[2] or for the fact that the name Aethericus regularly appears as Atticus in his version.[3]

Seeing then that a certain number of errors can be charged to the account of the Syriac translator and proved against him, it is not too bold to assume in a few passages similar mistakes.

Finally, three other passages where the Greek and Syriac texts diverge may be mentioned. On p. 119 the Greek δείκνυντος ἡμῖν implies ܠܢ ܡܚܘܐ '(The Gospel) declaring to us' for the Syriac ܡܚܘܝܢܢ 'we declare'. On p. 242, instead of the Syriac ܐܘܬܒܗ ܕܝܢ ܥܡ ܐܒܐ 'caused it to dwell with the Father', the Greek has συνεκάθισεν ἑαυτῷ...ὁ πατήρ 'the Father caused... to dwell with himself', apparently reading ܕܝܢ 'indeed' and not ܥܡ 'with'. On p. 270 the Greek has τοῦ δήμου, i.e. ܕܥܡܐ 'of the people' where the Syriac has ܕܓܒܐ 'of the parties'.

There seem also to be two passages where the double negative οὐ μή in Greek has led the translator into error. On p. 259, for the Syriac 'For I have not denied that Christ is not God', the context requires 'For I have not denied that Christ is God' (i.e. οὐ γὰρ ἤρνημαι τὸν Χριστὸν μὴ οὐκ εἶναι Θεόνλ; or the like); on p. 324, for the Syriac 'how do they escape from saying that the human attributes do not belong to the *ousia* of God the Word?', the context requires 'how then do they escape from saying that the human attributes belong to the *ousia* of God the Word?' (i.e. πῶς οὖν φεύγουσι μὴ προσνέμειν τὰ ἀνθρώπινα τῇ τοῦ Θεοῦ λόγου οὐσίᾳ; or the like).[4] Another Greek

---

[1] Cp. Germ. *meine Wenigkeit*.
[2] See p. 200, n. 1.   [3] See p. 355, n. 3.
[4] Cp. Syr. ܡܣܠܐ ܕܠܐ ܢܣܓܘܕ = Gk. ἀρνεῖται μὴ προσκυνήσειν (Syr., p. 89). For the imitation of the redundant Greek negative after verbs of denying, refusing, &c. in the Syriac version see also p. 371, n. 2.

Value of the Syriac Translation

construction over which the translator seems to have blundered is that of the double accusative. So on p. 156 the context requires that the Syriac ' to regard a *prosôpon* as a hypostasis ' should be changed into ' to regard a *hypostasis* as a *prosôpon* ' (*i.e.* τὴν ὑπόστασιν ἡγεῖσθαι τὸ πρόσωπον or the like, where the Greek does not indicate which word is the predicate).

Against these errors there can be set a few passages where the Syriac version is clearly superior to the Greek original, and several others where it can be used to decide between alternative readings. In the first class come such passages as that on p. 234, where for the Greek ὑπόστασις the Syriac substitutes πρόσωπον in conformity with the regular usage of Nestorius; again, the Syriac rightly assigns the quotation on p. 244 to St. Luke, where the Greek has St. John.

In the second category fall the following passages:

Pp. 131-2: The Syriac confirms the reading τύπον against the *v.l.* τόπον.

P. 236: The Syriac confirms the reading ταφέν against the *v.l.* φανέν.

P. 270: The Syriac confirms the reading παρὰ τὸν καιρόν against the *v.l.* περὶ τὸν καιρόν.

P. 295: The Syriac confirms the reading οὐδαμοῦ against the *v.l.* οὐδαμῶς.

Pp. 299-300: The Syriac confirms the *v.l.*, omitting the particle οὖν.

P. 311: The Syriac confirms the reading κακοδοξία against the *v.l.* κενοδοξία.

In two places the Syriac suggests a correction of the Greek text. On p. 223 ἀμιγῆ σώματος καὶ τῶν ὅσα σώματος is clearly preferable to the original καὶ τὸν ὅσα σώματος, and on p. 242, in the quotation καί μοι σκόπει τὸ ὅμοιον, ἐκ τῶν ἐν ἔργοις καιρῶν ἀρξάμενον (*v.l.* ἀρξάμενος), the Syriac translator seems to have had ἀρξαμένων before him.[1]

---

[1] The occurrence of the transliterated word ܐܘܦܪܟܝܘܣ = ὑπαρχικοί on p. 107 (Syr., p. 163, l. 3) confirms the existence of this adjective in Greek. Hitherto it had only been found, according to Dr. Darwell Stone, in Eusebius, *Vit. Const.* 4, 1, 2 οἱ μὲν χρημάτων, οἱ δὲ κτημάτων, περιουσίας ἐτύγχανον, ἄλλοι ὑπαρχικῶν ἀξιωμάτων, οἱ δὲ συγκλήτου τιμῆς, οἱ δὲ τῆς τῶν ὑπάτων, πλείους δὲ ἡγεμόνες ἐχρημάτιζον, κτλ., on which Heikel's note is ' ὑπαρχικῶν Cod. N.! ὑπατικῶν

The Syriac translation may therefore be accounted good after its kind. Though occasionally pedantically accurate, as when the see of Beroea of the original text is called by the translator that of Aleppo,[1] it aims generally rather at representing the sense of the original than at reproducing the Greek word for word; for the retention of the Greek redundant negative even against the sense in a few passages is due rather to the tendency of the Syriac language to model itself on Greek, regardless of the requirements of Semitic idiom, than to the slavish fidelity of the translator to his original. This is proved not only by the loose rendering of individual words and phrases—for example, of αἰδέσιμοι by 'beloved' (on p. 103)—but also by a certain laxity in regard to the translation of technical or semi-technical terms, due largely to the relative poverty of the Syriac language in comparison with the Greek; thus the preposition ܥܠ represents both ἀντί and ὑπέρ, ܒ means 'in', 'by', and 'with', ܦܪܫ stands for ἀποδιαιρεῖν, διαιρεῖν, ἀποδιϊστάναι, διϊστάναι, διορίζειν, μερίζειν, χωρίζειν, ܦܠܓ for διαιρεῖν, διανέμειν, μερίζειν, τέμνειν, and so on. Against this, the translator accurately renders ἐκκαπηλεύειν, 'to adulterate' (on pp. 323-4), according to its peculiar usage in the Cyrillian writings.

The present editors, therefore, mindful of the fact that they are translating into a third language a translation—and that one which possesses no grace of style or elegance of diction—of a lost work, whose meaning depends solely on the precise value assigned to a number of technical terms, have frequently sacrificed the English to an endeavour to render faithfully the Syriac version, keeping as far as possible the same English word for the corresponding Syriac even at the cost of a certain harshness or awkwardness in many passages; for they have regarded it as their aim not so much to present the reader with their view of what Nestorius said as to enable him to form his own opinion from a careful and accurate version of the Syriac text.

VJMBA; aber in A steht ρχ auf Ras. u. in B ist ein Buchst. ausradiert zwischen α u. τ'. The following οἱ δὲ τῆς τῶν ὑπάτων is clearly against the reading ὑπατικῶν, which must originally have been introduced by a scribe who was ignorant of the rare word ὑπαρχικός.

[1] See p. 330, n. 1.

iv. HISTORY OF THE CONTROVERSY.[1]

Date.	Events.	Refs. in *The Bazaar*. PAGES (English).
428. April	Nestorius becomes bishop of Constantinople	274-5
November	Anastasius preaches against *Theotokos*.	
Christmas Day	Nestorius begins a course of sermons	131
	Protest of Eusebius (afterwards bishop of Dorylaeum)	338
429. Lady Day	Proclus' sermon, replied to by Nestorius.	
Eastertide	Nestorius preaches three sermons in reply to Proclus.	
	Cyril sends his encyclical *Ad Monachos Aegypti*.	
	Photius replies to it.	
	Cyril stirs up accusers against Nestorius.	
	Caelestine of Rome makes inquiries.	
	Letters from Nestorius reach Caelestine	132
June	Cyril *Ad Nestorium I*	103 ff.
	Nestorius replies peacefully; his diocese is disturbed and he is not ready for war.	
	Nestorius is approached by the Pelagian exiles, Julian and Caelestius.	
	Basil and his monks petition Theodosius II against Nestorius, and ask for an Oecumenical Council	102
430.	Cyril *Ad Nestorium II* and *Ad Clericos Constantinopolitanos*	101 ff., 143-4, 149 ff., 218, 226, 243, 263
Lent	Nestorius replies to Cyril, this time more pugnaciously	141-2, 162, 257
	Cyril *De Recta Fide*, (1) *Ad Theodosium*, (2) *Ad Arcadiam et Marinam*, (3) *Ad Pulcheriam et Eudoxiam*.	
April	Cyril *Ad Caelestinum*, sent by Poseidonius, with other documents enclosed	131-2
	Cyril *Ad Acacium* (of Beroea)—a fruitless effort to win over 'the East'.	
August	Nestorius is condemned at a Council at Rome. Caelestine writes to Cyril instructing him to carry out the sentence, and to Nestorius bidding him to submit and to renounce his 'novel doctrines' on pain of excommunication.	

---

[1] This summary is compiled from B. J. Kidd; *A History of the Church to A.D. 461* (Oxford University Press, 1922), vol. iii, chs. xi-xvi.

xviii INTRODUCTION

Date.	Events.	Refs. in *The Bazaar*. PAGES
430. August	Cyril writes to John of Antioch and Juvenal of Jerusalem.	
	John writes to Nestorius begging him to submit and accept the term *Theotokos*.	
November	Nestorius *Ad Caelestinum III*.	
	Theodosius II and Valentinian III summon a General Council to meet at Ephesus at Pentecost 431.	
	A Council held at Alexandria.	
	Cyril *Ad Nestorium III* (Synodical Letter), with the XII Anathematisms appended	268-9, 287-93, 325
December 7	Nestorius receives Cyril's 'synodical' letter and Caelestine's sentence of excommunication, which cannot be put into force owing to the Imperial Letter summoning the Council of Ephesus.	
Dec. 13 & 14	Nestorius preaches two sermons (xiii and xiv) and sends them to Cyril with counter anathematisms. He also replies to John of Antioch, and with the aid of Cyril's anathematisms wins him over.	
430-1.	Cassian *De incarnatione Domini contra Nestorianos*, written at the invitation of Caelestine.	
431.	Marius Mercator *Nestorii blasphemiarum capitula*, based on Nestorius' December sermons.	
	John of Antioch enlists Andrew of Samosata and Theodoret of Cyrus on the side of Nestorius.	
	Cyril *Apologia contra Orientales*, in reply to Andrew, and *Apologia contra Theodoretum pro XII capitibus*, and *Adversus Nestorii blasphemias libri V*.	
	Cyril writes to Caelestine asking what is to be done if Nestorius recants.	
431. May 7	Caelestine replies that 'God willeth not the death of a sinner', and Cyril is to do what he can to win Nestorius back.	
June 7	Whitsunday.	
	By 12th June there are assembled at Ephesus:	
	(1) Nestorius with ten bishops.	
	(2) Counts Irenaeus and Candidianus, the latter	

History of the Controversy

Date.	Events.	Refs. in *The Bazaar*. PAGES
431. June 12	representing the Emperor, who had given him a letter of instructions.	
	(3) Cyril with fifty bishops.	
	(4) Juvenal of Jerusalem with the bishops of Palestine.	
	(5) Flavian of Philippi with the bishops of Macedonia.	
	(6) Besulas, a deacon, representing the African Church.	
	Memnon closes the churches of Ephesus to the Nestorians	267, 269
	Conversations between Nestorius and (*a*) Acacius of Melitene, (*b*) Theodotus of Ancyra	136–141
June 21	Cyril receives a letter from John of Antioch saying that he hopes to arrive in five or six days. Alexander of Apamea and Alexander of Hierapolis bring a message from him, that the Council should not wait for him if he is delayed on his journey.	
	Nestorius and Candidianus wish to wait for John	106–108, 269
	But Cyril and Memnon, with the support of their followers and the populace of Ephesus, have Nestorius summoned, and proceed without delay	134, 312
June 22	Candidianus protests, reads his Imperial instructions, utters his *contestatio*, and on being overruled withdraws	106, 108–16
	The Gospels are placed on the throne, as representing the presence of Christ	119–21
	Cyril presides, claiming to do so in virtue of Caelestine's letter of August 430; but the force of his claim is doubtful since the imperial summons to a General Council had superseded Caelestine's commission to Cyril to deal with Nestorius, and Caelestine had himself sent legates to the Council.	
June 22	*Session I.* Nestorius refuses to attend. The following are read:	
	(1) The Creed of Nicaea	141
	(2) Cyril *Ad Nest. II*—received with acclamation	143-4, 149 ff.

Date.	Events.	Refs. in *The Bazaar*. PAGES
431. June 22	(3) Nestorius *Ad Cyrillum II*—rejected with anathemas	141 ff., 162
	(4) Caelestine's Letter to Nestorius of August 430.	
	(5) Cyril *Ad Nest. III* with the Anathematisms —received in silence	151, 268, 269
	(6) Testimonies of various bishops concerning conversations with Nestorius	136–41
	(7) Passages from certain Fathers, including Athanasius, Theophilus, Ambrose, Gregory Nazianzen, and Gregory of Nyssa	191–2, 223–265
	(8) Extracts from the writings of Nestorius	188–263
	(9) The letter of Capreolus, Primate of Africa. Nestorius is deposed and excommunicated	265
	Cyril, Nestorius, and Candidianus all write to Emperor	268
June 26	Arrival of John of Antioch and the Easterns	267
	John immediately holds a Council. Forty-three bishops are present, and Candidianus. They depose Cyril and Memnon, and excommunicate all their adherents who will not repudiate Cyril's XII Anathematisms	267–9, 286–7
	Candidianus sends reports to the Emperor	117, 124
June 29	An Imperial Rescript arrives in which Cyril is rebuked for his haste, and the bishops are commanded to await the arrival of an Imperial Commissioner in Ephesus	117–18, 128
July 10	Caelestine's Legates arrive—the bishops Arcadius and Projectus and the priest Philip	126
	In accordance with Caelestine's instructions they give their support to Cyril.	
	Session II. Cyril presides. Caelestine's Letter to the Synod, written on 8th May, is read.	
July 11	*Session III.* The minutes of Session I are read. Philip announces Caelestine's assent to the sentence passed on Nestorius. Letters are sent to the Emperor and to the Church of Constantinople.	
July 16	*Session IV.* John of Antioch and his supporters are summoned, but refuse to attend.	
July 17	*Session V.* John sends a message refusing to have anything more to do with the Cyrillians.	

History of the Controversy

Date.	Events.	Refs. in *The Bazaar*. PAGES
431. July 17	They excommunicate him and his adherents, and send reports to the Emperor and to Caelestine.	
	Events in Constantinople in July.	
	The Cyrillians cannot get their messages through to the Emperor owing to the activities of Candidianus and Nestorian agents. At last a beggar carries in a cane a letter from Cyril to the bishops and monks at Constantinople. With the aid of the abbot Dalmatius they enlist Theodosius' sympathies for Cyril	272–8
	Theodosius then gives hearing to Cyril's envoys, Theopemptus and Daniel.	
	Nestorius' letters, and his friend, Count Irenaeus, put the case for the other side, and Theodosius orders Cyril's deposition.	
	The arrival of John, Cyril's chaplain and physician, turns the scale. Theodosius decides to treat Cyril, Memnon, and Nestorius as all deposed, and to send a new commissioner to Ephesus	279
July 21 & 31	*Sessions VI and VII* are not directly concerned with the Nestorian controversy.	
August	Count John, the imperial commissioner, arrives at Ephesus	279, 280
	He announces the deposition of Nestorius, Cyril, and Memnon, puts them all under arrest, and reports the fact to the Emperor.	
	The Orientals write to the Emperor, to Antioch, and to Acacius of Beroea.	
	The Cyrillians send two professedly Synodical letters to the Emperor. Count John tries to persuade them to confer with the Orientals. They will not, but the Orientals draw up as a basis of reconciliation, and send to the Emperor, a letter including the formulary which is later known as the *Formulary of Reunion*. The Cyrillians ask to be allowed either to lay their case before the Emperor at Constantinople, or to go home. Their appeals stir up again the clergy of Constantinople and Dalmatius.	

Introduction

Date.	Events.	Refs. in *The Bazaar.* PAGES
431. August	Cyril writes from prison his *Explicatio XII Capitum.*	
September 11	Theodosius receives at Chalcedon eight delegates from each side	284, 287–8
	No agreement is reached, and Theodosius, despairing of a solution, dissolves the Council, sending Nestorius back to his monastery at Antioch, and ordering the consecration of a new bishop of Constantinople (Maximian)	281, 285
	The rival parties go home, the Orientals accusing Cyril of having won his case by bribery	279–82, 286
October 30	Cyril arrives in triumph at Alexandria	281
	Maximian deposes Nestorian bishops; the Orientals renew their condemnation of Cyril, and treat Nestorius as unjustly deposed.	
432. January 27	Caelestine dies, and is succeeded by Sixtus III	375
	Rabbula of Edessa and Andrew of Samosata show signs of going over to the Cyrillian side. Cyril writes to Maximian, and sends the Emperor his *Apologeticus ad Theodosium*, which placates him.	
April	The Emperor suggests as a basis of reconciliation that the Orientals should give up Nestorius and Cyril his XII Anathematisms. He sends letters to this effect to John of Antioch, Acacius of Beroea, and St. Simeon Stylites. The letters and the negotiations are entrusted to the notary Aristolaus	289, 329
	John, Acacius, Alexander of Hierapolis, Andrew of Samosata and Theodoret of Cyrus hold a Synod at Antioch to consider Aristolaus' proposals. They demand the dropping of Cyril's Anathematisms, but are willing to make peace on the basis of the Nicene Creed as explained by Athanasius. These proposals are embodied in a letter from Acacius to Cyril, and taken to Alexandria by Aristolaus. No mention is made of abandoning Nestorius. Cyril replies that if the Orientals will accept the	

History of the Controversy

Date.	Events.	Refs. in *The Bazaar*. PAGES
432. April	deposition of Nestorius there need be no trouble about the Anathematisms	286
	John and Acacius wish to agree on this basis	290–1
	Theodoret agrees on the doctrinal question, but dislikes the abandoning of Nestorius. Andrew wavers and Alexander stands out.	
Autumn	John and Acacius determine to go forward, ignoring the opposition of Alexander. They send Paul of Emesa as their envoy to Alexandria	318
	Meanwhile Cyril has been working hard to win over the Court at Constantinople. The clergy and monks of Constantinople, including Maximian, Dalmatius, and Eutyches, have approached the Empress Pulcheria, while Cyril has heavily bribed her maids of honour, important eunuchs, and the Grand Chamberlain Chrysoretes.	
Winter	Paul of Emesa arrives at Alexandria, bringing (i) The Propositions of the Synod at Antioch, (ii) The Formulary of Reunion, and (iii) A Letter of Introduction from John to Cyril, cordial but containing no mention of the deposition of Nestorius. When pressed, Paul agrees to accept that deposition together with the deposition by Maximian of four Nestorianizing bishops.	
December 18	Paul is received into communion at Alexandria.	
Christmas Day	Paul is admitted to preach in Alexandria as an orthodox bishop.	
433	Aristolaus and Paul return to Antioch, and persuade John to agree	290–1
	John announces his decision in a Circular Letter to Sixtus III of Rome, Maximian, and Cyril, and also sends two private letters to Cyril. Cyril replies with a letter (Ep. xxxix) afterwards given oecumenical authority at Chalcedon. The question of the XII Anathematisms is left unmentioned by both sides	291–2
	Synod of Zeugma. Theodoret, Andrew, and John of Germanicia acknowledge the ortho-	

xxiv   INTRODUCTION

                                              Refs. in *The*
Date.   Events.   *Bazaar*.
                                                  PAGES

433.   doxy of Cyril, but refuse to accept the de-
             position of Nestorius.
             Alexander and some Cilician bishops renounce
             both Alexandria and Antioch.

434.   Death of Maximian. Proclus becomes bishop
             of Constantinople.
             An Imperial Rescript orders the bishops of 'The
             East' to abandon their resistance to John
             and Cyril. Theodoret, Andrew, and others
             obey   292-3, 328-30, 338

435.   *The Tome of Proclus* is approved by both Cyril
             and John.

  April   Alexander and seventeen other irreconcileables
             are deposed and banished to the Egyptian
             mines.
             Some Cyrillians begin to think that Cyril has
             compromised the faith by admitting 'two
             natures'. Acacius of Melitene writes to Cyril
             of the general uneasiness, and receives letters
             composed to reassure him 180, 293-318, 323, 325, 329

  August   *Edict of Theodosius* proscribing the writings of
             Nestorius and meetings of his followers   374
             Aristolaus is charged to carry it out.

436.   Nestorius is banished to Arabia, but actually
             sent to Upper Egypt. Count Irenaeus is also
             sent into exile   117
             Nestorianism begins to spread in the East out-
             side the Empire, e. g. in Persia.

437.   John of Antioch writes to Proclus to say that all
             have now accepted the deposition of Nes-
             torius, and that peace is restored.

438.   Proclus has the relics of Chrysostom restored to
             Constantinople.

439.   The Empress Eudocia returns from her pilgrim-
             age to Palestine.

440.   John of Antioch dies, and is succeeded by his
             nephew Domnus.
             Sixtus III of Rome dies, and is succeeded by
             Leo.
             The abbot Dalmatius dies, and is succeeded by
             Eutyches.

441.   Eutyches' godson, the eunuch Chrysaphius,

Date.	Events.	Refs. in *The Bazaar*. PAGES
441.	gains an ascendancy over Theodosius, and Pulcheria's influence declines	342
444.	Cyril dies, and is succeeded by Dioscorus. The Empress Eudocia is suspected of unfaithfulness and banished	379
446.	Proclus dies, and is succeeded by Flavian, who neglects to placate Chrysaphius with 'golden eulogies'	336
447.	Count Irenaeus is recalled from banishment and consecrated bishop of Tyre. Theodoret *Eranistes seu Polymorphus*.	
448. February	An Imperial Rescript proscribes the works of Porphyry and Nestorius, and orders the deposition of Irenaeus. Dioscorus complains both to Theodoret and to Domnus of the former's unorthodoxy. Theodoret replies and protests to Flavian and others, but Theodosius orders him to be confined within his own diocese.	
May	Eutyches writes to Leo to say that Nestorianism is on the increase.	
June	Leo replies cautiously, asking for more detailed information.	
September	Photius is consecrated bishop of Tyre in place of Irenaeus.	
November	*Synod of Constantinople*. Eusebius of Dorylaeum accuses Eutyches before Flavian	340
	Eutyches is summoned, but does not appear till Session VIII, when after being examined he is condemned. He immediately writes in protest to Leo, and Chrysaphius procures a letter from Theodosius to Leo on his behalf	340
	Eutyches also writes to Peter Chrysologus, archbishop of Ravenna.	
	Flavian writes to Leo, giving his account of the trial, and asking the West to recognize Eutyches' condemnation.	
449.	Leo, receiving first the letters of Eutyches and Theodosius, writes to Theodosius and Flavian complaining that he has had no report from the latter, and asking for one.	
	Eutyches invites Dioscorus to take his part Chrysaphius promises his aid, and that of	340

INTRODUCTION

Date.	Events.	Refs. in *The Bazaar*. PAGES
449.	Eudocia. Dioscorus admits Eutyches to communion, and asks the Emperor for a General Council.	
March	Theodosius summons a General Council to meet at Ephesus in August	342
April	Eutyches persuades Theodosius to have the Minutes of the Synod of Constantinople verified, and to order Flavian to produce a written statement of his faith	343
	The Minutes are verified, and Flavian produces his statement.	
	The Eutychians procure the condemnation of Ibas of Edessa.	
May	Leo acknowledges the receipt of Flavian's letter.	
	Theodosius summons the abbot Barsumas to represent the abbots of the East at Ephesus, and tells Dioscorus that Barsumas is to be allowed to sit and vote.	
	Dioscorus is appointed to preside, Counts Elphidius and Eulogius to keep order	345
	Theodosius' summons to the Council reaches Rome. Leo promises Flavian his support.	
June	Leo appoints Julius, bishop of Puteoli, the presbyter Renatus, the deacon Hilary, and the notary Dulcitius to represent him at Ephesus	345
	They take with them letters to Pulcheria, the archimandrites of Constantinople, the Council, and Julian of Cos, and *The Tome* for Flavian.	
August	*The Latrocinium.*	
	The Council meets, charged by Theodosius to put an end to Nestorianism and the trouble stirred up by Flavian.	
	Dioscorus presides. Of Leo's legates, Renatus has died and the others, since they sit apart from one another and do not understand Greek, have little influence	345, 351
	Session I. Dioscorus refuses to allow bishops who had taken part in the deposition of Eutyches at Constantinople to take part in this Council	352
	He has the letters of Theodosius read, but prevents the reading of Leo's *Tome*	345–6
	The Minutes of the Council of Constantinople are read	353

Date.	Events.	Refs. in *The Bazaar*. PAGES
449. August	Eusebius of Dorylaeum is refused a hearing	352
	Eutyches and his followers are absolved and restored to their lost positions. Flavian and Eusebius are condemned, a protest being met by Dioscorus calling in the Counts and the soldiery, and obtaining the verdict by military compulsion	347, 354–5, 358–61, 369
	Dioscorus sends in his report to Theodosius.	
	Session II, a fortnight later. Flavian has died from the violence of Barsumas and his monks	343, 362, 376
	Eusebius, Domnus, and Leo's legates are not present.	
	Ibas, Irenaeus, Theodoret, and Domnus are all deposed	348–9
	Cyril's XII Anathematisms are solemnly ratified.	
September	While a Synod is sitting on other matters in Rome, letters are received from Theodoret and Eusebius protesting against the Ephesian decisions, and Hilary brings his account of the Council.	
October	In the name of the Roman Synod, Leo writes to Theodosius and Pulcheria protesting against the proceedings at Ephesus. He also writes to various Eastern bishops, bidding them stand fast.	
	The Eutychians Anatolius and Maximus hold the sees of Constantinople and Antioch.	
450. February	The Western Court visits Rome, and Leo persuades Valentinian III, his mother, Galla Placidia, and his wife, Eudoxia, to write to their Eastern kinsfolk, but it is all in vain. Theodosius confirms all that was done at Ephesus, and informs the West that all is well in the East.	
July	Leo offers to recognize Anatolius if he will accept Cyril *Ad Nest. II* and his own *Tome*. There is no response.	
	Theodosius dies from a fall from his horse	369
	He is succeeded by his sister, Pulcheria, who puts Chrysaphius to death and marries the senator Marcian.	

xxviii   INTRODUCTION

		Refs. in *The Bazaar.*
Date.	Events.	PAGES

450. July   Eutyches is put under restraint, and Flavian's body buried with honour in Constantinople.

Theodoret and others are recalled from exile, and many of the bishops who supported Dioscorus at Ephesus explain that they did so under compulsion.

November
to June 451   Correspondence between Pulcheria, Marcian, Anatolius, and Leo. Leo says the trouble is due to Dioscorus and Juvenal of Jerusalem, and can easily be settled without a Council, which would be difficult to arrange owing to the invasion of the Huns. Nevertheless, Pulcheria and Marcian summon a Council to meet at Nicaea in September.

Leo appoints legates. Bishops assemble at Nicaea.

Eutyches excommunicates Leo.

Marcian cannot go so far as Nicaea for fear of Huns in Illyricum, and orders the bishops to move to Chalcedon.

Strong measures are taken to exclude monks and laymen, and to keep order.

451. October 8   *Session I.* Dioscorus is treated as defendant and accused by Eusebius of Dorylaeum. Theodoret is admitted as a bishop.

The Minutes of the *Latrocinium* and of the Synod of Constantinople are read.

Flavian's memory is vindicated, Dioscorus and his supporters are deposed, and the assembly bursts into singing the *Trisagion*—the first occasion on which it is known to have been used   Cp. 365 ff.

October 10   *Session II*—mainly occupied with the discussion of Leo's *Tome.*

October 13   *Session III.* Dioscorus is formally deprived of his episcopal dignity   Cp. 375

October 17   *Session IV.* The Council accepts 'The Rule of Faith as contained in the Creed of Nicaea, confirmed by the Council of Constantinople, expounded at Ephesus under Cyril, and set forth in the Letter of Pope Leo when he

Date.	Events.	Refs. in *The Bazaar*. PAGES
451. October 17	condemned the heresy of Nestorius and Eutyches'.	
October 22	*Session V. The Definition of Chalcedon*, under Roman and Imperial pressure, is amended so as definitely to exclude Eutychianism, and as adopted includes the following words: 'Following therefore the holy Fathers, we all teach, with one accord, one and the same Son, our Lord Jesus Christ, ... who for us men and for our salvation, according to the manhood, was born of the Virgin Mary the God-bearer,[1] one and the same Christ, Son, Lord—only-begotten, confessed in two natures, without confusion, without change, without division or separation. The difference of the natures is in no way denied by reason of their union; on the other hand the peculiarity of each nature is preserved, and both concur in one *Prosopon* and one *Hypostasis*.'	
October 25	*Session VI.* Marcian and Pulcheria attend in state. The Definition receives civil sanction, and is promulgated.	

v. THE ARGUMENT OF *THE BAZAAR*.

Nestorius' *apologia* contains two lines of defence, historical and doctrinal. Although the one shades off into the other, as the doctrinal issues are called to his mind by the memory of the wrongs he has suffered, and *vice versa*, yet on the whole three sections of *The Bazaar* may be distinguished as historical sections[2] in contrast to the remainder of the book which is mainly occupied with theological discussion.

The references to the text in the Historical Summary above provide almost all the introduction needed for Nestorius' historical sections. His argument is twofold. He claims to show, first, that his own condemnation at Ephesus was unjust, and secondly, that the vindication of Flavian, who had suffered from the same causes and for the same faith as

---

[1] τῆς θεοτόκου.   [2] pp. 96–142, 265–93, 329–80.

himself, was the vindication of all that he had stood for. To this end he gives a detailed account of the two Ephesian Councils of 431 and 449, showing how at the first Cyril by violence and bribery won imperial and episcopal assent to a verdict which was no genuine verdict of a council constitutionally assembled, while at the second Flavian had suffered in similar fashion at the hands of Dioscorus. But there was this difference. The injustice done to Flavian had been recognized by the Church and redressed, while that done to himself had not. So he claims that he never had a fair hearing, but was condemned untried for defending the faith which was ultimately accepted by the Church.[1]

But though he is not lacking in a lively sense of the wrongs he has suffered, Nestorius realizes that the triumph of the truth is of more importance than his own fate. Indeed, in a notable passage he asserts his determination not to press his claim to have been vindicated in the vindication of Flavian lest the odium of his name should delay the complete victory of the true faith.[2] It is that victory for which he chiefly cares, and hence the main bulk of *The Bazaar* is occupied with the doctrinal discussion of the Christian faith in the Incarnation.

In Book I, Part I, Nestorius sets forth his views in contrast to those which he holds to be erroneous. The section, which is divided into ninety-three numbered sub-sections, to which titles have been added by the Syriac translator, is cast in the form of a dialogue with one Sophronius. Here Nestorius sets forth as it were the theme of his thesis, and the remaining doctrinal discussions are little more than variations on it. He begins by a brief review of errors. The heathen, the Jews, the Manichaeans, the followers of Paul of Samosata, of Photinus, and of Arius are described, and their doctrines criticized. The theories which deny either the true godhead or the true manhood of Christ, or which involve the changing of one into the other, or the production of a third nature by the combination of divine nature with human, are pilloried. In the fifty-fourth sub-section,[3] in passing over to the positive assertion of his own christological beliefs, he directly denies that he teaches

---

[1] See pp. 176, 374.   [2] P. 378, cp. p. 370.   [3] P. 47.

The Argument of 'The Bazaar' xxxi

that there were 'Two Sons' in Christ, and the remaining sub-sections are mainly occupied with a statement of his own position, though the last five are again devoted to criticisms of other views already mentioned. Similar criticisms compose the short Part II of Book I. Having thus laid down his doctrinal position, in Part III Nestorius begins his historical review of the controversy between himself and Cyril. The remaining doctrinal discussions, lengthy as they are, do not carry us farther. They are concerned with contrasting his own views with those of Cyril and his followers, and repeat over and over again two points. On the one hand his own doctrines are shown to be consistent with the Scriptures,[1] the faith of Nicaea,[2] and the writings of accepted Fathers of the Church;[3] on the other hand the teaching of Cyril is exhibited as self-contradictory[4] and, on the points at issue between Cyril and himself, as having affinities not with orthodoxy[5] but with the heretics described in the opening section of the book.[6] The place of that opening section in the plan of the book can therefore clearly be seen. In it Nestorius describes the general doctrinal issues in the field of Christology, and sets the stage for the discussion of the particular points of the controversy between himself and Cyril.

What precisely did Nestorius teach? This is the question over which controversy has raged since the discovery of *The Bazaar*. It is not the object of the present volume to enter upon the discussion of this problem, but to provide English-speaking theologians with the necessary material to study it for themselves.[7] The following summary of undisputed facts may, however, be given without entrenching upon the questionable ground. It will be well first to state what Nestorius denies, and what he asserts.

[1] Pp. 46–55, 64–70, 164–7, 188, 192–203, 207, 228–30, 256–9.
[2] Pp. 143–6, 168–71, 181–2, 263–5.
[3] Pp. 168, 191–203, 214–17, 220–2, 223–5, 261–3, 316.
[4] Pp. 150–6, 161, 169, 170, 303, 316–17, 322–3.
[5] Pp. 142–3, 146–50, 173–5.
[6] Pp. 129, 162, 176–81, 210–11, 240–1.
[7] A contribution to the discussion by one of the two editors is reprinted as Appendix IV, and it has not been possible entirely to keep his views out of the notes on the text, though this has been done as far as could be.

(i) He denies that the unity of Christ is a 'natural composition' in which two elements are combined by the will of some external 'creator'.[1]

(ii) He denies that the Incarnation was effected by changing godhead into manhood or *vice versa*, or by forming a *tertium quid* from those two *ousiai*.[2]

(iii) He denies that God was in Christ in the same way as in the saints.[3]

(iv) He denies that either the godhead or the manhood of Christ are 'fictitious' or 'phantasmal', and not real.[4]

(v) He denies that the Incarnation involved any change in the godhead, or any suffering on the part of the Divine Logos who, as divine, is by nature impassible.[5]

(vi) He denies that the union of two natures in one Christ involves any duality of sonship.[6]

(vii) He asserts that the union is a voluntary union of godhead and manhood.[7]

(viii) He asserts that the principle of union is to be found in the *prosôpa* of the godhead and the manhood; these two *prosôpa* coalesced in one *prosôpon* of Christ incarnate.[8]

(ix) He asserts that this view alone provides for a real Incarnation, makes possible faith in a real atonement,[9] and provides a *rationale* of the sacramentalism of the Church.[10]

It is clear that the *crux* of the question is to be found in the eighth of these points, and that the difficulty arises from the difficulty of determining the sense in which Nestorius used the word *prosôpon*. His own theory can be stated almost in a dozen words. It is this: Christ is the union of the eternal Logos and the Son of Mary, the principle of the union being

---

[1] Pp. 9, 36–43, 84–6, 161, 179, 294, 300–1, 303–4, 314.
[2] Pp. 14–18, 24–8, 33–7, 80, 182.   [3] P. 52.
[4] Pp. 15, 80, 172–3, 182, 195, 208.
[5] Pp. 39–41, 92, 93, 178–9, 181, 184, 210–12.
[6] Pp. 47–50, 146, 160, 189–91, 196, 209–10, 215, 225, 227, 237–8, 295–302, 314, 317.
[7] Pp. 37, 179, 181, 182.
[8] Pp. 23, 53–62, 81, 89, 156–9, 163–4, 172, 182, 207, 218–19, 227, 231–3, 245–8, 260–1.
[9] Pp. 62–76, 205, 212–14, 253.   [10] Pp. 32, 55, 254–6.

that the πρόσωπον of each has been taken by the other, so that there is one πρόσωπον of the two in the union. Did one know precisely what Nestorius meant by the word πρόσωπον, one would know precisely how he thought of the Incarnation, and would be able to decide whether the logical implications of his teaching are those of Nestorianism or of orthodoxy. It is certain that he himself did not wish to teach what is known as 'Nestorianism'. His denunciations of Paul of Samosata and his followers show that he had no sympathy with those who think of the Incarnation on adoptionist lines, and when accused of 'Nestorianism', as on pages 19 and 47, he indignantly repudiates any such views. The intention of his doctrine is accurately summed up in the heading inserted by the Syriac translator to the fifty-fourth section of the first part of *The Bazaar*—'Concerning this: that God the Word became incarnate and there were not two sons but one by a union.'[1]

Nestorius, then, accepted as a matter of religious belief the faith of the Church in a Christ who was truly God and truly man and truly one, and through reflection on this he produced a theological theory which he thought adequately related this belief to the knowledge of the universe gained by metaphysical investigation. The positive teaching of *The Bazaar of Heracleides* is simply an elaboration of this theory of a *prosôpic* union. With wearisome iteration it is put forward again and again, and is shown to be satisfactory when tested by reference to the teaching of Scripture, the doctrine of the Fathers, the needs of religion, and the demands of the intellect.[2] In contrast to this the 'hypostatic union' of Cyril is shown to be unscriptural, unorthodox, destructive of true religion, and unintelligible—unscriptural because it ignores the scriptural distinction between the use of the words 'Logos' and 'Christ';[3] unorthodox since it involves if not Arianism, then docetism or Apollinarianism;[4] destructive of true religion in that it abolishes the work of Christ as High Priest of the human race, undermines the doctrine of the Eucharist, and

[1] P. 47.
[2] *E.g.*, pp. 188 sq., 263, 33 and 213, 308-10.
[3] *E.g.*, pp. 188 sq.
[4] *E.g.*, pp. 150, 304.

empties the Atonement of its meaning;[1] and unintelligible to such an extent that sometimes one is simply baffled by the contradictions in his teaching,[2] and sometimes forced to conclude that he has confused the essential distinction between godhead and manhood, thus undermining the true humanity of Christ and dishonouring his divinity.[3]

It seems possible that in this last point lies the solution of the vexed problem of what was at issue doctrinally between Cyril and Nestorius. Perhaps the most difficult task for Christian philosophy is the thinking out of its doctrine of creation, in which it is essential that man be conceived both as owing his existence to God and 'made of nothing' other than God, and yet also as in a real sense distinct from and other than God. If sometimes we are tempted to abandon the quest as hopeless, it is well to remember that even if we give up our Christianity we do not thereby remove our difficulty. The relation of the temporal to the eternal is no less difficult a problem for the secular philosopher than for the religious. Now in the fifth century the implications of the doctrine of creation do not seem to have been thought out. In the struggle with Arianism the Church had been forced, it seems for the first time, openly to face the question whether or no God could create directly and not only through some intermediate being, and the assertion that the Logos 'through whom all things were made' is 'of one substance with the Father' denies the impossibility of direct creation by God Himself. Before the implications of this assertion had time to be fully assimilated, the Church was stirred by the Christological controversies. In these all parties seem to have assumed a conception of the relations between godhead and manhood which made impossible any union of the two in Christ such as the Christian religion demanded. It was not noticed that it would also have made impossible any such direct creation by God as the Fathers at Nicaea had asserted, and was, in fact, a conception belonging to certain strains of ante-Nicene thought which ought to have been abandoned

---

[1] *E.g.*, pp. 248 sq., 212. [2] *E.g.*, pp. 257, 297, 303.
[3] *E.g.*, pp. 232, 238–40, 250, 294.

through being found to require an Arian rather than an Athanasian Logos. But Apollinarius provoked reply too soon.

It is the heretics, Apollinarius, Nestorius, and Eutyches, who are the logically consistent upholders of this outworn conception of the relation between godhead and manhood. Cyril's teaching, no doubt without his realizing the fact, *was* inconsistent, for he had not consciously abandoned this ante-Nicene position, with the result that his positive teaching on the Incarnation, while consistent with the Nicene doctrine of Creation, demanded a revision of his conception of godhead and manhood, a fact which he does not seem to have realized. But, as has happened so often in the history of thought, the inconsistency of a thinker great enough to recognize truth at the cost of his system won for his thought a place in posterity far above that of the barren coherence of his rival.

Nestorius has been called a confused thinker, but careful study of *The Bazaar of Heracleides* makes it clear that, whatever he was, he was certainly not that. His few points are repeated again and again with monotonous consistency. His trouble was rather that that confusion in the apparent nature of things which is the challenge to thought was too many-sided for so narrow and precise a thinker as he. *The Bazaar* may be long, and full of needless repetition, but it never contradicts itself, and were it not for two facts might well be studied in an abbreviated edition. Only, first, when a man has been for centuries condemned unheard, it is hardly fair to enforce a closure on the time allotted to him for his defence; and, secondly, when there is difficulty in determining precisely what he is trying to say, it is possible that in the course of often repeating an argument some little variation of detail may give a clue to the meaning of the whole.

*The Book
which is called*
THE BAZAAR OF HERACLEIDES
*of Damascus
which was composed
by*
MY LORD NESTORIUS

TRANSLATOR'S PREFACE [1]

[2] . . . .
. . . apostolic [3] he was known and famous in the labours of . . . . [4] that your enthusiasm . . . . and in your fulness . . . . of earthly kings. So you undertook the labour of a long voyage from the East to the West to give light to the souls which were plunged in the darkness of the Egyptian error and intent [5] on the smoke of the blasphemy of Apollinarius; men, however, loved the darkness more than the light, since the eyes of their minds [were dimmed] by personal prejudice [6] . . . . for your pride . . . . only the darkness . . . . comprehended it; but, on the contrary, although . . . . they became old. They were not convinced; they were convicted of error and exposed. In this firm confidence in the might of your prayers mine Insignificance draws nigh to translate this book from Greek into Syriac; yet at least, the hope of the help of the living God being laid upon my tongue and confirmed in my thoughts, I therefore draw nigh to compose these eight chapters wherein the purpose of the book is made clear.

1. *Concerning the aim of the book.* The aim, therefore, which has been proposed by the writer for this writing is this: that, because many, thoughtlessly [led astray] by the multitude of men and by the desire of possessions, have fallen without examination into the slough of prejudice through hatred and through attachment to persons,[7] from which . . . . not . . . .[8] they have been condemned to that woe which was written by the prophet: *Woe unto them that call evil good,*[9] My lord the blessed Nestorius / [set himself] to write this book to be a remedy to heal souls labouring

---

[1] *Viz.* the Syriac Translator: this title is added by Bedjan.
[2] These lines are only fragmentarily preserved.
[3] Nau conjectures: [*dans sa carrière*] *apostolique.*
[4] Nau conjectures: *dans les travaux de l'esprit*; see crit. n., p. 398.
[5] See crit. n., p. 398.
[6] Literally: 'by the precedence of the *parṣôphâ* (= πρόσωπον)'.
[7] Syr. *parṣôphâ*.   [8] There is a lacuna here in the text.   [9] Isa. v. 20 (P.).

B 2

at this stumbling-block and plunged in the depth of impiety. For great, to speak as in truth, was the schism which the devil introduced into the Christian body of the holy Church, *such as, if [it were] possible, to deceive even the elect*;[1] and for this reason this remedy has necessarily been required [to be] a corrective and a healing of the sickness of their minds. This is the aim of the book.

2. *Concerning the utility thereof.* I suppose that, before [the beginning of] the text, the spiritual utility of [2] this book has been revealed to the reader from [its] aim. According to the punishment that comes upon the doers of injury who make the innocent guilty and the guilty innocent, it gives indeed light to the eyes of the souls by teaching concerning that Christian dispensation which is in truth the more excellent theory [3] concerning the divinity and the humanity. For through this we are both far removed from blasphemy about the divine nature and about the dispensation, and we are brought nigh unto knowledge through his manifold mercies. But, that our discourse may not be prolonged concerning the great assistance which we gain from this book, which succours us [4] . . . . let us state in a few words the proof that he clears away the thorns . . . . and causes the seed to sprout in [place of] them.

3. . . . . Much has been written concerning the manner of the union, but not even one of them [that have written about it] in this research makes it clear and establishes it in all truth; for they have delighted to make many distinctions, and there are others who have ventured to fuse [the natures] without examination. But this blessed [Nestorius] has undaunted delivered to us the knowledge thereof which is right.

4. *The cause of its title.* It is called indeed the Bazaar [5] of Heracleides, for this is evident that it is the bazaar of spiritual knowledge; but it is not evident who Heracleides [was]. This is apposite to the illumination thereof, O reader; namely, Heracleides was a man honoured for his conduct and

---

[1] Cp. Matt. xxiv. 24, Mk. xiii. 22.   [2] Literally: 'in'.
[3] Syr. tē'ōryā = Gk. θεωρία.   [4] Literally: 'which gives us a hand'.
[5] See n., p. xii.

esteemed for his knowledge, and he dwelled in the neighbourhood of Damascus. Now this man, in consequence of his superiority in these things, was famous even before [his] Majesty[1] for his truthfulness and the justice of his words; who, being superior to all the passions which remove [men] far from the truth, did everything without partiality. It seemed [therefore good] to the writer to entitle the book with the title of this man's name, lest on account of his own name, in that many abhorred it, they should not / be willing to read [it] and be converted to the truth—[a book] which he sets as a judge between him[self] and the impious Cyril, speaking and defending themselves. But the book, nevertheless, ...

5. [2]. . . . .
. . . .[3] as that of the dispensation and of the truth of the inquiry concerning the faith, and the fourth [kind of literature is that] of history; but this book is placed in the third class, that is of chapters concerning the faith, to be read after these two books which were made by the saint—and I mean *Theopaschites*[4] and *Tragoedia*, which were composed by him as a defence against those who blamed him for having wanted a council to be held.

6. *Into how many parts it is divided.* Now in the first place he composed one dissertation wherein he speaks of all the heresies against the Church and of all the sects that exist concerning the faith of the three hundred and eighteen,[5] arguing valiantly against those who are of greatest repute among them. And in the second part he assails Cyril, putting before [everything else] the inquiry touching the judges and the accusation of Cyril. And the third [contains] his own defence and the comparison of their letters; and with this he finishes the first book. But the second book he divides into two parts: the defence and the refutation of the blame for the things on account of which he was anathematized; and in the second

---

[1] Nau: *devant l'Empire (le pouvoir impérial).*
[2] Added by Bedjan.   [3] Several lines are here missing.
[4] Syr. *Tē'ōpasṭiqôs* by metathesis for Gk. Θεοπασχίτης (Payne-Smith, *Thes. Syr.* ii. 4367). For fragments from these lost works see Loofs, *Nestoriana*, pp. 203-211, and below, Appendix I.
[5] *I.e.* The Council of Nicaea, A. D. 325.

[part he recounts that which took place] from [the time] when he was anathematized until the end of his life.

7. *Concerning the literary form of the book.* The literary form of the book is . . . . and drawing inferences . . . .[1]

8. *Under what*[2] . . . .[1] Now for the most part it is theoretical, because it is teaching us the complete knowledge of the dispensation touching our Lord Christ. With these [words] we will therefore stop our address / and approach the body of the book, requiring of those who come by chance upon what has been written by us that they blame us not as fault-finders, if haply there be [defects] in the composition of our discourse, but [that] they display a ready will and correct what is deficient in us. But if he conceives the reverse about us, for us the prayers of those who labour not with this sickness are sufficient; while the former will prosper in their own affairs, knowing that we have made no innovations at all. The editor is blameless.

[Here follow the titles of §§ 1-93, which are omitted as they are repeated in italics in the text.]

Finished are the titles of the chapters which are [given] in the preceding dissertation. And unto Yah [be] glory! Amen.

---

[1] There is a lacuna here in the text.   [2] See crit. n., p. 398.

The beginning of the book, that is, the beginning of the Discourse of the Saint is from here.

THE BOOK OF
MY LORD NESTORIUS
PATRIARCH OF CONSTANTINOPLE
AND THE
CANON OF ORTHODOXY

BOOK I. PART I.[1]

/ *Preface.* Now in my opinion whoever is about to investigate the truth in all seriousness ought not to compose his discourse with preconceived ideas, but should bring forward and explain everything which is opposed to the truth. As those who have a knowledge of gold show the distinction between good gold and that which is poor by a comparison of the one with the other in the sight of those who wish to accept what is alloyed as though it were pure, and even in preference to the pure (for many choose evil instead of good and falsehood instead of truth, in that both are equal to them, and their readiness is the greater to dispute and to defeat one another [in argument] than to establish the truth); so, since different people confess different opinions about Christ and hold fast / only to the name, we ought to set out the fictions of each one of these heresies concerning Christ, in order that the true faith may be known by comparison with [these] heresies, and that we may not be shaken, falling into the one or the other like men who do not see.

1. *Wherefore the Heathen do not call Christ God* . . . .
The heathen indeed are not content to name Christ God because of the suffering of the body and the cross and the death, and they consider that the miracles were [accepted]

[1] Syr. 'Dissertation I'.

in error. And they are not differentiated in name, because there is indeed no distinction between them, in that all of them are heathen.

2. *Wherefore the Jews do not admit that he is Christ.*

But the Jews do not confess that he is Christ because of the Cross and the death, in that they look for the advent of[1] Christ in all great glory and dominion.

3. *Wherefore the Manichaeans do not admit that Christ is also man by nature, but only God.*

The Manichaeans also, and those who have sprung up from them and among them, declare that he is not man but only God/because of the miracles; but as touching his human [qualities], they place them in *schêma* and illusion and not in nature.

4. *Wherefore the Paulinians*[2] *and the Photinians profess that our Lord Christ himself is only a man and that he is not also God.*

But the Paulinians say that he is not God but only man because of the birth and death; but they attribute to him miracles as to any of the saints.

5. *Wherefore the Arians profess that Christ is neither God whole and without needs, nor yet a man, but half God and half man.*

The Arians confess that he is half God and half man of soulless body and of created divinity; deeming him inferior to men in saying that there is not a soul in him and again deeming him inferior also to God in saying that he is not uncreate and without needs. But because of the incarnation[3] and the birth of a woman and the death they consider that in his human [qualities] he became God, and they confuse his divine with his human [qualities], attributing his incarnation not to [his own] authority, but to an overruling command,[4] saying that the union with the flesh resulted in one

---

[1] Literally: 'expect to accept'.

[2] *Viz.* the followers of Paul of Samosata, Bishop of Antioch in A.D. 260, condemned at the Council of Antioch, A.D. 268 (or 269). Among them, the semi-Arian Photinus was condemned in 351. [3] Sc. ἐνανθρώπησις.

[4] This passage illustrates Nestorius' use of the phrase 'natural union', and

nature and not / according to the use of the *prosôpon* of the dispensation on our behalf, but even as the soul and the body are bound [together] in one nature and [the soul] suffers sensibly the sufferings of the body whether it will or not, even though it has not of itself [the means] to accept them in that it has not a body in which to suffer. So also they say that God has only one nature in the body, suffering of necessity, whether he will or not, the sufferings of that nature which he took upon himself, as though he was not of the nature of the Father impassible and without needs. And this they say in order that they may not show him alone to be endowed with authority and command, so that even the command which he accepted is a punishment, and from a punishment which lies in his nature there is no escape; and, while he wished it not, he suffered the sufferings of the body by virtue of the sensibility of the nature: he hungered and thirsted and grew weary and feared and fled and died, and he rose not by his nature but by the authority and the might of the Father; and in short they say that he naturally endured whatsoever appertained to the sensible nature which he assumed.[1]

6. *Which the sects are which agree with the Manichaeans.*

.... In the midst of these there sprang up heresies, some of the Manichaeans and others of them from the Paulinians.

7. *And which those are which agree with the Arians.*

---

explains his refusal to use that phrase to describe the relation of the two natures in Christ. A natural union comes into being where elements are combined into a whole by some external force. (This is the meaning of 'in virtue of a command'.) But the incarnation of the Word was not imposed on him from without; it was due to his own free choice, and his godhead remained a free co-operator throughout. See below, pp. 36–43, 84–86, 161, 179, 300–1, 303–4, 314.

[1] Nestorius' argument seems to be as follows: to speak of the Incarnation as a 'natural union' implies that union with the manhood was imposed on Christ's godhead from without, so that the godhead was imprisoned in the manhood like a criminal in gaol. This involves two impossible positions, (1) the denial of the freedom of Christ's godhead (hence the language about 'punishment'), and (2) the ascription of passibility to his godhead.

....¹ /8. *And wherein they are far removed from them, and in what again they adhere to them.*

They are far removed from them . . . .

9. *Wherefore he has not written [the names of] the chiefs of these sects but only their dogmas.*

But we wish to decline to [give] the names of their chiefs, so as not to prolong our discussion nor to be found to have omitted any point in the inquiry by first becoming entangled in [questions of] names.

10. *What the statements are of those who say that by nature God the Word became flesh without having taken a body.*

So they accused the Manichaeans of saying that the body of our Lord Christ was not truly a nature but a fiction and an illusion; but they tolerate miracles for the most part only of God, either as though it were impossible or even as though it were not decent that they should come about through the body.

*Sophronius.*² It appertains to the omnipotent and infinite nature to be able to do everything; by its will then all other things are limited while it is not limited by anything, and it, as God, can do what cannot be [done] by any one else. For it cannot be [created] by a nature or a cause greater than itself, by which it possesses [the property] of being / and of not being God. And on account of this they fear to confess that the flesh truly came into being, lest in saying this they assume that God is the flesh³; they say: How could this be, seeing that we confess that the body is God, for even that which is supposed to be flesh is the nature of God and is the same and nothing else?

11. *How water which becomes ice is in its nature ice,*

---

[1] Marginal Gloss. *There was not an answer to the seventh question in the original, nor was there even a place for it.*

[2] *Sophronius.* In the text *Sôfrônyôs*; in the margin *Sôfrînôs*. Sophronius was a common name in the time of Nestorius; but he seems here to be simply a rhetorical figure devised by Nestorius to enable him to cast his argument in the form of a dialogue. He is used indifferently to represent any heresy. Nau (*in loc.*) suggests a Nestorian Bishop of Tella and a Nestorian layman of that name as possible references. Cp. Bedjan, *op. cit.*, pp. ix, x. Cp. p. 378.

[3] See crit. n., p. 398.

becoming that which it was not without receiving it from outside: so they say that God the Word became a body without having taken a body from outside.

As, after running and flowing water is frozen and becomes solid, we say that it is nothing but water which has become solid, so God truly became flesh though he was by his nature God; and he was in everything and he acted as God. And, as touching [the operations of] the flesh, he both did [them] also in truth, and he suffered also as flesh, and he became flesh in the womb, and in that he became [it] he both was born and grew up truly as flesh; and, after he had chosen to become it, he both hungered and thirsted and grew weary and suffered and was crucified truly, seeing that he was truly flesh. For as water, which cannot be broken because it is frozen, can in truth be broken / and truly accepts the suffering of the nature which it has become, so also God who became flesh in truth accepted truly all [the sufferings of] the nature which he became without having been expelled from his [own] nature.

12. *As he was revealed in human form to Abraham and Jacob without having taken bodily frame from outside, so also was his incarnation.*[1]

As also he was seen of our fathers Abraham and Isaac and Jacob and the rest of the saints in truth in visible nature, walking in him who walked and talking in him who talked, and eating and drinking in him who ate [so also was his incarnation]; for nothing is done of God through deception, but everything in truth and in nature; for he is the creator and the creator does nothing in *schêma* and in illusion but in nature and in truth. But those things which were not in the nature of the creator are rightly said to be fiction and illusion, since they cannot be seen in [virtue of] their nature.

13. *How they take the [words] 'truly and not in nature', and in how many ways 'truly' is said.*

Nestorius. Truly then they say that God became flesh?

Sophronius says: We confess / that he became flesh truly but not by his nature, in that he who became, became [so]

---
[1] Sc. ἐνανθρώπησις.

in truth, and he is the nature but not in the nature. Indeed the flesh has not always existed, but, as flowing water when frozen has the nature of ice though it is not so in its nature but has become [so], thus also has God truly become flesh, and he is the nature of the flesh and not in his nature, in that he is not it always but he became [so] afterwards. For this is truly the Incarnation,[1] in his nature to become flesh and man and not in illusion nor in *schêma* nor in fiction without *hypostasis*, which truly would be no incarnation. He therefore who wants to suppose that it came about in fiction flees from the truth.

14. *Wherein those who say [this] agree with the Manichaeans and wherein they are supposed to be distinct from them.*

Has it then been revealed to thee wherein they are imagined [to be] the same and wherein they are supposed to have differences and abide by the same? And we ought to leave out the things which follow these, in order that we may not vainly suppress the truth in what is confessed.

Nestorius says: I for my part say: Let us not entirely neglect this point, although thou dost wish to run over it as one which is confessed. Since it has been so unscrupulously said as to/be accounted absurd by the hearers, I suppose that it is so also to thee. I will now explain this inquiry to any one who wishes in order that that which surely is supposed may come to explanation; for I do not see in it anything like or akin to anything [else]. For they are quite as far removed from one another as fiction is far from truth and [as] the body of fiction [is] from the body [of truth]. I see many who strongly insist on these [theories] as something [based] on the truth and ancient opinion. And for this reason I wish thee to examine them not cursorily but with all care, in order that the words of the faith may not be [treated] without investigation and lightly,[2] but may be clear and known to all men, as things which are somehow defined by definitions and natural likenesses, and not like things which are represented by their shadows [and] resemble this or that so long as they

---

[1] Sc. ἐνανθρώπησις.   [2] See crit n., p. 398.

are figured in the same likeness.[1] In what then dost thou say that they say the same thing, in that they are like the Manichaeans even in the things wherein they reprimand them?

Sophronius. Those who say this are not repudiated by them as though they hold our body in contempt, for both of them deny that the body was taken, but because they do not say 'in truth', but that the nature of the flesh is illusion. We see then also their readiness in these things, [in bringing forward] what plea is justly theirs, lest their blasphemies should extend beyond what is right.

/15. *The refutation of those who say that God the Word became the* ousia *of the flesh without having taken a body.*

Nestorius says: I say therefore generally [in reference to] what they say more [insistently] than those who depend on themselves, in order that they may not suppose that they have been condemned because they had not an advocate nor a helper: for you seem like to me to be fully convinced of what they say, and with many words you are capable of making their words prevail, so as to be able to make also the hearers believe that they are so. So then, constrain thou me also to speak unto them. Take each one of the words that has been spoken by me and thine also, and bid me give an answer to each one of them if I can. But I can, if God wills and gives me that which ought to be said [in order] to instruct according to my own ability. For I indeed am of no worth; but it is for the sake of those who knock and seek at the door of the truth, when it is the truth.

Sophronius. I say that what I have said is a proof of the divine power to be able to become truly flesh, being God. For he who says 'God in truth' attributes to him the [quality] of being able [to do] everything; for everything that he wishes he does. He wished indeed to become flesh and he became flesh, not the *schêma*[2] of the flesh / but the nature of the flesh, that is truly flesh. And thereby did he truly become incarnate,[3] because he was man by nature and not by anything else;

---

[1] This passage is translated in Bethune-Baker, *Nestorius and his Teaching*, p. 45, and referred to on p. 78 of that work.

[2] Syr. *'ĕskēmâ* = Gk. σχῆμα.   [3] *Sc.* ἐνηνθρώπησεν.

and the Trinity was the Trinity without having accepted the addition of another *ousia*.[1] Speak then in answer to these [assertions]: for they appear to use the common words and views in such a way that to dispute against them would be great boldness.

16. *Concerning this: that he who has become body in* ousia *ceases to be God and omnipotent and to be as God.*

Nestorius. In truth hast thou spoken, and we ought not to dispute what has been said in truth; for indeed [thou hast said] that God is all-powerful and does all that he wishes. And because of this his *ousia* became not flesh, for that which becomes flesh in its nature ceases to be able to do everything, in that it is flesh and not God.[2] For it appertains to God to be able to effect everything, and not to the flesh; for it cannot do everything that it wishes. But in remaining God he wills not everything nor again does he wish not to become God so as to make himself not to be God. For he is God in that he exists always and can do everything that he wishes, and not in that / he is able to make himself not to be God; for he into whose *ousia* the nature of the flesh has entered makes himself not to be God, and further cannot do everything that he wishes.

Sophronius. He is not able to wish not to be what he is, but only to be that which he is not. And for this reason he became in truth man, which he was not; that is, he became truly flesh and man, but not in nature. For that which he is, he is in nature; but that which he became, he became it not indeed in nature, but truly he was that which he became.

17. *Whether it is assumed by them that God the Word became truly a body in* ousia *or in illusion.*

---

[1] The importance of this point is discussed by Loofs in *Nestorius and his place in the History of Christian Doctrine*, pp. 126 sqq.; see also below, pp. 22-26.

[2] The non-possession of body or flesh (the two words seem to be interchangeable) is for Nestorius a distinctive characteristic of godhead, while the possession of body or flesh is essential to manhood. This antithesis was, of course, common to him and to his opponents, but he seems to have developed his doctrine by the strictly logical working out of such principles. They seem to be the leaven which leavens the whole lump of his thought. Cp. pp. 22, n. 2, 48.

Nestorius. Dost thou attribute 'truly' as 'in *ousia*' or 'in illusion and in fiction'?

Sophronius. [Yes,] for both of them can truly be assumed.

18. *Concerning this: If God the Word became flesh by nature and remained God as he was, then God the Word was two* ousias *naturally.*

Nestorius. If that which is supposed to be in *ousia* is [so]—thou sayest therefore that truly God is in *ousia* / and that he is according to the flesh—[then] after he became flesh there were two *ousias*, that in which he was by nature and that in which he became, the one of God and the other of the flesh.

Sophronius. There is not one *ousia* and another, but the same *ousia* of God, which became also the *ousia* of the flesh; and for this reason there is one *ousia*. Just as when water is running and when it is congealed there are not two *ousias* of water but one, which exists both in the liquid and in the solid state, although the solid is supposed [to be] the opposite of the running state, so also God: the same is body and without body, but in that he is body he is distinct from that which is without body.

19. *Concerning this: that those things which have no distinction in nature and are distinct, are said to be distinct in* schêma.

Nestorius. I say therefore that they[1] have no distinction in nature; and things which have no distinction in nature and are distinguished are distinct in the *prosôpon*. But [to be distinguished] by the *prosôpon* without nature is a *schêma* without *hypostasis* in another *schêma*.[2] Or dost thou say, like the Manichaeans, concerning the flesh and the things of the flesh that [they came about] in fiction and illusion, alleging that the incarnation[3] took place by deception? What then dost thou

---

[1] *I.e.* running water and water frozen.

[2] This must surely mean: 'is a change from one *schêma* to another *schêma* while the *hypostasis* remains unchanged.' The word *schêma* seems to mean the form or appearance of a thing at any given moment, *e.g.* water has one *schêma* when running and another when frozen. But *prosôpon*, whatever it is, must be a permanent element in the being of a thing, without which, or if it were other than it is, the thing would not be what it is. Might it be that the *prosôpon* is the unity of the successive *schêmata* of a thing?

[3] *Sc.* ἐνανθρώπησις.

suppose is true? That we should concede / that the flesh issued naturally from the *ousia* of God and [that] the two *ousias* become one, and become that which it is impossible that they should become, that is, that he is not God but flesh, or that he became flesh in illusion?

Sophronius. Things which should properly be received with faith you accept with 'natural logic' and reduce them to impossibilities. Then you deprive us in truth of the Christian faith as heathens or Manichaeans who stumble at the Cross of Christ.

Nestorius. And who are those who like heathens and Manichaeans stumble at the Cross of Christ? Are they not those who accept his humanity as a change of the *ousia*? For it appertains to the heathen to say that God works by a change in [his] likenesses in any *ousia* whatsoever and in . . . .[1] into the nature of which he has been changed; and further they set aside the nature, [even] that which was in the beginning. And the Manichaeans also have taken [these opinions] from them and say that the change of likeness resulted in a *schêma* without *hypostasis*. And you, in saying that, are following them, and you speak as those who stumble at the Cross of Christ.

20. *Concerning this: that those who say that the Incarnation*[2] *[lay in] a change of likeness confess that Christ is neither God nor man.*

/ You do not confess that he is God in *ousia* in that you have changed him into the *ousia* of the flesh, and he is no more a man naturally in that you have made him the *ousia* of God; and he is not God truly or God by nature, nor yet man truly and man by nature.

21. *Concerning this: that he who comes into being by* ousia *from a preceding* hylê[3] *is that which he has become and not that which he was before he became [so], as from a woman there came into being a statue of salt.*

And it is nothing else than this, that, as a man of wood and stone is not truly called man, being the nature of wood and stone, so also neither is he who has become man from the

---

[1] See crit. n., p. 398. [2] Sc. ἐνανθρώπησις. [3] See p. 17, n. 4.

ousia of God called man by nature, so long as the divine nature subsists.

Sophronius. Then, O admirable man, from stones God can raise up children unto Abraham,[1] and from a human bodily frame a pillar of salt,[2] and from the earth a man;[3] and nothing has prevented God nor yet is anything preventing him from doing that which he wishes, preventing him from becoming flesh.

Nestorius. First, then, investigate that which thou hast said. / Prove this to us, that God wishes it so. For the whole opinion of the world is agreed that God can do everything whatsoever he wishes. But again thou hast made use of proofs to the contrary. For he who becomes man from stone or from earth is the nature of man, in that he truly has become man, and not the nature of stone or of earth; and that which has become a pillar of salt from a human body is only the nature of whatever it has become. For things which are changed from their first *ousia* possess only that nature into which they have been changed. Therefore, if thou sayest that he became the nature of the flesh from the former *hylē*[4] of the nature of God, he possesses that *ousia* which he has become without having been [it]. And it is of no importance that, as I have said, the *ousia* of man issues from a stone or from earth or from the seed of man, for that which is from a former *ousia* is changed into the nature which it has become; and if he is not changed, he does not at all become flesh by nature.

Sophronius. Divine Scripture solves for us this problem and does not permit us to be obstinate and to speak arbitrarily. For the staff of Moses, when it became truly a serpent,[5] was a serpent as well as a staff; and the waters of the Nile, which became blood,[6] became the nature of blood as well as of water. The *ousia* was the same although it was changed and for this reason / the children of Israel used water which had become blood as the nature of the water, and Moses [used] a serpent as a staff, in that it was truly both of them. For God sustains natures as he will.

---

[1] Matt. iii. 9. [2] Gen. xix. 26. [3] Gen. ii. 7.
[4] Syr. *hūlē'* = Gk. ὕλη. [5] Ex. iv. 2-4; vii. 8-12. [6] Ex. vii. 14-25.

22. *Concerning this: that the waters of the Nile, when they were transformed into the* ousia *of blood, were only that* ousia *into which they were changed.*

Nestorius. Again thou usest proofs like these because, as I suppose, thou art bewildered. There were then two *ousias*; for the water which was taken by the Hebrews was blood and water and that which was taken by the Egyptians was both in the same way. But if the former was only water and the latter only blood, then they were afterwards changed; for when they were taken, those which were taken were changed and further were something else, namely that which they became. How then is it not seen that that which it became by nature is by all means that which it has become and nothing else?

Sophronius. And behold! we see that Divine Scripture / has said that from the same *ousia* there are two things by nature, when that which has become man by nature from dust and earth and is man by nature, says: *I am dust and ashes*,[1] if it be that thou mayest not revile Divine Scripture as though it has said things that are impossible, when it says of him who was man, by nature man, *I am dust and ashes*.

23. *Concerning this: that one* ousia, *which appears in two* ousias, *is in the one* ousia *by nature but in the other in* schêma *only.*

Nestorius. If Divine Scripture, in reiterating these things about the nature of man, says [that], and [if] every man is the nature of man and nothing else, then also God the Word, who truly became man in nature, is dust and ashes in nature and is not of the *ousia* of God but of dust and ashes. If it [were the divine *ousia*] from which he became [man], it indicates—if indeed every man is this [*ousia*][2] by nature while he is not this *ousia* but the *ousia* of God—[that] he was not man except in *schêma*, as the Manichaeans say; and the statements also concerning him are in *schêma*, that it may not be revealed to every one what he is; since one *ousia*, if it be recognized in two *ousias*, in the one / is *ousia* but [is] in the other in *schêma* or in falsehood and in illusion.

---

[1] Gen. xviii. 27 (P.).   [2] *I. e.* an *ousia* of dust and ashes.

Sophronius. So thou art attributing to God nothing more than that he should be God truly by nature and man by nature. It is the same nature in both of them, except that God is in man. And what is the Incarnation[1] except that he became man by nature in the nature of man and that he spoke to us in our nature and that he endured naturally all the things that are ours, since for this thing indeed he became incarnate.[1] But, further, you lay down that God did [this] by means of an intermediary[2] and the clothing of the *schéma*, and absurdities such as this, in that he likened himself to tragedians and singers who somehow disguise themselves.

24. *Concerning this: that he who can be visible by his nature has no need to become anything else in order to be visible in it.*

Nestorius. But, O admirable man, it remains to compare the things which have been said by thee, [namely] that he appeared to us in his own nature without an intermediary. For what reason then hast thou said that he became the nature of man while remaining God? For he who appeared in his nature had no need to become another *ousia* in which to appear. If he appeared in his own, then thou sayest an impossible thing, that he was a mediator for him[self]. / For *a mediator is not of one, but God is one*,[3] and consequently he cannot be God but the mediator of God.

25. *Concerning this: that if, when God appeared to the saints, he appeared in a change of* ousia, *he therefore became incarnate*[1] *in many* ousias *and not in one.*

But further be persuaded to consider this: dost thou predicate of God one incarnation[1] or many? What sayest thou of this? Then, since you say that he became the nature of man and was seen by Abraham and Jacob, and by each one of the saints in any *schéma* whatever, in whatever *schéma* he was, he

---

[1] Sc. ἐνανθρώπησις, ἐνηνθρώπησεν.

[2] Nestorius is here accused of Nestorianism. His reply is a somewhat ambiguous reference to Scripture, after which he confines himself to attacking Sophronius' position, leaving till later the task of making clear his own views. Cp. p. 47, n. 3.

[3] Gal. iii. 20 (P.).

was naturally changed into the nature in which he was seen and in the last days he was changed into the nature of man in order to become incarnate.[1] [Therefore] you predicate many incarnations,[1] if indeed you agree that the Incarnation [1] was to become incarnate [1] in his nature. There are many changes through which he appeared in *schêma*.

Sophronius. One incarnation [1] do we predicate, [affirming] that at that time he truly became incarnate [1] in his nature and appeared not to some men, as to Abraham and to Jacob, but to all men.

26. *Concerning this: that if the word incarnation[1] is employed of his appearing to all men and not to certain ones, as to the saints, / in that he appeared not to all men, he has not then indeed become incarnate[1] at all.*

Nestorius. [It follows] from [2] this statement that he became not incarnate [1] at all, in that he appeared not to all men, but [only] to those in Palestine. Why then was his incarnation [1] partial and not for all men? Or is this what thou callest the Incarnation,[1] that he became man in nature when he became incarnate [1] for all time and appeared to all men?

27. *Concerning what has been said about the Incarnation,[1] in that he appeared in human nature.*

If then the Incarnation [1] was truly one and for all men and not for some, both for those who saw him and for those who saw him not, both for those who were [present] and for those of old, and if the Incarnation [1] happened at the same time for all nature, we duly confess that God the Word was not the nature of man; for that is not the nature of man which is not the nature of man but of God. But in the *ousia* of man [he is] truly man, of the true nature of the true man in which he became incarnate [1] altogether for all and which he made his *prosôpon*, and he was revealed in the things of men in comporting himself in the nature of man, being God in human nature. As a king in the *schêma* of a soldier comports himself as a soldier and not as a king, / he is clad in the manner of a soldier against whatsoever has

---

[1] Sc. ἐνανθρώπησις and cognate words.   [2] Syr: 'in'.

need of correction, and it is said that in everything he is [so] clad, in that he has become the *schêma* of one soldier, even that which clothes all the soldiers. So he became incarnate[1] in one man for all men who are of the [same] nature, since he was in their nature, and in it he spoke to all men, as if he spoke in his own nature.

Sophronius. Then, when he was in the nature of man, it is said that he became incarnate;[1] and through it and in it for all men and not rather on his own account, in that he became a man in truth and thereby was associated with a man who was of their very nature. And in truth incarnation[1] took place in that by his own nature he became man and had no need of another nature.

Nestorius. The Incarnation[1] indeed lay not in this, as a king, in using as a king the *schêma* of soldierhood, becomes not a soldier indeed in the manner of a soldier; or perhaps [it is] as if one were to say that in name only he becomes a soldier. Thus no more did God become incarnate,[1] being not in human nature, but . . . .

Sophronius. What meanest thou by 'as a king' and 'as a soldier'?

Nestorius. Just as purple is the clothing of royalty but not of soldierhood and as the clothing of soldiers is the equipment[2] which belongs to soldiers and not to kings, when / therefore a king wishes to put on the clothing, that is the equipment,[2] of soldiers and to lay aside the purple of royalty, though [clothed] in the *schêma* of a soldier of which he has made use without descending from his royal dignity, he then remains in majesty and authority over everything, even in this *schêma*. But when he wishes to condescend and to become one of the soldiers, [wearing] the clothing of one of these soldiers, as if he had become a soldier, and not [that] of royalty, and concealing himself in it and talking with them on equal terms and persuading them without constraining them, he so performs the duties of royalty in the *schêma* of a soldier. Thus also God, when he wished to become incarnate,[1] if he had not

---

[1] *Sc.* ἐνηνθρώπησεν and cognate words.
[2] See crit. n., p. 398.

come in human nature but had become flesh in his own *ousia*, would not at all have become incarnate,[1] in that he would have become incarnate[1] for them in his own *ousia* and not in the nature of men.[2]

28. *Concerning this: that he who by a change of* ousia *becomes man is of another nature and not of the nature of men.*

He indeed who by a change of *ousia* becomes man is of another nature and not of the nature of men, in that he has another description of nature and not that of men; because he is God by nature, and the *ousia* of man is something[3] else than the nature of God, as both of them exist by nature: not that he passed from the nature of God to the nature of man nor [that he was] something else than these;/he is by nature in both of them, but the man is only man and God is only God.

Sophronius. And he had not so received the incarnation,[1] but [if it] took place in another human nature and not from the *ousia* of God, how does the Trinity not accept an addition in [its] nature, since it has accepted the *ousia* of another?[4] Or how is this God of the nature of men and not of the *ousia* of God?[5]

29. *Concerning this: that, in that he has become man in the* ousia *of man and has not become man in [his own]* ousia, *neither in nature nor in* prosôpon *does he accept any addition.*

Nestorius. As a king, who takes the clothes of soldierhood and is [so seen], has not become a double king, and as the king exists not apart from him, in that he is in him, and as, further, he is not revered[6] apart from him in whom he is

---

[1] Sc. ἐνανθρωπῆσαι and cognate words.

[2] See p. 15, n. 2. Nestorius is here developing further the argument on p. 15. He has there denied that the Incarnation means *merely* the taking of the *schêma* of humanity by God the Word; he now shows that it involves the taking of that *schêma* and more. But the most important point seems to be the establishing of the fact that *ousias* are mutually exclusive. Henceforward this must be assumed as one of the presuppositions of Nestorius' thought. If Godhead and manhood are to be united neither of them can be the basis of the union. They must be united in some *tertium quid*. Cp. pp. 14, n. 2, 48, 298.

[3] See crit. n. p. 398.   [4] See p. 14, n. 1.

[5] On this passage see Loofs, *Nestorius and his Place*, p. 127.

[6] Literally: 'he is not adored'.

known and whereby men also have known him and have been rescued; so also God used his own *prosôpon* to condescend in poverty and shame even unto the death on the Cross for our salvation; and by it he was raised up also to honour and glory and adoration. Wherein he was abased, in that also he was glorified. For the sign of salvation and victory is [a sign] of honour and not of abasement. Nor did he receive any addition of the *ousia*, because the *ousias* remain without change. For then there is/an addition in the *ousia* when it accepts another *ousia*, an equal *ousia*.[1] But also he received not an addition to the *prosôpon*, in that he took his own *prosôpon* and not another, not for distinction but for the union of his own *prosôpon* and that in which he became incarnate;[2] and also his *prosôpon*[3] is in him and not in another. For he is clothed in the likeness of a servant, and by it he emptied himself and has clothed it with his *prosôpon* and has exalted his name above all names. In the *prosôpon* then of the divinity is he adored and in no other, and in consequence of this the *prosôpon* is one and the name of the Son [is one].

30. *Against those who say not that God was changed into the nature of a man, but that he changed the* ousia *of man into the* ousia *of God.*[4]

Now for those who predicate the union in a change there follows in any case an addition in *ousia* as well as in *prosôpon*. The *ousia* indeed, which became flesh out of God the Word, was added to the Trinity, and it is evident that this *prosôpon* is a part detached and that it is conceived in detachment; or it became the nature of the flesh [emanating] from the *ousia* of God the Word in detachment, an addition took place . . . . Whence then is the origin of these things and in what are they distinct? Further, we have already said the same thing.

---

[1] Nau points out that the emphasis is on the otherness, not on the equality, of the added *ousia*. The Syriac phrase is equivalent to the Greek ἰσουσία.

[2] *Sc.* ἐνηνθρώπησεν.

[3] Nau suggests, probably rightly, that the human *prosôpon* is here meant.

[4] This heading refers to the sect mentioned at the beginning of p. 24, and should probably be transposed to the top of that page.

/Let us turn then to another sect which has sprung from these and is distinct from them and at the same time is confounded with them . . . .

Sophronius. They confess then that the body of our Lord is of his own flesh and therein they mock both at those who say that the flesh was in fiction and illusion and also at those who say that it was of the *ousia* of God the Word, saying . . . .

31. *What words those use who say that the nature of the body was changed into the* ousia *of God the Word.*[1]

He came not to change his unchangeable *ousia* and to make it the *ousia* of the flesh but to raise up our miserable and changeable [*ousia*] to his own unchangeable [*ousia*] and to make it divine and adorable, not of itself but in the union. And he deems it worthy of the union with his *ousia*, in order that it may become one *ousia* and one *prosôpon* of one *ousia* ; and the smaller has been mixed with and deemed equal to the great and unchangeable divinity. Even as things which are cast into the fire are made equal to the *ousia* of the fire and become the nature of the fire which has made them what they have become, so also the divine nature has accepted the human nature and has mingled it in its own nature, and has changed it and made it therefore one without distinction in *ousia* and in *prosôpon* ; / and neither in nature nor in *prosôpon* has there truly been an addition to the Trinity; and thus the Incarnation[2] also took place and is conceived.

32. *In what they are distinct from the Manichaeans and in what they confess [the same] as they.*

[*Nestorius*]. These indeed are distinct from the Manichaeans in that they confess truly that the flesh is of our own nature and that it is not the *schêma* of the flesh but the nature of the flesh. But some of the others who are with them [are distinguished] in that they confess that the flesh is true, not belonging to human nature but being divine and of the nature of the divinity. In this they are distinct and they strive

---

[1] Nestorius seems here to be dealing with the position afterwards held by Eutyches.

[2] *Sc. ἐνανθρώπησις.*

with all their might. And those who suppose that they serve the church confess that the flesh is of our own nature and *ousia* and so its distinction is known to all men. Generally then they dispute with all:[1] with the Manichaeans concerning the [point] that there was an *ousia* and an *ousia* in truth; and with the others that it was not of the nature of God but of our fathers; but with the church in that they change the flesh into the *ousia* of God. Therefore in that they do not allow the flesh to remain in its own *ousia*, they resemble the Manichaeans by destroying the *ousia* of the flesh, but diverge from them in that they say that God was altogether in the *hylê* of the flesh. But in that they immediately change [the flesh] into the *ousia* of God the Word and are unwilling to / confess that God was with the human body, they agree with the same opinion and feeling when they exclude the *ousia* of the flesh as if it existed not, insisting either on deifying the *ousia* of the flesh or, so to say, on making the *ousia* of God become incarnate[2] in the *ousia* of the flesh of the divinity.

33. *That those who change the nature of man into the divine nature do not say that God became incarnate* [2] *but that a man was deified.*

He then who is not the human *ousia* of the flesh and is called flesh is so called by homonymy, even as a man of gold or silver or of another *ousia* of whatsoever material[3] is not man by nature, since he has not the nature of man; and this is not the incarnation[2] of God but the deification of man.

34. *Concerning this: that those who change the nature of man into the divine* ousia *make an addition to the Trinity both in the nature and in the* prosôpon.

If therefore the nature of the flesh which has been deified remains in the *ousia* in which it has been deified, how has the Trinity not accepted an addition in the *ousia* and in he *prosôpon*? / For there is nothing of human nature in the Trinity, neither the Father, nor the Son, nor the Holy Spirit,

---

[1] Altering the punctuation of the Syriac text, which puts the stop after 'Manichaeans'.

[2] Sc. ἐνανθρωπῆσαι and cognate words.   [3] Syr. *hûlê'* = Gk. ὕλη.

but it is alone ; and in that which was not with it eternally but which has been [added] to it, it has received an addition. But how could an addition which is [made] to it not be an addition ? And this also is another story and a Manichaean fable.[1] But if that which was [added] became not what it was and the nature of men was harmed by the nature of the divinity as by fire, and [if] thereby the Trinity accepted not an addition, no more is this an incarnation,[2] but the extinction of the Incarnation.[2] For anything which results in the extinction of human nature and not in its preservation, is not named an incarnation[2] but [is] as something which exists in relation to that which exists not.

35. *Wherein those who change the nature of the body into the* ousia *of God agree with those who change the* ousia *of God into the nature of the body.*

And herein they agree with those who change the divine *ousia* into human nature ; for that is the same thing, that God becomes the *ousia* in the nature [of the body] or that he changes the *ousia* in man into the nature of God.

36. *Concerning this : that it is not possible that the nature of God should be changed into bodily frame either by mixture or by change, nor yet that the body should be changed into the* ousia *of God the Word.*

/ He indeed who changes the divine nature into human nature brings about its suppression, and he who changes human nature into the divine nature makes mock of it and makes of it a nature unmade, in declaring a nature [which is] made unmade, which cannot be. For of nothing the maker easily assembles the *ousia* and makes the *ousia* which is made by change of that which is made. But it is impossible that [he should make] that which is unmade[3] and that which was not from that which was, as thou sayest ; or else surely thou dost deprive it of being *ousia*. But there are no means whereby the *ousia* which was should cease to be nor whereby that which was made should become unmade, nor again [are there any means whereby] that which is not should become an eternal

---

[1] See p. 14, n. 1.   [2] Sc. ἐνανθρώπησις.
[3] V reads : ' that which is made from that which is unmade '.

nature and be with the eternal ; nor again whereby a nature which was not should come into being nor whereby that which is not eternal should become eternal either by a change of nature or by confusion or by mixture; or whereby from the *ousia* of the eternal [should come into being] that which is not eternally. For either by mixture or by confusion of the two *ousias* a change of *ousia* took place [making] for one nature which should result from the mixture of both of them ; or one *ousia* of them was changed into the other. It is not possible that the unmade [should become] made and the eternal temporary and the temporary eternal and that the created [should become] uncreated by nature ; that that which is uncreated and which has not come into being and is eternal should thereby become /made and temporary, as if it became part of a nature made and temporary ; nor that there should come forth a nature unmade and eternal from a nature made and temporary to become an *ousia* unmade and eternal ; for such things are not possible nor conceivable. For how can anyone conceive that the Maker, seeing that he is in every way other than that which is made, should change into his being the other which has been made? For in that he is the Maker, he is unchangeable ; since he works by an unchangeable nature, and when he is not that which he is he works not. In effect either he is what he is by nature, eternally God, and became not another nature while remaining in the *ousia* of God ; or, not being the nature of God, he was made and is not the Maker, which is absurd and impossible.

37. *Concerning this : that those also who say that the nature has been changed in part, and not all of it, say [what is] impossible.*

Although indeed anyone should grant that in part he changed his nature and in part was not changed, he who makes has in every way the lordship over him who is made and over him who is changed ; for there is nothing which is more lordly in its [whole] nature than [in] a part of it, but whatever all of it is the same also / is in its part. Even if then we accept absurdities as well-pleasing, a part being mentioned in speaking of a nature simple and indivisible, not even so does one avoid what is absurd and not eternal For wherein does that which is not the *ousia* come to be in the *ousia*? For in so far as he is God he is unchangeable, but when he is not God he does nothing. How then is that said which cannot even be conceived: that God is changed into another *ousia* or again that another *ousia* is changed into the *ousia* of God and becomes that which is the Maker, that is, that what was unmade and was not [became] that which was made and came into being? These [statements] are in fact contradictory. How then do the things which have been said appear to thee? Have both parties been sufficiently treated, those who stand by the statements of those men and [those also] who are of ours? Or is there still something lacking which they ought to establish?[1] Thou oughtest to fill it in, as though thou speakest on their behalf.[2] For if anything touching the faith has been omitted in their statements, we shall lend it our aid with all our might, in order that their discomfiture may be exceeding great, since they are supposed by many to be unshaken and unaltered, although they are not.

Sophronius. I suppose then that the statements of both parties have been well handled and there remains nothing for us [to do], and therefore / indeed I rejoice in an hour of silence, and I beseech thee also to desist; for I have no good or useful objection that can be raised against thee, except one word only which people confidently use in regard to what pleases them.

Nestorius. What [is that]? Speak confidently, undaunted, using manfully and adequately every one of their arguments even as they themselves [do]; for no one who is hesitating in his thoughts can strive manfully.

Sophronius. So must it be in regard to the union even as the bread, when it becomes body, is one and the same body and not two. And one also is that which is conceived as the nature of the body, and further it is no more conceived in its former nature but as itself in that which it has become; wherefore it is not that which it appears [to be] but that

---

[1] See crit. n., p. 398. [2] Syr. 'their πρόσωπον'.

which it is conceived [to be]. And consequently also the Apostle decreed a fearful punishment against those who supposed the body of our Lord to be common, when he said thus: *If he who has violated the law of Moses dies without pity out of the mouth of two or three [witnesses], how much more is he counted worthy of a severe punishment who has trampled underfoot the Son of God and has considered common the blood of his testament, whereby he was sanctified, and has scorned the spirit of grace.*[1] This he said / against those who regarded the blood and body of God as the blood and body of man, and who erred in supposing that the body and blood whereby we have been sanctified are common; and the spirit of grace they have scorned in confessing not that the Son of God is consubstantial with God and the Father, but that the body of the Son of God is the body of a man, whose body and blood he has raised to his own *ousia* and has not let them be upbraided and taunted with a human *ousia* but has [caused them] to be adored in his own *ousia*.

38. *Concerning this: that the Apostle speaks also against those who consider the blood and body of Christ profane and impure, not as though to imply that it*[2] *has certainly been changed into the nature of God the Word but as though they refuse to call the blood blood and to call the body body and [because they assert] that they are not able to save us, as the Manichaeans say.*

Nestorius. Is this proof, concerning which thou keepest silence, of small importance in thy opinion? They indeed insist much on it, and thou oughtest not to bring it forward negligently. It had indeed escaped my notice in the manner of those who see the mote but not the beam. [Now that] it has been revealed, let us examine it from all sides, [to see] how it is and how / Divine Scripture wishes us to understand [it], so that we incur not blame just and divine.

39. *In how many ways the word which in Greek is called* koinon *is used.*

And first, let us speak of the use of the word called *koinon* in Greek. Now in meaning it refers to [what is] polluted,

---

[1] Heb. x. 28, 29.   [2] *Viz.* the human *ousia*.

and [what is] common and to participation. [It refers to] what is polluted, as he[1] said in the Acts: *Never have I eaten that which is impure and polluted*;[2] but to what is common in *whatsoever they*—the Apostles—*had belonged to them in common*;[3] but to participation in *the cup of thanksgiving which we bless, is it not a participation in the blood of Christ? And the bread which we break, is it not a participation in the body of Christ?*[4] And again: *He who sanctifies and those who are sanctified are all of one; wherefore he was not ashamed to call them brothers, saying: I shall proclaim thy name to my brothers and in the midst of the assembly I shall glorify thee; and again: I shall put my trust in him; and again: Here am I and the children which God has given me* . . . . *Since then the children have participated in the flesh and the blood, he also has participated likewise in the same things.*[5] Since therefore this term is employed of a man who is impure and polluted and also of that which is common and further of participation, [did he[6] so use] this expression which covers three uses / and does not distinguish against what opinion the apostle meant it, when he laid it down that for this reason men *trample underfoot the Son of God?*[7] Which of these three [interpretations] is accurate?

Sophronius. [He employed this word] against those who think that he died not for us but was in his own death as all men, and that both living and dead he was an ordinary man and that he possessed nothing more [than ordinary men], for they know not that he is the Son of God and that his blood is the blood of God and not that of a man.

Nestorius. Do you say this, that the body and blood are the *ousia* of the Son of God, or that the body and blood are of human *ousia* and have become the nature of the divinity? For, as you say, the flesh is not flesh, because it has been changed by him into the *ousia* of God the Word by means of a mixture and a union. And it [is what] the blessed Apostle meant when he mocked exceedingly at

---

[1] *Viz.* St. Peter.   [2] Acts x. 14.   [3] Acts iv. 32 (P.).
[4] 1 Cor. x. 16 (P.).   [5] Heb. ii. 11–14 (P.).
[6] *Viz.* the author of the Epistle to the Hebrews.   [7] Heb. x. 29.

those who confessed his body and his blood and [yet] supposed it impure.

Sophronius. He said not this against those who by no means confess the body in truth, nor against those who change or corrupt the *ousia* as by fire or [who suppose][1] the *ousia* of the flesh impure through mixture, but against those who confess the flesh and the blood and [yet] think that it is common./

Nestorius. As it seems to me, the opinion to which thou dost cling is not more in harmony with [2] these, but with those who change the *ousia* into the nature of flesh and blood, without thinking that the *ousia* of the flesh and blood of our Lord is common, but that it is of God the Word and not of men.

Sophronius. Then one ought not to return answer to these but a reprimand for having used contradictory expressions. But speak of those who supposed that the flesh was of the *ousia* of God.

40. *How one ought to understand: 'He who sanctifies and those who are sanctified are all of one.'* [3]

Nestorius. Thou art mistaken, for the Apostle said not two contradictory things. For he wished to say that he who sanctifies and he who is sanctified are of one and brothers of one and not of different *ousias*, and his children as those who are sprung from him. Thus he said: *For he who sanctifies and those who are sanctified are all of them of one.*[3] The blood then whereby we have been sanctified and which has been poured out on our behalf is of one; thereby also are we his brothers, as if of one father, but again also his sons, [as those who] possess one *ousia*, wherein we are also sons. In God the Word in fact there is not anything whereby he and we should be of one,/ or whereby we should be called sons in his likeness, that for this [reason] we should become his brothers, in that we have no reason for such a likeness, as those who are brothers and of one father; nor further that we should become his sons, because we do not participate

---

[1] See crit. n., p. 398.
[2] Syr: 'against'; here the Syr. *lúqbal* 'against' probably represents the Gk. πρός.   [3] Heb. ii. 11.

in the same *ousia*. So then the blessed Paul said this, accusing those who are not persuaded to admit that the blood of men can sanctify and who suppose that it is impure as being the blood of a man and consequently regard as impure the blood of the covenant whereby we have been sanctified and rescued from death through the true death of a man. And thereby he tells us that we are of one, and thereby he calls us his brothers on account of the nature which is born of our fathers and died for us;[1] for in that he was born he is of our race and we are all of one; but, in that he died on our behalf and has renewed the future state by immortality and incorruptibility, we are his sons; for he is the father of the world to come.[2] Are we not all in consequence of that one body in one? For we all receive from this same one bread, whereby he makes us participate in the same blood and flesh, which are of the same nature, and we participate with him in the resurrection from the dead and in immortality. So we are to him his body just as is the bread; even indeed as the bread is one, / so are we all one body, for we all receive of this one bread.

41. *Concerning this: that, if in Christ the* ousia *of the body was changed into the divinity, we also are changed into the* ousia *of God the Word; for we are all one bodily frame and one body.*

We then also have been changed into his flesh and we are his body, and we are therefore not the body and blood of man, but his own body. The bread indeed is one, wherefore we all are one body, in that we are the body of Christ. *You indeed are the body of Christ and members in your parts.*[3] Is the bread the body of Christ by a change of *ousia*? Or are we his body by a change? Or is the body of the Son of God one with God the Word by nature? But if they are one by nature, there is then no more bread nor again is there [any] body. But to those who thought that the body of the Son of God was polluted the Apostle says that

---

[1] The Syriac preposition *ḥlāf* corresponds in the New Testament both to ἀντί and to ὑπέρ.
[2] Isa. ix. 6. (R.V. Marg.) Cp. Heb. ii. 5.   [3] 1 Cor. xii. 27; see p. 12.

they are *trampling underfoot the Son of God*[1] in rejecting him and denying him, against those who confess that the body is of our own nature and who regard it as polluted, although [they admit] that it was given for the salvation of us all because it was pure and unstained and saved from sins,[2] and that for all our sins he accepted death and became as it were an offering unto God. For if we are not of one, we are naturally not called/his brothers nor his sons, nor are we any more his bread and his bodily frame; but, if all these belong truly to Christ, we are his body and consubstantial with him, in that we are that which is also the *ousia* of his body. And these things are also known through the words of the dogma of those who are changed now into this and now into that, because they possess not the truth.[3]

42. *Against those who say that the union took place in the ousia of God the Word and that the nature of the divinity effected the transfusion of the nature of humanity.*

From these again another sect has arisen who in some things are like them and in others are distinct from them, while they indeed agree with the Arians but also dissent from them; but in another way they are clothed in the *prosôpon* of the orthodox, whereby again they keep aloof from the one but so fall into the weakness of the first. They confess indeed that the body of our Lord is of the nature of our fathers and therein they are to be likened to those against whom we have spoken a little before; but they are distinct from them in denying the change of the flesh into the *ousia* of the divinity and in accepting the union without mixture and without confusion. But they incline towards the Arians in saying that the union resulted in one nature, not by change

---

[1] Heb. x. 29.   [2] Heb. vii. 26.

[3] §§ 37-41. Nestorius' argument seems to be : In whatever sense the bread becomes the Body of Christ, in that same sense we become the Body of Christ by participating in the Sacrament. Since we can only participate in a human body, the Body of Christ must have been (and be) human.

In view of the charge commonly brought against Nestorianism that it destroys the universal significance for all men of the Incarnation of Christ, it is interesting to find that he defends his own view as alone safeguarding this significance.

of *ousia* but by combination and natural composition, as the soul and the body are combined in one nature, and by natural force the soul naturally suffers the sufferings of the body, / and the body the sufferings of the soul. That which each one of them by its nature cannot accept, such as the sufferings and the activity, it has accepted in the natural combination by mixture, by one sensibility. They place the union not in revelation[1] and in use, but by natural force in a passible nature, and they say that the union took place for this [purpose], that they[2] should naturally participate in their activities and in their sufferings. But, further, they are distinct from the Arians in saying that there was an animal body and soul and that God the Word is consubstantial with the Father and that he naturally endured union with the nature, not by command but of his own will in order to accept on our behalf all the sufferings of human nature, not in any other nature but in his own.

The Apollinarians. He has not surely made a pretence of[3] our salvation in *schêma*, either by a change of likeness or by a change of *ousia* in such a way as not to endure sufferings in his own nature; for this would be [the action] of him who wished not to become incarnate[4] because by nature he became man. But if, since he wished not or since he could not enter where there was an intelligence, he united himself by a natural union to the sensitive and vegetative soul and to the body so as to complete and fulfil the nature of man [and so as, starting] from impassibility and immortality, to suffer natural suffering naturally and to be delivered unto death naturally in the nature of the soul and of the body, from no / nature he became and he is the nature of a man.[5] He had not been in a man but he was man truly, in that he was with the nature of man

---

[1] The Syriac text reads 'revelation', for which Nau suggests 'will'; but in view of later passages this seems unnecessary. Cp. *e.g.* pp. 60-69, 200, n. 1. See crit. n., p. 398.   [2] *Sc.* God the Word and the Man Christ.

[3] The Syriac verb is a derivative formed from the Gk. σχῆμα.

[4] *Sc.* ἐνανθρωπῆσαι.

[5] If the text of this passage is right, the last words 'from no nature' must be the apodosis to the conditional clause beginning 'But if, since he wished. ...' The sense must be that out of something which, being incomplete, is no real nature the human nature was made by the addition of the Logos.

and he was bound to the soul and the body in order to complete [them] and not to dwell [in them]. For he who dwells [in anything] is far removed from that in which he dwells and accepts neither the nature nor the name of that wherein he dwells. Consequently, seeing that he dwelt in all the saints, he is not said to have become incarnate [1] and become man in any one of them, but only when he became truly man for the natural completion of the nature of man by constituting himself the intelligence ruling naturally in the body and the soul, and when he constituted a natural union. And therefore it was united without intelligence that he might not be supposed as it were to have dwelt in man, but to have been united for the completion of the human nature. That then is their [view]. But those who wish rather to adhere to the orthodox attribute to him a body and an intelligent soul and agree to the union in one nature for the completion of the nature. And as the body and the soul and the intelligence are the completion of the nature of man, so also the union of God the Word took place with the body and an intelligent soul for the completion of the nature. He became man in truth, since he had according to nature all [the properties] of a man; he was not the half of a complete [man], that is flesh only, or animal soul, for it is not in this that he became man,/ in possessing nothing of man except animal bodily frame and soul without reason, but [in possessing] a rational soul and a rational body and a rational life, and not [all these] without reason. For all that is combined for the completion of nature participates in the same things and in one nature, since it participates both in suffering and in activity.

43. *Against those who confess a body endowed with soul and a soul endowed with intelligence but [say that] the union of the divinity resulted in one nature by composition.*

Nestorius. According to the former the statements of the latter are well said, that neither the animal soul nor again the bodily frame of the irrational soul are the body of a man; nor consequently is he—neither soul, nor body, nor divinity—a man who has nothing of a man; for the nature of man is not

---
[1] Sc. ἐνανθρωπῆσαι.

constituted of an animal soul and divinity and body. How then did he become man by the combination of things which make not the nature of a man, unless perhaps he became by fusion another nature apart from our own nature? But nothing like that has taken place in anything nor in all natures which have aforetime existed; and now [forsooth], after all creation has been completed another nature has come into being apart from those which were when it existed not!

/ 44. *Concerning this: that if the union of the divinity and the humanity resulted in one nature, that one nature is neither that of God nor that of man, but another nature which is foreign to all natures.*

But generally the same things are said [in answer] also to these: that by man we understand and mean him who from the body and the rational and intelligent soul has become the nature of man in the combination of nature, but not him who from divinity and a rational soul and a human body has become man by a combination of natures; for this is impossible. For human nature is definite, and [the things] which he possesses who is man in *ousia* and in nature ought to be his who comes to be in the nature of man neither more nor less; since the [properties] of the nature are definite. Either then [he became] man in such a way that the union of God the Word with the body and the soul took place not with a view to [forming] one nature but in order to serve for the dispensation on our behalf; or he had the [properties] of another nature apart from that of men and of God, which is an animate body and God the Word, which nature is neither that of a man nor that of God, but a new nature, to which belongs [something] of all our natures.

45. *Concerning this: that if the union of God / the Word with the body resulted in one nature, he is not to be conceived apart from the flesh, in that it is [possible] for him to become this in his nature.*

God therefore is no more of an impassible but of a passible nature, being conceived as of that which he became by the natural union, while he became anew that which was newly created.

If then God the Word, who is consubstantial with the Father and the Holy Spirit, has been united in a natural union, and thereby has that which he is, he exists not apart from it, since in it and by it he is united and unites himself, like the body and the soul which are united in one nature of a man, and are not to be conceived apart from their nature—but the body [is] in the soul and the soul in the body together with their sufferings and their operations, the body being natural and [the soul [1]] not in a voluntary habitation, [both] mutually receiving and giving in a perceptible manner by natural mixture and fusion for the fusing of the nature.

46. *Concerning this: that in the union two natures are not conceived as one nature.*

What after all is the nature in this natural union which you predicate? Is it that of the Father and of the Son and of the Holy Spirit, an impassible nature, immortal, eternal and without needs? Or is it [a nature] mortal and passible and with needs, which came into being yesterday and to-day and which belongs neither to men nor to God nor to any other nature, but is mixed from two natures for the completion of one nature? If then they say / that it is the *ousia* of the Father and of the Son and of the Holy Spirit united by a natural union, this is not a natural union with the flesh but a voluntary, since they are united for the use of the *prosôpon* and not of the nature; since [those things] which are united in one nature are not united voluntarily but by the power of the Creator, who combines them and brings them to a fusion in such a way that whatever is not of and belongs not to each of them obtains it in virtue of a natural and not a voluntary union, by which it has been united in one nature. By whom then are these united in nature? It is evident that that which has been united has been so [united] by the creator of the nature.[2] If anyone says that anything is united of itself, I do not suppose that it is right; for when the natures are united in the *ousias* in one nature, it possesses also a certain kind of change of *ousia* and it is necessary that that nature which has been united should

[1] The word 'soul' seems to have dropped out of the Syriac text.
[2] See notes on pp. 8, 9.

be bound in virtue of an equality of nature and not by the will.[1]

47. *Concerning this: that natures which are united voluntarily are not said to be united naturally, but* prosôpically.

The natures indeed which are united voluntarily acquire the union with a view to [forming] not one nature but a voluntary union of the *prosôpon* of the dispensation. If then they say that the union of the natures resulted in one nature, even though we ourselves should concede to them that it took place voluntarily, / yet, after it took place, the union existed not voluntarily in that the natures have acquired it. And it suffers as being united, whether it will or not, and accepts the sufferings of that nature to which it has been united, since it is defined by it and not by impassibility nor by immortality nor by infinity. For the definition and circumscription of all nature is that in which it has to be. And if it has been united to a nature, it is in that [nature] that it has to be and also [has to be] as that which exists by the nature. And from this it is established that both the Father and the Holy Spirit, who are of the same nature, are of a passible and created nature; for that which the Son has accepted in his nature, the Father also can accept. For it is impossible that he[2] should be able to accept in nature that which he[3] is not capable of accepting. If the Son accepted in virtue of his acceptance of the union of this nature, whereas the former did not accept, how are they of one nature who are opposed to one another in accepting or not accepting? And after a change of nature you are compelled to take the word 'union' according to the interpretation of the Arians,[4] that the nature of the Son has been united by the Creator of nature, in the same manner as he who created and made the soul and the body also united them; for the very work of creation also requires that he should unite

---

[1] This seems to mean: If the divine nature is found in Christ in a natural union, it can only be so in virtue of having been reduced to the level of human nature. If it were remaining itself and freely co-operating of its own will, the union would be another kind of union.

[2] *Viz.* the Son.   [3] *Viz.* the Father.

[4] Literally: 'for you the word "union" necessarily takes the meaning of the Arians.'

the soul / and the body in one nature, in that to him also belongs the realization of the creation of each one of them.

48. *Concerning this: that a natural union is the work of a second creation.*

The union in fact in one nature of natures which have been united is the work of a second creation. That which is not of itself naturally united to each one of them receives this from a second genesis. For indeed to hunger and to thirst and to perceive sensations by the senses belongs not to the body of itself, nor to the soul of itself, but [1] comes to them from a second genesis. So if there had also been a union of nature with the soul and the body for God the Word, in such a way that he received from the union of nature that which he had not in his nature of itself: hunger and thirst and weariness and strife and fear and death, in the one genesis indeed of a second creation [would be found] the first creation both of his *ousia* and necessarily also [of] the Creator's, if he endured these things not in fiction but naturally. And vainly do you give the name of consubstantial to one from whom you were compelled anew to take it away and were compelled to join either the Arians or Manichaeans in such a way as to admit either that he suffered not naturally any one of these things or only in illusion and in fiction. Or, by granting that in nature naturally, by a passible sensibility, / he accepted sufferings, you evacuate him of impassibility and of immortality, and of being consubstantial with the Father, because he acquired a change of nature, seeing that [the Son] accepts and [the Father] accepts not [these sufferings]. Or if he had not had one change of *ousia* in his nature, while that of the Father and the Holy Spirit was without needs and accepted neither suffering nor death, he would have been deprived of being God in that he was not in everything of an *ousia* without needs.

49. *Concerning this: that things united by nature endure natural sufferings naturally and not voluntarily.*

By diminution indeed the nature without needs and impassible became a passible and needful nature. In the same

---

[1] See crit. n., p. 398.

way as one who by his own will does away with his hand or his foot or his eye no longer possesses them after they have been done away, in that he has truly put them away, so he also who by his own will does away with his immortality and impassibility for the completion of a passible and needful nature no longer has that impassibility and freedom from needs which were formerly his, in that he was made equal to a passible nature until he obtained anew impassibility by command[1] [apart] from nature together with the natural union, since after the resurrection from the dead he has been in a nature which is immortal and impassible, but not in virtue of his own nature which [was his] before he became a mortal man by a natural union; since / he accepted naturally all the properties of nature, he [accepted] also obedience unto death, even death upon the cross and also an uplifting of exaltation above which there is no glory, and the adoption of a name which by grace is above all names, *before which every knee in heaven, and on the earth, and beneath the earth bows, for the glory of God the Father*[2] to whom he was subjected and fulfilled all obedience. He did not empty himself nor yet was he the similar to the Father nor received he anew the similitude from the Father. For indeed he exalted himself and emptied himself to [the state of] mortal nature and he became that nature, and that which he had in his nature he took by grace. And from a nature unmade he became a nature made and created by addition and diminution of natural power; and the *ousia* which accepted neither sufferings nor death became mortal and passible, and he died through weakness and through the power of God he became alive, in that he became a weak nature and endured the painful sufferings thereof, being in pain and suffering in consequence of the equality in nature[3] of the soul and of the body, being torn apart and isolated from his nature; under constraint he was torn out of his nature and consequently he was not even corrupted by the parting[4] of the soul from the body. As the body endures the suffering of

---

[1] See p. 8, n. 3.   [2] Phil. ii. 8-11.
[3] The Syriac *shauyûth kyânâ* occurs in Cyril, *de Incarn* vii. 109 (ed. Pusey), as meaning τὸ ἰσοφυές (Payne-Smith, *Thes. Syr.*, col. 4082).   [4] Syr: 'distiction'.

death and is violently torn apart from any equality[1] [with the soul] and from the natural / union by division, so also God the Word who was united for the completion of the natural union must endure naturally all the natural sufferings of death; therefore also life and death belong in common to those who are united in nature. He then who concedes this concedes also the rest, whether he will or not, even if he says a thousand times that he is impassible in his nature; for he suffered in the nature which he became, whether of flesh or of man or of any thing else that we might mention. And let us not say that his nature does not accept sufferings, except that perhaps, as those who are able to die or not to die are not by their nature immortal, so also might we say of God the Word; for therein is God the Word conceived in his nature and he has nothing more. If thou sayest that his nature is not subject to death, in no way is it subject to natural death; the union took place not for nature but for the use of man according to the dispensation, so that the Incarnation[2] of God the Word, who is impassible and immortal, took place. What then do they say? I ought fully to treat two things: to set out their objections and to resolve them as best I can, since thou hast persuaded me to do both.

Sophronius. They say in fact as follows: how is he called man heavenly and spiritual, if he is neither spiritual nor heavenly? / He who has been united to human nature is God the Word by nature as God; and it is said: *As the first man was of the dust of the earth, so also is the Lord from heaven;*[3] and: *The first man became a living soul and the second man became a quickening spirit.*[4] And not apart from the *ousia* of the body of dust is he called a man of dust nor again without the soul is he called animate,[5] but in consequence of their combination, which results in the nature of man, is he so called[6] apart from the *ousia* of the heavenly and the spiritual, which has been united by nature to the nature of man.

[1] The Syriac has *shauyûthâ*, which is equivalent to the Gk. ἰσο- in ἰσοφυές (*supra*).
[2] Sc. ἐνανθρώπησις.   [3] 1 Cor. xv. 47.   [4] 1 Cor. xv. 45.
[5] The Syriac adjective *nafshānâ* here used is that derived from *nafshâ*, 'soul'.
[6] Nau reads with V.: 'in the same way as he is not called heavenly without . . .'

50. *Concerning this: that if 'the second man, the Lord from 'heaven',[1] is adopted of God the Word, then men are heavenly since they are of the nature of God the Word; for 'as is the heavenly, so also are the heavenly ones'.[2]*

Nestorius. Hear then also this, when you read the rest of the book, that *as is the heavenly, so also are the heavenly ones*,[2] and *as we have clothed ourselves in the likeness of one of dust*,[3] so also [are we] of dust, because all possess the same nature, and as he is heavenly, so also [are they] heavenly, because they have the same nature as the heavenly; [so] also all of us, who wait to become [so] in this sort. We men are of the *ousia* of God the Word, since our soul and our body have been combined for the completion of such a nature, and each of us becomes that which God the Word is by nature; / for *as is the heavenly, so also are the heavenly ones*,[2] and to the extent that they are heavenly men, they are Gods the Words, in that each single one of them is both of God the Word and of the human soul and body, not infinite in his nature, although in each one he exists [in some sense] infinitely except inasmuch as the nature of each single one of them is finite and apart from it his existence cannot be conceived. If you so understand the *Lord is from heaven*[1] and *the second man was a quickening spirit*,[4] how do you imagine the rest of it: *as we have been clothed in the likeness of him of dust, so shall we be clothed in that of him from heaven?*[3] How then have we been clothed in the likeness of him from dust? What do we become? And in what have we been clothed? Have we become heavenly and spiritual men, [formed] of the soul and the body and of God the Word? Or has the spirit without body and without soul been clothed in the likeness of him of dust, [who is] body and soul and who urges us to become the likeness of spiritual beings, that is, spirits without soul and without body, although indeed it is not our affair but [that of our] Maker? If this is according to the truth, how does he urge us to be clothed in the likeness of spiritual man, that is, [of] Christ, as though Christ were without soul

---

[1] 1 Cor. xv. 47 (P.).   [2] 1 Cor. xv. 48.
[3] 1 Cor. xv. 49.   [4] 1 Cor. xv. 45.

and without body? And how then is he man, if he has nothing of man? Or how is Christ called spiritual / man, he who has been constituted the *ousia* of God the Word to [become] the nature of man, [that is], of soul and body? And we shall come to be without bodily frame and without soul in becoming as he is, having nothing that he has not. But this cannot be so. It follows that those who confess that the nature of God cohered for the completion of human nature say these and such like absurdities, for a passible and created nature is the result of a natural union with a passible and created nature. And therefore they fall either into the opinion of the Arians, who say that by nature God the Word became the nature of a passible and mortal man, in enduring sufferings sensibly, or into the opinion of those who say that he became body and soul in fiction, or into [that of] both of them in inclining now to the one and now to the other side, because they suppose by such inclining to escape from these absurdities.

51. *Against those who suppose that Christ was a mere man.*

So far the argument has been against these. Let us look then also at the heresies of those who dissent and confess that Christ was only a man, [and see] wherein they are distinct and in what they resemble those above, in order that we may distinguish and demonstrate their heresies, so that we may not, on account of what has been wrongly said, again escape / that which has been fairly said and so that further we may not without distinction accept that which has been wrongly said. For to confess that Christ is man both by nature and in truth appertains unto the truth and is attested by the truth ; and therein is there no one who blames them. But in that they shun his divinity, though it exists in truth and in nature, they are to be repudiated, since they suppress the Incarnation [1] of God the Word.

52. *Concerning those who confess God the Word only in name.*

The Sabellians. Among them indeed are also those who deny that God the Word exists in *ousia* and who say only

---

[1] Sc. ἐνανθρώπησις.

that the name 'God the Word' is that command: *He spoke and it became.* But thus also they predicate the Father and the Holy Spirit in name alone; so in short they agree rather with the Jews than with Christians.

53. *Concerning those who say that God the Word exists indeed by nature, but that he has not been united by nature but in* schêma *and that there are two sons.*

The Paulinians. But others reprove them, confessing that God the Word is a nature or a *hypostasis*,[1] as also are the Father and the Holy Spirit. Concerning his incarnation[2] they agree not with the orthodox, but they approach those who say that Christ was only a man and that he comported himself in subjection to the law as one of the saints, and that by command he observed all the commandments and that by supreme observance he was without sin as a man, and thereby he is more excellent than all men, either because, after having been without sin, he appeared freed from death and rightly accepted immortality which is established for the honour of those who observe the law without sin, or because, having so comported himself in all these things, after he [had] observed all the commandments without fault, he accepted for himself to die for us and, in consequence of that greatness of his obedience, he received the honour and the name of Son by grace. He is not God the Word but he who has so comported himself and observed all the commandments. So they say.

The Paulinians.[3] What purpose indeed could it have served that God the Word also should associate himself with him in operations and should operate with him as though he could not of himself observe the commandments? And what is that which has been preserved without sin? Or what is the victory? It is not a high merit if, being unable to be victorious, he had need of assistance so as with assistance to be victorious, since he [himself] could not do it [otherwise]. For it is not to him that victory comes but to him that assisted him and was invincible. What then is a combat for God?

---

[1] See pp. 156, n. 2, 218, n. 3.   [2] Sc. ἐνανθρώπησις.
[3] The Syriac has only *Paule*'.

And what is the merit? That he who asks [assistance] of any one should be the saviour! / For what is he who sees that there is [nothing in common] between him and the prince who comes and finds nothing in him,[1] when it is discovered that the [divine] nature has assisted him? And before whom is he judged, when he who judges and is judged is the judge? Who is it who has accepted the offering for all men, when it is he who accepts and he who is offered? Who is it who propitiates and who is propitiated, when he is in both of them? [Who indeed], unless perhaps they break up[2] one sovereignty into two which are not like one another, and say that the Father was angry and the Son propitiated him when he was enraged, as they have learnt from the fables of the Manichaeans, who have foolishly invented them; or [unless] perhaps the Father manifested his anger in *schêma* against those who erred and appointed a term hypocritically by showing himself angry and able to be propitiated as by the Word?

Now in another way there adhere also to that which the [followers] of Arius imagine [men] who say that God has not been propitiated in any other way than by the death of Christ, who from in the beginning was God and he was God. What urgent need then was there for this foolish invention? For he who was in him did this not by the death of another; further also it is not justice that he who is not of one nature should accept death for another nature for the remission of the debt; nor also has a true remission been shown, but a *schêma*. / And they say that these things have been divided between two sons in such a way that some befit the one and others the other, in order that there may be neither contradictions nor schematisms in all the words that there are. There is one divinity and one lordship and one authority of the Father and the Son, who accept not any such *schêma*. These things and such like they say, insisting on their views, and call Christ and the Son double in *prosôpa* as well as in

---

[1] Jn. xiv. 30. There is no predicate in the Syriac text. The words 'nothing in common' are supplied from καὶ ἐν ἐμοὶ οὐκ ἔχει οὐδέν in Jn. xiv. 30.   [2] See crit. n., p. 398.

hypostases—in like manner as the saints have received the indwelling of God—and they speak also of his image in the same way.

Nestorius. Let us speak then also with every one of those who, decieved and deceivers, deny the incarnation[1] which took place for God the Word. And first let us use against them their very own words. Thou then lay before me their words, those which are persuasive and are of use in persuading many; and combat manfully for them, so that no cause at all for excuse may be granted unto them. Since then there is only one divinity and lordship and authority and knowledge and opinion and power of God the Father and of the Son, by means of whom everything came from the Father and without whom nothing at all which has come into being came into being, for what reason does he[2] apply only to God the Word *he became flesh*, not *he made the flesh* but *The Word became flesh*,[3] even he who was with / God?[4] And said he not of God the Father *he who is with the Father?* For *he became* and *he made* both belong unto him, since they make no division; nor is it [said] that the one is and that the other is not; but perhaps they confess that there are two Words as also two Sons and that the one is the divinity and the other the passibility in that it became flesh.

Sophronius. And what is there absurd in our confessing so? For this is evident; for the Evangelist said this also concerning him: *he dwelt among us*,[5] that is, concerning the Word, [but] of man this: *we have seen his glory, the glory as of the only begotten*,[6] and: *who is full of grace and of truth*[7] was not [said] of the only begotten, nor is it any more by nature, for he is full of glory, not by virtue of grace but by virtue of nature and he has no need of any addition.

Nestorius. When then the Father said concerning him *This is my Son*[8] and again *He has given his only begotten Son*[9]; and *the only begotten who is in the bosom of his Father has*

---

[1] Sc. ἐνανθρώπησις. [2] *Viz.* the Evangelist. [3] Jn. i. 14.
[4] Jn. i. 1. [5] Jn. i. 14. [6] Jn. i. 14 (P.).
[7] Jn. i. 14 (P.). Note the interpretation of 'full of grace' as meaning 'filled by grace' in contrast with 'by nature'.
[8] Matt. iii. 17 (P.); xvii. 5 (P.). [9] Jn. iii. 16.

himself told us,¹ did it speak of him who was in the bosom of his Father or did it speak of three only begottens, one who was from in the beginning God the Word and another who had the glory as of the only begotten without being / the only begotten, and a third apart from these whom he gave on behalf of the world?

Sophronius. What then? Did he give God the Word, consubstantial with him, who is immortal and impassible, unto death? And do not *He who is consubstantial, impassible and immortal* and *He gave him unto death* belie one another? Or is it perhaps so in *schéma*?

Nestorius. Thou wilt confess aloud with us that there are not two Gods the Words or two Sons or two only begottens, but one, and so on with all the rest of them. Investigation is made on both sides similarly and rightly how he became incarnate ² voluntarily, when he was by his nature immortal and impassible, and how it is said that the Son is dead in nature and in so far as he is not immortal by nature.

Sophronius. But we say these very things to show clearly, although thou dost not wish [it], that thou dost predicate two sons by nature, one impassible and immortal and the other passible and mortal.³

54. *Concerning this: that God the Word became incarnate ² and there were not two Sons but one by an union.*

Nestorius. It is not at all true; but if it is right in the first place to speak concerning this, from Divine Scripture itself will we learn that which we confess to one another. Let us see then what the Evangelist / says concerning God the Word. Does he speak of one God the Word or of two Words? *In the beginning was the Word and the Word was with God and the Word was God. He was in the beginning with God; everything came into being by him and without him came into being nothing whatsoever that came into being.*⁴

---

¹ Jn. i. 18 (P.). ² Sc. ἐνηνθρώπησεν.
³ See p. 19, n. 2. Sophronius again accuses Nestorius of Nestorianism, and this time he defends himself against the charges by directly denying what is alleged against him. See especially pp. 49-50.
⁴ Jn. i, 1-3 (P.).

Concerning whom can these things be said by the Evangelist, except concerning him who is consubstantial [with the Father] and without bodily frame?¹ And this: *In him was life and the life was the light of men and the same light shineth in the darkness and the darkness comprehended it not.*² Did he say it of another or of the very same? Therefore he called him both the life and the light, which indicate the immortal and quickening *ousia*, and [he said] *it shineth in the darkness and the darkness comprehended it not*, as if concerning things which had been in death and in darkness. But he is not dead, for he is the life and the light which are not extinguished, and he quickens those who are in death. Concerning what light does John bear witness, that all men should believe through it? Surely *it was the light of the truth which gives light unto every man who has come into the world; he was in the world and the world came into being by him and the world knew him not; he came to his own and his own received him not;* and *but to those who received him he gave authority to become the sons of God, to those who / believe on his name, who were born not of blood nor of the will of the flesh nor of the will of man but of God.*³ Did the Evangelist speak of another Word or of God the Word, by whom everything came into being, life and the true light, who came unto his own and his own received him not, who gave authority unto those that received him to become the sons of God, [who] were born not of blood nor of the will of the flesh but of God? And, further, whereby gave he to those who received him to become the sons of God? [Was it] to those who were born of the nature of God? [Or to those who] have been changed in nature into the nature of God and have become that which God the Word is in so far as he is born of the Father? Or have they⁴ remained in the same nature in which they are and have they become sons of God and have they been born of God by adoption⁵ and by acknowledgement? As they have received him as being God, who has become

---

¹ Cp. p. 14, n. 2.   ² Jn. i. 4–5 (P.).
³ Jn. i. 9–13 (P.).   ⁴ Syriac reads: 'has he...'
⁵ The Syriac root regularly represents οἰκεῖος, οἰκείωσις, and οἰκειότης.

[their] kin-by-adoption,¹ and as they have acknowledged that he is their God who has made everything and who has come unto his own, so also he has made them his kin-by-adoption¹ and has acknowledged them to be the sons of God, as sons who have entered into sonship but who possess not the nature.

55. *Concerning this: that God the Word is one by nature and is [so] named and that there are not many who have been [so] named by homonymy.*

Those who become sons by adoption and by acknowledgement [become the sons] of him/of whom they are born not by flesh nor by blood but by the will and the love of him who has no bodily frame but has become their body by adoption and by love and by acknowledgement like a father; so also God the Word who has come into his own has given authority unto those who have received him and confessed him and believed in his name; for he has not given to those, who are not born of blood nor of the will of the flesh nor of the will of the man,² to become the sons of God—for that should have been possessed by them beforehand in their natures—but they were born of God by adoption. Thus therefore he who came into his own and was received gave to those who believed in his name authority to become the sons of God, and he will be their flesh by the taking of the flesh and he will make it [his] by adoption and he will acknowledge it as his body by adoption. Consequently he³ has said: *The Word became flesh*;⁴ balancing *in the beginning was the Word and the Word was with God*⁵ and so on. He also adduced *the Word became flesh and sojourned*⁶ *among us*.⁷ As those who have received him have become voluntarily by reception the natural [sons] of God, so also he, in that he received the flesh and sojourned in it, became their flesh by adoption and not by change of *ousia*. Therefore also he adduced the peculiar property of God, saying *And we have seen his glory, the glory as of the only begotten of*/*the*

---

¹ See p. 48, n. 5.   ² Syr. *gabhrâ* = *vir* rather than *homo*.
³ *Viz.* the Evangelist.   ⁴ Jn. i. 14 (P.).   ⁵ Jn. i. 1 (P.).
⁶ The Syriac root probably corresponds to Gk. σκηνόω.   ⁷ Jn. i. 14 (P.).

Father.¹ He qualifies it not by likeness but as for confirmation, when he says 'full of grace', in calling that which is of the nature of the only begotten grace; for that is the fulness. For that which surely participates [in anything] is not full but is deficient in that of which the nature is altogether it, and he is *full of grace and truth*¹; not as one who has been changed but as one who is that which the beloved Son was; according as they have received him and according as they have believed in him, so also have they seen him who was revealed in flesh, [even] him and not another God nor again another Word nor another life nor another light nor again another only begotten, but the very same who was revealed in flesh. And *of his fulness have we all received*² that which was not in us; and *of his fulness have we received* but not his fulness; for the fulness consists in being deficient in nothing, as God. And consequently the only begotten who is in the bosom of his Father has expounded unto us God whom no one has ever seen; and no one else than he who was in the bosom of his Father came and became flesh and dwelt among us; and he is in the bosom of his Father and with us, in that he is what the Father is, and he has expounded unto us what he is in the bosom of his Father—it being evident that he has not explained the infinity and the incomprehensibility of the *ousia*. As he knows our nature he has expounded unto us in our very nature that which none of mankind has ever seen. How then is it possible that we should understand by him one Son and by Christ another Son, who is only such as a man is and who in the equality and the honour of sonship remains in the image of him whom you deny to have been sent and to have moved among us? By a kind of divine indwelling he who was in the likeness of God [so] dwelt, as the Evangelist clearly refers us back from God the Word to God the Word³ and apart from God the Word shows no other Word nor other only begotten of God, except him [who is] with his flesh.

¹ Jn. i. 14 (P.).   ² Jn. i. 16.
³ *I.e.* from v. 14 to v. 1 of Jn. i.

Sophronius.[1] But from what has been said understand what the Evangelist says: *No man has ever seen God; the only begotten Son who was in the bosom of his Father has expounded [him],*[2] speaking of him who has been taken up and sits on the right hand of the Father, who is the Son in the image and glory of the Son, who has been shown unto us, *who has come after me, who is mightier than I,*[3] on whom the Holy Spirit has come down and has remained in the likeness of a dove,[4] who is the elect of God, the Lamb of God, the Nazarene, the Son of Man; *you shall see the heavens opened and the angels of God ascending and descending upon the Son of Man.*[5] It is not he who in *ousia* is God the Word, consubstantial with the Father; for *no one has ever seen God,*[6] but he has been seen. But he spoke not of him but of the Son of Man, who by his grace was in the rank[7] of the image of the Son of God, and thereby he was the Son and the only begotten by good will; *in whom dwells all the fulness of the divinity in bodily frame.*[8] He is not the fulness, but all the fulness dwells in him in bodily frame as it has dwelt in every single one of the saints. For he who is the Son is not by himself apart nor again is the Father by himself apart, for the Son is in the Father and the Father in the Son. And consequently if the incarnation[9] which took place in the *ousia* is that of the Son of God, it is also that of the Father and of the Holy Spirit, if you say that he is the Son by nature and not by equality and honour; for he has been sent in the *prosôpon* of the Son of God and is clothed in his *prosôpon* and everything appertaining unto him is referred unto him, as God is in an angel and in a mediator, for he is *the mediator of God and of men, the Man Jesus Christ.*[10] And how then has there been one Son and

---

[1] Sophronius here seems to identify himself with Nestorius' point of view, but to deduce from it that he must go on to conclude that God was in Christ in the same way as in the saints. He is thus used to represent an accusation commonly brought against Nestorius by the orthodox, which Nestorius proceeds to rebut.

[2] Jn. i. 18.   [3] Matt. iii. 11; cp. Jn. i. 27.   [4] Jn. i. 32.
[5] Jn. i. 51.   [6] Jn. i. 18.   [7] Syr. *taksâ* = Gk. τάξις.
[8] Col. ii. 9 (P.).   [9] *Sc.* ἐνανθρώπησις.   [10] 1 Tim. ii. 5.

an incarnation¹ of God, unless perhaps it is said that there has been an incarnation¹ of God in every thing whereby God wrought the dispensation for men, and it is said that God has said and God has wrought and God has been seen in those things which have been said or wrought by Moses and by the prophets and by the angels./ Because in fact God by his nature is invisible and incomprehensible, he must have some mediator, through whom to provide these things, while to him are referred those things which are wrought or said by them by the doctrine of providence and of the dispensation and not in the course of nature. How is he who is man by nature God by nature, and not by grace and activity, as God can act at his will in the case of all nature, unless, perhaps, God be everthing in him? Some one will say that God and man are acting [alike] and that he is two natures. I turn then to those things on which the whole investigation hangs.

56. *Concerning this: that it is not said that God became incarnate² also in one of the prophets or saints, nor even that he made use of any of them in his own prosôpon.*

Nestorius. Since then, as they say, they adhere to the Divine Scriptures, the statement [of our case] against them causes us no labour. For never has any of the prophets nor of the angels been seen to make use of the *prosôpon* of God in his own *prosôpon*; but our Lord Christ said: *I and God are one,*³ and *whoever sees me has seen God,*⁴ and *that which God has done, that I also do, as he,*⁵ and *as God has life in his hypostasis and gives life to whom he will, I also, even I, give life to whom I will,*⁶ / and *if ye believe not on me, believe at least in my works, because I and God are one.*⁷ None further of the prophets nor of the angels dared to say these things; but, whatsoever they said or did, [they said] *the Lord said*, and not 'God or they'; and all that they said or did, [they said] that by their means God said [it]; they also said that God said [it], as the prophets

---

[1] Sc. ἐνανθρώπησις. [2] Sc. ἐνηνθρώπησεν. [3] See Jn. x. 30.
[4] Jn. xiv. 9. [5] Jn. v. 17, 36; x. 37-8.
[6] Jn. v. 26. Note that Nestorius, like the writer of the Peshiṭtâ version, uses 'in his *hypostasis*' for ἐν ἑαυτῷ. [7] Jn. x. 38, 30.

and as the angels. And wherein he took the *schêma* of a man or of fire, it is said that God appeared or that one saw God; and in another place, that *God gave the law*,[1] and again: *by means of the angels the law was given*.[2] They are not lies nor further are they contradictory one to another; it is not that he calls the angels God nor again that an angel calls himself God; but, because he appeared by means of the angels, both are truly said, both that God appeared by means of the angels in the fire of a bush and that by means of it God appeared unto him.[3]

57. *Concerning this: that according to the Divine Scriptures we have learned to confess Christ God by nature and Man by nature.*

Since then he called himself by the two [names], both the Apostles and the Evangelists say also that he exists in the two: [he is] both God by whom everything comes about, and he came into the world, and he made the world, and he was not received by his servants, and to those / who received him and believed in his name he gave [4] authority to become the sons of God, and he became flesh and sojourned among us,[5] he and none other. And since he became [flesh] and sojourned among us, he has drawn to himself the very flesh for [the purpose of] the adoption as for his own *prosôpon*, which is in both of them, in that on the one hand [there is] the *ousia* of God, but on the other the flesh by the union and the adoption; in such wise that the flesh, which is flesh by nature, is also Son by the union and the adoption of the *prosôpon*; although he exists in both of them, yet he is called one Son and one flesh. And consequently the only begotten Son of God and the Son of man, the same [formed] of both of them, is predicated in both of them, because he has made the things of their *prosôpa* his own *prosôpon* and is therefore acknowledged as his own *prosôpon* by the one as by the other; and he speaks with them now by virtue of the divinity and now by virtue of the humanity and now by virtue of both of them; as also the humanity used to speak now by virtue of the *ousia* of the humanity and now

---

[1] Ex. xxxi. 18.   [2] Gal. iii. 19.   [3] Ex. iii. 2.
[4] See crit. n., p. 399.   [5] Cp. Jn. i. 3, 11, 12. 14.

by the *prosôpon* of the divinity: on this account he both is the Son of God and the Son of man and has so spoken.[1]

58. *That as also God the Word is conceived to have become flesh and the flesh is one, and there are not two fleshes, so also the flesh is Son and there are not two Sons.*

/ Is it not as if the Word were Son only in so far as he became flesh? Since he took the flesh in his own *prosôpon*, he became flesh and the flesh was God because of the *prosôpon* of the Word, in such wise that God the Word is said to be flesh and man, while the flesh is called the Son of God. For until he took the flesh in his own *prosôpon* and was revealed therein, he was called Son on account of the divinity: *in the beginning was the Word and the Word was with God, and the Word was God; everything came into being through him, and without him also nothing whatever came into being.*[2] But since he became flesh in taking the flesh, he was named after both of them in both of them,[3] but as though he were one in both of them, not [in both] in nature, but in the one indeed in nature but in the other in *prosôpon* by adoption as well as by revelation. The Son was revealed in flesh, being similar to his Father: *I and my Father are one*, he says in a manner demonstrative of his own *prosôpon*. He who was seen speaks from him who was conceived as from his own *prosôpon*, as though he were one and possessed the same *prosôpon*. Through one is the other conceived, and he who is conceived discourses by him who was seen as by the very *prosôpon* of him who was seen. *If you do not believe on me, believe in my works, because I and the Father are one.*[4] / And all such things as these which have been said originally of the *ousia* [are to be said] accordingly also to speak and to understand and to operate in the very same way in the *prosôpon* as by adoption. For they are not far removed either in operation or in word or in *ousia*; nor are the things which are to be distinguished the one from the other in the *prosôpon* distinct in love, for they are conceived of his *prosôpon* in the love and the will of God in that he took the flesh; and therein he was revealed and therein he taught, and

---

[1] Cp. p. 86, n. 1.
[2] Jn. i. 1, 3.
[3] Omitted in S. and C.
[4] Jn. x. 38.

therein and by means thereof he acts as though present and
not as though absent. Of his own *prosôpon* he made use in
the flesh, in that he wished that he should become flesh and
that the flesh should become himself, so that those who see the
flesh [see] also God, as his own body is in the bread and those
who see the bread [see] also the body, because he has taken it
for his *prosôpon*. He who is the similitude of God has taken the
prosôpon of the flesh, the likeness of a servant, and he has given
unto him, unto the likeness of the servant [which is] his likeness, *a name which is more excellent than all names*, that is
'Son', *at which every knee shall bow which is in heaven and in
earth, and which is beneath the earth*.[1] And consequently there
must be two natures, that of the divinity and that of the
humanity, that which has emptied itself into the likeness of
a servant and the likeness of a servant which has been raised
into *the name which is above all names*. For he who does not
remain in his own *ousia* can neither / be emptied nor diminished
nor even raised above all names. Therefore has he said 'the
likeness' and 'the name' which it has taken, which indicates
a *prosôpon* as of one; and this same name and *prosôpon* make
the two of them to be understood; and the distinction of
nature, one *hypostasis* and one *prosôpon*,[2] is theirs, the one being
known by the other and the other by the one, so that the one
is by adoption what the other is by nature and the other is
with the one in the body. As a king and a lord, who has
taken the *prosôpon* of a servant as his own *prosôpon* and gives
his *prosôpon* to the servant and makes known that he is the
other and the other he, is content to be abased in the *prosôpon*
of the servant while the servant is revered in the *prosôpon* of the
lord and king, and for this reason, even though I should not
have said the one for the other nor the other for the one, it is so
with both of them who are one and possess the same *prosôpon*
—[so] are these things in regard to the two natures which are
distinct in *ousia* but are united by love and in the same
prosôpon.

59. *Concerning this: that the adoption and the indwelling*

---

[1] Phil. ii. 9–10.

[2] This presumably means that each nature has its own *hypostasis* and *prosôpon*. (So Nau.)

ought to be accepted as the will of God and that we ought not to avoid a name as though that which is profane were said in consequence of the homonymy.[1]

For although the humanity of ours[2] bears / as mediator the *prosôpon* only of God by adoption as well as by the indwelling of the *ousia* and not only by the indwelling of divinity, yet this indwelling is such as to result in one *prosôpon*, which is the same for him who is revealed as for him who is to be revealed. For the [words] *He is* and *He dwelt* are of necessity to be confessed and interpreted[3] by us according to the will of God. God indeed is in all creatures; for in him we are and thereby is it defined that, although thus he is verily in all, he is said to have dwelt in some men; but in regard to others it is even said that he is not their God. And it is not said that he dwelt in all men in like manner, but according to his love; in some of us it is said that he only dwelt in a composition[4] as in a house, as in the believers, while in others, although he is acting, yet [he acts] not in like manner but to a greater or less degree; in others as in all the apostles and in others as in the prophets and in others as in teachers and in others according to the division of gifts. In this one and in that and in another he dwells, and he acts also in all; and all of them are not equal to all nor like one another, but [all are] according to the love of him who dwells in them. Among them some hold the first place and others of them the second [rank] and in gradually descending order are they attached and joined one to another, in the same way as are the limbs / in the body. But *Christ is the head of all*[5] and in him are we bound together; but also God is the head of Christ, for whom, as he is for us the head and the *prosôpon*, is God so also his head and his *prosôpon* in[6] his incarnation.[7] Therefore we have received

---

[1] In this section Nestorius shows clearly that he is aware that in using words like 'adoption' and 'indwelling' he is in danger of being taken to teach psilanthropism, from which he is careful to distinguish his own doctrine.

[2] Syr. 'which [is] of us'; *om.* V.   [3] Literally: 'judged'.

[4] Syr. *rûkhābhâ*, 'composition', which is thought by Nau to be perhaps a rendering of the Gk. κατασκευή. Bedjan marks the word as doubtful in his text.

[5] Col. i. 18.   [6] Syr. 'and'. See crit. n., p. 399.   [7] *Sc.* σάρκωσις.

from him to become the sons of God, in that he is the only begotten Son; so that his flesh becomes that which also is the Son of God and of the Father so as to become the image of the Father, [being] the Son of the Father whose is the image; because this same is the *prosôpon* of the Son, it is he and none other which [exists] in the two *ousias* and is not distinguished.

60. *Concerning this: that we should not thus think of the Archetype as also of images or as of angels or as of ambassadors who take the place*[1] *of him who is absent, but [that we should think] that he has been united to the body by his own nature and by his prosôpon and that he has become incarnate*[2] *in their making use of the body in its own* prosôpon *and the body's [making use] of the* prosôpon *of God the Word.*

God[3] is not indeed among the things which are represented in effigy[4] for there things can be said to exist only in the visible shape, by visible shape and by likeness while far distant from the *ousia*, nor again as angels or ambassadors who take the place[5] of those who send them and are thereby their *prosôpa* in virtue of service and mere authority, / but hè himself has made use of his very [own] nature and his *prosôpon* in saying that 'I and the Father are one',[6] and he is whatever he is in *prosôpon* and whatever he is in *prosôpon* he is, not that he made his likeness in another likeness but in his own likeness, nor in any other likeness like unto the likeness of a servant but in the very natural likeness of the other, so that the one became what the other was and the other that which the one was, both the one and the other remaining.

61. *Concerning this: that through the nature of man he received a name which is more excellent than all names.*

This in fact is the chief greatness of the nature of humanity: that, since he remains in the nature of humanity, he accepts *a name which is more excellent than all names*;[7] neither in consequence of moral progress[8] nor in consequence of know-

---

[1] Literally: 'fill the *prosôpon*'.   [2] *Sc.* ἐνηνθρώπησεν.
[3] *i.e.* in the Incarnation.   [4] Syr. *yûqnâ* = Gk. εἰκών.
[5] Literally: 'fill the *prosôpa*'.   [6] Jn. x. 30.   [7] Phil. ii. 9 (P.).
[8] The Syr. *dûrāghâ ddûbhārē*' means literally 'the gradual progress of manners' or 'manner of life'; the word *dûrāghâ* here translated 'progress' probably represents the Gk. προκοπή.

ledge and faith, but therein[1] by virtue of his readiness to accept [it] has it come about that it should become his *eikôn* and his *prosôpon* in such wise that his *prosôpon* is also the *prosôpon* of the other. And he is both God and man, and the likeness of God in condescension and in *kenôsis* and in *schêma*, [and] the likeness of the flesh as man; and the man is by exaltation what God is, through the name which is above all names. Consequently in the *kenôsis* he humbled himself *unto death, even death / upon the cross*,[2] in that he made use of the *prosôpon* of him who died and was crucified as his own *prosôpon*, and in his own *prosôpon* he made use of the things which appertained unto him who died and was crucified and was exalted. And therefore [this] is said as of the one *prosôpon* of Christ, and the former things and the latter are each thus different, in nature, as the divine nature is different from the nature of man; so that Christ is two natures, the likeness of God and the likeness of a servant, that which has been exalted and that which exalts. If also he is called Christ because of the flesh which has been anointed, there is one *prosôpon* of the two natures, because also there is only one name which is more excellent than all names, [one for] both of them, if the divine nature is meant; for the names of the natural *prosôpa* are common in the condescension and in the exaltation.

62. *Concerning this: that the dispensation for our sake ought to have taken place by both of them.*

And it was congruous with the dispensation which is for our sake that both of them should be taken into the *prosôpon*; for, because God created the first man in his own image and in his likeness and the *prosôpa* of God the Maker—of the Father and of the Son and of the Holy Spirit,—were not revealed to us, so that we might also know the Creator and obtain completely the teaching of the Divine knowledge and receive in completeness a complete idea / of the image of God, he has renewed all creation in Christ and has made known and shown unto us what the Maker is: he who from the beginning was the Word with God was also God the Maker

---

[1] *Viz.* the humanity. [2] Phil. ii. 8 (P.).

of all; *everything came into being through him and without him also nothing whatever came into being.*[1]

63. *Concerning this: wherefore God the Word built for himself the temple of the body.*

Even as it must have been fitting that our renewal also should take place through the Maker of [our] nature, through him who also originally formed us and made us from the earth, he who took the body and made it in his likeness and constituted it in his *prosôpon* in everything as his own in the honour and glory of God, made use of the nature of the Divinity on the one hand and of the *prosôpon* of the Son on the other. For the honour of the Father and of the Son is one in such wise that those who honour the Father honour also the Son. He then has taught us that he who has created everything is God and that he created [it] with the Father and the Holy Spirit;[2] for in him he lived, showing the natural union, [to wit] that the Father is [Father] of the Son and that the Father is in the Son and that the Holy Spirit lives in them. And he created the body in a new manner [other] than from a man and a woman, and, since it was an act of creation, he tells of that which is to be created and of him who creates: *The Holy Spirit will come and the power of the Most High shall overshadow [thee]*[3]*/*—denoting the Creator. *Therefore he who shall be born shall be called the son of God*[3] —that is the Holy One who is to be created; so that in the creation he calls [him] 'holy' and 'Son', denoting the image and the likeness which the first man received in the Creation and which he kept not. For, as the image of God, he ought to have kept himself for God without spot and without blemish, and that by willing what God wills, since he had the *prosôpon* of God. For [to have] the *prosôpon* of God is to will what God wills, whose *prosôpon* he has.[4] Consequently the second man was created by the Holy Spirit and the power

---

[1] Jn. i. 3 (P.).   [2] See crit. n., p. 399.   [3] Luke i. 35.
[4] If this were a definition of what it is to have the *prosôpon* of God, it would lay Nestorius open to the charge of being a Nestorian. But that it is not is made clear by p. 62, ll. 14-16. This sentence therefore merely states that willing the same things as God is implied in having the *prosôpon* of God. Cp. pp. 70, 163.

of the Most High and he has received from him to be *holy* and the *Son of God*.

64. *Concerning this: that he*[1] *has received to become 'Son' from [the moment of] his formation and not by degrees.*

[In that he has received the title to be 'holy'] not as the rest of mankind by virtue of obedience in faith and in works, but from [the moment of] coming into being by the creation of the Creator, he has received his *prosôpon* as something created, in such wise as not originally to be man but at the same time Man-God by the incarnation[2] of God who in him is what God was in the first man.[3] He indeed was the Maker of all, the law-giver, without king,[4] the glory, the honour and the power; he was also the second / man with qualities complete and whole, so that God was his *prosôpon* while he was in God.

65. *Concerning this: how, in that he has not the* prosôpon *of his being, the* prosôpon *in the union ought to be understood.*[5]

As God appeared and spoke unto Adam in *schêma*, and as it was none other, so will God be [seen] of all men in the natural *schêma* which has been created, that is, that of the flesh, appearing and speaking in his own image and the image in the Archetype. So that on the one hand God appeared in the image, since he is not visible, on the other hand the image is conceived as representing him who appeared not. For it is not [the fact] that the image is his being, but that on the other hand the very image and *prosôpon* [are] the humanity of the divinity and the divinity of the humanity. The *prosôpon* of him who is conceived, *who was in the likeness and in the similitude of God*[6] *took the likeness of a servant and in* schêma *was*

---

[1] *Sc.* the man Jesus.   [2] *Sc.* ἐνανθρώπησις.

[3] For Nestorius' teaching on the relation of Christ to Adam see Loofs, *Nestoriana*, pp. 256-8, and Labbe (Mansi), iv. 1349 E-1351 C.

[4] See crit. n., p. 399.

[5] In this section Nestorius develops the idea that the Incarnation took place for the purpose of revelation, an idea very prominent in his thought. Cp. p. 34, n. 1, and references there. The section is also an important one for the determination of the meaning of *prosôpon*.

[6] Phil. ii. 6.

found as a man[1] in him who appeared. And he who appeared [is considered] as representing him who is conceived as touching the *prosôpon* and the name which is above all names and honour and glory and adoration. For *he gave unto him a name which is more excellent than all names, that at the name of Jesus every knee should bow which is in heaven and on the earth and which is beneath the earth, and every tongue should confess that Jesus is the Lord*,[2] [as it is] narrated. /

66. *How the flesh is adored in the* prosôpon *of the Son and how, since it is in nothing worthy of that adoration, it is adored in the* prosôpon *of God the Word.*

Man indeed is known by the human *prosôpon*, that is, by the *schéma* of the body and by the likeness, but God by the name which is more excellent than all names and by the adoration of all creation and by the confession [of him] as God. For thereby has he taken the likeness of a servant and has given his likeness to the likeness of the servant, that it might be equal with God, and that, as he has accepted it for himself to be his own *prosôpon*, no one might refuse to him on account of [his] nature the adoration of the Divinity in heaven and on earth and beneath the earth and [the confession] by every tongue, although by nature it is above all human nature. Who then would refuse him the adoration which belongs to the Lord of all and which belongs to his own *prosôpon* and his name? And who again refuses to prostrate himself before that before which formerly the Creator of all refused not[3] to prostrate himself? And he prostrated himself to such a degree that his own creation in its nature was not in honour nor in glory but in contempt and in abasement and in all humiliation unto death upon the cross; he humiliated himself unto death, even death upon the cross; there is nothing more scorned than death. It was not wrought / in the same manner as in Adam, to whom he gave his image in all glory and honour; for *he subjected everything under his feet*.[4] In the same way also he gave to the Second Man his image of glory both in honour and in power. But

---
[1] Phil. ii. 7.   [2] Phil. ii. 9-11 (P.).
[3] The negative is omitted in the Syriac text. See p. xiv, n. 3.   [4] Ps. viii. 6.

all these things came to pass in the opposite way; he surely gave the image of God and he surely took the likeness of a servant in *prosôpon* . . .[1]

67. *Wherefore, in taking the likeness of a servant, he took not that which was honourable but rather that which was contemptible.*

And consequently he took the likeness of a servant, a humble likeness, a likeness which had lost the likeness of God, not for honour nor for glory nor for adoration nor again for authority, although indeed he was the Son, but for the obedience which it should observe in the *prosôpon* of the Son according to the purpose of God; since it had the purpose of the latter and not its own nor anything that it wished, but that which God the Word wished. For this is the likeness of God, to have neither purpose nor will of its own / but that of him whose *prosôpon* and likeness it has.[2] And therefore the likeness of God took the likeness of a servant, without concealing aught of the humiliation of the likeness of a servant; but all these things it took, in order that the likeness might be in all of them in such wise that it might do so without diminution in its own likeness.

68. *Why he took voluntary obedience in the likeness of a servant and did not exhibit a mechanical [obedience] without volition.*

Because in fact he took this [likeness] in order to abolish the guilt of the first man and in order to give to his nature the former image which he had lost through his guilt, rightly he took that which had proved itself guilty and had been made captive and had been subjected to servitude, with all the bonds of scorn and contempt. Apart from his own *prosôpon* there was nothing divine or appertaining to honour or to authority. As a son, as long as he is young, possesses not the authority to inherit or be master of anything, except by obedience, so also the likeness of a servant which he took for his own *prosôpon* he accepted as the

---

[1] Only isolated words and letters have been preserved in the next five lines of the Syriac text.

[2] See p. 59, n. 4.

likeness of a servant, not for authority but for obedience, even all that obedience from which especially is born the obedience which is sinless, and he appeared / truly sinless. When then anyone is freed from all the causes from which disobedience comes into being, then obviously and without doubt it appears that he is sinless. For this [cause] also he took a nature which had sinned, lest in taking a nature which was not subject unto sins he should be supposed not to have sinned on account of the nature and not on account of his obedience. But, although he had all those things which appertain unto our nature, anger and concupiscence and thoughts, and although also they increased with the progress and increase of every age [in his life], he stood firm in thoughts of obedience.[1]

69. *Wherefore he accepted not obedience in some commandments, as Adam, but accepted all the commandments and not single ones.*

Now in all the primary commandments his inclination [was] towards obedience, but not in the others, in order that it might not be supposed that he was able to conquer on account of their easiness; nor again in obedience made he use of those wherein there was attraction in honour and power and glory, but of those which in misery and poverty and contempt and weakness could offend the thoughts of obedience,[2] those also wherein there was no attraction to obedience but rather to remissness and to negligence, / and in nothing was he helped; but for this only was he anxious, to obey God, and he loved that which God willed.

70. *Wherefore in the moral life there was no occupation in human affairs on the part of the divinity.*

And therefore, while he was poor in everything and was violently drawn away by the opposite, he in nothing deviated from the purpose of God, although indeed Satan made use of all these things to remove him far from the purpose of God. And Satan sought much after this because he saw that none was occupied with him. For also it did not appear

---

[1] In Du Bose, *The Soteriology of the New Testament*, chaps. xiii and xiv, there is a modern statement of a position remarkably similar to that of Nestorius in this section. Cp. below, pp. 72, n. 6; 75, n. 1. [2] See crit. n., p. 399.

that from the beginning he wrought signs nor again that he had authority to teach, but only to obey and to keep all the commandments. As he moved among all men, where all the commandments surrounded him on all sides and showed him the strength of disobedience, he comported himself valiantly in the midst of them all, in that he used nothing special or extraordinary for his support, but he made use, as all men, of those very things which are common so that it should not be supposed that through observance of these things he was preserved from sin and that without them he could not be preserved. Consequently in eating and drinking he observed all the commandments and, in whatsoever there was pain and vexation, he was firm / in his thoughts, because his will was bound to the will of God and there was nothing to draw him away and make him distinct from him. For he was living not for himself but for him whose *prosôpon* he was, and he kept the *prosôpon* without blemish and without scar and thereby gave victory to the nature.

71. *Wherefore he accepted the baptism of John after he had shown himself sinless.*

Because he had fulfilled obedience in every thing, he accepted the baptism of John as [some thing] supreme,[1] after the likeness of all men; and although indeed he had no need, since he was sinless, by reason of the greatness of his obedience he accepted it as one in need. For it belonged to supreme obedience that he should be not as befitted his honour and his glory but as owing obedience to a commander; and, more than this, not only that he should allow him to baptize [him] but also that he should be baptized by him as one who is guilty and requiring to be justified and in need of absolution. For this was universal obedience, to ask for and exact nothing in his own *prosôpon* but in that of him whose was the *prosôpon*, and to prepare his will; for the *prosôpon* was properly his own and he considered his *prosôpon* as his own *prosôpon*; and the *prosôpon* is one.[2] There-

[1] Syr. *rîshâyâ* = (Payne-Smith) *eximius, praecipuus, praestans, optimus, κυριώτατος, πρωτεύων, ἀκρότατος* (in ἀκροτάτη ἄνοια), *pretiosus*.

[2] Bethune-Baker discusses the references of the pronouns in this passage in *Nestorius and his Teaching*, p. 126.

fore the Father has declared it from on high, saying : / *Thou art my beloved Son; in Thee I am well-pleased*;[1] and the Holy Spirit came down in the likeness of a dove and remained upon him, and he says not that the Son came down, because it was the Son who possessed his *prosôpon* and made the things which were his his own *prosôpon* without becoming distinguished from him. Therefore he is one even in the birth of the flesh.[2] *The Holy Spirit shall come and the power of the Most High shall overshadow thee; therefore also the Holy One who shall be born of thee shall be called the son of God;*[3] and he said not at all that the Son should come, because he who has taken him in his *prosôpon* is no other, but the same as he who has given him the dispensation[4] which is on behalf of all of us, for those reasons which we have said before.

72. *Wherefore he made his manner of life with all men and afterwards was led to the wilderness.*

Because it was thought that he was more than all an observer of the commandments, on account of his manner of life among all men, and because if in many things he was left alone, [it might have been] easy [to fight] against him, where there was nothing whereby he could be helped, he went forth alone into the wilderness to be tempted of the devil, while poor in all the things of the world, even in that which is considered a burden and a distress. And [because of this] removal far from every thing / he attained to the utmost supremacy to which bodily power could be raised, and instead of vehement assaults from the concupiscence of the soul, he was bound by the things of God as though without bodily frame, since he was not busied with his body as though it were his own but [as if he were] apart from it. For this appertains only to the image of God and to him who preserves the image

---

[1] Matt. iii. 17.

[2] This unity '*in* the birth of the flesh' must surely be something more than the union with a man *from* the moment of birth commonly associated with Nestorianism.

[3] Luke i. 35.

[4] Here *mpharnsānûthâ* (formed from the Gk. πρόνοος), elsewhere rendered 'providence' and not, as usually in this work, *mdhabhrānûthâ* = 'economy', 'dispensation'.

of God, to will the same as God the Father; and because there was nothing else in all that the devil said, he put him to shame as one who stood apart from the will of God. He raised up his very soul unto God, conforming that which was according to his will to the will of God in order that he might be the image only of the Archetype, and not of his being; for the image according to its [own] being is without likeness and its own proper likeness is that of the Archetype, and they are indeed two, but it is one and the same appearance. Since in actions in bodily things he has preserved the likeness of God from all the sufferings of the body, it was preferable to him that the will of God should be done and not that of the flesh; and in actions he made himself a likeness to will that which he wills, that there might be one and the same will in both of them, and one *prosôpon* without division; the one is the other and the other is the one, while the other and the one remain. As he remained firm in all things,/in temptations of body and soul, in cities and in the wilderness, there was no distinction in his observance and in his obedience.

73. *Concerning this: that, when he preached unto us the kingdom of heaven, he received [this] honour, victory*[1] *without sin.*

As then to him who has conquered and been victorious in all things there has been given in return for the honour of his victory authority to preach and to announce the hope of the kingdom of heaven, saying: *Be of good cheer; I have conquered the world;*[2] *now is the judgement of this world, now is the prince of this world condemned, and I, when I shall be raised up from the earth, shall draw all men toward me;*[3] and *whatsoever the Son is, by fear and the suffering which he has borne he has learnt obedience and has been perfected and has become unto all those who obey him a cause of life in the world to come.*[4] And he was sent to teach all men and to work signs and wonders and healings with all other things. Not to delight himself in and be zealous for obedience, but

---

[1] From the next section it is clear that the victory was that of the Temptation.
[2] Jn. xvi. 33 (P.).   [3] Jn. xii. 31-2.   [4] Heb. v. 8-9.

with a view to the faith of those who were being taught, he made use of all these things with a view to the obedience of the disciples; for until the time of his victory he was striving to make firm in God the image which had been given unto him. But because he stablished his own image in all temptations perfectly and without failing / and without falling short in anything, he comported himself on our behalf, being zealous to rescue us captives from the violence of the tyrant and to draw us towards him and to make all of us the sons of his own kingdom, the associates and the heirs and the sons of God. For the defeat of the tyrant was being [accomplished] without pity, when he threw him down openly from his primacy and, after he had thrown him down, he took from him also his might; and when he had taken it from him, his own victory sufficed him not, but it must henceforth be also ours for which sake he strove; and those who are obedient unto him he then brings unto him voluntarily and not by force, and those who come he persuades of their own will to part from him[1] and not of their own will to become his . . . .[2] disciples—and what shall I say? enemy? well then, of the enemy.

74. *Concerning this: that, after the victory and after it was said of him: 'He is my Son', he began other hard battles on our behalf.*

Therefore, after his victory in every thing and [after] it was said from heaven: *This is my beloved Son*,[3] he again began other battles . . . .[2] the supremacy and the teaching and the working of miracles with authority. Further he comported himself with sublime obedience / in our things, that is, in things human and weak, in such wise that he possessed not any authority or superiority; he was persecuted and beaten and fearful [with] the fear that terrifies all men; and he had not as the birds and as the beasts a place to lay his head.[4] He went from place to place and was bruised and constrained in every way, for the sake of our obedience. He was not constrained by any one, but he fulfilled [everything]

---
[1] *Viz.* the devil.
[2] There is here a short lacuna in the text.
[3] Matt. iii. 17 (P.).
[4] Cp. Matt. viii. 20.

and taught with all zeal, and he endured all temptations for the sake of instruction ; and from wheresoever he was driven out, he was driven toward those to whom his gospel was not yet preached,[1] so that that for which he was zealous was accomplished by the zeal of his enemies, who foresaw not the issue of their work but who looked to hinder him by opposition and works full of contempt and scorn and fear unto death. And after his victory and after the choice of God that *this is my beloved Son in whom I am well-pleased*,[2] after he had received the authority of the Gospel, after it was revealed that by his authority he was working the divine works, after he had said *I and my Father are one*,[3] he was with all this weakness and contempt in human things, whose burden he could not endure / by reason of their weight but which on the contrary were a grief unto him and a negation of grace. And so then there were many things also which hindered him from preaching the Gospel; and hence also there arose, [claiming to speak] on behalf of God, accusers of him as one who was a cause of disobedience,[4] and they brought him into contempt and weakness.

75. *Concerning this: that he made use of supreme[5] obedience itself as of a supreme honour so that Christ became also truly man and rejected it not as contemptible.*

For for all men contempt which comes after honour is accounted contemptible; but for Christ, who was in the flesh, it is the contrary. And he possessed as a supreme honour *obedience unto death, even death upon the cross*,[6] and he showed unto Satan and unto every principality and unto every authority that the cause of honour is rather obedience abounding and not disobedience unto God, whereby Satan suffered, when he was equal in nature and in honour but endured not the obedience of men, in that he was judging honour and contempt by the distinction between his own nature and

---

[1] The Syriac word corresponds to the Gk. εὐηγγέλισται.
[2] Matt. iii. 17 (P.).   [3] Jn. x. 30 (P.).
[4] This passage is obscure, but possibly refers to such charges as casting out devils through Beelzebub; threatening the Temple; and blasphemy. Cp. Mark iii. 22; xiv. 56-64.
[5] V: *human*.   [6] Phil. ii. 8.

[that] of men and thought that this obedience was not due unto God. On account of this love of glory he cast down Adam also into suffering in persuading him not / to obey God. And Adam chose not to show gratitude [unto God] nor to be obedient in any thing; but, because he was made like unto his own image, when he was forbidden to eat of one tree, he suffered in that which was not worthy to be called a suffering and acted against the commandment of God and regarded God as jealous. On account of all these things God made the second Adam worthy of all this honour for having practised all obedience; he granted him an honour above which there was nothing, even as there was nothing surpassing [his] obedience; he accounted himself as nothing, except to become conformed to the will of God, to become as God willed that he should become.

76. *Wherefore he wrought the incarnation through his own* prosôpon *so that he also became incarnate.*[1]

Consequently also God became incarnate[1] in the man through his own *prosôpon* and made his *prosôpon* his own *prosôpon*. And there is no condescension comparable unto this, that the *prosôpon* of the man should become his own and that he should give him his *prosôpon*. And therefore he made use of his *prosôpon*, in that he took it for him[self]; but he took it in order to make it not honourable but contemptible, that he might show to whoever wished to serve [God] that all / greatness grows great by condescension and not in exalting itself, [that] *in that he took the likeness of a servant, he has been found in* schêma *as a man.*[2] The likeness of this servant served him altogether as he wished; but he wished [it to be] according to what appertained to the nature, not only that he should obey his own *prosôpon* for himself, so that there might be no doubt concerning him, that he is the Son of God, but also that he might comport himself on our behalf and die for our salvation: on our behalf, then, not as though we were just or good—for therein there would have been an attraction for anyone to die for those who are so—but for the unjust: *for*

---

[1] *Sc.* ἐνανθρώπησις and cognate words. [2] Phil. ii. 7.

hardly would anyone die for the impious, but for the good someone perhaps would dare to die.[1] Because then he condescended in every thing inscrutably with an incomparable condescension, there was further demonstrated one purpose, one will, one intelligence, indistinguishable and indivisible as in one. So also in manliness and in authority and in ordering of life and in judgement, as in all things, he was associated with God indivisibly as if each thing were in one by the distinguishing and by the choice of them both, so that he possessed nothing human of his own in human things, but the will of God became his own will, when he was made firm in the actions and sufferings of the nature.[2] Thus also, in things divine, nothing is his own apart from the human humiliation; but, while remaining God in all things, [he is] that which the man was by his nature in sufferings, even in impassibility. In the same way as he made use of the likeness of a servant in the *kenôsis*, so in exaltation he participated in the likeness of God, since he is in them both, in the likeness of the servant and in the likeness of God, and possesses the same *prosôpon* of humiliation and of exaltation.[3]

77. *Concerning this: that the incarnation*[4] *has been for the education of the whole nature of rational beings.*

For this reason it was necessary that the incarnation[4] of God the Word should take place for the whole nature of rational beings, that we might learn to participate in his grace, in virtue of which, in that he was lacking in nothing, he wrought everything and abhorred not to do aught, even what is contemptible, and moreover that he might make man participate in his image, in such wise that every man who is beneath him might not make use of the likeness for pride but for participation in the likeness, and that he might do everything according to his might in the sight of God.

---

[1] Rom. v. 6-7 (P.).   [2] See p. 163, n. 2.

[3] At the end of his work Nestorius claims that the Church finally approved a doctrine which was what he had always taught: cp. p. 378. It is in passages such as this that his orthodox intention is most clear. Though he never speaks *totidem verbis* of one *persona* or one ὑπόστασις in Christ, he seems to be asserting what that terminology was meant to express. Cp. further pp. 246-9, 312-5.

[4] Sc. ἐνανθρώπησις.

78. *Concerning this: that Satan, in jealousy*[1] *towards man, wrought everything with a view to misleading.*

/ Because then Satan for opposition made use of that which was given unto him by God and because he had fallen away from the purpose of God, he made use of the image of God not as a model and an example befitting God but, through jealousy towards man, for misleading away from God, and he deceived man and made him fall from his image, since he observed not the will of God, and he raised him up as an enemy and an adversary against God that thereby he might reprimand God as unjust for showing toward man a good purpose such as this—reprimanding him in that he took vengeance on man for his shame and punished him with such punishment as was right for what he had done towards him. Satan, in fact, because he acted in anger and without reflection, forgot that God acts in contrary wise to that which he wishes.

79. *Concerning this: that God has shown the height of his bounty and has laid bare the height of the wickedness of Satan.*

For by death God wrought not the destruction of man but his consolation and his succour that he might not sin nor any more consent to the counsels of the evil one which lead to destruction; for also it was not [an occasion] to slander God but for the increase of his grace. He who accounted man worthy of such honour, when he was nothing, reprimanded the tyrant for his cunning in planning the overthrow of man, / and he shows that he in no wise plans his overthrow but to preserve him by his grace and to care for him, in order that he may be restored again to that which he was. For Satan hoped that after all this love of God towards man, if again he should make him transgress the commandment of God, God would be angered by all means to destroy him and that he would have no cause to turn and be healed. But against those who have sinned and have been accounted worthy of salvation and yet have continued in the same sins,

[1] Nestorius apparently follows the legend that when the angels were ordered to serve the later creation, man, some of them fell into jealousy and became his enemies. Nau refers to the version in the seventh century Nestorian Patriarch George, in Chabot, *Synodes Nestoriens* (*Notices et Extraits* xxxvii. 495).

as though they had not hitherto been liberated from the former punishment, wrath without remission is stirred up without there being therefore any cause for salvation. Satan then first meditated of himself the things which he planned for the destruction of man and he persuaded himself and he condemned man to vengeance without leaving him any cause for pardon. And, since he[1] was envenomed by his[2] anger and his jealousy, he[1] understood not by himself the grace of God, and as a result, being so [placed]..., he destroyed not Satan himself, who was the deceiver, but endured his wickedness; and by reason of this also God is long-suffering as touching men who sin and act impiously against him, as though it were another who deceives them; and he is long-suffering as touching men's being void of understanding[3] and as touching /the boundless wickedness of the devil against them, of him whose whole motive was to mislead all and set all against God, that all our race may be blotted out by him, without any one remaining unto it to become an intercessor for it. And because Satan showed all this supreme wickedness, though he had not any cause of wickedness, even amid all this wickedness the grace of God appeared, and he showed his ineffable grace in doing his good works universally unto all men. Because of the height of his condescension to him who has been altogether sinful, he came in contempt and in scorn and in lowliness and he was not ashamed of the scorn for the sake of the advantage. And by means of his own *prosôpon* he became the *prosôpon* of the other and that of God in fulfilling all that appertains unto God, that is, the instruction of an instructive condescension. For the supreme condescension consisting in[4] a humanity, which seeks not its own but the things of God, has taken place for the teaching of humiliation. And he was united in one purpose, so that there was not the least room for Satan to introduce[5] disobedience;[6] and because there remained

---

[1] *Viz.* man. [2] *Viz.* Satan's.
[3] The Syriac phrase is that used in Prov. ix. 16. [4] Syr.: 'of'.
[5] See crit. n., p. 399.
[6] Nestorius here seems to teach that the union in the Incarnation was so close as to exclude the possibility of sin. Cp. p. 63.

only death to be [endured] for defeat and victory, he endured this also after every thing so as to have won the victory even over it, utterly annihilating it. And two things he wrought /thereby: he defeated Satan and he took away from him all hope of disobedience.

80. *Concerning this: that when Christ conquered, his victory sufficed him not, but he was also pleased to be oppressed for us that he might obtain the exaction [of ransom] for the oppression which was for us.*

And since many are brought low by the fear of death, he endured unto death and gave a just compensation for us in that he exchanged for our death the death which came unjustly upon him.[1] Therefore, after he had observed all the commandments in such wise as to be exempt from death and to receive the choice of victory for us, he yet took upon himself this manner of life for the instruction of those who were deceived and he died on our behalf as on the behalf of the deceived. And he brought death into the arena,[2] since it was necessary that it should be abolished; for he hesitated not that his own being should be cast down in death since he had the hope of its abolition. So also therefore he suffered in advance other trials, but not so as to die unjustly without exacting [the ransom]. In this very hope he obtained also obedience and immeasurable love, not that he might obtain victory for himself but that he might secure the exaction of our own [ransom] and conquer not only for himself but also for all men. In the same way as the defeat /of Adam caused the defeat of all men, so also the victory of the former made all victorious.

81. *Concerning this: that God has shown to all by very deeds, that there is no acceptance of persons as touching humanity, in that it has suffered in all things.*

---

[1] Literally: 'he changed our death into the death which . . . .' Nestorius' theology of the Atonement is somewhat obscure. He seems here to teach in accordance with the line of thought which looks on the death of Christ as a ransom paid to the devil. Cp. p. 173. But see pp. 45 (propitiation), 62-3, 183, 205, 212 ff. (renewing of fallen human nature), 66-7 (conquest of Satan). And cp. pp. 75, n. 1, 84, n. 2.

[2] Literally: 'into the midst'.

And through these two all rational powers have learnt that there is no acceptance of persons with God, but the love of a just judge. For that reason humanity has conquered and Satan has been defeated. And God has magnified his victory and given unto him an honour which is more excellent than all names; and so all rational powers together have wondered even at his victory, kneeling and adoring the very name which has been given, which has been justly given unto him, and every tongue confesses the just dispensation which has taken place on behalf of all, whereby he has made peace and concord to reign over the earth, even he who in all his actions brings them nigh [unto himself] by persuasion and not by force.

82. *Wherefore he accepted for himself to become incarnate.*[1]

Now God indeed perfected the dispensation, nor came it about by means of any other lest, when he fell into such contempt and weakness, his commandment should be considered worthy of scorn and further lest jealousy should straightway be aroused against man. But he received in his being him/who could endure every thing, and he raised up as witnesses of the humiliation of his humanity angels who should strengthen him, that none might say that it was suffering without suffering, since he strengthened it that it might not suffer, and therefore it had no reason not to obey. For everything whatsoever could without doubt be conceived or said concerning him and what he knew that people said concerning him—though they could not say it either because they feared or because they were obedient—that he did that he might leave no single cause of doubt; for they were not convinced of this mystery, but it was hidden even from principalities and authorities and from all powers and it was revealed unto them as a matter of knowledge[2] and all of them confessed, after this explanation, the design which has done away with all designs and conquered them. And he has shown that his incarnation[3] was a universal dispensation for all those who have been accounted equal with him in one

---

[1] *Sc.* ἐνανθρωπῆσαι. [2] Syr.: '(as ?) if in knowledge.'
[3] *Sc.* ἐνανθρώπησις.

purpose and in one persuasion, to stand against the enemy of them all, whom he has driven out and whose authority he has suppressed, so that there is no more place for his deception and for his jealousy.

83 *For what cause, when he defeated and convicted Satan, who is the enemy of all, he did not destroy him but allowed him again to act.*[1]

/ And he continues to deceive that it may be made manifest for his own condemnation and that of those who are persuaded by him, though he has no more such strength for his deception; and for the sake of the victory of those who are not persuaded by him; for *none will be crowned unless he strives lawfully.*[2] Therefore after the victory and after the bringing to nought of death Christ has remained [sharing] in the [same] state of life—a state of life which was brought to nought in Christ—in order that those who are in Christ might comport themselves after the likeness of Christ, not only by the grace of the Resurrection but also by the works and manner of life of each one of them; for the former is universal but the latter individual. And, that it might not be thought that the construction of the nature of Christ was unique and distinct, that it was constructed to be without sin and for that reason conquered, he brought it about that he should be conquered by many myriads, in our own nature in the state of life in which Christ [conquered], by those who keep the exact commandments in such wise that according to the law they comport themselves in the body almost after a manner of life without bodily frame; and in times of distress and afflictions and in all frailty they endure the provocations and the excitements of nature together with violent assaults from without. And thus they have conquered in all things, so that the increase of the defeat of Satan

---

[1] Three points of importance in Nestorius' theology of the Atonement seem here to emerge: (i) the universality of God's grace in atonement, (ii) the need of its individual appropriation by men, and (iii) the reality of Christ's moral struggle as man. Again his teaching is almost exactly reproduced in Du Bose, *The Soteriology of the New Testament*. See especially chaps. vi and xiii–xix in that work, and cp. above, pp. 63, n. 1, 73, n. 1.

[2] 2 Tim. ii. 5.

becomes an increase [in the observance] of the commandments, while the latter thought that the fall of men would become much easier by an identical [1] manner of life.

/ 84. *For what reason Satan attained unto all this exaltation so as to rise up openly against God and make himself equal with God.*

And therefore, as he ran to and fro, his defeat became great; and then in consequence of this he increases his wickedness and reveals it and displays an unbounded audacity in rising up openly against God and making himself comparable with God and likening himself unto his incarnation,[2] deceiving not through anything else nor by anything else than by his own *prosôpon* and by a sublime deception. And because Christ had done away with the deception as touching their gods and their incantations, the former also did away with the things of the latter by deceiving. He put under his own *prosôpon* all things appertaining to gods and sects and incantations and other such things, of which he is the controller, for the sake of making himself great, so that he alone might be considered God. For he makes use of man as an instrument [3] which he has drawn away and led up to boundless evil, making man even to participate in the privation of Divine knowledge, as enemies are wont to act; and of necessity and out of rage he does these things which shall be utterly undone and abolished together with all his primacy. And when it has come to an end and he has nothing else to do, it will remain / for him to pour forth all his wickedness [4] and to be revealed to all as having fought against his Creator, in return for having made him and having given him such might and having allowed him to make use of his might, and having endured him when he fought with all these things. [But] God gathers together all those who would blot out and bring to nought his tyranny. For he has then no device which can be devised against the elect of God, since all things have been in all things fulfilled, both his deception and his evasion of the commandments, and he has been conquered in every thing, in secret and openly,

---

[1] Literally: 'exact.' [2] Sc. ἐνανθρώπησις. [3] Syr. 'órgānōn = ὄργανον.
[4] Cp. Jer. xiv. 16.

both as to his persuasiveness and as to all his force of which he has made use in the weakening and humiliation of the body. And he acted also in regard to the saints in like manner as he acted in regard to Christ, in order by all means to cast them into cruel distresses, but they were not conquered thereby. But in that he ceased not of himself after he was conquered by Christ nor again after he was defeated by the saints, Christ brought his primacy to an end by the death which unjustly came upon him, and it was utterly brought to nought by the death of the saints, which by audacity and improperly he brought upon them.[1] And [God] made him submit to a just judgement for the sake of us whom unjustly he distressed and with whom he combated for our destruction, and because of all his devices and his deceptions and every kind of his ingratitude and his arrogance and his tyranny in opposition to God and to his saints. For all the time / of the long-suffering of God was given for repentance and that he might come to himself and know his folly and his boldness in things impossible.

85. *What thoughts Satan thought against God.*

Though he was able to afflict him passibly and to win him over to the exaction of the ransom, he did this not, but let him make use of his anger as he willed ; for long-suffering toward those who are envenomed by wickedness works an increase of their wickedness, so that, when they see it and are accurately convinced of it, they do the opposite to those who see it not ; for there is no repressing the increase of what is wicked in those who carry out their wishes in opposition to God; for either they think concerning the long-suffering of God that, because he is unable to cast them down into sufferings, in that they possess an immortal nature, he will on this account be long-suffering with them, and for this reason they do those things which are contrary to God, or else, although they grant that he is able to do everything, they do those things which are contrary to his will, because, when he wishes it, he will of his long-suffering cause them to change from their wickedness. Since he wills this, they rise up against his will, doing this or

[1] See p. 73, n. 1.

that which is contrary / to what he wills. They do not ask to have redemption by him on account of their enmity and their infinite boldness, but they embitter him exceedingly so that he destroys them, in that they ask neither to be under God nor to live. And we shall see [Satan] condemned by a condemnation apart from men in a just judgement, when he shall have neither defence nor [counter-]accusation. For God let him do everything that he willed in such wise that there is not any cause at all to rescue him; for he destroyed him not indeed in a single moment by caprice nor further did he let him go without condemnation. Since in fact God left him no single cause of deliverance, for this he prepared himself to be by all means beyond repression; as one then who is the prey of jealousy and ambition, he desists not from his jealousy till the object of his jealousy [is attained] according to his will, and he is an example to all who are ungrateful. For him and all those who after his likeness have fallen into this sickness God judges justly and examines them and condemns them in the sight of all; and they are hated by common consent, and in him [men] see all ingratitude and all boldness and arrogance and all wiles and all falsehood and all impiety which springs up and grows great and is brought to fulness, so that it cannot even receive any increase.

86. *Concerning this: that at the time of condemnation Satan will be hated by all / and even by his own, in so much as he has been unto them a cause of punishment.*[1]

For this reason all this time of long-suffering has been given unto him, and it is given unto him until the day of judgement to do whatever he will, lest there should be left unto him any cause for being able to do anything in it; but a time of long-suffering and of authority has been given unto him; and after that he will be fully judged and distinguished from the righteous together with all those who have participated with him in tyranny; by them also will he be hated and accused as having been the cause of their condemnation. As in purity of love, in word and in deeds each will love God as good and

[1] This and the next two sections show clearly Nestorius' thought on the problem of reconciling God's omnipotence with the existence of evil.

just, as wise and as mighty, and as the Maker and as God, and, since they will obtain an example of just judgement without respect of persons, of the good and of the wicked, all classes of rational beings will duly learn the examination of the arguments for good and for evil, and for what reason God allows each man to choose it according to his will, and lets those who choose the good endure evils and is long-suffering toward those who have chosen the opposite thereof and who fight against his will, that they may do whatsoever they choose. And in this wise / the administration of this world is carried on: thus will it be administered by God until the end.

87. *The Consummation.*

And after this, seeing that everything has been well [done], we shall be in the joy of the world to come, having no cause [to fear] deprivation thereof nor that we shall have further need of instruction.

88. *Concerning this: that it was needful that there should be a union of two natures, and that it was not right that it should take place otherwise.*

For these reasons, then, and for similar causes, the incarnation [1] of God took place justly: true God by nature and true man by nature. For there would not have been any [union] of these, if one of these natures had been left out. If God became not incarnate,[1] and if he became not [incarnate] in a man [formed] of the nature of men, [it is] in fact as if it took place in deception and the truth [would be] what the words of Satan would have been, that Christ surely rejected as contemptible his [physical] formation after his image. Therefore there would have been no teaching of humility and of obedience and of condescension: that he, who when he had not taken the likeness of a servant was the similitude and the likeness of God, *should be found in the likeness as a man.*[2] But there would rather be a justification of the words of Satan, who had contemned [him], because / he had seen him inferior in his nature to the image and the likeness of the honour of God. And as for all the angels, though they were

---

[1] *Sc.* ἐνανθρώπησις and cognate words.   [2] Phil. ii. 7.

convinced of him as of God and were not able to dare to speak against him, this reason forced them not to blame Satan in anything [but to treat him] as one who had been cast down into sufferings which were not right for him, for the sake of the boundless honour of human nature, though he was blamed for this that he ought to have obeyed any commandment whatsoever of God. And since there was this suffering in their soul, they served him for the sake of him who commanded them, though not with a good will.

89. *Concerning this: that, even if he were in the* schêma *of a man but not in the nature of a man, the doctrine of an incarnation*[1] *would not become established.*

Although a man were to grant that he became incarnate,[1] yet [in placing the Incarnation] in the *schêma* of a man but not in the nature of a man, he would predicate the same repudiation of human nature.

90. *Concerning this: that, even if he were to change his own nature into the nature of a man, the doctrine of the Incarnation would not have been established.*

And even if he changed his own *ousia* for the *ousia* of a man, it seems that he would have surely repudiated the nature of a man, since he would have been in his own *ousia* and not in the *ousia* of man; for this *ousia* is his, not of the earth but of the nature of God the Word, and therefore / God the Word appears to have grown in wisdom[2] in a human manner of life, so as to remain without sin as one who is a man while he is God the Word by his own *ousia*. Thus also he comported himself as a man though he was not man by nature but God the Word; both when he had combated and conquered the adversary and when he suffered, he who was impassible by his nature suffered, and similarly also in these other things. And even if we say that he took a man and that he changed the nature of the man into his own *ousia*, did he not set aside the victory of the things which are rejected, which constitute man? And for this reason he changed the nature of the flesh which was rejected for him, lest God should be abased in his

---

[1] Sc. ἐνανθρώπησις, &c.   [2] Cp. Luke ii. 52.

being in the nature of a man; and in this way neither were his manner of life and sufferings and death those of a man, nor again were they for the sake of men. And so it was no more through the death of God, nay rather,[1] if God had been condemned to death, if he had willed to avoid it he would have set it aside without his own death rather than through a *schêma* of death. But, since he was God and immortal, in his *prosôpon* which was not guilty he accepted death, that is, [accepted] the mortal and changeable [*prosôpon*], [so] that he was able to fight against defeat through the commandments and the observances, so that victory might fall to his image and to his likeness, that it might / be the same who accepted death as defeat and to whom [God] gave immortality as a release from guilt, in that he was preserved without stain in his own image. And as he condemned him when guilty, so also when he conquered he exalted the name which is above all names; and he obtained it not by commandments and through ordinances but by victory in his own right not to be taken away from him, just as a son, who was formerly under authority, on growing up and becoming adult, has authority to become a son, although he was already such as a son is.

91. *Concerning this: that, even if any one were to grant that the union was by natural composition, or by mixture, or by confusion, or by intermingling of*[2] *the natures,*[2] *the doctrine of an incarnation would not have been established.*

On account of this very thing, even if any one were to grant that God the Word accepted humanity in his own nature, either by mixture, or by confusion, or by participation of *ousia*, and sets at nought this nature of man, he shows that this human nature is to be rejected and that it could not be preserved without sin, since his nature conquered not, but he who came into being from both of them; and he shows that Satan, since he was incapable, was defeated, and [that] in having defeated at the beginning man who sinned, he defeated him who could not be without sin because he was not of the sinless nature of

---

[1] Syr. '*ellâ*.   [2] See crit. n., p. 399.

God the Word / but of the nature of sinful man. And Satan appeared to speak with man in judgement but was surely defeated by God, of whose nature it is to be defeated of nothing. And both of these [theories] are absurd, in that he commanded Satan and man to do impossibilities. But if the things which were commanded had been possible to do and had not been observed, justly would Satan have been condemned; for, when he could obey, he obeyed not but rose up against God by means of the *schêma* of a man and slandered God before man as jealous, and man before God as ungrateful; and he is the enemy of all and has received a just judgement and has been openly convicted. He has in fact been conquered by Christ through his humanity and by the saints, for openly he rose up and still is risen up against God, and he has shown that, if he had not been able to deceive the first man, he afterward would have fought against God openly and not in the *schêma* of this man or that, and although he could do nothing, he had it in his intention to do whatever he desired like the Lord,[1] as one who was in everything able to act and to persuade and to fight. And he was able to destroy him in that moment, since he was worthy of destruction. But others would not have learnt / that wickedness is powerful and extinguishes itself, unless they had by all means known that they received subjection [to God] as a grace and from this subjection obtained grace not to show themselves bold against God and thereby themselves also to be parted from God with the former. How then would he have made the Incarnation[2] a stumbling-block by mixture, or by confusion, or by natural participation, so that he might not be supposed [to be] God nor even man, but one who is of them both and is neither simple nor undivided? So therefore he is [combined] with humanity, as a judge in a judgement and in a true trial, possessing it in his own *prosôpon* and [having it] obedient unto himself in everything. And it is not he who combats and is judged, but to the extent of appropriation[3] he has

---

[1] Syr. *mārānā'ith* = Gk. κυριακῶs.
[2] Sc. ἐνανθρώπησις.
[3] Syr. *baithāyûthâ* = Gk. οἰκείωσις.

brought it[1] nigh unto his own image and not to the nature of the invincible and impassible *ousia* of the divinity. For Satan had no commission from God to make him[2] disobedient to him, but to convince God that his own man was disobedient to him. He, who in everything accepted obedience with a good intention, exalted his honour in his own image to show that he is a just judge.

92. *Concerning this: that, even if one were to grant one nature by natural composition, either with flesh without soul or [in flesh] animated by an animal / soul or by a rational soul according to a natural union, the doctrine of an incarnation*[3] *would not have been established.*

But in this way neither those who say, as the Arians, that the flesh was united to God by a natural composition and that it suffered by natural sufferings, nor again those who say that the union took place with the rational soul and the flesh in such wise that it suffered by a natural sensibility the sufferings of the body and of the unreasonable and irrational soul, establish in truth the doctrine of the incarnation.[3] Do they not say this, that by a deception Satan was conquered by him who had been conquered, and that the latter conquered not by his own might but had need of a champion,[4] that is of God who created him, who fought either openly or in secret? For in that Satan, having held no contest[4] with God, was conquered by God, he conquered by having shown unto all that the love of God toward man was unjust and that the exaltation of humanity resulted as it were in the scorn of all and the subjection and the prostration[5] of all supremacy and all authority. Now if he sought to do that for man, he could do it even without this deception and cunning, for that which he says he also does. Nor further indeed hid he himself when he made use of this *schēma;* for he who seeks to hide himself, so long as it escapes him not that, if discovered, he will surely be confuted, is himself / his own accuser. So they are con-

---

[1] *Viz.* the humanity.   [2] *Viz.* Christ incarnate.
[3] *Sc.* ἐνανθρώπησις.
[4] The Greek words ἀγωνιστής and ἀγών transliterated.
[5] An unusual use of Syr. *seghdtā* 'adoration'; so translated by Nau.

strained to say the contrary of what they seek to say, so that they accuse God and make excuse for the evil one, and they put forth all [their] might in vain and reason contrary to the incarnation [1] of God.[2]

93. *Concerning this: that things which are composed in one nature [are so] either that they may be supreme or that they may be under supremacy and especially under the soul, which is supreme in the composite nature, if God the Word is naturally composed.*

Those things indeed which are composed and brought to fullness to [form] a nature [are so] either that they may be constituted chief and in control or that they may be under a chief and a controller. If then, because the rational soul is in need of being controlled, it is in need of participation in God the Word that he may be controller either of the body or of the rational or of the animal soul, then by him [3] he [4] obtained the victory, if it is fair to call victory that of another nature which is distinct and unlike and unequal to men, its companions. It seems that he acts in *schêma* and forcibly subjects all to him[self] and brings [them] under his authority by force like God, so that he [4] who was defeated by his very own choice could not escape owing to his defeat nor observe the commandments in his own nature, except by God the Word who is the conqueror for all time. It is not, in fact, / wonderful and worthy of praise that God the Word became in the body and observed all the observances of the soul and of the body. For

---

[1] *Sc.* ἐνανθρώπησις.

[2] Cp. p. 73, n. 1. Here we seem to find that although Nestorius looks on the death of Christ as ransoming mankind from the devil, yet he rejects certain ways of explaining that theory of the Atonement. Is it not possible that he is denying such a doctrine as is found extant in Gregory the Great (*Moralia* xxxii. 12–xxxiii. 6), where the devil is cheated through ignorance of the Crucified being divine and therefore immortal? Nestorius argues that the Cross must be a real moral victory by the Man, not an unexpected triumph by a concealed *deus ex machina*. Such a triumph would really mean the defeat of mankind. The individual humanity of Christ might have been exalted, but the devil's fetters would be rivetted on the rest of mankind. It is interesting that according to the traditional account of Nestorius' teaching he is himself open to precisely this charge.

[3] *Viz.* God the Word.   [4] *Viz.* The Man Christ.

if he had not remained in his nature above the nature of the body or of the soul or of the intelligence, he would surely have been required [to do so], since the rational soul also sufficed to observe the commandments; but if the latter had not sufficed and for this reason there had been need of the incarnation[1] of God the Word that for all he might support the sufferings of the body and of the soul and of the intelligence in a natural union which would have united the nature, he would have suffered as the body, as the soul [and] as the intelligence in the mixture. But since he was not conquered as one of them, it appears that he was outside their nature and therefore was not caught[2] by those things whereby each one of them was caught. Together with this [there is] another absurdity which they predicate in limiting God himself by the necessity of nature and ascribing, as the Manichaeans, to *hylê* such might that it drags after it by authority and its own force whosoever receives it, and that he suffers in all ways the actual bodily sufferings [namely] whatever God the Word suffered when he condescended to the body and supported these bodily sufferings in his own nature when he was scourged by hunger and thirst, by the natural bonds of the body, though in his own nature he was exempt from these things; he desired and he was angered / and was fearful and was suffering, and suffered naturally all these sufferings of the body and the soul, because he was composed of [one] nature. For he, who is composed of [one] nature, of necessity adheres in the nature to all the nature's own properties, whether of a man or of God or of any other nature to which he is naturally united and combined. And however one would be willing to say that he is in nothing distinct from me, yet those who are composed of [one] nature support of necessity that nature's own proper qualities which are naturally and not voluntarily theirs. But that God the Word is so voluntarily and not by force: *I have authority over my life, that I should lay it down and I have authority to take it again.*[2] Therefore the words of the Divine Scriptures befit not Christ in any other manner than this; but as we have

---

[1] Sc. ἐνανθρώπησις.   [2] See crit. n., p. 399.
[3] Jn. x. 18.

examined and found, all refer not to the union of the nature but to the natural and hypostatic *prosôpon*.[1]

[1] This must surely mean that in considering each passage of Scripture we have to ask to which of the two natures in Christ it is appropriate; then the passage is to be referred to the *prosôpon* which belongs to that nature and hypostasis. Each passage thus refers to a 'natural and hypostatic *prosôpon*'. (Cp. pp. 54, 316 sqq.) The two 'natural and hypostatic *prosôpa*' then somehow combine to form the one *prosôpon* of the union.

Professor Bethune-Baker's interpretation of this passage in *Nestorius and his Teaching*, p. 99, seems to require an unjustified identification of *prosôpon* in Nestorius with 'person' in the modern sense of the word, and does not seem to be borne out by Nestorius' usage and argument in other passages.

BOOK I. PART II.

CONCERNING THE FAITH.

Sophronius says: Because then many accept the faith of the Three Hundred and Eighteen which was laid down at Nicaea, both persons who believe in various ways and those who understand the Divine Scriptures some in one way and some in another and in various ways *He was made flesh and was made man*[1] may it please thy Reverence to pass [in review] their intentions and their opinions; and do thou write and make known unto me how it appears unto thee and what thou dost approve as well-pleasing, and give no cause to them that seek cause to calumniate thee.

Nestorius. 1. [Some] of them in fact say that the Incarnation[2] of our Lord Christ took place in fiction and *schêma* and in order that he might appear unto men and teach and give the grace of the Gospel unto all men. And, as he appeared unto each one of the saints, so in the last times he appeared unto all men.

2. But others say that the divine *ousia* became flesh, so that it should become in its own *ousia* the *ousia* of the flesh for the nature of men, and that he should comport himself and suffer and set our nature free. For he who became man not in his own *ousia* but in *schêma*, has surely not set us free but has surely deceived us, since he appeared in *schêma* and to suffer for our sakes without having suffered.

/ 3. Others again confess that God was made flesh in the flesh as a complement of nature instead of the soul. He was made flesh naturally in the flesh to work and to suffer, and he naturally endured all the natural sufferings of the body, being by his nature impassible but by a natural incarnation[3] passible,

---

[1] *Sc.* ἐσάρκωσε καὶ ἐνηνθρώπησεν. As *Incarnation* has to be used for ἐνανθρώπησις, the Syriac verb corresponding to the Gk. σαρκοῦσθαι will be rendered 'to be made flesh' and that corresponding to the Gk. ἐνανθρωπεῖν, 'to be made man'.

[2] *Sc.* ἐνανθρώπησις.   [3] *Sc.* σάρκωσις.

even as the soul, which by its nature suffers not the sufferings of the body nor is pained nor hungers, through a natural economy suffers naturally the sufferings of the body, being united with it naturally, that he may naturally comport himself and suffer on our behalf. And not in fiction and in *schêma* or by any other nature but by his own nature he has set us free from death and corruption.

4. But others confess that in body and in soul he was made flesh for the completion of the nature and that God the Word was instead of an intelligence, so as to be instead of an intelligence in the nature in the body and in the soul, and to comport himself in the nature of men and to suffer on our behalf. For he came to suppress that intelligence which transgressed the commandment and obeyed not God and to be instead of intelligence in the soul and in the body, and not in a *schêma* without *hypostasis* nor in another nature nor again in a bodily frame without a soul.

5. But others [confess] as touching that flesh wherein God the Word was made flesh[1] that he was made flesh, animate flesh, that felt not in its nature / and understood not through the soul but understood and felt by the activity of God the Word. In God the Word this soul felt and also understood, and the body was a natural instrument[2]; and they divide not Christ into instrument and workman, since the instrument and the workman act together.

6. But others confess two natures in Christ before the union and that each of the natures should be conceived in its own nature: God the Word on the one hand in the Father and in the Holy Spirit and men in the flesh; but after the union [they are] not conceived as two natures in virtue of being united in *ousia*; and one [*ousia*] results from the two of them. They change them from nature to nature in such wise that the same is literally man and God, so that God comports himself as a man and dies for[3] us as God and rises by his own might.

7. But others say of the incarnation[4] of our Lord [that it

---

[1] Sc. ἐσαρκώθη.   [2] Syr. 'órgānôn = Gk. ὄργανον.
[3] The Syriac preposition can represent either ὑπέρ or ἀντί; see p. 32, n. 1.
[4] Sc. ἐνανθρώπησις.

was in] an animate flesh in a rational and intelligent soul, complete in its nature and in its might and in its natural activities, and not in *schêma* nor in a change of *ousia* nor again for the natural completion of the nature of the body and of the soul, or of the intelligence, or [that it was] mingled into one nature out of two of them or that they were changed from the one into the other, or / that [it took place] for the completion of the natural activities in such wise that the flesh should not act in its own nature; but [it was in] one *prosôpon* of both natures, both of them maintaining the properties of their own natures; and the *ousia* of the divinity remains and suffers not when it is in the *ousia* of the flesh, and the flesh again remains in the *ousia* of the flesh when it is in the nature and in the *prosôpon* of the divinity; for the body is one and both of them [are] one Son. For no other is called God the Word in the flesh apart from him who is in our own flesh; nor again [is anything else called] the flesh, but it is in the Son, in God the Word: that he should comport himself completely in the nature of men being man, and that he should rise as God being God by nature, that he in consequence of sinlessness and of having observed [the commandments] should be delivered to death for our salvation, that he might preserve the likeness of his own image. In order then to become so, he took not for [his] likeness[1] *a name which is more excellent than all names*[2] that the nature of men might be exalted; for the honour and exaltation has not been given to an *ousia* which henceforward is not of man but of God the Word. Our own nature has been honoured in another nature and not in our own nature; for the exaltation of our own nature to *a name which is more excellent than all names*[2] belongs generally to that nature[3] which is the

---

[1] On this passage Bethune-Baker has the following note (*Nestorius and his Teaching*, p. 152): 'The Syriac word *dmûthâ* is the natural equivalent for the 'two Greek words ὁμοίωσις (Gen. i. 26) and μορφή (Phil. ii. 6, 7). When there-'fore there is reference to the passage in Gen. we should understand that it 'translates the former Greek word, when to Phil. ii the latter. Now all through 'this work Nestorius appears to use μορφή in a strongly theological sense which 'is practically equivalent to the sense he gives to φύσις (*kyânâ*, "nature"), 'ὑπόστασις (*qnômâ*), and οὐσία (*ousia*). This is certainly so whenever there is 'a reference to Phil. ii.'

[2] Phil. ii. 9 (P.).   [3] See crit. n., p. 399.

exaltation of one who remains in his own *ousia* and can be that which / is in the *ousia* of God the Word; this in fact is properly the exaltation, like which there is not [any other]. For the change of *ousia* into *ousia* is the suppression of that *ousia* which ought to be exalted, and also of its own, of the exaltation;[1] and there has been no more condescension of God the Word when once he is changed into the *ousia* of the flesh, because he is not the nature which is capable of condescending but is that which has condescended. As a king, if he becomes one of the subjects, is said to condescend though he is truly king, and on account of the clothes of subjects which he has put on is said to have surely condescended; in place of his own he has made use of those of the latter in *schêma*, in such wise that, as those who are under the law of administrators,[2] so will he be voluntarily under the law though he is their own king, [and king] of the administrators and of their lords. For there is no more an exaltation in being exalted to his own nature, but in giving him what he had not, not in taking away from him what he had. For if exaltation and humiliation belong to that which was and which originally was, humiliation belongs to this nature which was and which originally was. Of whom is the exaltation? First he said the *ousia* which was exalted and afterwards that name wherein it is exalted, / which is above all names. For if thou takest away the *ousias* which accept humiliation and exaltation, there is no *ousia* which has been humiliated. Therefore he said *he humiliated himself* in reference to a voluntary union, the incarnation[3] and the kind of humiliation which he showed when *he took the likeness of a servant*, and again that which took place resulted in a voluntary and not a natural [union]; in *schêma* he was found as a man,[4] not in *ousia*; for in the likeness of God [was] the likeness of the servant. The likeness of God was in *schêma* as a man, for God was in his own *ousia*, in such wise that it was conceived also as an humiliation in him that he took the likeness of a servant, and as an exaltation in the likeness of the

---

[1] Perhaps an accidental transposition in the order of the words, for which ' of its own exaltation ' should be read.

[2] See crit. n., p. 399.   [3] Sc. ἐνανθρώπησις.   [4] Phil. ii. 7.

The Gospel emphasis on Christ's manhood

servant that it took *a name which is more excellent than all names*,[1] and [so that] it was not conceived as a change of *ousia* either into an *ousia* or into a natural composition of one nature, but as being a voluntary [union], as [being] one in humiliation and in exaltation ; for that of nature [2] is passible and changeable, since it is a nature created and made, not uncreated nor unmade nor unchangeable nor immutable.

Consequently this man [3] has attributed nothing in the Incarnation [4] to the conduct of the man but [all] to God the Word, in such wise that he made use of the nature of humanity for his own conduct. So Arius and Eunomius and Apollinarius say therefore that Christ is God in name but in reality deprive him / of being God, in ascribing those things in him which are human in nature to his own *ousia*, and suppress the genealogy of the family of Christ and the promises made to the patriarchs, of whose seed arose the Christ after the flesh. Therefore the Evangelists record all those things which in truth show the nature of man, lest on account of the divinity it should not be believed that he was also man nor be believed together with this that it was he who was affirmed by the promises. Therefore the Blessed Mary was recorded as a woman who was betrothed to a man, of whom he [5] has written both his name and his race and his trade and his place, in order that there might be nothing to raise a doubt leading to disbelief that she was a woman. Therefore also [he wrote] of his low estate and with all these things also of the annunciation of his conception and of his birth and of the manger, to make known him who was born together with her who bore him, that it might be affirmed that he is truly man, of [his] sleeping in the manger, of the swathing in swaddling bands such as are natural to infants, of the offerings which were offered for him for his progress, of his increase in stature and in wisdom with God and with men, of his manner of life in the world, of his observances, of his submission, of the prayers which he prayed, of all his fulfilment of the law, of the baptism and of the saying which was

---

[1] Phil. ii. 9 (P.). [2] *I.e.* a natural union. [3] *Viz.* Cyril.
[4] *Sc.* ἐνανθρώπησις. [5] *Viz.* the Evangelist.

said of him, that he / who from the womb was son by union was the Son, of the witness to the observance of the customs, of the word of the Father, of the appearance of the Holy Spirit, of his dispensation with all zeal on our behalf, not in illusion nor in the *schêma* of a man but in the human nature [formed] of the body of a man and a rational soul which thinks and reflects in the nature of men, that it may have everything which is in the nature of man without being deprived of the union with God the Word. For the union of the natures resulted not in [one] nature or in a confusion or in a change or in a change of *ousia*, either of divinity into humanity or of humanity into divinity, or in a mixture of natures or in the composition of one nature, being mixed and suffering together with one another in the natural activities of natures which are naturally constituted.[1]

For they suppress all these things through the natural and hypostatic union and they take everything which is in his nature and attribute them naturally unto God the Word: the human fear and the betrayal, the interrogation, the answer, the smiting upon the cheeks, the sentence of the cross, the way thereto, the setting of the cross upon his shoulder, the bearing of his cross, the removal [of it] from him that it might be set on another, the crown of thorns, the robes of purple, / the raising up of the cross, the crucifixion, the fixing of the nails, the gall which was offered unto him, the other distresses, the surrender of his spirit to the Father, the bowing down of his head, the descent of his body from the cross, the embalming thereof, his burial, the resurrection on the third day, his appearance in his body, his speaking and his teaching that they should not suppose him to be an illusion of the body but truly body which had also flesh. Because he was not by illusion and by deception a body and a soul but in truth all that by nature, there was nothing that was hid.

All the human things, which now men are ashamed to predicate of him, the Evangelists were not ashamed to predicate, those which without being ashamed they [2] make over to

---

[1] According to the Syriac punctuation the full stop and new paragraph come at 'God the Word' above.   [2] *Viz.* the opponents of Nestorius.

the divine nature through the union of the natural *hypostasis* : God suffering the sufferings of the body because he is naturally united in nature, thirsting, hungering, in poverty, in anxiety, meditating, praying so as both to conquer human things wherein he was naturally suffering and to fight against the nature of men, [they claim this] so as to bring to nought our glory and to bring to nought our salvation. And the properties of God the Word they set at nought and make them human; he would have acted naturally in nature and suffered in the sensibility of nature, accepting sufferings in his own *ousia* naturally, as the body [accepts those] of the soul and the soul [those] of the body. / Surely it is an awful and dreadful thing to conceive this and to tell men what and what sort of thoughts they have concerning the Son, that he is both made and created and that he has been changed from impassible to passible and from immortal to mortal and from unchangeable to changeable. Although one would make him the *ousia* of the angels and without suffering and say that he operated not by his nature nor by his activity nor by his might, but by that which he became, would he escape withal from suffering sufferings? But it is not possible for one who is naturally united to escape; for if he were not naturally to suffer the sufferings of the body, he would suffer them as the soul instead of the soul, because he is instead of the soul which reflected not as intelligence and whose [1] in its reflection he was instead of intelligence. And he was in *schêma* and by means of the schèma of a man he deceived, as though he had the things of the soul and of the body and of the intelligence and these were void of operation by their nature.

But by those who pass for orthodox these things are said, that he is of the very nature of the Father, impassible and without needs and unchangeable and immutable, and then, as the Jews mocked, calling him Christ, and surely crucified him, / so also the former attribute unto him in word [2] a nature unchangeable, impassible and without needs, and they ascribe unto him all sufferings and every need of the body and make over all the things of the soul and the intelligence to God the Word in

---

[1] See crit. n., p. 399. [2] Or 'with the voice'.

virtue of an hypostatic union. And, like those who change him from his nature, at one time they call him now impassible and immortal and unchangeable, and afterwards they prohibit him from being then called immortal and impassible and unchangeable, being angry against any one who repeatedly calls God the Word impassible. Once thou hast heard; it is then enough for thee. And they predicate two whole natures of the divinity and of the humanity and they predicate a change of natures by union, attributing nothing either to the humanity or to the divinity in making over the things of humanity to the nature and those of the divinity to the nature. And they preserve not even the things which belong to the divinity by nature, in making God the Word of two *ousias* in nature; and they dissemble the man and all that is his own, on whose account the Incarnation [1] took place and in whom it took place and through whom we have been released from the captivity of death. And they make use indeed of the name of orthodox, but in fact they are Arians. And thereby they misrepresent the fullness of God the Word, by all the human things of nature which they predicate of him as the result of the union of the natural *hypostasis*, that he might comport himself and suffer naturally in all / human things. He made use of humanity not that it might comport itself and suffer for our sakes, but that God the Word might comport himself not in the *prosôpon* but in the nature, for the union in *prosôpon* is impassible; and this is [the opinion] of the orthodox; but one which is passible is the fabrication of heretics against the nature of the only Son. Each man comes with whatever he will; for unavoidably one arrives at the opinion of the orthodox and not at the blasphemy of heretics. He [2] has irreverently written all those things that he has wished in favour of the *hypostatic* union in his own Articles [3] and much has been written thereon by many. We too ought not to make our book endless in busying ourselves with things that are evident, but above all we ought to reveal unto all men such increase little by little of impiety. Because I have shown

---

[1] Sc. ἐνανθρώπησις.   [2] *Viz.* Cyril.
[3] The twelve anathematisms attached to the third letter to Nestorius.

this beforehand, I have not renounced the just course of the orthodox nor shall I renounce it until death; and although they all, even the orthodox, fight with me through ignorance and are unwilling to hear and to learn from me, yet the times will come upon them when they will learn from those who are heretics while fighting against them how they have fought against him who fought on their behalf.[1]

[1] There is here a lacuna in the Syriac text, followed by a fragment (Syr., pp. 137–46), which seems to be misplaced, being apparently the beginning of Bk. II, Sect. 1. The present editors have therefore followed Nau in continuing here from p. 146 of the Syriac text and in placing pp. 137–46 after p. 270.

BOOK I. PART III.

WICKEDLY thou hast separated off a party and there was not any one to contend / against me; on my account thou hast obtained by [thine] authority the documents from a number of bishops, every one [of whom] was as one dumb and deaf. Thou hast assembled a company of monks and of those who are named bishops for the chastisement and disturbance of the church, and there is none of the chiefs who has hindered [it] that it might be prevented. An assembly such as this which was sent came and appeared as a guard against me in the Imperial Palace. Thou hast all the support of the Empire, whereas I [have] only the name of the Emperor, not [indeed] to overpower [1] [you] nor to guard [me] nor for my own help, but rather as if to [ensure] my obedience. Because indeed I made not use of the support of the church nor of the support of the chief men nor of the support of the Empire, I am come to this extremity.[2] But I, who had the chief men and the Emperor and the episcopate of Constantinople, I, who had been long-suffering unto heretics, was harassed by thee so as to be driven out; and thou wast bishop of Alexandria and thou didst get hold of the church of Constantinople—a thing which the bishop of no other city whatsoever would have suffered, though one wished to judge him in judgement and not with violence. But I have endured all things while making use of persuasion and not of violence / to persuade the ignorant; and I looked for helpers, not for those who contend in fight and cannot be persuaded.

You have further with you against me a contentious woman, a princess, a young maiden, a virgin,[3] who fought against me

---

[1] Nau: *pour me fortifier*; but see Payne-Smith, *Thes. Syr.* ii. 3005.

[2] Syr. '*ānanqē*' = Gk. ἀνάγκη.

[3] *Viz.* Pulcheria. Suidas, under *Pulcheria*, says ἡ Πουλχερία τοσοῦτον ἐμίσει τὸν Νεστόριον, ὡς τοὺς φιλοῦντας ἐκεῖνον διαθρύλλειν, ὅτι πορνείαν πρὸς τὸν ἀδελφὸν αὐτῆς Θεοδόσιον τὸν βασιλέα διέβαλε ὁ Νεστόριος καὶ διὰ τοῦτο οὕτως ὑπ' αὐτῆς ἐμισεῖτο, ἐλοιδόρει γὰρ αὐτὴν εἰς τὸν τότε μάγιστρον Παυλῖνον λεγόμενον. This passage

because I was not willing to be persuaded by her demand that I should compare a woman corrupted of men to the bride of Christ. This I have done because I had pity on her soul and that I might not be the chief celebrant of the sacrifice among those whom she had unrighteously chosen. Of her I have spoken only to mention [her], for she was my friend;[1] and therefore I keep silence about[2] and hide everything else about her own little self, seeing that [she was but] a young maiden; and for that reason she fought against me. And here she has prevailed over my might but not before the tribunal of Christ where all [will be] laid bare and revealed before the eyes of him in whose presence our judgement and theirs will come in the days that have been appointed by him.

But I return again to that point to . . . .[3] I shall meet Apollinarius and his dogma. What he holds thou knowest not. However to those who know not I say: Him[4] he confesses consubstantial with the Father and thereby he obtains the impression that he agrees with the Divine Scriptures. It is not possible to see his [views] exactly. In that, in fact, the Son is consubstantial with God the Father, he disputes / against the Anomoeans and is ignorant that he initiates a dispute against the orthodox on [the point] that he is not consubstantial. But he distorts it, [as may be seen] from this, since he says that there is a union of the nature of God the Word and of the flesh, as he has learned from the Arians, he agrees with that which the Arians say, that the Son is not like the Father in nature, in that he confesses that he suffered the sufferings of the body by natural sensibility; for the same could not be by nature impassible and passible, even though he were to unite a soul without intelligence to the body, for he is united to the nature in the body as well as in the soul and he suffers in very

---

is discussed by Neander, *Church History* (Eng. Trans. 1855), vol. iv, p. 160. See too the references to Pulcheria in the Letter to Cosmos of Antioch, in Nau, Appendix I.

[1] Pulcheria was famous for her orthodoxy, and in particular for her anti-Nestorian zeal. Cp. Labbe (Mansi), vi. 590 D. Presumably Nestorius is here thinking of her later support of Flavian against Eutyches, for he claims Flavian as the exponent of his own views. Cp. pp. 342, 353-5, 362.

[2] Literally: 'I keep in silence'.   [3] There is a lacuna in the Syriac text.
[4] *Viz.* the Son.

nature his own natural sufferings of the nature. Although they speak of mixture and change and composition and the completion of the nature, in every case they bring it to this very thing: for he who suffers in the natural union is not the same in *ousia* as he who accepts not sufferings; but, in consequence of the natural union, he also falls under sufferings, for he is the nature in which he has become through natural union. But he disputes against Paul [1] and Photinus, in that he is the Word in nature and in *hypostasis* and is eternal; but he erred in referring the things of the body to God the Word by a natural union. For in that he disputed against the Anomoeans, [saying] that the Son is consubstantial with God the Father, and against Photinus and Paul,[1] / [saying] that he is by nature and *hypostasis* homoousian with the Father, unwittingly [2] he was accounted as [one of] the orthodox; nevertheless by not having applied that which was befitting but, like an enemy, having brought to naught even that which was well said, he pulled down that which he was supposed to be building upon the faith.

And further he disputes on these two points with those who confess rightly, as though he was in charge of the company of the orthodox, and he exerted himself to bring his error into the church, and he has introduced controversy. Now this question came not about in the East and had long since vanished from the church which I found in Constantinople; and it began not in my days either in Constantinople or in the East, for I had not yet been born when the question arose concerning these things and was settled; and again the inquiry received not [its origin] in Constantinople from my words but in the time of my predecessors. Why then dost thou calumniate me, saying 'He has posed this inquiry', and call me an inventor of novelties and a cause of disturbance and war, me who have posed absolutely no such inquiry but, to be sure, found it in Antioch? And there I taught and spoke concerning these things and no man blamed me, / and I supposed that this dogma had long been repudiated.[3] But

---

[1] *I.e.* Paul of Samosata.   [2] See crit. n., p. 399.
[3] Apollinarianism had been condemned at the Council of Alexandria in 362.

in Constantinople, when I found that men were inquiring and in need of being taught, I yielded to their persuasion as the truth required. For factions of the people who were questioning this came together to the bishop's palace, having need of a solution of their question and of arriving at unanimity.[1] Those on the one hand who called the blessed Mary the mother of God they called Manichaeans, but those who named the blessed Mary the mother of a man Photinians . . . .[2] But when they were questioned by me, the former denied not the humanity nor the latter the divinity, but they confessed them both alike, while they were distinct only in name: they of the party of Apollinarius accepted 'Mother of God' and they of the party of Photinus 'Mother of man'. But after I knew that they disputed not in the spirit of heretics, I said that neither the latter nor the former were heretics, [the former] because they knew not Apollinarius and his dogma, while similarly the latter [knew] the dogma neither of Photinus nor of Paul.[3] And I brought them back from this inquiry and from this dispute, saying that: 'If indistinguishably and 'without extrusion or denial of the divinity and of the 'humanity we accept what is said by them,/we sin not; but 'if not, let us make use of that which is very plainly [affirmed], 'that is, of the Word of the Gospel: *Christ was born*[4] and '*the Book of the generation of Jesus Christ*.[5] And by things 'such as these we confess that Christ is God and man, 'for *of them*[6] *was born in flesh Christ, who is God above all*.[7] 'When you call her the Mother of Christ, [Christ] by union 'and inseparate, you speak of the one and of the other in the 'sonship. But make use of that against which there is no 'accusation in the Gospel and settle this dispute among you, 'making use of a word which is useful toward agreement.' When they heard these things, they said: 'Before God has 'our inquiry been solved.' And many praised and gave glory and went away from me and remained in agreement until

---

[1] Cp. Loofs, *Nestoriana*, pp. 185, 312.
[2] Bedjan here marks a lacuna in the text.
[3] *Sc.* of Samosata.
[4] Matt. i. 16.
[5] Matt. i. 1 (P.).
[6] *Viz.* the Jews.
[7] Rom. ix. 5.

they fell into the snare of those who were seeking for the episcopate.

Now the clergy of Alexandria, who were in favour of his [1] deeds, persuaded them [of Constantinople] as persons deceived that they should not accept the word 'Mother of Christ', and they were stirring up and making trouble and going around in every place and making use of everything as a help therein; for his clergy were sending word unto him, so that he also became their helper in / everything, because long since he had been wounded by me; and he was in need of an excuse, because he had not been helped with what are called 'benevolences': and he was frightened of me because I had not helped his clergy. For report went out concerning me and grew strong, that I was neglecting—which I was not—him who was being injured. If the report is true or if it is false is clear unto God. It stirred up, however, the accusers of this man [1] and made them take heart to utter against him before the Emperor charges that should and that should not be said, uttering [them] and asking for me to be judge. But because they were sent unto me and I had no cause to decline, I sent for his clergy, demanding to be informed what the matter was. But they grew angry, saying: 'Thou admittest every 'accusation against the patriarch and punishest not forthwith 'without examination the accusers as calumniators. Knowest 'thou also surely all these things, that it is easy for them in this 'way to accuse . . . .[2] of Alexandria; not without constraint 'have we taken away from thee such authority, for it would be 'nothing else than an incitement to bitterness in accusation, 'so long as it were advantageous unto thee to keep him as 'thy good [and] loving friend and not to have him as thine '/ enemy, [even] him who is renowned for greatness and who 'is [3] among the great.' Then I said unto them: 'I have not 'any need of affection which would make me guilty of injustice, 'but [only] of that which works the things of God without acceptance of persons.' This I said, and they said unto me:

---
[1] *Viz.* Cyril.
[2] There is here a lacuna in the Syriac text.
[3] See crit. n., p. 399.

'We will make this known then unto the patriarch'; and since then he has been mine enemy without reconciliation and has been ready for anything. And first he brought about a cause of enmity that he might renounce me as an enemy and, according to his custom, make use of fraud against his accusers and draw a veil over the accusations against him; and thus he, who had preferred a request that the judgement should be entrusted to others, did this. And you have learnt from this that the things which I have said unto you are true and not trifles. What he sent to his clergy who were meddling in my affairs in Constantinople is clear unto all men.

The letter of Cyril to his clergy in Constantinople.[1]

I have received and read the copy of the request which has been sent by you, as one which ought to be given to the Emperor and which you did not want to forward / without my consent. But since there are therein many accusations against one who is there, if he is a brother and if it is right that we ought to call him such, forward it not at the present time, lest he rise up against you and state before the Emperor my accusation [of him] as an heretic.[2] But otherwise at the same time as you renounce his judgement, you shall state also the nature of his enmity, and, if they are utterly roused up [to proceed] to judgement, you shall forward it to other chief men.

Nestorius. On account of these things this man became my enemy. But hear thou also the rest of the letter that you may see that he was acting not for God nor for the fear of God nor for the faith, but on the contrary, although he knew the faith, he passed over it because of his enmity

---

[1] Nestorius quotes only the end of the letter, which is given in full in Labbe (Mansi), vol. iv, col. 1003 sq.; the original of the passage here cited is as follows: τὸ δέ γε σχεδάριον τῆς δεήσεως τὸ παρ' ὑμῶν ἀποσταλέν, ὡς ὀφεῖλον ἐπιδοθῆναι μὲν βασιλεῖ, οὐκ ἄνευ δὲ γνώμης ὑμῶν (v. l. ἡμῶν), λαβὼν ἀνέγνων. ἐπειδὴ δὲ πολλὴν εἶχε καταδρομὴν κατὰ τοῦ ἐκεῖσε ἢ ἀδελφοῦ, ἢ πῶς ἂν εἴποιμι, τέως ἐπέσχον, ἵνα μὴ ἐπέρχοιτο ἡμῖν λέγων· κατηγορήσατέ μου ἐπὶ τοῦ βασιλέως, ὡς αἱρετικοῦ. ὑπηγορεύσαμεν δὲ ἑτέρως, μετὰ τοῦ καὶ παραιτεῖσθαι τὴν αὐτοῦ κρίσιν, εἰπόντες καὶ τῆς ἔχθρας τὸν τρόπον, καὶ τὴν δίκην μετασπάσαι, εἰ ἐνίστανται ὅλως ἐκεῖνοι, εἰς ἑτέρους ἄρχοντας (1008 B, C). See introd. p. xvii.

[2] V reads: 'my accusation [of them] as heretics'.

toward me; and he disturbed and troubled everything in order that . . . .[1] these things of his might vanish and be dispersed.

The rest of the letter of Cyril.[2]

Read then the copy, and its return . . . . . .[3] use; and if you see that he continues to wrong us, truly stirring up every kind [of trouble] against us, zealously inform us, that I may choose some pious bishops/and monks and send them in good time. For *I shall not give sleep unto mine eyes*, as it is written, *nor slumber unto mine eyelids nor rest unto my temples*[4] so long as I strive in the contest which is for the salvation of all.

Nestorius. You have heard clearly how he has confessed, even without any *schéma*; he supposes it in fact a wrong that there is any investigation against him; if I stir not up trouble against him to do him wrong, he also will not stir up trouble against me and he is striving in a contest for the salvation of all. But I am friendly and pious and blameless towards him in everything; but if for the sake of a just judgement I disregard thy[5] blaming thou then becomest embittered and callest me impious and an heretic. And thou callest up bands of monks and bishops and sendest [them] against me to the Emperor, and they accuse me, while thou art striving for thine own salvation and not for the contest of all, but rather in a contest against the salvation of all. And thou hast troubled and confounded and deceived all; and thus hast thou persuaded them to become thine instrument[s][6] of wrong, in

---

[1] A lacuna is here marked by Bedjan.

[2] Labbe (Mansi), iv. 1008 c, D : ἀναγνόντες τοίνυν τὸ σχεδάριον, ἐπίδοτε, εἰ καλέσειε χρεία· κἂν ἴδοιτε ὅτι ἐπιβουλεύων ἐμμένει, καὶ ἀληθῶς πάντα κινεῖ τρόπον τὸν καθ' ἡμῶν ὁρῶντα, σπουδαίως γράψατε. καὶ ἐπιλεξάμενος ἄνδρας εὐλαβεῖς καὶ φρονίμους, ἐπισκόπους τε καὶ μονάζοντας, ἐξαποστελῶ πρώτῳ καιρῷ· οὐ γὰρ μὴ δώσω ὕπνον, κατὰ τὸ γεγραμμένον, τοῖς ὀφθαλμοῖς μου, καὶ τοῖς βλεφάροις μου νυσταγμόν, καὶ ἀνάπαυσιν τοῖς κροτάφοις μου, ἕως οὗ ἀγωνίσωμαι τὸν ὑπὲρ τῆς ἁπάντων σωτηρίας ἀγῶνα. The last eight lines of the letter are not quoted.

[3] Two words are illegible in the Syriac text; V reads: *and he advised the return [of the letter]*, which is clearly incorrect. See the Greek text above.

[4] Ps. cxxxii. (Syr. cxxxi) 4.

[5] This rapid change of person is common when Nestorius is referring to Cyril.

[6] Syr. *'órgānôn* = Gk. ὄργανον.

order that they may neither see nor hear nor be convinced, although one should tell them myriads of times that thou busiest thyself to do these things not for the salvation of all but that thou mayest escape from thine accusers. For what enmity have I with thee, that thou dost suppose / that I do these things to wrong thee? For I have had no word with thee concerning anything, neither concerning things nor concerning possessions nor concerning judgement nor concerning [any] comparison nor about any other cause, neither before I became nor after I became bishop of Constantinople; but in all things were we distinct from one another, as Alexandria is distant from Constantinople, and the interests of the latter are distinct from those of the former. But there was one cause, which even he himself has clearly proclaimed: that I have not helped thee to rise up against thine accusers, whether they be truthful or not. Seeing then that thou art thus perplexed and hast thus made thyself ready, it is known that they are right. For thereby alone is this to be known, [and so] thou[1] mayest know that the enmity is his who is prepared for all these things; but also [thou mayest know it] from his letter unto me.

The letter of Cyril unto Nestorius.[2]

Our colleague, Nestorius, the reverend and godly, Cyril greets in our Lord. Some men, beloved and worthy of belief, have come unto Alexandria and have made known that your Holiness has been much angered against us and has stirred up all that was fair[3] in order to afflict us. / When I wished to learn the affliction of your Piety, they said

[1] Here clearly not Cyril but Nestorius' reader.
[2] Labbe (Mansi), iv. 884 B, c. Nestorius quotes the first quarter of the letter: τῷ εὐλαβεστάτῳ καὶ θεοφιλεστάτῳ ἐπισκόπῳ συλλειτουργῷ Νεστορίῳ, Κύριλλος ἐπίσκοπος ἐν κυρίῳ χαίρειν. Ἄνδρες αἰδέσιμοι καὶ πίστεως ἄξιοι παραγεγόνασιν ἐν Ἀλεξανδρείᾳ. εἶτα μετέδοσαν ὡσανεὶ καὶ τῆς σῆς θεοσεβείας ἀγανακτούσης σφόδρα, καὶ πάντα κάλων κινούσης εἰς τὸ λυπεῖν ἐμέ. βουλομένῳ δέ μοι τῇ[s] σῆς θεοσεβείας τὴν λύπην ἀναμαθεῖν, ἔφασαν ὅτι τὴν πρὸς μοναστὰς ἁγίους γενομένην ἐπιστολὴν περιφέρουσί τινες τῶν ἀπὸ τῆς Ἀλεξανδρείας, καὶ ἡ τοῦ μίσους ἀφορμὴ καὶ τῆς ἀηδίας (v. l. ἀδικίας) αὕτη γέγονε. τεθαύμακα τοίνυν, εἰ μὴ ἐκεῖνο μᾶλλον ἡ σὴ θεοσέβεια καθ' ἑαυτὴν ἐλογίσατο· οὐ γὰρ πρότερον ἐμῆς γραφείσης ἐπιστολῆς ὁ ἐπὶ τῇ πίστει γέγονε θόρυβος, ἀλλ' ἢ εἰρημένων τινῶν παρὰ τῆς σῆς θεοσεβείας, ἢ καὶ μή, πλὴν χαρτίων, ἤγουν ἐξηγήσεων περιφερομένων, κάμνομεν ἡμεῖς, ἐπανορθοῦν θέλοντες τοὺς διεστραμμένους. This was sent in June 429.
[3] See introd. p. xiii.

that a letter had come to some holy monks, and men from Alexandria were carrying it around, and that it was the cause of this hatred and affliction. I then was astonished that your Piety had not considered further; for no letter had formerly been written by us before the disturbance which took place concerning the faith. But whether things were said or were not said by your Piety we are not persuaded. There are in any case pamphlets on doctrine which certain men carry round, and we are wearied with making inquiry with a view to setting right those things which are distorted.[1]

Nestorius. This is the first letter of friendship which was written to me; and learn therefrom whatsoever had been previously deposed against me. Tell the cause for which thou hast spoken: 'this disturbance arose concerning my 'teaching, so that our works when read stirred up all Alexandria 'as well as all the monks of Egypt.' But I leave out both Rome and the cities which are under her; 'and I stirred 'up all the rest of the East,' so that thou wast constrained to compose the letter to the monks so that from there thy letter was dispatched also unto me in order that I might be afflicted thereby; thou knewest indeed that I was afflicted. Wherefore didst thou not write first unto me a letter of friendship,/which would have instructed me concerning the disturbance and concerning the cause of the disturbance and concerning its cessation, as a friend unto a friend, or as unto a bishop or as unto a brother, or as on account of a stumbling-block in the church, or as though thou wert convinced that the teachings were mine own, or as though thou hadst not known and hadst required to be instructed and wouldest have parted company with blasphemy and impiety or wouldest have counselled me what ought to be done? But thy letters[2] against us [were conveyed] to Alexandria and disturbed the monks, and they reached also Constantinople, and thou hast filled all the churches and all the monasteries with disturbance against me, so that even the unfeeling have been roused to feeling; but wouldest thou have wished that I should not be stirred? For what reason were these things, unless thou wert working and

---

[1] See p. xiii.   [2] See crit. n., p. 399.

making ready with all zeal to bring about enmity? For thou wrotest unto me a hostile letter which testified unto me that thou wast mine enemy, and not mine alone, since also thou hast divided and removed far from me whosoever rejoiced in disturbance; and others also there are whom thou hast withdrawn from me, either because of their lack of feeling or because of their ignorance or because of their simplicity without discernment; thou hast stirred them up / in order that under pretext of their souls thou mightest show thyself zealous to set them aright, because thou hadst pleasure in them, or that either I might desist from listening to thine accusers and those who were ready to accuse thee, who were already armed against thee, since, if that were to come about, it would then be easy for thee to do whatsoever thou wouldest in regard to the possessions, or otherwise in oppressing me thou wouldest make believe that for the sake of the fear of[1] God I was thine enemy and that for this cause I had declined mine office as judge. And this is not hidden but is evident unto all men and is spread abroad unto every place in consequence of that enmity which thou hast brought about, because thou didst want all men as witnesses; though indeed I say not anything nor blame any of the things that thou hast prepared. Every man is entitled to receive instruction. For also thou art risen against me as against an impious man and thou art bringing about every disturbance and every stumbling-block; yet thou dost consider all this as nothing and makest ready easy solutions, saying 'let us show kindliness and say this word whereat 'the Church has stumbled, that is, call the blessed Mary the 'mother of God'. For he says not 'thou art obliged' but 'thou wilt show kindliness': not on account of that very thing but on account of those who because of their weakness were not able to examine those things which were said by thee and who stumbled . . . . /. .
. . . . saying . . . .[2]

[1] See crit. n., p. 399.

[2] The Syriac scribe has here inserted a note: 'From here one page has been torn out from the original.' It is clear from what follows that the missing passage must have contained a summary account of the injustice done to

Sophronius. But we became worn out with waiting, since many were dead or sick and in want of many things, and thus we were constrained to assemble together and to lay down conclusions.[1]

Nestorius. How long? say I.[2] Until you had done those things wherewith you were engaged and labouring and [concerning which] you were afraid lest all the Council should be [assembled] and your judgement should be seen? Until then you were sick and dying and you were unable to take nourishment; but afterwards how remained you a long while without enduring any of these things, unless because you were free from the care of these things? For this reason you have disregarded and disdained Candidianus who would have hindered an incomplete Council from being [held]. For you had the strength to do these things, without having convinced by those means whereby you might have succeeded in convincing those who are not believers; and you have accounted as nothing the testimony and the oaths before God and before the Emperor whereby you have sworn to do nothing but to wait for the Eastern Council / which was nigh at hand. For there were some who were persuading the Emperor, and you did not keep the word of God. And then before the command of Candidianus you heard the testimony which the bishops who were not assembled in your incomplete Council addressed to you; they were sixty-eight in number, nor were any of them contemptible nor unknown,[3] but [they were] metropolitans; and Candidianus also came with them and had testified beforehand unto them concerning the things which had lately been done.

Testimony of the bishops who did not associate themselves with Cyril.[4]

The faith indeed of the true religion is known first from the preaching of many holy books and [then] by the

---

Nestorius at the Council of Ephesus through Cyril's refusal to wait until the whole Council was assembled before proceeding. This grievance of Nestorius is treated in detail further on.   [1] Syr. *ṭûphôs* = Gk. τύπος.

[2] See crit. n., p. 399.   [3] Literally: 'from unknown [ones]'.

[4] Latin version in Labbe (Mansi), v. 765: Dominis nostris fratribus & com-

assembly at Nicaea of the holy fathers, on whose limbs were the scars of sufferings according to their number. But by reason of diverse inquiries and disputes the faithful and very Christian[1] Emperor has summoned by his letters the priesthood of the orthodox from every place unto Ephesus, being zealous in this also, according to his custom, out of enthusiasm for the truth's sake, and we are all assembled by the grace of God, except that there is lacking unto our assembly the holy and godly John, bishop of Antioch,/whose coming also is close at hand, as his letters, which have just been written unto us, and the governor[2] [and] the prefects,[3] who have been sent by us unto him, have made known unto us, and other godly bishops from the West. But your Reverence has made known unto us that it is burdensome unto you to attend here and that you are anxious to hold any examination which the Emperor wills even before the coming of the godly bishops whom we have mentioned. For this reason we have sent this letter unto your Reverence that you

ministratoribus Cyrillo & Juvenali Episcopis Tranquillinus & Alexander & Helladius & reliqui Episcopi qui cum eis, in Domino gaudere. Nota quidem rectae glorificationis est fides quae a divinis & adorabilibus scripturis ab olim nobis est praedicata. Nihilominus haec ipsa nobis a sanctis patribus tradita est qui in Nicaena synodo congregati sunt, quorum tot passiones erant pro pietate quot membra. Quia vero propter nonnulla certamina piissimus & amicus Christi Imperator literis suis orthodoxos sacerdotes undique ad Ephesum convocavit, in hoc quoque imitatus proprium circa fidem zelum, & sumus pene omnes per divinam gratiam congregati, deest autem praesentiae sanctae synodi religiosissimus Joannes Antiochenus Episcopus, qui & ipse jam in januis est juxta quae nuper suis literis intimavit, & per eos quos praemisit praefectianos atque magistrianos nuntiata sunt. Similiter etiam nonnulli ex occidentalibus Episcopis synodo adfuturi, mandarunt autem vestrae reverentiae, tamquam qui graviter habent sustinere usque ad ejus adventum, & urgent de his quae visa sunt piissimo Imperatori, (ne audientia celebretur antequam praedicti Deo amicissimi Episcopi sint praesentes,) hujus (rei) gratia has ad reverentiam vestram direximus literas, ut sustineatis Deo amicissimorum comministrorum praesentiam, & nec eos qui depositi sunt suscipiatis quoquo modo, neque illos qui ab Episcopis suis vel olim sunt excommunicati vel nuper. Manifesta enim sunt quae de his definiunt regulae; & praevaricantibus se defixere increpationes non modicas, quae nullo modo queunt despici a sancta synodo. Et illud vero reverentia vestra cognoscat, quia omnia quae ab audacibus abrupte fuerint perpetrata, contra praesumentium retorqueantur audaciam & a Christo Domino & a divinis canonibus. (There follow the signatures of sixty-eight bishops.) Compare the Letter to Theodosius, Labbe (Mansi), iv. 1232-6.

[1] Literally: 'Christ-fearing'.
[2] Syr. *magēstryânós* = Gk. μαγεστριανός, cp. p. 343.
[3] Syr. *hûpharkīqó* = Gk. ὑπαρχικοί; see n. on pp. xv-xvi.

should await the coming of the excellent bishops our colleagues and that you should not receive at haphazard any whose deposition[1] has been enacted nor those who have been or are coming under sentence of suspension from their bishoprics. For it is known what the holy canons ordain on this account, and those who transgress them are condemned to no slight punishment, which cannot by any means be transgressed by the Holy Council. May your Reverence then know also this, that everything which is done in boldness by bold men will be found to recoil on your boldness through Christ the Lord of all and through the holy canons.

/ Signature of the bishops.

Nestorius. But read also the admonition which was given by the illustrious Candidianus, Count of the Household,[2] that you may learn also from this the violence which they wrought irreverently and shamelessly and that he[3] may no longer deceive [you]. But after the testimony of the bishops who took as their plea the [fact that] they to be sure were in difficulties in that the bishop of Antioch together with the Eastern bishops was close upon coming at the gate as the governors[4] who were sent to their provinces[5] who reported these things learned from the letters of John—when they heard [the testimony] they made disturbance as with one accord, crying out and shouting and hurling insults, in order to bring forth the bishops who had been sent unto them and to cast them out, so that even the blows with which they attacked them were heard by Count Candidianus. But after they had so reverently driven them out, they returned against him that they might capture him, laying hands upon those who in consequence of hunger and sickness were not able to stand up, and they heard not the things which he spake unto them nor even the letters of the Emperor which were

---

[1] Syr. *qāthārāsis*, a transliteration of the Gk. καθαίρεσις, as wherever ' deposition ' occurs, unless otherwise stated.

[2] Syr. *qômes dômastîqô*, which probably stands for the Gk. κόμης τῶν δομεστίκων (Nau).

[3] *Viz.* Cyril. [4] Syr. *magistryânê*.

[5] Syr. *hûpharkyas* = Gk. ὑπαρχίας, meaning either ' to their districts ' or ' on their missions '.

sent unto them all!/And he commanded them that the Council should not be [held] incomplete, but [that] the things which were [done] by the Council should be settled in common by vote. But, like a wise man in the midst of fools, he seemed surely to have become a fool in saying that, for they were not willing to hear. He commanded them to read this imperial command before them, which ought not to have been read before all the bishops had been assembled. When he had done this, account was kept of nothing.[1]

Of the contents of the letter, which were as follows: [2]

We have commanded Candidianus, the illustrious Count, to come unto your holy Council, without participating at all in those things concerning which inquiry takes place among you, since we have thought that he who is not accounted of the assembly of the bishops ought not to interfere in an inquiry touching ecclesiastical regulations [3] and in an inquisition concerning the faith.

He said not, in fact, that he should not participate in the assembly but in an inquisition touching the faith, being ordered not to allow the Council to be [held] incomplete before the assembly of all the bishops took place. Because then he was constrained to read this—it ought not to have been read before the coming of all the bishops—they drove out him who came from/this side with much outcry and hisses and threats that he should be delivered unto death if he participated in the common inquisition of the Council. And they then named themselves authoritatively a general Council, for that those who were present were to be sure so many; and those who had not participated with them in the inquisition testified unto·them, saying unto them : 'we 'ought to wait for those whose coming is close at hand'[4]—that is, for the chief of the Council. And that the Count who had been charged with the maintenance of order among them might not participate with them, they said that he

---

[1] Cp. the two *Contestationes* of Candidianus and his *Edictum* printed in Lupus, *Var. Pat. Epist.*, p. 33 sq., and Labbe (Mansi), v. 770 sq.

[2] Cp. p. 110, n. 2.

[3] Syr. *!aksē'* = Gk. τάξις. [4] Literally: 'nigh unto the door'.

110   THE BAZAAR OF HERACLEIDES I. iii.   [166–

should not be present at the inquiry touching the faith nor at the inquisition touching ecclesiastical things. But in everything they were acting by their own authority and were not obeying the imperial command which made known clearly unto them that he had been sent for this reason, that he might check the disturbances and the dissensions which were taking place. But hear also the letters of the Emperor which were sent by the hand of Candidianus.

From the writ[1] of the Emperor.[2]

Previously indeed we have written what was right, that your Piety should be assembled in the city of the Ephesians; but since it is right to provide also for the maintenance of order in the deliberation which will take place in your assembly concerning the inquiry for which you are assembled, /this also we have not overlooked but have admonished you to be in all things untroubled; and we are persuaded that your Piety is not in need of external assistance that you may be zealous for peace; but this has been our [duty], not to be neglectful in solicitude for an inquiry touching

---

[1] Syr. *saqrâ*, a transliteration of Lat. *sacra* [*epistola*], a translation of θεῖον γράμμα.

[2] Labbe (Mansi), iv. 1117 E: διά τοι τοῦτο πρώτην μὲν περὶ τοῦ συνελθεῖν τὴν ὑμετέραν θεοσέβειαν εἰς τὴν τῶν Ἐφεσίων μητρόπολιν, τὰ εἰκότα γεγραφήκαμεν. ἐπειδὴ δὲ χρὴ καὶ τῆς πρεπούσης εὐταξίας τε καὶ ἡσυχίας (v. l. εὐκοσμίας) τῇ διασκέψει τῆς ἁγιωτάτης ὑμῶν συνόδου δεόντως φροντίσαι, οὐδὲ τοῦτο παρήκαμεν· ὥστε αὐτῇ πανταχόθεν περιφυλαχθῆναι (v. l. ὑπάρξαι) τὸ ἀτάραχον. καὶ πεπείσμεθα μέν, ὡς οὐδεμίας τῆς ἔξωθεν βοηθείας εἰς τὸ καὶ ἑτέροις εἰρήνην παρασχεῖν δεῖται ὑμῶν ἡ θεοσέβεια. ἦν δὲ καὶ τοῦτο τῆς ἐμμελοῦς (v. l. ἐντελοῦς) ἡμῶν περὶ τὴν εὐσέβειαν προνοίας μὴ παριδεῖν.

Ἐντέταλται τοίνυν Κανδιδιανός, ὁ μεγαλοπρεπέστατος κόμης τῶν καθωσιωμένων δομεστίκων, ἄχρι τῆς ἁγίας (v. l. ἁγιωτάτης) ἡμῶν διαβῆναι συνόδου· καὶ μηδὲν μὲν ταῖς περὶ τῶν δογμάτων γινομέναις ζητήσεσι κοινωνῆσαι· ἀθέμιτον γάρ, τὸν μὴ (v. l. ἔξω) τοῦ καταλόγου τῶν ἁγιωτάτων ἐπισκόπων τυγχάνοντα τοῖς ἐκκλησιαστικοῖς σκέμμασιν ἐπιμίγνυσθαι· τοὺς κοσμικοὺς δὲ καὶ μονάζοντας, τούς τε ἤδη διὰ τοῦτο συνειλεγμένους, καὶ τοὺς συνάγεσθαι μέλλοντας, τῆς αὐτῆς παντὶ τρόπῳ χωρίσαι πόλεως. ἐπειδήπερ οὐ χρὴ τοὺς κατ' οὐδὲν ἀναγκαίους ὄντας τῇ μελλούσῃ τοῦ δόγματος διασκέψει, κινεῖν θορύβους, καὶ διὰ τοῦτο ἐμποδίζειν τοῖς εἰρηνικῶς τυπωθῆναι παρὰ τῆς ὑμετέρας ἁγιωσύνης ὀφείλουσι· καὶ φροντίσαι τοῦ μή τινα διχόνοιαν ἐξ ἀντιπαθείας ἐπὶ πλέον παραθῆναι· ὡς ἂν μὴ ἐκ τούτου ἡ τῆς ἁγιωτάτης ὑμῶν συνόδου παρεμποδίζοιτο διάσκεψις, καὶ ἡ ἀκριβὴς τῆς ἀληθείας ζήτησις ἐκ τῆς ἐγγινομένης τυχὸν ἀτάκτου περιηχήσεως διακρούηται· ἀνεξικάκως δὲ τῶν λεγομένων ἕκαστον ἀκροώμενον προστιθέναι τὸ δοκοῦν, ἢ ἀντιτιθέναι· καὶ οὕτως κατὰ πρότασίν τε καὶ λύσιν, τὴν περὶ τοῦ ἀληθοῦς δόγματος ἔρευναν δίχα τινὸς ταραχῆς διαλυθῆναι (v. l. διακριθῆναι), καὶ κοινῇ τῆς ὑμετέρας ὁσιότητος ψήφῳ ἀστασίαστόν τε καὶ τὸν πᾶσιν ἀρέσκοντα τύπον λαβεῖν.

the truth, that is to send Count Candidianus to your Council, without participating at all in those things concerning which inquiry takes place among you; since we have thought that he who is not accounted of the assembly of the bishops ought not to interfere in an inquiry touching ecclesiastical ordinances[1] and in an inquisition concerning the faith; but he will expel from the city those seculars and monks who are there assembled for this purpose and are with you, because such men ought not to be found in your assembly, lest they excite disturbance and thereby make void whatsoever you duly examine and rightly do. He will be careful too that no one shall introduce division so as to cause dispute, lest from this cause your inquiry and the sincerity of true deliberation among you be delayed. But with patience each shall hear whatsoever is said and each shall be ready to reply or for reply to be made to him and thus by questions and by replies and by solution the inquiry touching the true faith shall be judged without any dispute and by the common examination of your Saintliness it will reach a happy agreement without dispute.

/ *Nestorius.* They did not press for this to be read nor yet were they willing to hear him who was telling them that 'they 'should be careful that no one should introduce division so as 'to cause dispute, lest from that cause the inquiry concerning 'the true faith and the true deliberation among you should be 'delayed, but that with patience each should hear whatsoever 'was said and that each should be ready to reply or for reply 'to be made unto him, and thus by questions and by replies 'and by solution the inquiry touching the true faith should be 'judged without any dispute, and the common scrutiny of your 'Saintliness should attain a happy agreement without any dispute'. Because they knew these things, they allowed them not to be read, for they hid this word, which, as a divine prophecy, showed clearly the things which were being done by them. Or was it that the Emperor, owing to a sign of the things which had been done by him, divined what he[2] was ready to do and set it down beforehand in his letters? For even slight symptoms suffice to give a small indication of the habits of the soul, although things like these have not yet already been [done]

[1] Syr. *ṭaksē'* = Gk. τάξις.   [2] *Viz.* Cyril.

by him, while those from which it could have been known have not yet already been brought to light. God however has brought to light all that concerns him for that to become the judge of them for the things which / were about to take place, that they might not suppose that because they had done this in ignorance and were ignorant of the manner of the inquiry and of the inquisition, [therefore] they said incidentally the things which were [proved] false by what had been said. Will then a sincere inquiry be settled [even] by sincere inquirers through division and through that which causes dispute, or through impartiality and patience on the part of the hearers towards what is said? And [will a sincere inquiry be settled] by merely laying down the subject of inquiry, or by the giving and receiving of replies on either side, and their being examined by questioning and unravelling, until the inquiry which is being examined is [settled] without dispute? Shall we with haste or without haste find a solution and an answer in harmony therewith when we are asked a question? Which of these things has been said untruly? But this command was not pleasing unto thee[1] because thou didst wish to conquer and not to discover the truth.

But what shall I do now? Shall I accuse Candidianus of not having observed the imperial letters and of having caused such a disturbance of bishops against bishops their colleagues as well as against him who was charged with keeping watch over them and with the maintenance of order? But he strained himself to persuade with words those who were not inclined to hearken unto words, who were in need of some one who would control them against their will according to the imperial command, which was acknowledged by all men to be just; and otherwise it was not seemly more should be [done] than that he should / carry out his message, speaking and having answer made to him by question and answer. However that which was done with intent to deceive was considered by them as a sport. I have not anything more to say; for he called them to witness by his commands that they should do nothing before they were all assembled together according to the

---

[1] *Viz.* Cyril.

imperial command, but they were not willing to hearken even unto the command of the Emperor. Hear then also his own admonition.

The admonition which was uttered by the illustrious Count Candidianus that they should not assemble before all the bishops were assembled.[1]

To the holy Cyril, bishop of Alexandria and Metropolitan, and to the bishops who have assembled together with him,

---

[1] Labbe (Mansi), v. 770; Lupus, *Var. Pat. Epist.* p. 33 : *Contestatio Candidiani Comitis, quam publice, mane audiens synodum celebrari, in Epheso proposuit* : Sanctissimo Episcopo metropolis Alexandriae Cyrillo, et reverentissimis Episcopis qui cum eo sunt congregati, Flavius Candidianus magnificentissimus Comes devotissimorum Domesticorum. Quoniam ex quo in Ephesinam civitatem veni, nihil aliud deprecatus sum communem sanctamque synodum vestram nisi ut cum pace atque concordia quae ad fidem rectamque glorificationem nostram exponerentur (*v. l.* disponerent), sicut et Dominus noster jussit et piissimus Imperator, scit religiositas vestra; et sufficit mihi testimonium quod ipsa veritas praebet, quia nihil aliud egerimus praeter haec. Quoniam vero et dum congregandos vos esse in sanctissimam Ecclesiam praeter aliorum Episcoporum cognoscerem voluntatem, nondum veniente sanctissimo Episcopo Antiochenae metropolis Joanne vel his qui cum ipso sunt, non cessavi rogans ut id fieret quod dixi superius; et unumquemque sum contestatus ob hoc, ne forte particularis fieri synodus videretur. Extremo (*v. l.* externo) vero nihilominus, cum congregati essetis in sanctissima Ecclesia, occurrere festinavi, et ea quae visa sunt Domino nostro et piissimo Principi, licet videam (*v. l.* id jam) ex superfluo facere, dum semel nosceretis haec eadem ex literis divinitatis ejus directis ad vos. Verumtamen edocui dispositionem ejusdem Domini nostri et piissimi Principis hanc esse. Velle namque eum dixi fidem nostram absque ulla discordia ab omnibus idem sapientibus roborari, et nolle particulares quasdam synodos fieri, quod maxime in haereses et schismata convertere novit religionem nostram fidemque orthodoxam. Insuper dum reverentia vestra exigeret sacram Domini nostri et piissimi Principis, quae directa est ad sanctam synodum, relegi, prius quidem id facere non annuebam (nec enim dicere refutabo) eo quod non adessent omnes qui ad sanctissimam synodum jussi fuerant convenire; sed quia vestra religiositas inquit ignorare se quae praecepta sint a Domino nostro et optimo Principe, necessarium mihi visum est apparere, ut etiam non praesentibus aliis reverentissimis Episcopis omnibus relegerentur divinae atque adorabiles literae. Nihilominus vero et postquam vobis manifestavi quae sunt decreta divinitus, in eadem supplicatione permansi, deprecans reverentiam vestram et poscens nihil novum fieri priusquam cuncti sanctissimi patres atque Episcopi ad synodum convenirent, sed sustineretis quatuor tantummodo dies sanctissimum Episcopum Antiochenorum metropoleos cum aliis qui pariter sunt, necnon et illos qui cum sanctissimo Nestorio sunt; ut vestra religiositate pariter congregata, et omni sancta synodo collecta simul in unum, si qua essent quae forsan in dubitationem venirent, a quibus nos sumus extranei, cunctis vobis praesentibus judicarentur, et tunc cum consensu omnium vestrum ostenderetur quis prave ac

Flavius Candidianus, the great and illustrious Count of the most religious Household.[1] Since I reached the city of Ephesus, nothing else have I demanded of the congregation of the holy Council except that the [questions] of the orthodox faith should be settled in peace and unity as the faithful, the victorious [Emperor] also has commanded : of this your Piety is aware. And it suffices me to bear witness to the truth that I am not more desirous of anything else than of this. But when I learned that you were ready to assemble together in the holy church without the will of the other bishops, when John, bishop of Antioch, had not yet come nor / the bishops who were with him, since one day before that whereon you were prepared to do this, I rested not from persuading and invoking each one of you not to think of holding a Council incomplete; and again on the next day, after you had assembled together in the holy church, I hesitated not in [my] desire to come unto you and I testified unto you what the faithful Emperor willed, although that was superfluous since you were already acquainted therewith from the letters which had been written unto you by his Highness. But although it was indeed so, I instructed you in our pious Emperor's own will, saying his will was this, that your faith should be defined without delay and confusion by all and in unity, and that he willed not that the Council should be held incomplete, because our orthodox

praeter regulas ecclesiasticas credere videretur an certe recte omnes pariter confiteri, sicut sanctorum patrum religio habet. Haec igitur non semel sed etiam saepius admonens, et suppliciter postulans, nihil profeci. Verum quia nihil eorum quae a me sunt dicta servatum est, sed a vobis injuriose ac violenter expulsus sum, necessarium duxi hoc mea contestatione vobis constituere manifestum, et per hoc edictum clare dicere nullum vestrum novi aliquid facere, sed omnium sanctorum Episcoporum sustinere praesentiam, et sic communi consilio quae ad catholicam sanctamque fidem pertinent judicari. Si quis vero ex propria voluntate ductus ea quae ab immortali et optimo vertice jussa sunt commovere voluerit, sciat se sibi ipsi reputaturum quicquid evenerit, praejudicium vero se alii (v. l. ab alio) non inferre. Non enim pigebit me haec eadem denuo iterare. Quoniam vero, sicut vestra sanctitas novit, hoc placuit Domino nostro et piissimo Principi, ut sub praesentia simul omnium sanctorum Episcoporum quae ab ejus divinitate sunt convocati ea quae in dubitationem veniunt dissolvantur, propterea et sacra quae ad sanctissimum synodum vestram directa sunt, et quae ad me ipsum ab eorum divinitate sunt scripta, huic edicto praeposui ; ut per omnia cognoscentes quae a Domino nostro et optimo Imperatore praecepta sunt, a tali praesumptione cessetis. Cognoscite igitur quod scripti hujus exemplar etiam domino nostro piissimo Imperatori transmissum est.

[1] Syr. *qathsimôn dômastiqón*, a transliteration of the Greek phrase καθωσιω-μένων δομεστίκων.

faith would be turned thereby to discord and dissension.
And further, when your Reverence demanded that the faithful and godly Emperor's own writ, which had been sent unto the holy Council, should be read, at first I was opposed to doing so—and I decline not to say [so]—because those who had been commanded to be at the holy Council had not yet come and [were not yet] assembled. But when your Piety said that you were not persuaded of any of the things which the Emperor willed and had commanded to take place, it seemed / unto me that it was needful, although the presence of all the bishops was not [complete], to present unto you the august and illustrious letter. And further indeed, after the will of his Lordship was made known to you, I neglected not to exercise the same persuasion with you demanding of your excellency and testifying unto you that you should introduce no innovations before all the holy bishops were gathered together unto the Council, but that you should wait four days only for the holy John, bishop of Antioch, Metropolitan, and those who were with him, and those again who were with the holy and pious Nestorius, bishop of Constantinople, in order that, when you were together and all the holy Council was assembled together, if there were anything of which there was inquiry or anything else of which there was dispute, for which we were superfluous, you, when assembled, together might investigate it. And then, by the consent of you all, it would be known who was found to believe improperly and outside the canons, [and] if you all rightly confessed and if you revered the faith of the holy fathers. Not only then have I surely counselled [you] but I have also persuaded [you] concerning these things. But because you have not accepted aught of what has been said, while I also have surely been driven out by you, / I have considered it needful by means of this testimony to make known unto you and by this charge [1] to testify unto you that you should make no innovations, but that you should wait for the coming of all the holy fathers, the bishops, and that, when you were of the same opinion, that which concerned the holy Catholic Church should be judged. If any one, by the impulse of his own authority, should will to change anything of that which had seemed [good] to the pure and imperishable Principate, let him know that it is in his own self that he will be blamed and that he will prove no one guilty in aught. But I shrink not from saying these same things: that your Holiness is persuaded of and knows what-

---

Syr. *diṭaghmâ* = Gk. διάταγμα.

soever the pious Emperor wills: that in the presence of all the holy bishops who have been summoned by his authority everything whereof there has been controversy should be settled and the true faith revealed. But for this reason I have set at the head of this protest[1] both the writ which has been sent to your holy Council and the letters which have been written to me by his Lordship in order that by means of all this, when you have learned his will, you may desist from those things which you have been zealous to do. / And know also that a copy of this letter has been sent unto our pious lord the Emperor.

Nestorius. When these things were set forth and read before them, did not their fury wherewith they were maddened deprive [every] man of his reason? Or had they reverence for anything? Or feared they the blame and the testimony? Or respected they their chiefs who were over them and the Emperor himself and those who were ready to judge them by the divine laws and by the definitions of the fathers? Nay, they disdained them all; for they had the things which had been made known unto them by [his] Majesty and all those things which [they were doing] against me were regarded by them as a sport. And, as I suppose, Candidianus knew them and was frightened by them; and by words alone would he have hindered them, but he dared not proceed to deeds and to afflict those who did such things. Whereon hast thou[2] trusted to do what even the barbarians dared not do of old? For suppose that it was [the case] that thou wast not my enemy nor my accuser; thou wast at any rate my judge, as thou hast made thyself with the rest of the others; I say that thou wast even more. And the time of judgement also drew nigh, wherein it was right that we should be judged; but those who were judges with thee came not, and you / were constrained to summon them. Thou wast willing to bring over to thine opinion all who were present; but I, who was demanding that the judgement should take place, I was testifying unto them all that they ought not to judge me before those who were summoned to the judgement had been gathered together.

---

[1] Syr. *dimarṭūryā* = Gk. διαμαρτυρία.   [2] *Viz.* Cyril.

There would have been every ground even for thy judgement if thou hadst not judged on the ground that thou wast summoned [as a party to the case];[1] but, [thou wilt say], it would have been difficult for thee.—Thou hadst authority to go away and to do this, on the ground that thou wert not able to judge in thine own cause.—And '[it was] not that I came not' [you will say], 'but I was not able to go away'.—Thou oughtest to have instructed in this him who had the authority, and the office of judge would have been conferred by him; for no one believed that thou wouldst have conferred the office of judge on thyself. And so these things were done. Has not God constrained you to write those things when you excused yourself and accused Candidianus himself and John and Irenaeus,[2] a man·who lived in God and served him with his possessions and with his soul and with his body. And because the things that he did were not pleasing, they set themselves to accuse him—that you might learn from them their barbarous and savage and unrighteous boldness. When indeed those who had acted boldly against the law which Candidianus set forth unto them and the things which they had done against them had been referred to the Emperor, he made answer openly unto them all. It is / fair that you should hear it, in order that you all may learn therefrom at the same time how God has condemned them all for me out of their [own] mouth in the place of judgement.

Of the imperial letters which were sent by the hand of the governor[3] *Palladius.*[4]

Our Majesty has learned from what the illustrious Count

---

[1] *I. e.* 'There would have been every reason for thee not to have accepted the post of judge which had been offered unto thee.' Perhaps the text is out of order.

[2] Count Irenaeus, afterwards Bishop of Tyre. See Introd. pp. xxiv, xxv.

[3] Syr. *magestryānōs.*

[4] Nestorius quotes about the first half of the letter; see Labbe (Mansi), iv. 1377: τοῦ μεγαλοπρεπεστάτου κόμητος τῶν καθωσιωμένων δομεστίκων Κανδιδιανοῦ γνωρίσαντος ἡμῖν, μεμάθηκεν ἡ ἡμετέρα εὐσέβεια ταραχωδῶς τινά, καὶ παρὰ τὸ προσῆκον κατὰ τὴν Ἐφεσίων γεγονέναι μητρόπολιν, οὔτε πάντων, ὥσπερ ἐδέδοκτο, τῶν θεοσεβεστάτων ἐπισκόπων συνεληλυθότων· καί τοι τοῦ τῆς μεγαλοπόλεως Ἀντιοχείας ἐπισκόπου πλησιάζειν ἤδη σὺν ἑτέροις μητροπολίταις μέλλοντος· οὔτε τῶν ἤδη παραγεγονότων συσκεψαμένων ἢ ὁμονοησάντων ἀλλήλοις, οὔτε μὴν τὰ περὶ τῆς πίστεως καθ'

of the most religious Household,[1] Candidianus, has written unto us what has taken place in the midst of disturbance and improperly in the metropolis of Ephesus. when all the pious bishops unto whom I had sent [word] to assemble together had not yet assembled and the coming of the holy John, bishop of Antioch, with other metropolitans was very near; and, further, when even those who were present had not deliberated with them nor come to agreement with one another; and, further, when there had not even been inquiry concerning the faith as there ought to have been or according to the letters which have always been sent by us. But the enmity of certain persons for certain others is well known, and for this reason they were zealous to act according to their opinions, without being able even to make use of a veil, or that they might be thought by people to have done what they did after reflection. Consequently it has seemed [good] / unto our Majesty that there should be no place for boldness and that whatsoever has been [done] by them improperly should be void. And first let the words touching the faith be examined that they may henceforth prevail, as it has seemed [good] unto us and as it has been decided and has been pleasing unto the congregation of the Council, since our Majesty accepts not those things which have been cunningly brought about by a preliminary finding.

These [are the words] of the Emperor.

But hear also the report [2] which they sent unto the Emperor, wherein they accused Candidianus of having misinformed them out of friendship for me and of not having made the truth known unto the Emperor and maintained that which they have done against me. For thereby you will know full well their audacity at the same time as their puerility; they played as with a child and disdained to excuse themselves before him. For they were rebuked [and asked]: 'for what

ὃν ἐχρῆν τρόπον ἐξετασάντων, ἢ ὥσπερ τοῖς ἐγκαταπεμφθεῖσι (v. l. ἀεὶ καταπεμφθεῖσι) θείοις ἡμῶν περιείχετο γράμμασιν· ἀλλὰ ὥστε δήλην εἶναι τὴν τινων πρός τινας ἀπέχθειαν, διὰ πολλὴν τὴν περὶ τὰ ὁπόσων δόξαντα σπουδήν, οὔτε παρακαλύμματι χρήσασθαι δυνηθέντων. διὸ νομίσειεν ἄν τις λογισμῷ τὰ γεγονότα πεπρᾶχθαι· ὅθεν δέδοκται τῇ ἡμετέρᾳ θειότητι, χώραν μὲν τὴν τοιαύτην μηδαμῶς ἔχειν ἐξελθεῖν αὐθεντίαν· τῶν δὲ ἀνακολούθως γεγονότων ἀργούντων, τοὺς περὶ τῆς εὐσεβείας λόγους, ὥσπερ ἐδέδοκτο, πρότερον ἐξετασθῆναι, καὶ κατὰ τὸ κοινῇ πάσῃ τῇ συνόδῳ δοκοῦν εἰς τὸν ἑξῆς χρόνον κρατεῖν· οὐκ ἀνεχομένης τῆς ἡμετέρας εὐσεβείας τῶν ἐξ ἐπιτηδεύσεως προλημμάτων· κτλ.

[1] See p. 114, n. 1.   [2] Syr. 'anāphôrâ = Gk. ἀναφορά.

'reason have you held a Council incomplete before all the 'Council was assembled, inasmuch as you have shown thereby 'that not out of the fear of God but out of human enmity you 'did all this and you were not observant with a pure con-'science that all the Council should be assembled.' And they made no answer whatsoever to these things, but the accusation stands as it was.

/ *Of the report*[1] *of Cyril which was sent unto the Emperor against the report which Candidianus sent.*[2]

Hereby it is proved of us that no enmity whatsoever has stirred us up against Nestorius; but we have laid down the doctrine of the fear of God. After we have compared it with that of Nestorius, the latter seems to have met with refutation. And after the letters which have been written by Nestorius and after the interpretations which have been put forward by him, we have openly published the decision of the judgement, the holy Gospel having been placed in the midst, and we declare[3] that Christ Himself, the Lord of all, was present.

Nestorius. [This is] like those who, being rebuked for the violation of oaths, would convince by oaths that they have not violated oaths and make no convincing reply concerning their acts. For they were rebuked [and asked]: 'For what 'reason have you transgressed the general rule and not waited 'for all the Council, as also you were summoned all together?' And they returned not any answer to this; and: 'for what 'reason, in addition thereto, have not the bishops who were 'present taken counsel in common with their colleagues '/ who were with them as to whether you ought all to have 'waited?' To this also they answered nothing. 'For what 'reason have you not done this by common agreement, but

[1] See p. 118, n. 2.
[2] The Report is given in full in Labbe (Mansi), iv. 1421. Nestorius gives only a short extract: ἐν οἷς (*i. e.* ἐν τοῖς τῶν πραχθέντων ὑπομνήμασιν) δεικνύμεθα οὐδεμίαν κατὰ Νεστορίου δυσμένειαν γυμνάζοντες, ἀλλὰ αὐτὰ τῆς εὐσεβείας ἐκθέμενοι τὰ δόγματα· οἷς παραβαλόντες τὰ ὑπὸ Νεστορίου κηρυττόμενα, ἔχοντα τὸν ἔλεγχον ἐκ τῶν γραμμάτων Νεστορίου (*v. l.* αὐτοῦ), ἐπιστολῶν τε καὶ τῶν ἐν δημοσίῳ γενομένων διαλέξεων, τὴν ψῆφον ἐξηνέγκαμεν, τοῦ ἁγίου εὐαγγελίου ἐν μέσῳ κειμένου, καὶ δεικνύντος ἡμῖν παρόντα τὸν δεσπότην τῶν ὅλων Χριστόν. (Continued on p. 121, n. 1). According to Labbe the Report was dispatched on July 1, 431.
[3] See p. xiv.

'have divided and separated in one Council of bishops those 'who were present from those who were about to come, so that 'through examination with them [1] the judgement touching the 'faith might be defined?' Nor to this returned they answer, but by anticipation without discretion and by agreeing to that which was pleasing unto them, being unwilling that they [2] should be judges with them, they made them for themselves adversaries of the faith. For thou hast not refrained from thy boldness wherewith thou hast been occupied from the beginning and on account of which thou hast drawn also the bishop of Rome into the rebellion and hast made void the oecumenical Council. In the face of all these things they were deaf and speechless. For what reason heard you not this; that 'you shall not hold a Council incomplete before all 'the bishops are assembled'? For what reason did you not wait for them, [when] the Count who was sent was restraining you and persuading you to wait for the bishops who were near and not far off? And you made no answer unto any one of these things. If Christ had been sitting [there] and if you had been persuaded that he was sitting with you, would you have done these things, and would you have made a participation in your impiety—Christ on whom you thus / trample, as if he, who would have exposed you so openly, could not confute you? For how [in that case] would you have supposed that your unrighteous and hidden purpose would be surely revealed, you who were the first to testify unto the bishops of your impiety and also unto the Count who had charge over you of the things which he has in truth forwarded in the report [3] for the instruction of the Emperor?

But for all those who want to learn your reputation through the letters of [his] Majesty or through your own reports, all these things will confirm them as being without doubt true: that you participated not in the opinion of those who were present and that you detached yourselves from the bishops

---

[1] *Viz.* the former alone.

[2] *Viz.* Nestorius and the bishops who had demanded that the Council should not be held before the arrival of John, bishop of Antioch, and his companions.

[3] See p. 118, n. 2.

who were absent and from those who were present, in that you were not willing to wait fourteen days more. And I sat neither saying nor doing aught, and 'in your midst sat 'Christ', who compelled you all so to speak and to act in my presence. 'No enmity at all against Nestorius has stirred us 'up.' When I was not present, my own enemy judged my words and compared them with those that he wanted and as he wanted, and I should have accepted from them that they preserved no enmity at all against me! Who will dare to say / this when he sees all the impious and bold acts wherewith I have been oppressed by them? And will it not rather seem a sport? For do you say these things to him who would have convicted you for them and for having acted in enmity toward me? Nay, [you speak] after the likeness of those who smite a man and strip him and say unto him who would rebuke them to be sure for their sport: 'Surely 'we were making sport, and did this not in enmity but in 'friendship'; but they cast him out wounded and naked. Thus also have they done unto me, being reproached and reproaching; but the judge of all will not so make sport. For although in all this I have no human tribunal, I have that of Christ.

But we demand of your Highness that none of those who value the love of man above the fear of God should be accounted worthy to be received. For we have perceived that the reverend John, bishop of Antioch, has some such a wish as this, seeking rather to gratify friendship than to consider aught that is advantageous unto the faith; and that, in addition to this, not fearing the threat of your Highness and not being stirred by enthusiasm for the faith which has been delivered unto us from above, he has delayed the holy Council twenty-one days / beyond the appointed time which has been granted to us by your Highness, and we have been constrained, we of the orthodox party of the holy Council, who love only the faith, to inquire into those things which appertain unto the fear of God.[1]

[1] Labbe (Mansi), iv. 1424 A (see above, p. 119, n. 2): δεόμεθα τοίνυν τοῦ ὑμετέρου κράτους, μηδένα παραδοχῆς ἀξιωθῆναι τῶν προτιμώντων ἀνθρώπων φιλίαν (v. l. τὴν ἀνθρώπου φιλανθρωπίαν) τῆς εὐσεβείας, καὶ γὰρ τοιαύτης αἰσθόμενοι τῆς διαθέσεως τοῦ

Nestorius. Have they not openly made known their will without keeping [it] dark, [showing] that not because they were wearied and worn with sickness and with death and with the poverty of their lives did they not come for the judgement, but, because they feared judgement by all men and before all men, they made a judgement, before the bishop of Antioch came? For what advantage unto me was a delay of twenty days or what gain would it have brought unto you? For that which would have been done after twenty days could also have been done as well before as after them all. All the more, in fact, if he had entertained friendship toward me, he ought surely to have been the first to rejoin me, and he would have persuaded many of those who were turned away from me and he would not have let you do that which you have done, because you would have been restrained by him. But, in order that there might not be an examination, thou hast made use of all means that judgement might be corrupted. So let it be. You ought then rather to have waited for it, so that there might be an examination and that you might not give me a cause of escape; but not one whit of this is true. Suppose then that I concede / unto you that you waited for the judgement to take place, for what reason did you not act according to the command of the Emperor? For you would have shown that you did not wait for this reason;[1] but you waited not. Therefore your anxiety from the beginning is evident from all these things; since he acted so because he feared to come to examination and to judgement, and, because he was grieved thereat, he was devising means to arrange all these things. If then thou hadst been confident in what thou wrotest, and if those who would have testified for thee had been on thy side, that is, the Father and the Divine Scriptures, thou wouldest have rebuked me for having done

---

θεοφιλεστάτου ἐπισκόπου Ἰωάννου τοῦ Ἀντιοχείας, ὡς βουλομένου φιλίᾳ χαρίζεσθαι μᾶλλον, ἢ τὸ συμφέρον τῇ πίστει σκοπεῖν, ἐξ ὧν μήτε τοῦ ὑμετέρου κράτους ἀπειλὴν φοβηθείς, μήτε τῷ ζήλῳ κινούμενος τῆς θεοφιλοῦς πίστεως τῆς ἄνωθεν παραδεδομένης, τὴν ἁγίαν ἀνεβάλετο σύνοδον ἐπὶ εἴκοσι καὶ μίαν ἡμέραν μετὰ τὴν δεδομένην προθεσμίαν παρὰ τοῦ ὑμετέρου κράτους, καὶ ἠναγκάσθημεν ἅπαντες οἱ τῆς ἁγίας συνόδου ὀρθόδοξοι, καὶ μόνης ἐρῶντες τῆς πίστεως, ζητῆσαι τὰ περὶ τῆς εὐσεβείας.

[1] *I.e.* through fear of the discussion.

that which I have done in enmity and not in truth, and thou wouldest have blamed me for having disturbed the world for nothing, when I raised the inquiry of the heretics and of the orthodox. Thou oughtest to have written these things unto the Emperor and all the other things, if it is on account of this that thou dost suppose that the things which thou hast done have taken place, as well as that I fled from judgement because I was not confident in what I had written. But they have done this as things done in enmity and not in truth; they have fled from judgement, and fabricated a story, that[1] judgement and examination took place, when none of these things occurred. Let him come; let him be judged; let him make answer to the things wherewith he is rebuked and let him hear the answer to the things wherewith he rebukes, and let the judgement of both of them take place without hindrance. / Yea, before the Trinity, on whose behalf I have shown all zeal, for what reason indeed do others stumble at the things wherein I am confident? These things brought low thy might, for thou knewest that they were true and convincing; but thou spakest not and thou hadst not confidence nor didst thou feign to quote the fearful and terrible saying that 'there will be a judgement and account will be given 'and answer will be made by question and answer', for thy voice was enslaved to thy conscience. But what then?

We entreat and we beg of your Highness, in order that the weight of the burden of the Council, which is [filled] with enthusiasm for God, may be known, to send for the most noble Candidianus and five of the holy Council, that they may vouch for what has been done before your Piety. For those who imagine other things apart from the correct faith are clever at veiling the planning of their deception, so that certain even of the holy bishops, in that Nestorius has dissembled his deception, have been cajoled and made participators with him and have given their signature. But when they had asked exactly and had found that his blasphemy was evident, they withdrew from him and were present at the holy Council.[2]

[1] Literally: 'they have fabricated, saying that...'
[2] Labbe (Mansi), iv. 1424 D. There are about ten lines omitted between the passage on p. 121 and this passage (ἀλλ' ἐπειδὴ σαφῶς τὰ πεπραγμένα γνωρίζειν τῷ

Nestorius. Because he[1] fled from the Council, lo! were you not evidently in need that the Emperor should send for five of / the bishops to expound that which was done? But you said 'with Candidianus' and not 'with the bishops their 'colleagues' who would have rebuked you on equal terms; and [you demand] five against one, and that one a secular, in order that they may bring forth the holy Gospel and swear by it—they who are five and bishops—and that they may be accepted as truthful against one secular, for much has been made void by you in the examination of this problem. When, in fact, Candidianus has come, what more or less will he have to say than that to which you have previously testified and that which he has referred to the Emperor? Or what more have those five [to say] than that which you have written concerning him—that he entertained friendship toward him [2] and that for this reason he has referred false reports to you? But what need was there for you to swear to your opinion? Was it for this reason that you wrote concerning Candidianus and the five bishops and demanded that neither Nestorius nor Cyril should come? These were the very causes of the disturbance; and they ought to have answered one another, but thou wast not confident because there was no basis of truth in thy discourse. The fear of my words, in fact, was not due to anything else more than to the truth. Suppose indeed that Candidianus had come and had said that you waited not for all the Council, though you / knew that they were near, and that he had testified unto you beforehand and that he had read out before you the letters from the Emperor and that he had made a request of you but that you were not

ὑμετέρῳ κράτει κωλυόμεθα, ὡς ἔφημεν, τοῦ μεγαλοπρεπεστάτου κόμητος Κανδιδιανοῦ ἡμᾶς μὲν κωλύοντος γνωρίζειν τὰ κατὰ τὸν εὐσεβῆ λόγον πεπραγμένα, πᾶσαν δὲ σπουδὴν νέμοντος Νεστορίῳ,) δεόμεθα τοῦ ὑμετέρου κράτους, ὑπὲρ τοῦ γνωσθῆναι τὴν κατὰ θεὸν σπουδὴν τῆς ἁγίας συνόδου, καὶ μεταστᾰλῆναι μὲν τὸν μεγαλοπρεπέστατον Κανδιδιανόν, καὶ πέντε τῆς ἁγίας συνόδου συστησομένους τοῖς πεπραγμένοις ἐπὶ τῆς ὑμῶν εὐσεβείας, δεινοὶ γάρ εἰσιν οἱ ἕτερα παρὰ τὴν ὀρθὴν πίστιν φρονοῦντες συσκιάζειν τὴν πλάνην· ὡς καί τινας τῶν ἁγιωτάτων ἐπισκόπων, κρυπτομένης μὲν τῆς πλάνης παρὰ Νεστορίου, δελεασθῆναι, καὶ προσθέσθαι αὐτῷ, τοῖς τε ὑπ' αὐτῷ πραττομένοις ὑπογράψαι· ἐπειδὴ δὲ σαφῶς ἐρωτήσαντες αὐτόν, εὗρον ἀνακαλύπτοντα ἑαυτοῦ τὰς βλασφημίας, ἀποστάντες ἐκείνου, τῇ ἁγίᾳ προσῆλθον συνόδῳ . . .

[1] *Viz.* Cyril.   [2] *Viz.* Nestorius.

persuaded: what else would he have said? Wherein then would you have refuted him? Would you have refuted him for this, that he spoke a falsehood concerning you that he might entertain friendship toward me? It was not so.[1] You did not do so.[1] But if you have done so, let them come and let judgement take place, although Candidianus would have lied. But in your own Records[2] you have stated that the cause wherefore you waited not for all the Council to be assembled was that 'we were constrained',[3] as if you were there alone; but in the report which you sent unto the Emperor you said that 'we have perceived that the reverend 'John, bishop of Antioch, has this wish, to seek to entertain closer friendship'[4] and on this account you were constrained not to wait; so that, if you had known that he agreed with you, you would have waited for him, and there would have been no constraint [laid] upon you because of the place. And in your Records, which you drew up against me, you said that I stood by those very things which I had written and said from the beginning and had also written openly unto thee;[5] but in that report which you wrote unto the Emperor, you wrote on the contrary that 'he is indeed surely hiding 'under a shadow the impiety that he has', 'for those who 'imagine other things apart from / the correct faith are clever 'at veiling their plans, so that certain even of the holy 'bishops, in that Nestorius has dissembled his deception, have 'been cajoled and made participators with him and have 'given their signatures to the things which have been done by 'him'. How then was that which concerns me to be veiled?

---

[1] Nau treats these two clauses as interrogative, though they are not so marked by Bedjan in the Syriac text.   [2] Syr. *hûphāmnēmātā* = Gk. ὑπομνήματα.

[3] Cp. Labbe (Mansi), iv. 1237 A: καὶ οἱ μὲν τῶν ἁγίων ἐπισκόπων ὑπὸ γήρως πιεζόμενοι, τὴν ἐπὶ ξένης διατριβὴν οὐκ ἔφερον· οἱ δὲ ἐν ἀρρωστίᾳ ἐκινδύνευον· τινὲς δὲ καὶ τὸ τέλος ὑπεξῆλθον τοῦ βίου ἐν τῇ Ἐφεσίων μητροπόλει· ἄλλοι δὲ πενίᾳ σφιγγόμενοι, προσιόντες ἡμῖν, κατήπειγον τὴν ἀκρόασιν.

[4] Cp. p. 121.

[5] Cp. Labbe (Mansi), iv. 1240 A: οὐ γὰρ ἄδηλα ἦν, ἐν ταῖς ἐπιστολαῖς αὐτοῦ διαρρήδην κηρυττόμενα, καὶ ἐν βίβλοις, καὶ ἐν τοῖς δημοσίαις διαλέξεσι φανερῶς ἀκροώμενα, καὶ ἐν αὐτῇ δὲ τῇ τῶν Ἐφεσίων μητροπόλει πρός τινας τῶν εὐλαβεστάτων ἐπισκόπων ὑπ' αὐτοῦ φανερῶς εἰρημένα.

[6] Cp. p. 123.

And again you have openly said[1] that 'Nestorius has dis-
'puted; when we found that he manifestly imagined otherwise
'[than in accordance with the correct faith], we deprived him.
'For also even in Ephesus the metropolis he has not dissembled
'his purpose, so that he has no need of other accusers, but daily
'he proclaimed, in preaching the doctrine before many, that
'which was alien to the faith. And every one of these things
'we have entered in the Records which have been drawn up
'in order, that they might be made known unto your Piety.'

Nestorius. In the same [place] they say the contrary. He then who received all these things, that is, the Emperor, knew that they had acted contrary to his command, while that also which they said against me was a foolish and base mockery, for they have not returned answer unto that wherewith he blamed them: 'For what reason have you dared to hold a 'Council incomplete, contrary to what you were commanded, 'before the bishops of the whole Council were gathered 'together?'[2] They say / nothing else than that 'it was 'pleasing unto us', though they say it not openly because of the outcry [which would arise] against the word among those who chanced to hear of it. 'For what reason did you not wait for 'the coming of John, bishop of Antioch, when you knew that 'his advent was nigh?' They had nothing else to say than that 'we were unwilling to hold the examination with him'; but [it was] rather because they knew that he agreed not with them. But suppose that John ought to have been judged because he delayed and came not in time; he ought not to have been judged by thee but by the Emperor who had jurisdiction over him. And first the bishops from Rome ought to have been punished for not having come when they were summoned: how then dost thou adhere unto them? In the same way as thou hast treated the latter, so also thou shouldest have treated John. But thou demandest of John that he should do possibilities and impossibilities, when there

---

[1] Cp. p. 125, n. 4, and the end of the letter: πρὸς δὲ σαφεστέραν καὶ ἐντελεστέραν εἴδησιν τῶν πεπραγμένων, συνέζευκται καὶ τὰ ὑπομνήματα· καὶ ὑπέγραψαν πάντες οἱ προταγέντες ἐν τοῖς ὑπομνήμασι θεοσεβέστατοι ἐπίσκοποι (1240 E). Nestorius only gives a free paraphrase of the letter.

[2] Cp. p. 118.

was one cause for which he delayed which was accepted from him by all men, except by thee thyself, who art far from all affection for mankind and from all the sufferings of human nature. Thou blamest not thyself, not even when thou art rebuked by the Emperor, and dost thou feel no scruples that, when thou neededst to have waited four days at the most for them, in order that the Council might take place without dispute, thou didst not hear but didst rather choose of thyself to cause trouble? As the kind / of fishes which are called cuttlefish, which go from clear waters into troubled waters that they may not be caught, so hast thou also acted. [These methods] are laughable, when one gives any thought to them, and men are surely not deceived when they demand [satisfaction] from thee because of them, as when men, playing with little children who struggle with them, seem indeed to be surely struggling and yet let themselves be conquered by them. For these are not the words of one who excuses himself but rather of one who is surely playing; [yet] the Emperor is not one who would surely play with thee, and thou dost not persuade him who justly rebukes thee nor [reply] to the things wherefore he rebukes thee. His power is relaxed because there has been bribery.

But they say:[1] 'We, who have assembled and have canoni-
'cally issued in agreement a sentence of deposition against the
'heretic Nestorius, are more than two hundred bishops who
'have assembled from the whole world, the whole West being
'in agreement with us.' And what does that mean? You were, in fact, more than two hundred bishops who were in agreement with thee in all things whereof thou wast making inquiry; thou didst, in fact, demand of them by no means to tell the truth. For to the report of the bishops who are with me are affixed the signatures of bishops whose cities are known beyond doubt; how many of these / hast thou verified? For suppose that we were, as thou dost say, thirty bishops or, if thou wilt, ten or as many as thou dost wish; does the number establish the truth of the orthodox and a true Council,

---

[1] Labbe (Mansi), iv. 1425 c: καὶ οἱ μὲν συνεδρεύσαντες, καὶ κανονικὴν ἐξενέγκαντες κατὰ τοῦ αἱρετικοῦ Νεστορίου ψῆφον τῆς καθαιρέσεως, ἐσμὲν ὑπὲρ τοὺς διακοσίους, ἐξ ἁπάσης τῆς οἰκουμένης συνειλεγμένοι, συμψηφιζομένης ἡμῖν καὶ πάσης τῆς δύσεως.

or [ensure] its enacting and maintaining what is right? What then has the Emperor censured in thee and blamed in thee? 'We have assembled an oecumenical Council in order 'that generally and by general consent the inquiry concerning 'the faith may be confirmed before all men. And thou hast 'known our project and hast willed to divide the Council that 'there might not be a general examination, and that the faith 'might not be confirmed before all men clearly and accurately 'by the general consent of all men. But now all the pious 'bishops, to whom I have sent [word] to assemble, have not 'assembled, while the coming of John, bishop of the great city 'of Antioch, together with the other metropolitans, is very 'nigh. Further, even those who were present have not 'deliberated with them nor have agreed with one another; nor 'further has there been [held] the inquiry concerning the faith 'as it ought to have taken place or according to the letters 'which have been at all times sent by us.'[1]

You have written unto him either as unto one who has surely erred or as those who play or as unto one who was playing with you, since in whatsoever you have said unto him you have said nothing else unto him / than whatsoever he said of his own purpose: that you have done all things without waiting for those who were far off and without having deliberated with those who were present, but [that] you have separated yourselves from those who were with you, and by yourselves you have made examination. You have, indeed, separated yourselves from those who were ready to come for a general examination, and you have not examined the things which concerned the faith in the right manner, those things concerning which there was inquiry being brought forward by question and being solved; and so you would have exculpated yourselves in the eyes of all men. If then you had not done this, you would justly have made excuses in the report to the Emperor; but if you deny not the things which the Emperor has accused you of having unrighteously done, and if you put them in your defence, what else rather is to be conceived than

[1] Nestorius is here paraphrasing the document given on p. 117. No new paragraph is marked here in the Syriac text.

that which men think of an idle talker, or as if men told tales in play to their playmates and had the assurance to write them down? You call that an oecumenical Council which was separated from the bishops who were waiting until the whole Council should assemble, in defiance of him who has rebuked you because of it, and thou wouldest have persuaded them that all authority should be given unto those who by reason of their great numbers transgressed justice against those who observed / the [commands] of the Emperor and of the truth and of the whole Council, for no other reason than that owing to their great number they surpassed those who observed the commands. But you would not have dared to say this except to those who were your playmates for whatever reason it might be.

So I come to speak of the present. But perhaps some one will say: 'Busy not thyself much with that, but inform us how 'they deprived thee not justly, after what has been written ' by thee and by Cyril?' 'For if all those things which ought ' to be examined are examined, what art thou advantaged? 'For thou art rebuked even by these men, yea, even by all 'men. In this let us rather investigate above all what we 'ought properly to imagine, and let us not be turned aside 'from orthodoxy either by the premature decision of this man 'or by reason of thine own sufferings.' But I was not willing to recount and to tell my own concerns nor again to accuse others, and especially when the Council is named; but the faith also was corrupted and calumniated on account of mine own self[1] in such wise that that of the heretics was confirmed by the judgement and examination of the Council.

Constraint therefore is upon us to prove how their assembly and their judgement were carried out, and to prove unto all men from those things which all men confess to have been written that there was neither judgement nor examination, that we may not / be bound as by the judgement of a Council. The things which God has not allowed to be hidden but has laid bare by their own hand, by those who have done and have written down the things which happened—these [are the

---
[1] Syr. *parṣôphâ*.

things] which we also are writing down and are explaining unto those who rise up and dispute with us whether these things are so; so that, if one lights upon the documents of the Council which have been drawn up by them, one learns that they are so and not otherwise, and one knows the calumny which was [uttered] by the Council against the orthodox and [the things] which were repudiated by those who were in truth orthodox as [were] those which were [directed] against Athanasius and Eustathius and ten thousand others. Let us see then in order how the Records have been drawn up by them against me.

BOOK II. PART I

From the Records of the things which were done against me at Ephesus.[1]

Peter, priest of Alexandria and chief of the secretaries[2] *says:* 'When formerly the reverend Nestorius received consecration to become bishop of the holy church of Constantinople, and a few days were passed by, his homilies which disturbed those who read them were brought by certain men from Constantinople, so / that there arose on that account much disturbance in the holy church. When then the reverend bishop of Alexandria, Cyril, learned this, he wrote one letter and a second unto his reverence, full of counsels and warning; and in reply to these he wrote that he listened not, hardening himself and resisting the things which were written. And withal again, when the reverend bishop, Cyril, learned that letters and books of his homilies had been sent by him to Rome, he also wrote to the pious bishop of the church of Rome, Celestinus, by the hand of the deacon Poseidonius, whom he commanded, [saying], "if thou findest that the books and the homilies " and the letters have been delivered, give also these things

---

[1] Labbe (Mansi), iv. 1128: Πέτρος πρεσβύτερος Ἀλεξανδρείας, καὶ πριμμικήριος νοταρίων, εἶπεν. Ἔτι πρότερον τοῦ εὐλαβεστάτου Νεστορίου χειροτονηθέντος ἐπισκόπου τῇ ἁγίᾳ Κωνσταντινουπολιτῶν ἐκκλησίᾳ, καί τινων οὐ πολλῶν διαδραμουσῶν ἡμερῶν, παρηνέχθησαν ἀπὸ τῆς Κωνσταντινουπόλεως παρά τινων ἐξηγήσεις αὐτοῦ, ἐκταράττουσαι τοὺς ἀναγινώσκοντας, ὡς πολὺν ἐκ τούτου ταῖς ἁγίαις ἐκκλησίαις γενέσθαι τὸν θόρυβον. τοῦτο μαθὼν ὁ εὐσεβέστατος καὶ θεοσεβέστατος τῆς Ἀλεξανδρείας ἐπίσκοπος Κύριλλος, ἔγραψε πρώτην καὶ δευτέραν ἐπιστολὴν πρὸς τὴν εὐλάβειαν αὐτοῦ, συμβουλῆς καὶ παραινέσεως γεμούσας. πρὸς ταύτας ἀντέγραψεν ἀνανεύων, καὶ ἐναντιούμενος τοῖς ἀπεσταλμένοις. καὶ πρὸς τούτοις ἔτι μαθὼν ὁ αὐτὸς εὐλαβέστατος ἐπίσκοπος Κύριλλος, ὅτι καὶ εἰς τὴν Ῥώμην ἀπεστάλησαν παρ' αὐτοῦ ἐπιστολαί, καὶ βιβλία τῶν ἐξηγήσεων αὐτοῦ, ἔγραψε καὶ αὐτὸς πρὸς τὸν θεοσεβέστατον ἐπίσκοπον τῆς Ῥώμης Κελεστῖνον διὰ Ποσειδωνίου τοῦ διακόνου, ἐντειλάμενος αὐτῷ, ὅτιπερ εἰ εὑρεθείη ἀποδοθέντα αὐτῷ τὰ βιβλία τῶν ἐξηγήσεων αὐτοῦ, καὶ αἱ ἐπιστολαί, ἀπόδος καὶ τὰ παρ' ἐμοῦ γράμματα. εἰ δὲ μή, ἄγαγε αὐτὰ ἐνταῦθα μὴ ἀποδοθέντα. οὗτος εὑρὼν τὰς ἐξηγήσεις καὶ τὰς ἐπιστολὰς αὐτοῦ ἀποδοθείσας, ἀναγκαίως καὶ αὐτὸς ἀποδέδωκε· καὶ γέγραπται τὰ εἰκότα παρὰ τοῦ ὁσιωτάτου ἐπισκόπου τῆς Ῥωμαίων ἐκκλησίας Κελεστίνον, τύπον (v. l. τόπον) φανερὸν περιέχοντα. ἐπεὶ οὖν ἐκ βασιλικοῦ καὶ θεοφιλοῦς νεύματος ἡ ἁγία ὑμῶν συγκεκρότηται σύνοδος ἐνταῦθα, ἀναδιδάσκομεν ἀναγκαίως, ὅτι δὴ τοὺς ἐπὶ τούτοις χάρτας μετὰ χεῖρας ἔχομεν πρὸς τὸ παριστάμενον τῇ ὑμῶν θεοσεβείᾳ.

[2] Syr. *nuṭārē* = Lat. *notarii*.

"which have been written by me; but if not, bring them
"back hither without now delivering them." But when he
found that his letter and his homilies had been delivered,
necessarily also he delivered [those of Cyril]. And those
things which were proper, containing a well-known rule,[1] were
written by the pious [and] saintly bishop of the church of
Rome, Celestinus. Because then, by the injunction of the
godly Emperor, your holy Council has met here, we
necessarily inform you that we have in our hands the
papers concerning these things, with a view to [doing]
whatever is pleasing unto your Piety.'

/ *Nestorius*. Cyril then is the persecutor and the accuser, while I am the persecuted; but it was the Council which heard and judged my words and the emperor who assembled [it]. If then he[2] was on the bench of judges, what indeed shall I say of the bench of judges? He was the whole tribunal, for everything which he said they all said together, and without doubt it is certain that he in person took the place of a tribunal for them.[3] For if all the judges had been assembled and the accusers had risen in their place and the accused also likewise, all of them would equally have had freedom of speech, instead of his being in everything both accuser and emperor and judge. He did all things with authority, after excluding from authority him[4] who had been charged by the emperor, and he exalted himself; and he assembled all those whom he wanted, both those who were far off and those who were near, and he constituted himself the tribunal. And I was summoned by Cyril who had assembled the Council, even by Cyril who was the chief thereof. Who was judge? Cyril. And who was the accuser? Cyril. Who was bishop of Rome? Cyril. Cyril was everything. Cyril was the bishop of Alexandria and took the place of the holy and saintly bishop of Rome, Celestinus.

/ Who would have believed that these things happened so, if God had not obliged them to tell [them] and to write [them] down and to send [them] unto all the world? For all those

---

[1] Syr. *ṭûphôs* = Gk. τύπος. See p. xv.   [2] *Viz*. Cyril.
[3] Literally: 'his *prosôpon* was certainly for them for a tribunal'.
[4] *Viz*. Candidianus.

who were his [followers] read them and believe not that they happened so, and they doubt even about themselves, since they would rather trust things which happened in dreams than these, if they were thus as they did happen. What need was there for a Council, when this man was everything? That these things then were so you will learn from what happened at Ephesus; for Memnon says that: 'since the period which 'was fixed in the letters of the pious and most Christian 'Emperor, sixteen days have passed.'[1] And he, in that he was lord of the Council, made use precisely of [these words]: 'Cyril, bishop of Alexandria, says: This great and holy 'Council has been patient enough, waiting for the coming of 'the godly bishops, who are expected to come.'[2]

Nestorius. Is it not evident even to the unintelligent that he was in everything? By him then, who was busied in everything, I was summoned. And before what tribunal? To what judgement? To what inquiry? Tell me. 'This great 'and holy Council has been patient enough, having waited '/ sixteen days.' Thou sayest that it has waited enough; and you were not ashamed to have written this as an excellent reason whereby you were constrained not to wait for the bishops who were far off who were constrained to come, and who had been delayed in coming by an important reason and besought you to wait for them—those also who were near and whose coming was by no means unimportant. They were unavoidably delayed these days, if not more, in order that they might rest from their hardship in journeying by road and by ship, both for rest and for needful purposes and for the sake of visiting one another and those who were sick and were in need thereof, and especially because of those persons[3] who were taking the place of those who were absent from the Council, in those things wherein constraint had been laid upon

---

[1] Labbe (Mansi), iv. 1129 D : Μέμνων ἐπίσκοπος πόλεως Ἐφέσου εἶπεν. Ἀπὸ τῆς ὡρισμένης προθεσμίας ἐν τῷ εὐσεβεῖ καὶ θεοφιλεῖ γράμματι, παρῆλθον ἡμέραι δεκαέξ.

[2] *Id. ib.* : Κύριλλος ἐπίσκοπος Ἀλεξανδρείας εἶπεν· Ἀρκούντως ἡ ἁγία καὶ μεγάλη αὕτη σύνοδος διεκαρτέρησεν, ἐκδεχομένη τὴν ἄφιξιν τῶν ἥξειν προσδοκηθέντων θεοφιλεστάτων ἐπισκόπων.

[3] Syr. *parṣôphē'* = Gk. πρόσωπα.

them. Although it were indeed the day which was fixed and [on which] the convocation ought to have taken place, if anything were to happen so that it should be delayed, another additional day would rightly be granted, even as among men there are many causes which come upon them of necessity, so that things are not done in accordance with the strict provisions of the appointed period. But it was not the day of the convocation, but that of the coming; for the day of the convocation had been decreed by the authority of the Count. Thou didst thyself usurp [that authority], in that in thy senseless boldness thou hadst confidence in those who would justify thee perversely. For thou / lovest to persuade and thou art such that thou dost disregard those who are present and dost require those who are far off and dismissest those who are present at the Council and lookest for those who are far off; and thou holdest the Council without those who are far off having arrived. And he held a Council by himself, before the general Council and summoned those who participated not with him, that there might be a Council before the Council of all the bishops. And they testified unto him that he should put no confidence in this Council, to which he summoned me also, even making use of violence, and of such violence and force that it would not be believed, were any one to recount [it]; but it has been revealed by those who have written. Seditious persons indeed filled the city with idle and turbulent men, who were assembled together by Memnon, bishop of Ephesus; and he was at their head and was making them run about armed in the city, in such wise that every one of us fled and hid himself and had resort to caution and saved himself in great fear, as it is also easy to learn from the language of those who were sent. The latter came under the pretence indeed of summoning me unto the Council in order that it might be testified that we were not amongst those who recognized not the Council before the coming of all the bishops; but in reality they came to carry me off by assault and by violence and to spread the rumour about me that ' he has surely perished, / and his mouth has been closed over his blasphemies'; or to deprive me after I had been questioned.

Hear now from the language of Juvenalius that these things were said.[1]

Juvenalius, bishop of Jerusalem, says:[1] 'But because a crowd of Romans surrounded his house, and since the pious bishops came and said: 'Let none come nigh there'; it is known that with no good conscience did he decline to come unto the holy Council.'[2]

Nestorius. You see of how much tyranny I made use and how far I was liable to accusation, because, for the purpose of rescuing myself from the conspirators who rose up against me, I had need to post soldiers around my house to guard me, that they might not come against me with violence and destroy me! Thou accusest me of posting soldiers around my house: [it was] not that they might do any wrong unto you but that they might hinder you from doing wrong unto me. From the fact that you reproach us with posting soldiers, it is clear that if they had not first been posted around me and been a wall for me, I should have been destroyed by violent men. What indeed would you have called / those who adjured you beforehand that there should not be an unrighteous Council? Were you assembled for the [end] for which you were summoned? You made the Council for yourselves and not for us; you expelled those men from the Council and of yourselves you acted for yourselves just as you wished, and you listened not unto those who called upon you not to hold a Council but to wait for the bishops who had been summoned with you and who were nigh unto coming. Now therefore for what purpose did you summon us after all this violence? Who will hold out and not weep when he remembers the wrongs which were [done] in Ephesus? It is well [that] they were against me and against my life and not for the sake of impiety! For I should not have had need of these words as touching a man who was capable of retribution but only as touching our Saviour Jesus Christ, who is a just judge and for

---

[1] So marked in the Syriac text as the heading of a new section.

[2] Labbe (Mansi), iv. 1137 A, B: Ἰουβενάλιος ἐπίσκοπος Ἱεροσολύμων εἶπε· ... ἐπειδὴ δὲ σύστημα στρατιωτῶν περιστήσας τῷ ἰδίῳ οἰκήματι, ὡς οἱ παραγενόμενοι θεοσεβέστατοι ἐπίσκοποι κατέθεντο, οὐ συγχωρεῖ προσιέναι, δῆλός ἐστιν, οὐχ ἀγαθῷ (*v. l.* οὐ καθαρῷ) τῷ συνειδότι τὴν εἰς τὴν ἁγίαν σύνοδον ἄφιξιν παραιτούμενος.

whose sake I have been content even to endure patiently that the whole bodily frame of Christ may not be accused. But now they invent [stories] concerning me, because I have not been able to be silent when I am accused on the subject of the dispensation on our behalf, so that of necessity I am excusing myself and am persuading all men who say : 'he has been the cause of this disturbance and disorder'; and I prove myself sincere, because I have been vexed by him[1] and because of those who have written against me. But thou indeed / wast the first to sit in the midst of our judges, and because there were no accusers, in that they were judges, they put up to accuse me Theodotus, bishop of Ancyra in Galatia, and Acacius, bishop of Melitene, who was the interrogator.

Theodotus. But Theodotus first replied that he had indeed had some conversation with me but had not told him[1] the conversation, and the latter asked him not concerning what his speech was, in order that he might judge both conversations as a judge and accept the one and reject the other as having evidently fallen into impiety; but it was enough for him only that [there should be] an accusation.

Theodotus, bishop of Ancyra, says : ' I am grieved indeed for a friend, but verily I value the fear of God more than all love, and consequently it is a necessity for me, although with great sorrow, to speak the truth regarding those things of which there is question ; I think not, however, that our own testimony is required, since his opinion has been made known in the letters unto thy Godliness; for those things which he there said are not to be said of God, that is, of the Only-begotten, counting human qualities a degradation unto him, he says also in conversation here that it is not right to say of God that he has been suckled nor that he was born / of a virgin ; thus here also he has many times said " I say not that God was two or three months old ".'[2]

---

[1] *Viz.* Cyril.

[2] Labbe (Mansi), iv. 1181 B, C : Θεόδοτος ἐπίσκοπος Ἀγκύρων εἶπεν. Ὀδυνῶμαι μὲν ὑπὲρ φίλου. πλὴν πάσης φιλίας προτιμῶ τὴν εὐσέβειαν. διὸ ἀνάγκην ἔχω καὶ μετὰ πολλῆς ἀθυμίας, περὶ ὧν ἐρωτῶμαι, τὴν ἀλήθειαν ἐκφάναι (*v. l.* ἐκφράσαι). οὐκ οἶμαι χρείαν εἶναι τῆς ἡμῶν μαρτυρίας, τοῦ φρονήματος αὐτοῦ δῆλου γεγενημένου ἐκ τοῦ γράμματος τοῦ πρὸς τὴν σὴν θεοσέβειαν. ἃ γὰρ ἐκεῖ ἀπηγόρευσε περὶ τοῦ Θεοῦ λόγου λέγεσθαι, τουτέστι τοῦ μονογενοῦς, ὀνειδίζων αὐτῷ τὰ ἀνθρώπινα, ταῦτα καὶ ἐνταῦθα διαλεγόμενος ἔφη· μὴ δεῖν περὶ Θεοῦ λέγειν, γαλακτοτροφίαν, μηδὲ γέννησιν

Nestorius. They have not examined these things as judges, nor further has he spoken as before examiners and judges, but he stood forth as the witness of a judge-accuser.

Theodotus. 'The things indeed which he there rejected as not to be said of God, that is, of the Only-begotten, counting human qualities a dishonour unto him, he says also in conversation here—that it is not right that one should say of God that he has been suckled nor that he was born of a virgin ; thus here also he has said that " I say not that God was two or three months old ".'

Nestorius. And he[1] accepted it without examination as a judge-accuser, without asking him anything, either: 'What 'said he unto thee when he said these things here ? ' or ' what 'didst thou say in reply to these things whereinsoever he 'seemed against thee ? Wait ; speak before us that we may 'know in what sense he has rejected these very things, in 'order that we may not accept without reason an accusation 'against him while he is far off and pass sentence against him 'without examination and without inquisition before those 'who need to learn exactly for what reason he has been con- 'demned. Thus also the accused will not be able to deny and 'he will have no cause / to accuse me of respect for persons. ' Therefore, O Theodotus,—thou hast conversed with him—if 'then thou art accurately acquainted with his opinion, since ' thou hast questioned him and he has returned answer unto ' thee, [thou knowest that] he says : " I do not say that God ' " is two or three months old ". Does he say [this] unto ' thee, as one who says that Christ is not God, that he was ' two or three months old, or does he confess that Christ is ' God but was not as God born nor [as God] became two or ' three months old ? '[2]

Thou[3] then, [dost thou confess] that God was born of a woman and that he was two or three months old, as though

τὴν ἐκ παρθένου· οὕτω καὶ ἐνταῦθα πολλάκις ἔφη, διμηναῖον ἢ τριμηναῖον μὴ δεῖν λέγεσθαι Θεόν.

This section of Nestorius' defence is discussed in Bethune-Baker, *Nestorius and his Teaching*, ch. v. Dr. Bethune-Baker's conclusions are anticipated in Neander, *Church History* (Eng. Tr. 1855), vol. iv, p. 175.

[1] *Viz.* Cyril. [2] No new paragraph is marked here in the Syriac text.
[3] *Viz.* Theodotus.

his own *ousia* were changed into the *ousia* of a man and he was born and became two or three months old, or [was he as] one who was changed in his likeness and in his *schêma* into the likeness and into the *schêma* of a man by means of the *ousia* and that Christ is to be conceived in the one *ousia* of God and not in two *ousias*; and if in two, [canst thou explain] in what way two [issued] from the one *ousia* of God the Word? Or [was he formed] of two distinct and unlike *ousias* and was he born with both of them? Or was he born one of these and did it become two or three months old, as though it had not existed before it was born and became two or three months old? Or did the *ousia* exist eternally and not have a beginning in being born and becoming two or three months old, whereas he had not in *ousia* that / which those who are born have of necessity? Or was he born by adoption of the *ousia* in the birth of the flesh? For if he[1] had thus been questioned, he would have confessed of necessity what he said before the Eastern bishops, when he was questioned in writing—that the Only-begotten Son of God created and was created, the same but not in the same [*ousia*]; the Son of God suffered and suffered not, the same but not in the same [*ousia*]; for [some] of these things are in the nature of the divinity and [others] of them in the nature of the humanity. He suffered all human things in the humanity and all divine things in the divinity; for birth from a woman is human but birth from the Father is without beginning, whereas the former [is] in the beginning, and the one is eternal while the other is temporal.[2]

Since he[1] was suffocated by the truth, he was not able to dissemble his opinion—he who was constrained by the result of the examination to set these things down in writing; and as is the manner of a dog which, being tied up by force, dissembles its bad habits and, as soon as it has escaped from its leash, flees to its hole with its companions and barks at those who caught hold of it and dares not come out and fight in the open but, remaining within, lays back its ears and puts its tail between its legs, thus also he dared not promise them that he would speak and conquer by reprimanding nor [do] any such

[1] *Viz.* Theodotus.   [2] No new paragraph is marked here in the Syriac text.

thing as those would normally do who were confident in their own cause, I mean [as any one] of them who should take his stand upon the Divine Scriptures and the traditions and the instructions of the holy fathers, and win the victory.

But hear these things, howbeit not as though I were speaking. He dares not speak openly of what he says nor establish from the Divine Scriptures nor from the fathers what they have spoken nor how they have spoken. Nor again was he constrained to agree to what he had said nor to set it down in writing. But it is right to tell what I consider to be the truth. He[1] was the first to withhold it in order that they[2] might not know all the conversation and all the inquiry which was [held] by us, recounting those things against which they could not say aught. For this reason they wrote them not down, not even in the Records, except only 'it was not 'right to say of God that he was suckled nor that he was 'merely born of a virgin'. They made examination [only] as far as was pleasing unto them; but we will indeed speak of these things presently.

After him came Acacius and recounted unto them the conversation which he had with me and which was considered by them [to contain] impossible things. But he recounted his question, accusing me and not by way of reprimand nor sincerely by means of those things wherein he was confident; but they accepted his questions as accusations. And lest you should suppose that I am creating[3] these things, hear from them their own Records.

The Conversation of Acacius, Bishop of Melitene.[4]

'As soon as I came to the city of Ephesus, I held [a conversation] with this man, who has been mentioned shortly before, and when I knew that he thought not

[1] *Viz.* Theodotus. [2] *Sc.* the bishops. [3] See crit. n., p. 399.
[4] Labbe (Mansi), iv. 1181 D : ... παραχρῆμα ἐπιστὰς τῇ Ἐφεσίων πόλει, ἐποιησάμην πρὸς τὸν εἰρημένον ἄνδρα διάλεξιν. καὶ γνοὺς αὐτὸν οὐκ ὀρθῶς (*v. l.* ὀρθὰ) φρονοῦντα, παντοίως αὐτὸν ἐσπούδασα διορθώσασθαι, καὶ ἀποστῆσαι τοῦ πονηροῦ φρονήματος. αὐτὸν δὲ ἐκεῖνον ἑώρων τοῖς χείλεσι συνομολογοῦντα, ὅτι δὴ μετατίθεται τῆς τοιαύτης ἐννοίας. ἡμέρας δὲ δέκα ἢ δώδεκα διαλιπών, πάλιν λόγου τινὸς κινηθέντος, ἀντελαβόμην τοῦ τῆς ἀληθείας λόγου· καὶ ἀντιπίπτοντα αὐτὸν τούτῳ ἑώρων. καὶ δύο ἀτόποις κατὰ τὸ αὐτὸ ἐγίνωσκον περιπίπτειν. πρότερον μὲν γὰρ ἐκ τῆς αὐτοῦ ἐπερωτήσεως ἀτόπου οὔσης ἀνάγκην ἐπετίθει τοῖς ἀποκρινομένοις, ἢ πάντῃ ἀρνήσασθαι

correctly, in every way the weight of the burden was upon me to set him correct and to lead him away from his opinion, and I saw that he confessed with his lips that he was abandoning any such opinion. But when I had delayed ten or twelve days, when again some discussion had been raised between us, I began to speak on behalf of the correct faith and I saw that he held what was contrary to this, and I perceived that he had fallen into two wrongs simultaneously. First indeed [in] his own question which was improper; he imposed on those who returned answer the necessity of either denying entirely that the divinity of the Only-begotten became incarnate or of confessing what is an impiety—that both the divinity of the Father and that of the Holy Spirit were found in body with the Word.'

Nestorius. Some questioned [and] others answered that these things consisted in absurdities and impiety; they confess and agree to the word / for which I have reprimanded them and, after what they have confessed, they will be condemned as impious. Would any one suppose that it was an [act of] oppression, when they have written down these things in their Records and make all the world testify against themselves? For suppose that my question was absurd: thou oughtest not to have accepted it but to have proved the absurdity of the question, in order that, as a result of correcting the question, thou mightest not fall into passing over impiety and absurdity; but, in accepting a question absurd for religion, thou hast therefrom in the next place come to the impiety of confessing either that God the Word, the Son of God, was not made man or that the Father and the Spirit also were made man; that then to which thou didst agree when thou wast questioned thou oughtest to have made void.[1]

Yet although, like the other, thou hast not corrected me, let us grant that thou hast not fallen into this absurdity voluntarily or involuntarily: for what reason dost thou not utter this

τὴν τοῦ μονογενοῦς θεότητα ἐνηνθρωπηκέναι, ἢ ὁμολογεῖν, ὅπερ ἦν ἀσεβές, ὅτιπερ καὶ ἡ τοῦ πατρός, καὶ ἡ τοῦ υἱοῦ, καὶ ἡ τοῦ πνεύματος θεότης συνεσαρκώθη τῷ θεῷ λόγῳ· . . .

[1] Nau makes certain additions to the text and renders: 'that which thou didst admit when thou wast interrogated thou oughtest [to establish and that which thou didst not admit thou oughtest] to bring to an end.' No new paragraph is marked here in the Syriac text.

absurd question whereby you wish to condemn me? But thou dost not utter it nor do the judges even require it. And if it is so absurd, how has it been left unconfuted, in such wise as not to be confuted by all your Council? And if you all leave it unconfuted and if there was none among you capable of confuting it, utter [this] absurd question, examine it, although you are judges [only] in *schêma*, and write down this question in *schêma* for those / who have intelligence and are ready to examine your judgement. But on account of your incapacity you remained in darkness, so that you were not even able to see things which were evident. But God rather helped you in your interrogation to write down these things that it might be evident unto all men that the enmity was without cause.

But from what can this be proved? From those things which they have set down in [their] cunning writings, in the judgement without condemnation. From now hear those things wherein they have placed the deposit of the faith of our fathers who were assembled at Nicaea, on two of which we shall rely as on testimonies which will not be declined by him; and we shall make use of them both against them, whether they act by examination, or in the likeness of those who accept them without examination, because they are the judges and they are the judged, like those who account themselves judges in fables and stories.

The faith which was laid down by the fathers at Nicaea.

'We believe in one God, the Father Almighty, Maker of all 'things which are visible and which are invisible, and in One 'Lord Jesus Christ, the Only-begotten Son of God, who was be- 'gotten of the Father, / that is, of the essence[1] of the Father...'[2]

.... and first laying down the names of the two natures which indicate that these are common, without the Sonship

---

[1] Syr. *'ithûthâ*.

[2] The Syriac scribe adds in a note: 'Here some leaves have fallen out.' Between the quotation from the Creed and that from Nestorius' letter, Nau inserts the title *Réponse et comparaison des lettres* taken from the Syriac translator's summary. Certainly Nestorius here passes from the historical section to a resumption of the doctrinal discussion based on a comparison of his own and Cyril's letters.

or the Lordship being separated and without the natures, in the union of the Sonship, coming into danger of corruption and of confusion.[1]

Observe then first who reduces and takes away from the deposit which has been laid down by the fathers, but lets not [anyone else] steal aught therefrom. This man [2] [it is] who has made no mention of the beginning and avoided the beginning and made a beginning which they laid not down but in this wise passed over the beginning and wished not to make a beginning therefrom, whereas [it is] I who have established the things which the fathers rightly said, and I said that we would make a beginning from here showing also the cause wherefore they first laid down the names which are common to the divinity and the humanity and then built up thereon the tradition of the Incarnation [3] and of the Sufferings and of the Resurrection, 'first laying down the names of the two 'natures which indicate that these are common, without the 'Sonship or the Lordship being separated and without the 'natures, in the union of the Sonship, coming into danger of 'corruption and of confusion.' Why then hast thou passed by these things as superfluous, as things which ought not to be said? Was it because thou didst suppose that it was the same and people ought not to speak thus, but that it was enough for them to begin thence whence thou didst begin and didst make a beginning and correct them? But those [fathers] anathematize those who make additions or diminutions, but they have done improperly and not according to the opinion of the fathers. But he gave a contrary explanation when I said unto

---

[1] For the reading of the Creed and Nestorius' Letter at the Council, see Labbe (Mansi), iv. 1137 and 1169; the text of the letter is in Labbe (Mansi), iv. 892 sq.; Loofs, *Nestoriana*, p. 173. The passage quoted is in Labbe (Mansi), iv. 893 B, C : ... ἵνα τῶν ὀνομάτων τῶν φύσεων ἑκατέρων (v. l. τῆς φύσεως ἑκατέρας / τῶν φύσεων ἑκατέρας) κοινῶν τινῶν σημαντικῶν προκειμένων, μήτε τὰ τῆς υἱότητος καὶ κυριότητος τέμνηται, μήτε τὰ τῶν φύσεων ἐν τῷ τῆς υἱότητος μοναδικῷ συγχύσεως ἀφανισμῷ κινδυνεύῃ.

[2] *Viz*. Cyril. Nestorius' point is that the Fathers at Nicaea begin by using the words 'Lord' and 'Son', which are applicable to both natures, while Cyril substitutes 'God the Word', which is not. Cp. Labbe (Mansi), iv. 888 D, 893 B.

[3] Sc. ἐνανθρώπησις.

him that 'this is the beginning and thence rather ought we to begin whence I have admonished thee'. But he was disputing against me as though in his wisdom he were teaching all men, lest through their ignorance they should fall short of this impiety. For what reason then, when thou didst lay down the faith, didst thou also not begin from here whence they began as touching that which was under inquiry? For we were searching how we ought naturally to understand and to speak of these properties of the flesh and of the rational soul and of the properties of God the Word, seeing that [either] they both belonged by nature to God the Word, or to Christ, so that both natures were united by the very union of one *prosôpon*. But I said and affirmed that the union is in the one *prosôpon* of the Messiah, and I made known in every way that God the Word was made man and that God the Word was at the same time in the humanity, / in that Christ was made man in it. And for this reason the fathers, in teaching us what Christ is, about whom they used to dispute, laid down first those things which constitute Christ; but thou [actest] in the reverse way, because thou wishest that in the two natures God the Word should be the *prosôpon* of union. Thou allowest these things [to pass] as superfluous and thou makest a beginning after them, as they do; and thou transferrest from the one unto the other all those things of which Christ is naturally [formed] and said. And since the Christ of the fathers is the opposite of thine, thou hast declined to acknowledge him and thou sayest with me, though thou wishest not, that Christ is in two natures but that God the Word is not in two natures.

But hear [an extract] from what he has written unto me, that you may know that there is nothing just in him but that he is arranging in everything that there may not be a judgement and an examination, which would make known his enmity toward me, which was not on account of the faith.

Diverse are the natures which have come unto a true union; but from them both [there has resulted] one Christ and Son, not because the diversity in the natures has been abolished by reason of the union, but because they have perfected for us rather one Lord and Messiah and Son.[1]

Not indeed as though the *ousia* of God the Word who remains eternally as he is and receives neither addition nor diminution, was perfected in a change of natures; / but owing to the concourse of the union of the divinity and of the humanity there came into being one Christ and not God the Word; for he exists eternally. Christ therefore is the *prosôpon* of the union, whereas God the Word is not of the union but in his own nature, and it is not the same thing to say and to understand [the one for the other]. And for this reason, O admirable man, the fathers also, adhering to the Divine Scriptures, have said 'One Lord Jesus Christ the only-begotten Son', on account of the *prosôpon* of the union, and then teach what those who are united are, and in whom. Who is he who was born of the Father only-begotten? Our Lord Jesus Christ. 'The only-begotten Son of God, that is, from the *ousia* of God 'the Father. God from God and Light of Light, Very God 'of Very God, born and not made, consubstantial with the 'Father, by whom all that is in heaven and in earth was '[made].' Of whom have you spoken, O fathers? Of something else or him [of] whom you have written before, 'One 'Lord Jesus Christ, the only-begotten Son of God'? Who is this and of whom? Of the Father, 'Very God of Very 'God, born and not made, consubstantial with the Father, 'through whom all was [made], who on account of us men 'and on account of our salvation came down.' Who is this? Tell me and him and all men, O fathers. What is he? Another / or the Only-begotten? Him we teach you and none other, who 'on account of us men and on account of our 'salvation came down and was made flesh of the Holy Spirit 'and of the Virgin Mary, who also was made man'. Thus far, then, that 'He came down, was made flesh and was made

---

[1] From Cyril's Second Letter to Nestorius, Labbe (Mansi), iv. 889 A, C, E: καὶ ὅτι διάφοροι μὲν αἱ πρὸς ἑνότητα τὴν ἀληθινὴν συναχθεῖσαι φύσεις, εἷς δὲ ἐξ ἀμφοτέρων Χριστὸς καὶ υἱός. οὐχ ὡς τῆς τῶν φύσεων διαφορᾶς ἀνῃρημένης διὰ τὴν ἕνωσιν, ἀποτελεσασῶν δὲ μᾶλλον ἡμῖν τὸν ἕνα κύριον Ἰησοῦν Χριστὸν καὶ υἱόν, . . . ἦν γὰρ ὁ ἀπαθὴς ἐν τῷ πάσχοντι σώματι . . . ἀλλ' ὡς ἕνα καὶ τὸν αὐτὸν προσκυνοῦντες, ὅτι μὴ ἀλλότριον τοῦ λόγου τὸ σῶμα αὐτοῦ, μεθ' οὗ καὶ αὐτῷ συνεδρεύει τῷ πατρί.

man', they have taught us about those things which concern the divinity of Christ: and in 'He was made flesh' about his union with the flesh; but for the rest, about the flesh wherein he was made flesh: ' One Lord Jesus Christ, the only-begotten Son of God.' For does not 'of the Holy Spirit and of the Virgin Mary' teach us concerning the birth of the flesh? 'One Lord Jesus Christ, the only-begotten Son of God.' What is his nature? That which his Mother also was, of whom the passible flesh was born. And 'He suffered 'and rose on the third day and ascended into heaven and 'will come to judge the living and the dead'. Who is this? 'One Lord Jesus Christ, the only-begotten Son of the Father.' They call him both things: 'consubstantial with the Father' and 'consubstantial with the mother, one Lord Jesus Christ', [speaking not of] God the Word as in both [*ousias*] by nature, but of ' one Lord Jesus Christ, the only-begotten Son of God'. For the union is in the *prosôpon* and not in the nature nor in the *ousia*, but a union indeed of *ousias*, namely, the *ousia* of God the Word and the *ousia* of the flesh; and they were united not in the *ousia*—for God the Word and the flesh became not one *ousia* and the two *ousias* became not flesh— [but] God the Word and the flesh [were so united]. And thou dost confess all these things with me / when thou sayest that the natures of the divinity and of the humanity are diverse and that the two natures remain in their own *ousia* and that their diversities are not made void by the union of the natures; for the two natures complete one Christ and not one God.

Of what then dost thou accuse me? Speak before all those who read our words. For I say this, and when thou hast spoken and confessed [this], thee too I have praised for what thou hast said, in that in thy discourse thou hast made a distinction between the divinity and the humanity and [hast united] them in the conjunction of one *prosôpon*; and [I have praised] thy saying that God the Word had not need of a second birth from a woman and that the divinity admits not of sufferings; faithfully hast thou spoken; and these [are the words] of those who are correct in their faith and are opposed to the wrong faith of all the heresies concerning the Lord's nature. Where then have I said that Christ was a mere man or two Christs and that there was not one Lord Jesus Christ, the only-begotten Son of God, of the union of the two natures one *prosôpon*? And even unto thee thyself I have said, as brother unto brother, that we should not distinguish the union nor the *prosôpon* which [results] from the union. Nor again do we begin from God the Word, as from a *prosôpon* of union, but from him from whom the fathers began, who were wiser than thou and who were excellently acquainted with the Divine Scriptures. And see how / they tear up as from the foundation and destroy all those things which effect a change. For if thou referrest all the properties of the flesh to God the Word, see that, after stealing, as thou hast said, the properties of the natures, thou dost not say those things which the three hundred and eighteen fathers have with one voice and with one mouth and with one conscience rejected: that there was when God the Word was not, that is, [that] when his flesh was not, then God the Word was not; that is, that, before his flesh was born, he was not. In that thou hast said that he made for himself all the properties, so then God the Word was born of things which were not, because his flesh was [formed] of things which were not, unless thou darest to say that the flesh itself has eternally[1] existed and sayest that God the Word was of another *hypostasis* and another *ousia*, and not of that of the Father but of that of which the flesh was, and [that] God the Word is changeable and corruptible on account of his flesh which is therein.[2] For the fathers anathematize those who predicate these of God the Father.

Now God the Word is not of them both in *ousia*, nor again is God the Word in flesh, nor is God the Word of two nor is God the Word two natures. / For herein only, in his being co-essential[3] with the Father, is God the Word conceived. For he was made flesh and was revealed in flesh; but if he was made flesh in the flesh, it is evident that [it was] in that flesh which had been made, and he who was made flesh in

---

[1] Syr. *'îthyâ 'îth = essentialiter, aeterne* (Payne-Smith, *Thes. Syr.*, col. 174).
[2] *Viz.* the *hypostasis* and the *ousia*.
[3] Syr. *bar 'îthûthâ* = 'coeternal' or 'coexistent'.

that which was made made not his own *ousia* the flesh, so as to make the properties of the nature of the *ousia* of the flesh his own properties, but with a view to the revelation he carried out all the operations of his *prosôpon*. For he made use of the likeness and of the *prosôpon* of a servant, not the *ousia* nor the nature, in such wise that he was by nature in them both, as being Christ. What[1] therefore has carried him[2] away to find another way and a beginning apart from that which the fathers had made, so that he came to anathematize all those things which had been said by them and of necessity to say all those things which had been anathematized by them? But he first laid down the [words] of the fathers, as though he wished to convince them, and to say 'I have said the same things as they', and then to accuse me as though I spoke not in the same way as they. But after he found that I said the same as they and that I maintained their own [views], he began to lay down laws and to substitute those terms which they had not said, and to introduce them into the faith, persuading [every one] that he ought to embrace the latter instead of the former. For thus it was said of God the Word, when he[3] said that he / existed before the worlds and was born of the Father and was born in flesh of a woman. But where have the fathers said that God the Word was born in flesh of a woman? Require him to state the deposit of the fathers which they have laid down for all men and to which also, thou hast well said, we ought to adhere in words and in faith. If then thou keepest thy promise in deeds, it is right; for he who has not spoken as the fathers have spoken is guilty. Prove then that the fathers have spoken this word, then condemn me with an anathema in the manner of one who has transgressed the books and the deposit of the fathers, although ten thousand times I have excused myself and said that I imagined not otherwise in mine imagination. Or if not, let not alone whosoever has defiled aught that the fathers have said in the terms which have been fixed by them. For those terms which

---

[1] Syr. 'wherefore'; the translation assumes that the preposition prefixed to *lmānā*, 'wherefore', is redundant (Payne-Smith, *Thes. Syr.*, ii, 1868, 8).
[2] *Viz.* Cyril.   [3] *Viz.* St. Paul; cp. Gal. iv. 4.

have been fixed by them ought by all means to be observed, although we have often neglected to explain them; for if any one otherwise makes use of them, such as they are, [he ought to do so,] not as with a view to suppression nor as with a view to change nor as with a view to transformation, but that he may preserve therein with me such an opinion as is correct, I mean, that of the fathers.

What then hast thou to prove concerning this? Did I make wrong use of the word which is in the deposit of the fathers and ought I to beg for an explanation? Prove unto me that God the Word was born / in flesh of a woman and then explain how thou understandest that he was born. For if thou presupposest it and if thou explainest what has been laid down by thee, thou art not accepted by those who accept the [words] of the fathers; they are without diminution and for this reason they admit neither addition nor diminution nor change. For he who explains also establishes those things which have been written and surely does not suppress them. And if I have made wrong use of the words of the fathers—I who would have persuaded [every one] by words not to call the holy virgin the mother of God nor would have called Christ God [1] and thou hast been constrained to come against me—prove unto me first that I said these things before certain men who duly examined us and not before those who inclined unto thy side; for thou hast conquered before the latter and thou hast made use of them as though they had neither reason nor soul; and thou hast not presented mine own letter, wherein I disputed against thee, as before men, lest thou shouldest confuse the words of the fathers; but that thou mightest confess one Lord Jesus Christ consubstantial with the Father, none other but one and the same who is one *prosôpon* of the two natures: of the divinity and of the humanity, Lord and Christ; and this also hast thou confessed. It was not therefore because I confessed not that Christ himself—who is also God, and none other than God the Word, consubstantial /—is God, but because I confess that he is also

---

[1] *I.e.* (presumably) would have objected to the use of 'God' and 'Christ' as interchangeable terms.

man. If it were that this is so and I had not thus confessed, in teaching I should have added that Christ is God and consubstantial with the Father and at the same time also man consubstantial with us. I should not have cursorily passed over the *prosôpon* of the union and the *ousia* of the divinity,[1] as if I were to begin from the common *prosôpon* of the divinity and of the humanity as if from one *ousia* of God the Word, which they both were; but I should have referred to him naturally all the things which concern him and which concern his flesh, since he is both of them by *ousia*.

Why then dost thou falsely charge the fathers with that which they say not? And why again dost thou persuade those who are unwilling to accept anything apart from the deposit of the fathers to accept thine own rather than that of the fathers? But recollect thyself and read and know and see that they have not said this and that we have not transgressed them as ignorant or as wicked men; but thou findest not that those who have written for thee have said that he who was born of the Father was born in flesh of a woman, if they have mentioned at all the birth from a woman. How then sayest thou, O calumniator, that ' we have found that the holy fathers ' thought thus and that they thus were confident in calling the ' holy virgin the mother of God. Thus we say that he both '/ suffered and rose'?[2] First prove unto us that the fathers called her the mother of God or that God the Word was born in flesh or that he was born at all and at the same time both suffered and died and rose, and explain unto us how they say that God suffered and rose. But if it has surely been fabricated by thee, and thou art calumniating [the fathers], how can any one without doubt admit the rest of these things? For thou hast made them all doubtful, because thou hast not said those things which the fathers have said but hast changed even the very term. For although thou hast supposed the same thing that they make known and there is no single distinction between 'the Lord and Jesus Christ' and 'God the Word', and though thou

---

[1] Altering the punctuation of the Syriac text which puts this stop after 'union'.

[2] From Cyril's Second Letter, Labbe (Mansi), iv. 892 B : οὕτως εὑρήσομεν τοὺς ἁγίους πεφρονηκότας πατέρας· οὕτω τεθαρσήκασι θεοτόκον εἰπεῖν τὴν ἁγίαν παρθένον.

makest known the same thing by this term or by that, thou oughtest not to have made changes but to have explained and made clear and to have made use of terms which have been laid down by the fathers. But thou couldest not by those terms prove God the Word passible and mortal, and for this reason thou makest use of this term whereby thou canst carry away those who know not what each one of them signifies.

Thus also we understand 'He died'; for God the Word is immortal indeed in his nature and incorruptible and quick and quickening; but, further, because his body *by the grace of God*, as Paul has said, *has tasted death for every man*,[1] it is said that he bore death for us.[2]

By / whom [is this said]? By thee or by the fathers? Speak, deceive not the hearers by means of the fathers, by thy statements that thou agreest with their words and their teaching. Read therefore: where have they said that God the Word suffered? But thou sayest that Divine Scripture has said that God the Word suffered; read and dissemble not. But it exists not for thee to read. For what purpose then dost thou calumniate the fathers? Or why dost thou take the faith of the fathers as a means for deceiving and forestalling those who believe simply and without investigating? Makest thou sport of those who read as men who reflect not? Or correctest thou the faith of the fathers, who have not written what they ought to have written? For thou first layest it down and thou sayest that we ought to agree thereto in words and in faith; but thou adherest not at all thereto and hast not even observed the order of the text nor begun whence the fathers began, and in addition to these things thou hast referred [to God the Word] all those things which have been said by them.[3] And thou hast neither feigned to make use of the same terms nor hast thou adhered to their teaching. For

[1] Heb. ii. 9.

[2] From Cyril's Second Letter, Labbe (Mansi), iv. 889 c: κατὰ τὸν ἴσον δὲ τρόπον καὶ ἐπὶ τοῦ τεθνάναι νοοῦμεν. ἀθάνατος γὰρ κατὰ φύσιν, καὶ ἄφθαρτος, καὶ ζωὴ καὶ ζωοποιός ἐστιν ὁ τοῦ (v. l. ἐκ) Θεοῦ λόγος. ἐπειδὴ δὲ πάλιν τὸ ἴδιον αὐτοῦ σῶμα χάριτι Θεοῦ, καθά φησιν ὁ Παῦλος, ὑπὲρ παντὸς ἐγεύσατο θανάτου, λέγεται παθεῖν ὑπὲρ ἡμῶν.

[3] In the Syriac text this sentence is given as a question with a mark of interrogation.

'created' and 'made' and 'passible' and 'mortal' and all such things as the fathers repudiate thou hast predicated of the *ousia* of God the Word, of whom are predicated all those things which belong unto the Father in his own *ousia* and who exists. For thou maintainest that we should so speak as those men who have not spoken, and then, to be sure, thou explainest / not, even though indeed thou wouldest preclude God the Word from being called passible and mortal, but so as to persuade men to say the things, the saying of which the fathers have refused. Thus we confess one Lord Christ who took his name at birth from the blessed Mary but is indeed man, yea even in the death, yea even in the resurrection, yea even in the ascension, yea even in his coming from Heaven; of all these things thou now strippest him. 'Thus', thou sayest, 'we confess one Christ and Lord', as thou thyself sayest. We shall then confess that which has not been confessed:

Not indeed as though we adore the man with the Word, lest thou shouldest introduce a semblance of separation in that we have said 'with', but we adore him as one and the same, because his body is not alien unto him, with which he also is seated with the Father.[1]

Either he has said it through the blindness of his intellect or he has been compelled by the necessity of God to fall into that whereat he is vexed in others and into [incurring] the same reprimand.

For he has used the [word] 'with' twice, in that he has said

[1] From Cyril's Second Letter, Labbe (Mansi), iv. 889 D: οὕτω Χριστὸν ἕνα καὶ κύριον ὡμολογήσαμεν, οὐχ ὡς ἄνθρωπον συμπροσκυνοῦντες τῷ λόγῳ, ἵνα μὴ τομῆς φαντασία παρεισκρίνηται διὰ τοῦ λέγειν τό, σύν· ἀλλ' ὡς ἕνα καὶ τὸν αὐτὸν προσκυνοῦντες, ὅτι μὴ ἀλλότριον τοῦ λόγου τὸ σῶμα αὐτοῦ, μεθ' οὗ καὶ αὐτῷ συνεδρεύει τῷ πατρί. With this should be compared the eighth anathema appended to Cyril's Third Letter, Labbe (Mansi), iv. 1084 B: εἴ τις τολμήσει λέγειν, τὸν ἀναληφθέντα ἄνθρωπον συμπροσκυνεῖσθαι δεῖν τῷ θεῷ λόγῳ, καὶ συνδοξάζεσθαι, καὶ συγχρηματίζειν θεόν, ὡς ἕτερον ἐν ἑτέρῳ· τὸ γάρ, Σύν, ἀεὶ προστιθέμενον, τοῦτο νοεῖν ἀναγκάζει· καὶ οὐχὶ δὴ μᾶλλον μιᾷ προσκυνήσει τιμᾷ τὸν Ἐμμανουήλ, καὶ μίαν αὐτῷ τὴν δοξολογίαν ἀναπέμπει, καθὸ γέγονε σὰρξ ὁ λόγος· ἀνάθεμα ἔστω. Nestorius' argument is obscure in detail, but its main tenor is clear. Assuming that Cyril does not hold an Apollinarian view of Christ's body, he argues that to speak of the Son sitting *with* his body with the father is open to the accusation of teaching 'two sons' just as much as anything that he himself has said. Hence Cyril is convicted of inconsistency and can himself be quoted as authority for doctrines that he denounces in Nestorius.

'*with* him who is seated *with* the Father'. For the [word] 'with' is not said of one but [of one] with another, and the one, who is with the other, is seated with the Father; how will he not introduce a semblance of separation? He says 'the body' and 'his own body' and 'seated with him' and causes not the semblance of a separation! By 'one and the same God the Word' he understands also his body; and he understands / the body and again he does not understand the body; and he understands that his body is with him and he does not understand that his body is with him but understands it [to be] alone; and he understands that he is seated with it with the Father and again does not understand that it is seated with the Father, but he understands him [to be] alone. Who could tell his ineffable wisdom? But he has taken it for him, not as though again two sons were sitting but one, owing to the union with his flesh.[1]

And further thou hast said: 'Thou hast[2] raised the semblance of 'a cleavage when thou givest to imagine one with another'. But [it is] in the union. Of whom? Of Christ? Then the *prosôpon* of the union is Christ, but thou sayest that he has taken for him that with which he also was seated with the Father. . . . Thou hast put a *prosôpon* in it itself; why therefore dost thou make [it] void, as if it had been unrighteously said that it also is seated with him with the Father? Or as if by this [word] 'with' thou hadst been forced to understand that he is so, and it were possible that thou understandest or imaginest correctly, in confessing that not two sons were seated but one owing to the union with his flesh. And thou makest void this [word] 'with', that men may not imagine two. But if that which thou hast said be impious for thee, return again to this chapter which thou hast omitted, for it is its aim. For what hast thou written? Hast thou not clearly disproved [thy statement] that we ought not to write 'with'; and hast thou written that 'He is seated / with it with the Father'? For he who says these things says that two sons are seated, but thou disprovest that men ought

---

[1] There is no new paragraph marked here in the Syriac text.
[2] Syr. 'thou hast said'.

not to imagine that two sons are seated. And thus in the deposit which has been laid down thou allowest that which signifies two sons, but thou sayest that we ought not to conceive two sons, but two are of necessity conceived, as it is supposed according to thine own opinion. But it is otherwise deposited and to be said, and two sons are not to be conceived. Of what dost thou accuse me, who say that two are united in one Son, whereby I wished to show the inconfusion of the natures in the union, in making use of the qualities of the natures? I seek not to make as it were two sons nor again the dissolution of the union, but I make use of one *prosôpon* of union as [formed] of the two *ousias*, as also Divine Scripture signifies.

But by one *ousia* thou signifiest two *ousias*. But if I were to say the things which thou sayest, it would appear to thee an impiety. But if thou didst have confidence to read the things, thou didst read them for thyself and not for them[selves], things which cannot be examined in that way, if in piety. Thou hast further shunned also an examination by the whole Council, because thou didst judge that these [views] had no accurate defence. And as I was not [there], / what thou saidest well unto them thou saidest for my sake, and what thou saidest wrongly against thyself [was] thus again also for my sake. For if this word 'with' hinders there being one Son and his being seated with his flesh with the Father, there are not two adorations of one Son because he is adored with it, since he who is seated with that which is alien is adored in one adoration; for there is a union in the natures—and thou also confessest [it] with me—but the distinction of the natures is not made void on account of the union. For it was right for me to say many times those words which have been well said; then thou art astonished, when thou hearest that which is mine in thine: that there was indeed no union which proved not a diversity, as [is shown by] the adoration of 'Him who is seated [at the right hand of the Father]'. But thou takest as the starting-point of thy narrative the Maker of the natures and not the *prosôpon* of union. Either then avoid saying two natures united without confusion; or confess and say these things, and it will not appear an impossibility unto thee to predicate one in the union and another in that which concerns the *ousia*, not in that which concerns the union of the *prosôpon*.

But if we decline the *hypostatic* union as being either incomprehensible or as unseemly, we fall into predicating two sons: for it is necessary to distinguish[1] and to say of man / alone that he is honoured with the name of son, but also of God the Word alone that he possesses the title and the functions of the sonship naturally. It is not right then to distinguish[1] two sons in one Lord Jesus Christ.[2]

I have said unto thee also in the letter that I do not know [the meaning of] the things which have been said by thee. And thou feignest to be repentant; thou hast not dissembled those things which thou wast fairly prepared to say afterwards. And when thou oughtest to have made answer concerning these things and to write and to persuade and to reprimand the calumniators openly, thou hast risen up against thyself and me and hast neglected the fathers and the Holy Scriptures. Why dost thou wish that there should be an *hypostatic* union, which makes us neither understand that there is [in the union] the *ousia* of man nor understand [that he is] man in nature but God the Word in nature, that is, God who is not in nature what he is in his nature through the *hypostatic* union, wherein there are no distinctions and definitions of the various [elements]. For this reason also this union is a union of those things which have been defined by the word *ousia*; and if it be void, there is no more a union; but [it is the result] of a union, yet not a union. And if every definition of the natures is made void, how will the union not make void the distinctions of the natures? And if they are conceived neither in nature nor in a union, how hast thou said that he has made / the property of the flesh his own, since thou sayest that [he is] in the one indeed by nature but in the other by union? And it is his to have suffered indeed

---

[1] The same Syriac root represents διορίσαι and διαιρετέον. Cp. p. 312, n. 3.
[2] From Cyril's Second Letter, Labbe (Mansi), iv. 889 E: ἐὰν δὲ τὴν καθ' ὑπόστασιν ἕνωσιν, ἢ ὡς ἀνέφικτον, ἢ ὡς ἀκαλλῆ παραιτούμεθα, ἐμπίπτομεν εἰς τὸ δύο λέγειν υἱούς. ἀνάγκη γὰρ πᾶσα διορίσαι, καὶ εἰπεῖν, τὸν μέν, ἄνθρωπον ἰδικῶς, τῇ τοῦ υἱοῦ κλήσει τετιμημένον· ἰδικῶς δὲ πάλιν τὸν ἐκ Θεοῦ λόγον υἱότητος ὄνομά τε καὶ χρῆμα ἔχοντα φυσικῶς. οὐ διαιρετέον τοιγαροῦν εἰς υἱοὺς δύο τὸν ἕνα κύριον Ἰησοῦν Χριστόν.

in nature and to have died, because he has made them his own. How then hast thou sought to establish the *hypostatic* union? What is this unintelligible *hypostatic* union? Or how shall we accept it, the unintelligible? Or how hast thou understood it? How is it raised up though incomprehensible? And again, unseemly? Instruct us. But thou art not willing to instruct me. Thou hast supposed[1] to thyself that the judges speak unto thee and persuade thee to instruct us and those who are like us, because we know not; and if not, instruct the whole Council. For neither thou nor the Council are capable of [understanding] the term 'union'. Because I also say 'union', yet thou acceptest not what I say, because I distinguish the union. If I say concerning things which have been united that they are corporeal in *ousia* and incorporeal in *ousia*, then [I say that] they are divided from one another: the one indeed as created, but the other as uncreated; the one indeed mortal and the other immortal; and the one eternal with the Father and the other created in the last times, and the one consubstantial with the Father and the other consubstantial with us; for the union makes not void the *ousias* which have been united in such wise that they are not to be known [apart].

/ Thou sayest unto me 'Thou distinguishest'; but verily thou also [dost likewise]; even in the very words to which thou hast recourse to accuse me, thou sayest as follows: 'Diverse are the natures which have come into a true union; 'yet from both of them [is formed] one Christ and Son, not as 'though the diversity of the natures had been removed because of the union.'[2] Dost thou give us to imagine this even concerning the *hypostatic* union? Or [dost thou not speak] as one who distinguishes, saying that as a result of their diversities the natures which have been united are diverse; and [then] rush headlong into thy profession that thou introducest not a semblance of separation? And what do I mean by 'thou introducest[3] a semblance of separation'? And what do I mean by 'a semblance'? Thou understandest the separation of the natures

---

[1] See crit. n., p. 399. [2] See p. 144, n. 1.
[3] Nau inserts here a negative which is not found in the Syriac text.

as expressing the natures and not as a confusion, since there is not in thy mind any semblance of definition of the natures whereby to understand that they were united without confusion, even as the fire was united with the bush and the bush with the fire and they were not confused. Thou therefore showest them without definition and without distinction, whereas I show them defined and distinct from one another. If thou then speakest of the *hypostatic* union, speak clearly; for I confess to not understanding either then or now; thou needest to instruct me in such wise that I may agree with thee. Or if I accept not thy opinion, say that I accept it not, and if the judges / accept [it] of thee, let them convince me or let them condemn me as one for whom there is no getting rid of his wickedness.

Say therefore [what] the *hypostatic* union [is]. Dost thou wish to regard a *hypostasis* as a *prosôpon*,[1] as we speak of one *ousia* of the divinity and three *hypostases* and understand *prosôpa* by *hypostases*? Thou callest therefore the *prosôpic* union *hypostatic*; yet the union was not of the *prosôpa* but of the natures. For 'diverse are the natures which 'have come into a true union, yet from both of them [is formed] 'one Christ'. Understandest thou the one *prosôpon* of Christ rather than the *hypostasis* of the *ousia* and of the nature, in the same way as thou speakest of the *form of his hypostasis*[2]

[1] Syr. 'a *prosôpon* as a hypostasis', apparently mistranslating the double accusative in the Greek original. See pp. xiv-xv.

[2] This surely represents the χαρακτὴρ τῆς ὑποστάσεως αὐτοῦ of Heb. i. 3, where ὑπόστασις is clearly synonymous with οὐσία (see Webb, *God and Personality*, p. 39). Nestorius argues that he can only understand Cyril's phrase ἕνωσις καθ' ὑπόστασιν if Cyril uses ὑπόστασις to express what Nestorius calls πρόσωπον.

This passage is a very important one for determining what Nestorius means by πρόσωπον. He seems to be willing to define it as χαρακτήρ, and this is consistent with the striking phrase below (p. 158, l. 18) '... as the πρόσωπον [makes known] the οὐσία'.

It would seem that Nestorius regularly uses ὑπόστασις as practically equivalent to οὐσία, and in Trinitarian doctrine would himself speak of three πρόσωπα in one ὑπόστασις (or οὐσία). But Cyril has the later usage in which the two are distinguished, and so speaks of three ὑποστάσεις in one οὐσία. Nestorius evidently appreciates this difference of terminology in Trinitarian doctrine, and tries to find in it a clue to the understanding of Cyril's Christology, asking whether after all Cyril always means by ὑπόστασις what he himself calls πρόσωπον. Cp. below, p. 208, n. 2.

and the union of the natures? But I say that; and I praised thee for having said it and having made a distinction of the natures in the doctrine of the divinity and of the humanity and coherence of these in one *prosôpon*. For hast thou not said 'diversities without confusion' and 'it remained without diversity whereby it would be separated'. But even if thou dost not concede a diversity and that a diversity of natures, thou dost concede a natural separation without knowing it. But it was not a diversity which became a union, since the things which are therein remain without confusion, as the bush in the fire and the fire in the bush. But it appears not that thou sayest this, and thou dost rebuke me as one who accepts not the *hypostatic* union. But I am not persuaded of any other / *hypostatic* union with other natures nor of anything else which is right for the union of diverse natures except one *prosôpon*, by which and in which both the natures are known, while assigning their properties to the *prosôpon*. It is well to confess and be conformable to the tradition of the Gospels that the bodily frame is the temple of the divinity of God the Word and that the temple has been united by the supreme adherence of the divinity in such wise as to make over to the one the things which are the other's by the appropriation of the nature of the divinity, but not that he made them [both] his own *ousia*. What other *hypostatic* union, then, dost thou wish to teach me, which consists in a supreme and divine and ineffable union? I know not unless [it be that] of one *prosôpon* where the one is the other and the other the one. And for this reason I proclaim eagerly in every place that the things which are said either about the divinity or about the humanity must be taken not of the nature but of the *prosôpon*, so that there might be no unreality [1] about the human qualities, [as there would be] if both of them were united in the *ousia*. For not in all things is he to be called in

There is a discussion of these points in Loofs, *Nestorius and his Place in the History of Christian Doctrine*, p. 69 sq. Dr. Loofs takes a somewhat different view, holding that Cyril too used ὑπόστασις as equivalent to οὐσία.

For the question of the distinction between οὐσία and ὑπόστασις in Nestorius, see below, p. 218, n. 3, and pp. 227, 228, 234, n. 3, 322.

[1] Syr. *panṭāsyâ* = Gk. φαντασία.

ousia that which was in the *ousia*, but all those things which indicate the *prosôpon* of [the *ousia*]. And it is known that God the Word is said to have become flesh and the Son of man after the likeness and after the *prosôpon* of flesh and of man whereof he made use to make himself known unto the world. For all the things which are naturally / called flesh are not to be called also God the Word: as that he should come into being when he was not or was [formed] of that which was not or whatever the flesh is said [to have been] before it came into being, when it came into being and after it came into being, in the changes of growth and corruption, and in short consubstantial with ourselves. Because he is consubstantial with ourselves in everything, the things which are said of the *ousia* are not said of anything else except only of this *ousia*, and he is called consubstantial [with us]; for in [the saying of] the things which are said of the *prosôpon* and of the likeness of the nature is said that which makes him known, as the *prosôpon* [makes known] the *ousia*. But that which exists naturally is not said [of God the Word], because the union took not place according to the *ousia* and the nature but according to the *prosôpon*. Thus also the flesh is not to be said [to be] all that God the Word is by nature; for it was not without beginning nor was it unmade nor was it incorporeal nor was it invisible nor was it consubstantial with the Father and with the Holy Spirit, although that which is called Son and Lord and God is also to be called flesh in this manner through the union, because the union came into being as touching the *prosôpon* of the Son of God, and neither the *ousia* nor the nature, but by means of the natures; and all things which belong to the *prosôpon* are its, except the *ousia* of the *prosôpon*, not according to the nature but according to the *prosôpon*.

/ What other *hypostatic* union, then, dost thou predicate, as if saying that I accept it not, either as incomprehensible or as unseemly, and [that] for this reason I have fallen into speaking of two Christs: the one man who is honoured under the title of Son and then apart [from him] God the Word, who possesses naturally the name and function of sonship? How can he who in the union speaks of one Son, one Christ, one Lord, distinctly speak apart of one Son, God, and one other, and thus of two sons? For again that would not be called a union but each one of the natures [by itself] in its own *ousia*. For neither is God the Word said to have become flesh in his own *ousia* but by union with the flesh, nor is the flesh called Son apart from the union with the Son of God. For this reason there is one flesh in them both and one Son in them both. For he whose it is by the union to exist and to be spoken of neither exists nor is spoken of in the definition and the distinction [of each] from one another. As God the Word is by his nature God incorporeal, nevertheless in the union with the flesh he is called flesh, and the flesh which is in its nature bodily frame and in its *ousia* also bodily frame, is yet God and Son by the union with God the Word the Son of God. There are said to be neither two fleshes nor again two sons: those which are distinct by nature and exist by the union of the natures. Among / men, in fact, many who are sons are [so] called by the distinction and by the division of the natures, those unto every one of whom [sonship] is given only by grace and adoption, as honour is given by the Emperor unto every one of the princes. For that which exists only in its own *hypostasis* belongs also unto many as by grace. For he exists in his *hypostasis* and has made it the likeness of his likeness, neither by command nor by honour nor simply by equality of grace, but he has made it his likeness in its natural likeness, in such wise that it is none other than that very [thing] which he has taken for his own *prosôpon*, so that the one might be the other and the other the one, one and the same in the two *ousias*, a *prosôpon* fashioned by the flesh and fashioning the flesh in the likeness of its own sonship in the two natures, and one flesh in the two natures, the one fashioned by the other and the other by the one, the same and the single likeness of the *prosôpon*.

I know not therefore in what sense thou predicatedst the *hypostatic* union in such wise that it is incomprehensible or unseemly, in order that I may admit or not admit [it]; and has he for this reason been

>defined and called solely man by the title or by the honour

of a son, and then again apart the Word which is from God, to which belongs naturally sonship and name and title?[1]

But what meanest thou by 'uniquely'[2]? / State clearly the deposit of the faith of the fathers and set down the things which are alike both for me and for every one to say, for thou hast not made clear the meaning which we ought to mean and to state. How sayest thou that the nature of man cannot be understood 'uniquely', especially apart from the *ousia* of God the Word, which is Son not by nature but by union? But also thou sayest that there are diversities in the natures which have been combined in the union of one Son; but the diversity is not voided through the union of the natures; it is not as though the diversity of the natures were made void because of the union. If then the distinctions of the natures have not been annulled, the nature of the flesh appertains solely to the nature of the humanity. But that which is Son consubstantial with God the Father and with the Holy Spirit uniquely and solely appertains to the divinity; for by the union the flesh is son and God the Word is flesh. And for this reason whoever speaks thus neither predicates two sons nor predicates two fleshes, nor predicates two fleshes in the nature nor yet of the flesh in the one and of the sonship in the other, but makes use of the same in the natural *prosôpa* of each of them in what is their own, as the fire was in the bush and the bush was fire and the fire bush and each of them was bush and fire and not two bushes nor two fires, since / they were both in the fire and they were both in the bush, not indeed in division but in union. From the two natures there come into being the natural *prosôpa*. Either then speak not of distinct natures when they remain in the distinctions of the natures and are not made void, or say that they have remained the diversity of the natures, or thou shouldest define them as a distinction of natures in an inseparable union, not indeed as diversities of nature made void by the union. . . .[3]

[1] Labbe (Mansi), iv. 889 E, and above, p. 154: ἀνάγκη γὰρ πᾶσα διορίσαι, καὶ εἰπεῖν, τὸν μὲν, ἄνθρωπον ἰδικῶς, τῇ τοῦ υἱοῦ κλήσει τετιμημένον· ἰδικῶς δὲ πάλιν τὸν ἐκ Θεοῦ λόγον υἱότητος ὄνομά τε καὶ χρῆμα ἔχοντα φυσικῶς.

[2] *Sc.* ἰδικῶς, translated above 'apart'. The Syriac has *lḥôdhā'ith* above and *yḥidhā'ith* here.

[3] There is apparently a lacuna in the Syriac text here.

For if then thou understandest them uniquely and not in the natures but in their mutual distinction, of what am I guilty who confess the indistinguishable union of the two natures in one *prosôpon*? And I am addressing my words unto thee as unto one who is in doubt concerning these things. But predicatest thou but one nature of the *hypostatic* union in such wise that after the union the natures preserve not their properties? And thou correctest the things which were formerly said by thee, but especially thou dost surely declare them void as a result of the examination against me, in wishing to say the contrary of the things which I say, because it has befallen thee to will to inquire into the cause of the distinction not as in sincerity but out of opposition as an enemy. For this [union] is as one that suppresses the natures, and I accept it not. / But out of opposition towards me thou hast occupied [thy mind] with definitions, with furious words, as robbers, that thou mightest conceal thy purpose and might not be discovered; and thou sayest this and that and all things, but thou speakest not of the *hypostatic* union for the making void of the natures but for the [establishing of] a natural union which [results] from the composition in one nature. As the soul and the body [result] in one nature of the man, so also God the Word is united with the humanity, and this thou callest the *hypostatic* union. But even then, though the natures were to remain, yet there would come to be a union [resulting] in a nature passible and made and created, for the natural union is a second creation. For those things which have not [a thing] in their nature receive it in their nature by the union of nature; but the things which are united in virtue of a natural union are united with the natural passibility of the other and accept not voluntarily mutual sufferings, as the body and the soul, receiving not in their nature their own mutual properties except by the union of nature, participate in one another and give and receive mutual sufferings by the necessity of nature in such wise that he suffers who would not have suffered of himself. For in the union the soul of itself neither hungers nor thirsts nor is pained by a cut or by a burn or by a blow, nor again is the soulless bodily frame sensible of any of these things; but by the natural union of diverse natures they suffer passively and participate in these mutual sufferings by the necessity of the union.[1]

If thou thus predicatest the *hypostatic* union of the nature, thou sayest, as the Arians, that it is natural and not voluntary, because he suffered with a natural passibility. He suffered as a result of the natural union, for the sufferings of the soul are the sufferings of the body in the natural composition. For he who is unmade, who is by his nature uncreated, was not composed that he might suffer as though created and made. For men prove not the one nature of the union by the fact that the soul is in the body and the body in the soul, for it [2] produces not the union in every bodily frame wherein there is a soul so as also to be able always to quicken it, but [it is in the body] by such a composition as has been constructed in one nature by the Maker, both subjected and involuntarily subject unto a natural limitation, both limited and unable to escape. And again they are released or bound by the construction in the union of the nature. If therefore the union of God the Word with the humanity was in one nature, although those natures remained without confusion but in a union of the nature, the Maker and that which was made would be constructed by a change either willingly or unwillingly since they have been so styled and it [3] is made and created. And he who can create everything, that is, God, will be the nature of the union, and it is not the *hypostasis* of the humanity which is known [to be] animal in nature, as even the body without the soul is not animal in its own *hypostasis*, but by the construction of the natural union it is its [property] to be animal. If it is so, it is also through God [the property] of man to be animal, but it is not his [property through] his own *hypostasis* and his nature,[4] but through the *hypostatic* union which establishes one nature.

For this purpose he declines to say that the man is man and that he is animal in his *hypostasis* and in his nature, and that

---

[1] See p. 8, n. 3.
[2] *Viz.* the Soul.
[3] *Viz.* their composition.
[4] See crit. n., p. 399.

God the Word is God the Word in his *hypostasis*, in order that he may maintain his nature in the union, and that it may not become animal as a result of the union. For he [1] received as a result of the construction of [all] creation by the Father and by the Son and by the Holy Spirit to become man, but to become the only-begotten Son he received from the union with God the Word, for it belonged not unto his own nature nor did it lie in the natural and *hypostatic* union. For that which it was his to become by the natural union was not his to become as a result of anything else than of the natural construction, as to become one animal results neither from the bodily frame nor from the soul nor from them both but from the natural construction. This [union] then is corruptible and passible, but the union of the *prosôpa* of the natures is neither passible nor corruptible as [having taken place] through a voluntary appropriation; and the union was not his involuntarily by condescension or by exaltation, by command or by subjection unto command. And such a conception as this consists neither in the making void / nor in the being made void nor in the extinction of one nature or of the properties of the two natures, but the several qualities in the natural qualities are distinct in purpose and in will, according to the distinction of the natures in the one equality, while there is the same will and purpose in the union of the natures, so that they may both will or not will the same things.[2]

And because also the *prosôpon* of the one is the other's and that of the other the one's, and the one [comes] from the other and the other from the one, the will belongs to each one of them. When he speaks as from his own *prosôpon*, [he does so] by one *prosôpon* which appertains to the union of the natures and not to one *hypostasis* or [one] nature. For the divinity is not limited by the body as each one of the natures which are

---

[1] *Viz.* (presumably) the human element in Christ, Jesus *qua* man.

[2] A passage such as this seems to show clearly that Nestorius did not teach merely a 'moral union', *i.e.* a union resulting from and consisting in the fact that the two natures in Christ both willed alike. Like the orthodox he makes that unity of will the consequence of the union, not its ground. Cp. pp. 59, 62, 70.

united in the *hypostasis*. For they are limited by the nature in that it limits them in their being and they exist not apart from them, as the soul and the body are bound together in their being and exist not apart from them[selves].[1]

If therefore thou thus sayest that God the Word and the flesh are united and thou callest this an incomprehensible and unseemly union, I decline not to say clearly: 'Those who 'say these things are impious, and this opinion comes not 'from the orthodox.' For if the Son, who is impassible, had come unto the necessity of a passible nature in order that he might sensibly suffer, it would prove that his own *ousia* was not impassible / but [was] a passible nature, whereof he had been constituted in the *hypostatic* union and wherein he suffered. For he to whose nature it appertains not to suffer, will not suffer in any way in his *hypostasis*, if he is impassible; for he who suffers in aught is not impassible in his *hypostasis*, but is impassible [only] in such manner as all those who, being passible, suffer in nature; they do not suffer in all ways, but in that way whereby it appertains to the nature itself to suffer. Everything suffers not in the same way, neither light nor air nor fire, nor the animals which are in the waters nor the animals which are on the dry land, nor birds nor bodily frames nor souls nor angels nor demons, but they are passible indeed in *ousia* and in *hypostasis*. But they suffer according to the disposition of their nature to suffer either of themselves or by another.

But thou sayest neither by confusion nor yet by change of *ousia* nor by corruption nor yet naturally, so that one *hypostatic* union takes place. Thou predicatest therefore this voluntary one wherein a union without confusion and without the suffering of the natures in one *prosôpon* is conceived, and not a natural union. For the *prosôpon* of a natural union is predicated of the two natures which have been united, as the man is neither body nor soul; for the union of these results in a nature and the *prosôpon* of the nature. But / God took upon himself the likeness of a servant, and that of none other, for his own *prosôpon* and for his sonship, as indeed are those who are

---

[1] *I. e.* each other.

united in nature.¹ He took the likeness of a servant : and the likeness of the servant was not the *ousia* of a man, but he who took it made it [his] likeness and his *prosôpon*. And he became the likeness of men, but he became not the nature of men, although it was the nature of a man which he took ; he who took it came to be in the likeness of man, whilst he who took and not that which was taken was found in *schêma* as man ; for that which was taken was the *ousia* and nature of man, whereas he who took was found in *schêma* as man without being the nature of man. For the nature he took not for himself but the likeness, the likeness and *schêma* of man, in all things which indicate the *prosôpon* : as touching the poverty of the *schêma*, he ² relates : *He condescended unto death, even the death upon the cross whereby he emptied himself,* in order to show in nature the humiliation of the likeness of a servant and to endure scorn among men ; for they shamefully entreated him, even him who displayed ³ infinite condescension. He made known also the cause wherefore he took the likeness of a servant when *He was found in the likeness of men in schêma as a man and humiliated himself unto death, even the death upon the cross.*⁴ But he suffered not these things in his / nature but made use therein of him who suffers naturally in his *schêma* and in his *prosôpon* in order that he might give him by grace in his *prosôpon a name which is more excellent than all names, before which every knee which is in heaven and on the earth and beneath the earth shall bow ; and every tongue shall confess him,*⁵ in order that by his similitude with God and according to the greatness of God he may be conceived as Son who *took the likeness of a servant and was in the likeness of a man and was found in schêma as a man and humiliated himself unto death, even the death upon the cross, and was exalted in that there was given unto him a name which is more excellent than all names* ⁶ in the *schêma* of the likeness of a servant

---

¹ Loofs suggests that the words 'as indeed are those who are united in nature' have been inadvertently transposed, and are the end of the previous sentence (*Nestorius and his Place, &c.*, p. **91**). Apart from such emendation Nestorius is here either inconsistent or more than usually obscure.

² *Viz.* St. Paul ; cp. Phil. ii. 7-8.   ³ Syr. ' who [was] in '.
⁴ Phil. ii. 8.   ⁵ Phil. ii. 9-11.   ⁶ Phil. ii. 7-9.

which was taken with a view to the union. But he was the likeness of a servant not in *schêma* but in *ousia*, and it was taken for the likeness and for the *schêma* and for the humiliation unto death upon the cross. For this reason it was exalted so as to take *a name which is more excellent than all names*.[1]

But to understand 'the likeness of a servant as *ousia*' he appointed Christ for the understanding; for Christ is both of them by nature. For this reason the properties of the two natures befit also one *prosôpon*, not [that] of the *ousia* of God the Word. And the *prosôpon* is not in the *ousia*, for it is not in the *ousia* of God the Word, nor is it the *prosôpon* of the union of the natures which have been united in such wise as to make two *ousias* befit the one *prosôpon* / of God the Word, for he is not both of them in *ousia*. God the Christ is not indeed as it were another apart from God the Word, but he is indicative of the union of the two *ousias* of God the Word and of man. But God and man—of them is Christ [constituted], as thou also hast said. The diversities of the natures are not destroyed because of the union, but they have rather perfected for us one Lord and Christ and Son, by an ineffable and incomprehensible concurrence of the divinity and of the humanity in the union. Although in the things which thou hast said well, where thou seemest to repent. . . . For the *ousia* of God the Word was not made perfect by the divinity and by the humanity, because it is not its [property] in virtue of the union to become God the Word, as Christ is [constituted] of the divinity and of the humanity. For the incarnation [2] is indicative of the humanity, for *He was made man* is all conceived not only of the divinity but also of the incarnation [2] which makes man.[3]

For this reason the Apostle lays down the *prosôpon* of the union and next the things wherefrom the union results. He says first *the likeness of God*, which is the similitude of God and next *it took the likeness of a servant*, not the *ousia* nor the nature but the *schêma* and the *prosôpon*, in order that he might participate in the likeness of a servant, and that the

---

[1] Phil. ii. 9 (P.).   [2] Sc. ἐνανθρώπησις.   [3] Sc. ἐνανθρωπίζει.

likeness of the servant might participate in the likeness of God, so that of / necessity there might be one *prosôpon* from the two natures. For the likeness is the *prosôpon*, so that it is the one by *ousia* and the other by union in respect to the humiliation and to the exaltation. How then dost thou bid us understand these diversities of the natures in the union? For the union has not removed the diversities of the natures, so that we should again understand these diversities anew. For *he who took the likeness of a servant* is the property solely of the likeness of God, whereas that which was taken concerns uniquely the likeness of the servant; but the one belongs to the other and the other to the one through the union of the *prosôpon* and not through the *ousia*, in such wise that, where the one is in *ousia*, the other is in union, and not another. That which is in *ousia* the likeness of God is consubstantial with this *ousia*, in that it is a natural likeness; but by union the likeness of God took the likeness of a servant and the likeness of God, which is naturally God's, became in *schêma* the likeness of a servant. But the likeness of the servant, which is naturally the likeness of a servant and in the union the likeness of God, is not naturally God's, so that we understand severally in nature the several qualities of each one of the natures and the natural distinctions of each single one of the natures; and the [properties] of the union we understand [as belonging] uniquely to the union and not to the *ousia*. How therefore dost thou bid us not to conceive any of these things apart in view of / the distinctions of the natures, things which thou hast said are not destroyed because of the union? But thou canst neither reply unto me nor convict me of the things whereof thou accusest me; but thou accusest thyself in the things whereof thou wouldest accuse me and thou speakest against thyself.

But you, O just judges, what have you examined of these things? Either concerning the things which we have subjected to inquiry or of the things which we have said and of the things which I have confessed and of the things which I have denied that I have imagined, convict him who has erred or instruct him who is ignorant. For not because of the things

that a man denies is he condemned as an heretic, but because
of the things that he confesses. Thus Arius, thus Eunomius,
thus Macedonius, thus each of the heretics was condemned
by the fathers because of the things which they confessed in
opposition [to the faith] and discussed and [which] were
subjected to scrutiny. What is there of that which I have
confessed and discussed against them for which they have
condemned me as an heretic? What have you found in my
letter that is contrary to the deposit of the fathers? Whether
I have said or have not said [it], speak. Thus he[1] has said
that all the things which are referred to Christ by the Divine
Scripture ought to be referred to God the Word: the birth
from a woman, the cross, the death, the burial, the resurrection,
the ascension, and the second coming when he shall come again.
It was not / from these things that the fathers began.... But
in regard to these things, I have stated why the fathers have
not said them; and for this reason also we ought not to begin
from here. I have also stated the argument, for they purposed
not to prove that God the Word is passible, mortal, and made,
and created, nor that he came into being from things which
were not—these [are the doctrines] which those who began
from there are constrained to state—but the opposite of the
things which Arius said and taught. For this reason they
placed the beginning of their teaching in the union of the
prosôpon of Christ in order that they might duly accept in
order the things appertaining to the divinity and those appertaining to the humanity, so that there comes about neither
confusion nor making void of the natures. But they combated
against all the heresies and were firmly confirmed in orthodoxy
when they answered and spoke these words: 'I believe in one
Lord, Jesus Christ, the only-begotten Son.'

    Examine, I said unto him, how they have placed first
'Lord' and 'Jesus Christ', and 'only-begotten' and 'Son',
common names of the divinity and of the humanity, as the
foundation, and next build thereon the tradition of the
Incarnation[2] and the sufferings and the resurrection, in order
that, placing first the names of the two natures which are

[1] *Viz.* Cyril.   [2] *Sc.* ἐνανθρώπησις.

indicative of the common [properties], the sonship and Lordship might not be separated and the natures in the union of the sonship / might not come into danger of corruption and of confusion. . . .[1]

How then does it appear unto you, O just judges? Because he has written the opinion which was pleasing unto him, and I also have written my opinion likewise, and further we have chosen you as judges, what think you of these things? What opinion have you of them? Who is just or who is unrighteous? And with what thought have you made examination? Tell us your opinion; write unto us as just judges. Have I lied and transgressed the faith of the fathers, because I have said unto him [2] that they began from here, and not with God the Word, but with one Lord Jesus Christ, the Son of God? You condemn me as one who has added thereto and you acquit him who has not entirely preserved their faith but has thought that they have made use of these terms fortuitously and without distinction. But I have said that they began from here not fortuitously but by the divine purpose. If I have done impiously therein, show me, and, if not, why do you repudiate as though the argument which I have made unto him were an impiety, [when I said] that they began from here because the [properties] of the divinity and of the humanity are common, as the names indicate, and that they wished to begin with these names / for the sake of complete and lucid instruction, as if the name of Christ existed truly in the two natures, man and God? But if for this reason, then you ought to condemn him also, for he has said that the natures which are combined to come together in union are diverse, but one Christ [is formed] of them both. There

---

[1] From Nestorius' Second Letter to Cyril. See above, p. 142, n. 1, and Labbe (Mansi), iv. 893 B: σκόπησον ὅπως, τὸ κύριος, Ἰησοῦς, Χριστός, καὶ μονογενής, καὶ υἱός, πρότερον θέντες, τὰ κοινὰ τῆς θεότητος καὶ τῆς ἀνθρωπότητος, ὡς θεμελίους, ὀνόματα, τότε τὴν τῆς ἐνανθρωπήσεως, καὶ τοῦ πάθους, καὶ τῆς ἀναστάσεως ἐποικοδομοῦσι παράδοσιν· ἵνα τῶν ὀνομάτων τῶν φύσεων ἑκατέρων κοινῶν τινῶν σημαντικῶν προκειμένων, μήτε τὰ τῆς υἱότητος καὶ κυριότητος τέμνηται, μήτε τὰ τῶν φύσεων ἐν τῷ τῆς υἱότητος μοναδικῷ συγχύσεως ἀφανισμῷ κινδυνεύῃ.

At the end of this quotation the Syriac copyist adds in a foot-note, 'Here there is a blank space, six lines'.

[2] *Viz.* Cyril.

resulted not one God the Word from them both, for the diversity of the natures is not removed because of the union. Therefore the two natures belong unto Christ and not unto God the Word. Either therefore condemn my words and his or, in accordance with his, consider me also innocent, since I confess all things. But if not, prove, either you or he, how he confesses that God the Word is in two *ousias*: of what divinity and humanity has God the Word been perfected by combination? For he has spoken of one Christ who is [formed] of diverse natures, of the divinity and of the humanity, and was perfected ineffably by the combination of the natures. And of what *ousias*? Of what divinity, of what humanity was God the Word perfected that God the Word should be in two natures? Either you or he, say unto us now also, although you have not said [it] before, say: God the Word is by *ousia* in them both, as you confess that Christ is in *ousia* in them both, [formed] from diverse natures. The union has not made void / the diversity of the natures. But you have said that God the Word is diverse natures. For if of one *ousia* there result two *ousias*, of the divinity and of the humanity, there has been a separation and not a union; but he says that Christ was in the union and existed in two natures. God the Word became flesh by union and not by *ousia*; how then does he indicate that the same is one, he who is two in the union and who is the nature? Or are nature and union the same thing, and ' in nature ' and ' in union ', and *prosôpon* and *ousia*? For although the *prosôpon* exists not without *ousia*, the *ousia* and the *prosôpon* are not the same.

How then have you judged, O wise judges? How then have you considered these [sayings] of the fathers? Do they agree with the Divine Scriptures in the terms and in the signification of the terms and have they made use of these terms zealously and clearly? And from here and from no other point have they been able lucidly to begin their teaching. But if [they began] from where the Holy Spirit guided them, that nothing might be abridged and that nothing might be superfluous and that they might do nothing in vain and by hazard, but everything with examination, [they acted] in such wise that the things which appear in Christ—all the [properties] of God the Word whose nature is impassible and is immortal and eternal, and all the [properties] of the humanity, which are / a nature mortal and passible and created, and those of the union and of the incarnation[1] since the womb and since the incarnation[1]—are referred to one *prosôpon*, to that common *prosôpon* of our Lord Jesus Christ, the only-begotten Son of God, whence the fathers began. And so by the distinction of language they have taught us ' The divinity ' is from God the Father, consubstantial with the Father, light ' from light, through whom everything was [made] which is on ' the earth and which is in heaven'. And then the incarnation[2] of God the Word and of the humanity—they have said ' He came down and was made flesh for the sake of us men ' and for the sake of our salvation '. And then they have said in regard to the things of the flesh, concerning the generation and concerning the formation, that he was made flesh; in teaching they have said ' He was made flesh of the Holy Spirit and of the Virgin Mary'; they have made known this union whereby he was made flesh and was made man. For until his incarnation,[1] they taught us everything in terms of[3] God the Word and after he was made flesh they speak of this union which [proceeded] from the Holy Spirit and the Virgin Mary, of the birth and the flesh which was made flesh, the sufferings and the death and the resurrection and the ascension and the operations which made known that the body was united unto him as being animate and intelligent in order that we might suppose that the union was without confusion and further without change of *ousia* and of nature, or mixture or / natural composition, so as to result in the coming into being of one animal, yet in one *prosôpon* in accordance with the dispensation on our behalf, in such wise as to participate in us through humiliation unto death, even death upon the cross. But we shall participate in him in *the name which is more excellent than all names, before which every knee shall bow which is in heaven and in the earth and beneath the earth and which every tongue shall confess.*[4]

[1] Sc. ἐνανθρώπησις.   [2] Sc. σάρκωσις.   [3] Syr. 'from'.   [4] Phil. ii. 10–11.

The soul was not without will nor without reflection in the nature of the humanity, nor was the soul without perception as regards the animal perception of its being, as a result of the natural union of the body and of the soul. All the natural things, both active and passive, are in the work of nature and of the unfailing might [of God]. For the union of God the Word with the humanity took place not in nature, in such wise that the intelligence of the humanity was without activity and that it reflected with the intelligence of God the Word, not with the intelligence of the humanity, and that it perceived not in the union of the living soul, but in the union of the divinity, and that it lived [its] life and that it perceived, not by the activity of the perception of the soul but by the might of the divinity; for such a union as this is passible; as the soul naturally gives perception unto the body, so by means of this perception is given unto it the perception of the sufferings of the body, / so that the perception of the sufferings of the body is given by the soul and unto the soul; for it is passible. For this reason the union is in the *prosôpon* and not in the nature, and we say not 'the union of the *prosôpa*' but 'of the natures'. But [there is only] one *prosôpon* in the union but in the natures the one and the other, as from the common *prosôpon* it is known that he took the flesh, the likeness of a servant, for his own *prosôpon*, and thereby he spoke in teaching and working and acting; and he gave his own likeness to the likeness of a servant and thereby he speaks as by his own *prosôpon* and by the divinity. For the *prosôpon* is common, one and the same. The likeness of the servant belongs unto the divinity and the likeness of the divinity unto the humanity. One and the same is the *prosôpon* but not the *ousia*. For the *ousia* of the likeness of God and the *ousia* of the likeness of the servant remain in their *hypostases*.

The union of the natures, in fact, was neither without will nor without imagination, as Arius and Apollinarius have said, but [it resulted] in the *prosôpon* and in the dispensation on our behalf and in the union of his image and of his likeness which is in our nature of soul and body, falling short of nothing except of sin alone. He comported himself [so] not for the sake of the divinity, but that thereby it might make him combat against guilt by fulfilling all the commandments of the law / and the chief observances, in order that he might appear without rebuke in the choice and in the observances of the commandments, and that he who was without sins might be given unto death because of us, the righteous for the impious. What indeed is this defeat? And what is this victory? What is this equality of recompense for the conduct of God and of man? For it is the controller[1] who is united in the *hypostasis* in such wise that he participates in the life and conduct and is overcome by death; the conduct also and the death and the resurrection are those of one who controls[1] and who is controlled.[1] For either God remains in his nature, as he was in nature, without sin, or those things which constituted the manner of life of Christ took place in deception since God the Word comported himself as a man. They both in fact were attracted and torn apart by one another, by the nature and by the will, and he also was torn apart. For the conduct [of his life] was by command: he was not of a nature unchangeable, unique and without master, which is not torn to and fro according to the will and plan of another; but, if there was in truth human manner of life and conduct, the conduct of God the Word was in nature, and in those [qualities] of the nature wherein he comported himself he indeed abode, in that he accepted the very nature and became changeable and variable. Therefore he comported not himself [after] the conduct of God but of that nature wherein he comported himself.

What then have you found in my letter, wherein I am impious / and [for which] you have condemned me and have regarded this man as one who fears God? First, then, I convicted him as one who lied concerning the fathers and abolished all the first principles of the faith, and of himself made a beginning whence of constraint he made even God the Word passible. Now 'God the Word' and 'Christ' do not indicate the same thing, either in the Divine Scriptures or

---

[1] Syr. *mdabhrānâ* (= Gk. οἰκονόμος) and cognate words, from the same root as that elsewhere translated 'dispensation'.

as he has said, although Christ exists not apart from God the Word. And I have neither instructed him in the custom of the Divine Scriptures nor shown him the things which happen from such and such terms. And I have praised him for the things which he has well said: that he has preserved without confusion the natures and their properties in such wise that God the Word was impassible even in the very union; and he makes his the properties of the flesh. I have proved unto him that they refer not unto his *ousia* but unto his *prosôpon*, so that his *prosôpon* is his own and so that all things indicate his *prosôpon*. All the things which [constitute] the *prosôpon* [constitute] not the *ousia*, for neither does God the Word exist in all the things of the *ousia* of the flesh, nor again also is the flesh said [to be] in all the things which belong by *ousia* unto God the Word, but in all the things which indicate the *prosôpon* and which are [therein], in such wise that the union without confusion is preserved also in the diversity of the natures / and the *prosôpon* of the union of the natures is undivided. And I have said unto him and have not dissembled that which I have not understood and about which I have disputed, and I have propounded the cause and the doubt which has been born in me, that I might not permit him to say aught of those things which he has formerly said.

For what then have you condemned me? Because I have convicted him of not having adhered to the words of the Fathers and of having, in opposition to their intention, made God the Word passible and created and made, and of having caused him [to issue] from things which existed not, having begun with him and having referred unto him all the properties —and I taught him all things. For this reason do you deal harshly [with me]? Or because I have convicted him of lying concerning the Fathers, of having said that the Fathers called the holy Virgin the mother of God, without even making mention of the birth itself? For the sake of these things have you treated me as an adversary? Let none show favour unto any man. But if this phrase[1] has been employed in the discussion about the Faith by the Fathers at Nicaea, with [the

---

[1] *I. e.* the term 'Mother of God'.

aid of] whom he combats against me, read it; or if it has been spoken by any other Council of the orthodox. For it is of the heretics, all of whom fight against the divinity of Christ, but it has not been spoken by those who have adhered to the faith of the orthodox. But if it were shown to have been said by a Council of the orthodox, then even I should confess / that I have been condemned as one who was on the opposite side. But if no one has used this phrase, thou hast risen up against them all to introduce into the Faith with boldness a new phrase which has not been accepted. And this it was that I required of thee in order to prove unto thee that it [1] was not laid down by the Fathers; but it is for the Council, which has been assembled for this purpose and for nothing else, to judge whether it shall be laid down or not laid down. For it is not for them to be persuaded by me in any case, but for me to be persuaded of those things which they examine and judge and select for acceptance. For I have called you judges and have made you all judges of a just judgement, but that which justly belongs to the Council have I not given unto one man, who has conducted [his case] with violence and prevailed on the whole Council to adopt the faith which seemed [good] unto him.

What then have you done of those things on account of which you have been assembled? You have not settled what you ought, and you have broken away from the Council and have not waited for those who were absent. Nor have you observed what you ought toward those who were summoned unto the Council; nor have you assembled together as you have been summoned, but the judges have been as the accused wished. Instead of [being] the accused you have made him sit as the judge of [his] adversary. And how shall I call him judge? You have made him sit / at the head of the Council. And what shall I say of those who were present? And of those who were absent and of those who were not yet come? And you have given him authority over all, both over those who were there and over those who were absent, and over those who were alive and over those who were dead. Who of

[1] *I.e.* the term 'Mother of God'.

those who have not chanced upon these things in the document which was [addressed] by them unto the Council in Ephesus, would believe them? Could a just judgement proceed from such a Council as this? Yet although I were supposed to say these things, because I have suffered, and not to have examined them with just deliberation, [and though] none were persuaded of my words, I would not indeed seek to have any help from men. *For I am already being offered, and the time of my departure is come*,[1] that I may be with Christ, on account of whom he[2] has fought with me. But [I am writing] that men may not be led astray from the right faith because of the name of the 'judgement of the Council'. For this reason have I said these things. I, however, have said less than the things which they have written; yet learn from those who have condemned me that there has not been a judgement and that I have not been condemned in judgement.

I indeed have spoken the [words] of the Fathers and have spoken those of the Divine Scriptures, and I first looked / into the plot which was being [made] against the Faith, and I first stated that it was the confirmation of the faith of the Arians on account of the *hypostatic* union, which resembled also [that of] the Manichaeans, in that he would have suffered being passible, and again [that of] Apollinarius, who agreed thereto with all his hands.[2] And he[3] was carried away by[4] all the heresies, since he declared it unlawful to predicate the properties of each of the natures in the union and referred them all, even those of the flesh, unto God the Word. And thereby you have thought that the orthodox were easily deceived by the heretics [into supposing] that they have none of those things whereof they ought to make use against them, since you have surrendered your mouths unto them, and you have bound your hands and your feet and have surrendered yourselves unto them. Either you will turn aside from your guilt or you will suffer wrongs without excuse for having, like irreverent persons, caused heresies to prevail against the orthodox. For supposing that he[2] be found [to be] an Arian, he will call you as witnesses against those who were assembled at Nicaea, as

[1] 2 Tim. iv. 6.   [2] Syr. 'with both his hands'.   [3] *Viz.* Cyril.   [4] Syr. 'to'.

though indeed they had openly risen up with audacity against Arius, to say what they ought not, namely, saying that he who is passible and mortal and made is consubstantial with him who is impassible and immortal and the maker of all created things. And supposing that he is a Manichaean, you will bear witness in his favour that, in that he suffered / impassibly, he suffered in *schêma*. For he, who, when he is supposed to be suffering, suffers not, suffers impassibly : for he who was not [man] by nature, has not even died. You have hardly confessed the truth, and you have reprimanded the three hundred and twenty-eight,[1] as not having spoken the truth through acceptance of persons. If in addition to this also you insist on saying: 'We do not say that God the Word died in 'nature, since the divine nature is immortal and impassible, 'nor in the semblance of the flesh, but in the nature of the 'flesh, which is passible and mortal, and that which God the 'Word became was flesh,' a heathen would accept this word, accepting [it] in the change of the likeness. And thou sayest that the Incarnation[2] took place through the change of the *ousia* without his own *ousia* and his likeness being changed: when he suffered in the passible nature, not before he came to be in the *ousia*. Why then do you not say the same things as we, when it is a question of the doctrine of the Incarnation ;[2] but why does he lead us astray with the birth of a material flesh,[3] with which God the Word was formed, and why have unconvincing and incredible fables been fabricated?

And if thou sayest against this, that the Incarnation[2] of him who became flesh and man took place neither through change of *ousia* nor through change of likeness, but [that] this man who was taken—who was born / of a woman and suffered and died and rose and is ready to come to judge the quick and the dead—was changed into the *ousia* of God and was no more considered a man, except in name alone, and [if] thou meanest by this that God died and rose, the heathen also, who practises a religion which predicates the change of men unto divinity and therefore propitiates and serves him as God, would stand

---

[1] Presumably a mistaken rendering of '318' in the Greek.
[2] Sc. ἐνανθρώπησις.   [3] Literally: 'a flesh of *hylē*'.

by thee. How then, sayest thou, is the opinion of heathendom yours? You, who have combated against me on these [points] until now, are deceived, and thereby have you also deceived men. And if thou sayest that the Incarnation[1] of God the Word took place neither by change of *ousia* nor by change of divinity and the body remained in the *ousia* without change, but [that] he[2] became man with a view to the *hypostatic* and natural union, Arius also, who mocks at the three hundred and eighteen, would accept this confession: and you accept it and are not scandalized, and you agree with heart and mind[3] to Arius who speaks truly when he claims that he became man in the natural *hypostasis* and was naturally united in *hypostasis*, suffering naturally by perception the sufferings of the body; him thou darest to call consubstantial, him who is the accepter of sufferings.

And if you decline this, as one who confesses not the soul and the body among the things whereof the Word has been constituted in the natural *hypostasis* nor [that] he suffered after becoming passible in a passible nature in regard to natural sufferings, he proclaims the / [doctrines] of Arius and Apollinarius. For Arius says: ' What does it serve thee that ' God should become a passible nature by the *hypostatic* union ' of the soul to suffer natural sufferings naturally in his body ' and in his soul?' Does he make him who is suffering all these sufferings consubstantial with an impassible nature? But Apollinarius condemns those who say these things while [otherwise] confessing like those who cleave unto his own faith, and commands them to keep aloof from those who say these things and to become his own partisans and to anathematize all those who dissent from him. If further he also is deposed for confessing neither the intelligence nor the will, for such reason as one who confesses not the Word in the flesh and in the soul and in the intelligence in the natural and complete union, you will not receive him, since he says all the [same] things as Arius. Let it be [granted] that he[2] is united to the soul and to the body and to the intelligence; but if it is an *hypostatic* and natural union, thou effectest an addition

---

[1] Sc. ἐνανθρώπησις.   [2] *Viz.* God the Word.   [3] Syr. ' with hands and feet '.

and not a diminution and thou avoidest a diminution of the sufferings of the body in such wise as to make subject unto the sufferings of many sufferings him who is consubstantial with him who is impassible ; great is the passibility of those who suppose this. For you give him the things which make [men] passible because of the *hypostatic* union, since he is united in a natural composition, so as to suffer without his will the sufferings of the body and of the soul and of the intelligence and [since] he is united in *ousia* and in nature, as the soul in the body endures / of necessity the sufferings of the soul and of the body. But thou makest him impassible. Then there has not been an *hypostatic* and natural but a voluntary union with the body and with the rational and intelligent soul which are united *hypostatically* and naturally in the nature of the man. But the union of God the Word with these is neither *hypostatic* nor natural but voluntary, as consisting in a property of the will and not of the nature. For the things which are united by the natural *hypostasis* have a natural and not a voluntary quality. For he took the likeness of a servant for his own *prosôpon* and not for his nature by change either of the *ousia*, of the *ousia* in the nature of the humanity, or of the humanity in the nature of the divinity, [so that] it was united and mixed with the human nature either by confusion or by a natural composition and a change of the activity of the nature ; for this quality is changeable and variable. But the voluntary [activity] is neither passible nor changeable ; it suffers not involuntarily in its natural *ousia* the sufferings of the soul and of the body. Those which are naturally united suffer indeed in *ousia* with one another, transmitting their own sufferings naturally and not voluntarily. For although he accepted them as sufferings voluntarily, when, however, he accepted them and suffered them, he suffered them naturally, in that he suffered them by a natural property and by perception.[1]

/ If you say these things thus, you have incited them all and have become heathens in saying that which he [2] has said who said these things with irreverent audacity; they have

---

[1] Cp. p. 8, n. 4.   [2] *Viz.* Arius.

anathematized him,[1] who said these things, and laid upon him punishment without remission and driven him out from the church and even from the inhabited world, as one who defiles the earth whereon he walks. How then do you say these things? But if he says concerning me: 'it is because he 'divides the natures into sundry parts and separates them and 'distinguishes them from one another, and not because he 'says these things clearly but because he distinguishes them 'into parts one from another and says: "one son of nature '"and one son of grace," as though there were two natures, 'and he distinguishes them, saying "I indeed distinguish the '"nature and I unite the adoration; because of him who is '"clothed I adore the clothing"'[2]—every one would say unto you 'O man, you have drunk mandrakes'.[3] If you understand also the Father by the things which have been said by you, how do you say also of him who has not been kept separate even by one word, that he took and was taken and made it his own, and [how] do you call [him] man and God? For all these things belong unto those in whose doctrine the natures are distinguished, and not unto those who say that there is one *ousia*; for the union destroys not the diversities of the natures; but if the diversities of the natures / remain in the union, they are kept separate by the diversities of the natures, in so far as they are diverse. But how do you say concerning me that I separate the union by distance of space, since I say:

[1] *Viz.* Arius.

[2] We have not been able to trace the source of this quotation. Nau refers to the following two passages: (1) Cyril, *ad Acacium* (Labbe (Mansi), v. 320 D): Ἑτέρα δὲ παντελῶς παρὰ ταύτην ἡ Νεστορίου κακοδοξία (*v.l.* κενοδοξία). ὑποκρίνεται μὲν γὰρ ὁμολογεῖν, ὅτι καὶ ἐσαρκώθη, καὶ ἐνηνθρώπησε Θεὸς ὢν ὁ λόγος, τὴν δέ γε τοῦ σεσαρκῶσθαι δύναμιν οὐκ εἰδώς, δύο μὲν ὀνομάζει φύσεις, ἀποδιαιρεῖ (*v.l.* ἀποδιΐστησι) δὲ ἀλλήλων αὐτάς, Θεὸν ἰδίᾳ τιθείς, καὶ ὁμοίως ἄνθρωπον ἀνὰ μέρος, συναφθέντα Θεῷ σχετικῶς, κατὰ μόνην τὴν ἰσοτιμίαν, ἤγουν αὐθεντίαν. ἔφη γὰρ οὕτως· ἀχώριστος τοῦ φαινομένου Θεός. διὰ τοῦτο τοῦ μὴ χωριζομένου τὴν τιμὴν οὐ χωρίζω· χωρίζω τὰς φύσεις, ἀλλ' ἑνῶ τὴν προσκύνησιν. (2) The following extracts from Nestorius' writings read at the Council (Labbe (Mansi), iv. 1201 B): . . . διὰ τὸν φορούντα τὸν φορούμενον σέβω. διὰ τὸν κεκρυμμένον προσκυνῶ τὸν φαινόμενον. ἀχώριστος τοῦ φαινομένου Θεός. διὰ τοῦτο τοῦ μὴ χωριζομένου τὴν τιμὴν οὐ χωρίζω. χωρίζω τὰς φύσεις, ἀλλ' ἑνῶ τὴν προσκύνησιν.

[3] For instances in ancient literature of 'belief in the soporific and narcotic quality of mandragora or mandrake' see Frazer, *Folklore in the Old Testament*, vol. ii, pp. 385-6.

'because of him who is clothed I adore the clothing'? For the clothing is not apart from him who is clothed nor he who is clothed apart from the clothing but it is conceived in the same likeness. And for this reason it is not possible to adore him who is clothed apart from the clothing upon him, clothed wherein he is seated with the Father; for he is not seated with him without being clothed in it and that which is seated with him receives also adoration with him. When it is seated with him it is by all means adored not for its [own] sake but for the sake of him who is clothed in it.

By all means therefore we shun those who predicate the Incarnation [1] [apart] from the union, either by a change of likeness which is [the view] of the heathen, or in hallucinations or in a *schêma* without *hypostasis* [which] suffers impassibly, or in predicating the natural sufferings of God the Word, as being either by *hypostasis* in the union or in flesh in the flesh either in an irrational or in a rational soul, and [in asserting] finally that the union resulted in an *hypostasis* of nature and not in a voluntary *prosôpon*, in order that we may not make the union of God the Word corruptible and changeable nor call it passible and necessary, but a voluntary union in *prosôpon* / and not in nature. Either they will renounce my words, admitting that the Incarnation [1] took place in the nature, and will make the union passible and changeable, as Arius, or [they will make it] impassible, as the Fathers. Partisans of which side do you seek to be? It depends on you: [you are] either on the side of the heretics or on the side of the orthodox Fathers, or on the side of those who say: '[He is] neither passible nor corruptible,' or on [that of] those who [say that] the union appertains unto the *hypostasis* or on [that of] those who [say that it appertains] unto the *prosôpon*. But I say that the union of God the Word is neither passible nor mortal nor changeable. For these things let him who would anathematize me! I have kept without blemish the faith of the three hundred and eighteen who were assembled at Nicaea, saying that God the Word is unchangeable [and] immortal, that he is continuously

[1] *Sc.* ἐνανθρώπησις.

that which he is in the eternity of the Father. He was not [formed] of things which existed not nor of any other *hypostasis*, and there was not when he was not. Eternally [exists] the Father, eternally the Son, eternally the Holy Spirit; but the flesh which was made flesh, which was of the Holy Spirit and of the Virgin Mary, exists not eternally, but there was when it was not; and it is of another *ousia* and of another nature and of another *hypostasis*, [to wit, of that] of men, and not of the *ousia* of God the Father—changeable and mortal and passible and corruptible. Not from [1] [being] the *ousia* / of God the Word was it changed into the *ousia* of the flesh, but [he had] an *ousiôdic* flesh and a natural flesh which was not changed from its own *ousia*. Nor again was he changed in his likeness from the *ousia* of God into the *ousia* of the flesh, he was flesh not in *schéma* and in semblance of flesh but in the *ousia* of the flesh, of the *ousia* of the flesh; the *ousia* of the flesh was not changed into the *ousia* of the divinity and made God; he was made flesh and made man neither by confusion nor by mixture, and he was composed neither in one plain *ousia* and uniquely after his kind nor according to a natural composition after one kind of animal. Nor further was he naturally united by a natural union in *hypostasis*, and suffered and was in a natural union, [the natures] participating in the same things for the sake of the natural participation in the sufferings.

For every natural composition, which participates by participation in one passible and changeable nature, and is completed in regard to the natures by the very nature of God the Word, [is completed] not in a natural change but exists voluntarily, in such wise that the union of the natures takes place in his own *prosôpon* and not in his own nature; yet the natures remain in their properties, and there is one *prosôpon* without separation and without distinction, having made them its own for the *prosôpon*. The divinity has obtained a likeness by the *ousia* of the humanity and the humanity has obtained / a likeness by the *ousia* of the divinity, so that there is one *prosôpon* of the union and so that the [properties] of the

---

[1] See crit. n., p. 400.

humanity belong unto God the Word and those of the divinity unto the humanity wherein it was made man [and so that] they were closely united unto one and the same with a view to the dispensation on our behalf, since men were in need of the divinity as for our renewal and for our formation anew and for [the renewal] of the likeness of the image which had been obliterated by us: but [men had need also] of the humanity which was renewed and took its likeness anew; for the humanity was congruous, so as to preserve the order which had existed. For he[1] who was honoured with the honour which he gave him and rendered not unto him his [due] honour for the honour which he received showed that he had lost the honour wherewith he had been honoured. For the one also was honoured as the other;[1] and he accepted him not for himself but regarded him as an enemy. When the other[2] was in these [circumstances] he thus preserved himself, making use of the things belonging to the other as if of his own; he truly preserved the image of God and made it his own: that [it is] which is the image and the *prosôpon*. For this reason there was need both of the divinity to renew and to create and to give unto it[self] the likeness, so that [it might be changed] from its own type to the likeness of a servant; and there was also need of the humanity, so that the likeness of a servant which was taken should become the likeness of God and God the likeness of a servant and that the one should become the other and the other the one / in *prosôpon*, the one and the other remaining in their natures; and he preserves an obedience without sin because of his supreme obedience, and because of this he was given unto death for the salvation of all the world.

Not indeed as Arius and Apollinarius are those who foolishly say that God the Word in his grace accepted an earthly mode of life and an obedience unto death through his Incarnation.[3] For this reason the Incarnation[3] took place in the nature of man by a natural union, in such wise that the divinity was made man naturally instead of the soul and comported itself and suffered truly by natural perception in

[1] *Viz.* Adam.   [2] *Viz.* Christ.   [3] *Sc.* ἐνανθρώπησις.

order to be given unto death on behalf of all men and in respect of death to accept naturally the passibility of the soul in the union of the natural *hypostasis*, being torn asunder by force. For this reason, the latter have attributed the Incarnation[1] of God the Word to one nature of man by a natural composition and to an incomplete man where the *ousia* of God the Word is instead of the things which are lacking from the flesh for the completion of the nature of the man, being commanded and performing the things which are comprised in the things commanded and enduring unwillingly the whole human conduct truly in observances difficult and painful and full of suffering, not doing what he willed through fear of transgressing the command, thirsting and hungering and fearing [with] human fear, willing / [with] a human will. And he is in the body, in all the things of the soul, making it in stature according to the formation and model of the sensibility, understanding, learning, being perfected in flesh in the nature of the soul by the natural and *hypostatic* union. And they make void the voluntary union in virtue of the *prosôpon* of the natures, establishing a natural and involuntary property in such wise that God the Word participates in the sufferings of the soul and of the body; the property [of participation] by force and not by will but natural[ly] by *hypostasis* is a union of the natural *hypostasis* naturally, so that the nature may become one which suffers.

But one ought to be neither Arian nor Manichaean, [according to] whom the Incarnation[1] took place in *schêma* or in the nature of God the Word and [who] refer all things to him in their doctrine: the manner of life and the sufferings and the death. For the nature of God the Word sinned not nor transgressed the commandment, so that God comported himself and observed all the commandments and died for us as one who was found without sin by reason of his manner of life. *Through man [came] death and through man the resurrection.*[2] For this reason also it was needful for the whole man, for the purpose of the Incarnation[1] of God the Word, being completed in body and in soul, to comport

---

[1] Sc. ἐνανθρώπησις. [2] 1 Cor. xv. 21.

himself in the nature of men and to observe the obedience and the moral life of human nature. And they long for and honour the name of the Mother of God, since they say that God has died. And, further, as for the Fathers who even unto death have withstood / the heretics who said 'Mother of God', they, however, have in no place indeed made use of these terms nor have they employed them in the documents of the Council. Was it because they knew not? Or because they hated it? Perhaps they had some such word in their thoughts whereby indeed to adhere to the divine teaching; and they heeded not the raving of [their] enemies and gave no opportunity to diminish the divinity by making it passible and mortal. For not he who is in name a theologian is to be called a theologian, but he who is a theologian in fact and in name does not leave alone those who are ready to make him made and created; it is not he who provides matter[1] for blasphemy nor does he admit that God the Word surely came forth from the Virgin Mary, as one who exists and has existed before, and he declines the [doctrine] that he was born a man from her as one who has not existed but has come into being. [Art thou] as one who says that God the Word is in two natures, God and man, and that the man, when he was born, was in the nature of God the Word, or [that] he was changed into another *ousia* of man; and sayest thou thus that he was born? For indeed [in that case] he would not have been of man, but of God the Word would he have been, and [that] in such wise as to make use of the *schéma* of a man but not of the *ousia* of a man.[2]

[1] Syr. *hûlê'* = Gk. ὕλη.   [2] Cp. p. 95, n. 1.

[BOOK II. PART I.][1]

YET some one perhaps will say, 'Thou hast read only the
'letter; but read / also thy blasphemies which [are found] in
'thine instructions; for the letter perhaps was written by thee
'with observance and caution as though it was written unto
'him,[2] whereas thine instructions, which were delivered
'authoritatively by thee, clearly explain thy purpose. And
'for this reason even thy letter has not sufficed us, but we have
'also examined thine instructions in order that we might be
'accurately instructed in all things concerning thee. Nor even
'so have we claimed authority for ourselves nor have we
'behaved boldly, but we have placed before ourselves also
'the instructions of the Fathers, and we have compared
'[thine] with them and, having thus made our examination
'with all accuracy, we have also pronounced sentence, making
'use of the Fathers against whom thou hast fought. For in
'that thou hast been summoned and hast not hearkened, we
'have done all these things rightly; we have condemned thy
'letter, we have examined thine instructions and we have also
'studied the instructions of the Fathers as law. What then
'ought we to have done and have not done? But he,[2] since
'indeed he was present, said and taught the things which he
'ought to say, whereas thou didst then decline [to come]; but
'now thou dost blame us, calumniating us. Why dost thou
'not rather accuse thyself than us? For we judge not things
'invisible but visible, and, if we have made omissions and if
'we have acted in ignorance, say now if things are such as they
'are; and if we were / not justly stirred up against thee, thou
'oughtest to have said it then and not now.'

But I have much whereof to convict them concerning those
many things which they have done and many things also
which they have omitted. But I pass this by now, lest any one

---

[1] See p. 95, n. 1. Nau suggests the addition of the words *Réfutation des Accusations* as the title of Book ii, part i.

[2] *Viz.* Cyril.

should say that he is now saying them because of the inadequacy [of his case]. But among those things which they have done against me, I convict them of having not justly condemned me, for they have told lies and have deceived many without having convicted me by examination, but according to what he[1] demanded. Now he demanded that the things should not be duly examined, lest the condemnation should be his, but he persuaded them all as God, as one who knows the secrets which are in the heart, and those who took part with him so presented him in the sight of many as [to seem] one who was the avenger of God, namely Christ, and he permitted me not to speak otherwise. And thereafter he carried every one with him against me, so that they were even unwilling to hear a word of mine, as one who, while declaring utterly void [the doctrine] that Christ is not man, spoke of Christ himself [as] man in *ousia* but God in equality of honour.[2] But he anticipated me and spoke against me as making God himself a man, / as if he conceived of Christ as nothing else whatsoever than God the Word. And of constraint I directed my words against him, [asserting] that he is also man, and I proved it from the Divine Scriptures and from the teachings of the Fathers; and he further made use of this against me, as one who said that Christ is only man, having dissembled whatever I had said and confessed as regards that which one required him to confess and [which] he was unwilling to confess. For I rebuked him not for not having confessed that Christ is God, but because he did not say that Christ was man whole in nature and in moral life and that God the Word became not the nature of man but in the nature and in the manner of life of man, in such wise that God the Word became both of them in nature. And these things I shall prove from the things which were written when he took [extracts] from my teachings and from[3] his teachings—whether they were thus the same as in the beginning or whether out of enmity towards me he has changed them into the opposite—and from the

---

[1] *Viz.* Cyril.
[2] Cp. *e. g.* Cyril's letter to Acacius of Melitene, on p. 180, n. 1 above.
[3] See crit. n., p. 400.

inventions [spread abroad] by the device of the heretics, but in reality [by men] such as Arius. When he speaks against the *ousia* of God, he refers all the human qualities to the nature of God the Word by the *hypostatic* union, so that he suffers in natural sensibility all human sufferings.

/ 'From the Book of Nestorius, from the sixteenth chapter, concerning the Faith.' From which book of mine? From which sixteenth chapter? What is it that you sought out, when there was none to argue against you? But this concerns me not much, whether it be clear or whether it be in need of investigation. I desire, however, to persuade you all concerning the things whereby he has deceived many and drawn them away from the Faith, as if indeed there had been an examination touching the Records [of the Council], concerning things whereof they have accused me by anticipation without examination, which they have accepted [as] mine and his without examination. . . .

When Divine Scripture is about to tell of the birth of Christ from the Virgin Mary or [his] death, in no place does it appear that it puts 'God' but either 'Christ' or 'Son' or 'Lord', because these three are indicative of the two natures, now of this and now of that, now of the one and now of the other. For example, when the Book relates unto us the birth from the Virgin, whom does it say? *God sent his Son.*[1] It says not that God sent God the Word, but it takes a name which indicates both the natures. Since the Son is man and God, it says that *God sent his Son and he was born of a woman*[1]; and therein thou seest that the name is put which indicates both the natures. Thou callest [him] Son according to the birth from the blessed Virgin, for the Virgin Mother / of Christ bare the Son of God. But since the Son of God is twofold in natures, she bare not the Son of God but she bare the humanity, which is the Son because of the Son who is united thereto.[2]

---

[1] Gal. iv. 4 (P.).

[2] Labbe (Mansi), iv. 1197 A : Ἐκ τοῦ βιβλίου τοῦ Νεστορίου, τετράδιον ιζ'. εἰς δόγμα, καὶ ἀνεγνώσθη οὕτως. "Ὅταν οὖν ἡ θεία γραφὴ μέλλῃ λέγειν ἢ γέννησιν τοῦ Χριστοῦ τὴν ἐκ Μαρίας τῆς παρθένου, ἢ θάνατον, οὐδαμοῦ φαίνεται τιθεῖσα τὸ Θεός, ἀλλ' ἢ Χριστός, ἢ υἱός, ἢ κύριος. ἐπειδὴ ταῦτα τὰ τρία τῶν φύσεών εἰσι τῶν δύο σημαντικά, ποτὲ μὲν ταύτης, ποτὲ δὲ ἐκείνης, ποτὲ δὲ ταύτης κἀκείνης· οἷόν τι λέγω· ὅταν τὴν ἐκ παρθένου γέννησιν ἡμῖν ἡ γραφὴ ἐξηγῆται (v. l. διηγῆται), λέγει·

I demand then of you to reflect accurately on these things; for I pass by the things which they have omitted, and they have clearly not preserved the coherence [of the argument]. And he accuses me of these things as if I were dividing Christ and making [him into] sundry parts, the divinity by itself and the humanity by itself, while making use of [the words] 'honour' and 'the equality of one' in such wise that they tend to bring together in love and not in the *ousias* things far apart. Thus he accuses me both as touching the divinity and as touching the humanity, [of saying] that God the Word is flesh and man but [that] the humanity is Son, Lord, and God, which has taken place through love and through coherence. This is his principal calumny, so that you, since you are judges concerning this, ought at all times to take heed that, if you find that I have imagined thus—condemn me and I too will condemn myself. And also I will beseech you to accept on tradition my condemnation, which is just, although I should have combated ten thousand times and cite convincing arguments to establish that I make use not of *ousia* but simply of love, / and that thereby he is called Lord and Christ and Son. But if I have said the contrary, let them prove that the union is [made] from nature and [that] the union belongs to nature. But, so far from a union in nature, I predicate one *prosôpon*, one equality, one honour, one authority, one lordship; and, in short, [I insert] these things also in virtue of the union of one *prosôpon* in all those things wherein the *prosôpon* of the one and of the other exists in nature; for the *prosôpon* of the natures is not one nature, but it is in nature and is not nature. For the Son of God the Father is by nature consubstantial with the Father and that which the Father is in his nature the Son also is; for that which the *prosôpon* is in nature, the Son,

---

ἐξαπέστειλεν ὁ Θεὸς τὸν υἱὸν αὐτοῦ· οὐκ εἶπεν· ἐξαπέστειλεν ὁ Θεὸς τὸν Θεὸν λόγον, ἀλλὰ λαμβάνει τὸ ὄνομα τὸ μηνύον τὰς δύο φύσεις. ἐπειδὴ γὰρ ὁ υἱὸς ἄνθρωπός ἐστι καὶ Θεός, λέγει· ἐξαπέστειλεν ὁ Θεὸς τὸν υἱὸν αὐτοῦ, γενώμενον (v. l. γενόμενον) ἐκ γυναικός· ἵνα ὅταν ἀκούσῃς τό, γενώμενον (v. l. γενόμενον) ἐκ γυναικός, εἶτα ἴδῃς τὸ ὄνομα τὸ προκείμενον, τὸ μηνύον τὰς φύσεις τὰς δύο, τὴν γέννησιν τὴν ἐκ τῆς ἁγίας παρθένου, υἱοῦ μὲν καλῆς· υἱὸν γὰρ ἐγέννησε Θεοῦ καὶ ἡ χριστοτόκος παρθένος, ἀλλ' ἐπειδήπερ ὁ υἱὸς τοῦ Θεοῦ διπλοῦς ἐστι κατὰ τὰς φύσεις, οὐκ ἐγέννησε μὲν τὸν υἱὸν τοῦ Θεοῦ, ἀλλ' ἐγέννησε τὴν ἀνθρωπότητα, ἥτις ἐστὶν υἱὸς διὰ τὸν συνημμένον υἱόν.

the Father also is not; for the Son, who is in nature, is not the Father nor is the Father the Son, who is in the nature of the Father and is the Son by nature; for in *prosôpon* he is something else. But they are not one thing and another but one only in *ousia* and in nature, without division, without separation, without distinction in all the things which appertain by nature unto the *prosôpon*; but he is other by the *prosôpon*. But certainly as regards the unity of the divinity and of the humanity it was not so. In whatsoever the *prosôpon* is by its nature, in those very things it exists by union as in one *prosôpon* even in another *ousia*. For he has taken him for the *prosôpon* and not for the *ousia* nor / for the nature in such wise as to become consubstantial with the Father or another son without there being one and the same Son. For the *prosôpon* of the divinity is the humanity and the *prosôpon* of the humanity the divinity; for it is the one in nature and the other in the union. Investigate therefore and see what it is that he has written: 'Whoever predicates two natures in the 'Son and who predicates each one of them by itself as in the 'remoteness of the distinction of God by himself and man by 'itself.'[1] For if I had said merely God and man and not 'two natures, one Christ', you would have had an opportunity to calumniate me for calling a man God and him man. Because of my having predicated two natures, man and God, I have not predicated two natures of man, though he is called God on account of the union, nor yet two natures of God, although he is called also flesh in the union. Thou hadst not [any ground] for the calumny, not even one, because I said that one Son and Christ indicate two natures; I said, however, that the Son is God and man. In the first place I said that the name of Christ and Son indicates two natures, and I came at the same time to speak also of 'the natures'; but since the Son is God and man, he is not predicated / solely but he is two natures. But thou art enraged against me because I have not called God the Word two natures by change of *ousia*; for it is not to be imagined otherwise than that I said that he came to be in the nature of the humanity and the Son was man in the union

[1] See p. 180, n. 1.

and not in nature. Has this that I said alarmed you, or that which he also has said, that the flesh, when it was born, was said to have been born? Because one considers the birth of his flesh clearly his; he too has thus said that the flesh was born but [that] he made it his own. What then have I said at all new, [in asserting] that it is said that, when it was born, there was born of the Virgin Mary a man, the Son of God, since this humanity was the Son of God by union with the Son and not by nature? For by the union God the Word made these [properties] of the flesh his own, not that the divinity was born in the birth of the flesh, nor again that the flesh was born naturally in the birth of the divinity, but [that] by the union with the flesh God is called flesh and the flesh by union with the Son, God the Word, is called Son; otherwise he has not been united, and we calumniate him [by denying his union]. Who has deceived you? For this is the agreement of men deceived. For there is this agreement concerning the two natures, that in fact [the word] 'Son' is indicative of two natures, indicating Christ and also Lord. 'The natures which have been combined in a true union are diverse, but the Son is one with them both,' the natures remaining without / confusion in the union : 'The diversities of the natures are not made void on account of the union.'[1] And again, it is by union that the flesh is son and not by nature . . .,[2] for 'that [3] wherewith he sits with the Father is not alien unto him'.[4]

Ambrose also has said :

> When the Son of God speaks by them both, because there are two natures in him, he speaks, but he speaks not continually in one manner. Reflect on him, now in glory and now in the sufferings of man, since as God he teaches the things of God, because he is the Word, but as man he teaches the things of man, since he speaks in our own *ousia*. He is *the living bread which came down from Heaven*;[5] this bread is the Body, as he has said: *This bread which I give unto you is my body.*[6] He it is who came down, he it is

---

[1] See p. 144, n. 1.   [2] The Syriac text indicates a lacuna here.
[3] *Sc.* the body.
[4] See p. 151, n. 1. There is no new paragraph marked here in the Syriac text.   [5] Jn. vi. 50 (P.).   [6] Jn. vi. 51.

whom the Father has sanctified and sent into the world. Does not the Scripture also teach you that not the divinity but the flesh has need of sanctification?[1]

How have you cited these things and anathematized mine? For I have not said anything else. . . .[2]

But Athanasius leaves thee not alone, saying:

These things did not take place artificially,[3] far from it! as some have supposed, but in reality, truly, our Saviour became man [and] the salvation of all men came about. For if he had been artificially[3] in the body, as they say— but that which is said [to be] artificially[3] is a fantasy— the salvation and the resurrection of men would have been found by him to have been fictitious as the impious Manes said; but our salvation exists not in fantasy [and our salvation takes place truly not for the body alone but for the whole man, for the soul and for the body].[4] Human therefore is that which [issued] from Mary, according to the Divine Scriptures and truly it belongs to our Saviour. . . .[5]

Let none admit the saying that God the Word is in the body artificially[3] but [that he is] God as [being] God the Word, who existed of old and exists eternally, and came to be in the bodily frame and exists also in the bodily frame, without having come forth out of his own *ousia* into the *ousia* of the

---

[1] Labbe (Mansi), iv. 1189-92; see below, p. 199, n. 1 (2).

[2] The Syriac copyist has here added a note to the following effect: 'From here twelve pages have been torn out and lost from the original by the troops of Bedr Khan Bey, when they captured the district of Dās in the year 2154 of the Greeks (= A. D. 1843).' See Introd. p. xi.

[3] Syr. *bash'ilû*, literally, 'metaphorically' (cp. Payne-Smith, *Thes. Syr.* 4008); the Greek version has θέσει and the Latin 'per extrinsecam Verbi praesentiam'.

[4] These words are added, as also by Nau, from the Greek text.

[5] Labbe (Mansi), iv. 1185 E: οὐ θέσει δὲ ταῦτα ἐγένετο, μὴ γένοιτο, ὥς τινες πάλιν ὑπέλαβον· ἀλλ' ὄντως ἀληθείᾳ γινομένου ἀνθρώπου τοῦ σωτῆρος, ὅλου τοῦ ἀνθρώπου σωτηρία ἐγένετο. εἰ γὰρ θέσει ἦν ἐν τῷ σώματι ὁ λόγος κατ' ἐκείνους· τὸ δὲ θέσει λεγόμενον φαντασίας ἐστί· δοκήσει εὑρίσκεται καὶ ἡ σωτηρία καὶ ἡ ἀνάστασις τῶν ἀνθρώπων λεγομένη, κατὰ τὸν ἀσεβέστατον Μανιχαῖον. ἀλλὰ μὴν οὐ φαντασίᾳ ἡ σωτηρία ἡμῶν, οὐδὲ σώματος μόνου, ἀλλ' ὅλου ἀνθρώπου, ψυχῆς καὶ σώματος, ἀληθῶς ἡ σωτηρία ἡμῶν γέγονεν· ἀνθρώπινον γὰρ φύσει τὸ ἐκ Μαρίας, κατὰ τὰς θείας γραφάς, καὶ ἀληθινὸν ἦν τοῦ σωτῆρος.

flesh, or having endured the birth of the flesh but from our *ousia*. . . .

For human is the nature which [issued] from Mary, as the Divine Scriptures say, and truly it belonged to our Saviour. For [as regards] the *ousia* of God the Word and as regards the *ousia* of man I dissociate myself from you, and not as regards the name; for I have said ' I object not to the appella-'tion of the Virgin, the Mother of Christ, but I know that she 'is to be honoured who received God, from whom the Lord of 'all came forth'.[1]

These things thou acceptest not; and how shall one leave thee alone / and believe thee, as one who sayest in this manner that God was born? 'Human therefore is he who [was born] of the blessed Mary,' although a thousand times thou wouldest dispute against Athanasius. God the Word existed in the body, in that which took the beginning of its coming into being from the blessed Mary; [yet] he took not the beginning of his coming into being. *In the beginning was the Word*, and God the Word exists eternally.

Confess that the natures exist, confess as thou hast been bidden, confess that God wished to rescue thee by means of the body and that the body was not changed from the *ousia* of God into the *ousia* of the flesh; it was formed and fashioned and grew and was perfected in the nature of men and was born, but from the bodily frame of our own form, of the seed of men; for it was of the seed of Abraham. Why dost thou treat these things of the body as hallucinations and makest void the things of the bodily frame and assignest them to God, in such wise as to bring the two generations[2] into doubt, in that thou makest even the generation of the bodily frame without beginning, from God the Father? For thou sayest that God the Father is body and man, both subject unto beginning and subject unto completion[3] and that he was

---

[1] Labbe (Mansi), iv. 1197 c: οὐ φθονῶ τῆς φωνῆς τῇ χριστοτόκῳ παρθένῳ· ἀλλ' οἶδα σεβασμίαν τὴν δεξαμένην Θεὸν, δι' ἧς προῆλθεν ὁ τῶν ὅλων Θεός (*v. l.* δεσπότης). No new paragraph is marked here in the Syriac text.

[2] *I.e.* the doctrine of the two generations, (1) that of God the Word 'begotten of the Father before all worlds'; (2) that of Christ, born in time of the Virgin Mary.   [3] Literally: 'under beginning and under completion'.

born of the Blessed Virgin, because he became man. How sayest thou 'the birth of the body'? For to God the Word alone thou dost attribute a generation from God the Father and from the Virgin. Speak clearly and confess the human nature, / [born] of the Blessed Mary, as the Divine Scriptures say. And that whereof inquiry was made is solved, that the *ousia* of God is not subject unto beginning and growth and completion, although it is so said through the revelation which [was made] little by little.[1] Wherefore makest thou void the names indicative of the humanity, but wouldest at the same time make us believe in the divinity, as if it were not unbelief [to say] the divinity came forth from her, just as thou makest void that which indicates that it derived not [its] beginning from her? And thou makest void the humanity which was born of the blessed Mary, for thou sayest that she bare not the man; since, as demons that deceive, showing that man is not man, thou confessest the man but [it is] God the Word and [then] thou confessest God the Word but [it is] the man. For thou deceivest men, changing the *ousias* from the names, for thou sayest 'man' and assertest the *ousia* of God the Word; and again thou sayest 'God the Word', and assertest the *ousia* of man, and then thou exaltest it with the name of God the Word. They have nought to say. 'It is the human nature which is from the Blessed Mary'; she is then the mother of the man who derived beginning from her and gradually advanced and was perfected. 'He is not by nature God, 'although he is so called on account of the revelation which '[was made] little by little....'[1] She is therefore on the one hand by nature the mother of the man, by revelation on the other hand she is the mother of God, if by revelation / and not by nature thou sayest that he was born of her; he then came forth united to him who was born of her in flesh. Wherefore dost thou in part assert and then make void these things, like miracle-mongers, who make visible things invisible and in semblance make things which are visible invisible?

---

[1] Nestorius here uses language drawn from a passage of Gregory of Nazienzum which was read at the Council, and which later he quotes frequently as supporting his arguments. See pp. 195 and 200 for the text.

Christianity exists in truth: deceive not . . . . ' He is human 'who was born of the Blessed Mary . . . .' ' He who took his 'beginning and gradually advanced and was perfected, is not 'by nature God, although he is so called on account of the 'revelation which [was made] little by little . . . .'[1]

Do you believe that they who say these things are [to be regarded] as truthful? Do you believe that which you have written—for you have written these things—or do you not believe them? Or do they say that Christ was a mere man, because they say these things concerning him? They say that God was not in the body artificially,[2] saying of God that he began and gradually advanced. For how is [either of] those which are united [to be] called mere? But thou considerest mere those which exist not both in *ousia*: the divinity which is not the humanity and the humanity which is not the divinity; but these things are foolish, as I suppose, in the mouth of one who[3] has said that the difference of the natures is not made void by the union. Thou sayest therefore that very thing which I also [say], commending [it]: that the divinity exists united to the humanity and the humanity exists in nature and united / to the divinity. And dost thou anathematize those things which [are found] in my [works]? Anathematize those which are thine, if it is right to call thine things of which thou art not confident that they are true, seeing that thou remainest in opposition to the Fathers and to the Divine Scriptures. For admirable and commendable is this discovery of heresy, wherein thou sayest [of] all these things that none confess them; thou alone hast set up thine own dogma in opposition to all men and thou dost suppose that they are held by all men. But, on the contrary, as one who has led all men through partiality, as partial thou art hated of all men.

In order that the truth which is preached by all men may be revealed, which surely indeed thou knowest, but which thou darest not say, it suffices therefore for those who seek to know thy mind to learn also of those things for which

---

[1] See p. 200, n. 1.   [2] See p. 192, n. 3.
[3] Literally: ' for one who . . . to say '.

thou blamest me, as though I were saying that the *ousias* are divided by remoteness in space, but participate together in equality by conjunction and by love and not by that whereby they naturally exist, [and as though] therefore we make a distinction in the doctrine of the natures,[1] for the divinity is one thing and the humanity another. But by the conjunction of these things there is not one and another in the *prosôpon*.[2]

Thus thou hast made men conceive of me, but it seems that I say the contrary of that which thou dost testify against me; for I indeed unite the *ousias*, but by the union / of the *ousias* I assert one *prosôpon* in one equality in everything whatsoever that appertains to the *prosôpon*, to which also both one *ousia* and another belongs, by separation and by being kept remote, but in the same [*prosôpon*]. Let us however also pass on as quickly as possible to other things, lest any one [there be for] whom in these things or by means of them there is blasphemy, and these also should be refuted . . . .
. . . .[3]

That therefore which we were saying: '*Fear not to take Mary [as] thy wife, for he who is born in her is of the Holy Spirit.*[4] For if thou sayest "was born in her" or "came "into being in her", that does no violence at all to the sense; for he who is born in her is of the Holy Spirit. Yet if we say that God the Word was born in the womb, it is indeed one thing [to say] "he was with him who was "born" and another "he will be born". For "he who is "born in her is of the Holy Spirit", that is, the Holy Spirit has created that which was in her. The Fathers therefore, in that they were acquainted with the Divine Scriptures, have seen that if "he who was born" is added to "he who was found in bodily frame", God the Word is found either [to be] the son of the Spirit or to have two Fathers. But if we say "He came into being", God the Word / is found to be the creature of the Holy Spirit. And, shunning the word "birth", they have laid down "He came down for us men and for our salvation and was

---

[1] Nau inserts a negative and translates: *ce [n'est pas] par la parole certes que nous séparons les natures.*

[2] There is no new paragraph marked here in the Syriac text.

[3] The copyist has added here in the margin the following note: 'Two lines have been left blank in the exemplar.' Nau suggests that they were so left for the title of the following section to be inserted in red ink, as elsewhere in the manuscript; cp. pp. 201, n. 3, 203, n. 2. [4] Matt. i. 20.

"found in bodily frame". What means "He was found "in bodily frame"? [Does it not mean] that he was not changed from the divinity into the flesh? For in "He was "found in bodily frame by the Holy Spirit" they concurred with the Evangelist. For the Evangelist also, when he came to the Incarnation,[1] shunned predicating the birth of the Word and laid down the being found in a bodily frame. How? Hear.

And the Word became flesh.[2] He said not that the Word was born through the flesh. For wherever indeed the Apostles and the Evangelists make mention of the birth they lay down that the Son was born of a woman.... Look well unto what has been written, I pray thee; where they employ the term "Son" and [the phrase] *He was born of a woman*, they lay down that *he was born*, but where they make mention of the Word, none indeed of them dares to say "the birth through the humanity". Hear the blessed John the Evangelist, when he came to the account of his Incarnation,[1] hear what he has said: *The Word became flesh*, that is, took the flesh, *and sojourned among us*, that is, put on our nature while living among us, *and we have seen his glory, the glory of the Son*; he said not "we have "seen the birth of the Word".'[3]

---

[1] Sc. ἐνανθρώπησις.   [2] Jn. i. 14.

[3] Labbe (Mansi), iv. 1197 E: ὁμοίως τοῦ αὐτοῦ, τετράδιον κδ'. Ὅπερ οὖν ἐλέγομεν· μὴ φοβηθῇς παραλαβεῖν Μαριὰμ τὴν γυναῖκά σου. τὸ γὰρ ἐν αὐτῇ γεννηθέν, εἴτε διὰ τοῦ ἑνὸν [? ἑνὸς ν], εἴτε διὰ τῶν δύο, τῷ νοήματι οὐδὲν λυμαίνεται· τὸ γὰρ ἐν αὐτῇ τεχθὲν ἐκ πνεύματός ἐστιν ἁγίου· ἐὰν εἴπομεν, ὅτι ὁ Θεὸς λόγος ἐγεννήθη ἐν τῇ σαρκί. ἄλλο γὰρ τὸ συνεῖναι τῷ γεννωμένῳ, καὶ ἄλλο τὸ γεννᾶσθαι· τὸ γὰρ ἐν αὐτῇ, φησί, γεννηθὲν ἐκ πνεύματός ἐστιν ἁγίου, τουτέστι, τὸ πνεῦμα τὸ ἅγιον ἔκτισε τὸ ἐν αὐτῇ. εἶδον οὖν οἱ πατέρες, ὡς ἐπιστήμονες τῶν θείων γραφῶν, ὅτι ἐὰν ἐπὶ τὸν σαρκωθέντα (v. l. τοῦ σαρκωθέντος) θῶμεν τὸν γεννηθέντα, εὑρίσκεται ὁ υἱὸς πνεύματος ὁ Θεὸς λόγος, ἢ δύο πατέρας ἔχων, ἢ δι' ἑνὸν εὑρεθήσεται ὁ Θεὸς λόγος κτίσμα τοῦ πνεύματος ὤν. φεύγοντες γοῦν τῆς γεννήσεως λέξιν ἔθηκαν· τὸν κατελθόντα δι' ἡμᾶς τοὺς ἀνθρώπους, καὶ διὰ τὴν ἡμετέραν σωτηρίαν, σαρκωθέντα. τί ἐστι σαρκωθέντα; οὐ τραπέντα ἀπὸ θεότητος εἰς σάρκα· τῷ σαρκωθέντα ἐκ πνεύματος ἁγίου ἠκολούθησαν τῷ εὐαγγελιστῇ. καὶ γὰρ ὁ εὐαγγελιστὴς ἐλθὼν εἰς τὴν ἐνανθρώπησιν ἔφυγε γέννησιν εἰπεῖν ἐπὶ τοῦ λόγου, καὶ τέθηκε σάρκωσιν. ποῦ; ἄκουσον· καὶ ὁ λόγος σὰρξ ἐγένετο. οὐκ εἶπεν· ὁ λόγος διὰ σαρκὸς ἐγεννήθη· ὅπου μὲν γὰρ μνημονεύουσιν ἢ οἱ ἀπόστολοι, ἢ οἱ εὐαγγελισταὶ τοῦ υἱοῦ, τιθέασιν, ὅτι ἐγεννήθη ἐκ γυναικός. πρόσεχε τῷ λεγομένῳ, παρακαλῶ· ὅπου μὲν λέγουσι τὸ ὄνομα τοῦ υἱοῦ, καὶ ὅτι ἐγεννήθη ἐκ γυναικός, τιθέασι τὸ ἐγεννήθη· ὅπου δὲ μνημονεύουσι τοῦ λόγου, οὐδεὶς αὐτῶν ἐτόλμησεν εἰπεῖν γέννησιν διὰ τῆς ἀνθρωπότητος. ἄκουε· ὁ μακάριος Ἰωάννης ὁ εὐαγγελιστὴς ἐλθὼν εἰς τὸν λόγον, καὶ τὴν ἐνανθρώπησιν αὐτοῦ, ἄκουσον οἷά φησιν· ὁ λόγος σὰρξ ἐγένετο. τουτέστιν, ἀνέλαβε σάρκα, καὶ ἐσκήνωσεν ἐν ἡμῖν, τουτέστιν, ἡμετέραν ἐνεδύσατο φύσιν, καὶ ἐνῴκησεν ἐν ἡμῖν· καὶ ἐθεασάμεθα τὴν δόξαν αὐτοῦ τοῦ υἱοῦ· οὐκ εἶπεν· ἐθεασάμεθα τὴν γέννησιν τοῦ λόγου.

So then I have stated the reason which I should have supposed satisfactory, / on account of which the Fathers said in their laying down of the Faith not that he was born of the Holy Spirit and the Virgin Mary, but that he was made flesh, in order that they might not say that the Holy Spirit was Father or that which was created [was] Son, but rather that he was made flesh by the Holy Spirit and of the Virgin Mary, in order that they might attach 'became' to the flesh, because he was made flesh. But as regards the history of [his] being made, what do you say? Speak openly. Reprimand those who have clearly blasphemed, [asserting that] 'He was born of the Holy Spirit'. If he was born, the Holy Spirit was the Father of the Son or the creator of God the Word; yet these, I have said, [are things] which neither the Fathers have said nor do I say. Have I blasphemed in saying these things? Or have I surely calumniated the Fathers? If it is [possible] for you to show that the Fathers have said these things, speak openly. Which of these things? Is God the Word a creature or the son of the Holy Spirit? And if he is not a creature, flesh which is fleshly, then is he no more a creature of the Holy Spirit; speak openly. 'He was made flesh' means that he was in every sense[1] made flesh in his nature, and it was not another who was made flesh; he is said to have been made flesh. But he was made flesh in his own *ousia*, in the flesh which came into being and was born of the Holy Spirit. For 'he was born', as thou sayest, is contrary to what thou hast said; since, when he was born, the flesh is said to have been born, as though he made it the birth of his own flesh, whereas he was not / made flesh in his [own] self but in its own *ousia*. Therefore 'he was made flesh' and 'he was born' do not signify the same thing, and for this reason they have laid down 'he was made flesh' and not 'he was born'. [This is clear], since they have taken the word 'became' for the flesh; and for this reason also the Evangelist said that he became flesh and said not that he was born, so that by 'became' he limited not God the Word. But, as touching the flesh which came into being, it became his flesh. And

---

[1] Literally: 'by every means'.

God the Word sojourned among us; God the Word 'became' not, for he existed.

And hear them; for you would not disclaim these men whom you have brought in accusation against me. Speak then, O Ambrose, disregard not him who is oppressed; be not at the beck and call of the calumniators,[1] and condemn not innocent blood before it has been heard. I say that the flesh came into being of the Virgin Mary [and] appertained not unto God the Word; for I confess him neither made nor come to be nor created. Yet all these rise up against me like swords, nor even are they willing to hear my speech entirely, and in regard to these things they cite thee among the witnesses. Of death I was not afraid, [I] who have been thus calumniated, but of having been condemned as impious in thy *prosôpon*, thine! I have spoken in accordance with Ambrose and I deny not aught that I have said, although they have drawn the sword against me. / This have I said: 'In consequence of these things he was ready to come into 'being of a woman, according to the [word] "became"'. Thou[2] limitest not the divinity, but the body which was

---

[1] Syr. 'in the mouth of the calumniators', probably a literal translation of the Gk. ἐπὶ στόματος as used in 4 Kings xxiii, 35 (LXX).

[2] *Viz.* Ambrose. The following are the passages from Ambrose read at the Council to which Nestorius refers. See Labbe (Mansi), iv. 1189 D, E:

(1) Εἰ ἐμοὶ οὐ πιστεύουσι, πιστεύσωσι τῷ ἀποστόλῳ λέγοντι· ὅτε δὲ ἦλθε τὸ πλήρωμα τοῦ χρόνου, ἐξαπέστειλεν ὁ Θεὸς τὸν υἱὸν αὐτοῦ, γενόμενον ἐκ γυναικός, γενόμενον ὑπὸ νόμον· τὸν υἱὸν αὐτοῦ φησίν, οὐχ ἕνα ἐκ πολλῶν· οὐ κοινόν, ἀλλ᾽ αὐτοῦ· τῆς ἀϊδίου γεννήσεως τὴν ἰδιότητα ἐσήμανε. τοῦτον μετὰ ταῦτα γενόμενον ἐκ γυναικὸς κατασκευάζει, ὅπως τὸ γενέσθαι οὐ τῇ θεότητι, ἀλλὰ τῷ προσληφθέντι σώματι περιγράψῃ. γενόμενον ἐκ γυναικός, διὰ τῆς προσληφθείσης σαρκός· γενόμενον ὑπὸ νόμον, διὰ τῆς τοῦ νόμου φυλακῆς· ἡ γὰρ θεϊοτάτη αὐτοῦ γέννησις πρὸ τοῦ νόμου, αὕτη δὲ μετὰ τὸν νόμον.

(2) Σιωπήσωσι τοίνυν αἱ ἀπὸ τῶν λόγων μάταιαι ζητήσεις, ὅτι ἡ τοῦ Θεοῦ βασιλεία, καθὼς γέγραπται, οὐκ ἐν πειθοῖ λόγων ἀνθρωπίνων ἐστίν, ἀλλ᾽ ἐν ἀποδείξει δυνάμεως. φυλάξωμεν τὴν διαφορὰν τῆς θεότητος καὶ τῆς σαρκός. εἷς ἐν ἑκατέρῳ λαλεῖ ὁ τοῦ Θεοῦ υἱός, ὅτι ἐν αὐτῷ ἡ ἑκατέρα φύσις ἐστίν. ὁ αὐτὸς λαλεῖ, καὶ οὐκ ἐν ἑνὶ πάντοτε διαλέγεται τρόπῳ. πρόσχες ἐν αὐτῷ νυνὶ μὲν δόξαν Θεοῦ, νυνὶ δὲ ἀνθρώπου πάθη. ὅτι ὡς Θεὸς διδάσκει τὰ θεῖα, ἐπεὶ λόγος ἐστίν· ὡς δὲ ἄνθρωπος, λέγει τὰ ἀνθρώπινα, ἐπεὶ ἐν τῇ ἐμῇ οὐσίᾳ διελέγετο. οὗτός ἐστιν ὁ ἄρτος ὁ ζῶν, ὃς κατέβη ἐξ οὐρανοῦ. οὗτος ὁ ἄρτος ἡ σάρξ ἐστί, καθὼς καὶ αὐτὸς ἔφη· οὗτος ὁ ἄρτος, ὃν ἐγὼ δώσω, ἡ σάρξ μού ἐστιν. οὗτός ἐστιν ὁ καταβάς. οὗτός ἐστιν, ὃν ὁ πατὴρ ἡγίασε, καὶ ἔπεμψεν εἰς τὸν κόσμον. οὐδὲ αὐτὸ τὸ γράμμα ἡμᾶς διδάσκει τοῦ ἁγιασμοῦ τὴν θεότητα χρείαν ἐσχηκέναι, ἀλλὰ τὴν σάρκα.

assumed: namely, he who descended is the same whom the Father has sanctified and sent into the world. Does not also the Scripture teach you that the divinity was not in need of sanctification but the flesh? If then they have deceived, they have deceived themselves and not me.

And thou also, O Gregory the divine, what then [sayest thou]? What opinion hast thou concerning these things? I ask, not that I know not, but because in thine own name they desire to crush the truth. What knowest thou of him who was by the Holy Spirit of the Virgin Mary, who began and gradually advanced and was fulfilled? I say not in the *prosôpon*, but in the *ousia*. What else at all wouldest thou concede except something which thou hast conceded unto them in written works? [To wit], that the man who was taken .... 'He indeed who begins and grows and is per-'fected is not God, although he is so called on account of 'the revelation which [was made] little by little.'[1] 'For one 'and another were those of which our Saviour was, if the in-'visible and the visible are not the same, God on the one hand 'who was man and man on the other who was made God.'[2]

But speak thou also, O wise Athanasius; for thou also hast been calumniated with many calumnies such as these and hast endured [much] at the hands of the Arians, on behalf of / the tradition of the Son, God the Word. What opinion hast thou concerning [the statement] that 'he was born of the Holy Spirit of the Virgin Mary'? In the nature and not in the *prosôpon* which [results] from the union ' we say 'that one and the same Son and none other was born of 'Holy Mary'. But [we call] this one and him only, who was born a son, Christ, God the Word together with his flesh, and the same one flesh with God the Word. But 'in *ousia* God 'the Word is of God the Father, and the flesh is the flesh

---

[1] Labbe (Mansi), iv. 1193 B: τὸ γὰρ ἠργμένον, ἢ προκόπτον, ἢ τελειούμενον, οὐ Θεός, κἂν διὰ τὴν κατὰ μικρὸν αὔξησιν οὕτω λέγηται. Nestorius throughout reads 'revelation' where the Greek text in Mansi has αὔξησιν and the Latin *incrementum*.

[2] Labbe (Mansi), iv. 1192 D: καὶ εἰ δεῖ συντόμως εἰπεῖν, ἄλλο μὲν καὶ ἄλλο τὰ ἐξ ὧν ὁ σωτήρ, εἴπερ μὴ ταὐτὸν τὸ ἀόρατον τῷ ὁρατῷ, καὶ τὸ ἄχρονον τῷ ὑπὸ χρόνον· οὐκ ἄλλος δὲ καὶ ἄλλος, μὴ γένοιτο· τὰ γὰρ ἀμφότερα, ἐν τῇ συγκράσει, Θεοῦ μὲν ἐνανθρωπήσαντος, ἀνθρώπου δὲ θεωθέντος, ἢ ὅπως ἄν τις ὀνομάσειε.

'which he put on from the Virgin' that it might come to be. We say not one and another, for there is one *prosôpon* of both natures. But he who by nature came into being by the Holy Spirit, what was he? And what was his nature? And of what nature was the Virgin, his mother? For inquiry is made of this. Hear them all. .... I have said he is man who was of Mary, according to the Divine Scriptures, and that he was truly our Saviour. 'For if artificially[1] the Word was in 'the body, as they say, he then who is said [to be] arti-'ficially[1] is a phantasy.[2] The salvation and the resurrec-'tion of men will be found to have been fictitious, as the 'impious Manes has said; but our salvation is not in phantasy 'nor in the body alone but in the whole man: to the soul 'and to the body truly salvation belongs. Human therefore 'was he who was of Mary, as the Divine Scriptures say, and 'he truly it was who .... [was] our Saviour ....'

/.... So indeed we name Christ as concerning the flesh, owing to the conjunction with God the Word, recognizing him since he is visible as man.

'Hear Paul, who says in two [passages]: *Of the Jews is Christ as concerning the flesh, he who is God over all.*[3] He confesses the man in the first place and then, owing to his conjunction with God the Word, he calls him who is visible God, that none may suppose that Christianity is the worship of a man.'[4]

That none may accuse me anywhere, take heed and look well, in what sense I say 'a mere man who is far removed from divinity'. I say 'Christ who [is] in flesh', as also I predicate the same in the divinity. For I have not said 'a fleshly Christ', but 'Christ who [is] in flesh', I speak of the flesh of Christ by reason of the conjunction with God the

---

[1] See p. 192, n. 3.   [2] Syr. *pantāsyâ* = Gk. φαντασία.   [3] Cp. Rom. ix. 5.

[4] Labbe (Mansi), iv. 1200 C: ὁμοίως τοῦ αὐτοῦ τετράδιον ιε'. εἰς δόγμα. οὕτω καὶ τὸν κατὰ σάρκα Χριστὸν ἐκ τῆς πρὸς Θεὸν λόγον συναφείας Θεὸν ὀνομάζομεν, φαινόμενον εἰδότες ὡς ἄνθρωπον. ἄκουσον τοῦ Παύλου ἀμφότερα κηρύττοντος· ἐξ Ἰουδαίων, φησίν, ὁ Χριστὸς τὸ κατὰ σάρκα, ὁ ὢν ἐπὶ πάντων Θεός. ὁμολογεῖ τὸν ἄνθρωπον πρότερον, καὶ τότε τῇ τοῦ Θεοῦ συναφείᾳ θεολογεῖ τὸ φαινόμενον, ἵνα μηδεὶς ἀνθρωπολατρείαν (v. l. ἀνθρωπολατρεῖν) τὸν χριστιανισμὸν ὑποπτεύσῃ.

Nau suggests that the space of four lines at the head of this quotation in the Syriac was left for the title to be inserted in red ink. Cp. pp. 196, n. 2, 203, n. 2.

Word, as being indeed united to and not distinguished from God the Word. Nor indeed with equality was it united but to God the Word himself. And of him who was visible in *ousia*, I said that he was of the Jews and not God the Word, since I confess that the man in respect of *ousia* and of nature is of the Jews and not God the Word in respect of nature. And I said ' man in nature apart from the nature of God the ' Word ' / but ' he is God by virtue of that union which came ' about in the *prosôpon* '. Art thou angered with me on account of this?

But hear what Athanasius proclaims unto thee: ' Human ' then is he who [was born] of Mary, according to the Divine ' Scriptures; neither in semblance nor in phantasy is he our ' salvation and the resurrection of men, as the impious Manes ' said; nor only of body but of the whole man, of soul and of body, became he truly our salvation.'[1] Human therefore was he who [was born] of Mary, according to the Holy Scriptures and truly was it he who was our Saviour. . . . . Why therefore deniest thou our salvation? Why therefore have you condemned as impious whosoever denies not but confesses [it]? You are then either denying that he is human, as the Manichaeans, or, if you deny not, you cannot condemn him who denies not but confesses [it]. Hear Gregory proclaiming that he who was taken was human; for ' he who begins ' and gradually advances and is perfected ' is not God ' although ' he is so called on account of the revelation which [was made] little by little '.[2] Seest thou that he says that he who was taken, who begins and gradually advances and is perfected, is man by nature but God by revelation? What then is the obscurity before your eyes, that you see not these things? But if you were to accuse these my [opinions], you ought not to contrast the one [statement] with the other, since it is [useful] in supporting them. / But if you accept these and such like things, it is not right to write of them as impious. I have brought these my charges against those who deny the humanity which has been taken from us and who confess as the Manichaeans; and not simply that, but I have laid down

---

[1] Cp. p. 192, n. 5. [2] See p. 200, n. 1.

the properties of the natures and of the one *prosôpon*: and [it is] moreover in some respects two, in that on the one hand which concerns the natures, but in other respects in the union. And thou hast accepted the *prosôpon* of those men,[1] as if indeed thou wert one of them, whereas thou art in everything the enemy of those who accept my words. For we take from these men and we cast before thee [our doctrine], proclaiming that our salvation has not taken place in phantasy, O men. 'Human is the nature which is of Mary, as the Divine Scrip-'tures say . . . . ' He indeed who begins and gradually 'advances and is perfected has not become God, although 'he is so called on account of the manifestation which [took 'place] little by little. . . . .'[2]

But even as we call God the Creator of all and Moses a god, for [it is written]: *I have made thee a god unto Pharaoh,*[3] and Israel the son of God, [for it is written]: *Israel is my son, my first-born,*[4] and as we call Saul the anointed, for [it is written]: *I will not put forth mine hand against him, seeing that he is the Lord's anointed,*[5] and [as we say] similarly also of Cyrus: *Thus saith the Lord to his anointed, to Cyrus,*[6] and [as we called] the Babylonians consecrated, [saying]: *I indeed / have commanded them; they are consecrated ones, and I shall bring them*[7]; so also we call our Lord Christ and God and Son and consecrated and Christ; yet, whereas on the one hand the participation in the names is like, the honour on the other is not the same.[8]

---

[1] *Viz.* Gregory and Athanasius.

[2] The copyist has here added the following note in the margin: 'These lines in the original are blank,' from which Nau supposes that the title of the following section has fallen out; cp. pp. 196, n. 2, and 201, n. 4.

[3] Exod. vii. 1.   [4] Exod. iv. 22 (P.).   [5] 1 Sam. xxiv. 6 (Syr. 7).
[6] Is. xlv. 1 (P.).   [7] Is. xiii. 3.

[8] Labbe (Mansi), iv. 1200 D : ὁμοίως τοῦ αὐτοῦ, τετράδιον κζ'. ἀλλ' ὥσπερ ἐλέγομεν Θεὸν τὸν πάντων δημιουργόν, καὶ Θεόν, τὸν Μωϋσέα· Θεὸν γάρ, φησί, τέθεικά σε τοῦ Φαραώ, καὶ υἱὸν τὸν Ἰσραὴλ τοῦ Θεοῦ· υἱὸς γάρ, φησί, πρωτότοκός μου ὁ Ἰσραήλ. καὶ ὥσπερ ἐλέγομεν Χριστὸν τὸν Σαούλ· οὐ μὴ γάρ, φησίν, ἐπιβαλῶ τὴν χεῖρά μου ἐπ' αὐτῷ, ὅτι Χριστὸς κυρίου ἐστί. καὶ τὸν Κῦρον ὡσαύτως· τάδε λέγει, φησί, κύριος τῷ Χριστῷ μου Κύρῳ· καὶ τὸν Βαβηλόνιον ἅγιον· ἐγὼ γάρ, φησί, συντάξω αὐτοῖς· ἡγιασμένοι εἰσί, κἀγὼ ἄγω αὐτούς. οὕτω λέγωμεν καὶ τὸν δεσπότην Χριστὸν καὶ Θεὸν καὶ υἱὸν καὶ ἅγιον καὶ Χριστόν. ἀλλ' ἡ μὲν κοινωνία τῶν ὀνομάτων ὁμοία, οὐχ ἡ αὐτὴ δὲ ἀξία.

Wherein do you blame these things, O calumniators and wise men? Because I have said that, even as we call God the creator of all and Moses a god, so also [have we called] our Lord Christ God of all and Maker? But, because Moses is called a god and Christ God and moreover Creator, we do not speak of Moses himself as of Christ; or, because Moses was a god unto Pharaoh, do we say that he was moreover the Maker of all? Far from it! For community of names constitutes not community of honour and equality. For the honour of the Creator of all and that of Moses are diverse: that of the one on the one hand [being] that of the creator, that of the other on the other hand [being] that of the creature which has been commanded to become the chief. Thus also both our Lord and Israel are called son; yet the community of names constitutes not a community of honour: but thus[1] [the one] is by nature God, consubstantial with the Father, Creator and Maker of all; but not the other. So also [with] every single one of the rest of them. As we say of God 'Creator of all', so also do we say of our Lord Jesus Christ 'God and Son and Christ'; for as regards each one of these things which are called by this name, there is therein a difference between the nature which created / all and the honours which are surely bestowed; for the rank and the honour which is more excellent than all is the [divine] nature. For I have said that the name of 'Christ' and [that] of 'Son' are indicative of the two natures, of the divinity and of the humanity—[a thing] with which there is nothing equal in those things which have been said—in such wise that it is not right to take heed of the name but of that which it indicates. Christ on the one hand is God of all and Creator; on the other hand Moses also is called a god, but he is not called in the same way a god nor is he conceived as God.

But they suppose, then, to overwhelm me on the subject of the humanity, [saying] that, if he, who was of Mary, was human nature, as the Holy Scriptures [assert and] yet was God by manifestation and not by nature, thou callest one of them by grace God and Son and holy. But in answer to you

[1] See crit. n., p. 400.

I say this only, that, if you, like Gregory and Athanasius, confess him who was of Mary and who began and gradually advanced and was perfected, [to be] human nature, while [he was] God by revelation and distinct from all men through the purpose concerning that name[1] whereof he made use for the distinction, to the same extent the Creator is [one] with the creature because there is one *prosôpon*—thus I also confess. But if you confess not the human nature which began and gradually advanced and was brought to fullness, as Athanasius and Gregory have said, / then you are not to be excused as [one of the] orthodox, but stand forth with the Manichaeans. But Gregory, Athanasius and Ambrose ask you if the flesh is consubstantial with us and if the soul is consubstantial with us. Whatever it is, it is also in the *ousia* of man; therefore it is man, distinct from us in honour and in rank. In such wise as Israel is called son and as Moses is called a god, so likewise Christ [is to be called] God, [but] not by nature, and Son of God, [but] not by nature. And as God himself was made man but in the nature of men, he was made man in him who [issued forth] from Mary.[2] But if he has not been made man in man, he has saved him[self] and not us; but if he has saved us, he has been made man in us and has been in the likeness of men and has been found in *schêma* as a man and has not himself been man.

Say then these and such like things openly. Why then do you make pretence of not speaking of these things, although you dispute concerning them as if [they were] the things which you are saying, whereas you are not saying them? And those things which you say you say in *schêma*, and you are unwilling to call him who was of Mary human nature, as is said in the Scriptures. Him who calls him not human nature, like one of

---

[1] *Viz.* the name which he took for the purpose of exalting it above all other names.

[2] This is one of the very few passages in which at first sight Nestorius seems to suggest something very like 'Nestorianism' as commonly understood; cp. p. 224, n. 3. But that this was not his intention is clear from pp. 225, 312-15. It is interesting that here, immediately after the suspicious passage, he claims for his doctrine that which 'Nestorianism' has usually been held to lack—the provision for a universal atonement.

men, of the natural body of our fathers, whence we also have come in soul and in body—and he has / all [the qualities] of the rational part of the soul except sin—him Gregory accuses [in the same way] as the Manichaeans: for 'he who begins and 'gradually advances and is perfected is not God, although he 'is so called on account of the revelation which [was made] 'little by little'.[1] In that which concerns the humanity he is not by nature divine but by revelation. But in the nature of the divinity there exists a great difference between those who are called gods or lords or christs, but in the humanity he is like them all, and there is one *prosôpon* in two natures. He is God and he is Lord and he is Christ; for he makes not use of a *prosôpon* which has undergone[2] a division but makes use of it as of his [own] *prosôpon*. For all the things appertaining to the *ousia* are his by virtue of the union and not by nature. Or do you not admit that Christ in his divinity is God and maker of all? He is not like Moses, although Moses is called a god. For community of names constitutes not community of honour; for there is one honour of the servant and one of the lord, although in that which concerns the body he is distinct[3] from the servants.

But if thou sayest that the body and the nature of the body and the soul, rational and intelligent, abide without change and without transformation, but dost not admit the things which indicate the soul and the body, [some] of them in the union and [others] of them in the nature, taking / all of them of one nature, thou beliest the truth, making yea nay and nay yea. And in order to deceive thou callest him who was of Mary human nature, as the Divine Scriptures [affirm], and accountest not among his own [qualities] according to nature those of the humanity. But in virtue of the *prosôpon* thou raisest him above all humanity, in such wise that he on the one hand, who is eternally even as he is and began not nor gradually advanced nor was perfected, is one, but he who began and gradually advanced and was perfected both in the

---

[1] See p. 200, n. 1.   [2] Literally: 'has acquired'.
[3] Bedjan so prints the Syriac text, adding *sic* in the margin: Nau inserts a negative and translates: *il ne diffère pas des serviteurs*.

union and in the manifestation in one *prosôpon*, is another, God who was made man and man who was made God. He was not transformed and changed from his divinity, just as also the humanity of Christ is not changed in nature from [that of] men except in honour and in *prosôpon*; for he is God of all and Lord and Son; and in all the things which are the divinity in *ousia*, in them exists the humanity in honour, not by another honour but by the same as that of him who took the *prosôpon*: the humanity making use of the *prosôpon* of the divinity and the divinity of the *prosôpon* of the humanity, since for this it has been taken and for this he has taken it, not indeed so that we should not confess him who was taken but that we might confess him. Confess then the taker as he took, and the taken as he was taken, wherein [each is] one and in another, and wherein [there is] one and not two, after the same manner as the manner of the Trinity.

/ *Likewise from the same, from the fifteenth roll.*
Have this mind in you which was also in Jesus Christ, who, being in the likeness of God, emptied himself and took the likeness of a servant.[1] He says not: 'Have this mind in you which was also in God the Word, who being in the likeness of God took the likeness of a servant,' but he puts the name 'Christ', which is indicative of the two natures, avoiding all risk,[2] and he names him the likeness of a servant which he took and [that] of God, those things which are said in regard to the duality of the natures being divided without blame.[3]

It is also right after this to examine the opinion of every one and first mine; [to ascertain] if it is, as he[4] says, that I say one thing and another and distinguish the divinity somehow as it were by remoteness of place, and confess not that he is one and the same. Yet, avoiding all risk,[2] I have said that he

---

[1] Phil. ii. 5–7.   [2] Literally: 'without risk'.

[3] Labbe (Mansi), iv. 1201 A: ὁμοίως τοῦ αὐτοῦ, τετράδιον ιε΄. τοῦτο φρονείσθω ἐν ὑμῖν, ὃ καὶ ἐν Χριστῷ Ἰησοῦ· ὃς ἐν μορφῇ Θεοῦ ὑπάρχων ἑαυτὸν ἐκένωσε, μορφὴν δούλου λαβών. οὐκ εἶπε· τοῦτο φρονείσθω ἐν ὑμῖν, ὃ καὶ ἐν τῷ Θεῷ λόγῳ, ὃς ἐν μορφῇ Θεοῦ ὑπάρχων, μορφὴν δούλου ἔλαβεν. ἀλλὰ λαβὼν τὸ Χριστός, ὡς τῶν δύο φύσεων προσηγορίαν σημαντικήν (v. l. ὡς τῆς τῶν δύο φύσεων προσηγορίας σημαντικόν), ἀκινδύνως αὐτὸν καὶ δούλου μορφὴν ἀναλαβεῖν, καὶ Θεὸν ὀνομάζει, τῶν λεγομένων εἰς τὸ τῶν φύσεων ἀλήπτως μεριζομένων διπλοῦν.

[4] *Viz.* Cyril.

named 'the likeness of a servant' and 'God'; we understand neither that which took nor that which was taken in distinction but that which was taken in that which took, while that which took is conceived in that which was taken; for that which took, therefore, is not conceived of itself, nor again that which was taken, so that he is not [conceived to have been] in the very *prosôpon* of that which took and of that which was taken.[1]

/ Thou dost censure me, therefore, not for this but because I distinguish the properties of the union which belongs to each of the natures, in such wise that each one of them subsists in its *hypostasis*, and I say not that they are referred to God the Word as one who is both of them in *ousia*; or that the [properties] of the flesh were taken upon God without [their] *hypostasis*,[2] that he might be revealed only in the likeness of the flesh and that he might make use of and suffer all the [things] of the flesh, whether he was changed into the nature of the flesh or they[3] were mixed in one nature, or [whether] the [properties] of the flesh are referred to the *ousia* of God by confusion or by alteration or by natural composition for the fulfilment of the natural composition, in order that he might suffer passibly the sufferings of the body, without the bodily frame's fulfilling any purpose in its own nature in the dispensation on our behalf, and without its performing human actions, either by the will of the soul or by the human imagination, or by the sensibility of the body, but by the imagination and by the will of God; still by the sensibility of God he is sensible of all human things. But in name alone he has a body, without *hypostasis* and without activity; and for this reason thou callest him man as something superfluous only in word and in name, in that thou art not content to predicate the

---

[1] The phrase 'so that he is not' must clearly be taken as expressing a corollary of the view which Nestorius is rejecting.

[2] Here Nestorius refuses *totidem verbis* to deny the human *hypostasis* of Christ; but see p. 156, n. 2. This passage surely makes it all the clearer that Nestorius used the word *hypostasis* in its older sense as practically equivalent to what Cyril called *ousia*. The two words are evidently synonymous in the sentence below beginning: 'But in name alone he has a body...' See too p. 218, n. 3.

[3] *Viz.* the two natures.

ousia and activity of man or the existence of two natures, each of them with properties and *hypostases* and *ousia*.

But some one perhaps will say: 'It is because thou con-'fessest not that / God the Word and Christ are the same 'thing.'

For this reason then thou [1] dost censure those who say that Christ is one [thing] and God the Word another, apart from Christ. If then I said 'Christ' and 'God the Word another, apart from Christ', or 'Christ apart from God the Word', you would have said well; but if I have not said and do not say this but confess otherwise, still now saying this same thing, pervert not that which I say, and in the very same thing thou wilt find the distinction of whatsoever it [2] indicates. Now I have said that the name 'Christ' is indicative of two natures, of God indeed one nature [and of man one nature [3]]. One indeed is the name which indicates two and another [that] which indicates one which is not anything else. Even as if a man were to say of man too that the name 'man' indicates one thing and 'rational soul' another. [It is] not that man is one thing and the soul another apart from man. For he who says 'man' speaks not of him [as] without a soul, because except for a soul he is not man. But the [name] 'man' on the one hand is indicative of the union of two natures, of the soul and of the body, but that [4] of a nature, for the nature is one thing and the union of the natures another. What then? God the Word is nothing else apart from Christ, nor Christ apart from God the Word. Why dost thou make use of the names indistinguishably, as though the same thing were indicated by this or / by that? [5]

But 'Thou makest a division, so that one says not "God the Word" but "Christ", as though "Christ" were one thing and "God the Word" another.'

But hear also from us: He is not one thing and another; for he would be one thing and another if Christ were apart

---

[1] *Viz.* Cyril.
[2] *I.e.* the name 'Christ' as used by Nestorius.
[3] These words are added by Nau to complete the antithesis.
[4] *Viz.* the soul.
[5] There is no new paragraph marked here in the Syriac text.

from God the Father. But, if there is not the very same thing in *ousia*, [this] indicates one thing and another, [for example], the visible and the invisible; and those things from which Christ is [formed] exist in their own *ousias* and God the Word is not in the nature of both of them. But thou confessest distinct natures of the divinity and of the humanity but one Christ from them both; thou sayest not that God the Word himself has different natures but one; but there is a distinction between him and his concomitant. Thou sayest therefore that Christ himself is one thing and another, because thou predicatest of him the different natures of divinity and of humanity. But the nature of God the Word is one, not different natures. Or, as I have said, [the truth is] that he is not one thing and another, in that Christ exists not apart from God the Word nor again God the Word apart from Christ, but he indicates one thing and another, because Christ is of God the Word and of humanity by union, whereas God the Word is one nature and not of both natures, and it is not his by union to become God the Word.

/ And thou too bearest witness, albeit unwillingly, to these words which I say; but forsooth thou bearest witness when thou sayest that the natures which have been combined in the union are different, whereas one Christ [issues] from them both. For if thou indicatest not the one and the other, wherefore hast thou not been the first to make bold to say that which thou wouldest persuade me to say: that one [issues] from them both, God the Word? But thou wast unable to speak or I was unable unmistakably[1] to hear thine impiety, and for this reason thou hast passed it by without indicating it; thou hast been constrained clearly to confess the truth, so that thou art thereby [proved to be] without reverence and hast no place of refuge. The one and the other indicate one thing and another, but it is not one thing and another: for it is one thing and another from which our Saviour [issues], but he is not one thing and another—far from it!—as he also is in respect to the Trinity. But thou referrest to God the Word the things of the flesh, so that he sees and speaks and suffers

---

[1] Literally: 'nakedly'.

the things of the flesh, but only as surely making use of the flesh, as the Arians say when they attribute the activities and the sufferings to the divinity naturally, and as Apollinarius [says when he maintains] that instead of the intelligence it [1] performs naturally the operations of the soul and of the body. Thus this man [2] also makes use of God the Word in all of them, both in the body and in the intelligent soul, that he may suffer the sufferings of the body and perform the activities of the rational soul, [making them] the manner of life and conduct of God the Word. And the properties of his own *prosôpon* thou dost attribute to the nature / of God the Word and not to the *prosôpon* of the humanity, which is moved to and fro by the humanity in accordance with the nature of man, but [according to you] by God the Word.

But what is [this] whole man who neither acts nor is acted upon in accordance with the nature of man? In name indeed alone is he man and in name body and in name rational soul, he who is not moved to and fro in the nature of his being, neither as soul by purpose and will nor again as body by sensibility of soul, but [in whom] God the Word has been established to become the will and the purpose and the sensibility in the body and in the soul in such wise that God the Word should act and suffer sensibly these bodily [sensations] and those of the soul: anger and wrath and lusts and fear and dread and thoughts and operations and judgement and voluntary choice; all these things he does and suffers in the place of the soul and in the place of the body, in such wise that by the victory of God the Word won in suffering and nature that nature which had been guilty was victorious, since he had given unto it his own victory, in order that it might be victorious through and by him who had assumed it for his nature. All these things are changes of the nature of God the Word, being naturally given to him that he might suffer, and [that] thou mightest predicate of him a nature passible and changeable and variable. For he, who by his nature was impassible but who through a passible nature became the nature of the other, was passible and corruptible

---

[1] *Viz.* the Word.   [2] *Viz.* Cyril.

and variable; for he, who by nature is impassible and / unchangeable and invariable, does not even suffer in any manner in the human nature, since it is not his to suffer in his nature. But if thou sayest that the one, whose it is not to suffer in his nature, has suffered in nature, it is a folly to say that he has suffered in another nature; but he who comes to folly surely deceives, and like the Manichaeans makes our very salvation to have taken place in deception.

Speak; what say you? Which is the party of the orthodox: [that] of those who teach that God the Word is unchangeable and invariable or [that] of those who predicate of him the human nature [received] from Mary, who consider him a rational and intelligent soul and a whole man and then deny the properties of the humanity and confess not that they are such as they[1] are in the nature of the man, but attribute to God the Word all things as to a changeable and variable [being]: birth and growth and upbringing and gradual advance in stature and in wisdom and in grace and the commandments and their observance and their fulfilment and the suffering and the Cross and the death and the resurrection? What say you? Instruct men. How ought they to think and to confess? Is God the Word two *ousias* in nature, or dost thou imagine that man is in his nature two *ousias*, of divinity and of humanity? Or is God the Word one *ousia*, and has his own *ousia* received no addition / as that which has existed eternally, and is the *ousia* of man one, of the nature of men, and was it also like the nature of the sons of man and did it [so] comport itself? Thou confessest not these things, nay more thou deniest them.

God the Word was made man that he might therein make the humanity the likeness of God and that he might therein renew [the likeness of God] in the nature of the humanity; and thereupon he renewed his material elements[2] and showed him [to be] without sin in the observance of the commandments, as though he alone sufficed for renewing him who had origin-

---

[1] Syr. 'there is'.
[2] The Syr. *gbîltâ*, elsewhere translated 'formation', corresponds to the Gk. φύραμα as used by Philo (i. 184) of the human body.

ally fallen by the transgression of the observance of the commandments. Otherwise he gave himself for him to observe them because he sufficed not to keep himself without sin. In that case our fall remains untended as a paralytic man who tends himself and remains incapable of walking, but for whom the attendant walks or whom he carries, saying not to him: 'Arise, walk, since thou hast indeed been healed that thou mayest walk.' For this reason he took the likeness of a servant which was without sin in its creation in such wise as even in the observance of the commandments to receive a name which is more excellent than all names and so that whatsoever came into being through the renewal of his material elements[1] might be confirmed by observances and by prudence; for which reason also the renewal of the material elements[1] took place through the incarnation[2] by means of which he might contend against defeat. But if the purpose also of his having been made man / had not been fulfilled, it[3] also would surely not have taken place at all, but all things would be fictitious and foolish, both the disobedience of the first man and the things which made him guilty unto death; for he who had not a nature which could observe [the commandments] would also have been unable to observe them. For this same reason the second man also observed [them] not, but God lived[4] in his stead[5] and observed the commandments, because he was in that nature which sins not. And if this is so, what was the need for the life[4] of the humanity to show that he who was God the Word was able to observe those human things which he who was man was unable to observe? But [there was such need] that he might show that he had not authority, when he wished, to rescue him[self] from death, because the Father wished it not;[6] for all [men] he comported himself and kept himself without sin and, as one who has not sinned, he gave himself for salvation on behalf of all men.

These are [the doctrines] of the orthodox, who confess one

---

[1] See p. 212, n. 2.   [2] *Sc.* ἐνανθρώπησις.

[3] *Viz.* the Incarnation.

[4] Syr. *'ethdabbar*, and the cognate substantive, elsewhere rendered 'comported himself' and 'manner of life' respectively.

[5] Or, 'on his behalf'; see p. 32, n. 1.   [6] See Matt. xxvi. 39.

ousia of the Father and of the Son and one will and one power; these are [the doctrines] of those who confess that the things of Christ are neither folly nor fiction. He did nothing in *schêma*, in hungering and thirsting and fearing, in learning, in not knowing, and [in] all those things which could convince [one] that he was a man, because / he was God in nature [and] in truth and man in nature and in truth. And because of this it was needful for the divinity to renew the humanity and for the humanity to be renewed and to take the very image [of him] who created it but not his own *ousia*; and it was needful that it should observe prudently the conduct of the man who had fallen, because especially for that it was created, to conduct itself according to the law which is in the nature of men and to preserve the very image of the Creator by the observance of the commandments without fault, the divinity making use of its own *prosôpon* in the likeness of a servant in order that the humanity by means of that *prosôpon* wherein it contended might be victorious, its victory being thereby confirmed. For since the renewal of its material elements[1] it had the image of the sonship from him who created it; but it[2] had need also of a recompense for the observance of the commandments, in order that the *prosôpon* might be common to him who gave and to him who for the sake of his obedience received the image which, because Adam preserved it not when it was given to him in his material elements,[1] was taken from him. Destroy not therefore the pattern of the Incarnation,[3] but concede the properties of the divinity and concede the properties of the humanity and concede one *prosôpon* of the union, and all of them [will be] true and all of them orthodox. If you are willing to hear, hear the same things concerning them according to the witnesses which you have cited.

'I said: *Have this mind in you which was also in Jesus ' / Christ, who, being in the likeness of God, emptied himself ' and took the likeness of a servant.*[4] He said not: " Have this ' " mind in you which was also in God the Word, who, being

---

[1] See p. 212, n. 2.   [2] *Viz.* the divinity.
[3] *Sc.* ἐνανθρώπησις.   [4] Phil. ii. 5-7.

' " in the likeness of God, took the likeness of a servant ", but 'he took the name " Christ ", as a title indicative of two 'natures, avoiding all risk,[1] and named therewith [both] the 'likeness of the servant which he took and God.'[2] I said: 'one and the same Christ, two natures,' 'the likeness of the servant which he took and God,' without distinction. Quote these words of Gregory: '[There are] indeed two natures, 'God and man, but not two sons; for one and another are 'those from which our Saviour is, but not one and another— 'far from it!—but one by mixture, God who was made man and 'man who was made God';[3] and again: 'He who begins 'and gradually advances and is brought to fullness is not God, 'although he is so called on account of the revelation which '[was made] little by little.'[4] He predicated not two natures of God the Word and he came not into being of two natures, neither has the man two natures nor is it [the case] that he is of two natures, but God and man are two natures. For he took a name common to the natures, Son and Saviour, and without separation he is named God and Son; and he[5] divides this twofold [Son and Saviour] into those two natures, from which our Saviour [came into being]; and by the union that which is one thing is called another: thus / 'God who was made man and man who was made God '—not because he was changed in respect to his divinity. And 'He who 'begins and gradually advances and is brought to fullness is not 'God, although he is so called on account of his revelation which [was made] little by little.'[4] Whom then does he call one? And whom two? And whom in *ousia*? And whom by union?

But Ambrose also has said the same and not strange things concerning the union of God and of the flesh: 'The Son of 'God speaks in both of them, because in him there were two 'natures. Regard in him on the one hand the glory of God, 'on the other hand the sufferings of the man.'[6] For he also predicates the union of the two natures, not that two natures

---

[1] Literally: 'without risk'.
[2] See p. 207, n. 3.
[3] See p. 200, n. 2.
[4] See p. 200, n. 1.
[5] *Viz.* Gregory.
[6] See p. 199, n. 2 (2).

[were] one nature but that two natures [were] in the one *prosôpon* of the Son:—'the glory indeed of the divinity, but the sufferings of the humanity.' For he calls not the one son and God the Word another son, but he indicates something else by *prosôpon* and *ousia*. As then is the name 'God', so is the name 'son', the one indeed indicative of the natures but the other of the *prosôpon* of the Son. The same is God and Son, and there is one *prosôpon* of the two natures and not of the one *ousia*. For this reason both of them [are] one Son and in one Son are both the natures. One God the Word is not both natures nor is one divinity both natures; for there has not been confusion nor has there been mixture nor again a change of *ousias* resulting in one nature of the *ousia* nor again also a natural composition[1] resulting in a composite nature. / What then have you heard [that is] strange in my words—and you have condemned me, and you have laid down these things? For the former has laid down the name 'Son' and the latter 'Saviour' and Athanasius 'Lord'. But how have they who are called Christians dared to doubt whether the Lord, who was born of Mary, is son in the *ousia* and in the nature of God the Word, but was born in flesh of the seed of the house of David? For the flesh was of the Virgin Mary. For thou also knowest that he who was of the Virgin Mary was human nature, in nature indeed and in *ousia* Son of God, in the *ousia* and in the nature of God the Father, but in flesh human nature from Mary. For he[2] lays down the common name 'Lord', which is conceived of nature and in nature, as well as the things which are indicative of the properties of the natures, indicating them both, the divinity and the humanity, the one from God the Father in nature and the other of a woman in nature. In calling him who was of God the Father 'human', he calls him not of God the Father in his nature, but rather in the human properties he indicates two natures. He is not making the human nature nor the divine without *prosôpon* and without *hypostasis*. Nor has the Incarnation[3] taken place on our behalf as something

---

[1] Syr. 'in a natural composition'. [2] *Viz.* Athanasius.
[3] *Sc.* ἐνανθρώπησις.

superfluous, unreal,[1] in such wise as to refer human [attributes] to God, as the Arians say that he suffered in nature our own sufferings, in his own nature and in his own *prosôpon*, the flesh adding not anything [thereto]. But since the humanity is understood completely as the nature of man, it has completely / all [the qualities] of the sons of man, [acting] and suffering, as the nature of men is wont [to do].

Likewise from the same, from the sixteenth roll.
 ' That at the name of Jesus every knee should bow-which is
' in heaven and on earth and which is under the earth and
' every tongue should confess that Jesus Christ is Lord.'[2]
' Because of him who is clothed I honour him wherewith he
' is clothed, and because of him who is invisible I adore him
' who is visible. God is not distinguished from him who is
' visible ; for this reason I distinguish not the honour of him
' who is not distinct ; I distinguish the natures and I unite
' the adoration.[3]

I seek and would persuade you prudently to look well in every place, lest he [4] blame me for breaking up into several parts and dividing the divinity and the humanity in the likeness of things which are distinguished in place from one another. How is he who is clothed distinguished from his clothing and one who is concealed from one who is revealed? As we have added in our very words : ' God is not distinct from him who is visible.' . . .

But thou sayest unto me that I distinguish the natures. How then are those natures which are indistinguishable distinguished? For in the formula they are known as *ousias* without confusion, without mixture, in such wise that in the

---

[1] Literally : ' not fulfilled '.   [2] Phil. ii. 10-11 (P.).
[3] Labbe (Mansi), iv. 1201 B : ὁμοίως τοῦ αὐτοῦ, τετράδιον ιϛ'. ἵνα ἐν τῷ ὀνόματι Ἰησοῦ, φησί, πᾶν γόνυ κάμψῃ, ἐπουρανίων, καὶ ἐπιγείων, καὶ καταχθονίων· καὶ πᾶσα γλῶσσα ἐξομολογήσηται, ὅτι κύριος Ἰησοῦς Χριστός· διὰ τὸν φοροῦντα τὸν φορούμενον σέβω. διὰ τὸν κεκρυμμένον προσκυνῶ τὸν φαινόμενον. ἀχώριστος τοῦ φαινομένου Θεός. διὰ τοῦτο τοῦ μὴ χωριζομένου τὴν τιμὴν οὐ χωρίζω. χωρίζω τὰς φύσεις, ἀλλ' ἑνῶ τὴν προσκύνησιν.
In what follows, the words ' distinguish ', ' divide ', etc., do not represent the translators' idea of what the meaning demands, but are used, as throughout the work, for the constant equivalents of certain Syriac words. For the looseness of the Syriac on this point see pp. 154, n. 1, 312, n. 3.
[4] *Viz.* Cyril.

union both the natures are preserved with their natural attributes and naturally with the properties / of the *ousia*, so that the divine nature is conceived in nature of God and the human nature is conceived in the nature of the humanity in the *ousia*. He [himself] distinguishes in several parts, he who says that the humanity is conceived by nature in the divinity but that the humanity is not conceived to be the divinity, and that God the Word was not in both the natures either in *schêma* or without the substance of the flesh or in passibility or in the action of the sensibility and in the nature of the flesh. For if he[1] were not so conceived, neither is he to be otherwise conceived without limiting by distinction him who is infinite and unlimited. For this idea he has also in the very thing which he says in his letter : 'The diversities of the natures are not made void by reason of the union ';[2] for in the natural differences he distinguishes the things which are united, having distinguished [them] indistinguishably, for he has made the distinction by the word *ousia*. For the word and the idea of divinity are one thing and that of humanity another, since things which are distinguishable are distinguishable. But I predicate two natures, that he indeed who is clothed is one and he wherewith he is clothed another, and these two *prosôpa* of him who is clothed and of him wherewith he is clothed. But thou also confessest 'of two natures'. Neither of them is known without *prosôpon* and without *hypostasis* in the diversities of the natures. There are not two *prosôpa* of the sons conceived nor again two *prosôpa* / of the men, but of one man who is moved in the same manner even by the other. For the union of the *prosôpa* took place for the *prosôpon* and not for the *ousia* and the nature. It is not indeed that one *ousia* without *hypostasis* should be conceived, as if by union into one *ousia* and there were no *prosôpon* of one *ousia*,[3] but the

---

[1] *Viz.* God the Word. [2] See p. 144, n. 1.

[3] In Christian doctrine ὑπόστασις was first used as practically equivalent to οὐσία, *e.g.* in Trinitarian definition. But there was always a shade of distinction between the two words, the germ of their being later set apart as in the formula τρεῖς ὑποστάσεις ἐν μιᾷ οὐσίᾳ. For a full discussion of this question see Webb, *God and Personality*, Lecture II. Professor Webb concludes his discussion of the earlier use of ὑπόστασις as follows : 'Thus it is that ὑπόστασις comes

natures subsist in their *prosôpa* and in their natures and in the *prosôpon* of the union. For in respect to the natural *prosôpon* of the one the other also makes use of the same on account of the union; and thus [there is] one *prosôpon* of the two natures. The *prosôpon* of the one *ousia* makes use of the *prosôpon* of the other *ousia* in the same [way]. For what *ousia* seekest thou to make without a *prosôpon*? That of the divinity? Or that of the humanity? Therefore thou wilt not call God the Word flesh nor the flesh Son.

But if thou predicatest God the Word [to be] in the two natures, God and man, but the man [to be] nought, it is not right to think aught else of thee [than] that either thou speakest only of the name and the *schêma* of man without the nature at all, after which God the Word was named, or [thou speakest] as though the humanity added not anything in nature to the *prosôpon* of the dispensation on our behalf; or, in order that God the Word might be able to be revealed and suffer human sufferings involuntarily, so that while the humanity was suffering without sensibility, God the Word was suffering the sufferings of the body / and the sufferings of the soul and the sufferings of the intelligence and was acting and being acted upon—so for this reason thou makest all of them God the Word's and dost expel the humanity. If after this thou dost decline to confess two natures with me, by the same argument decline also to say that God the Word was made flesh and [renounce] the flesh in which he was made flesh and was made man. [It is] likewise both in regard to the man and in regard to God. But he who speaks so[1] makes

into use as a philosophical term, often equivalent to οὐσία, which for Aristotle is most properly used of the concrete individual of a certain kind; but of Aristotle's two notes of real being, its *intelligible character* and its *concrete independence*, emphasizing the latter, as οὐσία emphasized the former. This difference of emphasis between the two words οὐσία and ὑπόστασις sufficiently accounts for the use made of them respectively by the Christian Church in the eventual formulation of her theology.'

This description seems precisely to fit Nestorius' usage. For him ὑπόστασις has its earlier sense, representing Cyril's οὐσία rather than his ὑπόστασις (see above, p. 156, n. 2, p. 208, n. 2). Nevertheless there is a distinction between the two words, as the passage here shows. Only that which is both οὐσία and ὑπόστασις actually exists and has a πρόσωπον (see below, p. 228).

[1] *I.e.* as Nestorius.

not two Gods the Words nor two fleshes, but makes confession completely, without diminution, of the divinity, and of the humanity in which it was made man, that the humanity might not be conceived [to be] fictitious, nor further that by a change of *ousia* and by a change of likeness the nature of God the Word might even so become the nature of a man. Neither by mixture and confusion nor by a change of *ousia*, nor again by a natural change of composition of the humanity, is he conceived; for all these things are rejected and corrupt and such as befit paganism and heretics and corrupt the properties of all natures.

But, O excellent judges, do you wish to cite the witness which [was borne] by the Fathers, which was written by them, that I may make use of it; that in my making use of indubitable witnesses you may learn that I too have said the same things, and [that] you have condemned me as one who says them not and have condemned me in raging anger and in darkness? For whatever / else have I said other than that which Gregory has said? 'One thing indeed and another are 'the things of which our Saviour is [formed], if the invisible is 'not the same as the visible and that which is timeless as that 'which is time; yet he is not one thing and another—far from 'it!—for they two are one by mixture, God on the one hand 'who was made man, man on the other hand who was made 'God.'[1] See then that he calls the clothing visible but him that is clothed invisible. For God is one thing and man another, but Christ is not one thing and another but one in *prosôpon* by union: [that] of God who was made man and [that of] man who became God. By man indeed is it said that God was made man, and by God is it said that man was made God. It was not that he was changed from the divinity; God indeed remained God and was made man, and man remained man and was made God; for they took the *prosôpon* of one another, and not the natures. Therefore [they are] one thing and another, and [he is] not one thing and another in *prosôpon*. For in that same doctrine by which it is said that man was made God men by all means attribute unto him

[1] See p. 200, n. 2.

adoration and service. In him, through whom and by whom it befell him to be made God, [he is adored] with one [and] the same adoration although he is conceived as one thing and another in the natures. And he is without distinction in the union, but in view of the natures which are distinct he both is and is conceived one thing and another.

Now Athanasius also has said things which agree with this: 'Now that the Word has become man and has made the 'properties of the flesh his own, / the same are not therefore 'imputed to the body because of the Word which has come to 'be in it.'[1] For he said that God the Word has come to be in the body as one who is clothed in the clothing and the invisible in the visible, not as though they had been confused nor as though they had been changed, but as though remaining in both their natures and making the very properties common to him who acts[2] and to him who is in his own *ousia*,[3] and he[4] possesses all those things which are made [the common] properties. And it is evident that he says two: 'God the 'Word and the body in which he was and whose [properties] 'he made his own in order that those of the one might become 'the other's and those of the other the one's.' But this God the Word remained impassible even in the body, nor yet was the suffering of the flesh brought nigh unto him, because God the Word who was in him was born of God; because of the heavenly Word which was in him he became heavenly, but because of him wherein he was he also was adored with God the Word who is adorable. Because of him who was clothed I honour the clothing, for he was clothed in the likeness of a servant, as Gregory said: 'The King of Kings and Lord of Lords is clothed in the likeness of a servant.'[5]

Why then have you accepted these things but accused of

---

[1] Labbe (Mansi), iv. 1185 B: νῦν δὲ τοῦ λόγου γενομένου ἀνθρώπου, καὶ ἰδιοποιουμένου τὰ τῆς σαρκός, οὐκέτι ταῦτα τοῦ σώματος ἅπτεται διὰ τὸν ἐν αὐτῷ γενόμενον Θεὸν λόγον.

[2] *Viz.* the man who suffers and obeys.

[3] *Viz.* God the Word.   [4] *Viz.* Christ.

[5] The previous quotations from Gregory have been from Gregory of Nazianzum. This one is from Gregory of Nyssa, Labbe (Mansi), iv. 1193 D: ὁ βασιλεὺς τῶν βασιλευόντων, καὶ ὁ κύριος τῶν κυριευόντων τὴν τοῦ δούλου μορφὴν ὑποδύεται.

impiety my words and not those also of them who have confirmed my own words? [Is it] either because you suppose that even these which in letter and in spirit are the same / are not to be rejected in [the rejection of] mine own words? Or [is it] because you make void [both] the former and the latter, that they may not be spoken, and further employ these of mine, having destroyed him who spake them? And you too, though involuntarily, are witnesses unto me and you bear witness unto me by those [words by] which you suppose that you undo these of mine, since you also are in agreement with them and undo yourselves, because you are speaking against yourselves. And if I were able to have judges unlike you, I should have had no labour to convince [them] that it is the same idea, and so on; and I do not suppose that it would be right to toil much.

Likewise, from the same, from the seventeenth roll, concerning the faith.

God the Word indeed was Son and God, and was with his Father even before the Incarnation,[1] but in the latter time he took the likeness of a servant. Yet having been formerly son and having been [so] called even after the taking he could not be called son by distinction, lest we should introduce two sons into our faith; but because he adheres to him who has been son from in the beginning, we cannot make him who adhered unto him distinct in the honour of the sonship—in the honour / of the sonship, I say, and not in the nature. For this reason the Word also is called Christ, because he has continuously adherence in Christ.[2]

But in order that we may not say the same things [and] tire the reader with the same [subjects], let us pass on to

---

[1] *Sc.* ἐνανθρώπησις.

[2] Labbe (Mansi), iv. 1201 c: ὁμοίως τοῦ αὐτοῦ, τετράδιον ιζ'. ἦν μὲν γὰρ ὁ Θεὸς λόγος καὶ πρὸ τῆς ἐνανθρωπήσεως υἱός, καὶ Θεός, καὶ συνών τῷ πατρί· ἀνέλαβε δὲ ἐν ὑστέροις καιροῖς τὴν τοῦ δούλου μορφήν. ἀλλ' ἦν (v. l. ὤν) πρὸ τούτου υἱὸς καὶ καλούμενος, μετὰ τὴν ἀνάληψιν οὐ δύναται καλεῖσθαι κεχωρισμένος υἱός, ἵνα μὴ δύο υἱοὺς δογματίζωμεν. ἀλλ' ἐπειδήπερ ἐκείνῳ συνῆπται τῷ ἐν ἀρχῇ ὄντι υἱῷ τῷ πρὸς αὐτὸν συναφθέντι, οὐ δύναται κατὰ τὸ ἀξίωμα τῆς υἱότητος, οὐ κατὰ τὰς φύσεις, διὰ τοῦτο καὶ διαίρεσιν δέξασθαι. κατὰ τὸ ἀξίωμά φημι τῆς υἱότητος, οὐ κατὰ τὰς φύσεις (v. l. οὐ δύναται κατὰ τὸ ἀξίωμα τῆς υἱότητος διαίρεσιν δέξασθαι· κατὰ τὸ ἀξίωμά φημι υἱότητος, οὐ κατὰ τὰς φύσεις). διὰ τοῦτο καὶ Χριστὸς ὁ Θεὸς λόγος ὀνομάζεται, ἐπειδήπερ ἔχει συνάφειαν τὴν πρὸς τὸν Χριστὸν διηνεκῆ.

their testimony which they have chosen, as they suppose, against me, and which they have set down as seemed good to them; whereby I have proved and shall prove that nothing strange has been said by me [and] that I have been condemned in this judgement without examination. Hear what Gregory, bishop of Nazianzum, says of the things which the former have written. . . .

For we [distinguish] not the man from the divinity; we call him one and the same thing; for [we call him] not originally man but God and Son and only-begotten before the ages, who was not mixed with the bodily frame nor with the things which are in the bodily frame [1] but in the end took also the man.'[2]

How then does it seem to you? That it is against [me]? Compare them both with one another. 'For God the Word, 'even before the Incarnation,[3] was son and God and was with 'the Father.' Set down the [words] of Gregory: 'Originally indeed not man but only God and Son.' These [are statements] which are supposed contradictory by you; quote those which have been spoken by me [to see] if they are applicable. 'But in the last times he took the likeness of a servant.' Set over against them [those] of Gregory: 'But at the end he took also the man.' Lest / they should be supposed to be contradictory by you, set down those things which have been said by me: 'But he was before the other and he was called Son, but 'after his taking he could not be separated nor distinctly dis-'tinguished nor be called Son.' Cite [the words] of Gregory: 'For also we separate not the man from the divinity.' Quote the rest of mine (which thou cuttest short) as having been laid down by me: 'That we may not speak of two sons.' Set down

[1] See p. xv.

[2] Labbe (Mansi), iv. 1192 B : μὴ ἀπατάτωσαν οἱ ἄνθρωποι, μηδὲ ἀπατάσθωσαν, ἄνθρωπον ἄνουν δεχόμενοι τὸν κυριακόν, ὡς αὐτοὶ λέγουσι, μᾶλλον δὲ τὸν κύριον ἡμῶν καὶ Θεόν. οὐδὲ γὰρ τὸν ἄνθρωπον χωρίζομεν τῆς θεότητος, ἀλλ' ἕνα καὶ τὸν αὐτὸν δογματίζομεν· πρότερον μὲν οὐκ ἄνθρωπον, ἀλλὰ Θεὸν καὶ υἱὸν μόνον καὶ προαιώνιον, ἀμιγῆ σώματος, καὶ τὸν (?τῶν) ὅσα σώματος· ἐπὶ τέλει δὲ καὶ ἄνθρωπον προσληφθέντα ὑπὲρ τῆς ἡμῶν σωτηρίας· παθητὸν σαρκί, ἀπαθῆ θεότητι· περιγραπτὸν σώματι, ἀπερίγραπτον πνεύματι· τὸν αὐτὸν ἐπίγειον καὶ οὐράνιον, ὁρώμενον καὶ ἀόρατον (v. l. νοούμενον), χωρητὸν καὶ ἀχώρητον. ἵν' ὅλῳ ἀνθρώπῳ τῷ αὐτῷ καὶ Θεῷ, ὅλος ἄνθρωπος ἀναπλασθῇ πεσὼν ὑπὸ τὴν ἁμαρτίαν.

[3] Sc. ἐνανθρώπησις.

those of Gregory: 'But we say that he is one and the same.' Quote the rest of my [words]: 'But because he adheres unto 'him who was in the beginning son; he who adhered unto him 'cannot receive in distinction the honour of sonship, by honour, 'I mean, and not by nature.' Set down the words of Gregory: 'There are indeed two natures, God and man, as also [there 'are] soul and body, but the sons are not two; for those from 'which our Saviour is [formed] are one and another; yet he is not one and another. Far from it! For both of them are one in the union.'[1] So he has made the distinction in the nature and not in *prosôpa*, in saying 'One and another, but one son'. And again: 'by nature' is other than 'by union', as he is called 'other' in *prosôpon* and not in nature. For after the flesh God the Word is flesh, but after the divinity the flesh or the man is called Son, in such wise that also after that flesh which has been taken God the Word is called Christ. Read those [words] of mine even as they have been written. . . . 'For this reason also God / the Word is named Christ, because he has continuously adherence in Christ.'[2] Quote those of Gregory: 'For [there are] two of them in the union, God who was made man and man who was made God.' For by adherence unto man God the Word is said to have been made man, even as also man is said to have been made God by union with God the Word. For he calls the union a 'mixture'.[3]

Quote the [words] of Ambrose: 'Does not also the very 'Scripture teach you that not the divinity needs sanctifica-'tion, but the flesh?'[4] After the flesh therefore which has been anointed or after man God the Word is called Christ, as Ambrose has said. But after the flesh he is named flesh or after man man; is not Christ to be named after the flesh which has been anointed? And after the flesh he is named

---

[1] See p. 200, n. 2.   [2] See crit. n., p. 400.

[3] In passages such as this Nestorius seems to approach most nearly to teaching Nestorianism as usually understood; indeed it may be argued that such teaching is logically implied in the language he uses. But that it is not his own intention to imply it he shows clearly almost immediately in the paragraph on p. 225 beginning: 'And thou dost concede . . .'

[4] See p. 199, n. 2 (2), *ad finem*.

flesh; yet they make not two fleshes nor two men after the man who is named God the Word. Because God is named Christ after Christ, does it make two Christs? Or preserve harmony between you and the Fathers as regards 'in the union' and as regards 'in nature', and as regards 'in *ousia*', and as regards 'the property of the *prosôpon*', seeing that he has given us his and taken ours.[1]

And thou dost concede unto him all the properties of the flesh and the sufferings and the cross and death and dost not concede that he should be truly Christ by reason of the man who was in truth anointed, without there being two Christs, since also [there are] neither two fleshes nor two men. / But let us add also the rest: [there are] neither two births nor two sufferings nor two crosses nor two deaths nor two resurrections from the dead nor the rest [of them], nor everything else which thou referrest from the flesh into God the Word. He[2] then changes it from the flesh [only] in name and makes all of them [the property] of God the Word naturally and is grieved with those who speak the truth, as though they were making two sons. But when thou speakest, thou dost shun change and transformation and illusion and supposition, and thou dost pretend to be suspected of saying these things with intent to deceive. But when I say these things, thou leapest from thy place as if I were speaking of two sons; and again thou deniest and pretendest not to deny.[3]

In this indeed lies the distinction between us, as touching what is in the natures and what in the union, in order that we may not deny the things appertaining to the natures on account of that which is predicated in the union, and again that we may not suppose that to be nature which is predicated of the union on account of that which is in the natures. In [regard to] the things which thou dost agree not to be predicated of the union, thou claimest as though they were in the nature and permittest not the mention of the union. But, being unable to speak of it when thou excusest thyself, thou settest therefore about accusing me and regardest me as

---

[1] A gap, not a new paragraph, is marked here in the Syriac text.
[2] *Viz.* Cyril.
[3] See p. 224, n. 3.

impious, although in excusing thyself from the things whereof I rebuke thee thou bearest witness unto me that I am pious; / and the same things are taken as impious in me but fair in him. Or perhaps they issue from thine own knowledge, that thou mayest strive and labour on their behalf! Yet, for all that [thou admittest them] of necessity and by constraint, hardly dost thou admit it and confess in him these human qualities. In what other things then more than these art thou confident of a just judgement? Even however in the following you have the same examination that by the same means you may confirm these my [words].

Likewise from the same, from the seventeenth roll: Concerning the Faith.'
Let us keep without confusion the adhesion of the natures. Thou therefore confessest God who is in man, but I worship the adhesion of the divinity [where]by man is adored together with [1] God Almighty.[2]

But that we may not make use of the witness of any other, it is fair that we should make use of his own testimony concerning these our [questions, of his] who says: 'We are keeping without confusion the adhesion of the 'natures, in that the diversity of the natures is not made void 'by reason of the union.'[3] Thereby he indicates one and the same, and further he indicates God who was in man. God indeed was impassible, in a passible bodily frame. Therein lies the diversity, nor does it indicate / identity. 'I worship 'the adhesion of the divinity where[by] man is adored together 'with [1] God Almighty,'[2] and 'the body indeed wherewith he 'too is seated with the Father is not a stranger unto him';[4] we have not quoted [these] that thou mightest disclaim them, but that thou mightest not blame the things which have been well said by thee. But you, O admirable judges without justice, you have not understood these things when they were

---

[1] Literally: 'in'.

[2] Labbe (Mansi), iv. 1201 D: Ὁμοίως τοῦ αὐτοῦ, τετράδιον ιε΄. εἰς δόγμα. ἀσύγχυτον τοίνυν τὴν τῶν φύσεων τηρῶμεν συνάφειαν· ὁμολογῶμεν τὸν ἐν ἀνθρώπῳ Θεόν· σέβωμεν τὸν τῇ θείᾳ συναφείᾳ τῷ παντοκράτορι Θεῷ συμπροσκυνούμενον ἄνθρωπον.

[3] See p. 144, n. 1.   [4] See p. 151, n. 1.

read before you; or else they have surely not been read or you have only been careful of this, that you might anticipate those who were about to come to the examination.

Now I pass by the [words] of Ambrose who says that the union of God and of the flesh is without confusion: 'In both 'of them there spake the Son of God in whom there are two 'natures, man and God.'[1] But Athanasius also says: 'If 'God the Word were in the body as it were artificially,[2] as 'these men say, that indeed which is said artificially[2] would 'be a phantasy; in regard to him both the salvation and the 'resurrection of men would be found a phantasy'.[3]

But let us again speak of the divine adhesion,[4] since thou shunnest indeed the term 'adhesion' as impiety, thou who sayest also this, that whoever says ['adhesion' says] that it has adhered to him as in the prophets or by grace and not that it adhered by *ousia*, that is, that it will be adored with him in virtue of the union. And again from Gregory: 'God indeed who was made man, but man who was made God.' For this was not / his on account of his own nature, but in virtue of the union of the divinity; for in the adoration of the divinity which is united unto him he is adored with it, not in his own adoration. Just as 'He was made God' is not 'He was changed into the divinity', so he was not made God of his own nature but by the union of the divinity. For he is adored with the adoration of the divinity which is united unto him and not with his own adoration. As being made God is not to vacate humanity, so he was not made God of his [own] nature but by the union of the divinity. Things indeed which are diverse in *ousia* but are adored with a single adoration are said to be adored together; but when they are mentioned as though in the union of the *prosôpon*, since there is no distinction in the *prosôpon*, how can one be separated and be said to be adored [apart]? But when mention is made of the *ousias*, on account of the distinction which exists between them, it is said: 'He is adored with it' because [he is adored] as if in both *ousias*, just as it is said also of the

---

[1] See p. 199, n. 2.
[2] See p. 192, n. 3.
[3] See p. 192, n. 5.
[4] Sc. συνάφεια.

Father and the Son and the Holy Spirit, in so far as they are in the union of the divinity, that ' God is adored ', and, in so far as they are distinguished in the *prosôpon*, although they are not distinguished in nature but remain always in their being, we say that the Son is adored with the Father and with the Holy Spirit, in order that we may not, like Sabellius, make the *prosôpa* without *hypostasis* and without *ousia*.[1] For he who would suppress [the saying] that the Son is adored with the Father / suppresses [the saying] that the Son exists in *hypostasis*. So also concerning Christ : when we speak of the *prosôpon*, we say that the Son of God is adored, concerning also the flesh as united with him ; but in discussing the natures and speaking of two natures, we say that the humanity is adored with the divinity which is united with it. And he indeed who would hinder the saying of 'two natures' and 'him who is adored with it' would suppress [the saying] that ' the humanity and the divinity exist in *ousia* and in *hypostasis*', even as has been our argument also concerning the Trinity, as also Gregory says. Our [words are] like those indeed of the Fathers. Therefore look well into the judgement which has been [passed] on these things, as they have been doing everything at haphazard, fleeing from the examination as from fire.

Likewise from the same, from the sixth roll. Ponder the things which follow immediately thereon: *That he may be merciful and a faithful chief priest in the things which concern God. In that indeed he has suffered and been tempted he is able to succour them that are tempted.*[2] Therefore he who has suffered is the chief priest, but the temple is passible, not God the impassible who has quickened the passible temple.[3]

Who indeed can undertake the advocacy of blasphemies such as / these? I called the temple passible and not God

---

[1] See pp. 156, n. 2, 218, n. 3.   [2] Heb. ii. 17, 18.
[3] Labbe (Mansi), iv. 1201 D : ὁμοίως τοῦ αὐτοῦ, τετράδιον ϛ'. σκόπει καὶ τὸ τούτοις εὐθὺς συναπτόμενον· ἵν' ἐλεήμων, φησί, γένηται, καὶ πιστὸς ἀρχιερεὺς τὰ πρὸς τὸν Θεόν· ἐν ᾧ γὰρ πέπονθεν αὐτὸς πειρασθείς, δύναται τοῖς πειραζομένοις βοηθῆσαι. οὐκοῦν ὁ παθών, ἀρχιερεὺς ἐλεήμων. παθητὸς δὲ ὁ ναός, οὐχ ὁ ζωοποιὸς τοῦ πεπονθότος Θεός.

the quickener of the temple which has suffered. For this you have condemned me like the priests for blasphemies, because I have said that God is incorruptible and immortal and the quickener of all. Or contrariwise [can he be] corruptible and mortal and in need of life? 'For does not also the Scripture 'teach you that the divinity has not need of sanctification, 'but the flesh?'[1] All this Ambrose proclaims unto you and you hearken not, or rather, you hearken and hearken not, you see and you see not, and you accept things which are inconsistent. How therefore do you accept these and have not accepted mine? Naught that is strange have I said, nor again have I written aught that differs [even] in small details from his own[2] [words]: *In that he has suffered and been tempted he is able to succour them that are tempted.*

Now he proclaims the nature which has suffered, and you have no need to learn of me or of others. 'The Scripture 'proclaims it: "Confess therefore the glory of God and the '"sufferings of man."'[1] Ambrose tells it unto all of you. Why are you frightened of accepting these [words] of Ambrose? And in that you ban my words [you ban] his also. These things he has said; for these things you have condemned me; then not me but him also, for I have said the same things as he, those which you have quoted. Who among men will / change these things and be able to accept them as the reverse? I should have had no need of much examination to establish my [words], if they had come up for examination and for judgement, and I should have been teaching in no other manner but by means of what they have said and what they used in [their] witness. Who had confidence in the judgement? And who [was it] that fled from him and carried him off by force, and wherefore? And it was by all means evident even to the unintelligent.

Thou hast said that he was impassible in a passible body, and thou accusest me as if I were speaking impiety [in saying] that the temple of God is passible and that the quickener of the temple is not passible. If thou art saying with truth that

---

[1] Cp. p. 199, n. 2.
[2] *Viz.* the author of the Epistle to the Hebrews.

God is impassible in a passible body, then hast thou not made use of this term 'impassible' merely [1] with intent to deceive, in order that men may let thee by all [means] say and maintain that God is passible and mortal, while thereof accusing me who say that the temple of God is passible and that the quickener of the temple has not suffered? But you have learned how wise is the judgement of the judges, and I have made you know for what cause I have been judged. But the rest of these things also it is fair [2] to read.

/ *Likewise from the same, from the twenty-seventh roll.* That you may learn how close [3] was his adhesion unto God, [know] that even in the infant the flesh of the Lord appeared; for the child and the Lord of the child were the same. You have praised my argument, but [beware] lest you laud it without examination; for I have said that the child and he that dwelleth in the child are the same.[4]

Suppose, then, that I have spoken thus; I turn not back from 'the child and the Lord of the child are the same'. I have said that he is the child and he that dwells in the child, but I [will] explain in what manner the child and the Lord of the child are the same, in order that thou mayest not suppose of me that I predicate them both of God the Word in *ousia*, as if he were in the two *ousias*. But, inasmuch as he appeared a child, he was of our own nature, made and created; inasmuch as he was concealed, he was Lord and Maker of the child which had been revealed; for there was one *prosôpon* of them both and not one *ousia*. Therefore have I said that he was one in the *prosôpon* and one and another in the *ousias*: the child and the Lord of the child; for 'he who begins and gradually 'advances and is brought to fullness is not God, although on 'account of his manifestation which [took place] little by

---

[1] Or, 'profanely'. [2] Literally: 'are fair'. [3] Literally: 'strongly'.

[4] Labbe (Mansi), iv. 1201 E: ὁμοίως τοῦ αὐτοῦ, τετράδιον κζ'. ἵνα μάθητε, φησίν, ὡς σφόδρα τις τῆς θεότητος ὑπῆρχε συνάφεια, καὶ ἐν βρέφει τῆς δεσποτικῆς καθορωμένης σαρκός. ἦν γὰρ ὁ αὐτὸς βρέφος, καὶ τοῦ βρέφους δεσπότης. ἐπῃνέσατε τὴν φωνήν, ἀλλὰ μηδὲ αὐτὴν ἀβασανίστως κρατῆτε· εἶπον γάρ, ὁ αὐτὸς ἦν βρέφος, καὶ τοῦ βρέφους οἰκήτωρ.

'little / he is so called'.[1] Gregory also, explaining that God is predicated in them both, who is in one *prosôpon*, lest we should suppose that there is one nature, says: 'He who begins 'and gradually advances and is brought to fullness is not 'God, although on account of the manifestation which [took 'place little] by little he is so called.'

Theophilus also says: 'This master-craftsman, the Word of 'God, living and making everything, who has disposed every-'thing in fitting order, put not on a body of an honourable 'nature and of heavenly attributes and came unto us, but he 'showed in the clay the greatness of his craftsmanship in re-'shaping[2] man who was formed from the clay,'[3] He hid not that he was made and that he was also the Maker. He has not made the Maker the made and the Lord the servant in the same *ousia*, as thou arguest with us. For the earthly and the heavenly, the visible and the invisible, the limited and the illimitable, are the same, as Gregory has said: 'The child 'and the Lord of the child are the same, yet the same not in 'the same [*ousia*], but in the *prosôpon*; but the child and the 'Lord of the child are in the natures one thing and another, '[even] those of whom is Christ; but [he is not] one and 'another—far from it!'[4] What then makest thou of the things of the *prosôpon* of the *ousia* and of the nature? Thou dost transport the *ousia* of God / into two *ousias* and then removest our own nature and the firstfruits which [are] of us in attributing neither to the child nor to the Lord of the child diversity of natures but saying that the *ousia* of the child and the *ousia* of the Maker of the child exist in the same *ousia* of God the Word, as if [it was] he who made his own *ousia* and God the Word was the two *ousias* [issuing] from the one *ousia* of God the Word, or as if the *ousia* of man was changed into the

---

[1] See p. 200, n. 1.   [2] Literally: 'in correcting anew'.

[3] Part of the passage read at the Council from the sixth Paschal Epistle of Theophilus of Alexandria, Labbe (Mansi), iv. 1189 A: οὕτως ὁ πάντων ἀριστοτέχνης, ὁ ζῶν καὶ ἐνεργὴς τοῦ Θεοῦ λόγος, τάξεως ἁρμονίᾳ διακοσμήσας τὰ σύμπαντα, οὐχ οἵας τινὸς τιμίας ὕλης, οὐρανίου λαβόμενος σώματος, πρὸς ἡμᾶς ἀφῖκται· ἀλλ' ἐν πηλῷ τὸ μέγα τῆς ἑαυτοῦ δείκνυσι τέχνης, τὸν ἐκ πηλοῦ πλασθέντα διορθούμενος ἄνθρωπον, αὐτὸς ἐκ παρθένου καινοπρεπῶς προϊὼν ἄνθρωπος.

[4] See pp. 230, n. 4, 200, n. 2.

ousia of God the Word. For if thou shrinkest from speaking thus, why censurest thou one who speaks clearly and accountest him impious and accusest him of impiety?

Wherefore then, O judges, you who have been [involved] in folly and in deception and in violence, have you not examined the testimony which has been written by the Fathers? You would have proved to him [1] indeed from his own [statements] that he indeed confesses two natures, one and another, of one and another *ousia*, as the holy Fathers have said. And thou also sayest that 'the natures are diverse, but that Christ [is] ' one of them both, [yet] not as though the union made void ' the diversities of the natures '.[2] These things it appears that thou hast said; and 'The child and the dweller in the child', which thou hast said, is also the same. I say that he was impassible in a passible body, that he has a rational soul inasmuch as he is a child, for he is man as well as child. How therefore, in saying these things and persuading / us to agree with the truth of the faith, condemnest thou this man [3] on these same [points]? Is not the injustice evident? Thou callest the natures diverse in Christ, and this man makes the same confession and accepts thy statement of these things; and [thou sayest] that there is one *prosôpon* in the diverse natures, while he too confesses this and accepts thy confession concerning these things. And thou speakest of property and appropriation in consequence of the union, and admittest that that which exists is one thing and that which is called another, while this man also speaks of property and appropriation without his [4] having come into being by [passing] from [his] appropriate and voluntary property into a nature that was without volition, that he might suffer the natural sufferings. But thou gatherest together the things which have been said, so that indeed there is neither he who made them his properties, nor those things which have become his own, but there is one, not [one] *prosôpon* but [one] *ousia* indeed, so that thou makest void all those things that we have confessed together.

If thou callest this correct and not different from the truth,

---

[1] *Viz.* Cyril.   [2] See p. 144, n. 1.
[3] *Viz.* Nestorius.   [4] *Viz.* Christ.

you ought not to have maligned either the [doctrine] of one *prosôpon* or again that of two natures. For naught have you condemned me, not that I do not confess one *prosôpon* in having said 'The child and he that dwells in the child are the same'; for 'is the same' indicates one and the same *prosôpon*; nor is it as though I confess not two natures, for 'he who dwells' indicates / the nature, as though it was in the child as in the bodily frame, that the *ousia* of God might not be supposed to be the same as the *ousia* of the child. If then neither thou preachest this, nor this man who has written these things, thou oughtest not to have accused me and calumniated me as not confessing one *prosôpon* in two *ousias* or as defining them individually[1] in distinction and in division, as things which are distant from one another. For I have called the 'dweller' one who by all means dwells in the nature; and the dweller is he who dwells in him in whom there is dwelling, and he has a *prosôpon*, while he in whom there is dwelling has the *prosôpon* of him who dwells. So by the use of their *prosôpa* as though they were making use of their own authoritatively, the one is the other and the other the one, the one and the other abiding just as they are in their natures. He is truly God, we confess truly that he [is so] also in his nature and is complete, in naught falling short of the nature of the Father; and we confess that the man is truly man, completely in his nature, in naught falling short of the nature of men, neither in body nor in soul nor in intelligence; all these things he has in our likeness, apart from sin. He was not without activity in his own nature; for although God makes use of these things in his own *prosôpon*, he makes use of them as of things appertaining unto man, in such wise also / as the humanity makes use of the divinity in the things appertaining to divinity; for they have a union in *prosôpon* and not in *ousia*.

For this reason it is right to lay down and to confess that, as he is confessed [to be] the archetype by reason of the image, since it is therefrom that he is called that which he is, so also, when God the Word is called flesh, he is confessed

---

[1] Literally: 'by parts' or 'in parts'.

[to be] flesh, that from it he is called flesh and the flesh is God and Lord and Son of God, that from it it is said that the Lord is in these things, that he may be conceived without either confusion or change or phantasy in respect to the divinity and in respect to the humanity. But if a man changes the things appertaining to the image and predicates them of the archetype, necessarily is he acting foolishly in regard to both of them, both in regard to the divinity and in regard to the humanity: in regard to the humanity in assigning unto it the nature of the divinity, and in regard to the divinity because he attributes the things appertaining to the divinity to the nature of the humanity and changes them both. But these things indeed would have been so when they were to be examined by the judges, if there had been judges and they had consulted the [interests] of the orthodox without inclining to the side of the heretics and had not let them be brought to pass against the rules. But you would not have been the judges, yea, I would add that [you would have been] not even orthodox, if you had not also obscured these things. And what shall I say? All of you have one and the same opinion; but read too what follows.

/ *Likewise from the same, from the first roll.* Common indeed is the activity of the holy Trinity, and they are distinct only in the *prosôpa*; for the majesty of the glory of the only-begotten applies sometimes to the Father, for *It is my Father that glorifieth me*,[1] and sometimes to the Holy Spirit: *The Spirit of truth will glorify me*,[2] and sometimes to the might of Christ.[3]

What, pray, is there finally in me to rouse them? [Is it] because I have said: 'The activity of the Trinity is common and the division lies only in the *hypostases*.'[4] Or perhaps it

---

[1] Jn. viii. 54 (43).   [2] Jn. xvi. 14.

[3] Labbe (Mansi), iv. 1204 A: τοῦ αὐτοῦ, τετράδιον α'. κοιναὶ γὰρ αἱ τῆς τριάδος ἐνέργειαι, καὶ μόναις ὑποστάσεσι τὴν διαίρεσιν ἔχουσαι. ἡ γοῦν τοῦ μονογενοῦς εὐδοξία ποτὲ μὲν τῷ πατρὶ περιῆπται· ἔστι γάρ, φησίν, ὁ πατήρ μου ὁ δοξάζων με· ποτὲ δὲ τῷ πνεύματι· τὸ πνεῦμα γάρ, φησί, τῆς ἀληθείας ἐμὲ δοξάσει· ποτὲ δὲ τῇ τοῦ Χριστοῦ δυναστείᾳ.

[4] This use of ὑπόστασις is quite unusual in Nestorius (see p. 156, n. 2). The curious thing is that, whilst the Syriac above represents Nestorius' regular usage, this passage accurately represents the Greek text (cp. p. 242). See p. xv.

is yours to suppose that I have said unto you otherwise concerning the Trinity that the Son is glorified by the Father and by the Holy Spirit. Not that he suffices not for his own glory, but I have formerly borne witness abundantly and for this reason I have laid down 'sometimes indeed by the might of God' as being sufficient unto his own glory and not in need, because he is not in need. Who then has deceived you? But perhaps you conceive that I am speaking of the humanity which has been glorified by the Father and by the Holy Spirit and by God the Word himself.

You fight hard, and you are unwilling to name aught of the dispensation. And suppose that it has been so said by me; for I disclaim not that on behalf of which you are fighting, but now I establish my theme openly. For naught / else is your fighting by all [means] against me than this: you confess not that the flesh of the Incarnation[1] is created and [that] the second Adam is of our own nature and that he is created. You concede not that he is the creature of the Father and of the Son and of the Holy Spirit and that further he is glorified by the Creator. Why doubtest thou? What do we make this man? Either you do not confess that the flesh is made, or you confess that the flesh is made but is not of an *ousia* other than [that] of God the Word? So, in order that he may not be the creature of the Father or of the Holy Spirit, you make him the creator of himself. For you are very cautious therein, and you make him the maker of himself and say that he is made of none other than himself. All this is fair and just in your opinion when it is so said; wherefore do you not say clearly whatever you suppose to be true? But [this] in name indeed you shun but revert to it in fact, and refer to the nature of God the Word naturally the attributes of natural flesh. That two natures should be united in one *prosôpon* makes not two Sons or two Christs, the diversities of each one of the natures being preserved.

/ Thou knowest him who by all means somewhere has said these things. Thou hast in fact said that the diversities subsist and are not made void by reason of the union of the

---

[1] See crit. n., p. 400.

natures of the divinity and of the humanity. Say one *prosôpon* in two natures and two natures in one *prosôpon*, as Gregory and as Ambrose and as Athanasius, as all the Fathers, as thou too hast said, that we may not [again] write the same things. If you had been just judges, he would not have been confident. But he would have made you all participate in impiety, that you too might shun equity of judgement, because you were afraid of reprimand for that which you have wrought against me. Are you willing that we should examine the other things too which they have written? Let it not be tedious unto you to hear the same thing many times; but you shall compulsorily, of necessity, attend to the things which are to be said.

Likewise from the same, from the sixteenth roll, speaking of the Son. He it is who said: *My God, my God, why hast thou forsaken me?*[1] He it is who endured death three days, and him I adore with the divinity. 'And after three days': on account of him who is clothed I adore the clothing,[2] on account of him who is concealed [I adore] him who is revealed, who is not distinguished from the visible. For this reason I distinguish not the honour of him who is not distinguished; / I distinguish the natures and I unite the adoration. It was not God by himself who was formed in the womb nor again was God created by himself apart from the Holy Spirit nor yet was God entombed[3] by himself in the tomb; for, if it had been so, we should evidently be worshippers of a man and worshippers of the dead. But since God is in him who has been taken, he also who has been taken is called God with him after him who has taken [him].[4]

Readers ought not to break off, as if they had no more any need of reminding, but to be willing to go through in the book of their words those which they have set down close

---

[1] Mk. xv. 34 (P.).

[2] Nau: *à cause de celui qui revet le vêtement j'adore celui-là.*   [3] See p. xv.

[4] Labbe (Mansi), iv. 1204 B : ὁμοίως τοῦ αὐτοῦ, τετράδιον ιϛ'. περὶ Χριστοῦ λέγοντος. οὗτος ὁ λέγων· θεέ μου, θεέ μου, ἵνα τί με ἐγκατέλιπες ; οὗτος ὁ τριήμερον τελευτὴν ὑπομείνας· προσκυνῶ δὲ σὺν τῇ θεότητι τοῦτον, ὡς τῆς θείας συνεργὸν αὐθεντίας. καὶ μεθ' ἕτερα. οὐ καθ' ἑαυτὸ Θεὸς τὸ πλασθὲν ἀπὸ μήτρας· οὐ καθ' ἑαυτὸ Θεὸς τὸ κτισθέν ἐκ τοῦ πνεύματος· οὐ καθ' ἑαυτὸ Θεὸς τὸ ταφὲν (v. l. φανὲν) ἐπὶ μνήματος. οὕτω γὰρ ἂν ἦμεν ἀνθρωπολάτραι, καὶ νεκρολάτραι σαφεῖς. ἀλλ' ἐπειδήπερ ἐν τῷ ληφθέντι Θεός, ἐκ τοῦ λαβόντος ὁ ληφθείς, ὡς τῷ λαβόντι συναφθείς, συγχρηματίζει Θεός. For the passage omitted see p. 217, n. 3.

at hand in opposition to me, that 'the bodily frame exists not by itself'. This [it is] concerning which they have unjustly belied me, as though I were speaking of a mere man and distinguishing him into part[s], as those things which are distinguished from one another in space. And again contrariwise to this they accuse me, [demanding] from what reason I call him indistinguishable and infinite, since they hear 'he 'came into being by himself, not even for one moment, but 'God too is in[1] him ever since his coming into being, since 'also God is in[1] him that he may come to be in[1] him'. 'For 'he is impassible in a passible body who in the fulness of the 'times assumed the man that he who assumed might come to 'be indistinguishably in him who was assumed.' And it was not artificially[2] that he came to be in the body, but truly he came to be in the body and was / not distinguished from the body. 'The nature which [was born] of Mary was human and our salvation came not to pass in phantasy.'

From the things which they say, you also know my [words]: ' And he who has been assumed is named God after him who assumed.' This was not his of his own nature; for he who has been assumed is the passible man in whom the impassible existed, [that is] the human nature in which God existed not artificially,[2] the clay wherein the cunning craftsman has proved his craftsmanship. By the union with the divinity it is his to become Son and to become God. For 'he who begins 'and gradually advances and is perfected is not God, although 'on account of the manifestation which [took place] little by 'little he is so called',[3] and he is called that whereunto God is united in nature. For 'one thing and another are those 'things whereof our Saviour is [formed], yet [he is] not one 'and another—far from it!—but one by adhesion, God on the 'one hand who was made man and man on the other who 'was made God'.[4] By his adhesion he was made God and not by his nature; by the union of the divinity and of the flesh he became one Son, for both the natures existed in him. Therefore 'The man is called God by the union of the

---

[1] The Syriac proposition means 'in' or 'with' indefinitely.
[2] See p. 192, n. 3.   [3] See p. 200, n. 1.   [4] See p. 200, n. 2.

divinity and is said to be one Son'—[he is said] to become one son—by this doctrine he is adored with the adoration of the divinity and is adored with him; yet there are not two adorations, but one. For in the / one adoration of this one *ousia* the other also is adored, because he who is adored with the other is not adored in his own adoration, but both of them together. In the adoration indeed of the one, the other who is with him, who is adored in the adoration, also [is adored]; of necessity he is united and not distinguished. For also he who is adored is not capable of not being adored, nor again [is he] to be adored apart from him in whom he exists, nor yet again [is he] to be adored in him without the latter also, in whom he receives adoration, being adored. For he is not adored in his own *prosôpon* but in that *prosôpon* to which he is united, which is common on account of the union for the union took place in the *prosôpon* in such wise that the one [became] the other and the other the one. From him therefore who assumed the *prosôpon* it is his who has been assumed to become the *prosôpon* of him who has assumed it. For this reason the flesh of God the Word bears the same title with him, and it is not according to the flesh that God the Word becomes God and Son and Lord; for God the Word is called God and Son in his nature and not after another in the things derived from the nature. But the flesh has received from God to be named that which he is called, being called God when bearing the same title with him, making use with him of the name of God; it is not its after its nature. Otherwise then thou art dividing the union and predicating two things of him.[1]

And censure one who says that the body is by itself and according to whom the [properties] of the divinity belong not to the divinity which [is] in the body. / And before everything censure [2] thyself who hast so spoken; and if indeed thou darest not to deny that owing to the union the flesh had the *prosôpon* of the divinity, but referrest to God the Word alone the [attributes] of the humanity and of the

---

[1] *Viz.* God the Word.   [2] Inserted by Bedjan in the Syriac text.

divinity but to the humanity neither those of the humanity nor those of the divinity, thou yet dissemblest in that thou namest God the Word in them both; thou art like unto me in being [too] reverent to suppose that the humanity is not worthy of the *prosôpon*, and thou overthrowest the union which thou confessest in *schêma*, where[by] two natures are one *prosôpon*, laying down that it is God the Word who is united to the flesh or to the man and that he is said [to be] in both of them in the nature of God and [to be] man in the union, but a man who is neither united to the divinity nor even exists.[1] And for this reason man is named Son neither after his nature nor through the union of God the Word. But thus thou seemest to set up God the Word in both of them but man [in] neither of the two of them, whether in the nature or in the union with that

[1] This sums up Nestorius' dissatisfaction with the Cyrillian conception of the 'impersonal manhood of Christ', and the question at issue is whether he misunderstood that conception, or rightly criticized it as unintelligible. See e. g. Loofs, *Nestorius and His Place*, p. 73. Consistently with this Nestorius suspects Cyril of treating Christ's manhood as something less than human ; cp. p. 260. On the general question the following statement may be quoted: 'From Locke's definition of "person" as "a thinking intelligent being that has reason and reflection, and can consider itself as itself" modern psychology has proceeded in a fairly regular course to identify " personality" as the potentiality of self-consciousness, or, more precisely, of conscious activity. The *persona* of Latin theology, as defined by Boetius, would certainly have this quality of self-consciousness, but would not be constituted by it. Thus St. Thomas Aquinas, following the definition, was able to say that a discarnate soul, which he held to be self-conscious, is not *persona*.... Thus : (1) when the Council of Chalcedon taught that our Lord is but one *hypostasis* (Latinized as *persona*), and that Divine, it is extremely improbable that there was any reference to personality as understood in modern psychology. If there was not, the dogmatic definition does not preclude the supposition of a " human personality" in our Lord. (2) When the Council proceeded to attribute to our Lord two natures—Divine and human —it is at least possible that " human nature" was taken as including all that is now called "personality". In that case, the Council implicitly affirmed the "human personality" of our Lord. (3) When the Sixth General Council, in the year 680, affirmed, as against the Monothelites, that there were in our Lord two wills and two *energeiai*—Divine and human—it seems fairly clear that the human *energeia* (Latinized as *operatio*) corresponds closely to that conscious activity which is the basis of the modern idea of personality. Therefore, what may have been implicit in the definition of Chalcedon now becomes explicit. The Council definitely attributes to our Lord " human personality" in the modern sense of the words' (T. A. Lacey, in *The Guardian*, Dec. 23, 1921). Cp. further pp. 218, n. 3, 321, n. 1.

which is united. 'God on the one hand who was made man, 'man on the other who was made God.' 'For he who begins 'and gradually advances and is brought to fullness is not 'God, although on account of the manifestation which [took 'place] little by little he is so called.'[1]

And all the things which are called after the union in respect to both of those / things which are united come to be with reference to the one *prosôpon*. And thou sayest that the union of the natures took place in one *prosôpon*, but in fact with all thy might thou settest up the Incarnation[2] of God the Word of the Arians and of the Apollinarians, and thou provest to those who have eyes to search thee out that he made use of the body and of the soul as of an instrument[3] without soul and without reason and without will as if for his own nature, doing and suffering the sufferings of the body which became consubstantial. And for this reason thou countest it not with him and thou referrest to God the Word, even as to a craftsman, all these [properties] of the instrument,[3] but thou dost attribute to the instrument those of the craftsman, since he was not assumed for this, that he might do and suffer voluntarily in his nature, but that God the Word might suffer all human things and do them, while he had not his own will or feeling or sufferings or humanity; but thou dost attribute unto God the Word feeling and willing and suffering in all the things of humanity in his nature. And for this reason thou declinest to say that there was aught [added] to the humanity itself owing to the union with the divinity, apart from what God the Word is in *prosôpon*, that is, God and Lord and Son of God; for except the *ousia* he[4] has all the [properties] of the *ousia* owing to the union and not by nature. For the divinity makes use of the *prosôpon* of the humanity and the humanity of that of the divinity; and thus we say one / *prosôpon* in both of them. Thus God appears whole, since his nature is not damaged in aught owing to the union; and thus too man [is] whole, falling short of naught of the activity and of the sufferings of his own nature

---

[1] See p. 200, ns. 1 and 2.
[2] Sc. ἐνανθρώπησις.
[3] Syr. 'órgānôn = Gk. ὄργανον.
[4] *Viz.* 'the man'.

owing to the union. For he who refers to the one *prosôpon* of God the Word the [properties] of God the Word and those of the humanity and gives not in return the *prosôpon* of God the Word to the humanity steals away the union of the orthodox and likens it to that of the heretics. For you have learnt of the orthodox in the testimonies which they have written, that they give in compensation the [properties] of the humanity to the divinity and those of the divinity to the humanity, and that this is said of the one and that of the other, as concerning natures whole and united, united indeed without confusion and making use of the *prosôpa* of one another.[1]

How therefore has he swept you away to everything that he wishes, O wise judges? Either then refute the [sayings] of the Fathers which you have cited in testimony, or else otherwise it is of necessity [incumbent] upon you to receive one who says on their own side according to their teaching: 'Two indeed in nature and one *prosôpon* in the union, in 'mixture, in revelation, in adhesion, God who was made man, 'man who was made God, the one is said after the other 'to have been made man and the other said after the one 'to have been made God.' Whatever therefore have I said which is alien from them, for which you have condemned me? Was it not right to confess two natures? Was it not right to confess one *prosôpon* belonging to two natures, / of the divinity and of the humanity, that of the divinity and of the humanity? But although you deny that which you have written you are to be reprimanded.

Read therefore what follows:

Likewise from the same, from the third roll: against heretics, concerning the Holy Spirit. For how is that a

---

[1] This statement of the doctrine of the *communicatio idiomatum* is surely in accordance with that elaborated in Leo's *Tome* and accepted as orthodox at Chalcedon. For an estimate of Nestorius' teaching on this point drawn from other sources than this work see T. H. Bindley, *Oecumenical Documents of the Faith*, p. 113: 'Leo drew out this at length in the *Tome*. Nestorius would not or could not see the validity of this method of speech, nor allow that the Son could enter the sphere of human life while still remaining within the Divine sphere.'

servant who [works with the Son and the Father? And, if any one inquires concerning the Spirit what are his acts, he will find that he][1] is with the Father and with the Son, and falls not short of them in aught. It is not indeed as though one divinity were divided, but the Divine Scripture, for the proof and the likeness of the Trinity proves that [there is] one power and that it is distinguished for each single one of the *hypostases*.[2] And search out likewise from the works which at sundry times have begun [as follows[3]]: *God the Word became flesh and dwelled among us*[4] and caused the humanity which was taken to abide with the Father. *The Lord said unto my Lord: Sit thou on my right hand*,[5] to that likeness which was taken, the Holy Spirit has come down and shown his glory.[6]

The reader therefore has not need that we should go back to each one of the things which have been said before, and that we should say the same things. But we will say unto them: Is the flesh created or not created? Speak clearly; if thou sayest that it is created, in whatever manner it be, thou concedest that it has been made by the Father and by the Son and by the Holy Spirit, for they are entirely distinct in nothing in the making and all things are wrought by one and the same / will and wisdom. But if thou distinguishest not between these and separatest [not] the Son from the Father and from the Holy Spirit, but even [sayest] that he has become flesh in virtue of the flesh and has dwelled among us and that all the dispensation on our behalf has been effected by one and the same will and wisdom and

---

[1] The passage in brackets is restored from the Greek. See crit. n., p. 400.
[2] See p. 234, n. 4.   [3] See p. xv.
[4] Jn. i. 14.   [5] Ps. cx. 1 (P.).
[6] Labbe (Mansi), iv. 1204 c: ὁμοίως τοῦ αὐτοῦ, τετράδιον γ΄. κατὰ αἱρετικῶν περὶ τοῦ πνεύματος λέγοντος. πῶς γὰρ εἴη δοῦλον, φησί, τὸ μετὰ πατρὸς καὶ υἱοῦ ἐργαζόμενον; κἄν ζητοίη τις τὰς τοῦ πνεύματος τάξεις (v. l. πράξεις), εὑρήσει τῶν τοῦ πατρὸς καὶ υἱοῦ κατ' οὐδὲν λειπομένας· οὐχ ὡς τῆς μιᾶς μεριζομένης θεότητος, ἀλλὰ τῆς θείας γραφῆς τὰ τῆς μιᾶς ἰσχύος καὶ καθ' ἑκάστην μεριζομένης ὑπόστασιν, εἰς ἀπόδειξιν τοῦ τῆς τριάδος ὁμοίου. καί μοι σκόπει τὸ ὅμοιον, ἐκ τῶν ἐν ἔργοις καιρῶν (v. l. καιρίων) ἀρξάμενον (v. l. ἴσως, ἀρξάμενος.—N.B. The Syriac text implies ἀρξαμένων)· ὁ Θεὸς λόγος ἐγένετο σάρξ, καὶ ἐσκήνωσεν ἐν ἡμῖν. συνεκάθισεν ἑαυτῷ τὴν ἀναληφθεῖσαν ἀνθρωπότητα ὁ πατήρ· εἶπε γάρ, φησίν, ὁ κύριος τῷ κυρίῳ μου, κάθου ἐκ δεξιῶν μου. τὴν τοῦ ἀναληφθέντος τὸ πνεῦμα κατελθὸν συνεκρότησε δόξαν· ὅταν γάρ, φησί, τὸ πνεῦμα τῆς ἀληθείας ἔλθῃ, ἐκεῖνο ἐμὲ δοξάσει.

might even as also it has been effected, I myself also and all the company of the orthodox say [the same], according to the Holy Scriptures. If therefore this is worthy of accusation, let care be taken by thee that naught is left without accusation. And yet sayest thou that it is created? Say it clearly and suppress the [doctrine] that God the Word became flesh; for if he became not, how is it said that he became? For thus he is not admitted [to be] as an act,[1] the work of the Father and of the Son and of the Holy Spirit. For thereby it appears that thou art constrained to say that the flesh of God the Word has need of the Father and the Holy Spirit, the [flesh] which in its own *ousia* is naught else than God the Word. But it is not God the Word, who has not need of the Father and of the Holy Spirit.

If thou conceivest the flesh thus, thou well definest it to be so. Look well however in the Fathers who imagine the opposite concerning the flesh, from whom you have cited testimony, when they say: 'It is indeed the human nature which [is] of Mary,'[2] and again: / 'He who begins and 'gradually advances and is brought to fullness is not God, 'although on account of the manifestation which [took place] 'little by little he is so called.'[3] For both natures of which our Saviour is [formed] are one thing and another, even as thou hast formerly agreed with them to say the same things: ' Diverse are the natures which have been combined in the 'union, but of both of them [there issues] one Christ, not 'indeed that the diversity of the natures is to be made void 'on account of the union; for God is impassible in a passible 'body; for his body, which also is abiding with him, with 'the Father, is not alien unto him.'[4] What then is there to do with the things that I have said, which confirm the [words] of the former and those of the latter? And they make void thine, while thou settest aside all those whom thou hast cited as thy testimony. For these reasons the judges have not come to the examination, lest they should

---

[1] See crit. n., p. 400.   [2] See p. 192, n. 5.
[3] See p. 200, n. 1.   [4] See p. 144, n. 1.

hear these and such like things and be condemning themselves. But I will cite again the rest of the things which are like unto them and we will run over them, that you may see through all of them the cause of his declining the judgement.

Likewise from the same, from the sixth roll: in speaking of Christ. He has been sent forth *to preach release to the captives*[1] as the Apostle [says], and cites: 'He [it was] who was trusted of God and was made chief priest;'[2] for he surely became and existed not eternally from aforetime. He it is who gradually advances little by little to the honour of the high / priesthood, O heretic! Hear the voice which clearly proclaims unto thee: *In the days of the flesh he offered up a prayer and a supplication with strong crying and with tears and was heard for his righteousness and, though he was rightly Son, learned obedience by the things which he bore and was made perfect and became unto all them that obey him the cause of eternal life.*[3] Being surely brought to fullness and made perfect he gradually advanced little by little, [O] heretic; concerning whom also Luke proclaims in the Gospel that *Jesus increased in stature and in wisdom.*[4] Paul also has said things agreeing therewith: *He was made perfect and became unto all them that obey him the cause of eternal life and was named of God chief priest after the order of Melchizedek,*[5] and, after other things, he was proclaimed chief priest. Why therefore dost thou interpret against Paul, thou that dost mingle God the Word impassible with an earthly likeness and makest him a passible chief priest?[6]

[1] Luke iv. 18 (P.).   [2] Cp. Heb. ii. 17.   [3] Heb. v. 7-9.
[4] Luke ii. 52. See p. xv.   [5] Heb. v. 9-10 (P.).
[6] Labbe (Mansi), iv. 1204 D: ὁμοίως τοῦ αὐτοῦ, τετράδιον Ϛ'. περὶ Χριστοῦ λέγοντος. ὅτι ἀπεστάλη κηρύξαι αἰχμαλώτοις ἄφεσιν, καὶ τυφλοῖς ἀνάβλεψιν· ὡς ὁ ἀπόστολος ἐπιφέρει, καί φησιν· οὗτος ὁ πιστὸς τῷ Θεῷ πεποιημένος ἀρχιερεύς. ἐγένετο γὰρ οὗτος, οὐκ ἀϊδίως προῆν. οὗτος ὁ κατὰ μικρὸν εἰς ἀρχιερέως, αἱρετικέ, προκόψας ἀξίωμα· καὶ ἄκουε σαφεστέρας σοι τοῦτο διαβοώσης φωνῆς· ἐν ταῖς ἡμέραις ἐκείναις, φησί, τῆς σαρκὸς αὐτοῦ δεήσεις καὶ ἱκεσίας πρὸς τὸν δυνάμενον σώζειν αὐτὸν ἐκ θανάτου, μετὰ κραυγῆς ἰσχυρᾶς καὶ δακρύων προσενέγκας, καὶ εἰσακουσθεὶς ἀπὸ τῆς εὐλαβείας, καίπερ ὢν υἱός, ἔμαθεν ἀφ' ὧν ἔπαθε τὴν ὑπακοήν, καὶ τελειωθείς, ἐγένετο τοῖς ὑπακούουσιν αὐτοῦ (v. l. αὐτῷ) πᾶσιν, αἴτιος σωτηρίας αἰωνίου. τελειοῦται δὲ τὸ κατὰ μικρὸν προκόπτον, αἱρετικέ. περὶ οὗ καὶ Ἰωάννης ἐν τοῖς εὐαγγελίοις βοᾷ· Ἰησοῦς προέκοπτεν ἡλικίᾳ, καὶ σοφίᾳ, καὶ χάριτι. οἷς σύμφωνα καὶ Παῦλος φθεγγόμενος· τελειωθείς, φησίν, ἐγένετο τοῖς ὑπακούουσιν αὐτοῦ (v. l. αὐτῷ) πᾶσιν αἴτιος σωτηρίας αἰωνίου, προσαγορευθεὶς ὑπὸ τοῦ Θεοῦ ἀρχιερεὺς κατὰ τὴν τάξιν Μελχισεδέκ. καὶ

I imagine therefore that all of you, since you constantly say these things and since the latter brings them forward in his testimony, are like those who make mock of them that are heavy with sleep and answer differently to different things to those who cry out and ask them. For this reason, when thou settest aside thine own testimonies, thou dost not understand. For thy witness Gregory says: 'He who begins 'and gradually advances and is brought to fullness is not 'God, although on account of the manifestation which [took 'place] gradually / he is so called.'[1] But then he is not thy witness but my advocate, who has laid down these things in his discourses. Why then dost thou mingle these [arguments] of one who has laid them down in his very discourses? But Ambrose too [says]: 'Does not the Scripture also 'teach you that the divinity has not need of sanctification, 'but the flesh? Confess the glory of God and the sufferings 'of man.'[2] [Thou claimest] that he is on thy side, but knowest not what thou sayest. Whatever then has this man[3] said unto thee other [than this]? For he who accepts these disputes not against those. If thou accusest the latter as one who predicates the two *ousias*, accuse also the former who predicates two natures, one thing and another.

But thou sayest that he who confesses two natures, one and another, of necessity makes two *prosôpa*; for it is not possible that two *prosôpa* should become one *prosôpon*; but, if it is right to confess one *prosôpon*, refer them all to the one *prosôpon* of God the Word, in order that they may be predicated of one *prosôpon* and not of two; just as thou sayest that he [it is] who suffered, and dividest [it] on thy two fingers and makest proof as if concerning things [that are] divided. In this indeed thou hast naught [to do] with me, O admirable man. He, who in word accepts the Fathers and the words of the Fathers, accepts also my words at the same time. He, who says: 'Does not / the Scripture itself

μεθ' ἕτερα. ἀρχιερεὺς κεκλημένος. τί οὖν ἀνθερμηνεύεις τῷ Παύλῳ, τὸν ἀπαθῆ Θεὸν λόγον ἐπιγείῳ καταμιγνὺς ὁμοιώματι, καὶ παθητὸν ἀρχιερέα ποιῶν; Cp. Loofs, *Nestoriana*, p. 235.

[1] See p. 200, n. 1.   [2] See p. 199, n. 2 (2).   [3] *Viz.* Nestorius.

'also teach you that the divinity has not need of sanctification, 'but the flesh?'[1] predicates one *prosôpon* of the flesh and of the divinity, and that the one has need of sanctification, while the other has not need. And 'He who begins and gradually 'advances and is brought to fullness is not God, although 'on account of his manifestation which [took place] little 'by little he is so called'[2]—and the latter too predicates two: he who has begun and he who has not begun, and he who gradually advances and is brought to fullness, and further he who eternally is such as he is; he who is not God in his nature, although through the manifestation he is called God, and he who is [so] in his nature. For in the natures thou dividest also the *prosôpa*: man and God. [There are] not two sons nor two men; but hast thou not been informed that the Fathers confess one *prosôpon* of two natures, and that the diversities of the natures, either of the divinity or of the humanity, have not been made void by reason of the union, because they are thereby combined in one *prosôpon* which belongs to the natures and to the *prosôpa*? For the diversities subsist, since there has not been confusion or even suppression, so that thou mightest refer the diversity of the natures naturally to one nature and to one *prosôpon* of the same nature and mightest suppress that which is without *prosôpon* and without its own *ousia*, that is, the humanity, and mightest name God and man God alone.

For he, who thus names the one *prosôpon* of the two natures / God the Word, further attributes not the [properties] of the divinity to the *prosôpon* of the humanity in such wise that there should be one *prosôpon* of the divinity and of the humanity: the *prosôpon* of the divinity and the *prosôpon* of the humanity are one *prosôpon*, the one on this hand by *kenôsis*, the other on that by exaltation. Either thou confessest the confusion of the natures and the absolute suppression [of the humanity], or thou confessest the instrumental[3] and natural union of the heretics, whereby he is united to all the [properties] of men, in order that he may be able to comport himself and to suffer according to human nature. And the [attributes]

[1] See p. 199, n. 2 (2).　　[2] See p. 200, n. 1.　　[3] Syr. *'ôrgānāyâ*.

of the humanity [are] as the instrument[1] to the craftsman; that is, thou referrest them to God the Word and dost not attribute to the instrument,[1] that is, to the humanity, those of the craftsman; and the [properties] of the humanity, as by an instrument,[1] thou referrest to God the Word, but thou dost not attribute those of God the Word to the humanity. Thou therefore deceivest, in that thou makest use of the things which we say in our own name alone and in our own *prosôpon*, whereas in fact on the contrary thou suppressest them; and thou makest God the Word himself passible, in suppressing the sensibility and the will of the humanity, which [according to thee] 'is not indeed sensible in its nature', but is sensible in the nature of God the Word, nor became willing in its own nature but became willing in the nature of God the Word. And for this purpose, as regards the humanity, thou attributest the things of the humanity to the nature and not to the *prosôpon*.[2] But thou attributest the things of the humanity unto God but dost not attribute those of the divinity to the humanity. But we / speak of one and another in natures but of one *prosôpon* in the union for the use of one another: God on the one hand who was made man, man on the other who was made God.

But further, as in the Trinity, [there is] there one *ousia* of three *prosôpa*, but three *prosôpa* of one *ousia*; here [there is] one *prosôpon* of two *ousias* and two *ousias* of one *prosôpon*. There the *prosôpa* exist not without *ousia*, nor here again does the *ousia* exist without a *prosôpon*, nor also the nature without *prosôpon*, nor yet the *prosôpon* without nature. For of the *prosôpon* of the one *ousia* and not of another the other *ousia* makes use in the same manner on account of the union. It has indeed made our own [properties] its very own properties, conceding its own to him to whom all these things belong completely, except sin. For he has come to aid our nature, not to take that which belongs to him, and to save and renew in him[self] our nature through a sublime obedience, and not to remove it from obedience, being obedient in its stead to all human sufferings, while it is obedient in naught,

---

[1] Syr. *'órgānón*. [2] *I. e.* of God the Word.

and not to participate in the human nature of men. Nor [according to Cyril] did he come into being of men nor again of the [things] of divinity, but he attributes to the divinity the [properties] of the humanity without attributing those of the divinity to the humanity; but he was taken as something to serve as an instrument,[1] not having voluntarily practised obedience as / a rational nature, with thought and with examination and with the choice of good and with the refusal of evil.

But if thou callest the nature of men in him whole, attribute unto him completeness also in the operations wherein it seems that it exists, that is, that he trusted in God and was made chief priest. And *he offered up prayer and supplication and entreaty unto him that was able to preserve him alive from death and rescue him with strong crying and with tears and was heard on account of his righteousness; and though he were a son, he learned obedience by the things which he had borne and became the cause of eternal life unto all them that obey him*;[2] and again 'he who begins and gradually advances and is 'brought to fullness is not God, although on account of his 'revelation which [was made] little by little he is so called';[3] and again: 'Does not the Scripture also teach you that the divinity has not need of sanctification, but the flesh?'[4] Although he was a son, by reason indeed of the union of the divinity and of the flesh, the Son of God speaks in them both because both the natures exist in him: 'Now indeed the glory of God and now the sufferings of the man.'[4] For in saying 'God' and in saying 'in nature', we conceive him not without the man; and so again in calling him 'man' and in speaking of him as 'in nature', we speak not of him apart from his being God, but / we name the man God indeed on account of the union of the divinity but man in nature; yet similarly once more also God the Word is God indeed in nature, but we call God man by reason of the union of the *prosôpon* of the humanity. The [properties] therefore of the natures change not the union nor those of the union the natures and deprive [not] both

---

[1] Syr. *'ôrgănôn*.
[2] Heb. v. 7-9.
[3] See p. 200, n. 1.
[4] See p. 199, n. 2 (2).

of them of the properties of the natures or of those which are caused by the union in the dispensation on our behalf.

But let other things also be written for the confutation of the condemnation which the judges have pronounced against me.

Likewise from the same, from the seventh roll. Wherefore, holy brethren who have been called by a heavenly calling, behold this Apostle and chief priest of our confession Jesus Christ, who [was] faithful unto him that hath made him as [was] Moses in all his house.[1] *And after other things*: Since you have this chief priest who suffers with you and [is] your kinsman and sustains your people, fall not away from the faith; for he, by means of the blessing which was promised unto him, was sent of the seed of Abraham in order that he might present himself as a sacrifice on his behalf and on behalf of his kinsmen. It is to be remarked that I have confessed, that they all had need of sacrifices, and that I have excepted Christ as one who has not need; but he offered himself as a sacrifice on his own behalf and on behalf of his race.[2]

Who then [is he] that is faithful / unto him that made him chief priest? Make answer. God the Word? For of him it says that he was made chief priest unto him who made him. Who is he that made him chief priest? [Was it] he who was faithful unto him, or did he make himself or [was he made it] by the Father? But if he made himself chief priest, if thou sayest that that [took place] in the union in the same manner as the Word also became flesh, thou art constrained to give a nature of our own *ousia* unto the flesh, after which he also is called flesh in the union and not in the nature. He is truly chief priest, he who is consubstantial with us and our kinsman, on account of whom God the Word also is called chief priest.

---

[1] Heb. iii. 1-2.
[2] Labbe (Mansi), iv. 1205 B: ὁμοίως τοῦ αὐτοῦ, τετράδιον ιζ'. ὅθεν, ἀδελφοί, κλήσεως ἐπουρανίου μέτοχοι, κατανοήσατε τὸν ἀπόστολον καὶ ἀρχιερέα τῆς ὁμολογίας ἡμῶν Ἰησοῦν, πιστὸν ὄντα τῷ ποιήσαντι αὐτόν. καὶ μεθ' ἕτερα· ὄντος οὖν ἡμῖν τούτου μόνου ἀρχιερέως συμπαθοῦς καὶ συγγενοῦς καὶ βεβαίου, τῆς εἰς αὐτὸν μὴ παρατρέπεσθε πίστεως. αὐτὸς γὰρ ἡμῖν τῆς ἐπηγγελμένης εὐλογίας ἐκ σπέρματος Ἀβραὰμ ἀπεστάλη, ὡς ὑπὲρ ἑαυτοῦ καὶ τοῦ συγγενοῦς τὴν τοῦ σώματος θυσίαν συνεπαγόμενος. σημειωτέον, ὅτι ὁμολογήσας πάντα ἀρχιερέα δεῖσθαι θυσίας, καὶ ὑπεξελὼν τὸν Χριστόν, ὡς μὴ δεόμενον, ἐν τούτοις ὑπὲρ ἑαυτοῦ φησὶ προσφέρειν, καὶ τοῦ συγγενοῦς, θυσίαν. Cp. Loofs, *Nestoriana*, p. 240.

For there is none that says that the one was of the other and denies that the other was of the one. Confess therefore in the first place this one who exists in the nature and next [him] who is said [to exist] through the union; for if this is not confirmed, there is not even place for it.

For each one of the names of an *ousia* indicates concerning him in the first place the *ousia* whose name it is. Bring it before the hearer, and then afterwards thou comest to the fact that they are said otherwise also and not in *ousia*. Consequently also when in that which is said men take first a name which is [used] of a nature, and afterwards of things which [are said] otherwise, however it may be, they are named either in the manner of homonymy or even not by nature; for this reason they cover them over as things concealed and forgotten. When therefore we speak of the things of the union, / thou sayest 'and is made man', but thou assignest this not to the union but as to the nature. But thou dissemblest the things appertaining to the nature and thou hinderest those who speak [them] as persons committing impiety. Thou allowest naught else than to take the [words] 'he became' and 'he was made' of the nature of God, although ten thousand times thou sayest [that he is] unchangeable; and thou confessest that he who made was made and exists in his nature and is called what he became; or speakest thou on the contrary in phantasy [words] which confess two natures of which Christ is [formed] and diverse natures which are diverse natures? How can men speak otherwise of the natures, unless they make use of the name of the natures, of the one and of the other?

But this [is] weighty. For this reason also I have said that it is to be remarked: he indeed has been sent unto us of the seed of Abraham through the blessing which was promised, that he might offer his body as a sacrifice on his behalf and on behalf of his kinsmen. Remark indeed that I have confessed, that all the chief priests have need of sacrifices, while Christ, as one who had no need thereof, offered himself as a sacrifice on his own behalf and on behalf of his race. Suppose that it has been so said by me; for I decline not to refute the change in your words, lest it should be supposed that, after I have been refuted, I have set myself to accuse [you] because of [your] inadequacy. For even in these things God has not left me without / excuse for my thought, which is clear unto all men. For I have said that all the chief priests have need of sacrifices for their sins, except Christ; whereas I have said that Christ has offered the sacrifice of himself for himself and for his race, for his race, indeed, that he may release them from the condemnation of the signed bond of sin.[1] While he was free from sin, [he] yet [offered himself] for himself that there might be given unto him a name which [is] more excellent than all names, and he was obedient unto death, and accepted death upon the cross, he who was free from sin. For he who was not found with sin and was obedient that he might die for us, received a name which is more excellent than all names, which was his since the beginning, from birth, since he was a little child. And although he was indeed Son and there was neither more nor less in him in authority in his sonship, yet was he made perfect that he might become a Son with authority; similarly the humanity, which from birth had to become the Son through the union and which had not authority but obedience, yet through obedience was perfected in authority and received a name which [is] more excellent than all names. Therefore he was neither passible nor yet mortal but both in authority and in honour. He was / in them all; apart from the *ousia* he had all the [properties] of the *ousia*; he is one Son who exists in the union.

And every chief priest has need of sacrifices for his sins, but Christ had not need [thereof] for his sins but for his race, that he might release them from sin. But this was also so for his own sake; because of his unlimited obedience [it was] that he died for sinners. Both in his will and in his thought he acquired, in short, naught else than to wish and to will whatsoever God willed in him. For this reason God also was in him whatsoever he was himself, in such wise that he also became in God whatsoever God was in him for the forming of his coming into being in his likeness, [to wit] the *prosôpon* of God; and whatsoever the humanity became

---

[1] Cp. Col. ii. 14.

by the obedience which it observed was not for his *prosôpon* therein, but for the *prosôpon* of God in God. This *prosôpon* will be his and [he will be] also God, in such wise that, wherein he is one, having acquired no distinction in the *prosôpon*, [it is] necessary to give unto him a distinction of the complete natures. But in the *prosôpa* of the union, the one in the other, neither by diminution nor by suppression nor by confusion is this 'one' conceived, but by taking and by giving,[1] and by the use of the union of the one with the other, the *prosôpa* take and give one another but not the *ousias*. The one we conceive as the other and the other as the one, while the one and the other abide. For when God the Word is called God and man, there are not two *prosôpa* of God the Word / because the two of them are not said [to be] in *ousia*, but the one is said [to be] in *ousia* and the other in the union, and in the use of the one with the other which came about through both the natures. But he is predicated in them both, in the one and in the other: in the one indeed by *ousia* and in the other by union. And so also, when by reason of the very union we concede to the humanity the being said [to be] in both of them, in the *ousia* and in the union, we make not of necessity two *prosôpa* of the union, in that there is [only] one belonging to both the natures, belonging to the divinity and to the humanity as to the humanity and the divinity. In saying 'God indeed who was made man', he[2] has not however left out the compensation, as thou conceivest this in the union, since the union with the humanity is congruous with God the Word, in such wise that he is called God in both of them. Nor again [is] the man also man and God; thou takest away the compensation from the union of the two *ousias*. For this reason he goes back on his word and [adds] 'the man who was made God' as depending on the union which makes the *prosôpa* and not the natures common.

And hear also from the same[2]:—'He who begins and 'gradually advances and is brought to fullness is not God,

---

[1] Cp. p. 262, l. 27. For Loof's interpretation of this phrase see *Nestorius and his Place in the History of Christian Doctrine*, pp. 92-4.

[2] *Viz.* Gregory.

'although on account of the manifestation which [took place] 'little by little he is so called.'[1] Because he is called God through the manifestation, he is not to be conceived as man without *prosôpon* and without nature; because he is man in nature, he is for this reason God in the manifestation, in order that it may not be supposed / that he is called God for the suppression of the natures and of their properties owing to the union, or that the union of God took place only with a view to the man. Wherefore whatsoever God is by nature is said also by [reason of] the union in whatever is united, that is, man. For the man, who, as not united, was not what he is by nature, [namely] man,[2] is called God through that which is united.[3]

For all these things make thy protests absurd; if indeed it be that another man says that he was man who began and therefore was not God, although by reason of the union he is so called, he is not foolish; for it is the other who begins and gradually advances and is brought to fullness, and not God, and he offends your hearing in naught. But if I say that the other is he who gradually advanced and was perfected for the chief priesthood, thou rebukest me as though I were introducing another *prosôpon*; there is, however, no distinction between a man's saying 'the man who begins' and his saying 'he who begins', for all these indicate the same thing, that is, the man. 'Speak of the glory of God and the sufferings of man': 'Does not the Scripture also teach you that the divinity has not need of sanctification, but the flesh?'[4] Why dissemblest thou these things as one who is ashamed of them and makest the sufferings of him who suffered for our sakes those of the impassible, in such wise that the debt on behalf of our salvation was paid and settled without sufferings, since / he took nothing? But thou hast done all things in

[1] See p. 200, n. 1.
[2] This is surely a reference to Nestorius' view that the manhood of Christ was united to the Logos from the very moment of conception; it therefore never existed by itself, but only in the union. With this interpretation there is no need to follow Nau in removing the negative from the sentence.
[3] There is no new paragraph marked here in the Syriac text.
[4] See p. 199, n. 2 (2).

schêma and in fiction and agreest neither with thyself nor with the Fathers. For you are not fighting against me, but through me you are fighting against these. Further, among the things whereof you accuse me, let us hear these things also:

Likewise from the same, from the fourth roll. Hear then, you who are inquiring into the words: *He that eateth my body.* Recollect that he speaks of the body, and [that] I have not added the term 'body', in order that it may not be thought by them that I am interpreting it contrariwise: *He that eateth my body and drinketh my blood abideth in me and I in him.*[1] *And, after other things*: But on the present subject he has said: *He that eateth my body and drinketh my blood abideth in me and I in him.* Recollect that he says of the body something which he says: *as the living Father hath sent me.*[2] The former then has said these things of the divinity, but I of the humanity; let us therefore see who it is that interprets [them] contrariwise. *As the living Father hath sent me*, as they say, I then too am living, I the Word by reason of the Father. And now after this [it is written]: *So he that eateth me, even he shall live.*[2] Whom do we eat? The divinity or the flesh?[3]

Therefore, although they are willing to say that I have not interpreted contrary to the divine / scriptures, they are to be reprimanded by all men. However, since I have asked, you have considered my request impious: [was it] then that I ought not to have said whatever divine scripture says, that 'the flesh was eaten'? But divine Scripture has said simply flesh, whereas you have condemned me, since by 'flesh' I

---

[1] Jn. vi. 56 (P.). [2] Jn. vi. 57.

[3] Labbe (Mansi), iv. 1205 c: ὁμοίως τοῦ αὐτοῦ, τετράδιον δ'. ἀκούσατε τοίνυν, προσέχοντες τοῖς ῥητοῖς. ὁ τρώγων μου, φησί, τὴν σάρκα. μνημονεύετε ὅτι περὶ τῆς σαρκός ἐστι τὸ λεγόμενον, καὶ ὅτι οὐ παρ' ἐμοῦ προστέθειται τὸ τῆς σαρκὸς ὄνομα· ὥστε μὴ δοκεῖν ἐκείνοις παερμηνεύειν· ὁ τρώγων μου τὴν σάρκα, καὶ πίνων μου τὸ αἷμα· μὴ εἶπεν· ὁ τρώγων μου τὴν θεότητα καὶ πίνων ταύτην; ὁ τρώγων μου τὴν σάρκα, καὶ πίνων μου τὸ αἷμα, ἐν ἐμοὶ μένει, κἀγὼ ἐν αὐτῷ. καὶ μεθ' ἕτερα. ἀλλ' ἐπὶ τὸ προκείμενον· ὁ τρώγων μου τὴν σάρκα, καὶ πίνων μου τὸ αἷμα, ἐν ἐμοὶ μένει, κἀγὼ ἐν αὐτῷ. μνημονεύετε, ὅτι περὶ τῆς σαρκὸς τὸ λεγόμενον, καθὼς ἀπέστειλέ με ὁ ζῶν πατήρ· ἐμὲ τὸν φαινόμενον. ἀλλ' ἐνίοτε παρερμηνεύω· ἀκούσωμεν ἐκ τῶν ἑξῆς· καθὼς ἀπέστειλέ με ὁ ζῶν πατήρ. ἐκεῖνος λέγει τὴν θεότητα, ἐγὼ δὲ τὴν ἀνθρωπότητα. ἴδωμεν τίς ὁ παρερμηνεύων. καθὼς ἀπέστειλέ με ὁ ζῶν πατήρ. λέγει καὶ ὁ αἱρετικός, ἐνταῦθα τὴν θεότητα λέγει· ἀπέστειλέ με, φησί, τὸν Θεὸν λόγον. καθὼς ἀπέστειλέ με ὁ ζῶν πατήρ. κατ' ἐκείνους, κἀγὼ ζῶ ὁ Θεὸς λόγος διὰ τὸν πατέρα· εἶτα τὸ μετὰ τοῦτο· καὶ ὁ τρώγων με, κἀκεῖνος ζήσεται. τίνα ἐσθίομεν; τὴν θεότητα, ἢ τὴν ἀνθρωπότητα; Cp. Loofs, *Nestoriana*, pp. 227-8.

conceive the flesh and not the divinity, as though I [were] one that makes distinctions, conceiving the one as flesh and the other as divinity. I distinguish not the union of the natures but the natures which are united in reference to the *ousias*, even as being without confusion of the one with the other. I have said the flesh and the divinity. Suppose that I was not speaking with precision; I condemn my lack of instruction and my own impiety. Only wait for me, that you may say this clearly: that the flesh and the divinity are one and the same in *ousia* as well as in *prosôpon* ;[1] and we denounce all those who think otherwise than this as impious. If you do not say this clearly, for what reason have you condemned me before God?

But some one will perhaps say: Wherefore art thou downcast? They have confessed the death of God and have condemned thee also to death. Whatever else hast thou thought in opposition to those who stand up for these things, and do not permit men not to attach death unto God and in fact defy those who confess [it] not? I know then that they have been / doing this for a long while, but now I am addressing this my discourse to those who in truth seek to be instructed lest they be deceived by the name 'Council' [and believe] that I have been condemned by the judgement of the Fathers and by the testimonies which they have cited. From all this I shall prove that there was no judgement, because they made no examination, neither amongst themselves nor with the others, nor have they been content even in *schêma* to divest themselves [2] of the depth of their impiety.[3]

'For the flesh of our Lord is one thing in *ousia* and the divinity is another,' says Gregory; for the things whereof our Saviour [was formed] are one thing and another, the visible and the invisible are not the same and 'he who 'begins and gradually advances and is perfected is not God, 'although by reason of the manifestation which [took place] 'little by little he is so called';[4] and 'not artificially'[5] was he

---

[1] The Syriac text gives this sentence as interrogative.   [2] See crit. n., p. 400.
[3] There is no new paragraph marked here in the Syriac text.
[4] Cp. p. 200, ns. 1 and 2.   [5] Cp. p. 192, n. 3.

in the body': and 'human was the body which [was] born of Mary', and the flesh [was] of the holy Mary. Athanasius said this: 'he took from the virgin a body in the likeness of the latter.' 'For he took not a body of an *hylê* precious and 'heavenly and came among us, but of clay, to show the great-'ness of his craftsmanship, in order that he might re-shape the 'very man who was formed of clay,' as Theophilus has said.[1]

But Ambrose speaks of the union of the divinity and of the flesh: 'The Son of God speaks in both of them, since in him 'were / the two natures. He is *the living bread which came* '*down from heaven*;[2] this bread is the body, the body whereof 'he himself has said: *This bread that I will give unto you is* '*my body*. He [it was] that came down, He [it is] that the 'Father has sanctified and has sent into the world. Does not 'Scripture also teach you that the divinity has not need of 'sanctification, but the flesh?'[3]

Did I alone say this? Why have I need of other witnesses for protesting that the flesh is not in the same [manner] God the Word? or that it is [not] for it to become what God the Word is, or that it is [not] God the Word's to become flesh, although the other is predicated in the union? If you yourselves are not persuaded and believe not all these things and defy all men, what have you [to do] with me [and] with all of these? Let him who injures me injure me and him who persecutes me persecute me and him who kills me kill me; and we consider it a great favour to be deemed worthy to endure the scars of Christ on our body. If [it is] pleasing unto you to hear, hear also other things and judge if they are worthy of the judgement [which has been passed] and if these things are not [the work] of men who look askance at heaven and contend against God.

/ *Likewise from the same, from the sixteenth roll.* If thou examinest well all the New [Testament], thou canst not anywhere find that death is imputed unto God but either unto Christ or unto the Son or unto the Lord. For the name of Christ or of Son or of Lord, which is taken

---

[1] Cp. p. 231, n. 2. [2] Jn. vi. 58. [3] See p. 199, n. 2 (2).

for the only-begotten from the divine Scriptures, is indicative of two natures and indicates sometimes the divinity, but sometimes the humanity and sometimes both of them. When Paul, who was sent forth to preach,[1] says *We were enemies, but God has been reconciled with us through the death of His Son*,[2] he proclaims the humanity by the name of the Son. When the same [Apostle] says unto the Hebrews *God hath spoken by his Son, by whom He made the worlds*,[3] he indicates the divinity; for the flesh was not the creator of the worlds, the [flesh] which has been made after many worlds. And, after other things: Nor indeed was James the brother of the divinity, nor do we preach the death of God the Word—eating the Lord's body.[4]

Can it be believed that there is in these things [a ground of] accusation wherewith I should be accused and [for] which I should suffer what I have suffered? Because I have said that not God the Word, whose nature is immortal, died but the flesh, for this reason have I been accused? I suppose that not even the demons and they that [are] in enmity with God, have dared to say or have taught this with their voices. Or is it not because of / those who fear not God and respect not men that I have said 'If thou examinest all the New '[Testament] together, thou wilt find no place where death is 'imputed unto God the Word, but either unto Christ or unto 'the Lord or unto the Son; for the name of Christ or of the 'Lord or of the Son, which is taken for the only-begotten 'from the Scriptures is indicative of two natures'. Have I lied? Thou hast the Divine Scriptures: read [them].

---

[1] See pp. xiii–xiv. [2] Rom. v. 10. [3] Heb. i. 1–2.

[4] Labbe (Mansi), iv. 1205 E: ὁμοίως τοῦ αὐτοῦ, τετράδιον ιϛ'. καὶ ὅλως, φησίν, εἰ πᾶσαν ὁμοῦ τὴν καινὴν μεταλλεύεις, οὐκ ἂν εὕροις οὐδαμῶς παρὰ ταύτῃ τὸν θάνατον τῷ Θεῷ προσαπτόμενον, ἀλλ' ἢ Χριστῷ, ἢ υἱῷ, ἢ κυρίῳ. τὸ γὰρ Χριστός, καὶ τὸ υἱός, καὶ τὸ κύριος, ἐπὶ τοῦ μονογενοῦς παρὰ τῆς γραφῆς λαμβανόμενον, τῶν φύσεων ἐστὶ τῶν δύο σημαντικόν, καὶ ποτὲ μὲν δηλοῦν τὴν θεότητα, ποτὲ δὲ τὴν ἀνθρωπότητα, ποτὲ δὲ ἀμφότερα· οἷον, ὅταν Παῦλος ἐπιστέλλων κηρύττει· ἐχθροὶ ὄντες, κατηλλάγημεν τῷ Θεῷ διὰ τοῦ θανάτου τοῦ υἱοῦ αὐτοῦ, τὴν ἀνθρωπότητα βοᾷ τοῦ υἱοῦ· ἂν λέγῃ πάλιν ὁ αὐτὸς πρὸς Ἑβραίους· ὁ Θεὸς ἐλάλησεν ἡμῖν ἐν υἱῷ, δι' οὗ καὶ τοὺς αἰῶνας ἐποίησε, τὴν θεότητα δηλοῖ τοῦ υἱοῦ. οὐδὲ γὰρ ἡ σὰρξ δημιουργὸς τῶν αἰώνων, ἡ μετ' αἰῶνας δημιουργηθεῖσα πολλούς. καὶ μεθ' ἕτερα. οὐδὲ θεότητος ἀδελφὸν τὸν Ἰάκωβον ἔσχεν. οὐδὲ τὸν τοῦ Θεοῦ λόγου καταγγέλλομεν θάνατον, τὸ δεσποτικὸν αἷμά τε καὶ σῶμα σιτούμενοι. Cp. Loofs, *Nestoriana*, pp. 269–71. For a similar argument cp. Nest. *ad Cyr. II*, in Labbe (Mansi), iv. 896 c, D; Loofs, *Nestoriana*, p. 177, ll. 8 ff.

What urgent need is there that we should speak cursorily? He has said: 'God the Word has suffered'; or else: 'Christ is not God and man of two natures and two natures.' Read. Either thou sayest [that] God the Word [is] in *ousia* in the two natures, of two natures and two natures, and, concerning the one *ousia* of God the Word, [that] it has been divided into two *ousias*, in such wise that, whatever is the nature of which we say that it has suffered, we attribute unto God the Word having suffered in nature in both of them; or both natures, distinct from one another, have been combined in the one *ousia* of God the Word, so that, of whichever we say that it has suffered, we say that it is one *ousia* and the same, which has been combined, that has suffered; or the *ousia* of the humanity has only been taken for use, that he might see and suffer, nor was it that they might make use one of the other at the same time, and to this reason the latter has contributed naught with the former to the dispensation on our behalf. And he made use thereof according to his own will / as though [it were] without feeling and without reason and without soul, without gaining aught, as the Arians say. For he who receives these things is not constrained to refer them to the *prosôpon* of him who endured these things, because he made not use of it in order that it might aid him, but that he might be able to suffer and fulfil all human things naturally, without that wherein he suffered or whereby he suffered being reckoned with him who suffered. Say clearly whatever thou dost wish; only [say it] clearly. Why censurest thou me as an impious person, because I have said 'If thou examinest all 'the New [Testament], thou wilt not find therein that death 'is imputed unto God the Word, but unto Christ or unto 'the Son or unto the Lord. For the name of Christ or of 'Son or of Lord, which is taken for the only-begotten in the 'Divine Scriptures is indicative of two natures and indicates 'sometimes the divinity and sometimes the humanity and 'sometimes both of them'? These things I have said, concerning them I am judged, and you are the judges of the things which are said. Speak thou!

For I ought to depose these things of thine also, as thou

too hast deposed against me, and to hide naught; nor indeed shall I show myself like you, who have judged my words without examination and without comparison. I have said this: 'In saying that God has not suffered and that 'Christ has not suffered, thou then inferrest naught else 'therefrom than that Christ is not God, while if thou sayest 'that God the Word suffered, thou confessest that Christ is 'God.' / So then you ought not to depose the whole section, but [only] as far as to bring forward those things which can make it known that I say these things; but the rest you ought to hide. How so? 'If thou readest all the New '[Testament], thou canst not find therein that death is 'imputed unto God the Word, but either unto Christ or 'unto the Lord or unto the Son.' For thus far he can extract them and make believe that I confess not Christ [as] God; but the rest of the things which have been deposed by you clearly dispose of this supposition. For 'Christ or Lord or 'Son, which is taken for the only-begotten in the Divine 'Scriptures, is yet indicative of two natures, sometimes indeed 'indicating the divinity, but sometimes the humanity, and 'sometimes both of them'. For I have not denied that Christ is not God,[1] but [I have said] that He is also God and God by nature; since I have said that it indicates two natures, the divinity and the humanity. It is not therefore possible that I should be accused of not confessing Christ [as] God through what I have written.

But perhaps [I am accused] because I have called Christ both man and two natures, of the divinity and of the humanity, one passible and the other impassible, and have not confessed that God the Word suffered in both the natures and in *ousia*, God the Word who became the *ousia* of man, [with the result] either that he who died lived as if he existed in *schêma*, and we refer / unto God the Word and not unto the *ousia* of the man the sufferings, in whatsoever manner it be, and that the

---

[1] If this, the literal rendering of the Syriac, be retained, 'not God' must be taken together as meaning 'human'. But it is much more probable that the 'not' of the Syriac represents the οὐ of the Greek μὴ οὐ after a negatived verb of denying and should therefore be omitted in English. See p. xiv.

humanity contributed naught to the dispensation, or that he is manifested and is able to suffer in the very human nature—for this reason it is not reckoned with the divinity—and we refer all these attributes of the divinity and of the humanity to the divinity, as those of the instrument[1] [are referred] to the craftsman, whereas he attributes not those of the divinity unto those of the humanity, in the same way as also those of the craftsman, without whose will nothing is done, are not attributed unto the instrument.[1] This man's meaning is not evident in the things whereof he accuses me. But the judges sit deaf and speechless, without having examined aught. Again constraint [is laid upon me] to make use of the same testimonies against them in establishing mine own [theories] and in reprimanding those who for this reason have fled from judgement, because they had no defence. But otherwise let him who has extracted my words say in passing that the name of Christ or of Son or of Lord is not indicative of two natures, of the divinity and of the humanity. I say naught else.

Read, O man, what thou hast amongst thy testimonies and contend not with a shadow: 'two natures indeed, God and 'man, but not two sons; for one thing and another are those 'things whereof our Saviour [is formed]; yet [he is] not one 'and another—far from it!/—but one in the mixture: God 'who was made man and man who was made God.' 'He 'who begins and gradually advances and is perfected is not 'God, although by reason of his manifestation which [took 'place] little by little he is so called.'[2] Have I written these things? Have I inserted aught in them all? Have you not written them? Wherefore then are you accusing me, as though I have predicated two natures of our Saviour? [He is] one thing indeed in nature in the divinity, but another however in nature in the humanity; the divinity [is] not two natures nor [is it formed] of one thing and another, neither are they by mixture in God the Word, but they are two in nature and in the union [there is] one *prosôpon* belonging to both of them. Yet again [it is] not as if the *prosôpon* of the humanity, of God

---

[1] Syr. 'órgānón, and see p. 239, n. 1.   [2] See p. 200, ns. 1 and 2.

who was made man, were rejected in the Trinity. 'He who
'begins and gradually advances and is brought to fullness is
'not God, although by reason of his manifestation which [took
'place] little by little he is so called.'[1] Neither does he say
that God the Word is both of them in *ousia*, nor does he
distinguish the humanity from the divinity in such wise that
God the Word should suffer even the sufferings of the flesh
and accept them in his nature in his *prosôpon*; for the flesh is
outside, participating not in the [properties] of the divinity
in its own *prosôpon*; but by a compensation consisting in [2] the
taking and the giving of their *prosôpa* he speaks of the
union of the divinity and of the humanity.[3] Of God on
the one hand he says that he was made man out of humanity
by union; / on the other hand he says of the humanity that
it was made God from the union with the divinity, whereas it
was not that it issued forth from the divinity; for 'he who
'begins and gradually advances and is brought to fullness is
'not God, although by reason of the revelation which [took
'place] little by little he is so called '.[1]

Ambrose too says the same of the union of the divinity and
of the flesh : 'the Son of God speaks in both of them, because
there were in him both the natures.'[4] Athanasius too says
this, that our Lord, and not the divinity, came forth from
Mary, and predicates also the two natures, calling indeed that
of the divinity one thing and the flesh another, and predicating
a union thereof. Therein there are both the natures, not in
God the Word but in the Son; not indeed that the Son is one
and God the Word another, but the one indeed indicates the
union and the other the *ousia*. For the *prosôpon* is one thing
and the *ousia* another, even as [it is] in respect to the Father
and the Son, [who are] one thing and another indeed in the
prosôpon but not one thing and another in the divinity.
Further, in respect to the union of the divinity and of the
flesh, in the *prosôpon* of the divinity of God the Word [he is]
not one thing and another but the same; yet in the natures
of the divinity and of the humanity [he is] one thing and

---

[1] See p. 200, n. 1.   [2] Literally : 'of'.   [3] Cp. p. 252, n. 1.
[4] See p. 199, n. 2 (2).

another. And for this reason Divine Scripture speaks lucidly of the *prosôpon* of the divinity and indicates them both in the *prosôpon* of the union. But of the *ousia* of the divinity and in the *ousia* of God / the Word there are not both of them; for the things which are said of the *ousia* are conceived in one something in so far as they are predicated only of the *ousia*.

For this reason Ambrose also speaks of the union of the divinity and spoke not of the union of the Son, although not another but out of the same. But the one indeed is indicative of the *prosôpon*, while the other is indicative of the nature; and for this reason, in that there has been a union of the *ousias*, he speaks of the union of the divinity and of the flesh, and, because the union of the natures resulted in one *prosôpon*, he added that the Son of God speaks in both of them, since in him are both the natures, [and] not God the Word. For God the Word is one and not two. That therefore which is known by the *ousia* is one thing and that which [is known] by the *prosôpon* is another, and that which [is known] by the natures is another, and that which indicates the union is another. For this reason I have said that 'Divine Scripture nowhere at all 'imputes death unto God, but either unto the Son or unto 'Christ or unto the Lord', in order that none may suppose that the union took place in the *ousia* and not in the *prosôpon*. And the *prosôpon* is not distinct,[1] so that one nature, [that] of the humanity, would be superfluous, since the Incarnation[2] is conceived [to consist] in the mutual use of taking and giving,[3] but Divine Scripture sometimes after the *prosôpon* of the divinity and sometimes after the *prosôpon* of the humanity, / names him Son and Christ and Lord. Gregory has said this, Ambrose has said this, Athanasius [has said] this: 'The 'Lord who [was born] of Mary is indeed the Son, by *ousia* in 'the nature of the Father, but by flesh of the seed of the 'house of David; for [he is of] the flesh of the Virgin Mary.'[4]

---

[1] *I.e.* presumably separable from the nature in such a way that the human πρόσωπον might have been assumed by the Logos without the human nature. Cp. pp. 170, 218-19.

[2] *Sc.* ἐνανθρώπησις.   [3] Cp. p. 252, n. 1.

[4] Labbe (Mansi), iv. 1185 D: πῶς δὲ καὶ ἀμφιβάλλειν ἐτόλμησαν οἱ λεγόμενοι

Have I said anything new? [Have I said] not the same things in the same words, and in the same sense? For what have you condemned me? Is it possible to imagine for what reason you have done these things by yourselves and have not waited to make your examination with all the bishops? But also it is not [possible] to flee from their accusation which they have brought against me; that which they have finally written without protest ought [here] to be written.

Likewise from the same, from the twenty-fourth roll. Now I observe in [the case of] our own people that they have acquired a great reverence and fervour of piety but have lapsed from the rest of the faith of the knowledge of God. Yet this is not [to be attributed] to the impiety of the people, but, that I may speak justly, [it is] because the very teachers have not had time at all to set before them the teaching of the exact faith....[1] This man has openly said therein that none of the teachers before him has spoken before the people / aught that he has spoken.[2]

But hear also concerning this—for this discourse is not very difficult and arduous—and ask these very persons; for they will tell the truth, though unwilling. In what treatise are these things said by me? [Is it] not in the deposit which was laid down by the holy Fathers who were assembled in Nicaea?[3] And what was my aim? [Was it] for the reprimanding of those who have taught wrongly or [of those] who have taught correctly and holily and with piety? And I have proved to the people that my own teaching and the teaching

χριστιανοί, εἰ ὁ ἐκ Μαρίας προελθὼν κύριος, υἱὸς μὲν τῇ οὐσίᾳ καὶ φύσει τοῦ Θεοῦ ἐστί· τὸ δὲ κατὰ σάρκα ἐκ σπέρματός ἐστι τοῦ Δαυείδ, σαρκὸς δὲ τῆς ἁγίας Μαρίας ;

[1] Nau, following the Greek, inserts: *Pierre, prêtre d'Alexandrie et premier des notaires, dit.*

[2] Labbe (Mansi), iv. 1208 B : ὁμοίως τοῦ αὐτοῦ, τετράδιον κγ΄. προσέχω, φησί, τοῖς ἡμετέροις δήμοις, εὐλάβειαν μὲν πολλὴν κεκτημένοις, καὶ θερμοτάτην εὐσέβειαν, ὑπὸ δὲ τῆς περὶ τὸ δόγμα θεογνωσίας ἀγνοίᾳ ὀλισθαίνουσι. τοῦτο δὲ οὐκ ἔγκλημα τῶν λαῶν· ἀλλά, πῶς ἂν εὐπρεπῶς εἴποιμι ; τὸ μὴ ἔχειν τοὺς διδασκάλους καιρὸν καί τι τῶν ἀκριβεστέρων ὑμῖν παραθέσθαι δογμάτων.

Πέτρος πρεσβύτερος Ἀλεξανδρείας, καὶ πριμμικήριος νοταρίων εἶπεν· ἰδοὺ φανερῶς ἐν τούτοις φησίν, ὅτι τῶν πρὸ αὐτοῦ διδασκάλων οὐδεὶς ταῦτα ἐλάλησε τοῖς λαοῖς, ἃ αὐτὸς ἐλάλησε. Cp. Loofs, *Nestoriana*, p. 283. For Cyril's comments on this passage made at an earlier date see Labbe (Mansi), iv. 1005 B, C.

[3] Cp. Loofs, *Nestoriana*, pp. 284, 285.

of these men [are] in agreement. Because they have not known the teaching of the Fathers they have been fighting with me, as though I were teaching outside the deposit of the Fathers. And I reprimanded them after the deposit of the Fathers, for not making known that whatsoever they were condemning is constantly in their mouths; and, lest I should reprimand them with excessive censure and vex them, I withheld myself from the accusation and I said concerning a person [1] against whom there was no accusation: 'the teachers ' of the faith have no time to set before you the exactitude of ' the faith.' [2] I said [it] simply without definition. How therefore have I accused all the Fathers before me as not having taught any of these things which I have taught the people, when my own aim and my work was this, namely, the teaching of them and the proving, after the deposit, that they taught these things and that I have said naught else apart from the deposit of the Fathers? But, from the ignorance and lack of instruction of the accusers they have supposed / concerning me: 'He is teaching us outside the teaching of these Fathers who have taught all of us.'

I have not then said that the teachers of sundry times have taught otherwise. How therefore should I have said that [they so taught], if [they taught] rightly? But I have said that they did not intelligibly and distinctly deliver to the people the deposit of the Fathers in order that they might hear and admire these things. For it [is] one thing for us to say that they have taught contrariwise, and another thing for us to say that they have delivered the very words without explanation, and another thing that, since they had not leisure, they could not teach according to what their intention was, and another thing that they were ignorant, or that I have been accusing them as heretics. For if I had finally accused the teachers before me thoroughly, I should also have accused the three hundred and eighteen on whose deposit [together] with the Fathers before me I was taking my stand. For none will say that I have said and taught these things apart from the teachers who [were] before me. I have said naught,

[1] Syr. *parṣôphâ*.   [2] See Fragm. 262, p. 289.

neither in word nor in thought nor [so as] to teach against those teachers who [were] before me. And yet if they have not read [it], you have written [it]. But you have nothing against me, because I have not said aught of those things whereof you have accused me. To this only, the chief point, have you clung; for this have I reprimanded you all. And you ought not also to believe these other things, since they have thus irreverently accused me, as persons who fear not God / and respect not men. But you have been abundantly convinced by him who was sitting with you in your assembly, as though indeed you could not otherwise escape than by quarrelling and by calumniating.

Those things which were done after the selection of these Chapters.

Yet after they have examined [my words] with all exactitude, as though Christ were seeing [them], they have condemned me without having found difficulty over anything or having quarrelled and without having established anything by question or by answer; but they were hastening in order that those who were about to come might not overtake them, that is, the Council of the East, which was near, and those from Rome. Neither have they examined nor even have they read; and, as I indeed suppose, even the things too which they have written they have written afterwards; the days and the time itself sufficed not for the writing and the signing. For it was apparent that they were signing against me gladly and freely, even without a cause; for not one indeed of them has written the cause on account of which they have deprived me, except only this man [who is] wise and intelligent above all men and able to say something intelligible, that is Acacius of Melitene: ' Because he has not confessed that God the Word ' died, he was worthy to be deprived, since he has made ' Divine Scripture to lie and further because he has calum- ' niated Cyril with having said that God the Word died, / when

'he has not [so] said; and he has also made the Scripture to
'lie, teaching that the birth and the suffering concerned not
'the divinity but the humanity, and he has calumniated also
'the very writings of the holy and godly bishop, Cyril, as
'though they call God the Word passible, a thing which
'neither he nor any other of those who think piously have
'dared to say. . . .'[1]

Now on one of these [points] and not upon two of them it was right that I should be accused; but they were accepting against me contrary [charges] and in the greatness of their preoccupation they were not willing to break off that with which they were engaged, but they were zealous to withdraw themselves and to dissent, that they might not come under the judgement of the judges. But they disclaimed [us] as enemies in such wise as to prove their preoccupation and their anxiety and to be thought fearful by the bishops who were present and who were absent; and they did all things such as take place in wars. And the [followers] of the Egyptian [2] and those of Memnon, by whom they were aided were going round the city, girded and armed with rods, stiff-necked men, who rushed upon them with the clamour of barbarians and forcibly emitted from [3] their nostrils a spirit of anger with fearful cries at no great distance, breathing [anger] without self-control, with all pride, against those whom they knew to be not in agreement with the things which were done by them. / They were taking bells round the city and were kindling fire in many places and handing round documents of various kinds; and all those things which were taking place were [matters] of astonishment and of fear, so that they blocked all the ways and made every one flee and not be seen,

---

[1] Labbe (Mansi), iv. 1172 C: καὶ θεοφόρων ἐπισκόπων φωνὰς ἀφελών, μόνῃ τῇ σαρκὶ τὰ τῆς σωτηριώδους περιῆψεν οἰκονομίας, ψιλὸν τὸν ναὸν τοῦ Θεοῦ γέννησίν τε καὶ τελευτὴν ὑπομεῖναι εἰπών. καὶ κατεψεύσατο μὲν τῆς γραφῆς, ὡς καὶ αὐτῆς τὴν γέννησίν τε καὶ τὸ πάθος οὐ τῆς θεότητος, ἀλλὰ τῆς ἀνθρωπότητος διδασκούσης. κατεσυκοφάντησε δὲ καὶ τῶν τοῦ ἁγιωτάτου καὶ θεοφιλεστάτου ἐπισκόπου Κυρίλλου γραμμάτων, ὡς παθητὸν λεγόντων τὸν Θεόν. ὅπερ οὔτε αὐτός, οὔτε ἄλλος τις τῶν εὐσεβῶς φρονούντων ἢ ἐνενόησεν εἰπεῖν, ἢ ἐτόλμησε. διὰ πάντων δὲ ἔδειξεν ἑαυτόν, ὀνόματι μόνῳ τὴν ἑνότητα τοῦ Θεοῦ πρὸς τὴν σάρκα ὁμολογοῦντα, τῷ δὲ πράγματι ταύτην πάντῃ ἀρνούμενον. . . .

[2] *Viz.* Cyril, archbishop of Alexandria. [3] Literally: 'in'.

and were behaving arbitrarily, giving way to drunkenness and to intoxication and to a disgraceful outcry. And there was none hindering, nor even bringing succour, and thus [men] were amazed. But all of it was being done against us, and for this reason we made use of the succour of the Emperor and of the authority of the Strategi, who were angered at the things which were done, though they let them be.

But there came the bishop of Antioch with many other bishops, whom they were seeking to win over to agree with them in what was unjustly and boldly done; and they named themselves an Oecumenical Council. And after they[1] knew the things which were being boldly done and their disgraceful audacity and their sudden war and the vehemence of the madness wherewith they were intentionally doing all things, they degraded from[2] their episcopal rank the organizers of this disorder, who had raised up all this evil; yea, I mean Cyril and Memnon. But for the rest / of their organizers, they laid them under anathema, because they had discharged naught of the work of the episcopate, as persons who have made use not of the object and traditions,[3] but [only] of the authority of the episcopate. And, in order that they might not deny or dissemble what was done against them, they wrote their deprivation in all parts of the city, that there might be for all of them witnesses that they had deprived them and for what reasons they had deprived them. They made these things known unto the Emperor through the letters of the Council, and their boldness in all of them and the war which had taken place after the fashion of barbarians.[4] And for this reason also they allowed them not to pray in the apostolic church of Saint John, but [brought it about] that persons stoned them, and they hardly escaped and were rescued, and they said also the cause wherefore they made bold to do this: that whatever had caused this disturbance and division in the churches might not be examined by the Council; I mean

---

[1] Viz. the new-comers.
[2] Literally: 'removed from'.
[3] Syr. *nishâ* and *qânônâ*.
[4] Cp. the account given by Nestorius and his adherents in Labbe (Mansi), iv. 1232 E-1236 A.

indeed the twelve Articles which were written irreverently and shamefully against God the Word,[1] immortal and incorruptible; and that great forethought ought to be shown that such blasphemies as these, which not even the party of Arius have dared to speak openly against God the Word, should not be left without examination.

But Cyril also and his fellow-conspirators wrote to the Emperor, blaming John for many things, as though / he had boldly deprived Cyril by reason of the love which had been vowed by him toward me. And they were in need of their confirmation of my deposition and the setting aside of that of Cyril and of Memnon; for they dared not write the [acts] of John and of the Council that [sat] with him and their words: 'That, as it has been ordained by the letters of your 'Piety, they have been assembled in common with us and we 'have been examining the things required dispassionately and 'accurately in order to confirm the faith of the religion of the 'Fathers'—which has been commanded by the Emperor and required also by the Easterns, who also were constantly expecting these things. Those who had confidence in the Divine Scriptures and in the teaching of the Fathers dared not say, though [it were] in *schêma*: 'Let there be a judgement!'—not even in order that they might escape a slanderous accusation. They indeed dared not hold an inquiry and a judgement concerning the things which were required to be [judged], because they had not confidence in the things which they wrote. So [that you may perceive] that I say them truly, read the report[2] of the latter and of the former, in order that you may know that the latter were always demanding that there should be a judgement, while the former were shunning [it].

[1] These are the twelve anathematisms appended by Cyril to his third letter to Nestorius, printed in Labbe (Mansi), iv. 1081 *sqq*. Together with Cyril's letter they were read at the Council, and inserted in the Acts, but whether they were formally approved is doubtful, though the Easterns and the Chalcedonian Council assumed that they were. See Labbe (Mansi), vi. 937, 972.

The anathematisms, with Nestorius' counter-anathemas, the comments of Theodoret and the Easterns, and Cyril's replies, are printed in Bindley, *Oecumenical Documents of the Faith* (2nd ed.), pp. 144 *sqq*.

[2] Syr. *'anāphôrâ*.

/ *The letter which was sent to the Emperor by John, bishop of Antioch, and by the other bishops who were assembled with him.*

Being commanded by your letters, we have reached Ephesus, the metropolis, and have found all [kinds of] turbulent fellows and the business[1] of the churches hampered with civil wars.[2] For Cyril of Alexandria and Memnon of Ephesus have gathered themselves together and have assembled a vast assembly of country-folk and have not allowed the feast of Holy Pentecost nor the office[s] of morning and of evening to take place ; and withal they have also closed the churches and the *martyria* ; but they have assembled with themselves and with those whom they have deceived and have committed ten thousand iniquities and have trodden [under foot] the canons of the holy Fathers together with your commands : and that when the most illustrious count Candidianus, who was sent by your most Christian authority, testified unto them in writing and without writing that they should await the coming of all the holy bishops, and that then there should be [done] whatsoever seemed [good] unto the whole assembly, according to the letters of your Piety. Cyril also the Alexandrian sent [word] unto me by letters two days before that we should hold an assembly, as all the Council were awaiting my coming. For this reason we have caused the deposition of those two who have been mentioned above, of Cyril and of Memnon, and interdicted them / from every spiritual ministration. But the rest of them, who have participated with them in iniquity, we have inhibited until they anathematize the Articles which have been sent by Cyril which are full of wicked purpose and are in accord with the teaching of Apollinarius and of Arius and of Eunomius, and [until] according to the letters of your Piety they have assembled themselves together unanimously with us in tranquillity and have scrutinized accurately with us aught that is required and have confirmed the true faith of the Fathers. But as for my own insignificance,[3] your Majesty knows that, in view of the length of the way and withal that we are journeying on land, we have advanced quickly and rapidly ; for we have travelled forty stages[4] without even one rest being taken by us during our journey ; and [this], it is within the authority of your most Christian

---

[1] Literally: 'with which the operations of the churches are full'.
[2] See p. xiii.   [3] See p. xiv.
[4] Syr. *masyônin* = Lat. *mansiones*, one *mansio* being equivalent to ten parasangs.

Majesty to learn from the inhabitants of all the cities through which we have passed. Withal however, both owing to the famine which has occurred in Antioch and owing to the daily brawls of the [diverse] parties[1] and owing to the great and continuous rains which have taken place out of season[2] and owing to the danger which came about through a flood[3] which approached the city, we were detained also not a few days in the city itself.[4]

But after the Emperor had seen these things, he was angered at what was being done against me without examination and without judgement, and he swore that there should be naught else except whatever had been before laid down to take place, that is, a judgement and an examination of the things which were required, so that for this purpose indeed the Oecumenical Council / was assembled, that it might at the

[1] See p. xiv.   [2] See p. xv.

[3] Nau, *un cyclone*; the Syr. *tauphānā* (= Gk. τυφῶν) is however rendered *inundatio, diluvium* by Payne-Smith (*Thes. Syr.* col. 1446 b).

[4] Labbe (Mansi), iv. 1272 : τοῖς εὐσεβέσιν ὑμῶν κελευσθέντες γράμμασι, κατελάβομεν τὴν Ἐφεσίων μητρόπολιν, καὶ εὕρομεν πάσης συγχύσεως καὶ ἐμφυλίου πολέμου γέμοντα τὰ ἐκκλησιαστικὰ πράγματα, Κυρίλλου τοῦ Ἀλεξανδρείας καὶ Μέμνονος συμφραξαμένων, καὶ πλήθος ἀγροικικὸν συναθροισάντων, καὶ μήτε τῆς ἁγίας πεντηκοστῆς τὴν πανήγυριν ἐπιτελέσαι συγχωρησάντων, μήτε τὰς ἑσπερινάς, ἢ τὰς ἑωθινὰς λειτουργίας· πρὸς δὲ τούτοις καὶ τὰς ἁγίας ἐκκλησίας, καὶ τὰ ἅγια μαρτύρια ἀποκλεισάντων. καθ᾽ ἑαυτοὺς δὲ σὺν τοῖς ἀπατηθεῖσιν ὑπ᾽ αὐτῶν συνεδρευσάντων, καὶ μύρια παράνομα ἐργασαμένων, καὶ τούς τε τῶν ἁγίων πατέρων κανόνας, τά τε ὑμέτερα πατησάντων θεσπίσματα, καὶ ταῦτα τοῦ μεγαλοπρεπεστάτου κόμητος Κανδιδιανοῦ, τοῦ παρὰ τῆς ὑμετέρας φιλοχρίστου κορυφῆς ἀποσταλέντος, παρεγγυήσαντος αὐτοῖς καὶ ἐγγράφως, καὶ ἀγράφως, ἀναμεῖναι τοὺς πανταχόθεν ἀφικνουμένους ἁγιωτάτους ἐπισκόπους, καὶ τότε κοινῇ τὸ συνέδριον ποιῆσαι κατὰ τὰ γράμματα τῆς ὑμετέρας εὐσεβείας· καὶ αὐτοῦ δὲ Κυρίλλου τοῦ Ἀλεξανδρέως, ἐπιστείλαντός μοι τῷ τῆς Ἀντιοχέων, πρὸ δύο ἡμερῶν τοῦ γενομένου ὑπ᾽ αὐτῶν συνεδρίου, ὡς ἡ σύνοδος πᾶσα ἀναμένει μου τὴν παρουσίαν. διὸ ἀμφοτέρους τοὺς προειρημένους καθείλομεν, Κύριλλον καὶ Μέμνονα, καὶ πάσης ἐκκλησιαστικῆς λειτουργίας ἀλλοτρίους πεποιήκαμεν. τοὺς δὲ λοιπούς, τοὺς ταύτης τῆς παρανομίας αὐτοῖς κοινωνήσαντας, ἀκοινωνήτους πεποιήκαμεν, ἕως ἂν τὰ κεφάλαια τὰ παρὰ Κυρίλλου ἐκπεμφθέντα, τῆς Ἀπολιναρίου, καὶ Εὐνομίου, καὶ Ἀρείου κακοδοξίας γέμοντα, ἐκβάλωσι καὶ ἀναθεμιτάσωσι, καὶ κατὰ τὸ τῆς ὑμετέρας εὐσεβείας γράμμα, κοινῇ σὺν ἡμῖν συνεδρεύσαντες, ἡσύχως καὶ ἀκριβῶς τά τε ζητήματα σὺν ὑμῖν ἴδωσι, καὶ τὸ εὐσεβὲς τῶν πατέρων βεβαιώσωσι δόγμα. περὶ δὲ τῆς ἐμῆς βραδύτητος ἴστω ὑμῶν ἡ εὐσέβεια, ὡς πρὸς τὸ χερσαῖον διάστημα τῆς ὁδοῦ, διὰ γῆς γὰρ ἡμῶν ἡ ὁδὸς γεγένηται, σφόδρα ἐπεταχύναμεν. τεσσαράκοντα γὰρ μόνας ὡδεύσαμεν, μηδεμίας ἀνακωχῆς κατὰ τὴν πορείαν ἀπολαύσαντες, ὡς ἔξεστιν ὑμῶν τῇ φιλοχρίστῳ βασιλείᾳ παρὰ τῶν τὰς κατὰ τὴν ὁδὸν πόλεις οἰκούντων μαθεῖν· πρὸς δὲ τούτοις καὶ ὁ λιμὸς κατὰ τὴν Ἀντιόχειαν γενόμενος, καὶ αἱ καθ᾽ ἑκάστην ἡμέραν ταραχαὶ τοῦ δήμου, καὶ ἡ παρὰ (v. l. περὶ) τὸν καιρὸν σφοδροτάτη γενομένη ἐπομβρία, ἥ καὶ κίνδυνον ἐκ τῶν χειμάρρων ἐπήγαγε τῇ πόλει, οὐκ ὀλίγας ἡμέρας ἡμᾶς εἰς τὴν προειρημένην ἐπέσχε πόλιν.

same time be convinced concerning the examination which should duly take place. But when the followers of Cyril saw the vehemence of the Emperor who was eager for this, thenceforth they roused up a disturbance and discord among the people with an outcry, as though the Emperor were opposed to God; they rose up against the nobles and the chiefs who acquiesced not in what had been done by them and were running hither and thither. And of such effrontery and boldness [were they that] they took also with them those who had been separated and removed from the monasteries by reason of their lives and their strange manners and had for this reason been expelled, and all who were of heretical sects and were possessed with fanaticism and with hatred against me. And one passion was in them all, Jews and pagans and all the sects, and they were busying themselves that they should accept without examination the things which were done without examination against me; and at the same time all of them, even those who had participated with me at table and in prayer and in thought, were agreed, [and] bound themselves together indistinguishably in affection and in visits to one another and by entertainment in [their] houses, and by covenant and by the confirmation of the things [done] against me, and were vowing vows one with another against me. Those too were willing who would surely not formerly have been supposed to be giving a welcome to heretics, although they were supposed / to be orthodox; in naught were they divided.

There is indeed much to say on the subject of the dreams which they recounted, which they say that they saw concerning me, while others [saw] other things. And they amazed the hearers by the saints to be sure whom they saw and by the revelations which were recounted by them and by a prophecy which was fabricated.[1] For there was none of them who was unaffected nor [any] that was distinct from their communion; I speak not only of Christians but also [of] pagans. For they were persuading all men of all the things which they were seeing, likening themselves to angels of light; and in all these

[1] A monophysite account of such phenomena as these, written in Syriac between 512 and 518 A.D., has been edited by Nau with a French translation; see Jean Rufus, Évêque de Maïouma, *Plérophories* (Patrologia Orientalis VIII. i, Paris, 1912).

things they had first calmed[1] and [afterwards] roused up the mind of the Emperor, that the inquiry which had been required and for which the Oecumenical Council was assembled might not take place. But when he was against their disgraceful [and] irreverent request in requiring that the judgement should not take place, they gave abundance of money to those who were nigh unto him. I have naught to say; for the Emperor allowed everything to take place in practice contrary to that to which he had clung in *schêma*; for they were not frightened by him nor [feared] to cause sedition and to run about unto all men.

But there was added thereunto also the plotting of evils: for they held assemblies of priests and troops of monks and they took counsel / against me, helping them in this purpose. And they had as helpers in these things all the ministers[2] of the Emperor who used to probe into his very purpose, and they gave confidence to the former. As indeed the *schêma* of the monks was very dear unto him, so all of them were unanimous in the one purpose of persuading him that there should be no judgement, while the things which had been done without examination against me should stand. And all the monks participated in the one purpose because of me, [even] those who in the rest of the other things were without love among themselves, [some] being envious and [others] envied, especially for the sake of the praise of men. And they took for them-[selves] as organizer and chief, in order to overwhelm the Emperor with amazement, Dalmatius the archimandrite, who for many years had not gone forth from his monastery; and a multitude of monks surrounded him in the midst of the city, chanting the offices,[3] in order that all the city might be assembled with them and proceed before the Emperor to be able to hinder his purpose. For they had prepared all these things in advance in order that there might not be any

---

[1] Apparently the 'aph'el of the Syr. *bhel*, 'was quiet', though it might be that of the Aram. *bathēl*, 'disturbed'.

[2] Literally: 'trusted ones', 'intimates'. Nau renders *eunuques* (see Payne-Smith, *Thes. Syr.* i. 233-4.

[3] Literally: 'ministering', of which the precise connotation is shown by the Greek original, ψάλλοντες ἀντίφωνα. Cp. Labbe (Mansi), iv. 1428 c. For the part played by Dalmatius, see Labbe (Mansi), iv. 1257-60, 1397-8, 1427-30, and Lupus, *Var. Patr. Epist.*, p. 419.

hindrance and they went in with [the chanting of] the office[1] even to the Emperor.

But when the Emperor saw Dalmatius, he shook his head and put up his hand as one who is in astonishment at the sight of a person;[2] and he said: 'What is the cause which 'has constrained thee to break thine own pact? For we were 'coming unto thee, but now why hast thou come unto us? 'And especially in the midst of the city! Thou, one that not 'even / in thy monastery hast been seen outside thy cell nor 'usest to let thyself be seen of all men, hast now made thyself 'as it were a spectacle both unto men and unto women. For 'why should there not have been many constraining causes 'which would have needed thy coming forth? [For example], 'mine own sickness even unto death and [that] of my relatives, 'the disturbances and the tumults which have been in the city 'and which had need of the intervention and the prayer of 'some one that they might not extend unto blood and unto 'death; wars and destruction and ruin and famines and earth-'quakes, which could have been stayed by prayer unto God 'alone—and has not one of these persuaded thee to come 'forth from thy monastery?'

Dalmatius says: 'Yea, Emperor, it was by no constraint 'such as this among these things that there was need of my 'coming forth. For this reason indeed God has not made me 'to know [aught of these difficulties], for he has settled them 'otherwise. But now God has commanded me, [even] me, to 'counsel thy Majesty, and I have been commanded to bear 'thee witness that thou transgressest against thyself in trans-'gressing against the Council and perverting its judgement. 'Thou hast assembled the Council for judgement and it has 'judged; it knows how it has judged; it is responsible unto 'God.'

The Emperor said unto him: 'I too find no impiety in this 'man nor any cause worthy of [his] deprivation. I testify 'unto thee and unto all men: I am innocent; for through no 'human / inclination have I loved this man and done the 'things which have taken place, so that he has been judged

[1] Literally: 'with the service' or 'ministering'. [2] Syr. *parṣôphâ*.

'and condemned, as those who rise up against God and usurp
'for themselves the [prerogatives] of the priests. Neither
'now nor formerly was I zealous for this ordination in such
'wise that I should be thought to be surely avenging myself
'and seeking retaliation on account of his election; but in
'participation with you all I caused this man to come by force,
'though his fathers' house and his race were loved by him.
'You have been the cause of these things, and not I. When,
'O Dalmatius, I was entreating thee to be [my helper] in this
'affair and was requesting thee with many [entreaties] not to
'decline the service of God, thou yet didst decline and didst
'beseech me on the contrary, [saying]: "Constrain me not
'"because I am a recluse."[1] And I also requested another of
'the monks, one who was supposed to be some one and illustrious
'for piety, and he too declined as one that knew not [how] to
'carry out this service, because he was a recluse.[1] For all of
'you said that Constantinople was in need of a bishop, one who
'[would be] loved by all men for his words and for his manner
'of life and who would be a teacher of the churches and the
'mouth of all men in everything. But when I declined for
'these reasons, [was it] that I did aught by my authority?
'Did I not again request of you to choose one who is such as
'this man? / Did I not even likewise beseech the clergy[2] of
'Constantinople to choose whosoever was suitable? Did I not
'say the same things unto the bishops, "It is yours to choose
'"and to make a bishop". And you too in like manner I
'besought; did I not leave [it] in your hands all this time,
'having waited patiently that you should choose peaceably,
'lest by haste there should be a mistake in him who was
'chosen? However, you chose, and did I not accept your
'choice? Requirest thou [that] I should say aught concerning
'[the rest of] you? Have I spoken of their zeal and their
'running about and their gifts and their promise and their oaths
'and everything [of] those who were seeking to become
'[bishops] as by purchase? Among the latter whom would
'you have sought to be [bishop]? But I pass over these
'things; which choice would you have sought to be [ratified]?

[1] Syr. *hedhyōṭā* = Gk. ἰδιώτης.   [2] Syr. *qlīrōs* = Gk. κλῆρος.

'Thine own or that of the former or of another? For some
'would have chosen [one and others] another, not as by choice
'as making their choice [fall on] the more excellent ones but
'on those who were evil; and each was glorifying him who
'had been chosen by himself and was speaking evil of the one
'who was chosen by the others and accusing him with evil
'accusations. But you have not agreed upon one and were
'not agreeing upon him upon whom the people agreed. I have
'read before you the utterances of the people concerning each
'one of those who have been chosen. What then ought I to
'have done and have not done? You / monks agreed not with
'the clergy, nor had the clergy one purpose, and the bishops were
'divided and the people were likewise divided, and one was striv-
'ing for [one and another for] another. Nor even so gave I myself
'authority, but I left the choice with you. But after all of you
'were found at a loss, all of you came and gave me [authority]
'to choose whomsoever I wanted. But thereupon, after I was
'hardly convinced, though all of you besought [me], I bethought
'me that none ought to be made [bishop] from here, lest there
'should be enmity against him and he should be hated; for
'you were all hating one another and were hated of one an-
'other, seeing that you were all zealous about this affair. But
'I had wanted a stranger who was not known by those here
'and knew them not, one who was famous for his preaching
'and for his manner of life. For people had informed me that
'there was [one] such as this in Antioch, [speaking] of
'Nestorius. This man I sent [and] fetched, though I grieved
'all that city; notwithstanding everything had been like this,
'I yet caused him to come for the sake of your own advantage
'which was more precious unto me than theirs. But when it
'happened, it was not supposed by you to be such. What then
'is it right to do unto the man? You have not examined him
'that he may make a defence of that wherewith he is reproached,
'nor has your bishop been judged by one consent, but the
'bishop of Alexandria / and [the bishop] of Rome have judged [1]
'that he was one that believes not correctly and ought to be
'convinced of their decision. But he requested and awaited the
'judgement as if an injustice were done unto him and blamed

[1] See crit. n., p. 400.

'them for not having accused him correctly, because he was
'a bishop and ought to be summoned to the judgement of the
'bishops and not to my judgement. Nor was it [the case] that
'any one whatsoever was a judge nor ought the bishop of
'Constantinople to have been heard before [any] one man.
'Did I judge as [was] pleasing unto me? I authorized
'the Council. Who is it that requested a judgement and
'submitted not thereto? Who is just? He that submits unto
'judgement and requests [it]? Or he that flees from the
'judgement? Could he liken himself unto the former, to do
'unto them whatsoever he himself suffered, and assemble the
'bishops who were under him and those of the East who were
'convinced by him, even so as to judge him guilty and accuse
'him himself? But he has indeed done this. But he has
'submitted unto the judgement, especially [with a view] to
'putting an end to these divisions. For there is no law that
'the bishop of Alexandria or of any city whatsoever should not
'be judged when he is to be judged. But also, when the
'Council assembled and sat, they required him [to present
'himself] once or twice, and he refused even to answer them.
'For what reason? Speak, dissemble not. For the things
'which took place are not forgotten by me; thus have they
'been irreverently done / so that the plotting which they
'plotted could not be hidden. For he has not declined the
'judgement but the preparation of the Council which has been
'[but] incompletely assembled to judge [him], a thing which
'pleased not us ourselves. Neither is that wherein an enemy
'sits among the judges a Council, nor have we ourselves com-
'manded that aught should take place before all the Council
'should be assembled; for an assembly of all of them, and not
'of some, we call a Council. Because we saw aforetime the
'plotting and the trickery which took place, we ordered that the
'Council should not be [held] incomplete but that they should
'await the assembly of all the bishops that the examination of
'the thing required might take place by question and by
'answer. They then dissolved the Oecumenical Council and
'the law of the tribunal; [it was] they who reckoned our will
'as nothing. And the bishop of Antioch has done well in

'regard to them, since he has deprived them of their episcopal 'rank lest, in remaining in their same ranks, they should 'dishonour their rank. Wherein therefore has he acted 'foolishly, who required of them that they should wait for 'those who were distant and that the rule which had been 'given should not be infringed and that there should be no 'dissension in the Council? Ought he, who did none of those 'things which it had been decided should be carried out, but 'was content to be judged by every one without declining, to 'have been deprived for this?'

/ After he [had] finished saying these things, he added and said: 'Neither do I find any cause of blame in this man; I and my empire and my race are guiltless of this impiety.' And the others agitated themselves at this very reply and seized upon it, as [if] to be sure he let pass and left alone those things which had been wrought against me in whatsoever they wrought. And Dalmatius and those with him cried out: 'On 'me let this impiety be, O Emperor; I rebuke thee and thine 'on account of these things; I will make my defence for these 'things before the tribunal of Christ, as having done this very 'deed' .... And after he [had] received this promise, that the responsibility for the impious deeds committed against me should not be [his], he decreed and confirmed the things which had been wrought against me. Thus I was judged and thus too was the examination [carried out].

And after the things were finished which were wrought against me by them, the impious band went forth from [his] Majesty and some spread abroad [some things and others] other things against me; and they carried Dalmatius around, reclining on a couch which was spread with coverlets, and mules bare him in the midst of the streets of the city, in such wise that it was made known unto all men that a victory had been gained over the purpose of the Emperor, amidst great assemblies of the people and of the monks, who were dancing and clapping the hand[s] and crying out the things which can be said against one who has been deprived for iniquity. But after it was known that the intention of the Emperor had been overcome by them, / all the heretics, who had formerly been deprived by me, took part with them, and all with one mouth were alike proclaiming my anathema, taking courage from anything that had taken place, in every part of the city, but especially in the parts by the sanctuary, in such wise as to add unto them[selves] crowds of the people to commit iniquity without reverence; and thus they took courage, clapping the hands and saying naught else except 'God the Word died'.

And there was not any distinction between heretics and orthodox, all of them together rising up against God the Word. And they were fighting without mercy against those who were not persuaded to predicate the suffering of the nature of God the Word, saying, not that the immortal adhered to the mortal to cause the mortal to die without its [being itself liable unto] mortality, but on the contrary that the immortal adhered to the mortal that it might become mortal and [that] thus it rose, having died with him, in the immortality of him who rose, and everything like this in that the immortal became mortal, that indeed again the mortal might become immortal in such wise that it might in its nature be receiving the [attribute] of immortality and that of mortality according to the might of him that commanded whereby he can make the immortal mortal and the mortal immortal. And these things were said openly by these and by those and by other heretics, being chanted and applauded / in the houses and in the streets and in all the churches, in consequence of which things thou couldest not distinguish the things which were being said in the churches or know whether the very churches belonged to the heretics or to the orthodox, such was the agreement and the zeal to embrace the faith and to confess God passible. And they were making use of demonstrations such as these while they were being accused for the same things and were making a defence thereof in the same [terms]. And they all had one mouth and one heart and one agreement against God the Word, in such wise that the services in the churches and in the monasteries were forgotten and they were busied with sedition and persecutions and affairs such as these. As for those who were furnishing them with money and supplies and provision, by all those things which they were giving they were both preparing them and demanding of them to be ceaselessly engaged in these things.

It therefore seemed [good] to the Emperor that I should be under [sentence of] deprivation and that both Cyril and Memnon likewise should be under [sentence of] deprivation. It would then have been supposed that he did this in order that he might constrain all of us to come to an agreement and to be accepted and to accept one another and that he bore patiently my deprivation that he might make us of one purpose. And further he was waiting without a reconciliation with the others in order that he might cause me, even me, by all means to come in, as well as through their zeal and their request on behalf of Cyril, that it might be supposed that the wisdom of [his] Majesty [had] defeated / their intentions. But this was not so; but, either because his purpose, which had been correctly [formed] from the beginning, was changed or because this had been his purpose from the beginning, he was indeed [only] in *schêma* on my side, until he found patience enough to sell [me] for money. But, howsoever all has happened, I have arrived at this.

But when Count John, who was set over the Treasury, was sent to Ephesus, it was then supposed that he had come that I and Cyril might speak with one another, all the Council having been assembled and [that] therefore it was an affair not to be declined. In everything there had been [cause] for fear and amazement unto the others, such had been their fear and trembling at speaking with me and at having judgement [passed] according to our words concerning the things about which inquiry was made. He, however, carried not his vehemence to the full but slackened, because that which is dear unto men [had] fallen upon him,[1] that which also was thenceforward mentioned as in a rumour; yet at the end he that reveals hidden things revealed it and brought it to light and made it known unto the eyes of all men. And it made him ashamed during his life, and after his death he was convicted: both he who sold the truth, that is John, and he who [did] more than he, that is Cyril, when the gold of iniquity was / exacted.

[1] *I. e.* he was bribed.

But let these things be set down in the midst and [such things] as they proclaim and prove with their voice that they may teach all men.

For, after John had come to Ephesus, he commanded each one to come, and Memnon fled from the things which were taking place; and when they were bringing him forth from the altar, he[1] both summoned him as to a friendly conference[2] and handed him over to be guarded that he might not be found wanting in aught of those things which ought [to be submitted] to the examination of the authorities, of those which all men ought to do. But after we were all assembled in order to hear in common the letters of the Emperor, his purpose to such an extent slackened and became altogether different that he made himself ridiculous rather than be zealous about the things which were thus worthy of zeal. For when the letter of [his] Majesty, which had been written unto all men, was about to be read, Cyril persuaded him and those with him that I should not come into their presence but that I should hear what the Emperor wrote from the curtain. He brought this about without letting aught of the things which were right enter into his purpose, because he had already been bribed. And when they perceived that the things which concerned me were being read, they praised the Emperor with many praises; but when it came to the [affairs] of Cyril, they cried out and swore that those things should not be read. Of such childish / licence as this used they to make use, who were formerly in trepidation and were zealous, if it were possible, to bury themselves in the earth, when they had no single defence, neither concerning the things which they [had] dared and carried out outside the command [of the Emperor] nor concerning the examination of the faith. But after I had been given into custody, so then [was] Cyril also,[3] as though on the supposition that we should not enter and approach our cities, and—a thing which also occurred aforetime by the command of the Emperor—that we should not be received by the chiefs and by those who were charged with the care of the cities. But finally he commanded

---

[1] *Viz.* John.   [2] Literally: 'a conference of love'.
[3] Cp. Lupus, *Var. Patr. Epist.*, pp. 47–9; Labbe (Mansi), iv. 1396–8.

me to dwell in my city where it was pleasing unto me, not by permission but in consequence of mine own request. For I had requested many times and I [had] requested of those, who had freedom of speech[1] with the Emperor and who were supposed [to be] my friends,[2] [as] a favour that they would inform the Emperor that for me indeed it was not a question of the human glory of the episcopate, but that I was longing for mine own cell—this favour he has done me; but before this, that there should be [held] even without me an examination of the faith so that they might not be deprived of the faith by reason of their passion against me. For I had seen the snares and the wars which had formerly taken place against me; and when there was no cause for accusation against my *prosôpon* so that they should send me forth and deprive me from Constantinople, they came on [the pretext of] the faith. And by reason of their passion against me, they were impassioned also against the faith. So it seemed unto me that this [was] advantageous and helpful, that I / should disregard myself that that might take place for which rather there was need; for whenever enmity is dissolved, how often do men come to themselves?

But he[3] gave unto me the dowry[4] of [his] favour, even that which he had sold unto Cyril, as this too was revealed after the death of the latter by the confession concerning me which was found in [his] writings; for immediately that this confession had been [made], there came that death which confutes all men and spares not; of such aids as this used I to make use. But while I on the one hand was dispatched in such honour as this, Cyril on the other hand was kept under guard for a while; but he who was being guarded with all caution hid himself from them that were guarding him in Ephesus and from the chiefs who had been commanded not to let him cross over unto Alexandria and set out from Ephesus and gained his [own] city without being hindered by any one. For this too had been prepared beforehand and bought by him with money; for he came not out of the city by force but

---

[1] Syr. *pārehsyâ* = Gk. παρρησία.
[2] Cp. Lupus, *Var. Patr. Epist.*, pp. 43-6, 67, 68; Loofs, *Nestoriana*, 190-6.
[3] *Viz.* John.   [4] Syr.: *pĕrnîthâ* = Gk. φερνή.

transgressed the letters of [His] Majesty against the will of the Emperor. He also [brought it about] that he escaped from the constraint and the punishment for his transgression of the command of [his] Majesty. But it was surely granted that all these things should occur thus by reason of that rage which was against him as it were in the folly of deception, in the likeness of which was also [his] friendship for me, since on account of this that, which was supposed / friendship for me, was always [a source of] harm unto me, because it was not [friendship] for me but [a desire] to sell [me]. For the enmity towards the other recoiled in fact upon me.[1]

Thus then these things against me were carried out from the beginning, and they left nothing undone which could convict me of having told a lie, and they were convicted by those [things] which they wrote. For [it is] in the power of every one, who wishes to examine [these things] with all exactitude and not in anticipation to pass over the things which were written by the others at Ephesus, to understand by reflection consequently from their writings who it is that has stirred up all these things and for what reason he has stirred them up and for what reason he has not consequently acted as a brother towards his brother, reprimanding, counselling, demanding, looking into these things by himself, but was the first to reveal them and spread abroad abundantly trouble and war and enmity by the letters which he had written. For what reason, when I have written an answer to his letter and when I have accepted [part] thereof as correctly stated and have made known unto him the things concerning which I doubted whether they were well stated as well as the purpose wherefore I accepted them not, either instructing or as if on the one hand he understood not or [as if] on the other hand it were so,

[1] The story of Cyril's bribery is continued below, p. 349. The other evidence for it is contained in the letters of Acacius of Beroea and Epiphanius the Archdeacon and *Syncellus* of Cyril ; see Labbe (Mansi), v. 819 and 987–9. The list of gifts referred to by Epiphanius is reprinted from *Florilegium Casinense* by Nau in an appendix. These documents are discussed in Hefele, *History of the Church Councils*, §§ 130 and 156. Nestorius uses the following language in a sermon reported by Marius Mercator : *Quid me latenter sagittis aureis iacularis ? quid in me sagittas aureas absconditus mittis ? . . . Noli me sagittis aureis vulnerare ; non sunt mihi sagittae aureae* (Loofs, *Nestoriana*, pp. 299, 308).

that he might establish that which was written—for what reason has he stirred up the Egyptian and the Roman Council about the things which [are] against me? / Hast thou requested me to establish mine own points as brother[1] to brother?[2] But thou didst wish by thyself to select these [writings] of mine and bring about a verdict against me when I was far away from thee. Wherefore hast thou not come unto me with thine own Council as one requiring [something] of me or as one reprimanding me, as they that [were] before thee did in regard to those whom they saw to be in need of their own coming: as Alexander against Arius and as Timothy[3] against Gregory[4] or as Theophilus against John?[5] For there was none to hinder thee nor yet to deprive him that was accused of [the right to] defend himself. There is none far away and requiring to be judged and [yet] judging another; there is no accuser to be the judge of his enemy far away. For what reason, when thou wast calling[1] an Oecumenical Council, didst thou together with the incomplete Council decline to come and defend the things [of] which thou didst accuse me and condemn me, when I was not present? For what reason, when thou camest, didst thou not wait for the Council which was required but wast frightened thereof? Wherefore, when I was requesting thee and hindering thee and adjuring thee to wait for the Council, didst thou refrain from [awaiting] the coming of the Eastern bishops, and didst not await the Count who was / charged with the duty of the maintenance of order but didst despise all of them together? For what reason, after all the bishops came and the Emperor commanded that indeed, since there had not previously been an inquiry and an examination, inquiry should be held into them between me and thee and the bishops of the East, didst thou do all [these] things that there might not be examination and judgement?

One was his aim and one his purpose from the beginning even unto the end: that there should not be a judgement and an examination on the subject of the things whereof he accused me, while mine [was] that there should be a judgement and an examination on the subject of the things whereof he accused

---

[1] See crit. n., p. 400.   [2] Cp. Labbe (Mansi), iv. 892 B.
[3] *I.e.* Timothy I (ἀκτήμων), bishop of Alexandria, A.D. 381.
[4] *I.e.* of Nazianzum.   [5] *I.e.* Chrysostom.

me, though not because the flight and the haste of this man had been victorious. For what reason was I zealous whereas thou didst decline, if thou wert confident in the proof which thou hadst from the Scriptures and from the Fathers? But he feared me, [some one will say,] because of the help which [I received] from the Emperor. He [it was], as men know, who was rather in actual fact for surrendering me and not for helping; but [granted] that this was [so], who then was hindering the judgement from taking place without the help of the Emperor? For after it had taken place, after I [had] already departed from Constantinople and the Council of the East was requiring that there should be a judgement and an examination of the faith, even without me myself, the Emperor too had also commanded that the two deprivations of those, whosoever [they were], who had been deprived by the Council, should be retained without [further] examination, but that they should choose each seven bishops[1] and [that] they should be sent by both the / Councils to Constantinople in order that they might speak before the Emperor concerning the things required and [that] the rest of the bishops might be dismissed from Ephesus.

Have they spoken with one another? Yet, since they [had] proceeded to Chalcedon in Bithynia in accordance with the letters of [his] Majesty, he[2] received[3] the two parties of the bishops who were sent by the Council. But after he [had] asked of the Easterns the cause of the division which had taken place, they said that they were introducing a passible God and that they themselves were not persuaded to agree before inquiry was made into these things, [adding] 'Even if 'the Emperor treats us with violence, we shall not be per-'suaded to admit a passible God; for he that has not a nature 'that suffers suffers not, while he that has such a nature as this 'is not consubstantial with one who has one such as the former; 'but if he who suffers not is consubstantial with the one who 'suffers, even he who suffers not can suffer'. And the Emperor

---

[1] For the names of those chosen by the Orientals see Lupus, *Var. Patr. Epist.*, p. 65; Labbe (Mansi), iv. 1400 A, B. In Labbe the number is eight.

[2] *Viz.* the Emperor.   [3] See crit. n., p. 400.

was in trepidation as it were at this supposition, and even his ears could not endure these blasphemies, and he shook his purple robes, saying: 'I have no part at all with such men as that.'[1] However, he commanded not to constrain them by violence but, on the contrary, that [the question] should not be left but that inquiry should be made into the truth in every manner whatsoever concerning the things to be examined; and with these [words] he dismissed them with many praises, having commanded them to make ready this examination.

/ But after this was heard, the others again stirred themselves up that there might not be a judgement and an examination of these things. But the authority of your Majesty sent away the Easterns, but commanded you[2]—and by 'you' I mean thine own sympathizers, them that were executing thy vengeance—to enter into Constantinople and to establish another bishop in mine own place.[3] Where then had been the judgement? And before whom? Say, in whose presence? Although it was a farcical judgement, say, you who have written the things that took place, how was it brought about? For they were many; be ye not persuaded by any of them that [are] my own [followers], lest you say that he wrote out of human love. Lean upon your own [followers], who have written of the things that were brought about. But you cannot efface what happened thus and was written at that time.[4]

But perhaps some one will say that whatever was brought about was clearly a farce. But it was an unscrupulous thing to bring about things which were unbelievable and in need of much indulgence. For the things which were done thus are unbelievable; but they have indeed been thus prepared not only against me but also against the faith, on account of which I was stirred up and was diligent to write and to teach the things which were taking place just as they were taking place, lest men should suppose that the judgement and the examination took place and should believe without a reason and depart from the faith. For the providence / and the judgement of

---

[1] Cp. Lupus, *Var. Patr. Epist.*, p. 70.   [2] *Viz.* Cyril.   [3] *I. e.* Maximian.
[4] Cp. Labbe (Mansi), iv. 1401–7. No new paragraph is marked here in the Syriac text.

God have been revealed unto all men, although there are [some] that see and see not, who have arisen against me out of enmity from the beginning, though now he [1] is willing to be the first to drive every one to evil against me who have been condemned without judgement. And at the same time he has put a barrier before all men that there might be no further return for me, and has thereby hemmed in the party of the Easterns and of the rest of the countries which had not taken part with them in what they brought about and [which] had given help unto me. Nor was I acquainted with any of the things which were taking place nor was I the first to think of rebuking and accusing them for the judgement [conducted] without justice.

And I summoned an Oecumenical Council against the Council which had been [held] incompletely, in order that it might be shown in the sight of all men for what reason they did what they did; since it was not for the faith that he was confident and enthusiastic but that his own [affairs] and mine might not be examined, while by means of letters and various other means he had corrupted those who were nigh unto the Emperor and unto the Empresses and was persuading [them] that there should not be a Council. And this was told unto the Emperor and he was much reprimanded by letters, lest he should be able to dissemble; for he ought to rejoice at a judgement, if all these things were not [uttered] in semblance, so that he might be zealous in proving to the Emperor that his purpose was straightforward and just. For this was done in such wise / that he should have no defence, as one that knoweth not the things of which he is rebuked and denies [them]; and he hindered the judgement not once nor twice but even unto death. But the Emperor had acted contrariwise toward him who was blamed by him and condemned me, even me who was honoured and praised, while many were testifying that I was injured. Thus absurdities were growing so many that they were not kept dark; but that their oppression might be revealed, he [2] properly made even him [1] a witness and a judge for me, so that [their] oppression might be indefensible.

[1] *Viz.* Cyril.   [2] *Viz.* the Emperor.

For all of them testified that we were not found doing iniquity and that they condemned me without reason. And while I was in the same [condition] without examination and without judgement, the others worked amongst them[selves] and changed all the things that concerned me.

Concerning the things which were done when Cyril and the Easterns met together and †before†[1] seven of each party[2] were sent [to Chalcedon].

But let us speak as in a few words: perhaps some one will ask: 'How therefore did the Eastern Council also condemn 'thee in such wise, that then not even a single cause of 'defence was left unto thee?' For by the persuasion of [his] Majesty, and by this [Council] every one is the more convinced, even so that none can hide it. For one and the same was the word concerning every one of those who were in accord with me and were accepting / me and were contending with me and [concerning every one] of those who were being accused with me and were being insulted with me, since those who were changed over with them had not a single cause to change over from me. Tell thou us the cause for which they changed over from thee; for [it is] thy boldness which was against me and thy writings and the Articles which thou hast composed. They anathematized thee and deprived thee in Ephesus; and thou canst not deny neither thou nor they, what you have done in your writings. When therefore they were doing these things, they were testifying about me in two things, both in respect to orderliness and in respect to piety; but thee on the contrary they were accusing both as a bold man and as an heretic, and they summoned thee to judgement to reprimand thee for them both and they judged that thou wast worthy of deposition. And when you were summoned by the Emperor as to judgement, they were the first to accuse thee;

---

[1] Altered rightly by Nau into 'after', on the grounds that Nestorius has just spoken of the dispatch of the seven bishops to Chalcedon and that this section deals with the agreement of Cyril with John of Antioch.

[2] Literally: 'seven of the one and seven of the other'.

for they were persuaded of your boldness and of your tyrannical behaviour and of all the evils which you caused in Ephesus. For in Chalcedon also you closed all the churches against them before the judgement should be [given], in order that they might not enter to pray, and you blocked the roads [leading] to the Emperor and were meeting them with stones and clubs and were driving them into narrow places as into places whence men [that were] strangers, being not acquainted with the roads, had not [any means] of escape, / since they were coming in the hope of order [being maintained] by the Emperor; and thus they were hardly rescued from those who were distressing them, until the Emperor sent the help of the soldiers to rescue them.[1]

But there was an assemblage of those who were practised in sedition without number,—then was I summoned from Ephesus,—[consisting] at that time of Egyptians and of monks from [2] Constantinople and of those who were renegade from monasticism and all those who by reason of any cause whatever had been driven out and were zealous for the work of agitators [3] and were supposed on account of the habit [4] of monks to be acting with enthusiasm. Then they were taking from the monasteries robes together with food and provisions, which were being given unto them as the wages of the fervour of love, and they were fattening their bodies therewith instead of [practising] continence.[5] From the things which thou wast sending and bringing from the granaries and the stores of wine and of oil and of vegetables and all kinds of clothes, thou didst fill the monasteries which were being set apart for this and other places, in such wise that even the holy places of prayer were being encumbered, and the issues and the entries of every place which could receive [them] were full thereof. These things [it was] which were taking place before every one and thou wast paying for them with the things which

---

[1] Cp. Labbe (Mansi), iv. 1392-3, 1404 D; Lupus, *Var. Patr. Epist.*, pp. 60-2, 89.
[2] Literally: 'in'.   [3] Syr. *'estāsirē* = Gk. στασιῶται.
[4] Syr. *'eskēmā* = Gk. σχῆμα.
[5] Cp. Labbe (Mansi), iv. 1405-6; Lupus, *Var. Patr. Epist.*, pp. 91, 92.

are called 'benedictions',[1] which were being given instead of wages thereof, a thing which heretofore / thou hast not done nor [wilt do] hereafter. And thou wast carrying out these things so that thou mightest not be supposed to be sending these things so as to cause sedition, but that, as they were coming into the monasteries and were being received by the monasteries, the recipients might not be convicted for having indeed received them and for acting irreverently as disturbers and causers of tumult, in being supposed [to be] enthusiastic. For thou wast letting them bring about anything at all and wast doing everything that men might not believe that they were doing these things.

Tell me therefore for what reason thou wast letting these things be done and for what thou wast driving out them that were suffering these things, so that they were not even accounted worthy to be heard concerning aught whereof they were being driven out. What was their purpose about thee and what about me when they returned to the East? Indeed every one of them warned his city not to agree to what was carried out against me. For what reason was a decree sent by the Emperor, by the hand of Aristolaus,[2] to constrain them to accept whatever was carried out against me? And was it sent unto them as unto persons who were and because they were [inclined] toward me? For what reason was he commanding them to accept thee among the bishops? And what [was] the reason that persuaded them / to accept thee among the bishops? You saw not one another and you spoke not with one another, nor have you said nor have you heard for what cause you were divided; and it was for you to accept without judgement and without examination and without

[1] Syr. *búrktâ*, 'blessing', a euphemism for 'presents' or 'gifts'; see Payne-Smith, *Thes. Syr.*, col. 614 b.

[2] Cp. Kidd, *History of the Church*, vol. iii, pp. 256-62. In April 432 the Emperor sent Aristolaus, a tribune and notary, to John of Antioch, Acacius of Beroea, and St. Simeon Stylites. He was to endeavour to make peace by persuading the Easterns to abandon Nestorius and Cyril to give up his Twelve Articles. After some negotiations, in which Paul of Emesa joined Aristolaus, Cyril and most of the Easterns came to an agreement before the end of the year, Nestorius being abandoned but without the explicit withdrawal of Cyril's Articles. Cp. Labbe (Mansi), v. 277-84, 312, 347-51, 663-6, 827, 828; Lupus, *Var. Patr. Epist.*, pp. 385, 386. Introd. pp. xxii, xxiii.

a Council what you accepted not in judgement, and for the others to accept what they accepted not! But of yourself you thought that you were reconciled with the others concerning the things whereof you were justly blamed in order justly to confirm the two Councils either through fear or by patience or by partiality[1] or by all of them together. What defence have you [to make] before those who are blaming you for having made a secret agreement in partiality and by deceitful means? 'The Emperor's command. It is the Emperor who has commanded us and who has prepared this for us.'

Say! why then dost thou ask me how they have accepted my deposition who formerly accepted it not? Ask me not, but I [will ask] thee; how hast thou accepted the faith which formerly thou didst not accept? How hast thou hidden thy Chapters[2] on account of which thou hast been deprived? How have they accepted thee who accepted not thy [writings]? But how have they, who accepted not thine impious Chapters, accepted the deposition which was [pronounced] against me? These [questions] need asking and[3] answering. For / the affair wherein thou wast openly judged by every one, willing and unwilling, made me not defenceless, but on the contrary it caused me to need no other defence. These things therefore cause those who are wanting to examine to know how they happened, as you too will confess with me therein. For the others deprive themselves and condemn themselves by their own judgement, since they have accepted not what was examined by the Council but what you have accepted in the participation of both of you,[4] willing and unwilling, in the settlement, apart from the rest of the others, in such wise as not to settle in the name of the Council things which they wanted [to have settled] once for all for better or for worse but to prove that they did things pleasing unto the Emperor in accepting what was carried out against me, though formerly they were not accepting [it]; but they were zealous, however, to shun [all] mention of the Articles.[5] And they were [attached] to these two parties, [some to one and] others [to the other]

---

[1] *Sc.* προσωπολημψία. [2] Lat. *Capitula.* [3] Literally: 'or'.
[4] *Viz.* Cyril and John of Antioch. [5] Gk. Κεφάλαια.

against one another: thou [being inclined] to my deprivation and the others to the denunciation of thy Articles, on account of which we have accepted every burden. But I have accepted all sufferings and have not agreed nor—but let this be said with the aid of God—shall I agree until my last breath. For this reason, in that they have accepted / what formerly they accepted not, they are the causes of their own condemnation and are suppressing also the things which were carried out against me. For by the suppression of the Articles my deposition also is suppressed with them; or was it not because I accepted them not [that] my deprivation has taken place? For other cause there was not for my deposition.

But thou sayest: 'I have not suppressed the Articles, but 'I have accepted John who has confessed with me and has 'agreed with me on the faith as against thee.' John also has said the same: 'I have accepted thee, Cyril, who hast confessed with me on the words of the faith.' Who then [is] he that has accepted his companion? And who [is] he that has been accepted? For both of you say them and are persuading those who have separated themselves and have distinguished [themselves] from the deceptive peace which you have made: thou indeed, in that the others have accepted my deprivation which they were not formerly accepting, [and because] thou wast supposing that they accepted also these Articles which I was not accepting; and he, because he accepts not the writing of thy Articles in the deposit of the faith—men of whom thou wast determined that they should agree with thee in the things whereof men were correctly accusing them. Or did not our inquiry and our war and our strife take place that we might not accept them?

But it is [possible] to say that it was not because they were suppressed [that] they were not written in the deposit of the faith, / when an agreement had been effected, but because they had been without division and without inquiry. If all our inquiry and dispute had been for the purpose of the suppression and the refutation of these things, for no other reason were they not written when the agreement was effected, than that they had not been accepted by common opinion and agreement. How then dost thou cling to them as though they were accepted, things which were not accepted in your confessions [of faith]? For in the course of coming to terms these things were not to be left alone, so that thou and thine own [followers] made not use of them as [being] orthodox nor the Easterns as [being] heretical; for that would not be any coming to terms on the faith, but disputes and divisions.

For what reason, however, was there no suppression of these things in confession [of faith] in the written documents? However, they were left alone. First indeed because they were giving way to the vehemence of [his] Majesty and men were requiring that every one so ever should make peace; after this, because they were wanting to do him the favour of not anathematizing his Articles in written documents, since it sufficed for them not to accept them and not to write in the written documents those things, which formerly he vehemently wanted to be accepted. But for what reason did he accept [the proposal] that they should be left out of the written documents, if he wished for this—as indeed [was] what he was wishing—that they / should be accepted as orthodox? In the first place indeed [it was] lest he should come to the necessity of a disputation and should fall and the Easterns should arise against him and require before everything that he should be deprived for these things, as one who was condemned—a thing which he feared, for, when he was being constrained and pressed, it was necessary for him clearly to say what he believed; since he would either seem to believe what was [written] in the Articles and in his letter or, otherwise, actually to have imagined as even the Easterns. In both [cases] he would be accused: either of saying the same things and having appeared as a wrongdoer or of clearly having revealed himself as an heretic. Yet in order that he might not suffer this, of his own will he agreed and adopted [their views] in order that they might have peace without the written documents and the Articles[1]; and next that they might concede unto him that which concerned me, which he was demanding, that is my deprivation, in order that I might have no further [opportunity

---

[1] See crit. n., p. 401.

of] making answer, in that all of them were come together at the same time against me, a thing for which he had been eager from the beginning. Yet notwithstanding he succeeded not, because it came about by the vehemence of [his] Majesty and not through a just judgement.

/ *The letter of Cyril to Acacius, bishop of Melitene.*[1] *Unto those who were blaming him for the agreement which he made with the Easterns, and how I made [my] defence before those who were blaming the agreement which came about.*
The one[2] indeed made [his] defence as though he [had] not accepted thy Articles but discarded them, while all of you were zealous for them. But the other[3] says that he had not been content to anathematize them, though they were very zealous that they should anathematize the Articles. The latter however [says]: ' I have brought about what was indeed 'needful for you but incredible; [to wit] that they have of 'their [own] will accepted the deposition of Nestorius, whereby 'they have also accepted the Articles.' But the former[2] denies not that he has accepted the deposition, but [it is] because thou hast accepted and confessed in written document the faith whereby the deposition is set aside; saying that thy faith is not a [matter of] dispute between thee and us in the written documents according to the certainty of our words, since thou distinguishest the natures and the divine utterances concerning both the natures. What we were all zealous to confess and thou confessedst not, has now come to pass. For he was the first to establish in every possible manner what was needful for the faith; but we have not hindered the establishment also of those things wherewith they were calumniated, but rather have we made [ready] the way.

/ And the one[3] indeed says: 'I have made them say " Mother of God", which they used not formerly to accept.'

[1] Although the first actual quotation from the correspondence between Cyril and Acacius does not occur till about two pages further on, the section dealing with that correspondence seems to begin at this point. There is therefore no need to follow Nau in regarding this heading as a later insertion in the text.
[2] *Viz.* John.   [3] *Viz.* Cyril.

Moreover he prides himself and extols himself against them that were disputing against this confession. But the other has confessed that I accepted quite simply [the name] 'Mother of God'. There is then need to state the meaning, according to which the *hypostatic* and the natural union of God and the natural birth from a woman is excluded. For he says that we confess Saint Mary the mother of God because God the Word was made flesh and was made man from her and, since the conception, he therein united himself unto the temple which was taken. And it was not that he was born but that he was united unto the temple which was taken and was born of her. For we decline not the term 'birth' but the '*hypostatic* union of God the Word'. For this reason we have caused it to be excluded. And the one[1] indeed predicates of God the Word God whole and man whole who in *ousia* is both [*ousias*];[2] and for this reason he has written, saying, 'He was born of the 'Father before the worlds in his divinity, but in the last days 'the same for us and for our salvation was born of the Virgin 'Mary in his humanity'.[3] He says that the same was born of the Father and of the Virgin Mary in the humanity, here again also because he has not examined clearly with a view to establishing the things which were required or which are required, that is, one Lord Jesus Christ, whole man [formed] of a rational soul and of a body, in such wise that Christ / and the Son and Jesus are in the two *ousias*. And in everything he is God as well as man by nature and in everything he is by nature man in the same way as God the Word; both of them exist in *ousia*, [and] for this reason each of them [exists] by himself.

Because these things have been laid down without comparison he drags them in to [serve his own] purpose according to his own aim and defends [them] to his sympathizers and deceives them, there being none indeed that is not surely calumniated, and each attracts his companion to his own aim. And he accuses me of not having correctly said that which was said by the Easterns, who [according to him] say that

---

[1] *Viz.* Cyril.   [2] See crit. n., p. 401.
[3] Labbe (Mansi), v. 317 B; see p. 297, n. 2.

God was born of a woman, whereas I say [it] not; and he states my own words according to hearsay; for he says:

He[1] says that God passed through the Virgin, the mother of Christ, [as] we have learned[2] from Divine Scripture; but we learn not indeed anywhere[3] that he was born of her. And elsewhere in his interpretation he has said: 'And nowhere 'therefore does Divine Scripture say that God, but Jesus and 'Christ and the Son and the Lord, came into being from the 'virgin, the Mother of Christ.' For by saying these things he divides our Lord into two sons, so that the one is uniquely Son, Son and Christ and our Lord, he that was born of God the Father, God the Word, and again the other [was] uniquely Son and Christ and Lord, he that was born of the holy virgin.[4]

How dissemblest thou the truth? Not only does the one[5] say this clearly, but the others[6] / name the holy virgin the mother of God because they speak of one Son and Christ and Lord, whole in his divinity and whole in his humanity.

But add what thou hast accepted and confessed, that there has been a union of two natures and that for this reason we confess one Christ, one Son, one Lord.[7] And deceive not the wise Acacius and through him the rest; for it would not escape such a man as he—in such wise as to be blamed for the faith to which he was reconciled against thee—that perhaps thou clingest also to these [theories] of mine or rather to those of orthodoxy, which thou hast accepted in all this trouble. For I have confessed two natures united, but thou wast denying [them]: that there is of the divinity and of the humanity one Christ and one Lord and one Son; he was not born of woman in the divinity, but in the humanity; not as he is God

---

[1] *Viz.* Nestorius.   [2] See p. xiv.   [3] See p. xv.

[4] Labbe (Mansi), v. 316 E–317 A: ἔφη γὰρ οὕτω· τὸ παρελθεῖν τὸν Θεὸν ἐκ τῆς Χριστοτόκου παρθένου, παρὰ τῆς θείας ἐδιδάχθην γραφῆς· τὸ δὲ γεννηθῆναι Θεὸν ἐξ αὐτῆς, οὐδαμοῦ (v. l. οὐδαμῶς) ἐδιδάχθην. ἐν ἑτέρᾳ δὲ πάλιν ἐξηγήσει· οὐδαμοῦ τοίνυν ἡ θεία γραφὴ Θεὸν ἐκ τῆς Χριστοτόκου παρθένου λέγει γεγενῆσθαι, ἀλλὰ Χριστὸν Ἰησοῦν, υἱόν, καὶ κύριον. ὅτι δὲ ταῦτα λέγων εἰς υἱοὺς δύο μερίζει τὸν ἕνα, καὶ ἕτερον μὲν ἰδικῶς εἶναί φησιν υἱόν, καὶ Χριστόν, καὶ κύριον, τὸν ἐκ Θεοῦ πατρὸς γεννηθέντα λόγον, ἕτερον δὲ πάλιν ἀνὰ μέρος τε καὶ ἰδικῶς υἱόν, καὶ Χριστόν, καὶ κύριον τὸν ἐκ τῆς ἁγίας παρθένου, πῶς ἂν ἐνδοιάσειέ τις, αὐτὸ δὴ τοῦτο σαφῶς μονονουχὶ βοῶντος ἐκείνου;

[5] *Viz.* Cyril.   [6] *Viz.* the Eastern bishops.

[7] Cp. Labbe (Mansi), v. 292 B, C.

is he one Son of two natures united, but he is one as man. Where then do I speak of two natures, one indeed solely Son and Christ and Lord, God the Word who was born of the Father, but the other solely Christ by himself [born] of the holy virgin? Thou also understandest not these sections which thou hast written down: 'We have learned from Divine 'Scripture that God has passed through the holy virgin, the 'mother of Christ', of which thou hast written / that I say them. How then proclaimest thou that I call God the Word who was born of the Father one Christ uniquely but the man who [was born] of Saint Mary another Christ? Of whom then sayest thou that I have said that God passed through her? For it is evident that [I spoke] of him who was born of the Father, [namely] of God the Word. How therefore do I call Christ any other than God the Word, him who was born of the Father? I have said that he passed through even the blessed Mary, because he derived not the origin of [his] birth from her as the bodily frame which was born of her. For this reason I have said that he who is God the Word has surely passed through but was surely not born, because he derived not his origin from her.[1] But there both exists and is named one Christ, the two of them being united, he who was born of the Father in the divinity, [and] of the holy virgin in the humanity, for there was a union of the two natures.

And we ought to say unto thee, Acacius, that I have confessed in one Christ two natures without confusion. By one nature on the one hand, that is, [by that] of the divinity, he was born of God the Father; by the other, on the other hand, that is, [by that] of the humanity, [he was born] of the holy virgin. How then canst thou name her 'Mother of God', when thou hast confessed that he was not born of her? For if thou hast said that in the divinity he was born of the holy virgin, she would be called the mother of God after the nature which was born of her; but if thou, even thou, confessest that

---

[1] There is surely here a confusion in Nestorius' thought. Would not the divine nature, which prevents us from thinking of God the Word as being born, prevent us also from thinking of Him in any way as moving through space, *e. g.* passing through the Virgin?

he was not born [of her] in the divinity, in / that thou confessest that he was not born, how dost thou confess her Mother of God? How canst thou accuse him of saying two Christs, [who said that] which thou also hast confessed—that Christ is two natures, one nature of the divinity which is called Christ and one nature of the humanity which also thou namest Christ? Either thou dost confess two Christs owing to the diversity of the natures, one indeed the humanity which was born of the holy virgin, but the other God the Word who was born of God the Father, or thou dost say, as the other says, 'one in the union' and nothing more? And on account of what hast thou brought thyself to all this and brought the others with thee to do these things against a man who was saying this?

Cyril. But God the Word who [proceeded] from the Father is not one son, while he again who [was born] of the holy virgin is not another, as was supposed by Nestorius, but one and the same. For it is made clear and explained afterwards; for he cites [1] that which signifies God whole and man whole, him who was born of the Father before the worlds in his divinity but in the last days for us and for our salvation of the Virgin Mary in the humanity, the same consubstantial with the Father in the divinity, the same consubstantial with us in the humanity. Therefore they divide not the one Son and Christ and Lord / and Jesus, but they say that the same existed before the worlds and in the last times; but [it is] known that he who [has proceeded] from God the Father [is] God and [he who was born] of a woman in the humanity [is] man.... How then is he conceived consubstantial with us in the humanity since he was born of the Father, I have said, in the divinity, if the same is not conceived and called God and man?[2]

---

[1] So the Syriac text; but the true sense is given by the Greek, where the verb is in the plural, the subject understood being the Easterns with whom Cyril has come to agreement. See pp. xiii, 401.

[2] Labbe (Mansi), v. 317 B: ὅτι γὰρ οὐχ ἕτερόν φασιν εἶναι υἱὸν τὸν ἐκ Θεοῦ πατρὸς λόγον, ἕτερον δὲ πάλιν τὸν ἐκ τῆς ἁγίας παρθένου, καθὰ Νεστορίῳ δοκεῖ, ἕνα δὲ μᾶλλον, καὶ τὸν αὐτόν, σαφὲς ἂν γένοιτο, καὶ μάλα ῥᾳδίως διά γε τῶν ἐφεξῆς. προσεπάγουσι γάρ, τίς ἂν εἴη, σημαίνοντες· ὅτι τέλειος ὡς Θεός, τέλειος δὲ καὶ ὡς ἄνθρωπος· τὸν πρὸ αἰώνων μὲν ἐκ τοῦ πατρὸς γεννηθέντα κατὰ τὴν θεότητα, ἐπ' ἐσχάτων δὲ τῶν ἡμερῶν δι' ἡμᾶς καὶ διὰ τὴν ἡμετέραν σωτηρίαν, ἐκ Μαρίας τῆς ἁγίας παρθένου, κατὰ τὴν ἀνθρωπότητα· ὁμοούσιον τῷ πατρὶ τὸν αὐτὸν κατὰ τὴν θεότητα, καὶ ὁμοούσιον ἡμῖν κατὰ τὴν ἀνθρωπότητα. οὐκοῦν ἥκιστα μὲν εἰς δύο διαιροῦσι τὸν ἕνα υἱόν, καὶ Χριστόν, καὶ κύριον Ἰησοῦν, τὸν αὐτὸν δὲ εἶναί φασι τὸν πρὸ αἰώνων, καὶ ἐν

Now if it [is true] that the one *ousia* of God the Word, which was born of the Father and of the Virgin Mary, [was] the same, for what reason dost thou confess two natures in the union and not [that] there was one belonging to the same who was born of the Father and of the Mother, as thou wantest and even constrainest us to suppose and to let thee also suppose? But they that have accepted this confession do not allow thee to lead them whither thou wantest, but constrain thee and induce thee as a deceiver to abide by the things which thou hast confessed with them.

For thou hast confessed the union of the divinity and of the humanity, since of two natures was the union. Two thou hast confessed, and thou sayest that the others have confessed one. Thy cunning [is] great: so thou hast confessed the union, and thou sayest that the others have confessed the division of the union, so that the one same *ousia* is divided into the two *ousias*, unlike one another, of the divinity and of the humanity, so that the one *ousia*, which is divisible into *ousias* unlike and of another kind / one from another, is consubstantial. For one *ousia* cannot be conceived as two *ousias* unlike and of another kind one from another,[1] but[2] which are alike [in the sense] that they are consubstantial one with another, as is that likeness. In which nature then is the Son consubstantial with the Father and in which [is he] consubstantial with us? For the *ousia* of God the Father and our own *ousia* are alien one to another. He therefore too would be alien unto his being and would be of two natures alien one to another. How then is it to be conceived that he is consubstantial with us ourselves in the humanity when he exists not in the *ousia* of the humanity? But how is he consubstantial with the Father, when he exists not in his *ousia*? Or how [is] the same in *ousia* of the *ousia* of God the Father and of our *ousia*? And [how] is it the same *ousia*? And [how] are two *ousias* alien one to

ἐσχάτοις, δῆλον δὲ ὅτι (*v. l.* δηλονότι) τὸν ἐκ Θεοῦ πατρὸς ὡς Θεόν, καὶ ἐκ γυναικὸς κατὰ σάρκα ὡς ἄνθρωπον. πῶς γὰρ ἂν νοοῖ τὸ πρὸς ἡμᾶς ὁμοούσιος εἶναι κατὰ τὴν ἀνθρωπότητα, καίτοι γεννηθεὶς ἐκ πατρός, κατά γέ φημι τὴν θεότητα, εἰ μὴ νοοῖτο καὶ λέγοιτο Θεός τε ὁμοῦ, καὶ ἄνθρωπος ὁ αὐτός;

[1] Literally: 'other than one another'. [2] Literally: 'and'.

another one, so that each one of the *ousias* both is and is conceived in one *ousia*? But if this is impossible, [it is] also inacceptable that it should be conceived in the word of truth. It is not a nature [which is] in its nature of the *ousia* of the Father and of the *ousia* of the humanity, so as to become consubstantial with both of them; but in the *ousia* of God the Word only is he consubstantial with God the Father, whereas he is consubstantial with us ourselves in our *ousia*; and the same both is and is named one, who [is formed] of the nature of God and of our nature, in the *prosôpon* indeed of the union. For in the natures he is naturally / distinct according to the diversity of the natures which participate not in one another according to the doctrine of the *ousias*. And thou canst not unloose aught that thou hast bound,—to wit, the union of two 'natures; and two natures are not one nature'. For a union of the diversity of the diverse natures and not of the diversities of its very own *ousia* is conceived and said to have taken place; for the coming into being appertains to the one *ousia*, while the union is the combination of the *ousias*.

Cyril. But these things appear not so unto Nestorius, but [it seems to him] rather that the aim thereof tends in the opposite direction in every respect. He used then to say in the church when interpreting [these doctrines]: 'For this 'reason too God the Word is named Christ, because he has 'adhesion constantly with Christ'; and again: 'He has 'preserved the adhesion of the natures without confusion, and 'we confess God in man; we honour the man who is adored 'with God Almighty through the adhesion of the divinity.' Seest thou[1] how far [from the truth] his word [is]? For it is full of great impiety; for he says that God the Word was named Christ singly, but that he has adhesion constantly with Christ. Does he not in effect speak of two Christs? Does he not confess that he honours the man who is adored with God? Do these things then, O our brother,[2] seem to be akin to those which have been said by the former?[3] They have not even any coherence[4] / with one another; for he on the one hand predicates two natures in operation in him, they on the other hand one; that is, they confess

---

[1] See p. xv.   [2] See p. xiii.   [3] *Viz.* the Easterns.
[4] Literally: 'one power of thought'.

and adore one Son and Lord and God, the same [proceeding] from the Father in the divinity and from the holy Virgin in the humanity; [we] say that a union indeed of two natures took place but we confess clearly one Christ and one Son and one Lord.[1]

Nestorius. We ought to say unto thee, wise Acacius: why deceivest thou us? For thou hast confessed the union of two natures unlike one another and, wherein thou accusest Nestorius himself, thou seemest to confess [the same] with him, although thou sayest not that two Christs are predicated; for Nestorius too seems not to have confessed two Christs. But, after what thou spreadest abroad concerning him, that he says so, though he confesses not that two Christs are predicated therein, thou too seemest to predicate two Christs; for thou speakest not of Christ in one nature but [sayest] that he is in two natures whole in their *ousia*, unlike one another; Christ exists in the divinity and in the humanity; for in that he is two, the two natures also are named two Christs by one and the same name of Christ. For when two natures, unlike one another, are named by the same name, they are called two /by homonymy. But thou sayest one in the union; this also Nestorius says: that two natures [result in] one Christ, which are self-sustaining[2] in their natures and need not, for the support of one another, that they should be supported by

---

[1] Labbe (Mansi), v. 317 C : ἀλλ' οὐχ ὧδε ταῦτ' ἔχειν Νεστορίῳ δοκεῖ· τέτραπται δὲ μᾶλλον ὁ σκοπὸς αὐτῷ πρὸς πᾶν τοὐναντίον. ἔφη γοῦν ἐπ' ἐκκλησίας ἐξηγούμενος· διὰ τοῦτο καὶ Χριστὸς ὁ Θεὸς λόγος ὀνομάζεται, ἐπειδήπερ ἔχει τὴν συνάφειαν τὴν πρὸς τὸν Χριστὸν διηνεκῆ. καὶ πάλιν· ἀσύγχυτον τοίνυν τὴν τῶν φύσεων τηρῶμεν συνάφειαν· ὁμολογῶμεν τὸν ἐν ἀνθρώπῳ Θεόν· σέβωμεν τὸν τῇ θείᾳ συναφείᾳ τῷ παντοκράτορι Θεῷ συμπροσκυνούμενον ἄνθρωπον. ὁρᾷς οὖν (v. l. om. οὖν) ὅσον ἔχει τὸ ἀπηχὲς ὁ λόγος αὐτῷ ; δυσσεβείας γὰρ τῆς ἀνωτάτω μεμέστωται. Θεὸν μὲν ἰδικῶς ὀνομάζεσθαί φησι τὸν τοῦ Θεοῦ λόγον, ἔχειν δὲ τὴν συνάφειαν τὴν πρὸς τὸν Χριστὸν διηνεκῆ. ἆρ' οὖν οὐ δύο Χριστοὺς ἐναργέστατα λέγει ; οὐκ ἄνθρωπον Θεῷ συμπροσκυνούμενον σέβειν, οὐκ οἶδ' ὅπως, ὁμολογεῖ ; ταῦτ' οὖν ἀδελφὰ τοῖς παρ' ἐκείνων ὁρᾶτε ; οὐκ ἀντεξάγουσαν ἔχει πρὸς ἄλληλα τῶν ἐννοιῶν τὴν δύναμιν ; ὁ μὲν γὰρ δύο φησὶν ἐναργῶς, οἱ δὲ Χριστὸν ἕνα, καὶ υἱόν, καὶ Θεόν, καὶ κύριον ὁμολογοῦσι προσκυνεῖν, τὸν αὐτὸν ἐκ πατρὸς κατὰ τὴν θεότητα, καὶ ἐκ τῆς ἁγίας παρθένου κατὰ τὴν ἀνθρωπότητα. δύο μὲν γὰρ φύσεων ἕνωσιν γενέσθαι φαμέν, πλὴν ἕνα Χριστόν, καὶ ἕνα υἱόν, καὶ ἕνα κύριον ὁμολογοῦμεν σαφῶς.

[2] Syr. *nṯîrîn* : (1) 'protected', (2) 'abiding', (3) *sibi cavens, sibi curam habens* (Payne-Smith, *Thes. Syr.*, col. 2354). For Nestorius an element which can only exist in combination with others (*e.g.* soul or body in human nature) is not in itself a nature. See pp. 9, 37, 304, 314, etc.

the union; but they have established the dispensation on our behalf. The divinity [is] not in need of the humanity, nor yet [is] the humanity in need of the divinity, because in their own nature they need naught. For it was not for the very divinity through the union with the humanity to become God without need, nor again was it for the very humanity to become man through the union with the divinity; but [it was that] from [its] creation by divinity in [its] ordinary[1] nature, although the union also was its as a result of its creation. For the union of the divinity came about not for the completion of the one *ousia* but for the *prosôpon* of the dispensation on our behalf. Nor again [as to] the divinity, was the humanity for the completion of its nature, but for the *prosôpon* of the dispensation on our behalf. For they uphold the *prosôpon* of one another, and for this reason there makes use of the *prosôpon* of the one nature the other nature, as of its own. Both of them make not use of the one and the other in common nor of composition for the completion of the nature, as the soul and the body [are composed] for [the formation of] the nature of man, but there makes use of the *prosôpon* of the one nature the other nature [as though it were] the same as its own. And for this reason the divinity also on account of the union is named Christ after the humanity which was anointed, and there exists / of two natures, of divinity and of humanity, Christ, one Son, one Lord; through the union of the divinity and of the humanity the same is Son and Lord and God. For[2] the things which have been called one in the union—a 'one' which exists united in nature—are indeed not predicated distinctly as things which are predicated by homonymy; yet, if thou dividest them, the 'one' is not divisible with them. For in its own nature the *ousias* are together and it is named after both of them owing to its own nature. Thus [it is] that the soul and the body which are united are named one living being and are not called two living beings. The soul and the body [constitute] one living being, because the

[1] Literally: 'common'.
[2] The rest of this paragraph seems to be a statement of the characteristics of a 'natural union' designed to show that that form of union is inapplicable to the 'Union of the Nature' in Christ.

body lives not in its own life but in the union with the soul; and for this reason, if they are divided, the life is not divided but there is [left] only [that] of the soul, since both of them are named after its nature one living being.

Let it then be assumed for demonstration also concerning the divinity and the humanity that there is one *prosôpon* in two *prosôpa*; that cannot be conceived [as] one without the union, but man [is] man and God God. Both of them [are] one Son, one Lord. For when they are distinguished it is not theirs that the latter should be called that which the former is; for this reason thou too confessest the union of two natures, and of two natures unlike one another; of the divinity and of the humanity, / complete divinity and complete humanity, one Christ, one Son, one Lord. Or callest thou perhaps one nature Christ and [sayest] not one Christ in two natures, and the union without confusion of the natures is superfluous? But if two natures are one Christ, thou sayest, as Nestorius, in [respect to] the union, that one is named after the other. And why hurriest thou outwardly to pursue the others, when thou makest [thy] defence on their behalf and the two [opinions] are found in thee, the former and the opposite thereof? . . . .

And further he[1] shows the same things:

We suppose not in fact, as some of the former heretics have supposed, [that] the Word which [proceeded] from God took a nature, that is, [that] he constructed by means of the divinity a bodily frame for him, but, in following everywhere the Divine Scriptures, we affirm that he took [it] from the holy Virgin. Therefore, as we accept in the understanding those things whereof was [formed] only one Son and Lord and Jesus Christ, we predicate two natures united; but after the union, as though the diversity of two natures was now abolished by him, we confess [that] the nature of the Son is of one, but that he was made man and was made flesh; but if it were said that he who was made flesh or was made man was God the Word, [all] supposition / of change would be far removed[2]; for he remained that which he was; but let the union also without confusion be confessed by us.[3]

---

[1] *Viz.* Cyril.   [2] See p. xiii.

[3] Labbe (Mansi), v. 317 E: οὐ γάρ τοι κατά τινας τῶν ἀρχαιοτέρων αἱρετικῶν, ἐξ ἰδίας λαβόντα φύσεως, τουτέστι τῆς θεϊκῆς, ἑαυτῷ κατασκευάσαι τὸ σῶμα τὸν τοῦ

Nestorius. Thou confessest then those things whereof Christ is [formed], that is, the divinity and the humanity, and thou hast confessed a diversity in the *ousias* and that they have remained without confusion; but they have remained without confusion, as are the natures; even then in the union they have remained thus. How therefore do the natures remain without confusion, since they remain not after the union such as they are in nature? . . . . 'For after the union 'the distinction between the two is suppressed, and we confess 'that the nature of the Son is one.' For if the natures have not remained even in the union such as they were, but their own distinctions, whereby they were conceived as two, though remaining even in the union without confusion, are suppressed, there comes about a confusion, a confusion of change and of transformation, a coming to be in one nature. How then seems it unto thee? 'The union which was united in the natures took place without confusion.' Two then [are] they whereof was [formed] only one son and Lord and Jesus Christ, two also in the union; and the natural diversities, wherein they are conceived as two, are not suppressed, since the one is not the other in *ousia* nor the other the one in *ousia*. For surely thou conceivest not so, but sayest not as / thou conceivest. How then in thy thoughts acceptest thou two [natures] whereof Christ is [formed], whereas after the union thou predicatest one nature of the Son as though suppressing the distinction between two natures? Above thou sayest that those whereof one son is [formed] are two and later that the nature of the Son is one, as though the union of the natures resulted in the nature and not in the *prosôpon*. For the natures of both of them which have been united have become one. For this union, being variable and changeable,

Θεοῦ λόγον ὑπονοήσομεν. ἑπόμενοι δὲ πανταχῇ ταῖς θεοπνεύστοις γραφαῖς, ἐκ τῆς ἁγίας παρθένου λαβεῖν αὐτὸν τὴν σάρκα διαβεβαιούμεθα. ταύτῃ τοι τά, ἐξ ὧν ἐστὶν ὁ εἷς καὶ μόνος υἱός, καὶ κύριος Ἰησοῦς Χριστός, ὡς ἐν ἐννοίαις δεχόμενοι, δύο μὲν φύσεις ἡνῶσθαί φαμεν, μετὰ δέ γε τὴν ἕνωσιν, ὡς ἀνῃρημένης ἤδη τῆς εἰς δύο διατομῆς, μίαν εἶναι πιστεύομεν τὴν τοῦ υἱοῦ φύσιν ὡς ἑνός, πλὴν ἐνανθρωπήσαντος, καὶ σεσαρκωμένου. εἰ δὲ δὴ λέγοιτο σαρκωθῆναι, καὶ ἐνανθρωπῆσαι Θεὸς ὢν ὁ λόγος, διερρίφθω που μακρὰν τροπῆς ὑποψία. μεμένηκε γὰρ ὅπερ ἦν. ὁμολογείσθω δὲ πρὸς ἡμῶν καὶ ἀσύγχυτος παντελῶς ἡ ἕνωσις.

in that it takes place for the nature and for the completion of the nature, is not of two complete but of two incomplete natures.

For every complete nature has not need of another nature that it may be and live, in that it has in it and has received [its whole] definition that it may be. For in a natural composition it seems that neither of those natures whereof it is [formed] is complete but they need one another that they may be and subsist. Even as the body has need of the soul that it may live, for it lives not of itself, and the soul has need of the body that it may perceive, whereas otherwise it would see, even though it had not eyes and would hear, even though the hearing were injured, so too with the other senses. How then dost thou predicate one nature of two whole natures, when the humanity is complete, needing not the union of the divinity to become man? / For it is its to become man not through the union with the divinity but by the creative power of God, who has brought into being all that which existed not, although the union took place with its very creation.[1] Nor was the divinity in need of the humanity as if for the knowledge or as if for the perceiving of human [perceptions]. How then resulted the union of the Son in one nature? Suppress then entirely the [theories pointing to] two natures and there will be room for that of one nature without soul, as Arius said, and without intelligence, as Apollinarius said; and thou attributest unto man one nature outside all the natures and afterwards [thou sayest] this, that God the Word is not without need, because he is not a complete nature in that he needs the nature of man. But now in the same [place] thou sayest the opposite to all this: both [that there are] two whole natures whereof the Son is [formed] and that the union resulted in one nature of the Son. Nor has it therefore been conceived that there is one Son [formed] of these [two natures], and thou hast spoken of two natures united, and further [thou hast said] that [they resulted] in one nature of the Son and dost abolish that of the flesh. And for this reason after the union thou suppressest the

---

[1] *I.e.* the union of Christ's divinity with his humanity took place simultaneously with the creation of the latter. Cp. p. 237.

distinction between two [natures] in that the nature of the flesh has thereby been suppressed either because it has been corrupted or because it has been changed, and thou believest, however, in 'one nature of the Son who was made man and was found in body'. Whom and what, whereof one Son is [formed], callest thou the nature? And what is / the one nature of the Son? But the things which are united from two natures into one nature are conceived [to be composed] of both the natures which have been united in like manner as [something] composed of simple [elements]. Therefore the one nature of the Son is composite, and for this reason thou hast said: '[He is] furnished however with a bodily frame.' How further will the distinction between both be suppressed, that he[1] may not be conceived [to be] with the flesh? And thou speakest of two and [sayest] that it is not right that they should be conceived [to be] two after the union, as though indeed suppressing the distinction between both. And thou speakest of one nature of the Son and attributest unto them the necessity of being conceived as two, in that thou sayest that he was furnished with a bodily frame after the union; for he was furnished with flesh in the flesh which was by nature flesh. Thou attributest therefore two natures unto the Lord after the union, one the nature of the Son and one the flesh wherein he was furnished with flesh; or before the union two distinct natures, of the divinity of the Son and of his humanity, are to be conceived, and then they were combined for the suppression of one nature. And thus too, neither before the union nor after the union, is the Son conceived as [formed] of two natures; or thou sayest this, that they continue disunited and undistinguished, and the nature of the Son remains alone [apart] from the nature of the humanity, as though suppressing the distinction between both; and thou castest before Acacius himself, as before a dog that is excited and infuriated against thee, the [view] that after the union the distinction between both is suppressed, and thou sayest that we believe that the *ousia* of the Son is / one; and again [thou proclaimest] before the Easterns that he however was furnished with flesh, in order

---

[1] *Viz.* the Word.

that they might not be excited. Thou hast also said this, that the union took place entirely without confusion, and thou concedest unto every man as he requires.

Acacius.[1] Yet verily and often indeed opponents will say: 'Lo! evidently these, in making confession of the 'correct faith, name two natures and distinguish the sayings 'of the theologians according to the diversity of the natures. 'And lo! how is it that these [theories] are not opposed to 'thine, for thou art not persuaded that [one ought] to divide 'the sayings unto two *prosôpa* or *hypostases*?'

Cyril. But, O wise man, I say that there is written in the Articles that that man who divides the sayings between two *prosôpa* or *hypostases*, some of them as if to the man who is known outside God the Word and others of them as though suitable to God the Word alone, who [proceeded] from God the Father, should be condemned. But we have not in any way abolished the diversity of the sayings, although we have ruled out the [phrase] ' we divide them ' as [dividing] the Son alone, the Word from the Father, and again as [dividing] the man known [as] the Son of a woman. For truly the nature of the Word is one, for we know that he was found in body and was made man.[2]

Nestorius. By reasoning and the train of examination did he persuade / Acacius of these words and did he not lead him, as one that was bridled, to follow whithersoever he required? For he said that there was a union of two natures whence there was [formed] only one Son and Lord and Jesus Christ and [that] the union took place entirely without confusion. How then is the nature of the Son one, that which thou hast

---

[1] The whole passage is taken from Cyril's letter, and follows immediately on p. 392, n. 2; Nestorius has added the name 'Acacius'.

[2] Labbe (Mansi), v. 320 B: ἀλλὰ γὰρ ἴσως φαῖεν ἂν οἱ δι' ἐναντίας. ἰδοὺ δὴ σαφῶς οἱ τῆς ὀρθῆς πίστεως τὴν ὁμολογίαν ποιούμενοι, δύο μὲν ὀνομάζουσι φύσεις, διῃρῆσθαι δὲ τὰς τῶν θεηγόρων φωνὰς διατείνοντα κατά γε τὴν διαφορὰν αὐτῶν. εἶτα πῶς οὐκ ἐναντία ταῦτα τοῖς σοῖς; οὐδὲ γὰρ ἀνέχῃ προσώποις δυσίν, ἤγουν ὑποστάσεσι, τὰς φωνὰς διανέμειν. ἀλλ', ὦ βέλτιστοι, φαίην ἄν, γεγράφαμεν ἐν τοῖς κεφαλαίοις· εἴ τις προσώποις δύσιν, ἤγουν ὑποστάσεσι, διανέμει τὰς φωνάς, καὶ τὰς μέν, ὡς ἀνθρώπῳ παρὰ τὸν ἐκ Θεοῦ λόγον ἰδικῶς νοουμένῳ προσάπτει, τὰς δὲ ὡς θεοπρεπεῖς μόνῳ τῷ ἐκ Θεοῦ πατρὸς λόγῳ, οὗτος ἔστω κατάκριτος. φωνῶν δὲ διαφορὰς κατ' οὐδένα τρόπον ἀνῃρήκαμεν, εἰ καὶ ἀπόβλητον πεποιήμεθα τὸ μερίζειν αὐτάς, ὡς υἱῷ καταμόνας τῷ ἐκ πατρὸς λόγῳ, καὶ ὡς ἀνθρώπῳ καταμόνας πάλιν υἱῷ νοουμένῳ τῷ ἐκ γυναικός. μία γὰρ ὁμολογουμένως ἡ τοῦ λόγου φύσις· ἴσμεν δὲ ὅτι σεσάρκωταί τε, καὶ ἐνηνθρώπησε, καθάπερ ἤδη προεῖπον.

said is two natures—that is, [is] in the natures, [being] that which is of them. For there is not a nature which should be two natures whence there should be one and not two. 'But', [thou wilt say], 'through the union it is his to become one, and 'yet he became not one through the union, and [it is right] that 'we should conceive two without confusion with the diversity 'of the *ousias* and further that we should not conceive two 'but one' .... Who understands confusion without confusion, and [how] to divide the sayings unto two *prosôpa* or *hypostases*? These things need much examination, an exact examination of identity and of difference. 'If one divides the sayings unto two *prosôpa* or *hypostases*,' [he says], and again : 'Nor [is it right] that we should abolish the diversity of the sayings even in any single way.' He who says that it is not right to divide the sayings into the *prosôpa* or the *hypostases* further abolishes not even in any way the two diversities of the sayings. For in what way is it by no means right to divide the sayings unto the *prosôpa* or the *hypostases*? From / two thou keepest us afar off ; how therefore hast thou not even in any single way abolished the diversity of the sayings? 'Although we have ruled out the [phrase] '" we divide them ", as [dividing] the Son alone, the Word from 'the Father, and again as [dividing] the man who alone is 'known as the son of a woman. For even truly the nature of 'the Word is one, for we know that he was found in body and 'was made man.' In what way then hast thou not suppressed the diversity of the sayings ; whereas thou sayest that the eternal Son is by nature God the Word? Say [that] thou givest [unto him] also the flesh even in union and not in remoteness, what is the diversity of the sayings which thou hast not abolished ? For the diversities are [those] of the operations which are set before us and these diversities are based on the sayings ; for when there is no diversity [in the operations], the diversity also of the sayings is suppressed. Thou confessest two natures of one Christ and Son, even two diversities, and thou makest the diversities of the sayings in accordance with the diversities of the natures and thou dividest also the sayings of the theologians. How hast thou joined together the very things which are divided, thou that acceptest with a joyful voice him that divides them? How confessest thou two natures of the union of one Christ and one Son and again one nature of God the Word? For thou hast said that we confess / one nature of God the Word and not two united. Thou sayest one Son, because thou predicatest of the Son two natures without distinction, and thou attributest again one nature only nor yet two without distinction unto God the Word and sayest that he is the Son found in flesh and yet that he is not in the flesh. But, lest thou shouldest predicate one Son of God the Word in one nature found in flesh and another Son of two natures united, of one Christ and one Son thou darest not predicate one nature found in flesh, but thou confidently determinest the one nature of God the Word found in flesh. Why then? There is one Son, God the Word, [with] one nature and another Son with two natures whence proceeded the one Son alone! For the nature of God is not said to be two natures but one nature, in such wise that thou callest Christ one Son in two natures. And thou sayest all these things, [to wit,] both two natures of one Son and one nature of God the Word; and thou speakest of the Son [as formed] of two natures unlike one another and further removest [one of them] from him and attributest one nature alone unto him; and thou removest one [from him]—I mean the humanity—so that it becomes not the Son in the union, and thou art constrained by the word 'natures' to distinguish the properties of each one of them, whether thou art willing or whether thou art unwilling.

/ For for what reason hast thou spoken of one nature of God the Word and not of two united? And further [for what reason] hast thou dared to say that there is only one God the Word [resulting] therefrom, as thou hast said that only one Son [results] therefrom? Let it be, as thou hast said, that two natures, which men would call united, are accepted in imagination; say thus also of God the Word, that thereby only one God the Word is two. I indeed predicate two natures united, following the Divine Scriptures and the divine teachings, and [I say] that God the Word is indicative of the nature but the Son of the *prosôpon*, but [that] he is one [and] the same God the Word. Thus [it is] that God is indicative of the nature but the Father and the Son and the Holy Spirit of the *prosôpa*. For this reason the divinity indeed [is] one but the *prosôpa* three; for God is Father and God Son and God Holy Spirit. The *prosôpa* are not without *ousia*. But again in the same way—thus also concerning Christ [there are] two natures, one of God the Word and one of the humanity, but one *prosôpon* of the Son, that whereof the humanity also likewise makes use, and one [of] the man, that whereof the divinity also likewise makes use. It is not of the nature but of the natural *prosôpon* of the natures [whereof they make use]; for even in the union the natures remain without confusion. Neither [are] the natures without *prosôpa* nor yet the *prosôpa* without *ousia*, nor as in the nature of an animal has the union resulted in the completion of one animal; it has derived from both of them / the [power] to become complete. Yet of two complete natures the one is predicated of the other by appropriation and not in the nature, but in the natural *prosôpon* of the natures and not in another nature. That which is another is [so] called by nature; for by the nature the Son of God [is] God the Word, in such wise that the humanity also makes use of the same through the appropriation of the union and not through the nature. For *Christ the same yesterday and to-day and for ever*[1] [is] the same in *prosôpon*, not in the same nature.

Why congratulatest thou thyself and confessest that the humanity and the divinity are not the very same in *ousia* or, as thou sayest, in natural quality,—if it is right to call the quality nature?[2] And further thou confessest that the nature of the divinity and [that] of the humanity are united without confusion; thou understandest two which are unconfused and which are combined with one another. Thou confessest also [these qualities] in respect to the natures because they remain without confusion. And by the nature of each one of them they are conceived as one, though thou confessest not by the *prosôpon* but by the nature. So thou suppressest both that are confessed without confusion by thee; for thou confessest

[1] Heb. xiii. 8.   [2] Cp. p. 321, n. 1.

that both were united without confusion, and further two are not to be conceived—as though suppressing the distinction of both—as that which [is] one. If the inconfusion of both the *ousias* had not been in thy mind, how then sayest thou of that which was combined in one *ousia* / that one ought to confess this union [to have taken place] without confusion? And again let us suppose that those [natures] which have been united without confusion have not been united without confusion[1] or, like the [view] which thou hast said, that the union took place for [the forming of] one Son from two natures. But after the union thou removest the humanity from the union which [resulted] in one Son, and it has been put far away from the union which [resulted] in one Son and is henceforth conceived apart from the union. But this *ousia* of the Son is conceived uniquely, nor yet are those [natures] whereof he is [formed] Son, but only one nature, conceived in the Son. Yet thou sayest that there is only one nature.

[*Cyril.*] But when the manner of the Incarnation[2] is investigated, the human intelligence sees inevitably two things which [are united] ineffably and inconfusedly in one union; yet it distinguishes not entirely what has been united but believes that of two there is [formed] one, both God and Son and Lord and Christ.[3]

Wherein sayest thou 'one'? That they have been united in the *prosôpon* of the union of the natures? Thus then the human intelligence sees those things which are united without confusion; but they are without confusion in their own natures and in their own *ousia* and thus they remain and are conceived. The one is not conceived as the other in *ousia* nor the other as the one. For in the matter of the *ousias* there is a distinction in the nature of each one of them: it both is conceived and exists. But in the combination of the natures there exists / in the same one *prosôpon* without distinction and without division.

[1] Syr. 'Let us not suppose .... have been united ....'
[2] *Sc.* ἐνσωμάτωσις.
[3] Labbe (Mansi), v. 320 D: ὅταν τοίνυν ὁ τῆς σαρκώσεως πολυπραγμονῆται τρόπος, δύο τὰ ἀλλήλοις ἀπορρήτως τε καὶ ἀσυγχύτως συνηνεγμένα καθ' ἕνωσιν ὁρᾷ δὴ πάντως ὁ ἀνθρώπινος νοῦς, ἑνωθέντα γε μὴν διΐστησιν οὐδαμῶς. ἀλλ' ἕνα τὸν ἐξ ἀμφοῖν καὶ Θεόν, καὶ υἱόν, καὶ Χριστόν, καὶ κύριον εἶναί τε καὶ πιστεύει καὶ ἀραρότως εἰσδέχεται.

In the natural *prosôpon* [there is] one nature, making likewise of the *prosôpon* of another nature. Thus therefore the natures which have been united are without confusion and are never to be divided in the same, in that in the matter of the natures they are conceived in the distinction of their own natures.

Cyril. But the wrong opinion [1] of Nestorius is [something] entirely other than this; for he proves that he confesses that the Word which is God was found in body and was made man; but, knowing not the force of 'was found in body' he names two natures and distinguishes them from one another, setting God solely by himself and likewise the man by himself, who has been joined unto God in proximity and in equality of honour only, and in authority. For thus he says: 'God is not distinct from him that is visible. For 'this reason I distinguish not the honour of him that is not 'distinguished; I distinguish the natures and I unite the adoration. . . .' But these our brothers in Antioch, accepting simply, as though in imagination only, the things whereof Christ is known [to have been formed], predicate the diversity of the natures—because the divinity and the humanity are not one thing in natural quality, as I have said,—as well as one Son and Christ and Lord; and, as indeed he is truly one, they say that his *prosôpon* / is one but distinguish not in any way at all the things which have been united.[2]

Nestorius. And verily, if this had been truly [said], thou too wouldest have been more confident in this word, while I should not be able to feel confident of being known thereby, but, as thou sayest, I should be making use [thereof] in *schêma*, and thou oughtest to have confuted me before all the Council;

---

[1] See p. xv.
[2] Labbe (Mansi), v. 320 D: ἑτέρα δὲ παντελῶς παρὰ ταύτην ἡ Νεστορίου κακοδοξία (v. l. κενοδοξία). ὑποκρίνεται μὲν γὰρ ὁμολογεῖν, ὅτι καὶ ἐσαρκώθη καὶ ἐνηνθρώπησε Θεὸς ὢν ὁ λόγος, τὴν δέ γε τοῦ σεσαρκῶσθαι δύναμιν οὐκ εἰδώς, δύο μὲν ὀνομάζει φύσεις, ἀποδιαιρεῖ (v. l. ἀποδιΐστησι) δὲ ἀλλήλων αὐτάς, Θεὸν ἰδίᾳ τιθείς, καὶ ὁμοίως ἄνθρωπον ἀνὰ μέρος, συναφθέντα Θεῷ σκετιχῶς, κατὰ μόνην τὴν ἰσοτιμίαν, ἤγουν αὐθεντίαν. ἔφη γὰρ οὕτως· ἀχώριστος τοῦ φαινομένου Θεός. διὰ τοῦτο τοῦ μὴ χωριζομένου τὴν τιμὴν οὐ χωρίζω· χωρίζω τὰς φύσεις, ἀλλ' ἑνῶ τὴν προσκύνησιν. οἱ δέ γε κατὰ τὴν Ἀντιόχειαν ἀδελφοί, τὰ μὲν ἐξ ὧν νοεῖται Χριστός, ὡς ἐν ψιλαῖς καὶ μόναις ἐννοίαις δεχόμενοι, φύσεων μὲν εἰρήκασι διαφοράν, ὅτι μὴ ταυτόν, ὡς ἔφην, ἐν ποιότητι φυσικῇ θεότης καὶ ἀνθρωπότης. ἕνα γε μὴν υἱόν, καὶ Χριστόν, καὶ κύριον, καὶ ὡς ἑνὸς ὄντος ἀληθῶς, ἐν αὐτοῦ καὶ τὸ πρόσωπον εἶναί φασιν· μερίζουσι δὲ κατ' οὐδένα τρόπον τὰ ἡνωμένα.

nor, when I had required [aught] of thee by request, oughtest thou to have kept it dark but to have waited for the whole Council; and again, when I was summoned to the Council, thou oughtest not to have declined. For how often hast thou not done this very thing and wast refuting my wrong opinion, whereas I was not able to make use of any defence. For he who is confuted of imagining the contrary of that to which he clings in hypocrisy[1] condemns with all condemnations the wrongness of his opinion. Yet perhaps it is not so, but the opposite. Whence knowest thou that I confess that God the Word was made flesh and was made man and yet say not that he was made flesh and was made man? For he who was made flesh was made flesh in the flesh, while he who says that they[2] are divided and distinct[3] from one another does not even confess the incarnation[4] at all; unless perhaps he confesses / the [view] that he who was not made flesh was made flesh. For how are those things made flesh which are apart from one another without being united? If therefore I confess two natures and that he was made flesh, from what [cause] have I been supposed to say that the natures are distinct and far removed from one another, without conceding the being made flesh[4] and the being made man[5] of God the Word?

For thou hast said that I say[6]: 'God is not distinct from 'him that is visible. For this reason [as regards] him that is 'not distinct I distinguish not the honour.' How does he who says that God is not distinct from him that is visible distinguish [the two]? For thou hast said that thou distinguishest not him that is visible from him that is invisible, and also that the honour of God is not to be distinguished; nor, if I distinguish not God himself from him that is visible because he is not to

---

[1] Sc. προσωποληψία. [2] Viz. the natures.

[3] The specific meanings of the words 'divide', 'distinguish', 'separate', etc., cannot be pressed in this translation. The editors have appropriated one English word to each Syriac word, but the result is at times unsatisfactory, as here. The sense required is clearly 'separate', while the Syriac word is that rendered throughout by 'distinct'. See the definitions on pp. 313-16. The Syriac translator seems to have used these words very loosely and without any precise discrimination of meaning. Cp. p. 154, n. 1.

[4] Sc. σάρκωσις. [5] Sc. ἐνανθρώπησις, elsewhere translated 'incarnation'.

[6] See crit. n., p. 401.

be distinguished, do I distinguish also the honour. 'Who', hast thou said, 'is not to be distinguished? And from whom 'is he not to be distinguished? And for this reason I dis-'tinguish not even the honour of him that is not to be distinguished.' But I say that I distinguish the natures but unite the adoration. Just as thou too hast accepted the union of the natures without confusion either in truth or in *schêma*, thou distinguishest also the natures in the matter of the *ousias* whereof Christ is conceived [to have been formed], whether thou art willing or whether thou art unwilling. Thou predicatest also the diversity and [admittest] / that the divinity and the humanity are not the same in natural quality, as thou sayest. For he that says that the divinity and the humanity are not the same makes by a natural diversity the distinction that the one is not the other nor the other the one. But the natural diversity is a distinction. The distinction therefore in the diversity and in the *ousia* of the natures is one thing and the distinction in the distance apart of the *ousias*, which have been combined and united in the combination, is another thing. Therefore I have predicated the union of the combination of the natures, of the divinity and of the humanity without distinction, [saying] that God is not distinct from him that is visible; yet I have said that according to the union without confusion the natures are distinguished by a natural diversity, but I have called the adoration of those [natures], which are thus not to be distinguished and are to be distinguished, one, seeing indeed that they have been combined in one *prosôpon* and not in one *ousia* nor in one nature, because the union of the natures took not place in confusion; nor further [did there take place] a confusion for the completion of one nature, because the union resulted not from incomplete but from two whole natures.[1]

For every union which results by a natural composition in the completion of the nature results from incomplete natures, but that which [results] from complete natures results in one

---

[1] Here Nestorius gives the most concise summary of his position. He then goes on to contrast it with 'Nestorianism' as commonly understood; see p. 314, n. 1.

prosôpon and subsists therein. For God the Word made not use of a bodily frame without soul nor / of a soul without will and without mind, nor of a bodily frame and of a soul instead of a soul and an intelligence. But thereby is distinguished the church of the Arians and [that] of the Apollinarians, which accepts not two whole natures which have been united. Neither do I distinguish the natures which have been united by abstraction and by isolation from one another, nor do I speak of an adhesion through love and through proximity, as though it were between those which are far apart [and] those united by love and not in the *ousias*; nor again do I speak of a union in equality of honour and in authority but of the natures and of whole natures, and in the combination of the *ousias* I concede a union without confusion; but in respect to one honour and to one authority I predicate the union of the natures and not of the honour and of the authority. Otherwise, prove [it] by what I have said: 'God is not to be distinguished from him 'that is visible; for this reason I distinguish not the honour of 'him who is not distinguished.' Where then have I said in these things that I distinguish the natures from one another and speak of God the Word by himself and the man by himself, [saying] that they adhered together by proximity of love and by equality of honour or by authority? For, I have said, I distinguish not God from him that is visible. [I spoke] not of the proximity nor the equality of honour nor of the equality, but I said that I distinguish not God the Word himself in his nature from the visible nature, and by reason of God who is not to be distinguished I distinguish not even the honour; for he is one thing and his honour is another, and his *ousia* is another / and whatsoever the *ousia* is is another. But, although I have said that I distinguish the natures and unite the adoration, I have not said that I distinguish the natures from one another by a distinction of distance, as thou accusest me in thy calumniation.[1]

For if there had not been [any] other manner of distinction between natures than that only of distance apart, thou wouldest

---

[1] Here Nestorius most directly repudiates 'Nestorianism' as usually understood; see notes on pp. 205, 224.

have well found fault with me for distinguishing them thus. But if there were many others, and especially [if], in the matter of the natures which all our inquiry concerns, the union of which natures, whereof I have spoken, took place without confusion or change, how is this to thy thinking?[1] And [yet] thou examinest up and down, as though I [had] said in this sense that I distinguish the natures?[2]

And thou bringest [word] that the others[3] divide not even in a single way the [natures] which have been united. In the first place thou wast the first to say that they are distinguished. But these our brothers in Antioch accepting simply, as indeed only by reflection, the things whereof Christ is known [to have been formed], predicate the diversity of the natures, because the divinity and the humanity are not any one thing in natural quality, as I have said, but one Son and Christ and Lord; and as indeed he is truly one, so we say that the *prosôpon* is one. But thou sayest that they divide not even in a single way the natures which have been united, while they have spoken of the diversity, / [saying] that the natural quality of the divinity and the humanity is not the same; and thou sayest that we ought not to divide the diversity, nor is it that there are the same things in nature, and therein thou predicatest the diversity. For in every way thou makest distinction, saying that there is a diversity and that the divinity and the humanity are not the same in natural quality; yet [thou makest the distinction] not in distance apart but in the matter of the natures, nor by means of a distinction consisting in a differentiation of functions,[4] but with an obvious meaning. How then do they not distinguish even in a single way those things whereof Christ is united and predicate the diversities in the *ousia*?

And further thou sayest:

> They accept not even the distinction of the natures, as it seems to have been imagined by the exponent of [these] paltry inventions, but they define and distinguish only the sayings concerning our Lord, saying that [some] of them are

---

[1] Literally: 'before thy face'.
[2] There is no new paragraph marked here in the Syriac text.
[3] *Viz.* the Eastern bishops.
[4] See crit. n., p. 401.

suitable not to the Word which [proceeded] from God the Father as to the Son solely and [others] also of them again to another Son who [was born] of a woman, but [some] of them to his divinity and [others] of them again to his humanity; for the same indeed is God and man; but they say that there are also others which [are] common, because they regard both of them—I mean, [the natures of] the divinity and of the humanity. . . .[1]

I indeed suppose that he does not even know what he says: however, what I suppose [is] that he says the opposite / of whatever he says in *schêma* that he confesses with the Easterns. For, if there were not a distinction between the natures, how hast thou said that they have predicated a diversity of natures? And how are not the divinity and the humanity the same in natural quality, since they are divided in nature according to [their] diversity? For therein, if it is supposed of me that I predicate a natural distinction, it belies [me] not; they are not however [derived] from the exponents of [these] paltry inventions, for they are not my own inventions, but the apostolic faith and the teaching of the Fathers and thy own confession also, since thou art constrained and turnest it hither and thither that thou mayest say it without saying it.

And thou hast confessed that those whereof Christ is [formed] are two natures and [that they are] alien to one another in *ousia*: 'We do not conceive that God the Word 'has taken [aught] of his own, that is, divine nature and 'has constructed for him[self] a bodily frame, following 'everywhere the Divine Scriptures, since we affirm that he 'has taken [it] from the holy virgin. We accept as by reason 'those things whereof [there is formed] only one Son and 'Lord and Jesus Christ, confessing two natures which have 'been united.'[2] And the natural distinction is not overlooked, for the indication of the natural distinction consists in their

---

[1] Labbe (Mansi), v. 321 A: οὔτε μὴν φυσικὴν παραδέχονται τὴν διαίρεσιν, καθὰ φρονεῖν ἔδοξε τῷ τῶν ἀθλίων εὑρημάτων εἰσηγητῇ· διαιρεῖσθαι δὲ μόνας διατείνονται τὰς ἐπὶ τῷ κυρίῳ φωνάς· πρέπειν τέ φησιν αὐτάς, οὐ τὰς μὲν ὡς υἱῷ καταμόνας τῷ ἐκ Θεοῦ πατρὸς λόγῳ, τὰς δὲ καὶ ὡς ἑτέρῳ πάλιν υἱῷ, τῷ ἐκ γυναικός· ἀλλὰ τὰς μὲν τῇ θεότητι αὐτοῦ, τὰς δὲ πάλιν τῇ ἀνθρωπότητι αὐτοῦ. Θεὸς γάρ ἐστιν ὁ αὐτὸς καὶ ἄνθρωπος. εἶναι δέ φασι καὶ ἑτέρας κοινοποιηθείσας τρόπον τινά, καὶ οἷον ἐπ' ἄμφω βλεπούσας, θεότητα καὶ ἀνθρωπότητα λέγω. [2] See p. 302, n. 2.

being called two; but, in respect to the natures, they are called two, for there is a natural distinction between the natures whereby thou confessest two but [addest] that they are united without confusion; for this reason also [they are] two.

/ Thou sayest again some thing else to the contrary, that after the union [there is] one nature, because the distinction of the two, both of them his own, has already been abolished for him. Therein it is not [possible] for him to come to terms with the Easterns. Thou sayest however that there is even no indication of the distinction between the two, not, [that is], the distinction of the union but [that] for the diversity of the *ousias*. But thou, O wise man, with all thy wisdom dost even confess two after the union and determinest to confess that after the union there are no more two natures. For thou predicatest two natures united; it is evident that they are united before the union and not after the union. How then confessest thou two natures after the union and forbiddest us to confess two natures after the union? Which should we believe? The first or the second? Or thine? Since thou confessest with the Easterns who confess two natures, but Acacius does not,[1] [saying] that it is not right to confess two natures but one after the union, because the distinction into two has already been suppressed. Thou concedest unto every man as he requires. . . . 'But 'they accept not the natural distinction,[2] but define and ' distinguish only the sayings concerning our Lord, saying that ' they are suitable, yet not saying that [they are suitable ' some] of them solely to the Word which [proceeded] from ' God the Father as to a Son and [others] of them again ' as to another Son / who [was born] of a woman, but [some] ' of them to his divinity and [others] of them again to his ' humanity, for the same is God and man.' . . . . And me, lying, he calumniates as though predicating two Sons; and those things also which he has cited against me therefrom as well as from the letters and from these interpretations

---

[1] See crit. n., p. 401.
[2] *I.e.* the distinction of natures; see p. 316, n. 1.

which have been excerpted by him proclaim [it]. But [as regards] his having said that now they accept not the natural distinction[1] but define and distinguish only the sayings concerning our Lord, let us see what those that [are come] from the East have said, and in what way he makes use of these things: 'As for the sayings of the Gospels concerning our 'Lord, we know certain theologians who make [some] of 'them that [are] common relative to one *prosôpon*.'[2] Hearest thou how they have confessed? 'Relative to one *prosôpon*' and not to one nature. Why changest thou their confession, when they make those that [are] common, as thou hast said, relative to one common *prosôpon*? And thou makest naught common.[3] Whose do they make those that [are] common, since there is not [anything] common except [in the eyes of] those who make use of one *prosôpon*? Predicate then a common *prosôpon* and predicate of one *prosôpon* the things that they make common. It [is this that] makes his one *prosôpon* common; for that which is made of things [that are] opposite in anything is made common, so that it is therefore not sole but / common. As then a serpent receives a wound and coils itself up over the wound and conceals the wound itself and unwinds itself anew out of pain and shows it, though unwilling, thus thou also darest to hide what thou hast confessed and afterwards hast confessed, though unwilling, the things which have been confessed.

For hear thine own confession; for they have required thee to confess with them the things which thou hast written.

> But as regards the sayings of the Gospels and of the Apostles spoken concerning one Lord, we know that certain theologians make [some] of the things which are common relative to one *prosôpon* but divide [others] of them as between two natures; those which are suitable unto God they attribute unto the divinity of Christ and [others] of them, and those them that are contemptible, unto the humanity. . . . .[4]

---

[1] *I. e.* the distinction of natures.   [2] See below, n. 4.
[3] *I.e.* because Cyril only allows of one nature.
[4] From the letter which John of Antioch sent to Cyril by Paul of Emesa, Labbe (Mansi), v. 292 c: τὰς δὲ εὐαγγελικὰς καὶ ἀποστολικὰς περὶ τοῦ κυρίου

These things thou hast confessed [in such wise as] to imagine and to teach [them]; why art thou now keeping [them] dark? For thou hast said that the things which are distinct [are] relative to two natures and not to one nature, nor are the divinity and the humanity the same, but the [attributes] of the divinity indeed [belong] unto the divinity and [those] of the humanity unto the humanity. They call not by two names one nature, which is distinct only in the saying and not in the *ousia*, as thou imaginest. For thou sayest that the diversities of the sayings are not suppressed but they have indicated in saying the natures and the distinction / of the natures. And thou confessest [so far as] to say that there is a distinction of the natures; for thou hast said that they divide the sayings as [relative] to two natures, [attributing 'some] of them, those which are suitable unto God, unto the ' divinity of Christ' and not unto the same *ousia* in respect to the humanity but to the nature in respect to the divinity. For they call not the divinity two natures but one nature and the humanity one nature; for two natures are not named after one nature nor one nature after two natures. For concerning two natures they have said that a distinction should be made and not concerning two sayings which indicate one nature but which indicate two natures owing to the distinction of the diversity of the *ousia* of the two natures.[1] 'Those ' indeed which are made common [they attribute] as unto one '*prosôpon*, but others of them they divide as between two ' natures, [attributing] those which are suitable unto God unto ' the divinity of Christ.' The common *prosôpon* of the two natures [is] Christ, the same *prosôpon* whereof the natures make use even likewise, that wherein and whereby both of them, the divinity and the humanity, are known in *ousia* without distinction and with distinction. Neither the divinity nor the humanity exists [by itself] in the common *prosôpon*,

φωνὰς ἴσμεν τοὺς θεολόγους (v. l. θεηγόρους) ἀνθρώπους τὰς μὲν κοινοποιοῦντας ὡς ἐφ' ἑνὸς προσώπου, τὰς δὲ διαιροῦντας ὡς ἐπὶ δύο φύσεων· καὶ τὰς μὲν θεοπρεπεῖς κατὰ τὴν θεότητα τοῦ Χριστοῦ, τὰς δὲ ταπεινὰς κατὰ τὴν ἀνθρωπότητα αὐτοῦ παραδιδόντας.

[1] Cp. the passage from Cyr. *ad Nest. iii* quoted on p. 325, n. 1.

for it appertains to both the natures, so that therein and thereby both the natures are known; for it is one in the *ousias*.¹ For even the *ousia* of the humanity similarly makes use of the *prosôpon* of the *ousia* of the divinity and not of the *ousia*, and the *ousia* of the divinity / makes use of the *prosôpon* of the humanity similarly, and not of the *ousia*, as thou pretendest. And they 'predicate not [some] of them solely
' of the Word who [proceeded] from the Father as of a Son
' but [others] of them again of another Son who [was born]
' of a woman; but [they attribute some] of them unto his
' divinity but [others] of them again unto his humanity; for
' the same indeed is God and man' . . . .²

If thou sayest 'solely' in [the sense of] remoteness apart of the distinction of the natures, thou speakest not unto those who confess that the natures are united and that they have been united in one *prosôpon* and are two natures and indicate therein and thereby two natures which are known [as such]. But if thou callest him [one and] the same in nature so that the divinity, which was born of God the Father is one nature and likewise again [that which was born] of the woman, thou sayest that God is distinct from man only in the saying and [is] the same in *ousia*.³ And thou speakest outside thine own confession and further art hastening to wage war with thyself. For how hast thou confessed with the Easterns the division into two natures, [attributing some] indeed of the sayings which are suitable unto the divinity unto the divinity of Christ, and those which are contemptible unto the humanity of Christ, who is by nature the humanity and by nature the divinity. [They said] not unto the divinity of God the Word nor yet unto the humanity of God the Word, for God the Word is not two natures nor [formed] of two natures / or two names or many-named, [bearing names] which are the names of the one *ousia* itself. And [supposing that] the divinity is not conceived in the nature but only in the saying, wherefore embroilest thou with thyself Acacius, thy loving and intimate [friend], whom thou oughtest to have let go, whatever hap-

---

¹ See crit. n., p. 401.   ² See p. 316, n. 1.
³ See below, p. 325, n. 1.

pened, who only in the simple term and in the saying agrees with thee, who dividest the natures not in their *ousias*, but in respect to the sayings which subsisted only in the imagination as saying, which indicate no [real] definition and no [real] nature? In nature on the one hand and in the *ousias* they [would have] had no distinction because also they are not *ousias*; only in the sayings of the natures on the other hand they [would have] had a distinction, because therein it is theirs to subsist.

Thus also of Christ[1] thou hast predicated two natures, but thou sayest that the distinction between them is not in the natures and in the *ousias* but only in the understanding and in the sayings. 'Our brothers in Antioch call those 'things whereby Christ is known a diversity of natures, as 'though merely accepting [them] in idea alone, because the 'divinity and the humanity are not one thing, as I have said, 'in natural quality' . . . .[2] Thou hast said in quality and not in *ousia*. But the quality, however, is not the nature of the *ousia* but either the *schéma* of the *ousia* or of the nature or of [that which is] not *ousia* or a view in mere idea[3] only expressed concerning the natures. [As for] this quality, it has not the natural / diversity of the natures but a diversity of the natures without *ousia*; yet thou sayest that they[4] exist only in the sayings, in reflection[3] about the natures, without *ousias*. And this he says, that they call the things whereby Christ is known the diversity of the natures, as though merely accepting them in idea alone, because the divinity and the humanity are not one thing in natural quality, as I have

---

[1] 'Thus also of Christ . . . .' This passage seems to reveal an important difference of terminology between Cyril and Nestorius. Nestorius spoke indifferently of two 'natures' or two '*ousias*' in Christ, but he objects to Cyril substituting 'natural quality' for 'nature', assuming that a 'quality' is not necessarily a real element in an object of thought, but may be something said or thought about it existing only in the mind of the thinker. But if for Cyril 'nature' was the sum of the 'natural qualities' (φυσικαὶ ποιότητες) and they shared its reality, it is easy to see how there was room for confusion.

[2] See p. 311, n. 1.

[3] Both 'idea' and 'reflection' represent the same Syriac word.

[4] The Syriac word is fem. plur.; as, however, all the nouns mentioned in the context are masc., we have taken this to refer generally to 'the things under discussion'.

said. . . . But they of Antioch are not content either to say this or to hear any man that says [it]; but they say that, touching the sayings of the Gospels concerning Christ our Lord, we know certain divines who make [some] of the things that are common relative to one *prosôpon*, but divide [others] of them between two natures. . . . They have said that they surely divide; they have predicated the sayings of two natures and accept not the diversity merely in idea alone. It is not by sayings but by sayings concerning two natures that they draw a distinction in the matter of the *ousias*. Two natures, which are to be distinguished by the sayings indicative of them, are distinguished. The natures are not without *hypostases*,[1] nor in idea without the *hypostases* of the natures do they constitute [them] by sayings in reflection, but by reflection upon the natures with the *ousias*, if not upon the *ousias* and the natures, they establish the ideas and the natures.

For the one is very distinct from the other; for the one says that they accept merely in idea alone the sayings about the diversities of the natures / and accepts not the idea of the natures with the *ousias*, but [says that] they are without *hypostases* and not subsisting, [and that] their origin indeed is from reflection and [that] they are whole in [its] wholeness. The other says that the idea and the sayings about the natures are indicative of the *ousias* both at the beginning in the idea and [afterwards] in the natures and in the *ousias*, in such wise that there are three kinds arising out of the nature of the *ousias* which are required of him who considers: the *ousia* itself and the idea of the *ousia* and the saying indicative of the idea. But whoever says that they [are] merely in idea alone, says two kinds [of things]: merely the idea and its own saying. For this reason he attributes the diversity to the idea alone of the nature and not to the *ousia*, but to a quality [resting] upon an illusion and upon a supposition of the nature, upon a *schêma* of the nature and not upon the *ousia* of the nature. For [as to] the quality of the nature and the *schêma* as well as the appearance of the *ousia*, all these things indeed he deduces and infers that it[2] is without *ousia*. Who would

---

[1] See p. 156, n. 2.   [2] *Viz.* the natural quality.

take account of one who makes use of divine things so disdainfully? He has not one pure and confident idea and he reckons everything in this way and surely makes sport of those who are distressed in heart[1] and [who] are zealous to learn the truth.[2]

And he is like unto Origen who says everything so that he may be accepted of every one, laying up favour with every one in whatever / he says, and persuades all [men]; [it is] for these things that he is hated of every one, because he turns about and suppresses the things which he has prepared by means of the opposite. For he wants every one to persist in whatever things please any one, and whoever changes them as an enemy is as the enemy of every one. And they rejoice not and are [not] delighted at the things which they have prepared [so much] as contrariwise they surely blush at the very things which they have prepared. The others[3] rejoice not at the things which delight him, for they suppose that they are outside the truth. But he makes [his] defence against those who have exalted themselves against him as against an enemy of the truth, namely on behalf of the faith of the Easterns, and he has not kept their own defence, such as it is, without an admixture [of falsehood].

Cyril. For because the confederates of the impiety of Arius, in impiously adulterating[4] the power of the truth, say that the Word which [proceeded] from God became indeed man[5] but made use of a soulless body,—but they do this craftily, that, in distinguishing human sayings [as] his and proving to those whom they deceive that he was in a state of inferiority to the sublimity of the Father, they might say that he was [of] another nature than he— therefore the Easterns, fearing this that perhaps then the glory of the nature, of God the Word might be made inferior by reason of the things which are humanly spoken on account of the incarnation[6] with / the flesh, distinguish the sayings, not dividing the one Son and Lord into two *prosôpa*, as I have said, but distinguishing [some] of them indeed [as belonging] unto his divinity and [others] of

---

[1] Literally: 'in whose souls distress has arrived'.
[2] Note that Nestorius here charges Cyril's teaching with implied docetism.
[3] *Viz.* the Easterns. [4] Literally: 'mixing untruth with'.
[5] See n. on p. xiii. [6] Sc. ἐνανθρώπησις.

them again [as belonging] unto his humanity, but all of them however [as belonging] unto one.[1]

Nestorius. For if they attribute the divine and the human sayings unto the one nature of God the Word as diverse only in sayings, how do they escape from saying that the human [attributes] belong[2] to the *ousia* of God the Word? But concerning the human [attributes] thou hast said that they [exist] not solely, [and] that they are indeed alien to the nature of the Father, seeing that he is one. For he is not another in nature in saying [alone], but also in *ousia*. For the *ousia* of man, as thou hast said, is the *ousia* of God: 'He is God and man.' [He is] then alien to the Father in every way whatsoever and he is inferior in everything according to thy own imagination, since thou imaginest that he is man also in the one same *ousia*. For drive not by force, thinking yourselves wise, though you are not so in the truth.[3] They have distinguished the sayings, that they may be supposed to distinguish them as it were between two natures of *ousias*, and they are blamed for an attempt against God the Word [in saying] that these are imagined without *ousia* in respect to the natures in idea alone, as thou feignest to call the ones and the others. But the others distinguish these sayings / as though between two natures which exist by *ousia*, as in truth they exist. And they reject the calumny of the Arians against God the Word; for he who joins naturally the two [kinds of] sayings to the one nature and the same *ousia*, aids and abets the Arians in every way whatsoever, [teaching] that God the Word [is] alien to God the Father.

[1] Labbe (Mansi), v. 324 c: ἐπειδὴ γὰρ οἱ τῆς Ἀρείου δυσσεβείας ὑπασπισταί, τῆς ἀληθείας τὴν δύναμιν ἀνοσίως ἐκκαπηλεύοντες, τὸν ἐκ Θεοῦ φασὶ λόγον γενέσθαι μὲν ἄνθρωπον, πλὴν ἀψύχῳ προσχρήσασθαι σώματι· πράττουσι δὲ τοῦτο φιλοκακούργως, ἵνα τὰς ἀνθρωπίνας φωνὰς αὐτῷ προσνέμοντες, ὡς ἐν μείοσιν ὄντα τῆς τοῦ πατρὸς ὑπεροχῆς τοῖς παρ' αὐτῶν πλανωμένοις ἐπιδεικνύωσιν, ἑτεροφυᾶ τε αὐτὸν εἶναι λέγωσι, ταύτῃ τοι δεδιότες οἱ ἐκ τῆς ἀνατολῆς, μὴ ἄρα πως ἡ τοῦ Θεοῦ λόγου κατασμικρύνοιτο δόξα τε καὶ φύσις ἀπό γε τῶν ἀνθρωπίνως εἰρημένων διὰ τὴν μετὰ σαρκὸς οἰκονομίαν, διορίζουσι τὰς φωνάς, οὐκ εἰς δύο τέμνοντες, ὡς ἔφην, τὸν ἕνα υἱόν καὶ κύριον, ἀλλὰ τὰς μὲν τῇ θεότητι αὐτοῦ προσνέμοντες, τὰς δὲ τῇ ἀνθρωπότητι πάλιν τῇ αὐτοῦ· πλὴν τὰς ἁπάσας ἑνί.

[2] The Syriac adds a negative, presumably corresponding to the second negative in Gk. μὴ οὐ. See p. xiv.

[3] Literally: 'and you are not true'.

Cyril. This is not unknown to thy Saintliness, that, in casting upon my letters the faults of the idea[s] of Apollinarius, they have supposed also that I say [that] the holy body of Christ was without a soul and that there was a mixing and a confusion and an intermingling and a change of God the Word with the flesh, or that the flesh was transformed into the nature of the divinity so that naught was preserved pure and that [the flesh] was not what it is. But with this they have supposed that I was implicated also in the blasphemies of Arius in that I was not willing to acknowledge the diversity of the sayings and to say that [some] of them are suitable to God but [others] of them [are] human and suitable rather to the dispensation with the flesh. But thy Perfection bears witness for me unto the others that I am far from such things as these; but I ought however to defend myself before those who have been scandalized, and for this [reason] I have written unto thy Piety that I have never been reconciled to the [teaching] of the adherents of Arius or of the adherents of Apollinarius and that I say not that God the Word was converted into the flesh nor that the flesh was altered / into the nature of the divinity, because the Word of God is unchangeable and invariable and incomprehensible in all things. Nor again have I ever abolished the diversity of the sayings, but I know that our Lord speaks at the same time divinely and humanly, because he is at the same time God and man.[1]

---

[1] Labbe (Mansi), v. 324 D : οὐκ ἠγνόηκεν ἡ σὴ τελειότης, ὅτι τῆς Ἀπολιναρίου δόξης τὸν μῶμον τῶν ἐμῶν καταχέοντες ἐπιστολῶν, ᾠήθησαν, ὅτι καὶ ἄψυχον εἶναί φημι τὸ ἅγιον σῶμα Χριστοῦ· καὶ ὅτι κρᾶσις, ἢ σύγχυσις, ἢ φυρμός, ἢ μεταβολὴ τοῦ Θεοῦ λόγου γέγονεν εἰς τὴν σάρκα, ἢ γοῦν τῆς σαρκὸς μεταφοίτησις εἰς φύσιν θεότητος, ὡς μηδὲν ἔτι σώζεσθαι καθαρῶς, μή τε μὴν εἶναι ὅ ἐστιν. ᾠήθησαν δὲ πρὸς τούτῳ καὶ ταῖς Ἀρείου με συμφέρεσθαι δυσφημίαις, διά τοι τὸ μὴ ἐθέλειν διαφορὰν εἰδέναι φωνῶν, καὶ τὰς μὲν εἶναι λέγειν θεοπρεπεῖς, τὰς δὲ ἀνθρωπίνας, καὶ πρεπούσας μᾶλλον τῇ οἰκονομίᾳ τῇ μετὰ σαρκός. ἐγὼ δὲ ὅτι τῶν τοιούτων ἀπήλλαγμαι, μαρτυρήσειεν ἂν ἑτέροις ἡ σὴ τελειότης. πλὴν ἔδει σκανδαλισθεῖσιν ἀπολόγησασθαι. ταύτῃ τοι γέγραφα πρὸς τὴν θεοσέβειαν αὐτοῦ, ὡς οὔτε πεφρόνηκά ποτε τὰ Ἀρείου, καὶ Ἀπολιναρίου, οὔτε μὴν μεταπεποιῆσθαι τὸν τοῦ Θεοῦ λόγον εἰς σάρκα φημί, ἀλλ' οὐδὲ εἰς φύσιν θεότητος μεταφῦναι τὴν σάρκα, διὰ τὸ ἄτρεπτον εἶναι, καὶ ἀναλλοίωτον τὸν τοῦ Θεοῦ λόγον· ἀνέφικτον δὲ καὶ τὸ ἕτερον. οὔτε μὴν ἀνῄρηκά ποτε φωνῶν διαφοράς· ἀλλ' οἶδα τὸν κύριον θεοπρεπῶς τε καὶ ἀνθρωπίνως ἅμα διαλεγόμενον, ἐπεί πέρ ἐστιν ἐν ταυτῷ Θεός, καὶ ἄνθρωπος. Cp. the following passage from Cyril, *ad. Nest. iii*, Labbe (Mansi), iv. 1077 B : τὰς δέ γε ἐν τοῖς εὐαγγελίοις τοῦ Σωτῆρος ἡμῶν φωνάς, οὔτε ὑποστάσεσι δυσὶν οὔτε μὴν προσώποις καταμερίζομεν· οὐ γάρ ἐστι διπλοῦς ὁ εἷς καὶ μόνος Χριστός, κἂν ἐκ δύο νοῆται καὶ διαφόρων πραγμάτων εἰς ἑνότητα τὴν ἀμέριστον συνενηνεγμένος, καθάπερ ἀμέλει καὶ ἄνθρωπος ἐκ ψυχῆς νοεῖται καὶ σώματος, καὶ οὐ διπλοῦς μᾶλλον, ἀλλ' εἷς ἐξ ἀμφοῖν· ἀλλὰ τάς τε ἀνθρωπίνας, καὶ πρός γε τούτῳ τὰς θεϊκάς, παρ' ἑνὸς

Nestorius. How hast thou said all these things which are supposed against me because thou wouldest not acknowledge the distinction between the sayings, when thou hast not abolished the diversity of the sayings? How art thou supposed, after what thou hast not abolished, to be reconciled to the [views] of Arius or to those of Apollinarius: that God the Word was changed into the flesh or the flesh was changed into the nature of the divinity? For in that thou makest [it thy] defence that some persons suspect thee of being unwilling to acknowledge the diversity of the sayings, by the very cause of [this] defence thou accusest thyself, as though thou hast given cause for them to suspect thee. But in those things, whereby thou defendest thyself, saying 'I have not abolished the diversity of the sayings', thou accusest thine own self both in the eyes of those who suspected thee, and especially in the eyes of Acacius, without any occasion for suspicion, as indeed he had accepted these very sayings which formerly thou usest not to accept. Either how knowest thou of thyself that I have not abolished the diversity of the sayings, while thou art supposed [to have done] / the contrary? Or how hast thou said that God the Word was not changed into the flesh and the flesh not into God the Word and [that] the diversity is only [one] of the sayings and not indeed of *ousias*, and that the *ousia* of the divinity persisted in its very [1] nature and the *ousia* of the flesh persisted in the very *ousia* of the

εἰρῆσθαι διακεισόμεθα φρονοῦντες ὀρθῶς. ὅταν μὲν γὰρ θεοπρεπῶς λέγῃ περὶ ἑαυτοῦ Ὁ ἑωρακὼς ἐμὲ ἑώρακε τὸν Πατέρα, καὶ Ἐγὼ καὶ ὁ Πατὴρ ἕν ἐσμεν, τὴν θείαν αὐτοῦ καὶ ἀπόρρητον ἐννοοῦμεν φύσιν, καθ' ἣν καὶ ἕν ἐστι πρὸς τὸν ἑαυτοῦ Πατέρα διὰ τὴν ταυτότητα τῆς οὐσίας, εἰκών τε καὶ χαρακτὴρ καὶ ἀπαύγασμα τῆς δόξης αὐτοῦ· ὅταν δὲ τὸ τῆς ἀνθρωπότητος μέτρον οὐκ ἀτιμάζων, τοῖς Ἰουδαίοις προσλαλῇ Νῦν δέ με ζητεῖτε ἀποκτεῖναι, ἄνθρωπον ὃς τὴν ἀλήθειαν ὑμῖν λελάληκα, πάλιν οὐδὲν ἧττον αὐτὸν τὸν ἐν ἰσότητί τε καὶ ὁμοιότητι τοῦ Πατρὸς Θεὸν Λόγον καὶ ἐκ τῶν τῆς ἀνθρωπότητος αὐτοῦ μέτρων ἐπιγινώσκομεν. εἰ γάρ ἐστιν ἀναγκαῖον τὸ πιστεύειν, ὅτι Θεὸς ὢν φύσει γέγονε σάρξ, ἤγουν ἄνθρωπος ἐμψυχωμένος ψυχῇ λογικῇ· ποῖον ἂν ἔχοι λόγον τὸ ἐπαισχύνεσθαί τινας ταῖς παρ' αὐτοῦ φωναῖς, εἰ γεγόνασιν ἀνθρωποπρεπῶς; εἰ γὰρ παραιτοῖτο τοὺς ἀνθρώπῳ πρέποντας λόγους, τίς ὁ ἀναγκάσας γενέσθαι καθ' ἡμᾶς ἄνθρωπον; ὁ δὲ καθεὶς ἑαυτὸν δι' ἡμᾶς εἰς ἑκούσιον κένωσιν, διὰ ποίαν αἰτίαν παραιτοῖτο ἂν τοὺς τῇ κενώσει πρέποντας λόγους; ἑνὶ τοιγαροῦν προσώπῳ τὰς ἐν τοῖς εὐαγγελίοις πάσας ἀναθετέον φωνάς, ὑποστάσει μιᾷ τῇ τοῦ Λόγου σεσαρκωμένῃ. (Quoted from Bindley, *Oecumenical Documents of the Faith*, 2nd ed., p. 127; cp. Labbe (Mansi), *loc. cit.*) [1] See crit. n., p. 401.

flesh, if their *ousias* were not changed? Or how assignest thou human and divine [attributes] unto the one nature of God the Word, in such wise that God the Word is in the same [*ousia*] God and man and was not changed into the flesh or into man? For it is impossible that both of them should be in the same *ousia*, when the one *ousia* is not as also the other [is], or perhaps becomes not existent. And is it what it became and is it changed into what it became, that is, into the *ousia* of man, or [is] the *ousia* of man [changed] into the *ousia* of God? If God and man are in one and the same *ousia* and in one nature, while the distinction into two is suppressed, how are the *ousia* of the flesh and the *ousia* of God in their being without being changed, since they are not to be conceived in the natures wherein they are without change? Yet if indeed they are conceived without change, how are they which are two not conceived [as] two? How is the distinction into two abolished and suppressed? How would these, even though it were a stone or a demon to whom naught that was pleasing was pleasant, not move and sink / to the perception of their baseness?[1] For he proclaims that the work is his own and, like those that are surely mad, that he does all things and says this and that and other things and all things and nothing.

But he makes all men adhere, however, to absurdities such as these, though they understand neither what they are saying nor what they are affirming. For they have not one and the same idea concerning the same thing, but they deny and persist in those things which they deny that they confess, as though they are indeed the true faith and cling in [their] faith to the things which are not of the faith and believe not the things which are evident and are confessed by all men. For the faith is one thing and the nature is another; for he who says that the things which are evident and known in respect to the *ousia* are something else in respect to the faith, suppresses not the [properties residing] in the nature but seeks to persuade [men] of those which are not in the nature. But that which is in the nature is compulsorily [2] that which the *prosôpon* is. For example, [in] what he says of the bread: '*It is my*

---

[1] Or 'absurd behaviour'.   [2] Or 'in might'.

body,'[1] he says not that the bread is not bread and that his body is not a body, but he has said demonstrably bread and body, which is in the *ousia*. But we are persuaded that the bread is bread in nature and in *ousia*. Yet in believing that the bread is his body / by faith and not by nature, he seeks to persuade us to believe in that which exists not in *ousia* in such wise that it becomes this by faith and not in *ousia*. If it is [a question of the] *ousia*, what is the faith worth? For he has not said: 'Believe that the bread is bread,' because every one who sees the bread itself knows that it is bread, nor further does he make it be believed that the body is body; for it is seen and known of every one. But in that which it is not he requires us to believe that this is [so], in such wise that it becomes this by faith to them that believe. Therefore it is not possible that the [properties residing] in the *ousia* should be one thing and another in one [thing] of which we should believe that it is said to be another, though it exists not in its own *ousia*, that they may become two and be alien to one another in the *ousia*. But he who therein suppresses the *ousia*, therewith suppresses that too which is conceived by faith.

Therefore also it is not in any way pleasing that we should openly make use indeed of what he thus says; for surely he is deceiving [us], since he accepts and suppresses these things so that he proves to every one that there are [views] true and false, both of orthodoxy and of heresy, in him; and I have obeyed him as one [would do] in what he requires. Nor have they been able to prove in any of those things which have been said by me that I am an heretic, but he has proved me / in all the [doctrines] of orthodoxy. And the things which he stirred not up in the beginning, he had stirred up in the [arguments] wherewith he defended himself, as he has now also defended himself on behalf of the Easterns, howbeit boldly and cunningly. But some one will say: 'Why 'have the Easterns accepted the deposition of thine Impiety 'whereof they accuse thee,[2] although however thou hast taught[3] 'nothing at all alien [to the faith]? But they too seem to 'accuse [him] of the same things whereof thou accusest him

---

[1] Matt. xxvi. 26.   [2] Syr. 'it', *i.e.* thine Impiety.   [3] See crit. n., p. 401.

'and they set aside these things while accepting also those very
'things, and there is nothing more. . . .' For we ought to
ask the one[1] and the others[2] likewise concerning these things.
But if you are willing to learn even from me, I will speak of
that which [has become known] gradually unto every one,
not that I may be accepted and helped by men—for I neglect
for my part all human things, since I have died unto the world
and I am living unto whom I am living—but I will speak
because of those who have been scandalized, not of myself nor
after my own [words], but after this man himself[1] whom
Christ has constrained to make defence on my behalf. For
they have said naught else except that they have been
constrained by the command of the Emperor to accept all
these things.

Cyril. The bishops at Constantinople have said: 'The
'pious bishop John must anathematize / the teaching of
'Nestorius and confess in writing his deposition.'

Nestorius. Therefore until then, according to the bishop
of Antioch and according to the Easterns and according to
the orthodox bishops, I was bishop.

Cyril. As then the pious Emperor agreed with them
very joyfully therein, my lord the admirable tribune[3] and
secretary Aristolaus was sent for the correction of this
[business].[4] But when the command of the Emperor was

[1] *Viz.* Cyril.   [2] *Viz.* the Eastern bishops.
[3] Syr. *ṭribūnā* = Lat. *tribunus*.
[4] The Syriac text ascribes the words 'As then the pious … of this [business]'
to Nestorius, making the second quotation from Cyril begin at 'But when the
command . . .' The correction, accepted by both Bedjan and Nau, is based on
the Greek original, of which the whole section is here printed; cp. Labbe
(Mansi), v. 309 E : ὁ εὐσεβέστατος καὶ φιλόχριστος βασιλεύς, τὴν ὑπὲρ τῶν ἁγίων
ἐκκλησιῶν φροντίδα πλείστην ὅσην καὶ ἀναγκαίαν ποιούμενος, οὐ φορητὴν ἡγεῖτο τὴν
τούτων διχόνοιαν. μεταπεμψάμενος τοίνυν τὸν εὐλαβέστατον καὶ θεοσεβέστατον
ἐπίσκοπον τῆς ἁγίας Κωνσταντινουπολιτῶν ἐκκλησίας Μαξιμιανόν, καὶ ἑτέρους δὲ
πλείστους τῶν αὐτόθι κατειλημμένων, τίνα δὴ τρόπον ἐκ μέσου μὲν γένοιτ᾽ ἂν τῶν
ἐκκλησιῶν ἡ διαφορά, κεκλήσονται δὲ πρὸς εἰρήνην οἱ τῶν θείων ἱερουργοὶ μυστηρίων,
διεσκέπτετο. οἱ δὲ ἔφασκον, ὡς οὐκ ἂν ἑτέρως γένοιτο τοῦτό ποτε, οὐδ᾽ ἂν εἰς
ὁμοψυχίαν ἔλθοιεν τὴν πρὸς ἀλλήλους οἱ περὶ ὧν ὁ λόγος, μὴ προανατείλαντος αὐτοῖς,
καὶ οἱονεὶ προεισκεκομισμένου τοῦ συνδέσμου τῆς ὁμοψυχίας, καὶ ὁμοπιστίας· ἔφασκόν
τε, ὅτι τὸν τῆς θεοσεβείας ἔμπλεον ἐπίσκοπον Ἰωάννην τὸν Ἀντιοχείας ἀναθεματίσαι
δεῖ τὰ Νεστορίου δόγματα, καὶ ἐγγράφως ὁμολογῆσαι τὴν καθαίρεσιν αὐτοῦ. καί, τό γε
ἧκον, εἰς λύπας ἰδίας, ὁ τῆς Ἀλεξανδρείας ἐπίσκοπος ἀμνημονήσει τε διὰ τὴν ἀγάπην,

shown unto the Easterns, as though it had been [issued] by the will of the holy bishops who were assembled in Constantinople the capital, they were assembled—I know not what they thought—with the saintly and pious Acacius, bishop of Aleppo,[1] and made him write unto me about the manner of the reconciliation of the peace of the churches; [that] it ought not to take place otherwise except in so far as it seemed good unto them. But this demand was hard and serious; for they were requiring that all the things should be suppressed which had been written [by me] in letters and books and writings.

Concerning what had taken place after the enforced peace.[2]

Nestorius. Until then, when they wrote these things, the other[3] also was [to be found] among the heretics, when every one, and not [only] certain individuals, knew and was blaming the things which were written by him. The hand was [the Emperor's] which led them by force, while there was / nought at [my] disposal to be done against what they were requiring. For all those who hear us have understood—for [many a] one used to suffer with us owing to the violence which took place by the command of the Emperor—that they have brought me

καὶ παρ' οὐδὲν ἡγήσεται τὸ ὑβρίσθαι κατὰ τὴν Ἐφεσίων. καί τοι παγχάλεπόν τε καὶ δύσοιστον ὄν. συναινέσαντος τοίνυν, ἡσθέντος ἄγαν ἐπὶ τούτοις τοῦ εὐσεβεστάτου βασιλέως, ἀπεστάλη αὐτὸ τοῦτο κατορθώσων ὁ κύριός μου, ὁ θαυμασιώτατος τριβοῦνος καὶ νοτάριος Ἀριστόλαος. ἐπειδὴ δὲ τοῖς κατὰ τὴν ἑῴαν τὸ βασιλικὸν ἐνεφανίσθη θέσπισμα, καὶ ὡς μετὰ γνώμης γεγονὸς τῶν εὑρεθέντων ἐπισκόπων κατὰ τὴν μεγάλην Κωνσταντινούπολιν, οὐκ οἶδ' ὅτι, σκοπήσαντες, συνήχθησαν μὲν πρὸς τὸν ὁσιώτατον καὶ θεοσεβέστατον τῆς Βερροιαίων ἐπίσκοπον Ἀκάκιον, γράψαι τε πρός με παρεσκεύασαν, ὅτι τὸν τῆς συμβάσεως τρόπον, ἤτοι τὸν τῆς εἰρήνης τῶν ἁγίων ἐκκλησιῶν, οὐχ ἑτέρως γενέσθαι προσήκει, εἰ μὴ κατὰ τὸ αὐτοῖς δοκοῦν. ἦν δὲ δὴ ἄρα τοῦτο φορτικόν, καὶ βαρὺ τὸ αἴτημα· ἤθελον γὰρ ἀργῆσαι μὲν σύμπαντα τὰ παρ' ἐμοῦ γραφέντα ἔν τε ἐπιστολαῖς, καὶ τόμοις, καὶ βιβλίοις, μόνῃ δὲ ἐκείνῃ συνθέσθαι τῇ ἐν Νικαίᾳ παρὰ τῶν ἁγίων ἡμῶν πατέρων ὁρισθείσῃ πίστει.

[1] Nau points out that the name 'Aleppo' is due to the Syriac editor; for the Greek has 'Beroea'. The See of Beroea only changed its name to that of Aleppo in A.D. 638. See p. xi.

[2] According to Bedjan and Nau, these words are to be regarded, not as the closing words of the extract from Cyril's writings, but as the Syriac editor's heading of the following section. Bedjan proposes to place here the beginning of Bk. II, pt. ii, instead of on Syr. p. 459.

[3] *Viz.* Cyril.

to [such] an extremity as this. But some one will grow angry, [asking] for what reason they abode not by the things which they once judged. For they are but slightly busied, [in taking measures] against what has been carried out against me for the sake of the correction and the confession of the faith and the agreement of the churches. Like the manner, however, of a tyrant when he comes to capture and cannot take a city, but for the declaration of peace seeks to procure the death of him who is fighting for them against him, that, when he has procured it, it may be defeated, thus the latter too has asked for my deposition to be granted without judgement. Let this be [so]. It concerns not me [to busy myself] with what has been carried out against me, but only that there may be peace among the churches. And I endure all things for the ordering of the churches. But all things have happened to the contrary.

For after he [had] received that for which he was anxious, he both reduced them under his hand for the sake of an apparent peace [1] and knew that he profited naught by what was carried out against me; but the confession of the faith, for the sake of which there was war against me, was confirmed. And it had been evident that there was enmity and violence and that it was a proof of the things which were taking place and that it would be possible for them also easily to be kept secret. But, that this might not take place, and further that my own enemies / might not become his accusers, [namely] those who had formerly aided him in the things which were carried out against me, he began to be drawn towards the confession of the faith, showing himself wise and making sport of the two sides with contrary confessions [of faith]. But they accurately examined and knew that certain among them were become enfeebled and had suffered many things, without even having been accounted worthy of any aid. And for this reason they were not easily breaking the peace which they [had] made as a result of the writings which were written by them from one side and another, desiring to be left in the same [circumstances], that they might think thus. But

---

[1] Literally: 'a peace of *schéma*'.

because he[1] had been accused by those who were clinging to his [side] and were confessing [the same faith] with him as one who went beyond the common opinion and had destroyed alone the zeal of all of them by his authority and by his disdain of them, he feared lest they should be alienated from him or rise up against him, and he was zealous to perform more than they were requiring.

And like the manner of those who are taken in war, [who,] seeking to prove that they are like-minded with their captors, spare not friends nor sons nor fathers in order that they may make them believe that they hate their [own] race, so also he immediately inclined himself to rise up against the Fathers who aforetime had passed away, against Diodorus and Theodorus, who were the common Fathers [of all] both while they were living / and when they [had] passed away, both his own [Fathers] and ours the same. Although he designated them, with whom he used to participate, as the enemies of every man and was clinging to the very Fathers and to the orthodox, yet he had even obtained with all zeal their own labours on behalf of the faith and had commanded [them] to be sent unto all. Yet, while he sought however to persuade [men] that he held not back against me out of hatred, he was seeking to anathematize those against whom no one would have expected nor even [have made bold] to suppose that he would have dared any such thing. And, what is baser[2] than all things, he destroyed the sermons which were published[3] against Apollinarius and supported those of Apollinarius, saying, 'It is the faith of the Church'. [Do you ask] on which party one would lean: on the party of Apollinarius, or that of the holy Fathers in all the world whom also all the world glorifies and whom it has reckoned with the single zeal as [of] a common mouth against Apollinarius and Arius and Macedonius and Eunomius and all the heresies, or on the side of Apollinarius? Suppose that I, who have not been obedient in the things which thou hast required of me, have been an enemy unto thee; for what reason dost thou war on my account with those who have passed away in orthodoxy? Or perhaps thou

---

[1] *Viz.* Cyril. [2] Or, 'more absurd'. [3] Literally: 'made'.

warrest on account of them who [are] with me? / But, that I may speak the truth, thou warrest with every man because of thine impiety in all things.

Tell me: Were there not Basil and Gregory in the days of Diodorus? Were there not also at Alexandria bishops known for [their] conduct and for [their] words? Were there not at Rome accomplished men who would suffice to stand up on behalf of the churches? And were not they who were doctors in all the world [sufficient] to stand up on behalf of the churches, men who were not [living] in luxury and in glory and in honour and in pleasure, but in persecutions and in distress and in wars and in fear, who had preserved and kept the true faith without wavering, [rather] than he who was an heretic and deceived—that is Diodorus, who was in every man's mouth and is handed down in books and was a [cause of] fear unto heretics, who by the word of doctrine and by divine grace raised himself up against the commands of [his] Majesty for the people of God and let them not perish but increased them manifold, and the whole concord of the churches was won by him? Then he was not an heretic neither for them of that time nor yet for thee thyself nor for thy [followers] nor yet during the disturbance itself which thou madest against me. But after thou wast encouraged and wast entered [on the way] whereon thou wast entered and [hadst] reached this tyrannical agreement,[1] then were Diodorus and Theodorus and the rest of the others / become heretics in thine eyes. For the way was becoming [open] before thee also against Basil and Gregory and Athanasius and Ambrose and against the rest of the others who at the same time said the same things.

Who is there who would not groan that this idea was come [to pass]: that, encouraged by the commands of [his] Majesty and by fear and by punishments, they were constraining the Easterns and, after the peace, were dragging and bringing them like captives and pressing round them to make them anathematize their Fathers? They reached this peace and this unanimity: thus they thought one thought, thus they rested from the suffering of wrongs, when they [had] delivered me

---

[1] Literally: 'reached this tyranny of the agreement'.

over to my enemy. Because they were fearful, they were saying that it was better that one man should suffer injury and [that] the faith should prevail. But would indeed that this had been true! How this would not irk me! But on the contrary I should have surely rejoiced when aught for which they were eager was receiving correction. But on the contrary they had suffered for [the words] which they allowed me [to say] and for the things which they let be said and further [for those] which people allowed them not to say, though I myself was saying them, and for which they had cast me out. And after that they fought against Theodore and after him against Diodorus and then also against every single / one of the rest of the others, and they were intent on the same intention, having set themselves to drive them out with me, as indeed they were saying those very things and naught else. And they ought either to drive them out with me for the same [reasons] or to accept me, even me, and to accept them too. But they dared not say that I should be accepted, because they had once driven me out; and it would have been necessary also for them, though grieving, to drive them out and afterwards for these same [reasons] to drive out also the others themselves, because those others were imagining and teaching the same things, and [saying] that these things were true. And with this boldness he hoped to rise up against all the saints to accept [their doctrine] and thereupon to invert and to alter the things which he [had] received.

For this man himself[1] showed his [true] self after the original confession [of the faith], both gradually adding and subtracting and saying the same things; and he denied therein the compulsion and the authority, acting and scheming until he suppressed [the doctrine] that those whereof Christ is are two natures; and he placed the natures in the names and not in the *ousias* and imposed the confession of one nature as if by law.[2] Then, in striving to undo and to overthrow those who predicated two natures, [he attacked,] not indeed all of them at the

---

[1] *Viz.* Cyril.

[2] This is Nestorius' most concise summary of Cyril's position as he understands it.

same time, but / in the first place certain men, in order that, when he [had] prevailed against the latter, he might go to war little by little against the rest of them, as against persons who were saying these [same] things as the others. For those too of whom they were making use in [bearing] witness to what the others [had] said, were saying those very things—and this is not a new discovery—[and] he was driving them out as heretics. And I too say these [same] things as those [others], and thus they confess as heretics! And they and all of them at the same time were increasing this very depravity of impiety in the face of every one. For he was not citing the [words] of the orthodox and of those doctors who [were] before me so as to prove that I am an heretic, but on the contrary he was taking my own [words] against them that he might prove that they [were] heretics, because the things which were said by them were like unto mine. But let us show also the things which were coming to pass after these things and took [their] beginning therefrom.

BOOK II. PART II

Concerning what was done in the time of Flavian.

Now after Proclus Flavian became bishop of Constantinople, a man who was used to comport himself with uprightness and with reverence, but had not the ability to speak in public and to expound his discourses. He then who was accusing all the bishops, he who / was left behind alone of the rest of the others who had passed away, that is Eutyches, took heart, and, because he was not a bishop, set himself by means of the authority of [his] Majesty [to behave] otherwise—as bishop of bishops. For he was taking charge of the affairs of the church, making use of Flavian who, by reason of the greatness of his humility knew not the things which were being prepared, as of a minister in [the execution of] the things which were being commanded at Constantinople, while he was driving out of the church as heretics all those who were not holding these views of his; but those who were aiding him he raised up and aided. But apart [from this] he was making use of the authority of the Emperor, a reliable authority, and he was unwilling that two natures should be predicated of Christ even in saying, and was mocking at the Fathers who spoke thus, blaming them as hypocrites who by hypocrisy were dissembling the truth or [who] like heretics expressed these [views] of mine, since the doctrines of those men ought not to be embraced in the judgement of the faith. Thus, while he was confirming and preparing these things by the authority and by the commands of [his] Majesty, all the East was disturbed at these things and there was no place that had not been stirred up, because he had set aside all things as things / that were happening in *schêma*; and already he was openly constraining them either to say things which they wanted not or to suffer wrong and to receive punishment.

For Flavian had heard that the churches were disturbed

anew over these things and the monasteries were divided and the people were rising up in parties,[1] and that already the fire was kindling in all the world owing to those who were going and coming and were preaching various things that were full of impiety. And he[2] sent unto him,[3] as they say, requesting him and beseeching him to spare the churches of God which were much distraught by the disturbances which had taken place aforetime and for which those things sufficed which had been settled while there was peace, and not to stir up against him 'that which was not stirred up against those 'who were before me, lest it should be supposed that it was 'not stirred up against them out of fear, whereas [it was so] in 'my own days because of the greatness of [my] negligence; 'for I confess that I am a miserable man. But what couldest 'thou have befall thee more than others? Yet, on account 'of my humility, even thou directest the episcopate and I 'have done everything that thou hast commanded without 'declining.'

But the other[3] on the contrary was saying : 'I aid thee / in 'the episcopate and thou oughtest to rejoice in the change : that 'these things, as they were being [done] out of hypocrisy, 'against them that [were] before thee will take place in thy days 'without hypocrisy. For now, to be sure, it is supposed 'that men have been purified from these [heresies] of Nestorius, 'whereas they have clung to his [views]; and we are supposed 'to have had a personal enmity towards the man and not [one 'conceived] on account of his impiety, since we have indeed 'condemned him but have let his faith flourish. Yet we ought 'entirely to drive out the things which he has said and con-'fessed; for he was not sent away as confessing two natures 'distinguished from one another and [that] each of them was 'by itself Son, but because he confessed two whole natures 'and one *prosôpon* of two, which of constraint are called two 'natures in that the Son is named Son in each of the natures.'[4]

But when Eusebius of Alexandria, who was bishop of Dorylaeum [and] who was regarded as a confessor because of

---
[1] Literally : 'in division'.   [2] *Viz.* Flavian.   [3] *Viz.* Eutyches.
[4] There is no new paragraph marked here in the Syriac text.

the words which had been said [by him] against me,[1] had come unto Eutyches, he [2] indeed praised the freedom of speech which had been [taken] by him against me in the things which were done against me. He said :[3] 'It would be suitable to thy 'freedom of speech itself to extirpate those who are encouraged 'by the impiety of Nestorius, and for this reason God himself 'has sent thee, not indeed as though thou lackest aught, for 'everything has been prepared beforehand by the Emperor, 'but indeed so / that thou shouldest exult in thy affliction, if 'this too should come to pass by means of thee. But thus, if 'thou dost approach the Emperor in blaming those who need 'to accept two [natures], either therefore, thou sayest, that the 'things which were taking place at the Council in thy days 'may not be suppressed. . . .'

But the other, supposing that he was neither disturbed nor yet angered at these things, but that he was quite calm, says unto him : 'Be thou silent, and labour not in vain, ye who 'want impossible things to take place, while neither all the 'Council which was at Ephesus nor Cyril himself, howbeit he 'was in agreement with the Easterns, has suppressed them. 'And afterwards again an agreement was [reached] concerning 'these very things, and one let be the things which were well '[able] to be retained. For it is not possible that there should 'be taken from the church [the right] that two natures should 'be predicated of Christ without confusion, [those] of the 'divinity and of the humanity, consubstantial with his Father 'in the divinity and consubstantial with us in the humanity. . . .'

And Eutyches became perturbed against him and said : 'God 'confound thee, who [affirmest] that even formerly Nestorius 'had said naught against God, but that [he was] turbulent and 'vainglorious ! For how [is it] that he who says the [same] 'things as Nestorius, can rise up against Nestorius ? For these

---

[1] See B. J. Kidd, *A History of the Church to* A.D. *461*, iii. 202; Cyril, *Adv. Nest.* i. 5 (Migne, *P.G.L.* lxxvi. 41 D); and Evagrius, *H. E.* i. 9. For the text of Eusebius's alleged protest see Labbe (Mansi), iv. 1008.

[2] *Viz.* Eutyches.

[3] This is presumably the conversation to which Eusebius referred at Constantinople; see Labbe (Mansi), vi. 656 A. No other record of it seems to have survived.

'words are his whom you have delivered up with much labour.' But Eusebius said / unto him : ' I know not what thou sayest : ' for I dispute not with him because he has predicated two ' natures, [n]or has the Council blamed him for this, but ' because he distinguishes and places [them] in sundry parts, ' God by himself and man alike by himself who make use of ' and are spoken of similarly only in honour and in equality ' alike. And in this way thou sayest [that there are] two ' natures and that the holy Virgin is not the mother of God, ' because God made the very birth of his flesh his own.'[1]

And Eutyches says : ' Thou liest concerning it, because you ' hold his views without being supposed to be clinging unto his ' [views]. For he was proclaiming ten thousand times : " I say ' " not two sons, I say one ; I say not two natures, nor two sons, ' " for the Son of God is twofold in the natures. For this ' " reason she bare not the Son of God, but she bare the ' " humanity which is Son because of the Son united thereto." ' And again : " Since God is not to be distinguished from him ' " who is visible, how therefore do I distinguish the honour of ' " him who is not to be distinguished ? " It was not then ' because he had said simply two natures nor because he [had] ' said that the natures were not united, for [he said]: " I con-' " fess the twofold [nature], but I adore two in one because of ' " the union ", but that even after the union / he says [that ' there are] two natures and that the Son is twofold in the ' natures and says that the union resulted in one *prosôpon* and ' not in one nature. But you also, acting impiously, say this ' and nothing more ; and all hypocrites ought to be extirpated. ' For I acknowledge after the union not another *ousia* in our ' Lord nor even do I surely conceive that our Lord, who is our ' Lord and our God, is consubstantial with us ; but he is ' consubstantial with the Father in the divinity.'

And Eusebius says unto him : ' Does Nestorius speak thus, ' as thou sayest, or not ? I am not now for my part concerned ' to investigate, but this I say : that he who says these things ' speaks correctly and thou, who confessest not with the

---

[1] Here clearly Eusebius ascribes to Nestorius the teaching commonly known as ' Nestorianism ', and is shown to have been mistaken in so doing.

'orthodox and, speaking of the flesh which is consubstantial
'with ourselves, either suppressest it or changest it into the
'nature of the divinity, [dost not.] For this reason we ought
'to subject to inquiry those things which thou sayest [are the
'views] of Nestorius and whereof thou accusest the Council and
'Cyril of surely lying against him, since they imagine so; and
'thou confirmest the accusation of that man, that he imagines
'that the truth is so. Every one anathematizes this opinion
'as impious, and I shall prove [it] at a convenient time; for, if
'there is not a [human] nature in our Lord, / neither is he also
'consubstantial with us; the very *ousia* of the flesh has thereby
'been suppressed.' And Eusebius accused him of these things
before Flavian and before the Council which was assembled
with him at Constantinople and [Eutyches] confessed them
and continued making a show of his impiety, confessing that
the body of Christ was not consubstantial with us as though
[resulting not] in two natures but in one nature.

This had stirred up the Emperor, and he had not wanted
him[1] to be thrust out by deposition, but he was not heard.
He therefore prepared all things for the deposition of Flavian
and for the restoration of Eutyches. He commenced by
attaching to him[self] the bishop of Alexandria and the bishop
of Rome by written accounts of what was done against
Eutyches;[2] and one agreed and one agreed not [with him].
For the bishop of Rome had read the things which were done
against Eutyches and had condemned Eutyches for impiety;
but, when I found and read this account, I gave thanks unto
God that the Church of Rome was confessing correctly and
without fault, although they[3] were otherwise [disposed]
towards me myself. But he[4] caused also the rest of the
bishops to secede from him[5] and made them hasten unto
Eutyches, insulting those who [remained] with Flavian, and
without having vouchsafed liberty of speech before him[self]
and before the chiefs; and they were surely rebuked, yet were
they surely not heard / touching that for which they were

[1] *Viz.* Eutyches.
[2] The letter to Rome is mentioned in Leo, *Ep. xxiv*, Labbe (Mansi), v. 1341 B.
[3] *Viz.* the Roman   [4] *Viz.* the Emperor.   [5] *Viz.* Flavian.

rebuked; but men were rising up with insult against them and seizing them and constraining them. And he caused the clergy also to secede from him, constraining and persecuting them in what was not given unto them for their sustenance; and the [charges], which he had commanded should not be exacted of the churches when he respected the church and God, in furious anger he commanded should be exacted of them with implacable abuse. And prelates[1] were openly seized and rebuked before the crowds, and every bishop who was not of the party of Eutyches was seized; and he commanded every tax upon the possessions of their churches which had been remitted unto them by him and by the emperors before him, [even] the tax of all these years, to be exacted of them at one time; and of those who were nobles or of the family of noble persons he exacted openly, in return for the honour which was theirs, a quantity of gold—by which very [means] he commanded vengeance to be exacted of Eusebius, the accuser of Eutyches, without mercy. For these two [means] were employed [together] with all the assaults of hunger and of usury and of captivity, things which were innumerable, and he made the Roman nobility fall at his knees and groan.

/ And while Flavian was overwhelmed with all these things, he was keeping the feast of the Passover, during which the Emperor entered into the church. But he[2] looked not upon him as an enemy and he took the holy Gospel to have mercy upon them, while all the bishops and clergy were assembled with him and the [newly] baptized in their attire,[3] while the people were crying [aloud] with him. And he fell upon his face and prostrated himself in the church, beseeching them to accept him making his defence, since he supposed that he respected the Gospel. But the other[4] dismissed him with scorn, menacing him as having acted insultingly in that he did it, while the bishops and clergy besought [the Emperor] with him and the [newly] baptized prostrated themselves upon the ground amid the voices of the people; and they persecuted

---

[1] Syr. *rabbay bātte'* = (i) 'chiefs of houses', *i. e.* stewards, and (ii) 'prelates'; see Payne-Smith, *Thes. Syr.* ii. 378. 4.
[2] *Viz.* Flavian.   [3] Syr. *schêma.*   [4] *Viz.* the Emperor.

them as if [they were] acting insultingly towards [the Emperor], and he withheld himself from that time from entering into the church, and he commanded that whatever was due should be exacted with insult and [that] no respite should be granted unto him, so that he was consequently constrained to send [word] unto the Emperor that he had not possessions of his own, because he was poor, and that not even the possessions of the church, if they were sold, would suffice to [pay] the quantity of gold which was being exacted of him. But he had the holy vessels of the church, which he and the emperors his ancestors had placed [therein], and [he said] : 'I must melt them down, because I am driven [to do so] / by force.' But the Emperor then said : 'I want not to know [this], but the gold I do want in any way whatsoever.' And because of this he took out the vessels of the church and they were melted down openly, so that there was weeping and outcry among all who took part for these exactions that were being made, as though [they were being] subjected to persecution.[1]

But after the Emperor heard the things which were taking place, he was angered exceedingly and bitterly and furiously and as though indeed he [2] [had] brought about these things to scorn him. And he commanded that an Oecumenical Council should be assembled against him and that the deposition of Flavian himself should be undertaken. But Flavian, after he had been closely pressed by all sides and had seen that everything that he was doing and saying he was doing to his own blame and to his rebuke, and [because] he had no aid from [his] Majesty—for since, as they say, that came through the choice and zeal of his sister,[3] [and] she was unwilling to show authority in aught in internal affairs, he had been [filled] with suspicion that on her account he was being wronged—he purposed to resign from the episcopate and go unto his monastery and dwell there ; and he drew up a document of abdication and

---

[1] Cp. Evagrius, *H. E.* ii. 2 ; Nicephorus Callistus, *H. E.* xiv. 47.

[2] *Viz.* Flavian.

[3] *Viz.* the emperor's sister, Pulcheria. She was consistently favourable to Flavian, but from 441-50 she was out of favour with Theodosius who was under the influence of the eunuch Chrysaphius. Flavian had neglected to bribe Chrysaphius, as Eutyches was careful to do. Cp. p. 97, n. 1.

gave [it] in. And after the Emperor knew that he had done this, he sent for him to come back unto him, as though he had done it to slander himself and to blaspheme against him; and [he sent word] that, if he should not return unto his church, he would fall into danger, [saying]: 'For I have not / commanded 'a Council to be held as if to wrong thee, but for [the purpose 'of] a true examination and the satisfaction of the truth in the things that are required.'

But, when he came back, he[1] immediately suborned accusers to say that the records which had been [drawn up] in Constantinople[2] [of the things done] against Eutyches were false. But the accusers were those that took refuge with Eutyches [and] who were they that had written down the things which were done against him, and they were accusing themselves much more than Flavian, so as to be rather praised and not judged. By means of the liberty [accorded] by the Emperor they were doing all things by force, so that suddenly there came about the decease of Flavian, distressed so that he had no respite in all the accusations against him and was amazed and perished. But because he was capable of resisting, he[1] gave himself up to various absurdities and was doing all things desperately. For he anticipated also the bishops, who were undecided[3] and who ought to have sat on the bench of judges, and he won them over and made them his own, such as the Bishop of Ancyra [and] him of Caesarea in Cappadocia, sending for them and, as though he was vexed at what was done against / Eutyches, interrogating them whether what was done against him was in truth done; and he said that the things which were done by the Council were deficient and that they remained accusers, and [he added]: 'We want to examine them before the governor[4] and before your Pieties,' and he made them take heart thereby, so that they should not accept what was being [done] but should submit all things for arbitration to the wisdom of the Emperor.

But all these things were being done so that there might be no examination of the faith but [that] Flavian might be

---

[1] *Viz.* the Emperor.   [2] See crit. n., p. 401.   [3] Literally: 'in expectation' or 'in suspicion'.   [4] Syr. *magestryānôs*; see p. 107, n. 2.

deprived as a result of what was prepared outside [the Council] and [that] they might accept the [doctrines] of Eutyches, without examination. If Flavian then had said unto him these things, and that Christ is of two natures, and that the natures subsist after the union as things that have been united without confusion, and [that] he is consubstantial in the divinity with the Father and consubstantial in the humanity with ourselves through [his] mother, these then abbreviated his sayings and changed what the judges ought [to have heard], and condemned him as one that imagined the contrary. He was a man [worthy] of aid on account of his having been surely calumniated. But if they had deprived him as one that said not these things but as one that even then still persisted in these very [views] of his, confessing that he imagined thus and was attached unto the heretics who imagined not thus, wherefore do you abandon the examination concerning him and put into [the minds of] them that are outside [the thought] that there is in them / [cause for] suspicion, because they were brought about by the accusers? For they it was that wrote [against him] and they showed great zeal in what was being examined.

For suppose that something was deficient in the sentence of judgement by these or by those; perhaps even his[1] having been deprived by them was surely deficient. For what reason then have you not examined it in regard to its having been deficient, in [that for] which they have truly deprived him and in what he has not in truth agreed with them? For he who says: 'They have surely failed against me, who have been surely calumniated,' denies that he has said the things on account of which he has been accused and deposed. But if he has confessed that they were not two natures that were united and further [that] the bodily frame of our Lord was not consubstantial with ourselves, and even now is showing that he abides by the same [views], what is its having been defective, as though indeed these things are not sufficient to prove him possessed of a strange opinion? But by any means on the one hand he had denied the things that he said, on the other

[1] *Viz.* Eutyches.

hand he strengthened himself thereby against his accusers who deprived him. This then was already examined and he [had] also accepted the judgement. What other judgement or examination ought there [to have been] more than that which the bishop of Rome had pronounced[1]? For he, when he had accepted what was done by the two parties, praised indeed the one but condemned the other by divine / inspiration, and had not simply passed sentence on them. And because they felt scruples before the bishop of Rome, they turned back to the bishop of Alexandria as to one who liked to run with them and was an enemy of the bishop of Constantinople.

Concerning what was done in Ephesus against Flavian.

For again indeed they had reached Ephesus, which is appointed and destined for the deposition of the bishops of Constantinople; and further the bishops of Alexandria and of Ephesus consented together and were aiding one another against the bishop of Constantinople. The bishop of Rome was not [there], nor the See of Saint Peter, nor the apostolic honour, nor the primacy dear[2] to the Romans, but he of Alexandria sat in authority and made him of Antioch also to sit with him; and he of Rome—and we mean Julian, who represented the holy bishop of Rome—was asked if he was in agreement with the holy Council and wished to read in this account what was done at Constantinople. He,[3] as / one that had authority, then asked and spoke as though even passing sentence against them. Yet they[4] conceded however unto him their intended purpose, not that he should accept that which they wished nor yet that he should give unto them the primacy, but that, if the bishop of Rome should agree with him, he should accept him as an addition to his party, and otherwise, supposing[5] he were found [to be] against them, he might remove him afar as one that had not authority even in a single [thing], wanting to prove unto every man that they should not look unto the bishop of Rome, since he was not able to aid him of Constantinople. For after Julian had said: 'For this

---

[1] Literally: 'made'.   [2] See crit. n., p. 401.   [3] *Viz.* the bishop of Alexandria.   [4] *Viz.* the Romans.   [5] Literally: 'and if not and ...'

'do we wish, that the deed which was committed should be 'read out, if the letter of our father Leo has first been read,' afterwards indeed Hilary the deacon of the holy bishop of Rome said : ' After these records which you now want to read had been read before him, he [1] then sent that which he sent.' When he had heard these things and there was naught that he ought to say, he [2] passed the opposite sentence concerning them : that 'this indeed was a procedure pleasing [unto him], 'that the things which were done should be read out and then 'the writings of the pious bishop of Rome'.[3]

Wherein then is the procedure pleasing indeed [4] that in the first place these things / and then the others should be read and, when they are read, the decision that thou wantest should be passed upon them? For what [reason] hast thou afterwards commanded things to be read when thou leavest no room to read them? Then thou commandest them to be read whose purpose thou wantest to make void! For thou didst know, thou didst know accurately what was sent concerning these things unto the Emperor and unto the Empress [5] and

[1] *Viz.* Leo.
[2] *Viz.* the bishop of Alexandria.
[3] Cp. Labbe (Mansi), vi. 649 A: ἡ ἁγία σύνοδος εἶπε. πάντες θέλομεν ἀναγνωσθῆναι τὰ πεπραγμένα· ἀναγινωσκέσθω τὰ πεπραγμένα. Διόσκορος ὁ ἐπίσκοπος Ἀλεξανδρείας εἶπε· λεγέτω καὶ ὁ θεοσεβέστατος ἐπίσκοπος Ἰουλιανός, ὁ ἐπέχων τὸν τόπον τοῦ ἁγιωτάτου ἐπισκόπου τῆς Ῥωμαίων ἐκκλησίας Λέοντος, εἰ σύμψηφος γίνεται τῇ ἁγίᾳ ταύτῃ συνόδῳ, καὶ βούλεται καὶ αὐτὸς ἀναγνωσθῆναι τὰ πεπραγμένα ἐν Κωνσταντινουπόλει ἐπὶ τῇ ὑποθέσει ταύτῃ. Ἰουλιανὸς ἐπίσκοπος, ἐπέχων τὸν τόπον τοῦ ἁγιωτάτου ἐπισκόπου τῆς Ῥωμαίων ἐκκλησίας Λέοντος, ἑρμηνεύοντος αὐτὸν Φλωρεντίου ἐπισκόπου Λυδῶν, εἶπε· τούτῳ τῷ λόγῳ βουλόμεθα τὴν πρᾶξιν ἀναγνωσθῆναι, εἰ πρῶτον ἀναγνωσθῇ τὰ παρὰ τοῦ πάπα ἐπισταλέντα. Ἵλαρος διάκονος τῆς Ῥωμαίων ἐκκλησίας, ἑρμηνεύοντος αὐτὸν Φλωρεντίου ἐπισκόπου Λυδῶν, εἶπεν· ἐπειδὴ καὶ ὁ ἁγιώτατος ἐπίσκοπος Ῥώμης, ἀναγνωσθέντων αὐτῷ τούτων τῶν ὑπομνημάτων, ὧν νῦν ζητεῖτε τὴν ἀνάγνωσιν, ἐπέστειλεν ἃ ἀπέστειλεν. Εὐτυχὴς ἀρχιμανδρίτης εἶπεν· οἱ ἀποσταλέντες θεοσεβέστατοι ἄνδρες ὑπὸ τοῦ ἁγιωτάτου καὶ θεοφιλεστάτου ἀρχιεπισκόπου Λέοντος τῆς Ῥωμαίων εἰς τὴν ἁγίαν ὑμῶν σύνοδον, ὕποπτοί μοι γεγόνασι· κατήχθησαν γὰρ πρὸς Φλαυιανὸν τὸν θεοφιλέστατον ἐπίσκοπον, καὶ ἠρίστησαν παρ' αὐτῷ, καὶ συνεκροτήθησαν, καὶ πάσης θεραπείας παρ' αὐτοῦ ἠξιώθησαν· ἀξιῶ οὖν τὴν ὑμετέραν ἁγιότητα, εἴ τι παρὰ τὸ δίκαιον γένοιτο παρ' αὐτῶν κατ' ἐμοῦ, τοῦτο πρόκριμά μοι μὴ φέρειν. Διόσκορος ἐπίσκοπος Ἀλεξανδρείας εἶπεν· ἀκόλουθόν ἐστι, καὶ εὔλογον, πρῶτον ἀναγνωσθῆναι τὰ ἐπὶ τῇ ὑποθέσει πεπραγμένα, εἶθ' οὕτως τὰ γράμματα τοῦ θεοφιλεστάτου ἐπισκόπου Ῥώμης· ὅθεν κατὰ τὰ δόξαντα τῇ ἁγίᾳ ταύτῃ συνόδῳ, ἀναγινωσκέσθω τὰ πεπραγμένα. [4] See crit. n., p. 401.
[5] Presumably Eudocia. See Nicephorus Callistus, *H. E.* xiv. 47.

unto Flavian himself, and contrariwise thou wentest by the road which led towards the Emperor and whereunto thou wast subjected, and left that which conducted towards God, and didst concern thyself very little therewith. But I have said too little: that is, [I have omitted to say] that thou didst not reckon it anything at all and didst despise him.[1] And thou didst even sweep aside the adjurations of the bishop of Antioch[2] who adjured thee with frightful adjurations, by the holy mysteries, not to show thyself zealous for the deposition of Flavian nor for his harm. 'It is right to look not to what would be for the 'consolation of the Emperor but to what will arise therefrom.' 'For I will examine and I will gratify the Emperor; [it is for 'us] to be eager not for defeat but for victory, because other- 'wise we cannot aid him, however much we show ourselves 'eager, when the Emperor strives with him and is angered '[against Flavian]. And he is so altogether angered that he 'will turn unto chastisement unless we give [him] this room to 'appease his rage.' Thus by these words / he deceived him[3] and brought him under his control, and so he led him by this word which he had said as though with a bridle. And he[3] accepted him and took part with him in the rest of the other [affairs], and he warred on his side and also [helped him to] deprive him[4] and the others and whoever in whatsoever manner was supposed to think the [same things] as Flavian. And concerning these things it seemed thus unto the Emperor.

For I pass over the things, which were being directed against my own person[5] and [that] of Flavian, and all that they were wanting in order to drive out those who wanted not at all to anathematize us. However, they deprived him[4] too by the same [means as me]. But others, who were injured, were deprived without judgement; for they saw not the judgement nor the place of judgement, nor was [the right of] defence nor speech granted unto them. Except him who had been pleasing to the Emperor and to Eutyches, these were depriving and driving them out of their cities. And

[1] *Viz.* God.
[2] Domnus, nephew and successor of John of Antioch.
[3] *Viz.* the bishop of Antioch.
[4] *Viz.* Flavian.   [5] Syr. *parṣôphâ*.

those who [were followers] of him of Antioch, had much defence [to make] before men concerning him to whom this was not conceded; for he was therefore sore beset without [hope of] aid by the very [means] wherewith he [had] acted against others, suffering for the same things and not on behalf of others. And [conduct] which had not even any reverence, from which there was no escape, that is his injury and the transgression of his adjurations, brought him to all these things. For he[1] made him of Antioch,/who indeed was of such an opinion [as Flavian], an instrument against the bishop of Rome and against the bishop of Constantinople, since it was not quite forgotten by him[1] whether he held such an opinion; for they had written many times to one another concerning these things. Yet he made use however of the holy bishop of Antioch, such as he was, and he made use [of him] until he made him useless and unworthy of the work of the episcopate, and he cast him aside and deprived him, while [his] adjurations were still on his tongue, either [as] one that was useless to him or because he was frightened of him, seeing indeed that he had fallen into the temptation of having transgressed [his] adjurations. For this reason he had deprived him in this very [way] whereby he might be able even otherwise indeed to exact his vengeance. But he was frightened not only of him,[2] in case he had this [same] opinion [as Flavian], but also of the Emperor, and he was doing all things [possible] lest, after carrying out by [means of] him all these things according to his wish, he should afterwards turn round and hate him as untruthful and transgressing [his] adjurations and [as one] who was committing all things unjustly to appease him who was in authority, and then would also work against him and cast him aside.

For it was even like this [that he was behaving] for the sake of him whom he was appeasing [and] whom he was drawing nigh unto him[self], and he was both / aiding him and advancing him in what he wanted. And he was doing all things [possible] and persuading every man to believe that he had undying love for him, and, when he was supposed

---

[1] *Viz.* Dioscorus.　　　　[2] *Viz.* the bishop of Antioch.

to love him the more when he was gathering the fruit of whatever he wanted, straightway he cast the man aside and then came to hate him[1] and turned away from him and wronged him; and he delivered him unto his enemies to be insulted as a man that had done very wrong and had sinned against his will, and he insulted [him] and transgressed against his adjurations. And for this reason, since he had known him, he had also wished to tempt him that he might be sinned against [by the very means] whereby he [had] sinned, in such wise that he might thereby become [his] master and slander the man before every one. And a trial of these things was made by this very man; for these things took place no long time before.

Concerning what happened about Cyril when the gold was exacted from him.[2]

For Cyril, who had given many things because of us, when he had gathered the fruit for which he had given [them], because the Emperor knew that he still had money, was indeed pledged in written documents [to pay] two thousand pounds[3] [in] gold, as they say, that what was done against me might be confirmed. But because they had been confirmed / and he who had imposed upon him the condition that he should give [this sum] unto him,[4] that is, John[5] had passed away with insult and in contempt with him who had laboured with him for what was done against me at Ephesus, and because some thing which he had done in his writings [had] come unto him, that he should take also that which was left, and should release the man,[6] what did he[4] do, according to what men say? He wrote unto him[6] a friendly letter,[7] beseeching him to hear him and to come with him as far as Ephesus, because he was under a vow touching himself and touching what was done at Ephesus, to bring [it] and to complete [it] within [the church of] Saint John,

---

[1] Literally: 'and then was (or became) hating him'.
[2] See above, pp. 279-82.   [3] Syr. *li(rin* = Gk. λίτραι.
[4] *Viz.* the Emperor.   [5] *Viz.* Count John.   [6] *Viz.* Cyril.
[7] Literally: 'a letter of love'.

for the sake of an [holy] death through his intercession. And [he said]: 'If there is aught that I have not done well 'because I knew not, I want to be rebuked by thee and I will 'render unto thee the honour which I owe unto thee,' indicating his [1] flight from Ephesus and what he had done against him; and he wanted him to correct these things because of those who were rejoicing at his flight from Ephesus and who were supposing that he hated him and was striving on behalf of Nestorius. And he [2] required his return [unto Ephesus], so that every man might be convinced and not suspect these things, ' lest they that oppose [thee] should be [buoyed up] ' by a vain expectation, [and that] we may make them subject ' unto thee '.

But the other,[1] since he knew naught thereof, had zealously / done the work, and he filled ships with all [kinds of] things and presents, as though for the Emperor and for the Imperial family and for the chief persons as much as was sufficient according to their rank and according to their honour. And he had come unto Ephesus and had given his presents and was honoured and caused every man to be amazed, and according to his honour he was in the mouth of every man. He was so honoured with all honour that he sat with the Emperor upon the first throne—and I mean [that] of the Emperor—while the Emperor sat on the second; and this happened also within the palace and in the [imperial] chariot and in public, so that the seat of the Emperor might be sanctified by his sitting [therein]. And for this reason he caused him to enter also into Constantinople, so that the brothers of the Emperor and the household of the Emperor and the city might be sanctified by his coming. But after he had here also satisfied the cupidity of men with presents and consequently had nothing [left over], he [2] then commanded that the gold should be exacted, the two thousand pounds, which he was pledged by written documents [to pay] and which he could not deny without being further deprived of his honour if he were to deny [them] and be convicted. But after he knew and perceived that the suffering which

---

[1] *Viz.* Cyril. [2] *Viz.* the Emperor.

had come upon him [was] a great wrong, he gave pledges for these [two thousand pounds] and sailed across the sea amid storms and in a great disturbance / and fled, lest he should fall in with other wrongs by reason of the accusers who were accusing him. . . .

But again I revert there to the just judgement of Dioscorus, who had received from Cyril the primacy and a hatred for the bishop of Constantinople. For their aim was not this, to attain the truth, but in every way whatsoever to strengthen themselves. For before Flavian had entered into the assembly, as they say, the other[1] had taken the seat and the place of the bishop of Constantinople and had made the others precede him, so that he sat at the end, as if [treated] with contempt. But he thought indeed nothing like this and sat down; but the other himself,[1] wanting to make a show of his tyranny, in the first place made this stir—and thou didst it that it might cause suffering unto him of Rome, as they say—and he arose and constrained him[2] and made him come and sit upon his own throne. And then the Counts, who had been charged with this, restrained the bishops who were assembled and were wanting to speak for him[2] outside what was asked of them by the bishop of Alexandria, who had the power of authority. / And those that had come from outside to [bear] witness to all the things which happened aforetime and [who] were able, in respect to the conviction of Eutyches of having said these things also before his accusation, to prove that there had been no calumny—and I mean the enclosed [monks] in the monasteries and all those who were supposed to have come on behalf of Flavian—they made to hide themselves and be in alarm because of their coming, as though they had vainly and boldly given themselves up on behalf of him who had been deprived by the Emperor from Constantinople.

But all of those with Eutyches—they were monks—were in [the enjoyment of] great liberty and authority, in such wise that whatever men wished to be [done] by authority

[1] *Viz.* Dioscorus. [2] *Viz.* Flavian.

was done by means of them, so that also they delivered unto the chiefs themselves and unto the inhabitants of the city all those who were indicated unto them. For every man was made subject unto them, and they were ministering unto them whether they were willing or whether they were unwilling. For what was being done was displeasing unto many of them, but they were constrained and [were] weeping. And by every means they were doing the things which were commanded; and they were carrying off men, [some] of them from the ships and [others] of them from the streets and [others] of them from the houses and [others] of them while praying from the churches, and were pursuing [others] of them / that they fled; and with all zeal they were searching out and digging after those who were hiding in caves and in holes in the earth. And it was [a matter] of great fear and of danger for a man to speak with the adherents of Flavian on account of those who were dwelling in the neighbourhood and keeping watch and were as spies to see who entered in unto Flavian.[1] And on account of this they were going and taking part with the adherents of Eutyches, [some] of them indeed since they feared to bear ill-treatment, and [others] of them since they had been the first to depend upon his own aid, and were speaking and lying much; and all that they were saying unto him against the other[2] was approved and [such things] were said unto him as if for [his] pleasure.

But they had dissociated from him[2] Eusebius, bishop of Dorylaeum, who was the accuser of Eutyches, and they had neither let him come in nor defend himself;[3] and they had also dissociated [from him] all the Council which had heard [him] and which had set him[4] aside at Constantinople [and] which ought to have spoken with him and established the things which it did. And they isolated him from all sides and made all of them his accusers, who suffered from fear lest they should bear ill-treatment; for both if a man were not

---

[1] Cp. the speech of Eutyches quoted on p. 346, n. 3.
[2] *Viz.* Flavian.   [3] Cp. Labbe (Mansi), vi. 644 B–645 B.
[4] *Viz.* Eutyches.

persuaded and if he were persuaded, it was by all means certain / that he would bear ill-treatment if he did not belie Flavian and become a partisan of Eutyches. But thus they were beforehand in settling him [1] and stripping him on all sides and placing him [in a position] without hope and without freedom of speech, so that there was even no speech [left] in him. For all of them prepared themselves as if not to hear him but by all means to condemn him, and they brought him into the assembly, insulting him and not letting him defend himself against [the things for] which he was rebuked. And before the presence of the Counts, who were in charge, they were stirring him up and instigating him, commanding him not to speak. But hear however this speech also which was [extorted] by force and by constraint for [a proof of] the mockery of the trial of this man.

For when the records [of the things] which were [done] in Constantinople against Eutyches and the agreement and the signature[s] of the bishops opposed to Eutyches, and especially [that] of Seleucus, bishop of Amasia, who had condemned him, were read, they examined him neither by any judicial process nor by any [regular] procedure, so as to exact of him the acknowledgement [2] of his signature, [in order to discover] what his view was [3] and whether it had been correctly put by him; but they passed sentence without examination and as if as the result of a labour confused / [and] indiscriminate, which was uncontrolled and unruly. They were crying out '[These] things are not [the concern of] the bishop of Amasia; divide thou not the indivisible!' in such wise as thereby to dismay the man and so that he should agree with those who were accusing him.[4] And by this demonstration

---

[1] *Viz.* Flavian.   [2] Literally: 'establishing'.

[3] Literally: 'how it was supposed by him'.

[4] Cp. Labbe (Mansi), vi. 685 B: ὁ θεοσεβέστατος ἐπίσκοπος Σέλουκος τῆς μητροπόλεως Ἀμασείας εἶπεν· ἐπλήρωσε τὰς καρδίας ἡμῶν εὐφροσύνης τὰ ἀρτίως ἀναγνωσθέντα δόγματα τοῦ ἁγίου πατρός, καὶ ἐπισκόπου γεγονότος Κυρίλλου, καὶ ἡ σύνεσις τοῦ ἁγιωτάτου ἀρχιεπισκόπου ἡμῶν Φλαυιανοῦ, καὶ ἡ νῦν συγκατάθεσις τοῦ ἁγιωτάτου ἐπισκόπου Βασιλείου. ὅθεν ἀποστολικῶν, καὶ ὀρθῶν, καὶ εὐσεβῶν ὄντων τῶν τοιούτων δογμάτων, καὶ αὐτὸς συντίθεμαι, καὶ συναινῶ· καὶ τὸν μὴ φρονοῦντα οὕτως ἀναθεματίζω, καὶ ἀλλότριον ἐγκρίνω τῆς ἐκκλησιαστικῆς καὶ ὀρθοδόξου συναφείας. πιστεύομεν γὰρ καὶ ἡμεῖς εἰς τὸν ἕνα κύριον ἡμῶν Ἰησοῦν Χριστόν, τὸν ἐκ

they [wished also to] make others fear and deny the sentence which they [had] passed and calumniate Flavian in one and the same manner; for this [treatment] was common unto all those who accepted him and agreed with him.

There ought therefore to be also a common judgement [both] of those who had condemned him[1] and [of those who] agreed with him and had repented of the signature which had been signed against Eutyches, but they were however doing these things in order to show that they ought by all means to condemn Flavian, as though he had modified their words and the decision of their judgement, nor was it [possible] for them to make [their] defence otherwise. But, that they might accuse Flavian, Dioscorus, the instigator of this examination, while putting to silence the unruly crowd, was crying aloud in his [own] unruliness: 'Be silent awhile; let us hear also the 'other blasphemies. Why do we blame only Nestorius? 'There is many a Nestorius.'[2] Not one convicted him of holding these views of mine, nor yet did he allow [any one] to calumniate him in me,/ but indeed he[3] spoke of me as well as of him; for the other too—he was of them that speak correctly—was however saying: 'I speak in one way and he in another,' and was denying that I said these very things, either because thou knewest it not or out of fear. Without therefore having given unto him a chance to defend himself, he anticipated [him] and condemned him, lest, when he defended himself, the truth should be established concerning the things whereof he was accused: [that is,] that they were not the doctrines of Nestorius but of the Divine Scriptures and of the holy Fathers who [had lived] before the three hundred and eighteen and of those after them. For it was possible through him in all respects to prove that they[4] were orthodox.

Θεοῦ λόγον, τὸν ἐκ τοῦ φωτὸς φῶς, τὸν ἐκ τῆς ζωῆς ζωήν, ἐν δύο φύσεσι μετὰ τὴν ἐνανθρώπησιν, καὶ τὴν τῆς σαρκὸς τῆς ἐκ τῆς ἁγίας Μαρίας πρόσληψιν, δογματίζεσθαι· καὶ τὸν παρὰ ταῦτα φρονοῦντα, ὡς ἀλλότριον τῆς ἐκκλησίας ἀποκηρύττομεν.

Ἡ ἁγία σύνοδος εἶπεν· οὐδεὶς δύο λέγει τὸν κύριον μετὰ τὴν ἕνωσιν· οὐκ ἦν Ἀμασείας ἐπίσκοπος. τὸν ἀμέριστον μὴ μέριζε· ταῦτα Νεστόριος ἐφρόνησεν, οὐκ ἦν Ἀμασείας ἐπίσκοπος, οὐκ ἦν Ἀμασείας, Σινώπης ἐστίν. Διόσκορος ἐπίσκοπος Ἀλεξανδρείας εἶπε· σιωπήσατε ὀλίγον. ἀκούσωμεν ἄλλων δυσφημιῶν. τί μεμφόμεθα Νεστορίῳ μόνῳ; πολλοὶ Νεστόριοί εἰσιν.   [1] *Viz.* Eutyches.   [2] See p. 353, n. 4.
[3] *Viz.* Dioscorus.   [4] *I. e.* the views which he was accused of holding.

So therefore that these things might not be examined, in that they could not deny that they were [the views] of the orthodox, and that, in accepting them as [those] of the orthodox, they might not again let go that which they were zealous to do, [that is,] to condemn Flavian and acquit Eutyches, they passed over these words and went on to accuse him of other things, as though he was surely modifying the decision of the judgement. And they gave him [permission] to defend himself on this charge and not on that on account of which and by means of which Cyril and the Council of Ephesus were exposed. For among the things which they had said, the adherents of Cyril and of Eutyches culled / what was in agreement with them and chose what was pleasing unto them, and the partisans also of Flavian [acted] similarly in opposition to the former. But Cyril was the father of many heresies and used to say this and that and otherwise at the same [time], in such wise that, when they made use of what was contrary, [it was impossible that] they should not distort those things which happened in the time of Cyril and what happened at Ephesus. And of necessity they[1] supported my own words [so as] to suppress what was done against me and that there might be no chance for [the execution of] what was being done against Flavian on account of the accusation of Eutyches. For these reasons they[2] would not allow Seleucus himself to make [his] defence, nor even support what was written by him. But in short they had recourse to such an outcry that no one else dared to make a defence but [only] to say what they wanted against Flavian, [that is] that the things which were brought about by the decision of the judgement of Eutyches were [being] modified by him [and] that they would accept such a signature without a word. For thereby has their aim become known unto every man, but [even] is it known from the signature of Atticus.[3]

/ Now Atticus[3] was a countryman and a rustic unable even

---

[1] *Viz.* the adherents of Flavian.
[2] *Viz.* the adherents of Eutyches.
[3] So the Syriac text, reading 'Atticus' *passim* for 'Aethericus'.

to [understand] evident things; for he was a confidential servant,[1] and had been brought up within the house like slaves, and had been given to the great palace of the imperial household; and, since he had thus the licence of influence and greatness, he had been elected among the bishops, though he was not learned in nor understood ways and triflings and schemings such as these. And they had constrained him lyingly[2] [to] say that it was surely modified, and he constrained them to say and to make known unto him the violence, since he understood not what they were saying unto him. For Atticus the bishop had said: 'Immediately I entered Con-
'stantinople and looked upon the hearers and the monk
'who was saying: "Sign, my lord," I said unto him: "[Wait]
'"awhile; allow me to see." And I heard him reading some-
'thing lying. And after these things he said unto me: "Sign,
'"my lord." I said: "I cannot sign; truly indeed I know,
'"but I cannot say aught; I say however that if any one
'"believes not as the three hundred and eighteen Fathers at
'"Nicaea and those at Ephesus, let him be anathema in this
'"world and in that to come."' And Dioscorus, as before a child that is accused, commanded Atticus to deny [these charges] and to belie himself, and he said what he wanted [him] / to say, [that is:] 'These things therefore which have been read are lies and trifling.' And Atticus knew not what he wanted him to say and said: 'I know not,' because they had suggested unto him to say [that] they were lies and trifling, and Atticus knew not. Again he asked him otherwise, suggesting unto him: 'Hast thou not said these things?' and hardly, as they goaded him on, did Atticus know what he wanted him to say; and Atticus said: 'No.' And again they wanted to confirm what he wanted him to say. Dioscorus grew confident to ask him about the same things [and] he even said: 'I have heard what has therefore been said by thee.' He said what he wanted [him] to say and to teach, because he was afraid lest he should reply to him one thing for another. And Atticus says: 'I have heard.' And

[1] Literally: 'trusted', *i.e.* (probably) a eunuch; see p. 272, n. 2.
[2] See crit. n., p. 401.

Dioscorus suggested unto him, saying: 'Then thou hast not said them?' And Atticus, suggesting [the same thing] as he who was prompting him, said also the same things: 'Have I not said [1] [it]?' Thus both before the Emperor and before other men he made use of the same artifice so as [to ensure] that they would deny their own signature and act against Flavian irreverently and unjustly. He accepted indeed the things which [were said] by them / without examination and the things which had been said under [stress of] evidence, [that is] that they [2] had been modified, he accepted without hesitation.[3]

---

[1] See crit. n., p. 401.   [2] *I. e.* the ὑπομνήματα of Flavian.

[3] The following account of the conduct of Aethericus at the Latrocinium is given in the Minutes of the Council of Chalcedon in Labbe (Mansi), vi. 688-9:
ὁ θεοφιλέστατος ἐπίσκοπος Σατουρνῖνος τῆς Μαρκιανουπολιτῶν μητροπόλεως εἶπεν· εἴ τις ἑτέρως φρονεῖ παρὰ τὰ ἀρτίως ἀναγνωσθέντα ἐπὶ τῆς ἁγίας ταύτης συνόδου, οὗτος κατὰ τοὺς τύπους τῶν ἁγίων πατέρων ἀλλότριος ἤτω, καὶ ἀκοινώνητος ἡμῖν, ὡς μὴ ἐμμένων τοῖς καλῶς θεσπισθεῖσι παρὰ τῶν ἁγίων πατέρων. ὁ θεοφιλέστατος Αἰθέριχος τῆς Σμυρναίων πόλεως εἶπε· καθὼς οἱ πατέρες οἱ παρόντες συνέθεντο, κἀγὼ συναινῶ, καὶ συντίθεμαι, καὶ πρὸ τούτου, καὶ νῦν, καὶ μετὰ ταῦτα, καὶ εἰς τὸν μέλλοντα αἰῶνα.
Αἰθέριχος ἐπίσκοπος Σμύρνης εἶπεν. ἐγὼ ταῦτα οὐκ εἶπον. Διόσκορος ἐπίσκοπος Ἀλεξανδρείας εἶπε· τί λέγει; Ἰωάννης πρεσβύτερος, καὶ πρῶτος νοταρίων, εἶπε· πλαστοῦ ἐπιλαμβάνεται. Διόσκορος ἐπίσκοπος Ἀλεξανδρείας εἶπε· διδασκέτω ὁ εὐλαβέστατος ἐπίσκοπος Αἰθέριχος, ἃ βούλεται. Αἰθέριχος ἐπίσκοπος Σμύρνης εἶπεν· αἰφνιδίως ἐπεισῆλθον ἐν Κωνσταντινουπόλει· προσέσχον δὲ τοῖς ἀκροαταῖς· εἶτα τοῦτον αὐτὸν τὸν μονάζοντα μετ' αὐτῶν, καὶ λέγει· κύριε ὑπόγραψον. λέγω κἀγώ· τέως κἂν ἄφες ἴδωμεν· ἐπηκούσαμεν· ἐπηκούσαμεν αὐτοῦ φανερά τινα. μετὰ ταῦτα λέγει, ἔκθου. ἐγὼ λέγω, ἐκθέσθαι οὐ δύναμαι. ἀληθῶς μὲν οἶδα, ἀλλ' οὐ δύναμαι εἰπεῖν· πλὴν λέγω· εἴ τις οὐ πιστεύει καθὼς οἱ τριακόσιοι δέκα καὶ ὀκτώ, καὶ οἱ ἐν Ἐφέσῳ, ἀνάθεμα ἔστω καὶ ὧδε, καὶ εἰς ἐκεῖνον τὸν μέλλοντα αἰῶνα· Διόσκορος ἐπίσκοπος Ἀλεξανδρείας εἶπε· ταῦτα οὖν τὰ ἀναγνωσθέντα πλαστά εἰσιν; Αἰθέριχος ἐπίσκοπος Σμύρνης εἶπεν· οὐκ οἶδα ἐγώ. Διόσκορος ἐπίσκοπος Ἀλεξανδρείας εἶπε· περαιτέρω τούτων οὐκ εἴρηκας; Αἰθέριχος ἐπίσκοπος Σμύρνης εἶπεν· οὔ. Διόσκορος ἐπίσκοπος Ἀλεξανδρείας εἶπεν· ἐπήκουσας δὲ τῶν δῆθεν παρὰ σοῦ εἰρημένων; Αἰθέριχος ἐπίσκοπος Σμύρνης εἶπεν· ἐπήκουσα. Διόσκορος ἐπίσκοπος Ἀλεξανδρείας εἶπεν· καὶ οὐκ εἴρηκας αὐτά; Αἰθέριχος ἐπίσκοπος Σμύρνης εἶπεν· οὔ. Διόσκορος ἐπίσκοπος Ἀλεξανδρείας εἶπεν· δῆλα τὰ κατατεθέντα παρὰ τοῦ παρόντος. ὅθεν ἀναγινωσκέσθω τὰ ἑξῆς.

Καὶ ἐν τῷ ἀναγινώσκεσθαι, Αἰθέριχος, ὁ εὐλαβέστατος ἐπίσκοπος Σμύρνης, ἀναστὰς εἶπε· τὰ πρῶτα συνεθέμην, καὶ ὑπέγραψα μόνον, ἀπῆλθον. ἐκολλήθη μοι Διόσκορος εὐλαβέστατος ἐπίσκοπος, καὶ λέγει· διὰ τί ὑπέγραψας κατὰ Εὐτυχοῦς; λέγω ἐγώ, ὑπέγραψα, ὡς πάντες οἱ πατέρες ὑμῶν· εἰ δέ ἐστι τί ποτε ἄλλο, εἴπατέ μοι. λέγει· τί ὑπέγραψας; λέγω, ὑπέγραψα, ὡς προσήνεγκαν μοι. ἀνάθεμα, εἴ τις οὐ πιστεύει τοῖς τριακοσίοις δεκαοκτώ, καὶ ὡς ἐν Ἐφέσῳ, οὗτος ἀνάθεμα ἔστω. ὕστερον τί ὑπέγραψαν, οὐκ οἶδα, ἐπὶ πάντων εἶπα. Διόσκορος ὁ εὐλαβέστατος ἐπίσκοπος Ἀλεξανδρείας εἶπεν· ἐνέγκῃ δύο μάρτυρας. Αἰθέριχος ὁ εὐλαβέστατος ἐπίσκοπος Σμύρνης εἶπεν· ὡς Κύριλλος, φρονῶ· οἱ ἐνδοξότατοι ἄρχοντες, καὶ ἡ ὑπερφυὴς σύγκλητος εἶπε· τίνος

But he wanted Flavian to speak against them, and they allowed him not, since he was quite [overcome] by constraint such as this and by violence, but they wounded him, as the Counts say, so that he should surely not speak until the signature against him was complete and the [affairs] of Eutyches were thus confirmed, and that for which they were zealous wholly attained[1]; for they were therefore assembled as for a dead man. For when that which was done against Eutyches was read in the records and Flavian had spoken against them, they said: 'He is surely lying about our own signature,' and they wounded him, as men say. Then, after the decision of the judgement and the sentence against him had been promulgated, as was pleasing unto them, Dioscorus had commanded him to speak, and he said: 'If the godly 'bishop Flavian knows aught that would aid him, let him say '[it] in written documents.'[2] What ought he, who knew that in all things his just words had been repudiated with violence such as this, to have said? And they were therefore commanding him as in sport to say, in addition to what he had said: 'Thou hast inhibited my just words, in that thou hast accepted every calumny against me without hesitation.

/ Yet in order that this too might be proved to have been [done] in sport, they had set down in the records for [our] instruction, even though they were unwilling, in what way they [had] checked all his just words: that Dioscorus said unto Flavian: 'The holy Council knows if I have inhibited thee,' and Flavian spoke openly of the violence which had been [done] unto him, [saying:] 'I have not been let alone nor is it permitted unto me even to speak,' so that it was also known that these things which were said were [said] in mockery. He[3] said: 'Say what would aid thee,' and he said that there

παρόντος ταῦτά σοι εἶπε Διόσκορος ὁ εὐλαβέστατος ἐπίσκοπος; Αἰθέριχος ὁ εὐλαβέστατος ἐπίσκοπος Σμύρνης εἶπεν· ἐπὶ πάντων. Θαλάσσιος ὁ εὐλαβέστατος ἐπίσκοπος Καισαρείας Καππαδοκίας εἶπε· ταῦτα, ἃ γέγραπται, εἶπες ἐκτὸς ἀνάγκης, τί θέλεις ἄρτι καταστρέφειν; Διόσκορος ὁ εὐλαβέστατος ἐπίσκοπος Ἀλεξανδρείας εἶπεν· συκοφαντήσας οὐδὲν πάσχῃ; εἰ ἤμην καταγνωσθείς, οὐκ ἔπασχον; According to Hefele, the first paragraph, as far as τὸν μέλλοντα αἰῶνα, refers to the Synod of Constantinople; the second, as far as τὰ ἑξῆς, to the Latrocinium; and the rest to Chalcedon. [1] Literally: 'attained wholeness'.
[2] See p. 360, n. 1. [3] *Viz.* Dioscorus.

was no trifling or lying in the affair of the records; and 'both 'my lord Eusebius and my lord Thalassius, who signed and 'examined [them] with me knew [it]'. And Thalassius and Eusebius repudiated his statement, [saying] that they had not examined [them]. Then consequently, in that they were addressed only in mockery, namely, after the sentence, Thalassius said these [same] things as Dioscorus: 'There is no one restraining thy Saintliness from speaking,' and Dioscorus mockingly replied unto each one of the bishops who perceived this artifice, saying: 'My lord Eusebius, say whether these 'things have not taken place, and examine, so that he may be 'found guiltless. But hast thou indeed restrained him from 'speaking, and, further, dost thou urge him to speak?' And, after he had spoken unto him, he [1] again said the same things :/ that this affair had been before my lord Thalassius and my lord Eusebius, when also my lord Magnus the privy councillor [2] was present, and had been examined, and naught such as this was found [in it]; every single one of the bishops who were there present [and] those who heard [the case] would say as before God whether it had been said lyingly.

Dioscorus again mocked him, [saying] that this to be sure was no defence, and the other supposed that he was in truth offering him [leave] to speak, having let him examine these things. And again, deriding, he [3] turned to face Stephen and said unto him: 'Hast thou prohibited him?' and unto all of them: 'Speak, all of you.' And thus he made sport of the man himself who was not versed in nor knew the wickedness and the wiles of the Egyptians but supposed that they were [filled] with piety and were eager to speak more than the truth in the interests of those who were misrepresented by slander. And consequently, after he [1] knew what they were doing and that there was not [any] urgency at all for defence nor for proof, he became quiet and bore witness before every man, saying: 'By the aid of God I am not affected by aught of what you 'have done unto me; for I have neither confessed aught and 'thought at all otherwise, [n]or do I confess [otherwise now].' And he then was silent [and ceased] to answer / a word unto

---

[1] *Viz.* Flavian. [2] Syr. *sĕlanṭāryós* = Lat. *silentiarius*. [3] *Viz.* Dioscorus.

him as if unto an evident heretic.[1] And for this reason he had incited him to speak, and he[2] persisted in this confession. He suffered naught that he ought not, nor was he like unto the bishops of this world of his time who agreed in all that men were demanding of them, nor did he even change the likeness of his opinion but persisted in giving himself up to suffer; nor was he resolved nor even purposed to say: 'I[3] am a simple man 'and I am far from this exactitude; and also aforetime we 'were instructing and persuading Eutyches, and I have con-'demned him as indeed I was persuaded [to do] by his 'accusers who were supposed to know something, having been 'persuaded by the opinion of many and not by myself; and 'now, if it seems [good] unto all of you together and you have 'examined [and found] that these [opinions] of Eutyches are '[those] of orthodoxy, I too am persuaded of that whereof all

---

[1] Cp. Labbe (Mansi), vi. 832 D-833 D : Εὐτυχὴς ἀρχιμανδρίτης εἶπε· συνείδεν ἡ ὑμετέρα θεοσέβεια, ὅτι τῶν ἀναγνωσθέντων ἡ πρᾶξις ἔδειξε παραπεποιημένα τὰ πρώην ὑπομνήματα. ἔχομεν δὲ καὶ νῦν τὴν κατάθεσιν τοῦ θαυμασιωτάτου σιλεντιαρίου Μάγνου, τὴν γενομένην ἐπὶ τοῦ μεγαλοπρεπεστάτου μαγίστρου· καὶ ἀξιοῦμεν ταύτην ἀναγνωσθῆναι. Φλαυιανὸς ἐπίσκοπος Κωνσταντινουπόλεως εἶπε· ψευδής ἐστιν. Διόσκορος ἐπίσκοπος Ἀλεξανδρείας εἶπεν· εἴ τι ἔγνωκεν ὁ θεοφιλέστατος ἐπίσκοπος Φλαυιανὸς συμβαλλόμενον αὐτοῦ τῇ ὑπολήψει, λεγέτο ἐγγράφως. Φλαυιανὸς ἐπίσκοπος Κωνσταντινουπόλεως εἶπεν· ἀπέκλεισάς με πᾶσαν δικαιολογίαν. Διόσκορος ἐπίσκοπος Ἀλεξανδρείας εἶπεν· οἶδεν ἡ παροῦσα ἁγία σύνοδος, εἰ ἀπέκλεισά σου τί. εἴ τι οὖν οἶδας συμβαλλόμενόν σοι, εἰπέ· Φλαυιανὸς ἐπίσκοπος Κωνσταντινουπόλεως εἶπε· συνεχωρήθη μοι λαλῆσαι; Διόσκορος ἐπίσκοπος Ἀλεξανδρείας εἶπεν· οὐδείς σε ἐκώλυσεν· οἶδεν ἡ ἁγία σύνοδος. Φλαυιανὸς ἐπίσκοπος Κωνσταντινουπόλεως εἶπεν. ἡ δευτέρα πρᾶξις οὐδὲν ἔχει πλαστόν, οἶδε καὶ ὁ κύριος Θαλάσσιος, οἶδε καὶ ὁ κύριος Εὐσέβιος. Θαλάσσιος ἐπίσκοπος Καισαρείας Καππαδοκίας εἶπεν· οὐδεὶς ἐκώλυσε τοῦ λαλῆσαι τὴν σὴν ὁσιότητα. εἴ τι τοίνυν ἔχεις συμβαλλόμενον, εἰπέ. Διόσκορος ἐπίσκοπος Ἀλεξανδρείας εἶπε· κύριε Εὐσέβιε εἰπέ· ἐκώλυσα αὐτὸν λαλῆσαι; Εὐσέβιος ἐπίσκοπος Ἀγκύρας Γαλατίας εἶπεν· ὡς εἶδεν ὁ Θεός, εὐχόμεθά σε λαλῆσαι. Ἰουβενάλιος ἐπίσκοπος Ἱεροσολύμων εἶπεν· ἔτι καὶ νῦν, εἴ τι θέλεις εἰπέ. Φλαυιανὸς ἐπίσκοπος Κωνσταντινουπόλεως εἶπεν· ἐπὶ τοῦ κυροῦ Θαλασσίου, καὶ τοῦ κυροῦ Εὐσεβίου, παρόντος, καὶ τοῦ σιλεντιαρίου Μάγνου, ἐγένετο ἡ πρᾶξις, καὶ ἐξητάσθη, καὶ οὐδὲν τοιοῦτον ἀπεδείχθη. ἕκαστος τῶν τότε παρόντων ἐπισκόπων, ὡς ἐπὶ Θεοῦ, ἃ ἤκουσεν, εἶπε· καὶ ἀψευδῶς ἐρρέθη. Διόσκορος ἐπίσκοπος Ἀλεξανδρείας εἶπεν· κύριε Στέφανε ἐπίσκοπε εἰπέ, εἰ ἐκώλυσα αὐτόν. Στέφανος ἐπίσκοπος Ἐφέσου εἶπεν· ἰδού, ποῦ ἐστίν; ἐὰν ἐκώλυσας αὐτόν, εἴπῃ. Διόσκορος ἐπίσκοπος Ἀλεξανδρείας εἶπεν· εἴπατε πάντες, εἰ ἐκώλυσα αὐτόν. ἡ ἁγία σύνοδος εἶπεν· οὐκ ἐκωλύσαμεν αὐτόν. Φλαυιανὸς ἐπίσκοπος Κωνσταντινουπόλεως εἶπεν· ἐμοῦ τῶν πεπραγμένων οὐδὲν ἅπτεται διὰ τὸν Θεόν. οὐδὲν γὰρ ἑτέρως ἐδόξασα, ἢ ἐφρόνησά ποτε, ἢ φρονήσω. Διόσκορος ἐπίσκοπος Ἀλεξανδρείας εἶπε· δήλων ὄντων τῶν πραχθέντων, λεγέτω ἕκαστος τῶν παρόντων ἁγίων ἐπισκόπων, οἵως οἶδε πιστεύοντα τὸν ἀρχιμανδρίτην Εὐτυχῆ, καὶ τί περὶ αὐτοῦ τυποῖ.

[2] *Viz.* Flavian.   [3] See crit. n., p. 402.

'of you are persuaded, and I will sign with you in order to 'cling to those of orthodoxy; and reckon me also with the 'party of those bishops who need to be condemned!'

For all things would have been brought to an end by this discourse, as well as the anger of the Emperor who clung to the slander and was zealous for tyranny, for which reason indeed he had caused the Council to assemble. But he had not been persuaded, even in Constantinople, when all of them / were persuading and beseeching him to do this, nor yet in Ephesus, where consequently the wrong was nigh at hand, when he was on the verge of[1] death and it was being said by every man that only this was for him [a means of] escape from death, while he saw all of them fleeing from him and taking part with Eutyches and being rescued thereby. And I was a proof for him that neither deprivation from the bishopric of the city nor yet silence sufficed for me not to give them a cause for change, but [that] the cause wherefore I was suffering wrong [was] altogether that I was heard to be [still numbered] among the living. For, as long as thou art alive, expect death from the wicked; therefore, that thou mayest not surrender the faith, let all these things for [thine] endurance be [ever] before thine eyes. For immediately after [his] deposition was suspected, he was carried off as if by bears and by lions by the Counts before whom this deprivation took place in such a way that he was both dragged away and hurled down, and some were saying and even doing [one thing and others] another. And he was isolated and perturbed by all of them, and his spirit was vexed. And they delivered him up to the soldiers and commanded them to lead him away and remove him from the holy places. And they led him away and incarcerated him, / a man who was fainting, in prison. And before he came unto himself and was revived and was breathing fresh and pure air and taking nourishment that strength might be a little [restored] in him, they delivered him up unto the officer[2] and threatened to send the man away, bruised.

And he was unable to endure the hardship of the journey. The Emperor was as one that desired not his life but wanted

---

[1] Literally: 'he inclined towards'.   [2] Syr. 'arkôn = Gk. ἄρχων.

to punish him and not to keep him alive. And thus they brought him down by force and gave him to a man [that was] a murderer so as to destroy him and to send him without mercy, in word indeed unto his [own] place, but in reality unto destruction. And thus he was dragged away and led off, [with strength] sufficient only to survive four days, as men say, while every day his soul was being released from his body, and they counted his decease [as] a festival for them[selves]. And wrongs were being increased against all of them who agreed with him and his fellow believers. And further I [was] among the first in severe persecutions and in flight and in exiles and in commands whereby authority was given in every place unto them to do what they were purposing; since I and Flavian certainly thought the same things. And authority was given unto the people to lead off and to hale away and to deliver up. Slaves / were accusing their masters by the same [means], and authority was given unto them [to do so] by the command of the Emperor;[1] and all their eagerness was to lead their own souls into error as well as the souls [of those] who conceived or thought that God the Word is immortal. And they were saying things more impious than these in such wise as to constrain [men] to say that it was his *ousia*, [that] of God the Word, which died. And he[2] had given unto them authority against every man while the chiefs were not trusted nor the bishops nor all this world nor enemies nor slaves; but, as though they fell short of their cupidity and their zeal in regard to those who called God the Word immortal and impassible, they set up those who were more eager to scrutinize and to search out, to seek for those who were fleeing. And all these [terrors] overtook them; and the suspicion and the expectation of sufferings were worse for them than the sufferings; and it was evidently a Pharaonic struggle against God.

/ Enumeration of some part of the ills which happened in the world because of the transgression against the true faith of God impassible, with a prophecy.

But after these things began to take place concerning the

---

[1] Cp. the *Sacra Lex Theodosii* in Labbe (Mansi), v. 417 B. [2] *Viz.* the Emperor.

faith and in respect to the discussion against [the doctrine] that God the Word was not immortal and impassible, it therefore [came to look] as though the immortal God the Word himself had no care for them;[1] for those [who thought] therefore that God the Word was not immortal had begun to be overthrown and brought to subjection in one way and another and some of them in all ways and there was none to turn aside the wrath.

What happened in [the way of] earthquakes and wars.

1. They had been worn out with pestilences and famines and failure of rains and hail and heat and marvellous earthquakes and captivity and fear and flight and all [kind of] ills, and they came not to perceive the cause of ills such as these; but they were the more inflamed and embittered against any one who dared to call God the Word impassible, as though they were suffering these ills because men called God the Word himself impassible and immortal; and there was no place of refuge.

/ 2. A twofold upheaval on the part of the barbarians and the Scythians, who were destroying and taking every one captive, had shaken them and there was not even a single hope of rescue; and hitherto they understood not that all this was not simply human.

3. And therewith he[2] had also shaken the earth with earthquakes, the like of which there was none that remembered.[3] For thus the earth was shaken, as a thing that was being overturned and burst open or inevitably destroyed. But when again it ceased [from trembling] and was firm as aforetime, it was like unto a thing that a man had grasped, [torn] out of its natural place; he indeed who shook it was also shaken therewith. [It was] not only to the eyes that it showed its shaking which shook it and the stability that established it [anew in its place], but it brought all men themselves to perceive [it] and through the greatness of all

---

[1] *I. e.* for those who denied that God the Word was immortal.

[2] *Viz.* God.

[3] For these earthquakes see Evagrius, *H. E.* i. 17; Philostorgius, *H. E.* xii. 8-10; Nicephorus Callistus, *H. E.* xiv. 46.

[these] things it brought knowledge to the minds [of men] more than speech [would have done].

4. The barbarians indeed had drawn nigh and had assailed the Romans and reduced them to all despair.

5. But in Constantinople, the imperial city, the towers of the wall which were built with it had collapsed and left the wall [isolated], though it had not suffered any [injury] from the things whereby it had been shaken, and they remained as things that have not been shaken, while there was not even a single indication in them of the earthquake; and even [in some] of the places in the midst of the walls the stones had started out of the whole building and from the parts adjoining the building; even the lime had been shaken out.

6. And some things appeared openly in one part of the city [in one way, and others in another part] otherwise, and things had not been shaken by a common earthquake but to convince men that he who was doing these things was immortal and had authority over them.

7. *About the Forum of Theodosius the Great.* For even the stones which were bound with iron and lead had been torn up, being borne up into the air and remaining suspended awhile and then falling; and, when those that were about to meet them were coming out, they immediately fell. And ten thousand other things and many [there were] which were happening in other countries and were being heard of and were a great cause of[1] trepidation and fear, so as to bring men, though unwilling, to supplication and to the beseeching of God to have mercy upon them, not however as he wished; for some were beseeching him [for some things and others] for others, according to their [own] calculation, and were praying unto him for what they possessed. And this one was saying: 'God that has suffered and died for us' and was beseeching [him], while yet another [was praying] otherwise, as though they were saying that which was honourable unto them. For they were [filled] with wrath and with anger against those who dared to call [him] immortal and impassible; and for this reason did afflictions and fears which

---

[1] Literally: 'were full of'.

were very fearful crowd the more upon them, while their wrong deeds recoiled upon them, so that there was no time for them to have leisure to act wrongly towards the pious who were among them.

Concerning 'Holy God'.

But, since he wished to bring them to perceive their blasphemy and to desist therefrom, because they came not thereto, God himself gave unto them a manner of intercession —for he who should do this had not been found—whereby they should say: 'Holy God, holy [and] mighty, holy [and] immortal, have mercy upon us.'[1] And every one assented with one mind thereto and left off the things for which they had yearned [and] for which God had not yearned. And they wrote this down in the basilica and in public[2] and set it up thus: 'Glory and thanks to the holy one and to the immortal, God the saviour of all'; and they had almost succeeded in confessing God immortal; and that to which they clung they denied not, but this was sung in every place. But after the earthquake had ceased and a few wars were arising, they roused themselves again and revealed themselves against God; and they were dissembling the confession [of faith] in God, as persons that remembered not the [formula] 'God the holy one and mighty and immortal', who was able/to bring wars to peace even without human might, wherein was his might and except for which there was not [any kind] of preparation [for war]; and they have made trial of this thing in fact. Now indeed they have ceased even from [this] supplication.

But a little before their war with these barbarians the very cross alone used to teach them and bring them to believe in God, who more [than all] swept warriors away without a weapon. But before this, when the barbarian was stirred up by an army, he threw himself into holes and fastnesses.[3] For,

---

[1] The account of the miraculous revelation of the *Trisagion* is given in John of Damascus, *De Orth. Fid.* iii. 10, and in Niceph. Callist. *H. E.* xiv. 46, in a form consistent with Nestorius's references to the matter. For the use of the formula at Chalcedon see Labbe (Mansi), vi. 936 c.

[2] Syr. *bdēmōsyâ* = Gk. δημοσίᾳ.   [3] See crit. n., p. 402.

because the people of the Scythians were great and many and formerly were divided into peoples and into kingdoms and were treated as robbers, they used not to do much wrong except only as through rapacity and through speed; yet later they made them a kingdom and, after they were [established] in a kingdom, they grew very strong, so that they surpassed in their greatness all the forces of the Romans. And God showed them that he was not become weak, against whom they had already agreed together and whom they had made subject unto suffering and unto death. And they strengthened the persecutions against them that confessed God holy and mighty and immortal, and they let be him in whom they hoped and [by whom] they were rescued from death; and he gave them the knowledge / to repudiate the death of God but to acknowledge him and to confess that he is immortal.

But, because this had taken place and they had not been converted to glorify the God who rescued them but blasphemed and constrained every man to confess the death of God but shunned [the term] 'immortal' as impiety, the barbarian again was stirred up against them, massacring and swarming over all the land of the Romans and overturning everything. And they had no means [of escape] nor refuge but were stricken with fear and had no hope. And he had closed them in and made them insufficient in everything that they were doing for their salvation; and, because they understood not their former salvation, he had sent this man whom he had taken from pasturing sheep, who had protested against the privy [purposes] of the heart of the Emperor. And already he had been stirred up by God, and he commanded to make a cross; and as though indeed he[1] believed him not, he made [it of] wood with his own hands and sent [it] against the barbarians. But he had planted another cross also within the palace and another in the forum of Constantinople in the midst of the city that it might be seen of every man, so that even the barbarians, when they saw it, fled and were discomfited. And the Emperor himself, who was already

---

[1] *Viz.* the Emperor.

making ready / to flee, gained confidence to remain, and the nerves of the city, which was enfeebled, grew firm and all things happened thus.

For when the barbarians had fled in discomfiture, while none was pursuing them, and the Emperor was mightily heartened to engage in thought for his empire, and the city was mightily filled with encouragement, they found none other cause of [this] sudden change—because there was none else doing this: to discomfit the one and encourage the other —except only the cross, which had been set up, of him who was crucified in nature and in truth, that is, [of] the bodily frame which had been crucified naturally. And it is known unto us that we should not be ashamed to say that he died, and not God who made mighty the bodily frame, weak and passible and mortal, which suffered and died by lifting up [upon the cross]. For this reason also the wood whereon he was crucified was [a means] to salvation. For, as though for one that believed not and repudiated the crucifixion of the mortal body which can save, he commanded to make the cross of wood, to effect thereby salvation such as this in the city and amidst the barbarians, in such wise that it is not doubted that it is a crucifixion of the body which has given life to all the world, and not of God who by the lifting up of the body and the cross has effected such a miracle as this.

/ But because they had feigned themselves wise in this, as though the divinity was crucified and not the body, they were still left in opposition to the pious, who were saying that the crucifixion was not of the divinity but of the body of the divinity and [that] for this reason he saved us through the cross. Again God raised up anew the vehemence of the barbarians and earthquakes against this Pharaonic intention. And again, because he sought to restrain them from [the persecution of] the pious and from [inflicting upon them] the sufferings which they caused them to bear—for then only were they revived and set free—by both of them he taught [them] that the impious thought, wherein was [contained] the confession of [his] death, was not pleasing unto him.

For, although they supposed that that which [had been caused] by the barbarians was death [caused] by men, yet they could not suppose this of that which was being [caused] by the earthquake. But, after they had not even so come to a perception of the glory of God incorruptible, and were imputing death and suffering and weakness unto him in manliness and immortality such as this, he had then taught them by the words themselves [1] not to impute blemish and decay unto God, because he is holy and free from all sufferings and even without weakness, he who by a weak cross quitted himself manfully like a man and was [endowed] with all manliness. So then impute not death / unto him who is alone immortal and by our own death has proved that he is immortal by means of the confession of the holy and of the mighty and of the immortal.

But because they abode not by what they had been forced to confess and had not believed in God the mighty and immortal, who is able to make even wars to cease, they had [not only] become the slaves of the barbarians and been subjected unto slavery to tribute unto them by the confession of written documents, but were also giving [it] unto those who were warring on his side. And there was naught that he, who showed the barbarian [to be] master and the Romans slaves, did not. And thus the supremacy had changed over unto the barbarians, as though the Romans themselves had not God who [is] over all, holy and mighty and immortal. For this reason the rest also of the peoples fled unto him but fled from the Romans, so that they were not even able to rescue themselves. And because they had thus set up the supremacy, as though they had no urgent need for divine aid and had not come to themselves, they remembered not even the very confession of the holy one and the mighty and the immortal which they had taken into their mouths; but contrariwise they were again maintaining the sufferings of the divinity, by means of which they were showing that not one of these [attributes] was his. For with the sufferings and the death this also was assumed: that he was neither holy / by

---

[1] *I.e.* the *Trisagion.*

nature nor immortal by nature nor mighty by nature, until God had again restored [some] of them, whether they wanted or whether they wanted [it] not, for the reputation of their impiety and for the defence of those who had suffered wrongfully and for the instruction of those who in anticipation were praying unto Flavian and Eusebius, whom they would have killed.[1] Because men made compensation unto God, having confessed him [to be] both holy and mighty and immortal, both by law and by commands and by penalties they confirmed [their actions] against those who confessed God the Word [to be] holy and mighty and immortal and [punished them] with despoilment and exile and death, until Theodosius, who had raised himself up against God, was taken from [their] midst; and the mouth [of every man] was opened to confess and to glorify and to adore God the holy and mighty and immortal, speaking without fear.[2] For not he who calls Christ God passible and mortal confesses Christ [to be] God, but he who speaks of Christ in his divinity which he is in his nature and confesses God impassible and immortal and mighty and holy in his nature but passible in his humanity, in that he confesses that he is by nature man.

But some will say: 'What participation hast thou with 'Flavian and with what has been done against him and on 'his account? For / thee every man has anathematized and 'denounced, and what thou addest after this thou toilest to 'thine [own] evil name and to thine [own] accusation and not 'to a simple and just defence.' That which I say unto him above and below and always is that it concerns me not to

[1] Nau translates 'qu'ils avaient tués'; but see Nöldeke, *Syriac Grammar*, § 277. Eusebius of Dorylaeum had been deposed, but not killed. He was exiled and escaped to Rome where he was welcomed by Leo, who mentions his deposition in Letters lxxix and lxxx, dated 451. See Labbe (Mansi), vi. 907-36, 107 B, 110 B; Liberatus, xii (Galland. xii. 140); *Gest. de Nom. Acac.* (Galland. x. 668).

[2] Theodosius died on July 28th, 450, and was succeeded by his orthodox sister, Pulcheria, who took Marcian as her husband 'vir gravissimus, et non solum reipublicae, sed etiam Ecclesiae necessarius. Huius edictis apostolicae sedis auctoritatem secutis, synodus Ephesina damnatur, et apud Chalcedonem celebrari concilium episcopale decernitur; ut correctis venia mederetur, et pertinaces cum haeresi depellerentur.' Prosper, *Chron.* in Migne, *P. L.* li. 602; cp. *Chronicon Paschale* in Migne, *P. G.* xcii. 812.

have mercy upon any man such as these, but to be very anxious whether through my own anathema they are rescued from blasphemy and [whether] those who are rescued confess God holy and mighty and immortal, without changing the image of God who is incorruptible unto the image of man who is corruptible and mixing paganism in the midst of Christianity, but confessing God himself as is his image and confessing man as is his image, in such wise that the passible and also the immortal are confessed in the image of their natures, so that Christianity confesses not a change of God nor yet a change of man, [after] the likeness of the impiety of paganism. But let yea be yea and nay nay in truth, so that Christ in truth and in nature may be confessed to be the saviour and the saved, God and man, who is in nature immortal and impassible as God and mortal and passible in nature as man. He is not God in both the natures nor yet man in both the natures. Therefore my own aim and my zeal is that God may be blessed and glorified even on earth as in heaven. / But may Nestorius be anathematized; but may they say what I pray them to say concerning God. For I am of those who [are] with God and not of those who [are] against God, who scorn God himself in the *schêma* of piety and make void [the fact] that he is God. For he was for the things [for] which I war, and they that war with me against him; and for this reason on his account I am pledged to endure and to suffer everything, so that by my own anathema would that every man might be [ready] enough to be reconciled unto God, because there is naught greater or more precious unto me than this. Nor would I have declined to say the contrary of what I used to say, if I had known that they were wanting [me] to say the contrary of these things which I used to say in everything whatsoever and [that] they were of God, and [that] I should thereby be honoured before God on account of the [attributes] of God which I have regarded as God and not as man....

But otherwise again [it is the case] that I have not merely said the things touching Flavian, but I have cited them for a proof of what was done against me with impiety and with injustice, in such wise that certain men are not deceived by the name 'Council' but seek [to learn] the things which took place with all truth and judge [some] of them before God, although they took place otherwise. For Satan is disguised in the *schēma* of an angel of light[1] and deceives / men [in order] to remove them afar from God. But further, since I have judged in my mind that to hide the dispensation which came about through the might and the wisdom of God without showing and revealing them unto all men is a great peril and [fraught] with all impiety and ingratitude—for he had done them on their account, that he might undo the schemes of them that were confirming their impiety and causing it to shine forth, and expose them bare, while I was not believed in what I was saying, whereas they were doing and had also done this in their assembly in the Council—all of which [it was] that I was suffering, and they believed me not. But it was not possible to refute and to undo these things which had been done in the Council, but the will to impiety was [stronger] than the will of God, by means of which the impious were convicted of being impious and the pious of being pious; and they contended unto death and preserved that sincerity of mind which was owing unto God.

For when the time [was] not that under discussion which came by the patience of God [and] wherein some suffered and others caused them to suffer, the impious were not revealed [as] impious[2] nor they that were worthy of such forethought as this [as worthy thereof, forethought] which had turned them aside from the contest against God, in which operations he was warring and fighting against them and restraining them from kicking against / the pricks[3] of God; and yet not even so were they converted from their iniquity, while the pious had not been dispersed nor yet discouraged, while God was patient, from suffering throughout their whole lives, having adhered unto the purpose of

[1] Cp. 2 Cor. xi. 14.
[2] The Syriac has: 'as not impious', but the repetition of the negative is probably due to the influence of the Greek original. See p. xiv.
[3] Cp. Acts xxvi. 14.

God. For this reason one finds that diligence and aid have been relaxed by[1] those who had taken it[2] up, and they have neglected what has been [entrusted] to them and diligence has been [only shown] by them in making pretence without knowledge concerning what ought to have been corrected, things which were disregarded and set aside by them. For it would have been right to cut short the things which were wrongly [done] and not to hide them. Those things then which [came about] as for correction were of God; what concealed them was not of God but of those who were undoing his [work].

For for what reason do you suppose that they who possessed the inhabited world [as] their home became the spoil of the barbarians? Was it not because they made not use of the supremacy which was given unto them as was right, that the peoples might know the grace which was given unto them, in such wise that they might learn as slaves what was required, because they learnt not as masters? For what reason again heard they the word of the Gospel, not from the orthodox but from the worshippers of creatures?[3] They were / brought into subjection neither to the supremacy of the Empire nor yet under the religion wherein they were, that they might know that, when they took the supremacy of the Empire, they preserved not even in the Empire the supremacy of their religion in God; for this reason also they were not supreme in aught else, in that the supremacy changed over to [their] enemies. For whereby they neglected the Gospel, by these very things were they rejected from the supremacy; and they took part also in the faith of the worshippers of creatures and were distinct [only] in name and in the use of the term 'consubstantial'. As these[3] confess the created and the uncreated and say 'consubstantial' in one way as if in praise and attribute the nature in another way by the distinction of the created and of the creator, thus also those[4]

---

[1] Literally: 'departed from'.
[2] *I.e.* the discussion of the faith.   [3] *Viz.* the Arians.
[4] *Viz.* the Monophysites. Nestorius's point seems to be that in ascribing sufferings to God the Word, the Monophysites deny him consubstantiality with the Father, and thus resemble the Arians. So Nau.

attribute the nature in one way unto the passible and unto the impassible, the created and the uncreated, and say 'consubstantial' in another way in name alone as something [said] in praise, since they hold supremacy and religion[1] in opposite senses without straightforwardly[2] confessing the nature. For until even the [term] 'in nature' is freed from suspicion and has taken away the supremacy from the fear and the fear from the supremacy, [the supremacy] being supported by God, so that he may be glorified in heaven and on earth and [that there may be] glory in heaven and peace on earth[3] in the government of the affairs thereof, God ceases not to guide us and to teach us, just as those / who teach children, making use of plagues[4] and of protests which ought to teach us and to convince us that we err, and defending the silent and proving their victory.

For what have I done of these things which have happened as they have happened and not God himself? For because they have betrayed the tradition of the Fathers and have closed the mouth[s] of those who exacted the rights of the Fathers, so for this reason [some] of them have inclined unto Arianism according to what has been confessed [by them], and [others] of them unto Manichaeism, and [others] of them unto Judaism, and [others] of them unto other [errors, both] new and old. God has raised up of them and among them their own [judges], as he used to raise up judges from among the Jews, to confute them for their transgression against God, that is Flavian, who was representing me [in that] whereby he ought to have been my enemy, as indeed he was unto me both unwittingly or for some other reason, and Eusebius, who used to war against me. They have confessed without any cause for alarm, having warred against the adherents of Cyril, who were blaspheming and seeking to gain their ends.[5] And God abandoned them not until they showed hostility unto Cyril; since these indeed were citing his words against those, and those again were choosing those things / which were opposed to these and setting them against

---

[1] Syr. 'fear'.   [2] Syr. 'with *pār(h)ēsyâ*' (= Gk. παρρησία).
[3] Cp. Luke ii. 14.   [4] Literally: 'blows'.   [5] Literally: 'to prosper'.

them; and they were mutually disputing, the one [side] with the other. And these were saying that they were Manichaeans since they referred all things, even the properties of the flesh, unto God the Word. But these too were accusing those of holding my opinions, since I too say these [same] things, and of referring the properties of God to the nature of the divinity and the properties of the humanity to the humanity; and they admitted that the union took place in *prosôpon* and not in the nature. And every man was within a very little of disputing with his neighbour, protesting against him on my account, as though I was surely calumniated. And these my [words] were quoted with all zeal; and these were refuting them that were saying that I predicate two sons, as indeed was never said by me; and those were confuting them that were predicating one nature for calling God himself passible, as I was saying that they said.

Who was it that constrained them to say these [same] things as I, when through the commands [of the Emperor] their reading was prohibited,[1] since they were warring of themselves to discuss them with all zeal? And, when I was silent, and the authority to say them [had been] taken away from me, and I was not believed, God raised up those [men], who were believed when they said these [same] things as I, / which were the truth, without there being any suspicion therein of their having said these things out of friendship or out of love for me. And God brought not these things about on my account. For who is Nestorius? Or what is his life? Or what is his death in the world? But [he has brought them to pass] because of the truth which he has given unto the world, which was suppressed from deceitful causes, while he has also confuted the deceivers. And because they were [filled] with suspicion about me and were not believing what I was saying, as one that dissembles the truth and represses exact speech, God appointed for this [purpose] a preacher who was guiltless of this suspicion, Leo, who used to preach the truth undaunted. And, because the anticipation of the Council caused many to wonder and even the Romans them-

---

[1] Cp. Labbe (Mansi), v. 413-20.

selves,[1] [so] that they believed not the things which I was saying and which were left without examination, God allowed these things to come to pass contrariwise, that he might cause the bishop of Rome,[2] who was exercising the direction of the plotting of the Council in Ephesus against me, to pass away, and [that] he might make him [3] agree with and confirm what was said by the bishop of Constantinople.

And he who was able [to do] everything, that is Dioscorus, bishop of Alexandria, was reckoned as naught. I say indeed, as naught, since he had recourse to flight and was looking out [means] not to be deprived and banished into exile.[4] [These things took place] that through what they suffered / they might believe also what had been committed against me by the Egyptian in the former Council. And, because of the sham friendship of the Emperor and of the chiefs of the imperial household [toward me], I was suspected of constraining the Council, which stirred me not to be remiss in the truth, and of being constrained to agree with the Emperor because of what was committed against me, since, because they had held no examination about the truth, they suspected me of being a blasphemer. But God, in order that he might prove that the love which the Emperor had for me was treacherous, and [that it was felt by him] not for the truth but for the sake of [my] possessions, proved it by his [5] aid in [the affair of] Eutyches and in [that of] Flavian, whereby it was seen that he gave not [permission] for an assembly to be held, and those who were assembled permitted not aught to be said except what they were commanded [to say]; but they condemned themselves also in fear and in ignominy.

Again, because they supposed that my [doctrine] had been summoned to examination and to judgement, but [that] I was surely trifling [in saying] that they [had] summoned me not to judgement but to deposition and to a snare of destruction

---

[1] Literally: 'the *prosópon* of the Romans'.
[2] *Viz.* Celestinus. Nestorius apparently ignores Sixtus III.   [3] *Viz.* Leo.
[4] Syr. *'eksōryā* = Gk. ἐξορία. Dioscorus was deposed and exiled at the Council of Chalcedon. Nestorius shows no knowledge of this, but only mentions earlier precautionary measures. See introd. p. x.   [5] *Viz.* the Emperor's.

and of death, God, in protesting against them as being murderers, [even] God allowed Flavian to enter the Council and to suffer what he suffered at their hands; for it is evident that these were those things which the other had also committed against me aforetime. And, because it was supposed that those who had been bishops were disposed / to do naught outside the judgement which was pleasing unto them, either on account of the Emperor or out of fear or because of disturbances, God again exposed them as doing the contrary and confuted them before every man; and they let nothing be to which they bore not witness, but by all of them he had refuted the causes of error and preached them upon the roofs in such wise that there was not even a single excuse [left open] to those who feigned themselves without knowledge. Yet, just as Pharaoh was confuted by God by means of all things, and remained without excuse for not having been willing to be convinced either by the logic of words, or by the deeds themselves, or by the protest[s] of men, or again by the things of God, and for having died in his blasphemy, so also they remained without excuse. . . .

When therefore I had seen that these things were brought to pass by God, would you have wished that I should be silent and hide such a dispensation of God as all this? . . . . The prophets of God, who had been cursed as lying prophets by lying prophets as if by [true] prophets, would not have been distinguished [from the latter], unless they [had] consented to be cursed by lying prophets for the sake of God; the sons of those men would not have been worthy of the glory and the instruction of the prophets if they [had] kept agreement with the lying prophets. Nor would those of the Jews who became / Christians have been saved and rescued if they had kept to the oppressive judgement of their fathers against Christ as if [it had been delivered] by holy and righteous men. They would not have become the apostles of Christ if they had adhered to the whole crowd of Jews and to the priests and to the teachers of the law and to the chiefs as [unto true] teachers of the law and prophets. They would not have believed in Christ nor even have died for Christ, if they had supposed death and contempt [to be] not honour but contempt, nor yet would they have now been honoured by the crowds and by chiefs and by lords, if they had not endured death and shame at the hands of chiefs and peoples; they would not have been worthy of such as this on the part of emperors and chiefs and of powers, if they had kept the commands and the laws of emperors and of judges and of chiefs. Our fathers would not have been reckoned orthodox in this and doctors, if they had sought to flee from the condemnation of the Council of the heretics and to say the things which they were saying, and had been hypocrites. We should not have been worthy of the instruction resulting from the labours of these men, if we had accepted without examination the agreement [which was reached], as if by a Council, against them.

And, that I may speak briefly, Meletius and Eustathius [1] would not have been bishops of Antioch, if they had accepted the choice and the judgement / of the Council of the heretics against them, nor would Athanasius [2] be bishop of Alexandria if he were to accept the judgement of those who deprived him without hesitation and as [if it proceeded] from the orthodox. John [3] would not be bishop of Constantinople, if he were to accept the judgement and the deprivation which was [promulgated] against him without examination as [if it proceeded] from a Council; nor again would Flavian have been bishop of Constantinople, if he were to agree to the pronouncement of the Oecumenical Council which deprived him as a pronouncement [proceeding] from an [Oecumenical] Council. Every one, of whatsoever city it may be, who has suffered therein on my account, would not be giving light, even as the sun, if I

---

[1] Eustathius, Bishop of Antioch, 324-31, returned from Nicaea a strong supporter of the Nicene faith, and was deposed and exiled through the influence of Eusebius of Caesarea in 330 or 331. He died in exile at Philippi in 337.

Meletius, Bishop of Antioch, 361-79, was deposed by Arian influence; the Arian Euzoius was appointed in his place, and schism followed.

[2] Athanasius, Bishop of Alexandria, 326-73, was exiled in 336, 340, 356, and 362.

[3] John Chrysostom, Bishop of Constantinople, 398-404, was exiled in the latter year through the intrigues of Theophilus of Alexandria.

had looked towards my accusers and not towards God and [if] also I had not been deemed worthy to be [given a share] in those things, every single one of which had been [brought to pass] by God; for this affair was not mine but Christ's who made me mighty. But every man will give account unto God concerning the things which he has said or brought to pass or done to cause scandal, or [wherein] he has been zealous with all zeal to make scandals to cease; but if, when a man does everything, he who is scandalized is not to be persuaded, let him be scandalized on his own account and not on account of him who says and cries out unto him and is not heard by him.

But, because many were blaming me many times / for not having written unto Leo, bishop of Rome, to teach him all the things which were committed, such as came to pass, and the change of faith, as if unto a man who is correct in his faith, especially when there had been given unto me, [even] unto me, a part of the letter relating to the judgement concerning Flavian and Eutyches, wherein it was revealed that [he feared][1] not the friendship of [his] majesty, for this reason I wrote not, not because I am a proud man and senseless, but so that I might not hinder from his running him who was running fairly because of the prejudice against my person.[2] But I was content to endure the things whereof they accused me, in order that, while I was accused thereof, they might accept without hindrance the teaching of the Fathers; for I have no word [to say] concerning what was committed against me. And further I wrote not for the purpose that I, to whom for many years there was not one [moment of] repose nor human solace, might not be suspected of surely fleeing from the contest, fearing the labours [thereof]; for sufficient are the wrongs that have come upon the world [and] which are more able than I to make the oppression of the true faith shine forth in the eyes of every man.

But, because thou blamest me as though I have failed to say clearly the things which have occurred, O chief of the saints, / Sophronius,[3] hear therefore also the things which thou

---

[1] See crit. n., p. 402.   [2] Syr. *parṣôphâ*.   [3] See above, p. 10, n. 2.

knowest and testifiest concerning the truth of the things which are said. For immediately, as indeed thou art persuaded, thou hast first seen that death has carried off the daughter of him who was then reigning,[1] and thereafter, thou seest, that demon, the chief of adultery, who cast down the empress with insult and contumely.[2] Again [thou seest] that the cities of Africa and of Spain and of Muzicanus[3] and great and glorious islands—I mean Sicily and Rhodes and many other great ones—and Rome itself have been delivered over for spoil unto the barbarian Vandal.[4] Yet there will however be in the first place and at no longer distance [of time] a second coming of the barbarian against Rome itself, during which also Leo, who has indeed held well to the faith but has agreed to the things which these have unjustly committed against me without examination and without judgement, will deliver up with his own hands the divine vessels of the sanctuary into the hands of the barbarians and will see with his [own] eyes the daughters of the emperor who is reigning at that time led into captivity.[5] But I have endured the torment of my life and all my [fate] in this world as the torment of one day and lo! I have now already got me / to [the time of my] dissolution, and daily every day I beseech God to accomplish my dissolution, whose eyes have seen the salvation of God.

Conclusion. Rejoice for me, O desert, my beloved and my foster-parent and the home of my habitation, and my mother

[1] This cannot be Eudoxia, the daughter of Theodosius and Eudocia, for she was still living in 455 (see the *Chronicon Paschale* in Migne, *P. G.* xcii. 817 A), but must be her younger sister Flaccilla, who died in 431. See Du Cange, *Hist. Byz.* (Paris, 1680), p. 71.

[2] Theodosius had Paulinus executed in 444 on suspicion of adultery with the Empress Eudocia; see the *Chronicon Paschale*, Migne, *P. G.* xcii. 801-5.

[3] See crit. n., p. 402.

[4] According to the *Chronicon Paschale* (Migne, *P. G.* xcii. 797 C, 801 A, B). The Vandals entered Africa in 428 and Sicily in 439.

[5] John of Malala is probably wrong in placing the capture of Eudoxia and her daughters before the death of Theodosius (Migne, *P. G.* xcvii. 545). According to the *Chronicon Paschale*, they were taken by Gensericus who entered Rome in 455 (Migne, *P. G.* xcii. 816-17), but he was persuaded by Leo to spare the lives of the citizens and the buildings, though the city was plundered and the sacred vessels carried off which Titus had brought from Jerusalem (Prosper, *Chronicon*, Migne, *P. L.* li. 605-6).

[the land of] my exile, who even after my death will guard my body unto the resurrection by the will of God.   Amen.

Finished is the writing of the book which is entitled the Bazaar of Heracleides, composed by [him who is] illustrious among the saints and all-blessed, my lord Nestorius, bishop of Constantinople, a witness every day and the pride of orthodoxy, a true preacher of the glorious Trinity.   And unto Yahweh [be] unfailing glory.   Amen.

APPENDICES

I. *Fragments*

THE translation of the fragments is made from the text given on pp. 365-88 of F. Loofs, *Nestoriana: Die Fragmente des Nestorius* (Halle, 1905).

A. LETTERS

XI c. Fragm. 258. *From the letter to Alexander of Hierapolis.* But the property which [exists] in the nature of the divinity and [that which exists in that] of the humanity is indeed distinct from everlasting. For this reason Paul, the teacher of the churches, not in placing 'God' first and then adding 'in flesh', but in saying either 'Son' or 'Christ' first, makes 'in flesh' follow at the end: 'Concerning the Son who was of the seed of David in flesh' and again: 'Of whom [was] Christ in flesh,' nowhere at all saying God first, making 'in flesh' follow, but Christ or Son.[1]

XII. Fragm. 276. *From the letter to Theodoret, wherein he blames what was written by Cyril to the Easterns.* For what does he say? Although the diversity of the natures, from which the ineffable union was brought about, is ignored, this [phrase] 'from which' again [is] as if he were speaking in respect to the Lord's natures of parts of one another which became one. For he ought to have said not 'from these' but 'of those [it is] that we say that an ineffable union was brought about'. For the ineffable union is not of the natures but the things of the natures.[2]

Fragm. 290 is identical with Fragm. 276, except for slight differences in orthography.

Fragm. 310. *From what he wrote unto Theodoret from exile, speaking thus about Cyril.* For what does he say? Although the diversity of the natures is known, from which

---

[1] See *op. cit.*, pp. 196–7 and 365.
[2] See *op. cit.*, pp. 197–8 and 365–6.

Fragments

we say that an ineffable union was brought about: Behold! again 'from which' as if he were speaking concerning our Lord's.... which became one. For he ought to have said not 'from them'[1] but 'of those'.... for not of the natures....[2]

Fragm. 226. *For he wrote from exile unto Theodoret, blaming what had been written by the Holy Cyril unto the bishops of the East. And thus Nestorius concludes:* For what does he say: Although the diversity of the natures is known, of which we say that an ineffable union was brought about....[3]

Fragm. 243. *But then Nestorius, rebuking from exile the patriarch*[4] *Cyril, wrote unto Theodoret:* Here with a view to dissembling [the truth] he confounds the properties of the natures.[5]

Fragm. 253. *After the deposition of Theodoret took place, Nestorius wrote thus to him.* Surely I have borne what thou hast become; I have not left [it] alone. For not when I was far removed from the assembly of the impious did I then show myself an enemy to the throne of the fear of God. For not even Paul, when he was stoning Stephen with the stoning Jews, was then an Apostle but when he removed himself afar from stoning. When thou too seest proof herein, although thou wast brought up in godly learning, exult, I counsel [thee] and deck thyself out in this time which now is, being head and all with them that are victorious on behalf of religion and, exulting, say these [words] of David: 'Mine is Gilead and mine is Manasseh, and Ephraim is the support of my head.' But lay hold of the departure from Egypt and believe, since thou hearest, in God who now calls unto thy Piety with a loud voice: 'What hast thou to do in the way of Egypt, to drink the waters of Gihon?'[6] For the people [that is] striving with God is from the beginning and is warring with the holy fathers.[7]

---

[1] Frag. 219: from those.
[2] See *op. cit.*, p. 366.
[3] See *op. cit.*, pp. 197-8 and 366.
[4] Syr. 'father'.
[5] See *op. cit.*, pp. 198 and 366.
[6] Cp. Jer. ii. 18; the Hebr. text as well as the Pesh. have 'the waters of Shihor'.
[7] See *op. cit.*, pp. 201-2 and 367.

B. MISCELLANEOUS WORKS

II c. Fragm. 208. *Records which were forged by him in Ephesus, concerning which he wrote thus: About what took place at the Council at Ephesus and the cause which brought about its assembling Nestorius says these things:* This was not supposed by any one of the [followers] of Apollinarius or of Arius just as also these [believe: namely] the [fact] that they mingle the quality of the natures in one nature.[1]

Fragm. 305. *In these records which were forged by him at Ephesus he wrote thus:* This was not supposed; and not by any .... they mingle.[2]

III. Fragm. 225. *For in the book which is inscribed 'Unto the Theopaschitans or Cyrillians' he wrote in the form of question and answer things which have been taken up by us in what was investigated before, Nestorius [says]:* The Theopaschitan says: Now as we are rebuked [on account of] the dual composition of the natures, we who predicate one nature of Christ which is [that] of God made flesh—in regard to the reprimand [uttered] against thee thou hopest not for any defence against the reprimand which is uttered; for thou hast confessed that you obtained for Christ one nature out of what is without bodily form and [what is without] body and a one-natured *hypostasis* of the becoming flesh of the divinity. But such is the mingling of the two natures, that those natures are deprived of the *hypostases* which they solely possess, being mingled with one another; and yet above, as the foolish theory which he has forged necessitates,[3] he introduces the Theopaschitan who says these things: 'For the nature of the flesh is passible and changeable newly created;[4] yet [it is] thus on the contrary the godhead's very own, as both of them subsist[5] in one and the same nature.'[6]

Fragm. 307. *And in the homily [called] 'the Dialogue' against the Cyrillians, as he required, he introduced the Theo-*

---
[1] See *op. cit.*, p. 208.   [2] See *op. cit.*, p. 368.   [3] Literally: 'wishes'.
[4] Fragm. 307: and the nature [is] newly created.
[5] Fragm. 307: 'in an identity of natural quality' (*sc.* ἰσοφυία).
[6] See *op. cit.*, pp. 209, 210, and 369.

paschitan who says thus: For I have confessed .... mingled with one another. *And again before this, as was pleasing unto him, he brought in the Theopaschitan who says thus:* For the nature of the flesh is passible....¹

Fragm. 304. *Likewise, and in the work which [was addressed] to the Theopaschitans, namely the Cyrillians, he wrote thus:* If our dividing of these properties of the flesh or the Son and of his divinity is named a kind of addition of quaternity on our side, what prohibits also the incarnation² itself of the Son from being passed over in silence as far as concerns you, because the Trinity accepts not the *ousia* which makes the man³ as any addition. For without the *ousia* which was made man⁴ no one understands that which has made the man.⁵ *And again:* To confuse the properties of the nature of that which was made⁴ and of that which made the man⁴ is very impious.⁶

Fragm. 239. *Unto the Theopaschitans or ¦Cyrillians in the form of question and answer Nestorius [wrote] thus:* There is indeed one Son, equal in *ousia* to the Father, just as thou hast well said before; but the natures of the Son, in accordance with the identity of *ousia* of the Father and of ours, are divided by the distinction in the mind.⁷

Fragm. 220 is identical with Fragm. 239, except that the introduction is only: '*Nestorius [wrote thus].*'

Fragm. 309. *The homily [called] 'the Dialogue' against the Cyrillians: he wrote thus:* By 'Christ' or 'Only-begotten' or 'Jesus' or 'Son' or by other [terms] such as these we preach the term of the union, but by 'man' the *ousia* which was assumed and by 'God the Word' the property of the *hypostasis* which was made man.⁸

VI. Fragm. 205 a. *Again, from his distinct Chapters against those who say that Christ is God alone:* They say that Christ is God alone, and behold! God is the Trinity; therefore Christ is the Trinity. But, if Christ is God alone, while the Father

---
¹ See *op. cit.*, p. 369.   ² *Sc.* σάρκωσις.
³ *Sc.* ἀνθρωπίζει.   ⁴ *Sc.* ἐνηνθρώπησεν.   ⁵ *Sc.* ἠνθρώπισεν.
⁶ See *op. cit.*, pp. 210 and 369–70.   ⁷ See *op. cit.*, pp. 210 and 370.
⁸ *Sc.* ἐνηνθρώπησεν. See *op. cit.*, pp. 211 and 370.

is not Christ, we thus distinguish them in the nature. [So much the more is it] that Christ is the name not of the essence but of the dispensation. And Christ is God, but God is not Christ.[1]

Fragm. 205 b. *Again, his [Chapters]:* Unto him who asks who it was that walked upon the water we answer that it was the feet that were walking and the concrete bodily frame through the strength that dwelled therein. This [it is] that is a [cause of] wonder. For if God were walking upon the water, that is not astonishing, as also [it is] not in the air. And the [fact] again that the concrete body came in through closed doors—this too is [matter] for astonishment. But, if the divine nature came in, it is nothing that I should desist from what belongs to the infinite.[2]

Fragm. 205 c. *Again, his [Chapters]:* They ask, [saying] that it is written: 'My God, my God, why hast thou forsaken me?' What is this? Does he speak the truth or does he lie? If he is left alone, where then is the infinity of God? If he is not left alone, he has therefore lied. What then do we say—that he neglected to let it[3] suffer for its[3] sake, in order that he might leave him to adhere to us that the dispensation might be fulfilled?[4]

C. HOMILIES

VI. Fragm. 254. *From the books of Nestorius; blasphemies. From the homily against the Jews, of which the commencement is this:* 'How great is the might of him who was crucified,' cry out the devils who possess not that which they used to possess.

And after other things: Dost thou not hear what these say .... who are warring and falling and they convince him that is abhorred of the judgement concerning the people? We indeed rebuke not in anything; [but] dost thou not tremble to surpass the proper measure? Dost thou not judge that excess of praise exaggerated beyond what is proper is worthy of censure? Dost thou not hear what a child,

---

[1] See *op. cit.*, pp. 218 and 371.
[2] *I.e.* possibly 'the infinity'. See *op. cit.*, pp. 218-19 and 371.
[3] Fem. [4] See *op. cit.*, pp. 219 and 371.

Fragments

praising [thee], says on thine account? For they saw not him who was concealed in the visible.[1]

VIII. Fragm. 270-272. *From another homily, of which the commencement is this*: There is nothing harder to the souls of men than the sickness of ignorance.[2]

Fragm. 270. *And after other things*: But I know not how of a sudden they, being sick with ignorance, have been found [as those] who are equal with them that have not heard; and somehow they err with an astonishing error, not being placed with the heretics as were the lovers of the church, and have fallen away as heretics from the teachings of the church. But these are wretched rather than heretics; for these indeed make God the Word younger than the essence[3] of the Father, while they even make bold to blaspheme with similes; for in the nature of the divinity youngness of existence and age of days are not.[4]

Fragm. 271. Of the mediator then the mother is she that bore Christ, the Virgin; but the divinity of the mediator existed before she bare the mediator. How then did she bear one older than her[self]? Why dost thou prepare God the Word for the creation of the spirit? For, if God the Word is he who was born of her but he who was born of her exists according to the word of the angels from the Holy Spirit, God the Word is to be celebrated as a creation of the Spirit.[5]

And again: If thou conceivest of him who in the nature was born of the Virgin in the course of months, so [is] he man who was born of a virgin according to the word of him who was born, who said: 'Why seek ye to kill me, a man who has spoken the truth among you?' *And again*: 'One 'is God, one also the mediator of God and men, the man 'Jesus Christ, a man who was born of the race of David.'[6]

Fragm. 272. *And after other things*: Hear both things: Paul preaching: 'Of the Jews is Christ who was in flesh.'

---

[1] See *op. cit.*, pp. 243 and 372.
[2] See *op. cit.*, p. 372 (cp. p. 245, ll. 1-2).
[3] Syr. *'ithûthâ*.
[4] See *op. cit.*, pp. 245 and 373.
[5] See *op. cit.*, pp. 247 and 373.
[6] See *op. cit.*, pp. 247-8 and 373.

What then? A mere man is Christ, O blessed Paul? No; but 'a man on the one hand is Christ in flesh, in the divinity on the other hand God over all '.[1]

X. Fragm. 300. *An homily delivered by Nestorius against the Theopaschitans:* As in regard to the abuses [uttered] against the true and natural union—as that which we [2] say: that the flesh vanished and was transformed by the nature of the Word, as an eddy of water which the sea swallows up—*as Nestorius himself says:* A statue without bulk of water, which vanishes at once in the vastness of the sea.[3]

XII. Fragm. 297. *And in the homily which is inscribed 'The kingdom of heaven is like unto a certain king which made a banquet for his son',[4] and so on; and about the Incarnation, of which the commencement is:* Fearful and pleasant is the trumpet for the reading of the Gospel. *This he wrote.*

The union then of the natures is not divided: the *ousias* of these, which are united, are divided. This [consists] not in the annulling [5] of the union but in the understanding of the flesh and of the divinity.[6] Hear the same clearly:[7] Christ [8] is indivisible in that [he is] Christ [9] but double [10] in that [he is] God and man; in the sonship simple, [but] double [11] in that which he has put on and in that which is put on; sole in the *prosôpon* of the Son, [but], as in [the case of] the two eyes,[12] dissimilar in the natures of the divinity and of the humanity; for we know not two Christs or Sons or an original and a new only-begotten, nor a first and a second Christ, but one and the same who is visible in nature created and not created.[13]

Fragm. 308. For we know not two Christs or Sons or only-begottens or Lords; nor one and another Son nor an

---

[1] See *op. cit.*, pp. 248 and 373.
[2] *Viz.* the Monophysites.
[3] See *op. cit.*, pp. 131 and 374.
[4] Matt. xxii. 2 (Pesh.).
[5] Fragm. 221: divided, not in the annulling.
[6] Fragm. 221: in the consideration of the divinity and of the humanity.
[7] Fragm. 221: very evidently indeed.
[8] Fragm. 241: and Christ.
[9] Fragm. 221: in that he is Christ.
[10] Fragm. 221: twofold.
[11] Fragm. 221 and 241: but double.
[12] Fragm. 221: as in [the case of] two eyes.
[13] See *op. cit.*, pp. 279–80 and 374. Fragm. 241 has σύνθετος in the margin against 'double' and δυικός against 'twofold' (*v. l.*).

original and a new only-begotten nor a first and a second Christ, but one and the same who is visible in the invisible and the visible nature. Can a man, when he hears these things, say that something else was said by him and by those at Chalcedon and by Leo? For openly he is bold and knows the same Christ who is visible in the invisible and the visible nature nor has said two Christs and two sons and Lords. And the Council of Chalcedon said: 'One and the same 'Christ, son, lord, only-begotten, in two natures, not change-'ably, not confusedly, not divisibly.'[1]

Fragm. 312. For we know not two Christs or two sons or Lords nor original and new only-begotten nor a first and a second Christ but one and the same, who is visible in the uncreated and the created nature.[2]

Fragm. 292. Christ in that [he is] Christ is not divided; for we have not two Christs or two sons, for there is not with us a first and a second Christ nor one and another, nor again one son and again another; but the son is double not by authority but by nature. *And again:* Preserving then without confusion the adherence of the natures.[3]

Fragm. 285. Who is visible in the created and the uncreated nature.[2]

Fragm. 287 is identical except for the omission of one enclitic pronoun.

XIV. Fragm. 262-264. *From another homily which is called 'the Explanation of the Teaching', of which the commencement is this:* Not with clamour do I judge the love which is toward me but with longing for the teaching of the faith.[4]

Fragm. 262. *And after other things:* Again, I say it clearly: not an ordinary danger is ignorance of the teaching of the faith. And I see that many indeed in our assemblies have modesty and ardent piety but slip out of ignorance respecting the teaching of the faith. But this is no rebuke for the people but—[to speak] as one who will say it suitably—[it is] because

---

[1] See *op. cit.*, p. 375.
[2] See *op. cit.*, p. 376.
[3] See *op. cit.*, pp. 281 and 376.
[4] See *op. cit.*, pp. 282 and 376.

the teachers have not time to set before you the exact teaching of the faith.¹ Our Lord Christ then in his divinity is consubstantial with the Father and the creator of the blessed Mary; for he is the maker of all. But in his manhood he is the son of the blessed Mary; yet he is our Lord Christ, who is double in his divinity and in his manhood. But for this reason also I turn aside from ornate speech because [so] I shall be understood by [my] hearers. Our Lord Christ, who is double in his divinity and in his humanity, is one Son by adhesion. One then is he [who] was born of Mary that bare Christ, the Son of God. Many times do I say the same things, because [so] thou wilt not again, when thou goest forth, calumniate the Word. Remember, I pray, what is said by you; for there are many calumniators. I extol praise for piety, but I require the Trinity. He then who was born of Mary that bare Christ is one Son of God; but the Son of God is double in the natures: God and man. Here sharpen for me your hearing. For here is a [cause of] trespass for them on whom is laid the *prosôpon* of piety; for they say that the bishop calls Christ a mere man. Then behold! how many witnesses [there are] to what is said! Our Lord Christ is God and man. I call not Christ a mere man, O excellent [man], but one adhering to God the Word.²

Fragm. 263. *And after other things:* That then which I was saying: 'I believe in one God'—that belief possesses the common name of the natures: 'in one God Almighty, maker of all things made, visible and invisible.' Give heed therefore from here [onwards] with [all] exactness: 'and in one Lord Jesus Christ the Son of God.' Give heed, I would persuade [you], to what is said: The fathers were able to say: 'I believe also in one God the Word the Son of God, who was begotten of the Father.'³

And again: The blessed and holy company⁴ of the Fathers takes up the name of our Lord Christ and calls him the creator of all, consubstantial with the Father. None was able to rebuke [thee] and say: 'Thou sayest that he who

---
¹ See above, p. 264. ² See *op. cit.*, pp. 282-4 and 377.
³ See *op. cit.*, pp. 284 and 377-8. ⁴ Syr. *tegmâ* = Gk. τάγμα.

'was born yesterday is consubstantial with the Father. But
'the title which has been laid down, which indicates both the
'divinity and the humanity—but we mean that of "Christ"—
'makes the fathers hold both of them true. Consubstantial
'with the Father is Christ: this is true; for in the divinity
'he is eternal. Consubstantial with us [is he] naturally: this
'is true; for he too was a man as we also [are]. Again how
'many times is exception taken to the saying, if an heretic
'is near and says: "Behold!" he says "man as we also [are]"
'and introduces our Lord [as] a mere [man]!'[1]

Fragm. 264. *And after other things*: I believe in one Lord Jesus Christ the only-begotten Son of God; for God the Word is not distinct from him.

And after other things: Many times am I forced to say the same things. For I fear those who change the words 'in one Lord Jesus Christ the only-begotten Son of God who was begotten by the Father before all worlds'. Behold! thou hast [there] a birth before all worlds. Can what was born before all the worlds be born another time?

And after other things: Give heed to the words. Believe; I lie not in what I say. These things have been said of me by some of the reverent clergy: 'My lord bishop is blaming God.' Until I came none of us took notice of the words of the bishops of Nicaea, that we are saying these things.

And after other things: For this reason, where the Word is laid down, the birth from a woman is not laid down, but [it is laid down] thus: 'And the Word became flesh'; he says not: 'And the Word was born through the flesh.' For this would have been for us to introduce a second birth of the divinity.[2]

XXI. Fragm. 306. *'About the Faith' or 'the Deposit of the Faith'*. But if those Theopaschitans, while holding true the religion of Apollinarius, were to say that one nature showed itself after the union, is it proper for us with much indignation to turn our faces from them because they impiously alienate the two natures from their properties in consequence of the

---

[1] See *op. cit.*, pp. 284-5 and 378. [2] See *op. cit.*, pp. 285-8 and 378.

mixture and the confusion? They therefore as far as concerns them let neither the divine [nature] in that it [exists] nor the human persist in that each one of them falls away from its own *ousia* through the mixture and the confusion and is altered into the other. But if they say that the natures are of necessity neither mixed nor confused, they are constrained to concede not one nature of Christ but two, impassible and passible; and there is established the dogma, accounted true: [that the nature] of the Trinity is of the same *ousia*[1] with the impassible divinity.[2]

Fragm. 216. Not one nature but two are we constrained to concede in Christ.[3]

Fragm. 215. One and the same which is visible in the nature not created and created.[4]

And again: Not one nature but two are we constrained to concede in Christ.[5]

Fragm. 209. *But also in the homily which is inscribed 'About the Faith' or 'the Deposit of the Faith': that which is the commencement thereof we confess, [namely] the dogma 'of one* ousia'. *He wrote thus:* But if we were to say ... of both of them that there are before the union as in a story two natures. They are to be understood as if in a temporal comparison.[6] This [it is] which was said by the holy Cyril to Nestorius.[7]

Fragm. 291. 'About the Faith', namely 'the Deposit of the Faith'. Because in all of them those two natures also, complete and not transformed[8] nor distinguished, are seen in our Lord Christ and every nature acknowledges these things [as] its own. ...

And again: In consequence of these which are known as one Christ[9] in two natures, God and man, the visible and the

---

[1] Sc. ὁμοούσιος.
[2] See *op. cit.*, pp. 329 and 379.
[3] See *op. cit.*, p. 379.
[4] See *op. cit.*, pp. 330 and 379.
[5] See *op. cit.*, p. 379.
[6] Loofs: *wir verstehen, dass es zwei Naturen [seien] wie in einer Erzählung vor der Einigung, welche ist wie in einer zeitlichen Vergleichung.*
[7] See *op. cit.*, pp. 329, n., and 379.
[8] Fragm. 224, 228, and 229: confused.
[9] Fragm. 228 and 229: one son.

Fragments

invisible, he will hold the future judgement.[1] As there is one judge in the two natures,[2] so also in every one of the natures is there one Son, because according to the decision of the Apostles that invisible [nature], God the Word, is about to hold the judgement in a visible man whom he has raised even from the dead; and there is one judge in every one of the natures, just as also [there is] one Son in the two natures.[3]

Fragm. 277 is identical with Fragm. 291.

Fragm. 224. And each one acknowledges these things as its own. *And in another place:* What we have also laid down among the things which have been examined before: one and the same which is visible in the uncreated and the created nature.[4]

Fragm. 223. One and the same which is visible in the uncreated and the created nature; and because in everything those two natures also, complete and not confused and not far apart, are seen in our Lord Christ and every one acknowledges these things [as] its own. . . .[4]

Fragm. 228. But one and the same which is visible in the uncreated and the created nature.[4]

Fragm. 229. *And again in another homily which is inscribed 'On account of the Faith', namely 'the Deposit of the Faith' of which the commencement is: 'We confess the dogma " of one ousia ",' Nestorius [says]:* Because in all of them . . . .[5] (continued as in Fragm. 291).

Fragm. 280. *Concerning Nestorius' having said 'one* prosôpon *out of two [natures]': his own [words] from the homily which is called 'Concerning the Faith'.* For harm was not done to the uniqueness of the Son by the diversity of the natures. But in such wise as the corruptible body is one thing and further the immortal soul is another thing, yet one man is constituted of them both, so from the mortal and the immortal, from the corruptible and from the incorruptible, and from what is subject to beginning and from the nature which

---
[1] Loofs: *wird das zukünftige Gericht abhalten.*
[2] Fragm. 228 and 229: in each one of the natures.
[3] See *op. cit.*, pp. 330 and 380. [4] See *op. cit.*, p. 380. [5] See *op. cit.*, pp. 380-1.

has no beginning, that is of God the Word, I confess one *prosôpon* of the Son.[1]

XXII. Fragm. 256. *From another homily which is inscribed 'Concerning the Learning', of which the commencement is this:* Behold! already the time of the holy mysteries is nigh. *And after other things:* One is the temple which was made by the Holy Spirit and another is God, who sanctifies the temple; and the one indeed can be destroyed, while the other accepts not [its] destruction but even restores that which is destroyed, him who is hung upon the cross and after three days is built anew.[2]

XXIII. Fragm. 314. *From the homily which is inscribed 'When the [passage]: How many times, if my brother sins against me, shall I forgive him? is read:'*[3] But I, that is the person[4] of the Church for all of them,[5] unto whom I speak, before every man,[6] lay down[7] one and the same, naming Christ a whole[8] God and a whole[8] man, natures which are not mixed[9] but which are united.[10]

Fragm. 289. *In the homily which is inscribed 'About the [passage]: The kingdom of heaven (was) is likened unto a certain king' and so on, he said thus:* But I, that is the person[4] of the Church, for all of them unto whom I speak say the same unto every man, naming whole man and whole God, natures which are not mixed but which are united.[11]

XXIV. Fragm. 265-267. *From another homily, of which the commencement is this:* Although there is among men some great vehemence of impiety. . . .

---

[1] Or: that is, I confess that God the Word [is] one *prosôpon* of the Son (Loofs). See *op. cit.*, pp. 330-1 and 381.

[2] See *op. cit.*, pp. 331 and 381.

[3] Matt. xviii. 21 Fragm. 228 (as introduction): for he said in another book of his. Fragm. 217: as Nestorius has written.

[4] Syr. *parṣôphà* (= Gk. πρόσωπον).

[5] Fragm. 228: those; Fragm. 230 and 294: these.

[6] Fragm. 228: before all of them.

[7] Fragm. 228: I propose; Fragm. 217: I prove.   [8] Fragm. 228: complete.

[9] Fragm. 228: divided.

[10] Fragm. 228: not mixed but united. See *op. cit.*, pp. 332 and 382.

[11] See *op. cit.*, p. 383.

Fragm. 265. *And after other things: For there was seen by him,* I say, *an angel from heaven which strengthened him;*[1] but it strengthened him as many times as the picture of agony[2] was stirred up in our Lord who alone could [suffer] in the sufferings of him who was visible. *And after other things:* This one thing thou lackest only, that thou shouldest be led as a lamb to the slaughter and be silent as a sheep before the shearer.[3] This is the summit of thy [qualities] illustrious and divine and the height of honours worthy of adoration and the great mystery of the victories over Satan. For when thou tastest death, thou dost cause death to die, when thou goest down to Sheol, thou dost liberate the dead; when thou art crucified with robbers, through these thou dost seize the day of sinners. Thou desirest not, O Lord, death which is victorious; the cross [it is] which fills a short time, death fills a time, the grave three days. But the lordship of an everlasting kingdom in heaven—these are after the grave. All these things, O Theopaschitan, thou makest into parables and into 'he suffered an impassible suffering', as thou sayest. For he who suffers impassibly has no need of things to strengthen him; for why should it have been required that he who suffers not with suffering should need strengthening?[4]

Fragm. 266. *And after unimportant things:* For just as is my opinion concerning the suffering, such also is it concerning the resurrection; as [is the doctrine] that thou givest death to be destroyed, which is the truth, so is this: that thou givest also the resurrection which has destroyed death. For if the suffering of the divinity is an impassible suffering, so is the destruction of the suffering an indestructive destruction. For with the newness of the words [spoken] by them concerning the teaching of the faith I am forced to coin new words for new terms.[5]

Fragm. 267. *And after other things: Why are you disturbed and [why] do thoughts arise in your hearts? See my*

---
[1] Lk. xxii. 43.   [2] Syr. 'agónā (= Gk. ἀγών, ἀγωνία).
[3] Cp. Isaiah liii. 7, Acts viii. 32.   [4] See *op. cit.*, pp. 332-3 and 383-4.
[5] See *op. cit.*, pp. 333-4 and 384.

hands and my feet, that [*it is I who*] *have come; touch me and see. A spirit has not flesh and bones as ye see that I have.*[1] Why then, in letting the hands and feet of him who suffered be felt and teaching therefrom the resurrection as he has commanded, dost thou touch the nature that cannot be touched as though it has suffered? Why changest thou the sacrifice of the Lord? Why dost thou sacrifice instead of the lamb him who has raised up the sheep that was slain? Instead of the sheep thou slayest the divinity which has accepted the sacrifice of the sheep. If thou slayest the divinity as a sheep, thou makest the power of the sacrifice a dead thing. For this reason had John, when he saw our Lord, said: '*Behold! the Lamb of God*,'[2] not: 'Behold! the lamb God.' For he who is visible is the lamb and he who is concealed is God. These [properties] of the natures are distinguished.

And after other things: As lord of the hosts of the angels with God the Word is he who is visible; for *he has given him,* he says, *a name which is more excellent than all names, that at the name of Jesus every knee shall bow of those in heaven and of those on earth,* and so on.[3] But with him who [was] visible God the Word was not strengthened by the voice of an angel at the season of the suffering. The flesh possessed with God the Word the authority of a judge; *for God,* he says, *has appointed a day wherein he will judge the world in justice in the man whom he hath appointed, giving the faith to every man in that he has raised him from the dead.*[4]

XXV. Fragm. 257. *From another homily,*[5] *of which the commencement was:*[6] All hearts which longing for God has seized beforehand and which none of the things which are of this world either afflict or elate. . . .

And after other things: If he said: 'Who was born of Mary?' I return answer unto him at once: 'The man who adheres to God, the man who is honoured above all men on account of God who adheres to him.

---

[1] Lk. xxiv. 38-9.   [2] Jn. i. 29.   [3] Phil. ii. 9, 10.
[4] Acts xvii. 31. See *op. cit.*, pp. 334-5 and 384-5.
[5] Fragm. 313: from the homily.   [6] Fragm. 313: is.

And again: I have said 'the Son' and I have confessed the two brief [phrases], both 'the created nature' and 'the uncreated'. The power of the Lord's flesh and of his divinity [is] the same;[1] the same is the adoration of him who appears and of him who appears not.

And after unimportant [*things*]: But both of them[1] have one and the very same authority. The angels therefore see him who appears and with him adore him who is concealed in him who appears; for there is no distinction [of him] from him who appears with honour but only in the property of the nature.[2]

Fragm. 302. *For that unjust man in the exposition concerning the* [*passage*]: '*I have not spoken of mine own will*'[3] *and so on, wrote thus:* The Son is not to be entitled 'God the Word' distinctly nor yet man distinctly; for this is indeed nothing else than to construct two natures. But the term 'sonship' is common to both the natures. I have said 'the Son'; two natures have I indicated. I have said 'Christ' and have not divided either of the natures in the sonship.[4]

D. FRAGMENTS OF UNCERTAIN LOCATION

XIV. Fragm. 231. He who said: '*My God, my God, why hast thou forsaken me?*'[5] was human nature,[6] O wise man.[7]

Fragm. 237 b. *And again in another place he said, as I have deposed above:* He who said .... was human nature, O wise man.[8]

XV. Fragm. 210. *In the homily* '*On account of the Incarnation*' *Nestorius wrote thus:* I hold then to the two natures in the one title 'Christ', because the one[9] is not known apart from the other.[10]

XVI. Fragm. 242 a. *For if we were to have said, as Nestorius:* A man who, complete in his own *hypostasis*, in honour and by mercy only adheres to the Word.[11]

---

[1] Fragm. 286 and 313: is the same.   [2] See *op. cit.*, pp. 335–6 and 385.
[3] Jn. xii. 49.   [4] See *op. cit.*, pp. 336 and 386.
[5] Mt. xxvii. 46.   [6] Fragm. 233: the nature of the humanity.
[7] See *op. cit.*, pp. 360 and 387.   [8] See *op. cit.*, p. 387.
[9] *Viz.* the Word.   [10] *Viz.* the man Christ. See *op. cit.*, pp. 361 and 387.
[11] See *op. cit.*, pp. 361 and 388.

XVII. Fragm. 244 a. *But, as Nestorius, in predicating two natures in one Christ, began*: It is known to all of them who hear and are willing to speak the truth.[1]

[XVIII]. Fragm. 296. And simultaneously he shows in what capacities he calls Christ one, that is, in authority and in greatness; for they define the gift of sonship [as] the source[2] of authority.[3]

II. *Critical Notes*

P. 3 (2). Nau proposes ܪܘܚܐ 'of the spirit' for .. ܪܘ, which is all that can be read on the MS.

3 (2). As the verb ܪܓ 'gazed upon,' has no Pa'el, Mrs. Margoliouth suggests ܡܪܕܝ 'intoxicated (by the smoke)', *i.e.* asphyxiated.

6 (4). Read, ܐܝܢܐ 'what' for ܐܝܕܐ 'hand', which yields no sense (Bedjan).

10 (15). Read ܒܣܪܐ 'flesh' for ܒܪܐ 'son'.

12 (18). Read ܡܬܩܕܫܬܐ for ܡܬܩܕܫܬܐ, which is probably a misprint.

16 (23). Read ܩܢܘܡܐ 'hypostasis' for ܩܘܢܝܩܘ κυνικοί (Nau).

21 (31-32). The Syriac word ܡܙܘܢܐ 'rations' being here out of place, Nau takes ܡܙܘܢܐ here as a derivative of the Greek ζώνη 'girdle'.

22 (32). Nau reads ܗܘܐ 'is' for ܗܘܐ 'was'.

28 (41). The text has ܠܩܢܘܡܗܘܢ 'for their hypostasis', for which Nau reads ܠܩܘܡܗܘܢ 'for their establishing'.

31 (45). Owing to the difficulty of supplying 'who suppose' from the context, Nau changes ܕܒܣܪܐ 'of the flesh' into ܕܡܣܒܪܝܢ 'who suppose', as six lines above, translating it: 'or who suppose the *ousia* impure through mixture'.

34 (50). Nau proposes ܒܨܒܝܢܐ 'in the will' for ܒܓܠܝܢܐ 'in revelation'.

39 (57). Read ܐܠܐ 'but' for ܘܠܐ 'and not' (Bedjan).

45 (66). Read ܢܨܡܥܘܢ 'they rend asunder' for ܢܣܪܩܘܢ 'they make empty' (Bedjan).

[1] See *op. cit.*, pp. 361 and 388.
[2] Literally: head.
[3] See *op. cit.*, pp. 361 and 388; according to Loofs this fragment is a reference to, not a quotation from, Nestorius' own words.

53 (78). Read ܝܗܒ 'he has given' for ܝܗܒܘ 'they have given', as the sense requires; cp. p. xiii.

56 (83). Read ܒܡܬܒܣܪܢܘܬܗ 'in his Incarnation' for ܘܡܬܒܣܪܢܘܬܗ 'and his Incarnation' (Nau).

59 (86). The text has ܘܪܘܚܐ : ܕܒܪܢܫܐ 'and the spirit; of man', wrongly dividing the clauses and substituting ܕܒܪܢܫܐ 'of man' for ܕܩܘܕܫܐ 'of holiness' (Bedjan).

60 (87). The text has ܕܠܐ ܡܰܠܟܳܐ 'without a king' with a *v.l.* ܕܠܐ ܡܶܠܟܳܐ 'without counsel', for which Nau proposes ܕܠܠ ܡܶܠܟܳܐ 'counsellor' (cp. Is. ix. 6).

63 (92). Read ܕܡܫܬܡܥܢܘܬܐ 'of obedience', as above, for ܘܡܫܬܡܥܢܘܬܐ 'and obedience'.

72 (106). Read ܠܡܥܠܢܘܬܐ 'for the introduction' for ܠܡܥܠܝܘܬܐ 'for the exaltation' (Bedjan).

81 (119). The text has ܟܝܳܢܐ 'the nature'; V., according to Bedjan's *Errata* on p. 630, reads ܟܝ̈ܢܐ 'the natures'.

85 (124). V. reads ܐܬܚܝܕ 'united' for ܐܬܐܚܕ 'caught'.

89 (129). The text has 'the nature of Him (ܕܗܘ̇) who is the exaltation', which Nau adopts; V. has: 'that (ܗܘ̇) nature which is the exaltation'.

90 (130). The text has ܕܕܘܒܪ̈ܐ 'of morals', for which Nau reads ܕܕܒܘܪ̈ܐ 'of administrators'.

93 (134). If with the text ܕܠܗ̇ (fem.) is read, 'whose' refers to the soul; if ܕܠܗ (masc.), the reading of V., is followed, 'whose' refers to the body.

98 (150). The text has ܝܳܕܰܥ 'knowing', for which Nau proposes ܝܕܝܥ 'known'; cp. p. 345 (473).

100 (154). Read ܐܝܬܘܗܝ 'he is' for ܐܝܬܝܟ 'thou art' (Nau).

104 (159). The text has ܐܓܪ̈ܬܟ 'thy letters', for which V. reads ܐܓܪܬܟ 'thy letter', which Nau adopts.

105 (160). For 'the fear (ܕܕܚܠܬ) of God', the reading of the text, V. has 'the mother (ܐܡܗ) of God'.

106 (161). Read ܐܳܡܰܪ '(I) sa ' or 'sayest (thou)' (ptcp.), as Nau translates it, for ܐܶܡܰܪ 'say' (impt.).

139 (205). Nau proposes 'by confirmation (ܒܫܘܪܪܐ ܕܐܝܠܝܢ) of those things' for 'sincerely' or 'in truth (ܒܫܪܪܐ ܒܐܝܠܝܢ) by means of those things'.

139 (206). Nau proposes ܦܳܪܶܐ 'inventing' for ܒܳܪܶܐ 'creating'.

155 (227). The text has ܣܒܰܪܬ 'thou hast supposed'; V. and S. read ܣܒܰܪ (impt.) 'suppose', which Nau adopts.

162 (238). V. reads: 'the very own hypostasis of his nature

(ܘܟܝܢܗ)' for the text, which has 'his own hypostasis and his nature (ܘܟܝܢܐ)'.

182 (266). For 'not from (ܡܢ) the *ousia* of God the Word was it changed', the reading of the text, V. has: 'the *ousia* of God the Word was not indeed (ܡܢ) changed'.

187 (140). Read ܘܡܢ ܡܠܦܢܘܬܗ 'and from his teachings' for ܕܡܢ ܡܠܦܢܘܬܗ 'which were from his teachings' (Bedjan).

204 (285). The text reads ܗܟܢܐ 'thus', for which Nau appears to substitute ܗܢܐ 'the former'.

224 (312). Read ܠܘܬ ܡܫܝܚܐ 'with Christ', as on Syr., p. 310, for ܠܐ ܡܫܝܚܐ 'not Christ' (Nau).

235 (327). Read ܕܡܬܒܪܢܫܢܘܬܐ 'of the Incarnation' for ܕܬܠܝܬܝܘܬܐ 'of the Trinity' (Bedjan).

242 (335). The Syriac text has only: 'how is he an act which is with the Father and the Son and falls not short of them in anything?' The translator, having passed over from ܥܒܕܐ 'slave', which he omitted, to ܥܒܕܐ 'work', continued from there, reading only πῶς γὰρ εἴη τὸ μετὰ πατρὸς καὶ υἱοῦ ἐργαζόμενον (ܥܒܕܐ) 'work' being a mistake for ܥܒܕܐ 'working'), and then by another mischance omitted also ἂν ζητοίη τις τὰς τοῦ πνεύματος τάξεις εὑρήσει.

243 (336). The text has ܥܒܕܐ 'act', as on the preceding page, for which Bedjan proposes to read ܥܒܕܐ 'slave'.

255 (353). The text has ܕܢܣܬܡܟܘܢ 'that they should rely upon', which is impossible with the preposition ܡܢ 'from' and yields here no satisfactory sense; Bedjan therefore proposes ܕܢܣܬܟܡܘܢ and takes ܐܣܬܟܡ ܡܢ in the sense of the Greek ἀπο-σχηματίζεται 'divests of the monastic habit', which must be translated reflexively: 'that they should divest themselves of'.

275 (379). Read ܕܢ ܗܘܐ 'have judged' for ܕܢܗܘܐ 'that he should become', dividing differently the words in the text (Nau).

276 (380). Nau proposes ܘܠܐ 'and . . . not' for ܐܠܐ 'but'.

283 (390). Read ܐܚܐ ܠܘܬ ܐܚܐ 'brother to brother', almost as above, in place of ܚܝܐ ܠܘܬ ܚܝܐ 'living man to living man' (Nau).

283 (390). Nau appears to read 'when thou wast summoned (ܡܩܪܐ—pass.) to an Oecumenical Council' for 'when thou wast summoning (ܡܩܪܐ—act.) an Oecumenical Council'; cp. Nöldeke, *Syriac Grammar*, § 64.

284 (392). Read ܡܩܒܠ 'he received' for ܡܩܒܠܘ 'they received' (Bedjan); cp. p. xiii..

292 (403). Read with S. and C. ܘܡܐܡܪ̈ܐ 'and the Articles'; V. has ܕܡܐܡܪ̈ܐ 'of the Articles', which Nau appears to adopt in his translation : *sans écrire les chapitres.*

294 (405). For ܕܐܝܬܘܗܝ ܒܐܘܣܝܐ ܠܬܪ̈ܝܗܘܢ 'who in *ousia* is both of them' (*sc.* of the *ousias*) read probably, as below, ܕܐܝܬܘܗܝ ܒܐܘܣܝ̈ܣ ܠܬܪ̈ܬܝܗܝܢ 'who is in both *ousias*'.

297 (410). The text has ܐܝܟ ܕܐܡܪܬ 'as thou hast said', for which V. has ܐܝܟ ܕܐܡܪܬ 'as I said', in accordance with the Greek ; see p. 357 (489).

312 (430). Read ܕܐܡܪ 'that I say' or, with Nau, ܕܐܡܪܬ 'that I have said' for ܕܐܡܪ 'that he has said', the reading of the text.

315 (434). The text has ܦܘܪܫܐ ܕܡܪܚܩܘܬܐ ܕܐܝ̈ܕܝܐ 'a distinction of remoteness of hands', i.e. a distinction consisting in a differentiation of functions, for which Nau proposes to read ܦܘܪܫܐ ܕܒܡܥܒܕܢܘܬܐ ܕܐܝ̈ܕܝܐ *une séparation qui ait lieu à l'aide des mains.*

317 (436). For ܠܘ ܕܝܢ ܐܩܩܝܣ 'but Acacius does not (do so)' Nau proposes to read ܐܘ ܕܥܡ ܐܩܩܝܣ 'or with Acacius'.

320 (439). Read ܒܐܘܣܝ̈ܣ for ܒܐܘܣܝܐ, the same error as that on p. 294 (405).

326 (448). Read ܒܗ (masc., referring to 'nature') for ܒܗ̇ (fem., referring to 'the divinity'?).

328 (451). Read ܐܠܦܬ 'thou hast taught' for ܐܠܦܬ 'I have taught' (Nau).

343 (470). Read ܒܩܘܣܛܢܛܝܢܘܦܘܠܝܣ 'in Constantinople' for ܒܐܦܣܘܣ 'in Ephesus' (Bedjan).

345 (473). Read ܪܚܝܡܐ 'beloved' for ܪܚܡܐ 'loving' (Bedjan); cp. p. 98 (150).

346 (474). Read ܐܦ 'indeed', as above, for ܐܘ 'or' (Nau).

349 (478). Read ܪܡܝܗ 'he cast aside' for ܕܡܝܗ 'he likened' (Bedjan).

356 (488). Bedjan proposes 'that he should openly (ܕܒܓܠܝܐܝܬ) say' for 'he should lyingly (ܕܒܕܓܠܐܝܬ) say', the reading of the text; this gives an easier construction, by inserting ܕ 'that', and is in harmony with the Greek in the following passage (*v. infr.*). Cp. Engl., p. 356 (Syr., p. 489). For ܡܕܡ ܕܕܓܠܐ 'something false', the reading of S., which is given in the text, V. and C., following the Greek, have ܡܕܡ ܕܓܠܐ 'something which was open'.

357 (489). Read ܐܡܪܬ 'I have said' for ܐܡܪܬ 'thou hast said'; see p. 297 (410).

360 (493). Read ܐܢ 'I' for ܗܘ 'this' (Bedjan).

365 (501). The Syriac text has ܘܒܚܣܢܐ 'and into fortresses' or 'fastnesses', a word otherwise known only from citations in the lexicographers (Payne-Smith, *Thes. Syr.* i. 620), for which Bedjan proposes to read ܘܒܚܓܘܐ 'and in crevices (in the rocks)', a word in Syriac also cited only from lexicographers (*op. cit.*, i. 453).

378 (519). Read ܕܚܠ 'he feared' for ܕܚܠܘ 'they feared' (Bedjan); cp. p. xiii.

379 (520). For the unknown ܡܘܙܝܩܢܘܣ 'Muzicanus' Bedjan proposes ܡܘܪܝܛܢܝܐ 'Mauretania' and Nau tentatively [ܠܘܣܝܛܢܝܐ] 'Lusitania'.

III. *The word* πρόσωπον.

THE original meaning of the word πρόσωπον is *face, visage, countenance.* It is also used in classical Greek as equivalent to προσωπεῖον, a *mask,* and so for a *dramatic part,* or *character.* Other classical usages are *front* (as opposed to back), *outward appearance, beauty.* When used to denote a *person,* it is always simply *the person as regarded from the outside,* not the inner *ego* or personality.

In the Septuagint, the word is confined to translating Hebrew words signifying *face,* or *parts of the face used for the whole.* It is used both literally of the human face, and metaphorically of the surface of anything.[1]

In the New Testament πρόσωπον is used for *face* (both literally and metaphorically), for the *outward appearance* or *surface* (e.g. of the heavens or the earth), and so for *person* in such phrases as οὐ γὰρ βλέπεις εἰς πρόσωπον ἀνθρώπων (Mt. xxii. 16); οὐ λαμβάνεις πρόσωπον (Lk. xx. 21); θαυμάζοντες πρόσωπον (Jude 16). Three passages in 2 Corinthians should be quoted: (1) ἵνα ἐκ πολλῶν προσώπων τὸ εἰς ἡμᾶς χάρισμα διὰ πολλῶν εὐχαριστηθῇ ὑπὲρ ἡμῶν (i. 11). Here προσώπων seems to mean simply *people*; (2) κεχάρισμαι, εἴ τι κεχάρισμαι, δι' ὑμᾶς ἐν προσώπῳ Χριστοῦ (ii. 10)—in the *presence* of Christ; (3) πρὸς φωτισμὸν τῆς γνώσεως τῆς δόξης τοῦ θεοῦ ἐν προσώπῳ Χριστοῦ (iv. 6). Here the stress seems to be laid on the function of Christ as the visible revelation of the glory of God (cp. v. 4 ὅς ἐστιν εἰκὼν τοῦ θεοῦ).

In the Apostolic Fathers the usages are similar to those in the

[1] The following list of the Hebrew equivalents is given by Hatch and Redpath: פאה, מראה, עינים, פה, פנים, אף.

The word πρόσωπον

New Testament. The passages in which the word means *person* are as follows: [στάσις] ἦν ὀλίγα πρόσωπα προπετῆ καὶ αὐθάδη ... ἐξέκαυσαν (Clem. Rom. i. 1); ἐκκλησίαν δι' ἓν ἢ δύο πρόσωπα στασιάζειν (*Id.* xlvii. 6); ἐν τοῖς προγεγραμμένοις προσώποις τὸ πᾶν πλῆθος ἐθεώρησα ἐν πίστει καὶ ἠγάπησα (Ignatius, *Magn.* vi. 1); ἐκζητήσεις καθ' ἡμέραν τὰ πρόσωπα τῶν ἁγίων (*Did.* iv. 2; *Ep. Barn.* xix. 10); οὐ λήψῃ πρόσωπον ἐλέγξαι ἐπὶ παραπτώμασιν (*Did.* iv. 3; *Ep. Barn.* xix. 4). Elsewhere the word means *face, surface,* or *outward appearance*.

In the Apologists Justin Martyr and Theophilus there appears an extension of the dramatic use of the word which is afterwards common; it is used to denote the *person represented* by another, especially in biblical exegesis. Thus ἀπὸ προσώπου τοῦ πατρὸς ἐλέχθησαν διὰ Ἡσαΐου ... οἶδε οἱ λόγοι (Just. *Apol.* I. xxxvii. 1); ὁ Ἡσαΐας ὡς ἀπὸ προσώπου τῶν ἀποστόλων ... λέγει (*Id. Dial. c. Tryph.* xlii); ὁ Λόγος ... ἀναλαμβάνων τὸ πρόσωπον τοῦ πατρός (Theophilus, *ad Aut.* ii. 22). In this last passage πρόσωπον is clearly not used technically of a 'person' of the Trinity. It is so used by Pseudo Justin Martyr, but the fact that that writer also uses ὑπόστασις in the same sense shows his later date: τὸ Ἀγέννητον καὶ Γεννητὸν καὶ ἐκπορευτὸν οὐκ οὐσίας δηλωτικὰ σημαντικὰ δὲ τῶν ὑποστάσεών ἐστιν· ἱκανὰ γὰρ ἡμῖν διακρινεῖν τὰ πρόσωπα, καὶ τὴν Πατρὸς καὶ Υἱοῦ καὶ ἁγίου Πνεύματος ἰδιαζόντως δεικνύει ὑπόστασιν (*Exp. Rect. Conf.* iii; cp. *Resp. ad Orth.* xvii, cxxix, cxxxix).

Irenaeus and Clement of Alexandria make no advance in their use of the word, but two passages from the latter are worth quoting as they refer to the Incarnation: ὁ θεῖος λόγος ... τὸ ἀνθρώπου προσωπεῖον ἀναλαβὼν καὶ σαρκὶ ἀναπλασάμενος τὸ σωτήριον δρᾶμα τῆς ἀνθρωπότητος ὑπεκρίνετο (*Protrept.* xx, 109, 3); οἱ δὲ "διὰ παντὸς τὸ πρόσωπον τοῦ πατρὸς βλέπουσιν",[1] πρόσωπον δὲ πατρὸς ὁ υἱός, δι' οὗ γνωρίζεται ὁ πατήρ (*Excerpt. ex Theod.* x. 6). In the former of these προσωπεῖον, not πρόσωπον, is used.

The ordinary meanings of *face, outward appearance, dramatic part,* and *person* appear in Origen as in his predecessors,[2] but there are also passages which seem the extension of πρόσωπον to denote the inner mental and spiritual characteristics of personality. A metaphorical use of the literal sense of *face*, as

---

[1] Mt. xviii. 10.

[2] These meanings remain in constant use throughout; no further references will be given for them, except for special reasons.

ἐπίκειται τῷ ἔνδον προσώπῳ, ⟨τῷ⟩ ἡγεμονικῷ ἡμῶν, τὸ κάλυμμα καὶ ἡ ἀτιμία (*Hom. in Jer.* v. 9) may possibly have been the starting-point of this development, which is carried further in two passages of Origen himself and in one possibly quoted from Heracleon: κατὰ τὸ ἱερατικὸν καὶ λευϊτικὸν πρόσωπόν ἐστι μεθ' ἡμερότητος τὰ λεγόμενα (*Comm. in Ioh.* vi. 8[1]); Ὅμηρος μὲν ἐν πολλοῖς θαυμάζεται, τηρήσας τὰ τῶν ἡρώων πρόσωπα, ὁποῖα αὐτὰ ὑπέθετο ἀπ' ἀρχῆς (*c. Cels.* vii. 36); τὸ "Ἐὰν μὴ σημεῖα καὶ τέρατα ἴδητε, οὐ μὴ πιστεύσητε" λέγεσθαί φησιν οἰκείως πρὸς τὸ τοιοῦτον πρόσωπον δι' ἔργων φύσιν ἔχον καὶ δι' αἰσθήσεως πείθεσθαι καὶ οὐχὶ λόγῳ πιστεύειν (*Comm. in Ioh.* xiii. 60). There is possibly a similar use in the apocryphal Acts of Andrew: ἰδὼν τὸ σὸν πρόσωπον ἐν τῇ οὐσίᾳ σου (*Act. Andr.* vi).

The regular use of the word in Trinitarian doctrine begins with the Monarchian controversies. Hippolytus quotes Callistus as teaching that the Father, the Son, and the Spirit are ἓν πρόσωπον· οὐ γάρ, φησίν, ἐρῶ δύο θεούς, πατέρα καὶ υἱόν, ἀλλ' ἕνα. ὁ γὰρ ἐν αὐτῷ γενόμενος πατὴρ προσλαβόμενος τὴν σάρκα ἐθεοποίησεν ἑνώσας ἑαυτῷ καὶ ἐποίησεν ἕν, ὡς καλεῖσθαι πατέρα καὶ υἱὸν ἕνα θεόν, καὶ τοῦτο ἓν ὂν πρόσωπον μὴ δύνασθαι εἶναι δύο, καὶ οὕτως τὸν πατέρα συμπεπονθέναι τῷ υἱῷ· οὐ γὰρ θέλει λέγειν τὸν πατέρα πεπονθέναι καὶ ἓν εἶναι πρόσωπον, ⟨ἀλλ'⟩ ἐκφυγεῖν τὴν εἰς τὸν πατέρα βλασφημίαν ὁ ἀνόητος καὶ ποικίλος, ὁ ἄνω κάτω σχεδιάζων βλασφημίας, ἵνα μόνον κατὰ τῆς ἀληθείας λέγειν δοκῇ, ποτὲ μὲν εἰς τὸ Σαβελλίου δόγμα ἐμπίπτων, ποτὲ δὲ εἰς τὸ Θεοδότου οὐκ αἰδεῖται (*Ref.* ix. 12. 18); πνεῦμα γάρ, φησίν, ὁ θεὸς οὐχ ἕτερόν ἐστι παρὰ τὸν λόγον ἢ ὁ λόγος παρὰ τὸν θεόν. ἓν οὖν τοῦτο πρόσωπον, ὀνόματι μὲν μεριζόμενον, οὐσίᾳ δὲ οὔ (*Ref.* x. 27. 4). Hippolytus himself uses the word of the distinctions within the Trinity: δύο μὲν οὐκ ἐρῶ θεούς, ἀλλ' ἢ ἕνα, πρόσωπα δὲ δύο, οἰκονομίαν δὲ τρίτην, τὴν χάριν τοῦ ἁγίου Πνεύματος. πατὴρ μὲν γὰρ εἷς, πρόσωπα δὲ δύο, ὅτι καὶ ὁ Υἱός, τὸ δὲ τρίτον τὸ ἅγιον Πνεῦμα (*c. haer. Noet.* xiv). Two passages from Eusebius are similar: πῶς δὲ ἐταπείνωσεν ἑαυτὸν ὑπήκοος γενόμενος τῷ πατρί; τὸ γὰρ ὑπακούειν τόνδε τῷδε δυεῖν γένοιτ' ἂν προσώπων παραστατικόν (*De Eccl. Theol.* i. 20); τότε μὲν Χριστοῦ πρόσωπον, τότε δὲ πνεύματος ἁγίου, τότε δὲ τοῦ ἐπὶ πάντων Θεοῦ ἦν διὰ τοῦ προφήτου χρηματίζον (*Dem. Ev.* v. 13. 2).

In one passage Eusebius uses πρόσωπον for a human *person* with direct reference to mental and spiritual qualities: ἐντεῦθεν

---

[1] But possibly in this passage the word only means 'characteristic manner' as seen from the outside.

ὁρμώμενος καὶ ὁ τὴν πανάρετον σοφίαν εἰς αὐτοῦ πρόσωπον ἀναθεὶς ἔφη κτλ. (*Praep. Ev.* xi. 7. 521 d).

Cyril of Jerusalem interprets the πρόσωπον of Ps. civ. 15 as meaning τὸ τῆς ψυχῆς ... πρόσωπον (*Myst.* iv. 9).

Eustathius of Antioch, in speaking of the Trinity, says τριὰς ὁμοούσιος, μία θεότης ἐν τρισὶν προσώποις καὶ ὑποστάσεσι κηρύττεται (*All. ad Const.*, Migne, *P. G. L.* xviii. 676 A). This use of the word is a common formula in the fourth century, and is found in the Creed of Sirmium: δύο πρόσωπα ... πατρὸς καὶ υἱοῦ (*Hardouin* i. 705 c). Athanasius denies that the Father, the Son, and the Spirit are ἓν πρόσωπον (Migne, xxvi. 740 B), and speaks of an Arianizing creed as τρία ὁμολογοῦντες πράγματα καὶ τρία πρόσωπα τοῦ Πατρὸς καὶ τοῦ Υἱοῦ καὶ τοῦ ἁγίου Πνεύματος κατὰ τὰς γραφάς (Migne, xxvi. 729 B). But, on the other hand, the word can still be used in its non-technical sense so that Athanasius, in citing Jn. xiv. 9 (ὁ ἑωρακὼς ἐμὲ ἑώρακε τὸν πατέρα), can speak of the Son as πρόσωπον τοῦ πατρός (*In Psalm.* xx. 7). Cp. ἵνα ... καὶ ἐφ' ἡμᾶς μεταγάγῃ τὸ πρόσωπον τοῦ πατρός (*In Psalm.* xxii. 1). The old usages of the word for *person represented*, or *person referred to*, persist, e.g. ἐκ προσώπου τοῦ Ἰησοῦ λέγει (*Exp. Fid.* iii), τὰ πρόσωπα ... τῶν γεγραμμένων ἐρευνῶν (*De Decr. Nic. Sym.* xiv). Cp. *Or. I c. Ar.* liv; *In Psalm.* ii. 14, xiv. 2, xv. 8; *Ep. ad Marcellin* vii. In one passage πρόσωπον seems to mean *position in the eyes of the world*: καιροῦ καὶ προσώπου πρόφασις εἵλκυσεν αὐτὸν τοιαῦτα γράψαι (*De Sent. Dion.* iv). The predominance of this meaning of *person as seen from the outside* is interesting when it is noticed that there appear for the first time in Athanasius passages concerning the Incarnation which, in their use of the word πρόσωπον, seem to prepare the way for the later language of Nestorius: τὰ γὰρ τοῦ σώματος αὐτοῦ εἰς τὸ αὐτοῦ πρόσωπον λέγεται (*Lib. de Inc. et c. Ar.* ii); τὸ κοινὸν ὥσπερ πρόσωπον τῆς ἀνθρωπότητος ἀναλαβὼν τοὺς πρὸς Θεὸν καὶ Πατέρα ποιεῖται λόγους (*In Psalm.* xv. 1); σκόπει μοι πάλιν τὸ τῆς ἀνθρωπότητος πρόσωπον ἐν Χριστῷ παρακαλοῦν ἀπαλλάττεσθαι τῶν πταισμάτων (*In Psalm.* xxii. 1). Such language is definitely repudiated in Athanasian works of doubtful authenticity: ὁ δὲ ἄνθρωπος ἓν πρόσωπον ... ἀπό τε πνεύματος καὶ σαρκός· κατὰ δὲ τὸ ὁμοίωμα αὐτοῦ νοητέον τὸν Χριστὸν ἕνα καὶ οὐ δύο πρόσωπα (*Dub. de Incarn.* i); Χριστὸς ἓν πρόσωπόν ἐστιν συντεθὲν ἐκ Θεοῦ καὶ ἀνθρωπότητος ὡς πᾶς ἄνθρωπος ὁ κοινὸς ἐκ ζώου καὶ λογικοῦ (*De S. Trin. Dial.* v, Migne, *P. G. L.* xxviii. 1277 A).

As might be expected the word occurs in Basil most frequently in connexion with Trinitarian doctrine. He is mainly concerned to assert, as against the Sabellians, that each πρόσωπον in the Trinity implies a distinct ὑπόστασις, e.g. χρὴ ἕκαστον πρόσωπον ἐν ὑποστάσει ἀληθινῇ ὕπαρχον ὁμολογεῖν (*Ep.* ccx. 5. 317 A); οἱ δὲ ταὐτὸν λέγοντες οὐσίαν καὶ ὑπόστασιν, ἀναγκάζονται πρόσωπα μόνον ὁμολογεῖν διάφορα, καὶ ἐν τῷ περιίστασθαι λέγειν τρεῖς ὑποστάσεις, εὑρίσκονται μὴ φεύγοντες τὸ τοῦ Σαβελλίου κακόν, ὃς καὶ αὐτὸς πολλαχοῦ συγχέων τὴν ἔννοιαν, ἐπιχειρεῖ διαιρεῖν τὰ πρόσωπα, τὴν αὐτὴν ὑπόστασιν λέγων πρὸς τὴν ἑκάστοτε παρεμπίπτουσαν χρείαν μετασχηματίζεσθαι (*Ep.* ccxxxv. 6. 364 B). A passage in *Adv. Eunomium V*, which at first sight appears curious, probably means that St. Paul and the prophets when rightly understood proclaim the doctrine of the Trinity when only mentioning any one Person: Τριάδα τὴν μονάδα κηρύσσοντες, ἀλλ' ἑνότητα θεότητος εἰδότες, ἐν ἑνὶ προσώπῳ τὰ τρία κηρύσσουσι (315 B). Besides this frequently recurring use of the word, it is also found in Basil with its older meanings of *face, person represented, person referred to,* and *dramatic character.* He refers to the Jewish interpretation of ποιήσωμεν ἄνθρωπον in Gen. i. 26 as follows: πολλά, φασίν, ἐστὶ τὰ πρόσωπα πρὸς οὓς ὁ λόγος γέγονε τοῦ Θεοῦ. τοῖς ἀγγέλοις γὰρ λέγει τοῖς παρέστωσιν αὐτῷ (*Hex.* ix. 6. 87 E). The only reference to inner personality is a metaphorical use of πρόσωπον as *face*: ἀνάγκη ... τὸν ἀποθανόντα ... ἀναστῆναι διὰ τῆς ἐν Χριστῷ ... χάριτος, καὶ μηκέτι διὰ τὰς ἁμαρτίας τὸ πρόσωπον τοῦ ἔσω ἀνθρώπου ὡς πρόσκαυμα χύτρας ἔχειν (*De Bapt.* i. 10. 636 E).

What is true of Basil is true of the Gregories. A typical Trinitarian passage is χρὴ καὶ τὸν ἕνα θεὸν τηρεῖν, καὶ τὰς τρεῖς ὑποστάσεις ὁμολογεῖν, εἴτε οὖν τρία πρόσωπα, καὶ ἑκάστην μετὰ τῆς ἰδιότητος (Greg. Naz. *Or.* xx, Migne, xxxv. 1072 c). The older, non-technical, uses are also found. In one passage mental and spiritual qualities are implied: διὰ τὸ τῶν προσώπων ἀξιόπιστον (Gr. Naz. *Ep.* ci, M. xxxvii. 177 A); and in one place Gregory of Nyssa uses the word non-technically in reference to the Incarnation: ὑπὲρ τῆς ἀνθρωπότητος τὸ ἴδιον πρόσωπον προβαλλόμενος (*c. Ar. et Sab.,* M. xlv. 1292 B).

A very important development is found in Epiphanius. The common ancient use of the word in such phrases as ἀπὸ προσώπου τινός to denote the *person in whose name an utterance is made* is combined with the later Trinitarian use: πολλά ἐστι δεῖξαι ὅτι ἐκ προσώπου τοῦ Πατρός ἐστιν ἐν τῇ παλαιᾷ διαθήκῃ εἰρημένα. ἀλλὰ καὶ ἐκ προσώπου τοῦ Υἱοῦ πολλάκις, καὶ ἐκ προσώπου πάλιν τοῦ ἁγίου Πνεύματος (*Ancor.* xxxix, M. xliii. 88 A); οὐκέτι δὲ ἀπὸ προσώπου Πατρὸς μόνον, οὐδὲ ἀπὸ προσώπου Υἱοῦ μόνον, ἀλλὰ μεσαίτατα τῶν προσώπων Πατρὸς καὶ Υἱοῦ φησι... (*Adv. Haer.* II. ii. 74, M. xlii. 325 B). Further, this idiom is applied to the Incarnation in the exposition of the Gospel sayings of Christ, with the result that language is used similar to that in which Nestorius expounds his Christology: τί οὖν, φασίν, ἔστιν ὁ Λόγος οὗτος ὃν εἶπεν, ὅτι Θεέ μου, Θεέ μου, ἵνα τί με ἐγκατέλιπες;[1] τίνι δὲ οὐ σαφὲς εἴη ὅτι ἀπὸ προσώπου τῆς αὐτοῦ ἐνανθρωπήσεως ἀνθρωποπαθῶς προβάλλεται τὸ ῥῆμα (*Ib.* II. ii. 62, M. xlii, 305 c); εἰ δὲ ἀδύνατον ἦν κατασχεθῆναι διὰ τὴν θεότητα, πῶς ἄρα ἐκ προσώπου τοῦ αὐτοῦ θεότητος ἠδύνατο ῥηθῆναι τὸ Θεέ μου κτλ.; ἀλλ' οὗτος ἐκ προσώπου τῆς αὐτοῦ ἐνανθρωπήσεως ἀνθρωποπαθῶς ἐδείκνυτο ὁ λόγος, ἵνα μάθωμεν ἀληθινῶς εἶναι τὴν ἔνσαρκον παρουσίαν, καὶ οὐ δοκήσει ἢ φαντασίᾳ παρ' αὐτοῦ οἰκονομηθεῖσαν (*Ib.* II. ii. 63, M. xlii. 308 c).

Such language is never found in Apollinarius. For him Christ is ἓν πρόσωπον. He only uses the word as a technical term, as in the following passages, of which the first two refer to the doctrine of the Trinity, the rest to the Incarnation: ἀλλότριοι δὲ οὐχ ἧττον καὶ οἱ τὴν τριάδα μὴ κατὰ ἀλήθειαν ἐκ τριῶν προσώπων ὁμολογοῦντες, ἀλλ' ἐν μονάδι τὸ τριπλοῦν ἀσεβῶς κατὰ σύνθεσιν φανταζόμενοι καὶ σοφίαν ἐν θεῷ τὸν υἱὸν ὡς ἐν ἀνθρώπῳ τὴν ἀνθρωπίνην ἡγούμενοι, δι' ἧς ὁ ἄνθρωπός ἐστι σοφός, καὶ λόγον ὁμοίως τῷ κατὰ προσφορὰν ἢ διάνοιαν εἰσηγούμενοι οὐδεμίᾳ ὑποστάσει οὐδὲ μόνῃ (Lietzmann,[2] p. 167, 18); πρόσωπον μὲν γὰρ ἑκάστου τὸ εἶναι αὐτὸ καὶ ὑφεστάναι δηλοῖ, θεότης δὲ πατρὸς ἴδιον, καὶ ὁπότε μία τῶν τριῶν ἡ θεότης λέγοιτο, τὴν πατρὸς ἰδιότητα παροῦσαν υἱῷ τε καὶ πνεύματι μαρτυρεῖ· ὥστε εἰ μὲν ἐν τρισὶ προσώποις μία ῥηθήσεται ἡ θεότης, καὶ ἡ τριὰς διαβεβαιοῦται καὶ τὸ ἓν οὐ διακόπτεται καὶ ἡ πρὸς τὸν πατέρα φυσικὴ υἱοῦ τε καὶ πνεύματος ἑνότης ὁμολογεῖται· εἰ δὲ καὶ πρόσωπον ἓν λέγει τις ὥσπερ καὶ τὴν θεότητα μίαν, οὐκ ἔστιν ὡς ἓν τὰ δύο ἐν τῷ ἑνὶ (*Ib.* p. 172, 10); εἰ γὰρ ὅλος ἁγιάζει, τί τὸ ἁγιαζόμενον· εἰ ὁ σύμπας ἁγιάζεται, τί τὸ ἁγιάζον· ἀλλ' ὅμως φυλάττων τὸ ἓν πρόσωπον καὶ τὴν ἀμέριστον ἑνὸς ζῴου δήλωσιν τό τε ἁγιάζειν καὶ τὸ ἁγιάζεσθαι καθ' ὅλου τέθεικεν (*Ib.* p. 189, 14); εἰ γοῦν "εἷς" ὁ ἐκ τῆς ἁγίας παρθένου τεχθεὶς ὠνόμασται καὶ αὐτός ἐστι "δι' οὗ τὰ πάντα γέγονε", μία φύσις ἐστίν, ἐπειδὴ πρόσωπον ἓν ἔχον εἰς δύο διαίρεσιν, ἐπεὶ μηδὲ ἰδία φύσις τὸ σῶμα καὶ ἰδία φύσις ἡ θεότης κατὰ τὴν σάρκωσιν, ἀλλ' ὥσπερ ἄνθρωπος μία

[1] Mt. xxvii. 46.
[2] *Apollinaris von Laodicea u. seine Schule*, Tübingen, 1904.

φύσις, ούτω καὶ ὁ ἐν ὁμοιώματι ἀνθρώπων γενόμενος Χριστός (*Ib.* p. 257, 14); λέγομεν δὲ τὰ ἀμφότερα, καὶ ἐξ οὐρανοῦ τὸ ὅλον διὰ τὴν θεότητα καὶ ἐκ γυναικὸς τὸ ὅλον διὰ τὴν σάρκα, οὐκ εἰδότες διαίρεσιν τοῦ ἑνὸς προσώπου οὐδὲ ἀποτέμνοντες τοῦ οὐρανίου τὸ γήϊνον οὐδὲ τοῦ γηΐνου τὸ οὐράνιον (*Ib.* p. 259, 10).

There is no further light on the use of the word to be gained from Chrysostom. He makes use of it in many of its common non-technical meanings, and also as a technical term in Trinitarian doctrine, *e.g.* when he speaks of Arius as εἰς παραλλαγὴν οὐσίας ἔλκων τὴν ἐν τοῖς προσώποις διαφοράν (*De Sacerd.* iv. 410 A). The only passages in which the word occurs in connexion with the Incarnation are an obscure reference in Cramer's *Catena*, where the words δύο πρόσωπα δεικνὺς καὶ θεὸν καὶ ἄνθρωπον occur (on Heb. i. 8), and a sentence in a spurious treatise: μὴ ποιήσητε δύο πρόσωπα τὸ ἓν πρόσωπον τοῦ Χριστοῦ (Migne, *P. G. L.* lxiv. 35).

Macarius of Egypt seems to use πρόσωπον for *aspect*: εἰς δύο πρόσωπα νοεῖται τὰ πράγματα (*Hom.* xxvi. 10); ἐκκλησία ἐν δυσὶ προσώποις νοεῖται... τῇ συστήματι... καὶ τῇ συγκρίματι τῆς ψυχῆς. ὅταν οὖν εἰς τὸν ἄνθρωπον λαμβάνηται, ἐκκλησία ἐστὶν ὅλον αὐτοῦ τὸ σύγκριμα (*Hom.* xxxviii. 8). Sometimes he uses it simply to mean *thing*: τὰ δύο πρόσωπα χάρις καὶ ἁμαρτία (*Hom.* xl. 7); δύο πρόσωπα συναπτόμενα τέλειόν τι πρᾶγμα ἀπεργάζεται, οἷον δύο διαθῆκαι ... (*Hom.* xxxii. 6). In Palladius the word occurs once meaning *type*: Νῶε πρόσωπόν ἐστι τῆς ἀκτημοσύνης (Migne, *P. G. L.* lxv. 336 c).

So far the only usages suggestive of that which is common in Nestorius have been found in Athanasius and Epiphanius. But in Theodore of Mopsuestia, as might be expected, there is an exact anticipation of the teaching of Nestorius: ὅταν μὲν γὰρ τὰς φύσεις διακρίνωμεν, τελείαν τὴν φύσιν τοῦ θεοῦ λόγου φαμέν, καὶ τέλειον τὸ πρόσωπον· οὐδὲ γὰρ ἀπρόσωπον ἔστιν ὑπόστασιν εἰπεῖν· τελείαν δὲ καὶ τὴν τοῦ ἀνθρώπου φύσιν, καὶ τὸ πρόσωπον ὁμοίως· ὅταν μέντοι ἐπὶ τὴν συνάφειαν ἀπίδωμεν, ἓν πρόσωπον τότε φαμέν. τὸν αὐτὸν δὴ τρόπον κἀνταῦθα ἰδίαν φαμὲν τοῦ θεοῦ λόγον τὴν οὐσίαν, ἰδίαν δὲ καὶ τὴν τοῦ ἀνθρώπου· διακεκριμέναι γὰρ αἱ φύσεις, ἓν δὲ τὸ πρόσωπον τῇ ἑνώσει ἀποτελούμενον· ὥστε κἀνταῦθα ὅταν μὲν τὰς φύσεις διακρίνειν πειρώμεθα, τέλειον τὸ πρόσωπον φαμὲν εἶναι τὸ τοῦ ἀνθρώπου, τέλειον δὲ καὶ τὸ τῆς θεότητος. ὅταν δὲ πρὸς τὴν ἕνωσιν ἀποβλέψωμεν, τότε ἓν εἶναι τὸ πρόσωπον ἄμφω τὰς φύσεις κηρύττομεν, τῆς τε ἀνθρωπότητος τῇ θεότητι τὴν παρὰ τῆς κτίσεως τιμὴν δεχομένης, καὶ τῆς θεότητος ἐν αὐτῇ πάντα ἐπιτελούσης τὰ δέοντα (*Fragm. de Incarn.* viii). There is also the older non-technical use : ἄπαντα μέντοι τὰ τοῦ ψαλμοῦ ὡς ἐκ προσώπου τοῦ λαοῦ φησιν (*Exp. in Ps.* xv. 1).

In Theodoret, the contemporary and friend of Nestorius, there is a surprising absence of the Nestorian technical use. There is the original meaning of *face* : πρόσωπον θεοῦ τὴν εὐμένειαν καὶ τὴν τῆς ἐλευθερίας ἀπόδοσιν καὶ τὴν τῆς κηδεμονίας ἀπόληψιν (*In Dan.* iii. 41); τὸ μὲν τῆς ἐπιεικείας ἀπεδύσατο προσωπεῖον, τὰ δὲ τῆς δυσσεβείας ἐγύμνασε πρόσωπον (*H. E.* iii. 11). There is the technical use in Trinitarian doctrine : τὴν δέ γε ὑπόστασιν προσώπου τινὸς εἶναι δηλωτικήν, οἷον ἢ τοῦ πατρὸς ἢ τοῦ υἱοῦ ἢ τοῦ ἁγίου πνεύματος. τὴν γὰρ ὑπόστασιν καὶ τὸ πρόσωπον καὶ τὴν ἰδιότητα ταὐτὸν σημαίνειν φαμὲν τοῖς τῶν ἁγίων πατέρων ὁροῖς ἀκολουθοῦντες (*Dial.* i, Migne, *P. G. L.* lxxxiii. 36 A). But of the Incarnation he says : ὅτι μετὰ τὴν ἕνωσιν ἑνὶ προσώπῳ καὶ τὰ ὑψηλὰ καὶ τὰ ταπεινὰ προσάπτει ἡ θεία Γραφή ... πολλάκις ἔφην ὡς καὶ τὰ θεῖα καὶ τὰ ἀνθρώπεια τὸ ἓν δέχεται πρόσωπον. διά τοι τοῦτο καὶ οἱ τρισμακάριοι πατέρες, ὅπως δεῖ πιστεύειν εἰς τὸν πατέρα διδάξαντες καὶ εἰς τὸ τοῦ υἱοῦ πρόσωπον μεταβάντες, οὐκ εἶπον εὐθὺς " καὶ εἰς τὸν υἱὸν τοῦ θεοῦ ", καίτοι λίαν ἀκόλουθον ἦν τὰ περὶ θεοῦ καὶ πατρὸς εἰρηκότος εὐθὺς καὶ τὴν τοῦ υἱοῦ θεῖναι προσηγορίαν· ἀλλ' ἠβουλήθησαν ὁμοῦ καὶ τὸν τῆς θεολογίας καὶ τὸν τῆς οἰκονομίας ἡμῖν παραδοῦναι λόγον, ἵνα μὴ ἄλλο μὲν τὸ τῆς θεότητος ἄλλο δὲ τὸ τῆς ἀνθρωπότητος πρόσωπον νομισθῇ (*Dial.* iii, Migne, *P. G. L.* lxxxiii. 280 c).

In Cyril of Alexandria is found almost every sense of the word : *face* (Migne, *P. G. L.* lxviii. 236 D); *aspect* (*Id.* lxxiv. 336 A); *mask* (*In Act. Syn. Eph.* 218); *image, representation* (*In Ioh. Comm.* 302 c); *type* (Migne, *P. G. L.* lxviii. 235 D, 285 A, lxix. 596 A); *antitype* (*Id.* lxviii. 785 B, lxix. 568 B); *the person represented by a speaker* (*In Ioh. Comm.* 304 a ; *De Inc. Unig.* 703 a; *In Oseam.* v. 143 c, d ; *In Psalm.* ix. 1, &c.); *a person in the ordinary colloquial sense* (Migne, *P. G. L.* lxix. 752 B, lxxvii. 169 A). In at least ten passages πρόσωπον is used in its technical sense of the doctrine of the Trinity, *e. g.* μία γὰρ ἡ τῆς θεότητος φύσις ἐν προσώπῳ τε καὶ ὑποστάσει πατρός τε καὶ υἱοῦ καὶ ἁγίου πνεύματος (*In Ioh. Comm.* 806 a). The passages referring to the Incarnation may be divided into those in which he is reproducing Nestorian views, and those in which he is expounding his own. The former are as follows : εἰ κοινὸς ἄνθρωπός ἐστιν ὁ Χριστός, ἑνώσει μόνῃ τῇ κατὰ πρόσωπον τὴν συνάφειαν ἔχων πρὸς τὸν ἐκ θεοῦ

APPENDIX III

λόγον ... (*De Rect. Fid. ad Arc. et Mar.* 66 c); ... τὴν καθ' ὑπόστασιν ἕνωσιν τοῦ λόγου πρὸς τὴν σάρκα, καὶ οὐχὶ δὴ μόνην τὴν ἐν προσώποις, καὶ κατὰ θέλησιν ... (*Ib.* 103 e); ... ψιλῇ προσώπων ἐνώσει τετιμημένος (*Ib.* 22 d); ὠφέλησε κατ' οὐδένα τρόπον τὸν ὀρθὸν τῆς πίστεως λόγον εἰς τὸ οὕτως ἔχειν, κἂν εἰ προσώπων ἕνωσιν ἐπιφημίζωσί τινες (*Ep.* iv, *Ad Nest. Oec.* i. 24 d); ἀλλ' ἐπειδὴ σκοπὸς ἐκείνοις δύο λέγειν Χριστούς, καὶ δύο υἱούς, καὶ τὸν μὲν ἄνθρωπον ἰδικῶς τὸν δὲ Θεὸν ἰδικῶς· εἶτα μόνων τῶν προσώπων ποιοῦσιν τὴν ἕνωσιν, διὰ τοῦτο ποικίλλονται, καὶ προφάσεις πλάττονται ἐν ἁμαρτίαις, καθὰ γέγραπται (*Ad Cler. Const.* M. lxxvii. 65 B); οὐδὲ γὰρ ἀνέχῃ προσώποις δυσίν, ἤγουν ὑποστάσεσι, τὰς φωνὰς διανέμειν (*Ad Acac. Mel.* M. lxxvii. 193 A). In the following two passages Cyril is setting forth his own teaching: γέγονε γὰρ ἡμῶν μεσίτης ἐνανθρωπήσας ὁ υἱός, καὶ οἷον διαλλακτὴς εἰς εἰρήνην, οὐχ ἑτέρῳ προξενῶν τῶν ἐν τῷ κόσμῳ τὴν ὑποταγήν, ἀλλ' ὡς ἐν ἰδίῳ προσώπῳ, τῷ θεῷ καὶ πατρί (*De Rect. Fid. ad Pulch. et Eud.* 169 a); ἔσται τῆς ταπεινώσεως τὰ δουλοπρεπῆ ῥήματα, οὐκ ἀναβαίνοντα μὲν πρὸς τὴν οὐσίαν αὐτοῦ, ἀλλὰ τῷ τῆς ἐνανθρωπήσεως προσώπῳ περικείμενα (*Thes.* M. lxxv. 120 A). The dubious treatise *De Trinitate* contains the two following passages: ... ἵνα κἀντεῦθεν τό τε διάφορον τῶν φύσεων τοῦ Χριστοῦ, τό τε μοναδικὸν τοῦ προσώπου γινώσκομεν (xvii); τὸ ἡμέτερον τοίνυν οἰκειούμενος πρόσωπον, καὶ μεθ' ἡμῶν τάσσων ἑαυτόν, ταῦτα ἔλεγεν (xxv). This last sentence, with its suspiciously Nestorian language, is silently omitted by the Latin translator (see Migne, *P. G. L.* lxxvii. 1169 A).

This survey may be concluded by the following passage from the *Definition of Chalcedon*: ὁμολογοῦμεν ... ἕνα καὶ τὸν αὐτὸν Χριστὸν ... οὐδαμοῦ τῆς τῶν φύσεων διαφορᾶς ἀνῃρημένης διὰ τὴν ἕνωσιν, σωζομένης δὲ μᾶλλον τῆς ἰδιότητος ἑκατέρας φύσεως, καὶ εἰς ἓν πρόσωπον καὶ μίαν ὑπόστασιν συντρεχούσης, οὐκ εἰς δύο πρόσωπα μεριζόμενον ἢ διαιρούμενον, ἀλλ' ἕνα καὶ τὸν αὐτὸν Υἱὸν καὶ μονογενῆ Θεόν Λόγον Κύριον Ἰησοῦν Χριστόν.

IV. The Metaphysic of Nestorius.[1]

WHAT Nestorius really taught, and whether he was himself orthodox or a heretic, are questions which have been reopened by the discovery of his own defence of his position in the 'Book of Heracleides'.[2] So long as the first of these remains a mystery, the second cannot be answered; and this paper is put forward as a suggestion towards the interpretation of Nestorius' writing and the understanding of what he taught. It deals mainly with one point, the meaning of the word πρόσωπον in Nestorius' teaching; but as the argument in the *Liber Heraclidis* depends on his use of the word, it is a point which must receive our first attention.

The traditional view of Nestorius has been that he thought to solve the Christological problem by the theory of a 'moral union': 'The answer was found in the theory of a moral union, the association of Jesus the Son of Mary with the eternal Logos: an association the basis of which is the actual moral identity of the will of Jesus with the divine will of the Logos.'[3] Such a theory could only be satisfactory if it were based on a metaphysic in which the ultimate reality is identified with will: but, in the language of patristic theology, that would involve identifying will with οὐσία, and the slightest acquaintance with Nestorius' writings is enough to show that he never did that. Dr. Loofs has put forward the theory that Nestorius did not mean to teach any metaphysical union at all. He opposes what he calls a 'personal and moral' union to all kinds of metaphysical union, and holds that Nestorius cared nothing for the latter. We misunderstand him because 'we cannot free ourselves from metaphysics'. Without stopping to discuss the curious notion that any non-metaphysical Christology can be satisfactory, or whether such a conception can credibly be

[1] Reprinted from *The Journal of Theological Studies*, vol. xix, No. 73.

[2] Cp. Bethune-Baker, *Nestorius and his Teaching*, Cambridge, 1908; Loofs, *Nestorius and his Place in the History of Christian Doctrine*, Cambridge, 1914; and criticisms of them in the *Church Quarterly Review* by H. M. Relton (Jan. 1912) and A. C. Headlam (July, 1915). Also R. H. Connolly and A. J. Mason in *J. T. S.* xii. 486 and xv. 88.

[3] Weston, *The One Christ* (1914), p. 88.

ascribed to a patristic theologian, I shall hope first to show that Nestorius did, as a matter of fact, mean to put forward a metaphysical theory; secondly, to make a suggestion as to what that theory was; and, thirdly, to offer some few criticisms on what I believe him to have taught.

I

When we ask whether Nestorius meant to teach that Christ was one person or two persons, we are faced by the fact that there is in his terminology no word precisely similar to our 'person'. He shares with all his contemporaries an outlook not yet concerned with the psychological investigation which has produced the problem of the nature of personality as it appears in modern philosophy.[1] Still, if by 'personality' we mean the real centre of being of a person, that idea was rightly expressed by the use, which came to be generally adopted in Nestorius' day from the Cappadocian Fathers, of ὑπόστασις; which word, although commonly rendered in Latin by *persona*, itself really means *individua substantia*. It denotes some thing objectively existent, one piece of reality, so to say, which in the case of a human being will naturally be his personality, though in the case of a material thing we could not use that term to describe it. It is in this sense of ὑπόστασις, I am inclined to think, that Cyril bases the oneness of Christ on a ἕνωσις καθ' ὑπόστασιν.

Nestorius generally used ὑπόστασις in the older sense, as equivalent to οὐσία, though there are a few passages in which he shows himself to be acquainted with, and even accepts the newer usage.[2] Apart from these he has no word which, like ὑπόστασις in Cyril, may be looked on as expressing the germ of that conception of 'person' which is still growing to-day. When he wishes to emphasize the unity of Christ's essential (as we should say) personal being, he simply uses the number 'one', or denies that he makes Christ two. He teaches that Christ is one: he denies that he believes in two Sons or two Lords or two Christs.[3]

---

[1] Cp. C. C. J. Webb, *Studies in the History of Natural Theology*, pp. 143 sq.

[2] Cp. Bethune-Baker, *op. cit.*, p. 50.

[3] *E.g.* 'Dominum nostrum Christum secundum naturam duplicem dicamus, secundum quod est filius, unum', Loofs, *Nestoriana*, p. 341; and cp. *Heracleides*, pp. 47-50, 146, 160, 189-91, 196, 209-10, 215, 225, 227, 237-8, 295-302, 314, 317. (The references are to the pages of the present volume.)

This is in effect a claim not to be condemned as Nestorian in the traditional sense, and our object is to discover how he attempted to make good this claim.

It is a question, he says, of the *kind* of unity possible in the circumstances, and to describe it he uses the word πρόσωπον. We will call it provisionally *prosôpic union*. His argument seems to rest on two principles.

(1) Divine and human οὐσίαι being entirely different things, absolutely antithetical the one to the other, they must remain so in the union of them in Christ, if He is to be perfect God and perfect man: for if either the godhead changes into the manhood, or vice versa, one or other will not be there at all: and if the two are fused, Christ will be neither God nor man, but some new kind of being.[1]

(2) The union must be voluntary on both sides. We cannot think either of Christ's humanity or of His divinity as being constrained against its will as a result of the union.[2]

With these two principles in his mind he turns to consider the three kinds of unity which he finds have to be taken into account.

(*a*) There is the unity of the Persons in the Trinity.
(*b*) There is the unity of soul and body in man.
(*c*) There is the unity of godhead and manhood in Christ.

In the Trinity the Father and the Son are one in οὐσία and φύσις, but differ in πρόσωπον, while soul and body differ in οὐσία and φύσις, but are united φυσικῶς so as to make one human οὐσία with human φύσις. So he calls the first of these a unity of οὐσία, and the second a natural union (ἕνωσις φυσική). Now, the godhead and the manhood in Christ cannot be united like the persons in the Trinity, for their οὐσίαι are two and not one[3]: but neither can they be united like soul and body, for the union of soul and body is not a voluntary union; they are both created things held together by the will of their Creator, and besides, they are both by themselves, unlike the godhead and the manhood of Christ, incomplete things incapable of separate existence.[4] So there must be some third kind of unity,

[1] *Heracleides*, pp. 22, 26–7, &c., and cp. his accusation of Cyril on p. 320.
[2] Pp. 38, 179, 304, and cp. Loofs, *Nestorius*, p. 68.
[3] P. 189.
[4] Pp. 38, 179, 304.

exemplified in the third case, and this he calls a unity of πρόσωπον.

All the way through he confidently appeals to this conception of a *prosôpic* union as though it explained everything, and as though it were quite clear what the word πρόσωπον meant. What it did mean to him we shall consider below: the immediate point is that from his use of it in discussing these three kinds of unity we may surely conclude that to him it meant something parallel to οὐσία and φύσις. But these are elements in the metaphysical analysis of a thing, and so πρόσωπον, whatever the word means, must denote some other such element, and if so, then the phrase '*prosôpic* union' must represent an attempt to find a real metaphysical unity of the godhead and the manhood in Christ.

The belief that πρόσωπον denotes a real element in the being of a thing is strengthened by the consideration of such passages as these:

'Although the πρόσωπον exists not without οὐσία, the οὐσία and the πρόσωπον are not the same,' and

'In order that we might not, like Sabellius, make the πρόσωπα without *hypostasis* and without οὐσία.'[1]

It looks then as though in the metaphysic of Nestorius everything that exists may be analysed into οὐσία, φύσις, and πρόσωπον. We must now ask what in this analysis the word πρόσωπον is used to describe.

II

'For Nestorius', says Dr. Loofs, 'who ... was influenced by the manner of speaking common at that time, the main thing in his notion of πρόσωπον, according to the etymology of the word, was the *external undivided appearance*. ... In his opinion, I believe, everything had its πρόσωπον, that is its appearance, its kind of being seen and judged. In not a few places in Nestorius, it is true, the meaning of πρόσωπον coincides with our meaning of the word "person", *e.g.* "Cyril's πρόσωπον" means Cyril, "these πρόσωπα" means these persons, and εἷς καὶ ὁ αὐτός and ἐν πρόσωπον may be used alternately. Nevertheless ... I must lay stress on the fact that the notion of πρόσωπον in Nestorius grew upon another soil and, therefore, had a wider application than our

---

[1] *Heracleides*, pp. 170, 228.

The Metaphysic of Nestorius

term "person".[1] A similar account of the Syriac word *parṣôphâ*, which is used throughout the *Liber Heraclidis* to represent πρόσωπον, is given in a note added to Prof. Bethune-Baker's work.[2] These passages suggested to me that we should take this simple and clear meaning of πρόσωπον, a meaning which the word is undoubtedly able to bear, and, using it as parallel to 'essence' and 'nature' in the metaphysical analysis, see how far it would carry us in the interpretation of Nestorius' writing. The surprising thing was that throughout the *Liber Heraclidis* the understanding of πρόσωπον in this way gave an intelligible sense, and presented a coherent and consistent Christological theory sufficiently simple to explain how Nestorius could confidently appeal to it as the solution of all difficulty.

In modern times, of course, many thinkers have distinguished between a thing as it is in itself and as it appears to us. In this they have usually started by considering the fact of error in sense-perception, or by contrasting our 'mental image' or 'idea' of a thing with the reality it is supposed to represent. But neither of these lines of thought must be ascribed to Nestorius. If πρόσωπον for him means the appearance of a thing, it means that appearance not as opposed to the thing's reality, but considered as an objectively real element in its being; and the genesis of the conception must be sought along other lines. Two suggestions may be made. In the first place, an analysis of reality into οὐσία and φύσις almost demands such a completion. If the invisible οὐσία is that in which the various elements of the φύσις are united, a word is needed to describe the external undivided appearance of the whole. And secondly, the common conception of the Godhead as invisible but revealed in Christ who is the εἰκὼν τοῦ ἀοράτου πατρός is a conception akin to that which we are considering.

Supposing then that Nestorius analysed everything that exists into οὐσία, φύσις, and πρόσωπον, that is, into essence, nature (or sum of qualities), and appearance, how can this be applied to Christology?

The godhead and the manhood of Christ each has its οὐσία, φύσις, and πρόσωπον. Now for reasons given above we cannot find the centre of their union in either their οὐσία or their φύσις. But we *can* think of two different things, different in οὐσία and

---
[1] Loofs, *Nestorius*, p. 76.   [2] Bethune-Baker, *op. cit.*, p. 219.

φύσις, which nevertheless are identical in appearance. The appearances overlap, so to say. But two identical appearances will be one appearance. Surely here we have found that element in their being in which two οὐσίαι, complete with their respective φύσεις, can be united so as to be one without ceasing to be themselves.

At first sight this certainly does not look like any real union at all. Two things which look alike are not one thing. But such a criticism entirely misunderstands Nestorius' thought. For him the πρόσωπον is no *mere* appearance. It is a real element in the being of a thing, without which, or if it were other than it is, the thing would not be what it is. A πρόσωπον which was not the πρόσωπον of an οὐσία would be a mere illusion, a figment of the imagination, and neither the manhood nor the godhead of Christ was that. On the other hand, an οὐσία without a πρόσωπον was unthinkable.[1] And so a *prosôpic* union is a real union, and that kind of real union which is possible in the particular case we are considering.

The ordinary view of Nestorius' position is that he taught that the manhood and the godhead of Christ existed in two separate persons who were united by a 'moral union', that is, two persons whose wills were identical in content: the man Jesus being granted κατ' εὐδοκίαν complete unity with the Logos. Undoubtedly Nestorius did teach the existence of two wills which were one in that they willed alike.[2] But he taught more than this. The contents of the wills are alike, it is true, but also in one of the three elements of their being their owners are united in a real metaphysical union. So although he says '[To have] the πρόσωπον of God is to will what God wills',[3] yet he denies that he teaches a union of two separate persons united by love and by an equality of honour and power.[4] No; there is a real metaphysical unity, and he neither teaches nor believes in 'two Sons'.[5]

---

[1] 'Nestorius as an adherent of the Antiochian school could as little realize a really existent nature without πρόσωπον as without ὑπόστασις, for the whole of the characteristics which make the nature must, in his opinion, as necessarily have a form of appearance, *i.e.* a πρόσωπον, as a real being by which they are borne, *i.e.* a ὑπόστασις.' Loofs, *Nestorius*, p. 78. Cp. *Heracleides*, pp. 170, 219, 228.

[2] *Heracleides*, pp. 59, 62, 65–6, 70, 163. [3] P. 59.
[4] P. 314. [5] See p. 412, n. 3.

The Metaphysic of Nestorius

Passages which suggest the above interpretation of πρόσωπον will be found on pp. 20-1, 53, 146-7, 158, 165, 189-90, 218-19, 238, 246-7, 310-11, and 318 of the present volume.

These passages illustrate Nestorius' prevailing use of πρόσωπον and treatment of the subject. There are also passages of great significance in which the object of the sharing of the πρόσωπα is said to be *manifestation, e.g.* 'It is known that God the Word is said to have become flesh and the Son of man after the likeness and after the πρόσωπον of flesh and of man whereof He made use to make Himself known to the world.'[1] We must also note what a prominent place in his Christological argument is taken by the passage in Phil. ii. 7, where St. Paul speaks of the Son taking the 'form of a servant'.

One is apt to think that this interpretation of Nestorius' teaching cannot be right because it is so simple and obvious that he must have meant something more. If this was his doctrine, the doubt and confusion which exists as to what he taught could never have arisen. But I am not sure that the very simplicity of it may not have been both the ground of its attractiveness to Nestorius and the cause of its being overlooked by students of him. Certainly his language throughout the *Liber Heraclidis* is the language of one who believes that he is presenting a simple, clear, and satisfactory solution of the Christological problem, which removes all difficulty. Any one who turns from struggling to understand Dr. Loofs' interpretation of Nestorius to the study of the *Liber Heraclidis* itself must find it incredible that the theory which Nestorius presents with such confidence should be anything so obscure as his interpreter makes out. And yet its simplicity, on the interpretation suggested above, is based on a very acute subtlety of metaphysical thought, which might easily have rendered the theory unintelligible to many even in his own day; though Cyril may well have understood it when he wrote οὐ διαιρετέον τοιγαροῦν εἰς υἱοὺς δύο τὸν ἕνα κύριον Ἰησοῦν Χριστόν. ὀνήσει δὲ κατ' οὐδένα τρόπον τὸν ὀρθὸν τῆς πίστεως λόγον εἰς τὸ οὕτως ἔχειν, κἂν εἰ προσώπων ἕνωσιν ἐπιφημίζωσί τινες· οὐ γὰρ εἴρηκεν ἡ γραφή, ὅτι ὁ Λόγος ἀνθρώπου πρόσωπον ἥνωσεν ἑαυτῷ, ἀλλ' ὅτι γέγονε σάρξ.[2]

---
[1] *Heracleides*, p. 158. Cp. pp. 55, 172, 194.
[2] Cyril, *ad Nest.* ii, ll. 101-6 (Bindley), Labbe (Mansi) iv, 892 A.

III

In this brief sketch of a suggested interpretation of Nestorius' teaching I have concentrated attention on what seems to be the main point of his teaching as set forth in the *Liber Heraclidis*. It is true that he objected to the term θεοτόκος as implying the ascription of a human mode of existence to the divine οὐσία, though he was willing to accept it if properly safeguarded. It is true that he spoke of a unity of will owing to the divine and the human will in Christ willing alike. So far he is purely Nestorian in the traditional sense, and such teaching may be found discussed in any work on Christian doctrine. But if beyond all this he went on to explain the Incarnation as a union in πρόσωπον in the sense outlined above, then this will be really the keystone of his dogmatic edifice, and by this he must stand or fall.

Now, in the first place, as often in the case of philosophical theories, the almost immediate objection of the plain man is really justified. Two things which look alike are not really one, and in trying to show that they are Nestorius has fallen into a temptation which always besets philosophers. All metaphysical systems are attempts to describe reality, but unless at every step one's thought is tested by reference to the reality one is trying to describe, it is fatally easy to elaborate the system, but in doing so to wander farther and farther from the truth. So here, when we have analysed real things into οὐσία, φύσις, and πρόσωπον, it is tempting to play with these three elements of the analysis as Nestorius does, as though they were the real object of our thought. But if we go back to consider the real thing, and see how it is a unity whose elements are only separable in thought, we see that the πρόσωπον is so bound up with the οὐσία and φύσις that two different οὐσίαι and φύσεις must have different πρόσωπα. Two identical πρόσωπα would be indeed not two but one, and would imply but one οὐσία and φύσις. The Christology of Nestorius is only possible when his metaphysic has become thoroughly artificial.

Secondly, this statement that the system is artificial is borne out when we remember that there is in reality another kind of unity to be considered which is not allowed for by Nestorius. Where are we to place the unity of God and man in the prophets, of Christ and man in the Christian? The fact that

The Metaphysic of Nestorius

Nestorius was accused of Samosatene teaching shows that he was felt to be unsatisfactory on this point: although he himself repeatedly denies that he taught that Christ was a mere man, or that he had any sympathy with Paul of Samosata.[1] But surely there are only three possibilities:

(a) Christ and the Christian are united according to one of Nestorius' three kinds of union.

(b) That list of kinds of union is not exhaustive.

(c) They are not really united.

Nestorius' teaching really seems to have involved (c).[2] But if we are not satisfied with this we must choose between (a) and (b). Now for Nestorius (b) would destroy his main argument, In what can they be united except the πρόσωπον?; and he has ruled out (a) in teaching that Godhead and manhood cannot be united in οὐσία or φύσις, and that the *prosôpic* union does not make Christ a man like other men.

So we come to a third criticism. If Nestorius' theory after all does not provide a real union between the godhead and the manhood in Christ, nor allow for a real union between the Christian and God, then, from the point of view of religion, the One Mediator between God and man has not been found; from the point of view of philosophy the universe contains an unresolved dualism between two utterly opposed οὐσίαι, godhead and manhood. Here of course lies the importance of Christ for metaphysics: godhead and manhood finding their oneness in Him He is thus the guarantee of the rationality of the universe. The Christological problem is the problem of explaining that oneness, and the '*prosôpic* union' of Nestorius' theory is not strong enough to bear the strain it was designed to meet.

It is the conception of the complete and eternal antithesis between Godhead and manhood which prevents any satisfactory solution of the problem, but neither Nestorius nor any of his contemporary theologians would ever have thought of questioning the truth of this conception. The difference between Nestorius and Cyril is that whereas Nestorius is throughout perfectly consistent, and his theory a brilliant attempt to solve the problem on the basis of a principle which renders all solution impossible,

[1] Cp. *Heracleides*, pp. 194, 236-7, and Loofs, *Nestoriana*, pp. 182, 192, 222, 299, 303-12.

[2] *Heracleides*, pp. 48-9, 74-5.

Cyril's greatness lies in the very fact of his inconsistency. He would no more question the antithesis between godhead and manhood than would Nestorius, but where the truth was too much for his system, he preferred the truth to the system, and by his self-contradiction (which Nestorius exposes again and again) left room for further development of Christological doctrine in the future.

What, then, will be our judgement on Nestorius? If the above interpretation of his teaching be true, he surely represents a very gallant and ingenious attempt to explain the Incarnation without giving up the belief that in Christ is to be found a complete human person as well as a complete divine person.. He could not think of humanity except as existing in a distinct human person; for him, to deny the human ὑπόστασις of Christ was to teach an Apollinarian maimed humanity.[1] Cyril boldly gave up belief in a distinct human ὑπόστασις in Christ. Nestorius saw at once that this was inconsistent with the belief of both as to the relation between God and man, but in Cyril's inconsistency we have still a challenge to thought and to the search for a perfect Christology which is not to be found in the barren coherence of Nestorius. L. H.

[1] *E.g. Heracleides*, pp. 240-1.

INDEX

Abraham, 193, 250.
Acacius of Beroea, xxi–xxiii, 282, 289, 330.
Acacius of Melitene, xix, xxiv, 136, 139, 265, 293–318, 320, 326.
Adam, 60 ff., 81, 82, 183, 213, 214.
Adoption, 48, 49, 55 ff., 159.
Aethericus of Smyrna. *See* Atticus.
Aleppo (Beroea), xi, xv, 330.
Alexander of Apamea, xix, 107.
Alexander of Hierapolis, xix, xxii–xxiv, 382.
Ambrose, xx, 191, 199, 215, 224, 227, 229, 236, 245, 256, 261, 262, 333.
Anastasius, xvii.
Anathematisms, Cyrillian, xviii, xx, xxii, xxiii, xxvii, 94, 268, 269, 287, 290, 291, 292, 293, 306.
Anathematisms, Nestorian, 268.
Anatolius, xxvii, xxviii.
Andrew, Acts of, 404.
Andrew of Samosata, xviii, xxii–xxiv.
Anomoeans, 97, 98.
Apollinarianism, xxxiii, 151, 420.
Apollinarians, 34, 240, 314.
Apollinarius, xxxv, 1, 91, 97 ff., 172, 176, 178, 183, 211, 269, 304, 325, 326, 332, 384, 391, 407.
Aquinas, St. Thomas, 239.
Arcadius, xx.
Archetype and image, 233, 234.
Arianism, xxxiii, xxxiv, 373.
Arians, 8, 33, 34, 38, 39, 43, 45, 83, 94, 97, 162, 176, 184, 200, 211, 217, 240, 258, 314, 324, 372, 373, 377.
Aristolaus, xxii–xxiv, 289, 329.
Arius, xxx, 91, 168, 172, 177, 178, 181, 183, 188, 268, 269, 283, 304, 323, 325, 326, 332, 384.
Athanasius, xx, 130, 192, 193, 200, 202, 205, 216, 221, 227, 236, 256, 261, 262, 333, 377, 405, 408.

Atonement, the, xxxii, xxxiv, 32, 45, 59, 62 ff., 73, 75, 84, 93, 94, 171, 173, 183, 201, 205, 211–14, 247, 249, 250, 251, 253, 367.
Atticus (Aethericus of Smyrna), xiv, 355, 356, 357.

Babylonians called 'Anointed', 203.
Baptism of Christ, 64 ff.
Barnabas, Epistle of, 403.
Barsumas, xxvi, xxvii.
Basil, xvii, 333, 406.
Bazaar, xii.
Bedjan, P., xi, xii, 3, 5, 10, 56, 99, 102, 125, 206, 238, 329, 330, 398–402.
Bedr Khan Bey, xi, 192.
'Benevolences', 100.
Beroea (Aleppo), xi, xv, 330.
Besulas, xix.
Bethune-Baker, J. F., x, xi, 13, 64, 86, 89, 137, 411, 412, 415.
Bindley, T. H., 241, 268, 326, 417.
Birth of Christ, 59, 60, 65, 91, 92, 151, 168, 171, 174, 177, 191, 193, 196–8, 225, 237, 253, 294–7, 387, 390, 391.
Boetius, 239.
Braun, x.
Bribery, xxii, 127, 272, 279–82, 349.
Burning Bush, analogy of the, 156, 157, 160.

Caelestius, xvii.
Callistus, 404.
Candidianus, xviii–xxi, 106–125, 134, 269.
Capreolus, xx.
Cassian, xviii.
Celestinus, xvii–xxii, 131, 132, 275, 375.
Chalcedon, Council of, x, xxviii, xxix, 239, 241, 358, 365, 389, 410.

Christotokos, 99.
Chrysaphius, xxv, xxvii, 342.
Chrysoretes, xxiii.
Chrysostom, xxiv, 283, 377, 408.
Clement of Alexandria, 403.
Clement of Rome, 403.
Communicatio idiomatum, 241, 247.
'Community of names', 203 ff.
Connolly, R. H., 411.
Constantinople, Synod of, xxv, xxviii, 338, 340, 343, 346, 353, 358.
Cosmos, Letter to, ix, xi.
Creation, xxxiv, xxxv, 46.
Cyril of Alexandria, *passim*.
   ad Acacium, xvii, xxiv, 180, 187, 190, 293-330.
   ad Caelestinum, xvii, xviii.
   ad Clericos Constantinopolitanos, xvii, 101, 102.
   ad Monachos Aegypti, xvii.
   ad Nestorium I, xvii, 103.
   ad Nestorium II, xvii, xix, xxvii, 143-4, 149 ff., 191, 218, 226, 243, 417.
   ad Nestorium III, xviii, xx, 151, 268, 269, 319, 325.
   Adv. Nest. Blasphemias, xviii.
   Apologeticus ad Theodosium, xxii.
   Apologia contra Orientales, xviii.
   Apologia contra Theodoretum, xviii.
   de Recta Fide, xvii.
   Epistola xxxix, xxiii.
   (See also pp. 409-10.)
Cyril of Jerusalem, 405.
Cyrus, 203.

Dalmatius, xxi, xxiii, xxiv, 272, 273, 277.
Daniel, xxi.
Devil, the, 65 sq.
Dialogue, the, 384, 385.
Didache, the, 403.
Diodorus of Tarsus, 332, 333, 334.
Dioscorus of Alexandria, x, xxv-xxviii, xxx, 340, 345, 348, 351, 354, 356, 358, 359, 360, 375.
Docetism, xxxiii, 323.
Domnus of Antioch, xxiv, xxv, xxvii, 345, 347, 348.
Du Bose, W. P., 63, 75.
Dulcitius, xxvi.

Ebedjesu, ix, xi.
Elphidius, Count, xxvi.

Ephesus, Council of, ix, xix-xxii, xxix, 106 ff., 265 ff., 375, 384.
Epiphanius, Archdeacon and *Syncellus* to Cyril, 282.
Epiphanius of Salamis, 406, 408.
Eucharist, the, xxxiii, 28-33, 55, 254, 327-8.
Eudocia, xxiv, xxv, 346, 379.
Eudoxia, xxvii, 286, 379.
Eulogius, Count, xxvi.
Eunomius, 91, 168, 269, 332, 406.
Eusebius of Ancyra, 343, 359, 360.
Eusebius of Dorylaeum, xvii, xxv, xxvii, xxviii, 337-41, 352, 369, 373.
Eusebius of Pamphila, xv, 404.
Eustathius of Antioch, 130, 377, 405.
Eutyches, xxiii-xxix, xxxv, 24, 336-41, 343-5, 347, 351-5, 358, 360, 375, 378.
Euzoius, 377.
Evagrius, ix, x, 338, 342, 363.
Evil, Problem of, 78 sq.

Fall, the, 69, 71.
Flaccilla, 379.
Flavian of Constantinople, x, xxv-xxx, 97, 336, 337, 341-8, 351-62, 369, 373, 375-8.
Flavian of Philippi, xix.
'Formulary of Reunion', xxi, xxiii

Galla Placidia, xxvii.
Gensericus, 379.
Goussen, H., x.
Grace contrasted with Nature, 46.
Gregory of Nazianzum, xx, 194, 195, 200, 202, 205, 206, 215, 220, 223, 224, 227, 228, 231, 236, 245, 252, 255, 260-2, 333, 406.
Gregory of Nyssa, xx, 221, 406.

Headlam, Bishop A. C., 411.
Heathen, xxx, 7, 16, 177, 181, 370.
Hefele, 282, 358.
Heikel, xv.
Helladius of Tarsus, 107.
Heracleides, 4.
Heracleon, 404.
Hilary, xxvi, xxvii, 346.
Hippolytus, 404.
Homilies and Sermons of Nestorius, ix, xi.
Hylê, 16, 17, 25, 85, 177, 185, 256.

Index

Hypostasis, xv, xxix, 15, 16, 44, 46, 52, 55, 88, 93, 94, 98, 146, 156, 159, 162-4, 172, 173, 178, 181, 184, 208, 209, 216, 218, 228, 234, 242, 306, 307, 384, 385, 397, 412.

Ibas of Edessa, xxvi, xxvii.
Ignatius, 403.
Immortality, 32.
'Impersonal manhood', 239.
Irenaeus, Count (Bishop of Tyre), xviii, xxi, xxiv, xxv, xxvii, 117.
Irenaeus, St., 403.
Israel called 'God's Son', 203 ff.

Jews, xxx, 8, 373, 376, 386.
John of Antioch, xviii-xxiv, 107, 108, 114, 115, 117, 118, 120, 121, 125, 126, 132, 267, 268, 269, 287, 289-91, 293, 318, 329.
John, Chaplain to Cyril, xxi.
John Chrysostom, xxiv, 283, 377, 408.
John, Count, xxi, 279, 280, 349.
John of Damascus, 365.
John of Germanicia, xxiii.
John of Maïouma, 271.
John of Malala, 379.
Judaism, 373.
Julian of Cos, xxvi.
Julian of Eclanum, xvii.
Julian of Puteoli, xxvi, 345, 346
Justin Martyr, 403.
Juvenal of Jerusalem, xviii, xix, xxviii, 107, 135, 360.

Kenôsis, 58, 70, 246.
Kidd, B. J., xvii, 289, 338.
Kotchanes, x, xi.

Lacey, T. A., 239.
Latrocinium, the, xxvi-xxviii, 343-62.
Leo, x, xxiv-xxviii, 340, 345, 346, 348, 351, 369, 374, 375, 378, 379, 389.
Leo, *Tome* of, xxvi-xxviii, 241, 346.
Liturgy of Nestorius, ix, xi.
Locke, John, 239.
Loofs, F., x, 14, 22, 60, 99, 157, 165, 239, 249, 252, 254, 257, 263, 281, 282, 382-98, 411, 412, 414, 415, 416, 417, 419.

Macarius of Egypt, 408.

Macedonius, 168, 332.
Magnus, 359, 360.
Majority rule, 128, 129.
Manes, 192, 201, 202.
Manichaeans, xxx, 8-18, 24-6, 29, 39, 45, 85, 99, 176, 177, 184, 202, 205, 206, 212, 373, 374.
Maraba, x.
Marcian, xxvii-xxix, 369.
Marius Mercator, xviii, 282.
Mason, A. J., 411.
Maximian, ix, xxii-xxiv, 285, 329.
Maximus, xxvii.
Meletius of Antioch, 377.
Memnon of Ephesus, xix-xxi, 133, 134, 266-9, 279, 280.
Minorities, Rights of, 128, 129.
Miracles of Christ, 7, 8, 10.
Monophysites, 35-43, 372, 388.
Monothelites, 239.
Moses, 17, 203, 204, 205, 206.
Muzicanus, 379.

Nature as opposed to Grace and Adoption, 46, 49, 159.
Nau, F., xi, 3, 5, 10, 23, 41, 55, 56, 83, 96, 97, 108, 125, 141, 155, 186, 192, 196, 201, 203, 206, 209, 253, 263, 270-2, 282, 287, 293, 329, 330, 372, 398-402.
Neander, A., ix, 97, 137.
'Nestorianism', xxxiii, 19, 47, 65, 339, 374, 411, 418.
'Nestorianism' denied, 50, 65, 153, 158, 159, 189, 196, 204, 339.
Nestorius, *passim*.
  ad Caelestinum, xvii, xviii.
  ad Cyrillum I, xvii.
  ad Cyrillum II, xvii, xx, 141, 142, 168-9.
Nestorius' writings, ix, xi.
Nicaea, Council and Creed of, 87, 107, 141-50, 196-8, 263, 264, 354, 356, 377, 390, 391.
Nicephorus Callistus, 342, 346, 363, 365.

Omnipotence, 10, 14, 17.
Origen, 323, 403.
Ousia, xxxii, 13-43, 48-57, 80-3, 87-94, 98, 138, 144-7, 149, 151, 153-60, 164-7, 170-2, 174, 177-80, 182, 184, 185, 187-96, 198, 200, 202, 205-10, 212, 214-20, 225, 227, 228, 230-3, 235, 238,

240, 243, 245, 247, 249-52, 255, 258, 259, 261, 262, 294, 298, 299, 301, 305, 307, 309, 310, 313-17, 319-21, 324, 326-8, 334, 339, 340, 362, 366, 367, 385, 388, 392, 393, 412-16, 418.

Palladius, the governor, 117.
Palladius monachus, 408.
Passibility, 9, 34, 36-43, 47, 93, 94, 146, 150, 162-4, 172-4, 178, 179, 181, 182, 184, 188, 211, 212, 218, 228-30, 253, 255, 258, 278, 284, 362-73, 395.
Paul of Emesa, xxiii, 289, 318.
Paul, Nestorian patriarch, xi.
Paulinians, Paul of Samosata, xxx, xxxiii, 8, 9, 44 ff., 98, 99, 419.
Paulinus, 379.
Peter Chrysologus of Ravenna, xxv.
Peter, priest and notary, of Alexandria, 263.
Pharaoh, 376.
Philip, xx.
Philostorgius, 363.
Photinians, Photinus, xxx, 8, 98, 99.
Photius, xvii, xxv.
Porphyry, xxv.
Posidonius, xvii, 131.
Priesthood of Christ, xxxiii, 244, 248, 253.
Proclus, xvii, xxiv, xxv, 336.
Projectus, xx.
Prosôpon (non-technical), 3, 28, 33, 57, 129, 132, 133, 199, 203, 247, 264, 273, 281, 347, 375, 378, 390, 394, 402-410.
Prosôpon (technical), xxix, xxxii, xxxiii, 9, 15, 20-5, 37, 38, 45, 51-82, 89, 94, 143-9, 152-4, 156-61, 163-8, 170-2, 174, 179, 181-4, 189, 190, 196, 200-3, 205-8, 211, 214, 216-20, 224, 225, 227, 228, 230-6, 238-41, 245-7, 251-3, 255, 258, 260-2, 299, 301-3, 306-11, 313-15, 318-20, 322, 323, 327, 337, 339, 374, 388, 393, 394, 402-10, 413-18.
Psilanthropism, 43, 56, 146, 195, 237.
Pulcheria, xxiii, xxvi-xxix, 96, 97, 286, 342, 369.

Rabbula of Edessa, xxii.
Relton, H. M., 411.
Renatus, xxvi.

Resurrection of Christ, the, 75, 151, 168, 171, 177, 225, 395, 396.
Revelation, as the purpose of the Incarnation, 34, 60, 147, 158, 194, 200, 202, 205, 206, 253, 417.

Sabellians, 43, 406.
Satan, 68, 69, 71 ff., 395.
Schêma (non-technical), 102, 141, 205, 254, 255, 268, 272, 279, 288, 311, 313, 316, 331, 336, 341, 370, 371.
Schêma (technical), 8, 11-21, 34, 44-7, 53, 58-61, 69, 80-4, 87-93, 138, 165-7, 177, 181, 182, 184, 185, 205, 214, 218, 219, 239, 259, 321, 322.
Scythians, 363, 366.
Seleucus of Amasia, 353, 355.
Sheol, 395.
Simeon Stylites, St., xxii, 289.
Sinlessness of Christ, 172, 206, 213, 247, 250, 251.
Sirmium, Creed of, 405.
Sixtus III of Rome, xxii-xxiv, 375.
Socrates, *H. E.*, ix.
Sophronius, xxx, 10, 378.
Stephen of Ephesus, 345, 359, 360.
Stone, Darwell, xv.

Temptation of Christ, 66, 67.
Thalassius of Caesarea, 343, 358, 359, 360.
Theodore of Mopsuestia, 332, 333, 334, 408.
Theodoret, xviii, xxii, xxv, xxvii, xxviii, 268, 382, 383, 409.
Theodosius II, ix, x, xvii-xxvii, 96, 100, 101, 102, 106-29, 132, 267-77, 279-87, 289, 290, 292, 293, 329, 330, 336, 338, 340-3, 346-51, 357, 361, 362, 369, 374-6.
Theodotus of Ancyra, xix, 136, 137.
Theopaschitans, 384, 385, 388, 391, 395.
Theopemptus, xxi.
Theophanies in O. T., 11, 19, 20.
Theophilus of Alexandria, xx, 231, 256, 283, 377.
Theophilus (the Apologist), 403.
Theotokos, xxix, 99, 148, 149, 293, 295, 296, 297, 418.
Timothy, 283.
Tragoedia, ix-xi.
Tranquillinus of Antioch (Pis.), 107.

Index

Trinity, the, 14, 22-6, 37, 38, 45, 51, 59, 156, 182, 189, 207, 210, 228, 234, 235, 242, 247, 261, 309, 385, 390, 392, 404-10, 413.
Trisagion, the, xxviii, 365, 366, 368-70.
'Two Sons', 44, 47-50, 154, 159, 215, 222, 223, 225, 295-7, 300, 339, 374, 388, 389, 412, 416.

Union,
Hypostatic, xxxiii, 92, 94, 154-6, 161-4, 178, 179, 182, 184, 188, 294.
Instrumental, 246, 260.
Moral, 59, 62, 65, 70, 163, 189, 196, 314, 411, 416.
Natural, 8, 9, 34, 37, 84 ff., 91 ff., 98, 161-3, 178, 182, 183, 246, 294, 301, 303, 304, 309, 313, 388, 413.
Prosôpic, xxxii, xxxiii, 38, 51 ff., 70, 72, 89, 94, 143, 145, 146, 148, 157, 158, 163, 164, 164, 171, 172, 189, 196, 205-7, 211, 219, 220, 227, 230-3, 240, 248, 245, 246, 247, 252, 261, 262, 301, 309, 310, 311, 313, 314, 319, 320, 413-20.
Voluntary, 8, 9, 37, 38, 47, 85, 90, 91, 163, 179, 181, 182, 184, 413.

Valentinian III, xviii, xxvii.
Van, xii.
Virgin Birth of Christ, 59.

Webb, C. C. J., 156, 218, 412.
Weston, Bishop, 411.

Zeugma, Synod of, xxiii.